Mapping the Ottomans

Sovereignty, Territory, and Identity in the Early Modern Mediterranean

Simple paradigms of Muslim–Christian confrontation and the rise of Europe in the seventeenth century do not suffice to explain the ways in which European mapping envisioned the "Turks" in image and narrative. Rather, maps, travel accounts, compendia of knowledge, and other texts created a picture of the Ottoman Empire through a complex layering of history, ethnography, and eyewitness testimony, which juxtaposed current events to classical and Biblical history; counted space in terms of peoples, routes, and fortresses; and used the land and seascapes of the map to assert ownership, declare victory, and embody imperial power's reach. Enriched throughout by examples of Ottoman self-mapping, this book examines how Ottomans and their empire were mapped in the narrative and visual imagination of early modern Europe's Christian kingdoms. The maps serve as centerpieces for discussions of early modern space, time, borders, stages of travel, information flows, invocations of authority, and cross-cultural relations.

Palmira Brummett is Professor Emerita of History at the University of Tennessee, where she was Distinguished Professor of Humanities, and Visiting Professor of History at Brown University. Her publications include *Ottoman Seapower and Levantine Diplomacy in the Age of Discovery* (1994); *Image and Imperialism in the Ottoman Revolutionary Press, 1908–1911* (2000); *The 'Book' of Travels: Genre, Ethnology and Pilgrimage, 1250–1700* (2009), for which she was the editor and a contributor; and *Civilizations Past and Present* (2000–2005), for which she was the co-author of multiple editions. She has also written numerous articles on Ottoman, Mediterranean, and world history. She has been the recipient of NEH and ACLS fellowships, a Phi Beta Kappa Faculty Award for Scholarly Achievement, and a Bunting Fellowship at Radcliff University.

For Jim, again.

And in gratitude for the fellowship of the Folger Institute, where this book took shape.

Mapping the Ottomans

Sovereignty, Territory, and Identity in the Early Modern Mediterranean

Palmira Brummett

CAMBRIDGE
UNIVERSITY PRESS

CAMBRIDGE
UNIVERSITY PRESS

32 Avenue of the Americas, New York, NY 10013-2473, USA

Cambridge University Press is part of the University of Cambridge.

It furthers the University's mission by disseminating knowledge in the pursuit
of education, learning, and research at the highest international levels of excellence.

www.cambridge.org
Information on this title: www.cambridge.org/9781107090774

First published 2015

Printed in the United States of America

A catalog record for this publication is available from the British Library.

Library of Congress Cataloging in Publication Data
Brummett, Palmira Johnson, 1950–
Mapping the Ottomans : sovereignty, territory, and identity in the early modern Mediterranean /
Palmira Brummett.
    pages   cm
ISBN 978-1-107-09077-4 (hardback)
1. Cartography – Turkey – History – 17th century.   2. Cartography – Europe – History – 17th
century.   3. Turkey – History – Ottoman Empire, 1288-1918.   4. Religion and geography.
5. Christianity and other religions – Islam – History.   6. Islam – Relations – Christianity – History.
I. Title.
GA1303.5.A1B78   2015
526.0956–dc23   2014047990

ISBN 978-1-107-09077-4 Hardback

MM

Publication of this book has been aided by a grant from the Millard Meiss Publication
Fund of the College Art Association.

Contents

List of Images

Acknowledgments

This book evolved out of a long process of study, reflection, observation, and conversation with people and texts; and its creation and refinement were dependent on the intellectual space provided by libraries and their staffs. I wish to thank the Folger Shakespeare Library for sharing its wonderful space, hospitality, and resources, first at a symposium on the Ottomans and then during a period of research funded by the National Endowment for the Humanities. I have had the good fortune also to enjoy interludes of study in other great libraries: the Newberry Library, the Library of Congress, the British Library, Biblioteca Correr, Harvard Map Library, Houghton, the John Carter Brown, the Bodleian, John Hay, Library Znanstvena knjižnica Zadar, and the University of Chicago. In each case, their book people greatly facilitated my research. Special thanks to John Powell and James Ackerman at the Newberry, Kim Nusco at the John Carter Brown, Joanna Snelling at Corpus Christi College Library, and the whole gang at the Folger. These library collections, along with several others, have provided the images that are being recycled yet again for the perusal and interpretation of a modern audience. The University of Tennessee, especially the Department of History and colleagues Thomas Burman, Robert Bast, John Bohstedt, and Vejas Liulevicius, provided support and the congenial academic environment necessary for the production of scholarly work. Colleagues at my "new" institution, Brown, such as Rebecca More, Evelyn Lincoln, and Bill Monroe, have helped lend nuance to this work. Many individuals have been instrumental in the evolution of my thinking on maps and things Eurasian. To Tom Goodrich, a pioneering scholar whose generosity is unrivaled, I owe an unpayable debt. It was Jerry Brotton who suggested the idea of remapping the Ottomans in the first place. Further, I have benefited from the words and imaginations of many colleagues, including Virginia Aksan, Cristelle Baskins, Ebru Boyar, Robert Dankoff, Eric Dursteler, Katherine Ebel, Matthew Edney, Maria Pia Pedani Fabris, Caroline Finkel, Kate Fleet, Antonis Hadjikyriakou, Colin Heywood, Colin Imber, Sean Keilen, Dina Khoury, Tijana Krstic, Michael Kulikowski, Kathleen Lynch, Claire Norton, Victor Ostapchuk, Patricia Parker, Natalie Rothman, Goran Stanivukovich,

Fariba Zarinebaf-Shahr, and Madeline Zilfi. For the hospitality and collegiality provided by Zsolt Török at the ICHC conference in Budapest in 2004, many thanks for the inspiration. I also want to thank my editor, Will Hammell, at Cambridge University Press, for helping see this project through. To my companion and love, James L. Fitzgerald, this one's for you.

Earlier versions of parts of this work appeared as "The Lepanto Paradigm Revisited: Knowing the Ottomans in the Sixteenth Century," in A. Contadini and C. Norton, eds., *The Renaissance and the Ottoman World* (Farnham, Surrey: Ashgate), 2013; "The Fortress: Defining and Mapping the Ottoman Frontier in the 16th–17th Centuries," in Andrew Peacock, ed., *Frontiers of the Ottoman World* (Oxford: Oxford University Press), 2009; "'Turks' and 'Christians': The Iconography of Possession in the Depiction of the Ottoman–Venetian–Hapsburg Frontiers, 1550–1689," in Matthew Dimmock and Andrew Hadfield, eds., *The Religions of the Book: Christian Perceptions 1400–1660* (Houndmills: Palgrave Macmillan), 2008; and "Imagining the Early Modern Ottoman Space from Piri Reis to World History," in Virginia Aksan and Daniel Goffman, eds. *The Early Modern Ottomans: Remapping the Empire* (Cambridge: Cambridge University Press, 2007).

No person living or dead, except myself, bears any responsibility for errors contained herein. This is a literary convention that I think bears repeating. It is important to keep in mind, however, that in the early modern era, the publishing industry careened wildly beyond any fixed rules governing accuracy, censorship, copyright, or propriety!

Note on Transliteration and Translation

There is no one standard transliteration for Ottoman Turkish. That phenomenon is illustrated by the sources cited here in the footnotes, which employ at least four variations on Ottoman transliteration. Further, the style employed for indicating diacritical marks in modern Turkish has evolved since the language reforms of the 1920s and 1930s. This volume generally employs the transliterations used in the *Redhouse Türkçe/Osmanlıca–İngilizce Sözlük* (Redhouse Turkish/Ottoman–English Dictionary), with certain modifications and simplifications. Words such as 'tugh' (horsetail standard) and 'pasha' are not transliterated, as they have become standard in English language usage. English plurals have occasionally been used for select Turkish words in the text, for example kadıs (Islamic judges) rather than *kadılar* and beyliks (provinces) rather than *beylikleri*. For the few Arabic names employed, diacritics have been omitted (e.g., al-Malik al-Kamil rather than al-Malik al-Kāmil). İstanbul, with a dotted "I," is used only for citations of works published in that city; I have preferred "Istanbul" in the text. I have used both "Constantinople" and "Istanbul" to refer to the Ottoman capital because that is what early modern sources (including Ottoman sources) did. For other city names, which have multiple variants depending on the language (or time) of designation, I have preferred either the most familiar (but still relevant) English name or the contemporaneous name employed in the sources. Some cities are glossed with Italian, Turkish, and Slavic variants. Quotations for the most part employ the (often highly variable) spelling, diacritical marking, and capitalization found in the original sources, except when preserving the original proves unduly confusing or gives the appearance of a typographical error. In particular, because of the flexibility of spelling in early modern English sources, when one word might be confused with a similar word, I have updated the English spelling. The use or omission of accent marks in Italian and French works generally conforms to the usage in the original. It is important to note that I have preserved the capitalization used on the maps themselves and in early modern titles. Translations are mine except where otherwise indicated.

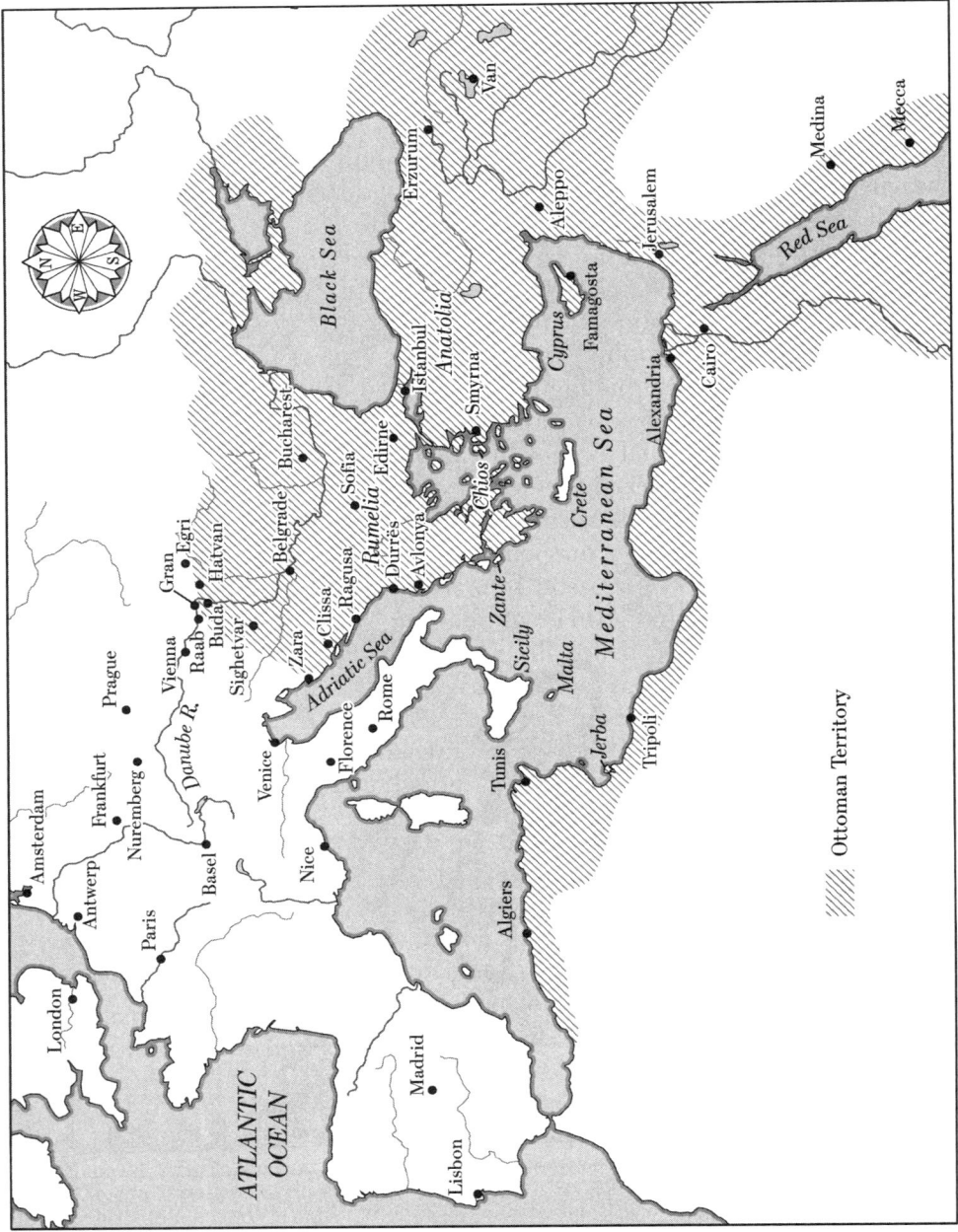

Map 1. The Ottomans in the Mediterranean world, c. 1600.

1

Introduction

Mapping Empire, and "Turks" on the Map

> *I will confute those blind geographers*
> *That make a triple region of the world,*
> *Excluding regions which I mean to trace,*
> *And with this pen reduce them to a map,*
> *Calling the provinces, cities, and towns,*
> *After my name and thine, Zenocrate.*

Christopher Marlowe, *Tamburlaine* 1 IV.iv. 81–9[1]

Thus Christopher Marlowe's theatrical Mongol ruler (Timur) proclaims that it is the sword (his "pen") that ultimately determines the mapping of empires. In his play, *Tamburlaine*, first performed c. 1587, Marlowe (1564–1593) created an artful counterpart to the maps of his day, a sovereign space concocted out of a rather indiscriminate mixing of myth, history, and fiction. He collapsed time and space to place Muhammad and Jove in the same firmament, meld the medieval with the early modern, and jumble the territories of the Afro-Eurasian oikumene into one great imperial backdrop.[2] Marlowe's English audience (elite and common) may or may not have known the historical figures of Timur (r. 1370–1405) and the Ottoman sultan Bayezid I (r. 1389–1402). But in the play these rulers' times, locations, compatriots, and identities were mutable, subject to the vagaries of drama, history, memory, education, artistic convention, and strategic interest. Just so, as early modern Europeans created representations of territory, they employed those same factors to delineate an Ottoman imperial space (and identity) that was as much a function of cultural imagination as it was a product of contemporary technologies of print and measurement. Such representations, particularly those

---

[1] Christopher Marlowe, *Tamburlaine* (Mineola, NY: Dover Books, 2002), 50; see also Jonathan Burton, "Anglo–Ottoman Relations and the Image of the Turk in Tamburlaine," *Journal of Medieval and Early Modern Studies* 30, 1 (2006): 125–56.

[2] Marlowe, *Tamburlaine*, 102–3.

found on maps, form the subject of this volume. It examines the rhetorical
construction of the Ottomans in the texts and images of the Christian kingdoms of early modern Europe and the inscribing of Ottoman territory,
sovereignty, and identity onto maps, employing Ottoman self-mapping as
a comparative foil. Maps, broadly construed, complicate the notion that representing the Ottomans was an evolutionary process that typed the empire
as terrible in the sixteenth century and domesticated in the eighteenth. If we
dismiss Marlowe's swirling of character, border, time, and space as merely
fanciful or theatrical, we miss the point. For, in the early modern era, mapping was both a pictorial narration of territory and events and a process by
which events were subordinated to history, memory, and desire.

With their conquest of the great Christian and Muslim capitals, Constantinople in 1453 and Cairo in 1517, the Ottoman Turks captured the
imagination of observers across the Afro-Eurasian world, asserting their
identity as one of the most powerful empires of the early modern era. The
Ottomans had become a European empire in the fifteenth century, crossing
the Danube into Wallachia and extending the territories under their dominion to the borders of Hungary. In the sixteenth century they became a world
empire, confronting the Muslim Mamluks and Safavids, in Egypt and Iran
respectively, and the Christian kings of Europe, in a broad frontier zone
stretching from the western Mediterranean to the Black Sea. Belgrade fell to
Ottoman armies in 1521, Rhodes in 1522, and, by 1541, Sultan Süleyman
I (r. 1520–66) had occupied Buda and could claim sovereignty over much
of Croatia and Hungary. See Map 1. This expanding empire was the object
of careful scrutiny and wild speculation in Christian Europe, its military
and spiritual prowess addressed in diplomatic reports, histories, sermon literature, compendia of knowledge, plays, essays, murals, broadsheets, and
maps, among other forms of communication.

In the Christian kingdoms of Europe the Ottomans were presented as
descendants of the "Scythians," the same "Turks" who swept out of Central Asia and confronted the "Saracens" in the crusading era.[3] The "Turks"
(a generic designation used to connote the Muslims in Ottoman territory)
were then mingled with all the historic Islamic 'marauders' who had tested
and trampled the borders of "Christendom."[4] A parade of witnesses passed
among the capitals of the Mediterranean world, circulating information

---

3   Nancy Bisaha, *Creating East and West: Renaissance Humanists and the Ottoman Turks* (Philadelphia:
    University of Pennsylvania Press, 2004), 174–5, 270 n. 62; Patricia Springborg, *Western Republicanism
    and the Oriental Prince* (Austin: University of Texas Press, 1992); John Michael Archer, *Old Worlds:
    Egypt, Southwest Asia, India and Russia in Early Modern English Writing* (Stanford, CA: Stanford
    University, 2001), 65–9, 73–4; and Samuel Chew, *The Crescent and the Rose: Islam and England
    during the Renaissance* (New York: Octagon Books, 1965), 55–99. See also Kiril Petkov, *Infidels,
    Turks, and Women: The South Slavs in the German Mind, ca. 1400–1600* (Frankfurt: Peter Lang,
    1997), 239–40, on the "German humanists' fondness for their neo-classical knowledge and strict
    adherence to the norms and requirements of puritanical classicism," in describing the conquests of the
    Ottomans.
4   See, for example, G. J. Reinink, "Ps. Methodius: A Concept of History in Response to the Rise of
    Islam," 149–87, in *The Byzantine and Early Islamic Near East: Problems in the Literary Source
    Material*, v. 1, Averil Cameron and Lawrence Conrad, eds. (Princeton: Darwin Press, 1992), 165, 170,
    174, who illustrates how this apparently late-seventh-century text collapsed time using both Biblical
    and classical references (especially to Alexander the Great) to create a vision of apocalyptic restoration.

about the Ottomans, their society, personnel, customs, beliefs, institutions, texts, identities, and material culture. The audiences for that information ranged from statesmen to merchants, and from scholars to illiterate parishioners, from the readers of cheap broadsheets to the consumers of lavish atlases (see Ch. 2). There was enormous demand for images and knowledge of "the Turks," whose successes, coinciding with the Renaissance and Reformation, were believed both to exemplify the effectiveness of a brutal, Islamic 'slave state' and to signal the wrath of an angry Christian God, perhaps even heralding the advent of the Last Days. For some observers, the Ottomans, with their ferocious gunpowder infantry, were poised to overrun Europe; for others, they were temporary squatters on classical and sacred space, the redemption of which awaited only the will and unity of the monarchs of Christendom.[5] Still others saw the rich and successful empire as a land of opportunity, a potential wellspring for products, patronage, and power. These varying perspectives are reflected in the texts and imagery of the time (roughly the mid sixteenth to the later eighteenth century), complicating and lending nuance to the enduring message of the Ottomans as a threat to Christendom.

Methodology, Historiography, and Objectives

The Ottomans, as an element of the historiography of early modern Europe, often appear in two standard forms: the "empire," a continent-spanning but rather amorphous imperial entity that functioned as a military great power; and the "Turks," an embodied plurality that "threatened Christendom," but was ultimately domesticated, exoticized, and dominated by an ascendant Europe as the early modern era came to an end. What the Ottomans did to or with early modern Europe has traditionally been couched in terms of the words "impact" and "difference"; and those terms are a logical outcome of the language of early modern texts. Indeed, Ottoman rhetorics of power and sovereignty, like those of their imperial predecessors and European Christian rivals, highlighted difference and military supremacy. But if we turn to the ways in which the Ottomans and their neighbors in "Christendom" visualized and designated space, then we find a rather more complex picture, one that included permeable borders, overlapping interests, and shared societies.

The historiographic literature on both the Ottoman empire and Christian Europe's reception of the "Turk" has become increasingly rich in recent years through the contributions of Ottomanist historians and scholars of European history, literature, and art.[6] So, too, considerable interest has been

---

See also Walter Kaegi, "Initial Byzantine Reactions to the Arab Conquest," *Church History* 38.2 (June, 1969): 139–49, esp. 144–5.

[5] Anthony Grafton, "The Humanist as Reader," 180–211, in *A History of Reading in the West*, Guglielmo Cavallo and Roger Chartier, eds., Lydia Cochrane, trans. (Amherst: University of Massachusetts Press, 1997), 187, writes of the simultaneous Renaissance impulse both to "bring the ancient world up to date," and to "reconstruct it as it was."

[6] For example: Virginia Aksan and Daniel Goffman, eds., *The Early Modern Ottomans: Remappping the Empire* (Cambridge: Cambridge University Press, 2007); Gerald MacLean, *The Rise of Oriental Travel:*

generated on the question of Ottomans on the map, a field that for a long time was limited to the pioneering works of Tom Goodrich, Svat Soucek, and a few others.[7] The publication of J. B. Harley and David Woodward's magisterial *History of Cartography* (hereafter *HOC*), along with the staging of cartographic exhibitions such as the 2008 "European Cartographers and the Ottoman World, 1500–1750" at the Oriental Institute in Chicago, have provided textual and visual inspiration on this theme to a wide audience.[8] Nonetheless, much of the work currently available on representations of the "Turk" still tends to proceed in well-defined channels (from a focus in cartographic studies on Piri Reis and major European mapmakers on one hand, to the examination of select travel accounts, diplomatic reports, or 'national' dramas on the other). Thus there remains much to be said regarding the ways in which those residing in the Christian kingdoms of Europe imagined, narrated, and visualized the Ottomans, their sovereignty, and the spaces they possessed.

   This work attempts one segment of that larger project. It traces out some of the historical and literary sources for representations of the Ottomans, plotting the dissemination of visions of the "Turk" and perusing the complex matrix of borders, interactions, and identities through which European audiences visualized Ottoman territory. It delineates specific categories (war space, historical space, travel space, and sacred space) employed to inscribe the Ottoman empire on maps. It also presents the iconography of the "Turk" as displayed on maps, an iconography that painted the Ottomans, alternately and in combination, as commercial partners, epic warriors, and objects of ethnographic scrutiny, as well as marauding barbarians, heretics, and harbingers of the Antichrist. This study devotes particular attention to the image/text interface (that is, the relationship between images and the texts with which they were associated). That interface is especially important because early modern maps derived their characterizations of Ottoman space from the rhetorics and imagery of texts, and because maps often involve an intricate layering (or collage) of text and image derived from other works.[9] Just as there was no definitive border between Europe and Asia, or Islam and Christendom, in this era, so too there was no definitive boundary between the map itself and the texts that surrounded, inspired, or were inscribed upon it. Further, this book contributes to the burgeoning literature on 'Eastern' travel. As mapmakers enclosed the land and seascapes of the Ottomans within the

   English Visitors to the Ottoman Empire, 1580–1720 (Houndmills: Palgrave Macmillan, 2004); and Natalie Rothman, *Brokering Empire: Trans-imperial Subjects between Venice and Istanbul* (Ithaca, NY: Cornell University Press, 2012).

[7] Thomas D. Goodrich, *The Ottoman Turks and the New World: A Study of Tarih-i Hind-i Garbi and Sixteenth Century Ottoman Americana* (Wiesbaden: Otto Harrassowitz, 1990); and Svat Soucek, *Studies in Ottoman Naval History and Maritime Geography* (İstanbul: Isis Press, 2008).

[8] J. B. Harley and David Woodward, eds., *The History of Cartography,* [hereafter *HOC*], v. 1–3 (Chicago: University of Chicago Press, 1992–2007); Ian Manners, ed., with M. Pinar Emiralioğlu, *European Cartographers and the Ottoman World, 1500–1750: Maps from the Collection of O.J. Sopranos* (Chicago: Oriental Institute, 2010).

[9] Leonora Navari, "Gasparo Tentivo's Il Nautica Ricercato. The Manuscripts," 135–55, in *Eastern Mediterranean Cartographies*, George Tolias and Dimitris Loupis, eds. (Athens: Institute for Neohellenic Research, 2004), 138.

map frame, they displayed early modern notions of space measured in terms of cities, fortresses, pilgrimage sites, provisioning stations, and accessible or inaccessible routes. Mapping was thus intimately connected to travel, both actual and imaginary. It had its own logics of possession, movement, and frontiers. The traveler, along with the diplomat and other types of intermediaries, was the eyewitness, the authority invoked by the mapmaker to legitimate his vision of space. Finally, this book, as it examines the diffusion of images of the Ottomans, their sovereignty, their mores, and their armies, adds to the growing historiography on the circulation of knowledge and the translation of culture in the early modern Eurasian world.

It is also important here to state what this book does not do. I am a historian of the intersections between the Ottoman world and surrounding territories; I am neither a cartographer nor an art historian. Thus it is not my intention here to trace the evolution of maps of Ottoman territory or the technical details of map production and artistry. Those tasks have been accomplished or are being accomplished by experts elsewhere, in the *History of Cartography* and in the journal *Imago Mundi*, among other sources. Rather than sorting out the direction of cartographic influences, or precedence in discoveries of mapping technology, what I want to know is how mapmakers in different places embodied and circulated ideas of the Ottomans and Ottoman space, and what their images might tell us about their milieu, their audiences, and things such as state power, historic memory, identity, worldview, borders, the visualization of land and sea, and the exigencies of getting from place to place.[10]

The early modern era was indeed a time when the technologies of charting, engraving, and depicting the world's spaces were evolving and improving. But technological capability and scientific knowledge were only two factors in the complex intellectual, political, economic, historical, and pictorial process that was mapping.[11] Early modern maps, like the texts from which they derive, do not follow a strict evolutionary pattern in depicting the Ottomans and their empire; they are, rather, the products of tropes of narration and conventions of representation, the technical constraints of printmaking, and the knowledge, education, imagination, and demands of a consuming public that is notoriously difficult to pin down, except anecdotally. Most of all, I want to know what Ottoman space looked like to that public. In seeking that objective, I focus on the map itself and its narrative contexts to demonstrate the ongoing tensions over truth-claims and illustrate some of the ways in which Ottoman space was experienced and constructed. The tales of individual narrators do not, of course, substitute for a close examination of each one of the numerous interpretative communities affected by these maps: how they accepted, misunderstood, acted on, or ignored the messages of the map. But it may be hoped that the traveler witnesses employed here will speak in some

---

[10] That is, I was more interested in the essential contexts for maps described so eloquently by J. B. Harley, *The New Nature of Maps: Essays in the History of Cartography* (Baltimore: Johns Hopkins, 2001), 35–8.

[11] Peter Whitfield, *The Charting of the Oceans: Ten Centuries of Maritime Maps* (London: British Library, 1996), 46, 56–7, for example, notes the adherence to old templates, "legend and imagination," despite the acquisition of new knowledge.

small way for their own reading communities, whereas I leave the project of assessing audience reception in specific communities to other scholars.

Neither do I propose to trace out the extent of geographic knowledge in the Ottoman world or to present in any comprehensive way the literary and historical contexts out of which mapped images of the Ottomans emerged. A database of cartographic literary allusions grouped by time and region would be a wonderful thing; but it is beyond my capabilities. What I hope to accomplish, rather, is a comparative commentary on the modes and types of representation of Ottoman space deriving from some of the Christian kingdoms of Europe. I place before the reader an array of mappings of the Ottomans (particularly those spaces on the European 'side' of the empire) in hopes that they will provoke discussion and refine and expand our sense of the ways in which the Ottomans were imagined and imagined themselves. This material is purposefully selected to range widely, unconstrained by strict chronology or 'national' designation. It crosses genres to present a mix of imagery of the "Turk," similar, perhaps, to that an educated reader might be exposed to. I hope thereby to illustrate the ways in which the map layered historical time and manipulated space, suggest those forms of representation that were enduring and those that were exceptional, and, further, propose that the mappings of the sixteenth and eighteenth century worlds were not as dramatically different as they might sometimes seem.[12]

This volume is divided into three parts comprising seven chapters plus an afterword. Part One (Chapters 1 and 2) sets the stage by addressing methodology, approach to space and time, categories of analysis, genres of mapping the "Turk," and the processes by which the Ottomans were made familiar to audiences in the Christian kingdoms of Europe. This first chapter serves as an introduction. It suggests a set of categories by which Ottoman space was understood and introduces some of the possibilities for comparisons to Ottoman self-mapping. It emphasizes the ways in which time and space were collapsed on early modern maps in order to convey political and cultural messages of entitlement and identity. Chapter 2, on "Reading and Placing the 'Turk,'" introduces some of the genres employed for mapping the Ottomans and speaks (through a set of illustrative examples) about the ways the Ottomans were represented and translated into text and image. It also addresses questions of the circulation of knowledge. Part Two (Chapters 3, 4, and 5) presents the mapping of Ottoman space in terms of borders, fortresses, and the iconography of triumph and submission. Chapter 3 is divided into three sections, which address conceptions of the ends of empire; the transimperial borders among the Ottoman, Hapsburg, and Venetian empires; and, finally, the roles played by Constantinople and the Holy Land as annexes of Europe and focal points for prophecy in mapping the division of "Christian" and "Turk" space. Chapter 4 examines the fortress (inland and coastal) as

---

[12] David Woodward, "Cartography and the Renaissance: Continuity and Change," 3–24, in *HOC*, v. 3, pt. 1, *Cartography in the European Renaissance*, David Woodward, ed. (Chicago: University of Chicago Press, 2007), 12, 23, provides a typology of the ways in which the nature of European maps changed (or did not change) in the Renaissance era, noting that the timing of changes varied from place to place in Europe. He lays out the arguments against any simple "progressive" model of mapmaking (6–7).

the quintessential marker of space and sovereignty, employing examples concentrated in the late sixteenth and early seventeenth centuries. The fortress was the centerpiece of possessed space and of the competition for hegemony in the transimperial zone linking the Ottoman, Venetian, and Hapsburg empires. Chapter 5 continues the examination of conflict imagery in historical texts and map imagery. Possession was counted not only in fortresses but also in images of the conquered foe, his head, his body, his arms, and his symbols. The fallen Turk, deployed on the map, delivered a powerful message of ownership. Part Three (Chapters 6 and 7) elaborates on the literatures and imagery of travel along with the various authorities invoked in an attempt to demonstrate the 'accuracy' and 'truth' of mapped space. Chapter 6 presents the stages by which travelers and maps charted the movement into and out of Ottoman space. This chapter highlights the journeys from Vienna and Venice to Istanbul by land and sea and illustrates the modes and measures by which Ottoman space was counted. Chapter 7 addresses the threefold foundation of authority (knowledge, text, and eyewitness testimony), used by travelers and transposed onto the map to certify the validity of descriptions of Ottoman domains. The knowledge and texts of 'classical' and Biblical pasts were front and center in the imagery of the early modern era. They constituted its history and memory. In this chapter, narratives by Italian and English travelers will be featured and then juxtaposed to the well-known travel narrative of the Ottoman raconteur Evliya Çelebi.[13] Additionally, in this chapter, I will use travelers' descriptions of women and their dress as a special element of claims to authority. By way of conclusion, the "Afterword" (Chapter 8) will take up some of the implications of mapping space and identity that have traced through both the volume and the historiography of Ottoman–European relations and that find resonance in both world-historical paradigms and contemporary world struggles.

Designations of Space

This work is about mapping Ottoman space. I employ the term *space* as an alternative to *territory*, because I want to suggest the Ottoman realm (conceptualized by early modern peoples) as a place imbued with attendant identities, cultures, and historical contexts, all of which could be enclosed within the map frame.[14] Ottoman space, in the European (and Ottoman) imagination, was not simply a block of territory circumscribed on a map. It was a place entangled in a set of histories and competing claims dating back to creation. It was full of peoples, faiths, languages, occupations, and cultural mores that transcended political reality, or endured as carefully preserved

---

[13] Italian and English travelers were certainly not alone, nor was actual travel a necessity, as Tom Conley, *The Self-Made Map: Cartographic Writing in Early Modern France* (Minneapolis: University of Minnesota Press, 1996), 135, has aptly noted.

[14] This is not to argue that "territory," a term that I employ as well, is not conceptually complex. Stuart Elden, *The Birth of Territory* (Chicago: University of Chicago Press, 2013), 7, speaks of "territory" as "a word, a concept, and a practice"; also as "a distinctive mode of social/spatial organization, one that is historically and geographically limited and dependent... (10)." In his discussion of early modern conceptualizations, highlighting the work of Gottfried Leibnitz (1646–1714), he focuses on "legal–political power" and the articulations of sovereignty (315–20).

artifacts of cherished past lives. Further, Ottoman space was not limited to those lands where the sultan's armies could readily be deployed. It included lands claimed by the sultan. It comprised those adjacent places where the threat of Ottoman arms held (or seemed to hold) sway. Nor was it limited to *terra firma*, including as it did the seascapes of the Mediterranean, Aegean, Adriatic, Black, and Red Seas onto which Ottoman power was projected. The notion of Ottoman space then presumes the sultan's domains as a complex form of possession and identity, dependent not entirely on what was actually there but also on what was imagined, remembered, depicted, hoped for, and then visualized in textual and pictorial sources such as maps and travel accounts.[15]

The idea of Ottoman space is complicated by terminologies of place and identity that defy the drawing of borders. The borders of Europe, in the early modern imagination, as we shall see in Chapter 3, ranged over a broad territory, despite what the continental divisions of ancient geographies or the national boundaries of contemporary atlases might suggest. Christendom and Europe on one hand, and Islam and Asia on the other, were not coincident. And finding precise terminology for designating Ottoman space in Europe is a vexed process and one with a long history. That dilemma is reflected in early modern European cartographic usage, which came to employ the designations "Turkey in Asia" and "Turkey in Europe" to suggest its own uncomfortable relationship to the cross-continental territorial holdings of the Ottoman sultans. I have used here (rather broadly) the terminology "Balkans" and "Greco-Balkan peninsula" to describe those European territories into which the Ottomans expanded and in which they operated in the fifteenth to eighteenth centuries.[16] That usage is a geographic convenience employed to avoid the repeated recitation of individual regions. But it fails to reflect the complex relationships among sovereign (or not so sovereign) lords, or among inland, coastal, and island territories. I cannot resolve these ambiguities of designation in any comprehensive way. "Europe" remains a term that designates continental space, with Constantinople as its evident eastern outpost, "before Asia."[17] And in this study I will employ that term because it is customary and familiar to denote the location from which 'outside' observers in the Christian kingdoms characterized the sultan and his territories. But the Ottoman empire was as European as it was Asian; its heartland and signature province, Rumelia, lay in Europe.

Another problem of designation resides in the fact that the territories of Europe were no more entirely Christian than the territories of Anatolia or Syria or Egypt were entirely Muslim, or Turk, as European sources of the

---

[15] For a discussion of some elements of the "spatial turn" in history, see Charles Withers, "Place and the 'Spatial Turn' in Geography and in History," *Journal of the History of Ideas* 70.4 (October, 2009): 637–58, esp. 648–9, on history as "mapping," and 656–8. Withers nonetheless points out the complexity and "metaphysical imprecision" of the usage of the terms "space" and "place" (637).

[16] Maria Todorova, *Imagining the Balkans* (New York: Oxford University Press, 1997), 21–37.

[17] See Norman Davies, *Europe: A History* (Oxford: Oxford University Press, 1996), 27–8, 44. Although pointing out that East and West in Europe were categories most durably based on the line between Catholic and Orthodox Christianity, he also notes that "In more modern times there is the Ottoman line, which marked off the Balkan lands which lived for centuries under Muslim rule (27)."

era might describe them. Ottoman sources customarily employed a we/they distinction: the "well protected domains" of the sultan as opposed to the "lands of the Christian kings." This juxtaposition separated the empire from the polities of European enemies and allies alike without suggesting that the whole continent of Europe was somehow necessarily "Christian." That division of space, relying on sovereignty rather than communal identity, is a useful one because it includes all those people (and readers) resident under either Ottoman rule or that of the Christian kingdoms. It takes up the enduring minorities (such as the Jews of Europe or Anatolia), that seem to be precluded in designations such as "Christendom" and "Islam," highlighting instead the communally legitimized power structures to which majority and minority populations alike were subject.

Time/Periodization

Various scholars have tried to periodize the representational relationship of the kingdoms of Christian Europe to the Ottoman empire. Some, such as Lucette Valensi, see European authors as moving by the turn of the seventeenth century from the vision of the Terrible Turk to a rather admiring notion of the Ottoman empire as a well-organized and efficient form of government.[18] A related notion, articulated by Joan Pau Rubiés, is that the depiction of the East in the seventeenth century became more systematic, more scientific, and more "secular."[19] Other commentators, such as Mustafa Soykut, argue that the Ottomans were domesticated in the European imagination, particularly after the death of Sultan Süleyman I in 1566, the Christian victory at the Battle of Lepanto in 1571, and the advent of the English in the Ottoman Mediterranean around 1580.[20] Conventions of representation, however, do not necessarily, or readily, transform in response to political changes, battles, or commercial developments. The ways in which the Ottomans were mapped in any period might thus have as much to do with aesthetic tastes, ideological positions, available print models, consumer demand, conventions of labeling, or modes of looking as with any given political episode or any given advances in technologies of writing, commerce, travel, or mapping. More broadly, the whole notion of the early modern as an era that anticipates the ideas, state formations, and hegemons of the nineteenth century suppresses a set of very powerful continuities that tie the sixteenth, seventeenth, and even eighteenth centuries to the long medieval era that preceded them. The ways in which the Ottomans were mapped was inevitably conditioned by the pull of the past. The English advent in the Mediterranean, for example, was important to the English, and to their

---

[18] Lucette Valensi, *The Birth of the Despot: Venice and the Sublime Porte*, Arthur Denner, trans. (Ithaca, NY: Cornell University Press, 1993); and Jean Pierre Amalric, "Une géopolitique de bénédictin: la Turquie d'Europe dans la Géographie historique de Dom Vaissète (1755)," 359–74, in *Byzance et ses périphéries: Hommage à Alain Ducellier* (Toulouse: Université Toulouse, 2004), 366, 372–3.

[19] Joan-Pau Rubiés, *Travel and Ethnology in the Renaissance: South India through European Eyes, 1250–1625* (Cambridge: Cambridge University Press, 2000), 388–91. But science had to contend with the known and remembered layers of history. And the "secular" retained at least a very healthy measure of the sacred.

[20] Mustafa Soykut, *Image of the "Turk" in Italy* (Berlin: Islamkundliche Untersuchungen, 2001).

competitors. But its significance has been greatly magnified by the much later ascent of that nation to the position of world seapower, and by the extensive scholarship on both the English mercantile investment in Asia and the English literary imagination of the 'East.'[21]

That said, the death of Süleyman, the Battle of Lepanto,[22] the founding of the English "Turkey" Company,[23] and cartographic innovations did all play important roles in the familiarization of Europe with the Turk. Indeed, *familiarity* (how it happened and what form it took) is perhaps *the* key concept in establishing a periodization for European representation of the Ottomans.[24] Although the Ottomans were certainly "domesticated" for European readers (or viewers) by the seventeenth century, that domestication was already well under way by 1548. And it was accomplished not simply through a rather ephemeral naval victory but through a blizzard of news and imagery that had already reached stunning proportions by 1571. In many ways the Ottomans were familiar to some European audiences long before Lepanto. That familiarity derived in part from a complex network of commercial and cultural relationships that spanned the Afro-Eurasian oikumene and predated the Ottomans.[25] It drew on the medieval constructions of the Muslim conquerors who were the Ottomans' antecedents. And it added new variants to the representational corpus as events, audience, and situation demanded and as narrative and visual modes allowed.

These demurrals are not meant to argue that there can be no logical periodization for early modern European mapping of the Ottomans. Indeed, that mapping was characterized increasingly by a movement from regional to state designation; a complementary movement to the marking of borders of various sorts; the employment of ethnographic vignettes; a willingness to

---

[21] Constance Relihan, *Cosmographical Glasses: Geographic Discourse, Gender, and Elizabethan Fiction* (Kent, OH: Kent State University Press, 2004), 45, links Lepanto to the notion of a turning point but also suggests the continuity in England of the consciousness of Ottoman threat. See also Nabil Matar, *Islam in Britain, 1558–1685* (Cambridge: Cambridge University Press, 2004).

[22] On Lepanto, see Niccolo Capponi, *Victory of the West: The Great Christian–Muslim Clash at the Battle of Lepanto* (Cambridge, MA: da Capo, 2008); and Andrew Hess, "The Battle of Lepanto and Its Place in Mediterranean History," *Past and Present*, 57 (November, 1972): 53–73. See also Palmira Brummett, "The Lepanto Paradigm Revisited: Knowing the Ottomans in the Sixteenth Century," 63–93, in *The Renaissance and the Ottoman World*, Anna Contadini and Claire Norton, eds. (Farnham, Surrey: Ashgate, 2013); John Guilmartin, *Gunpowder and Galleys: Changing Technology and Mediterranean Warfare at Sea in the Sixteenth Century* (Cambridge: Cambridge University Press, 1980), 221–52; and Halil İnalcık, "Lepanto in the Ottoman Documents," 185–92, in *Il Mediterraneo nella seconda metà del '500 alla luce di Lepanto*, Gino Benzoni, ed. (Florence: Leo S. Olschki, 1974).

[23] On the English "discovery" of the Mediterranean, see, for example, Archer, *Old Worlds*, 3; and MacLean, *The Rise of Oriental Travel*. This is an era that Daniel Vitkus, *Turning Turk: English Theater and the Multicultural Mediterranean, 1570–1630* (New York: Palgrave, 2003), 21, has called "a period of intensive intelligence-gathering" by the English on the Mediterranean and the Ottomans.

[24] Bronwen Wilson, *The World of Venice: Print, the City, and Early Modern Identity* (Toronto: University of Toronto Press, 2005), 147, has argued, rightly, that the Ottomans were "too familiar to be made exotic." See also Deborah Howard, "Cultural Transfer between Venice and the Ottomans in the Fifteenth and Sixteenth Centuries," 138–77, in *Cultural Exchange in Early Modern Europe*, v. 4, *Forging European Identities, 1400–1700*, Heinz Schilling and István György Tóth, eds. (Cambridge: Cambridge University Press, 2006); and Gerald MacLean and William Dalrymple, eds. *Re-orienting the Renaissance: Cultural Exchange with the East* (London: Palgrave, 2005).

[25] See Palmira Brummett, *Ottoman Seapower and Levantine Diplomacy in the Age of Discovery* (Albany: SUNY Press, 1994).

recognize the sovereignty of the Ottomans on the body of the map (in addition to its acknowledgment in legend or captions); the characterization of the sultan as analogous to European Christian rulers; greater sophistication in the depiction of fortresses and troops; enhanced claims (based on increased volume of contact) to the "latest" and most "scientific" knowledge in narrating the Ottomans; and the utilization of more advanced technologies of print and measurement.[26] The mapping of Ottoman space might also be characterized as moving from what was in part a medieval pilgrim mode to a later seventeenth century connoisseur mode, although the latter did not preclude the former.[27]

This study thus does assume a certain logic of beginning and ending points. I have chosen, somewhat arbitrarily, 1548 as a beginning date, the year in which the maps of Giacomo Gastaldi of Piedmont (fl. c. 1544–66), cosmographer of the Venetian republic, were published in a new and revised edition of Ptolemy's geography.[28] Gastaldi was a notable figure in the production of cartographic visions of the Ottoman world. And Venice was (as Levantine commercial emporium and translator par excellence of things Ottoman to the rest of Europe) the preeminent center for the circulation of such visions. Although it is clear that the evolution of mapping was a slow and intricate process, it is also the case that the second half of the sixteenth century was a time in which the mapping of Ottoman space geared up and the circulation of images of the Ottomans flourished in tandem with the expansion of both the empire and print.

As for an end point, Napoleon's 1798 invasion of Egypt and the European project of translating the East that it helped launch are often employed as a fitting beginning for both the "modern" Middle East and the "modern" consumption in Europe of knowledge about the "Orient." But the production of the monumental *Description de l'Egypte* (published in 1809) may well be a more suitable transition point for the history of mapping than Napoleon's invasion is for a new era of Middle Eastern political history. Closer to the center of Ottoman power, the treaty of Küçük Kaynarca signaling Russia's victory in the 1768–74 Russo–Ottoman war and the reform period of sultan Selim III (r. 1789–1807) have also been employed to map modernity onto Ottoman space.[29] Nonetheless, I have chosen a rather different theater

---

[26] Michael Biggs, "Putting the State on the Map: Cartography, Territory, and European State Formation," *Comparative Studies in Society and History*, 41.2 (April, 1999): 374–405, see 380, suggests that although "the basic principles and technique of cartography," were established by the early sixteenth century, "fundamental change would come only in the late twentieth century..." The pace and benchmarks of change are contested, but the subordination of science to story is ongoing.

[27] This notion derives in part from Edward Chaney, *The Evolution of the Grand Tour: Anglo–Italian Cultural Relations since the Renaissance* (London: Frank Cass, 1998), xvi, characterizing transformations in the modes of early modern English travel.

[28] Robert Karrow, *Mapmakers of the Sixteenth Century and Their Maps: Bio-bibliographies of the Cartographers of Abraham Ortelius, 1570* (Chicago: Newberry Library, 1993), 216, 246. Gastaldi was associated with Giovanni Battista Ramusio and produced maps for his *Delle Navigationi et Viaggi*, 1550–56, the model for other later European collections of voyages (227). See also David Woodward, "The Italian Map Trade, 1480–1650," 773–803, in *HOC*, v. 3, pt. 1, 781–91, on Gastaldi and Venetian successors.

[29] See Virginia Aksan, *Ottoman Wars, An Empire Besieged 1700–1870* (New York: Longman, 2007), 129–79; and Karl Roider, Jr., *Austria's Eastern Question, 1700–1790* (Princeton, NJ: Princeton

of mapping and war for my end point: the Ottoman conflicts with Austria (1788–91) under Joseph II and Russia (1787–92) under Catherine the Great. That great transimperial struggle, with its battlegrounds at Danube and Dniester, its transcontinental implications, and its backdrop the paroxysm of the French Revolution, provoked a surge of cartographic endeavor in Christian Europe on the scope of war and the necessity of new constructions of the "world." The "new" and the "news" were always an important element of the articulation of early modern mapping, as we shall see; but the decade of the 1780s produced its own variations on that consciousness.[30] And the war was one, as Karl Roider puts it, in which "there was hardly a hint of the old cry of gathering the Christians to strike the Moslems."[31]

Even so, the cartographic visions of the later eighteenth century, despite their claims to novelty and a clearer sense of the expansive nature of the world and its cultures, did not disown the past. Between 1783 and 1790, Thomas Stackhouse, in London, published four editions of his *New Universal Atlas:*

> *consisting of a complete set of maps, elegantly engraved and colored, peculiarly adapted to illustrate and explain ancient and modern geography; in which the ancient and present divisions, as also the subdivisions, of countries and various names of places, are exhibited to the eye at one view, distinctly and correctly, on opposite pages, the several parts of the earth, which were originally peopled by the descendants of Noah, pointed out expressly, and the geography of the Old and New Testaments rendered clear and perspicuous The Whole Being Particularly Suited to Facilitate the Study of Geography; To make that Science more generally known; and thereby the Knowledge of History, both Ancient and Modern, much more useful, instructive, and pleasant.[32]*

Those who wished to study and perfect history and geography needed to see the living traditions of the ancient and the Biblical stamped onto the expansive territories of the globe. Thus Stackhouse used ancient divisions and peoples, along with colored maps, to illuminate the current situation of the world. In that regard, his atlas echoed the new Venetian edition of Ptolemy that appeared in 1548.

Proclaiming itself "truly no less useful than necessary," that 1548 edition included "the usual antique and modern" plates, but boasted the addition of "an infinite number of modern names, of cities, provinces, castles, and other places, accomplished with the greatest diligence by the aforementioned

---

University Press, 1982), 135–96. When Austria planned to seize the Bukovina (which the Ottomans claimed) in 1774, the Austrian internuncio, Thugut, requested maps and information on the region, arguing that the Ottoman ministers "possess not the slightest knowledge of geography (147)." In 1786, the Hapsburg officer Wenzel Brognard "journeyed from Constantinople to Vienna via the Danube, mapping and describing Turkish military installations along the way (177)."

[30] Adrian Johns, *Piracy: The Intellectual Property Wars from Gutenberg to Gates* (Chicago: University of Chicago Press, 2009), 49–50, on the eighteenth century (in England). But my choice of periodization here is more concerned with transformations of scale and style and with enduring rhetorical continuities.

[31] Roider, *Austria's Eastern Question*, 179.

[32] T. Stackhouse, *A New Universal Atlas*, 2nd ed. (London: For Mrs. Stackhouse, 1785), title page.

Mr. Giacomo Gastaldi."[33] The modern was thus an adaptation of the ancient for both Gastaldi and Stackhouse, not a replacement. The true, the accurate, and the unusual constituted the rhetorical foundations for claims to the customer's attention and money, whereas "divisions," "names," "cities," and "castles" were the irreplaceable components of the mapmaker's art.

Thus, 1548 and the 1780s seem fitting temporal brackets for our consideration of the cartographic vision of early modern Ottoman space. And a fitting counterpart to Gastaldi's new map of Anatolia (presented as a transnational region rather than Ottoman sovereign territory) might be F.I. Maire's 1788 *"Carte générale des Limites entre les trois Empires,"* a Viennese map that demonstrated the expansive boundaries of war and the diminishing power of the Ottomans in the transimperial space (Figs. 1.1 and 1.2).[34] Maire's map traces the changes in imperial borders and power from the 1718 Treaty of Passarowitz (a major juncture in the Ottomans' struggle for supremacy with Hapsburg Austria) to the combat of the "present war." It provides an example of the complex and technical sorting out of imperial space and of eighteenth-century attempts to fix 'national' boundaries. But its modern, scientific qualities do not preclude its recycling the iconographies of the past. The sultans, after all, remained the self-described successors of Alexander and of the Byzantines.[35] They had conquered the "Holy Land" and "Rome." Maire's cartouche thus showed the Hapsburg eagles tearing apart the empire's turban and breaking its bow, to leave no doubt who represented the new Rome.

Layers of History

Early modern maps displayed space through a process of selecting from among available associations with the present or with proximate and distant pasts. Thus Ottoman cities, throughout our period, were mapped both as the sites of current events and as the cities of the Greeks and Latins, of Strabo, Pliny, and Mela, the "ancient *auctoritates,*" as Roger Chartier has noted, who were "continually cited and tirelessly commented upon."[36] The

---

[33] Giacomo Gastaldi, *La Geografia di Claudio Ptolomeo Alessendrino* (Venetia: Gio.a Baptista Pedrezano, 1548), title page. See Karrow, *Mapmakers of the Sixteenth Century,* 220, 30/C. See also Conley, *The Self-Made Map,* 105–8; and on the circulation of Ptolemy's "expanded geographical order," Francesca Fiorani, *The Marvel of Maps: Art, Cartography, and Politics in Renaissance Italy* (New Haven, CT: Yale University Press, 2005), 85–9.

[34] F.I. Maire, "Carte générale des Limites entre les trois Empires et leurs variations successives depuis l'année 1718 jusqu'à ce jour, ou Théâtre de la Guerre présente, Vienna, 1788," British Library, Maps K.Top. 113.34.a.11[Roll].

[35] Mr. C. [Henri Abraham Chatelain], *Atlas Historique, ou Nouvelle Introduction à l'Histoire, à la Chronologie & à la Géographie Ancienne & Moderne; Représentée dans de Nouvelles Cartes, Ou l'on remarque l'établissement des Etats & Empires du Monde, leur durée, leur chûte, & leurs differens Gouvernemens; La Chronologie des Consuls Romans, des Papes, des Empereurs, des Rois & des Princes, &c. qui ont été depuis le commencement du Monde, jusqu'à présent: Et la Généalogie des Maisons Souveraines de l'Europe,* 3rd ed., v. 4 (Amsterdam: Chez L'Honore & Chatelain, 1739), first published in 1705, makes these connections in a series of charts and a fold-out map (stretching from Spain to Iran) that place the Ottomans in the flow of imperial history and treat them as conquerors in a long list of conquerors.

[36] Roger Chartier, "Foucault's Chiasmus," 13–31, in *Scientific Authorship: Credit and Intellectual Property in Science,* Mario Biagiolo and Peter Galison, eds. (New York: Routledge, 2003), 16.

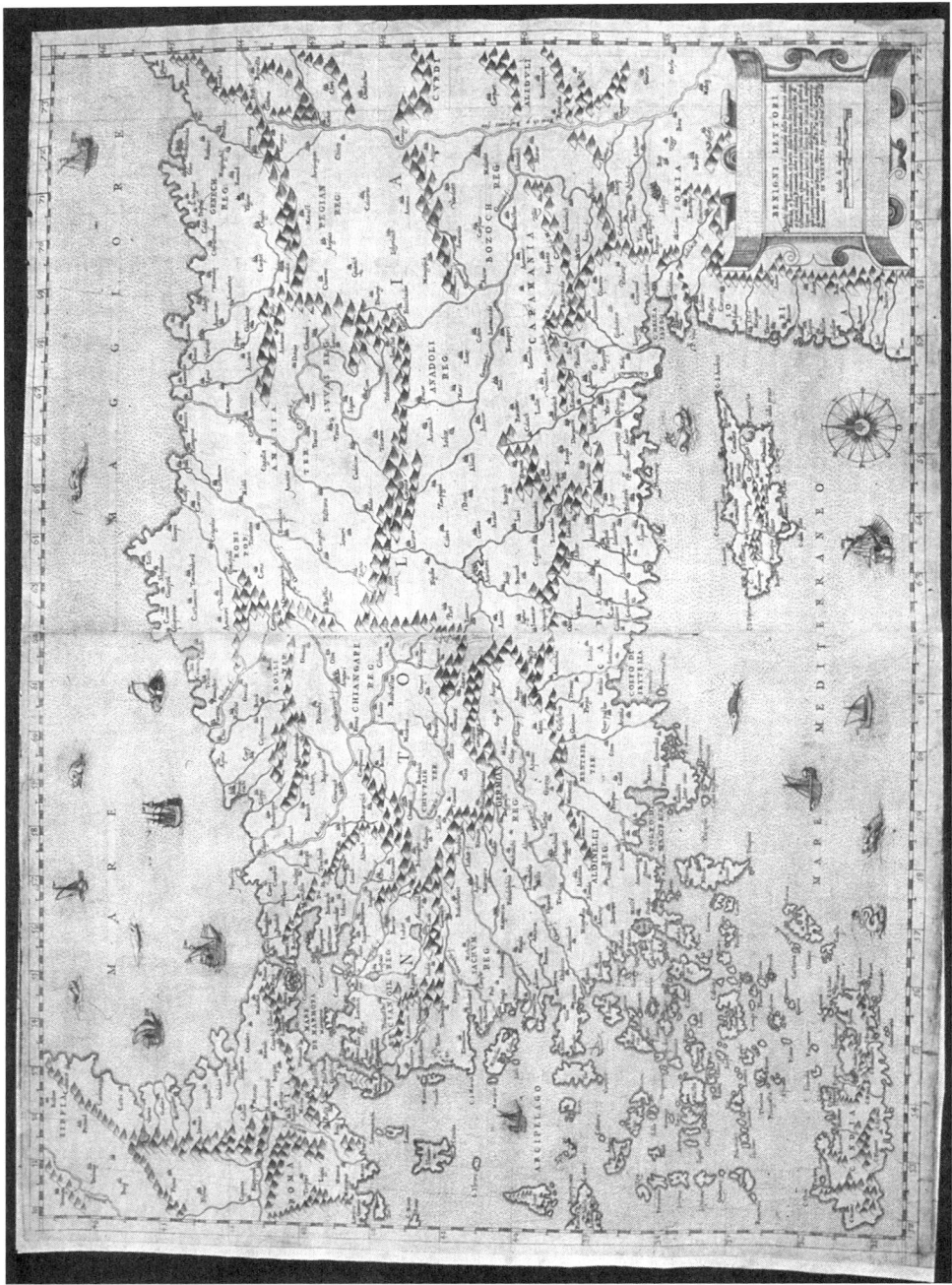

Figure 1.1. Giacomo Gastaldi, "Natolia," Venetia [1564, 1566]. Photo Courtesy of the Newberry Library, Chicago, Novacco 4F 377.

Figure 1.2. F.I. Maire, "Carte générale des Limites entre les trois Empires et leurs variations successives depuis l'année 1718 jusqu'à ce jour, ou Théâtre de la Guerre présente," cartouche, Vienna, 1788. The British Library Board, Maps K.Top. 113.34.a.11. (See color plate)

layers of the past also certified imperial claims to territory. The Venetian cartographer Vincenzo Coronelli (1650–1718), for example, charted the space stretching from Negroponte to Constantinople in a 1696 map entitled "Parallello Geographico Dell'Antico Col Moderno Archipelago" (Figs. 1.3 and 1.4).[37] The legend tells us that the map is intended for "instruction" in the history of the islands of the Archipelago. Constantinople is marked with a list of historical "owners": Constantine, the Latins, Venice and France in 1204, and the "Turks" in 1453. It was not 'national' borders that were important here; rather it was a vision of expansive space, ultimate victory, and the layers of memory to which the Archipelago was inevitably attached.[38] History,

[37] Vincenzo Coronelli, "Parallello Geographico dell'Antico col Moderno Archipelago per Istruzione dell'Istoria dell'Isole contenute in esso," in *Isolario* [*dell'Atlante Veneto*] *descrittione geografico-historica, sacra-profana, antico-moderna, politica, naturale, e poetica...di tutte l'isole...del globo terracqueo...ornato di trecento-dieci tavole...in supplimento dei XIV volumi del Blaeu...,* v. 1 (Venetia: A spese dell'autore, 1696). On Coronelli, see Ermanno Armao, *Vincenzo Coronelli: Cenni sull'uomo e la sua vita* (Firenze: Libreria Editrice, 1944); the introduction to Vincenzo Coronelli, *Ships and Other Sort of Craft Used by the Various Nations of the World, Venice 1690*, Mario M. Witt, ed. and trans. (London: Francis Edwards, 1970), v–xiii; Denis Cosgrove, "Global Illumination and Enlightenment in the Geographies of Vincenzo Coronelli and Athanasius Kircher," 33–66, in *Geography and Enlightenment*, David Livingstone and Charles Withers, eds. (Chicago: University of Chicago Press, 1999); and Annette Gerstenberg, *Thomaso Porcacchis 'L'Isole piu famose del mondo,' Zur Text – und Wortgeschichte der Geographie im Cinquecento (mit Teiledition)* (Tübingen: Max Niemeyer Verlag, 2004), 58–9.

[38] Daniel Smail, *Imaginary Cartographies: Possession and Identity in Late Medieval Marseille* (Ithaca, NY: Cornell University Press, 1999), 59, has used toponyms among other evidence to illustrate the ways in which "people convey an image of the past in the confines of the present."

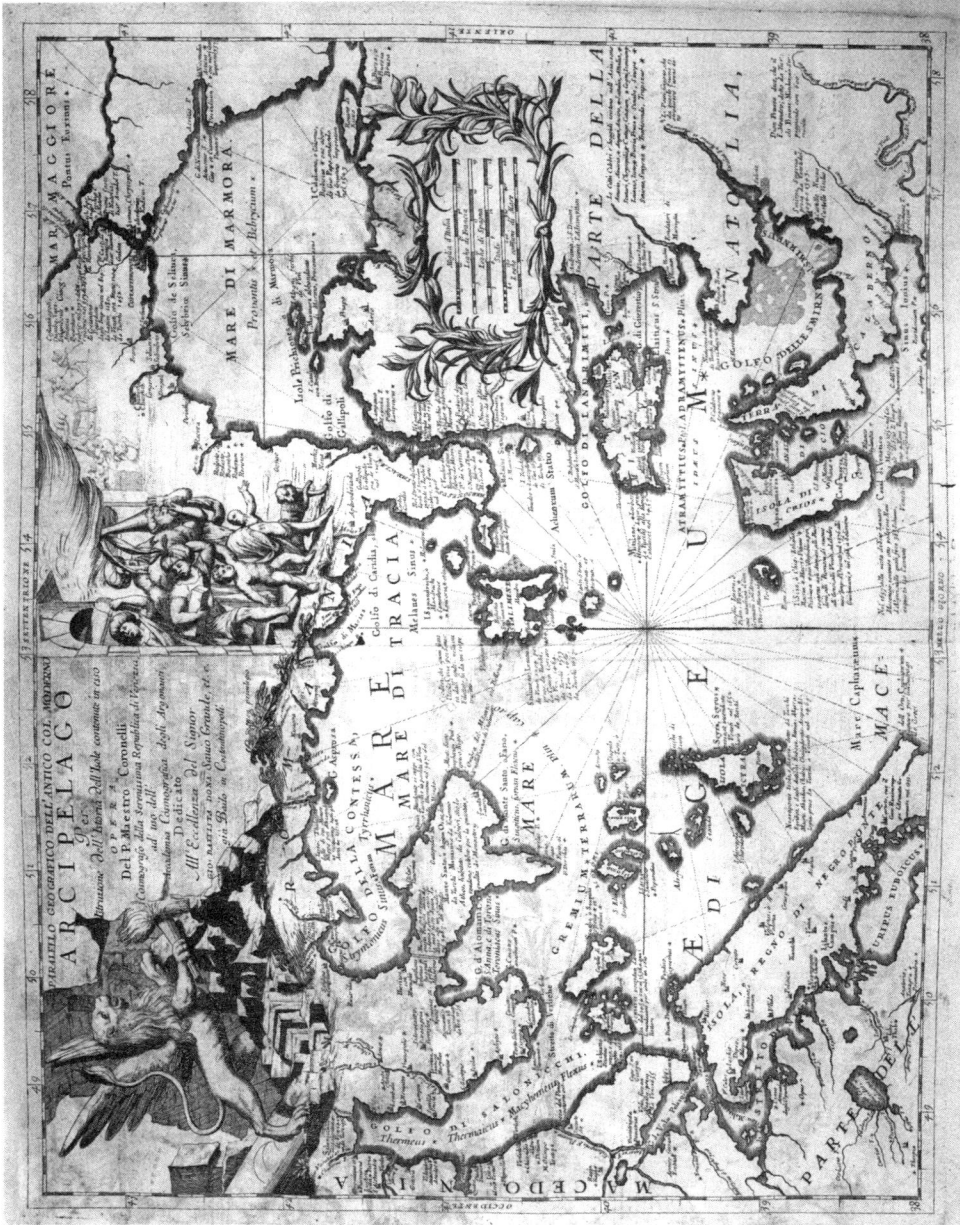

Figure 1.3. Vincenzo Coronelli, "Parallello Geographico Dell'Antico Col Moderno Archipelago," *Isolario [dell' Atlante Veneto]*, v. 1, Venetia, 1696. Photo Courtesy of the Newberry Library, Chicago, Vault Ayer 135.C8.

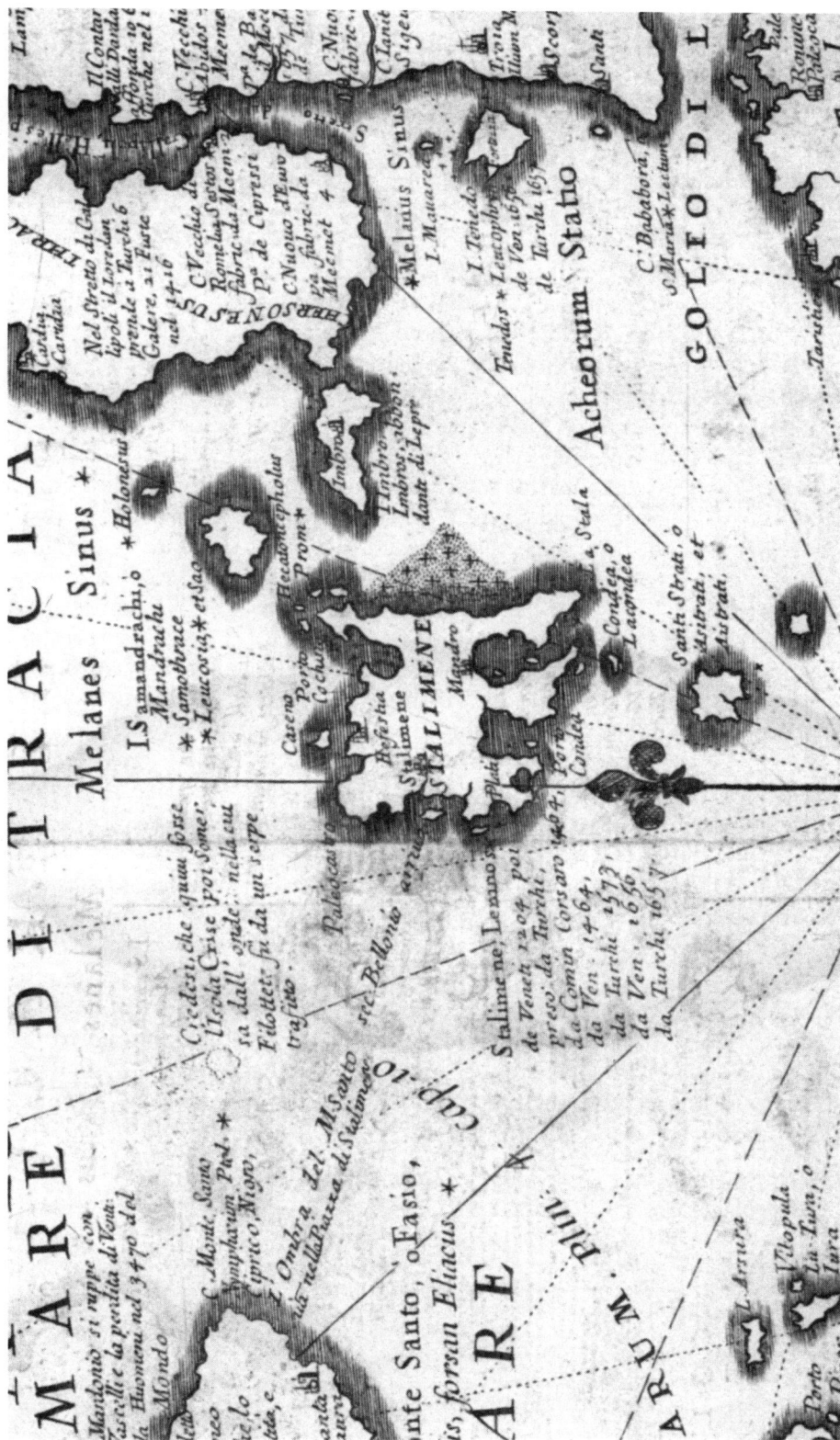

Figure 1.4. Vincenzo Coronelli, "Parallello Geographico Dell'Antico Col Moderno Archipelago," detail, *Isolario* [*del Atlante Veneto*], v. 1, Venetia, 1696. Photo Courtesy of the Newberry Library, Chicago, Vault Ayer 135.C8.

as Coronelli tells his readers in another context, is explained through the "collation of memories, both antique and modern."[39] And what better place to see that collation than on a map?[40]

Coronelli dedicated this particular map of the Archipelago to Giovanni Battista Dona, the Venetian bailo of Constantinople (resident ambassador and chief intermediary between the Venetian Signoria and the Ottoman Porte). It later appeared in an atlas of "the celebrated emporium of Venice," which was dedicated to the Holy Roman emperor Leopold I (r. 1658–1705), thus illustrating the transimperial options for patronage available to accomplished cartographers. In the atlas's dedication, the author imagines the Ottoman monarchy felled by the heavy blows of the emperor's sword. Having despoiled Asia, Africa, and Europe, and terrorized the West, the Ottomans, Coronelli suggested, would be subordinated to the "superior faith" of the emperor and his forces, who would restore to Christianity "all good things."[41] This claiming of the Archipelago as Christian space was impressed on the consciousness of the reader, not through physical lines but through a narrative of historical entitlement. The map harked back, as one Italian treatise in 1590 put it, to the imperial glories of the "ancient states already possessed in Asia and in Europe," which had to be "recovered for Christianity."[42]

And lest there be any doubt about the 'proper' associations for the Archipelago, history was inscribed onto Coronelli's seas through an elaborate system of legends on the body of the map. On the European side of the Straits of Gallipoli, a small text notes that it was in these waters that the Venetian commander Pietro "Loredano took from the Turks 6 *galere* and 21 *fuste* in 1416." And in the Aegean, northwest of the island of Stalimene, the sea is inscribed, "It is believed that here was the Island Crise [Chryse] later submerged under the waves; on which Filottete [Philoctetes] was stung by a serpent." The Archipelago of the present, with its Venetian–Ottoman struggle for supremacy, was thus rooted in the Archipelago of myth and history. So the mapmaker's waves restored Philoctetes and Chryse to the surface of the map. Coronelli was a scholar who prided himself on searching out the most up-to-date sources for his cartographic productions. But that inclination, even in the later seventeenth century, was never detached from the inclination to keep the past close at hand. The accuracy of his coasts was not more important to his audiences than the sense of place and attributions of "divine" right that his maps embodied.

[39] Vincenzo Coronelli, *Isola di Rodi geografica-storica, antica e moderna* (Venetia: n.p., 1702), "To the Reader," first unnumbered page.

[40] Woodward, "Cartography and the Renaissance," 4, 17, 23, proposes a phenomenon beginning in the 16th century by which contemporary and historical information were separated on the map, "favoring the idea that things represented in the map space should all have the same 'tense' (23)". Although that separation is clearly evident, I would suggest that it coexisted with an ongoing commingling of historical and contemporary space within the map frame.

[41] Coronelli, *Isolario*, 1696, v.1, unnumbered dedication pages 1–2.

[42] Gherardo Bergogni, *Le Discordie christiane le quali causarono la Grandezza di Cassa ottomana* (Bergamo: Comino Ventura, 1590), 1. See John Gillies, *Shakespeare and the Geography of Difference* (Cambridge: Cambridge University Press, 1994), 156–75, esp. 171, on the use of classical and Biblical references in the "new geography" of the Renaissance.

Various other artifacts suggest the role of the past in imagining the place of the Ottoman Turks in the 'Western' historic and geographic imagination. An unsigned mid-sixteenth century map, for example, shows a sea-based attack on a fortified port. This is the 1538 battle of Prevesa at the mouth of the Gulf of Artha on the western shore of the Greek peninsula. There the Ottomans, fighting for control of the Ionian islands, successfully battled a combined Christian fleet under the Genoese admiral Andrea Doria. The legend, in Italian, highlights what David Woodward calls the "storytelling role" of the map.[43] It informs the reader that this is the place where "at present one finds the navy of [Hayrettin] Barbarossa and that of the Christians" (Fig. 1.5).[44] Cannons roar and naked men leap from a burning ship into the water. The viewer can almost see the famous red-bearded Ottoman naval commander and hear the booming of the cannons. But the legend goes on to situate the map not only in the events of the time but also in the historic memory of its readers, showing these consumers where and how this space was important. This is the place, it reads, "called the Gulf of Artha; in ancient times it was called Ambracio da Ambra, the actual city of Pyrrhus, near the promontory of Actium where the memorable victory of Augustus over Marc Anthony and Cleopatra took place." Marc Anthony and Cleopatra, for the viewer, thus inhabit the same space as Barbarossa (c. 1478–1546). The Ottomans in this vision are one set of fragments in the kaleidoscope of rulers, battles, and ambitions that form the knowledge-picture of the reader.[45]

Space on the map, like time, was flexible. It had to be in order to facilitate the demands of historical consciousness and the need to see distant lands in their full measure of connectivity. In 1541 the Holy Roman Emperor, Charles V (r. 1519–56), lost his fleet in an effort to take Algiers and end the threat of Barbarossa to Spanish shipping in the Mediterranean. A map produced that same year visualizes the port-fortress of Algiers as lying in the back yard of Italy and Spain (Fig. 1.6).[46] The author notes this conscious distortion of space in the map's legend; it is a distortion that suggests a relationship. Algiers was a site where the history of Europe was being made. It was a site the emperor wanted to draw into the power sphere of the Hapsburgs. And it was a site of encounter with the "Turk," whose military successes mirrored those of Rome and confounded the continental division of the Christian and Islamic worlds. So the mapmaker drew Algiers in toward the coasts of Europe, demonstrating its potential for conquest by one 'side' or the other.

[43] David Woodward, "Cartography and the Renaissance," 16.

[44] Anon., "La dimostratione del luogo ... Artha," [c. 1538]. For a rather less dramatic Venetian map by Giovanni Camocio, see Ennio Concina and Elisabetta Molteni, *La fabrica della fortezza: L'architettura militare di Venezia* (Verona: Banco Popolare di Verona, 2001), 252.

[45] Vincenzo Coronelli, *Conquiste della Serenissima Republica di Venezia nella Dalmatia, Epiro, e Morea* (Venetia: 1686), second section, text on Prevesa, pages of volume unnumbered, described Prevesa as the place of the victory over Cleopatra and Marc Anthony, "the 723 year of the foundation of Rome, 29 years before the birth of Christ ... "

[46] A. S. [Antonio Salamanca], "Algeri," 1541. Spain had fortified Pignon islet in 1510; the city was taken by Aruj Barbarossa in 1516 and then controlled by his brother Hayrettin (Barbarossa). See Woodward, "Cartography and the Renaissance," 18, on proportion vs. exaggeration in Forlani's map of the siege of Algiers; and María Antonia Garcés, *Cervantes in Algiers: A Captive's Tale* (Nashville, TN: Vanderbilt University Press, 2002), 62–3.

Figure 1.5. The Battle of Prevesa. Anonymous, "La dimostratione del luogo . . . Artha" [n.p.], [c. 1538]. Photo Courtesy of the Newberry Library, Chicago, Novacco 2F 22.

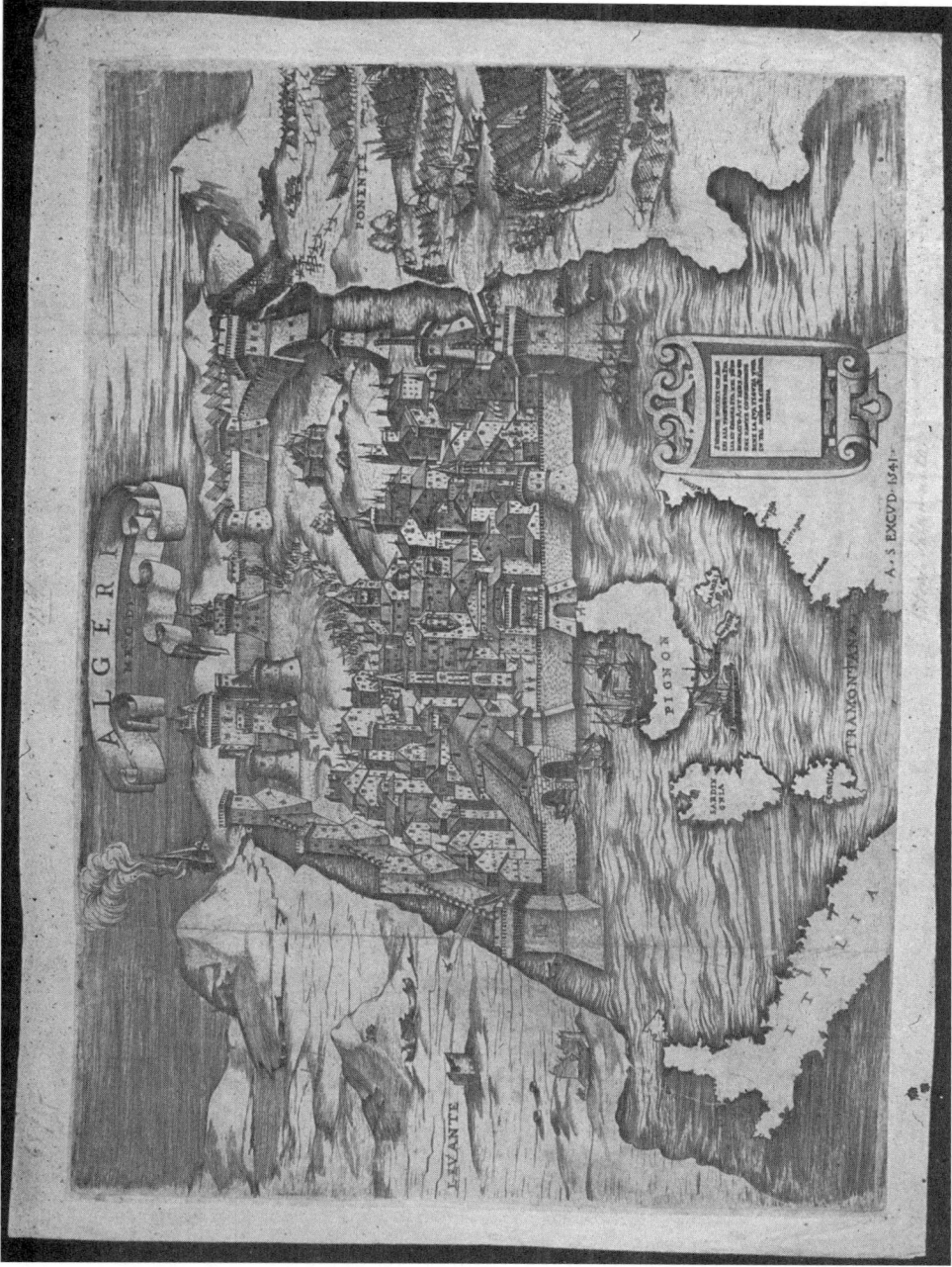

Figure 1.6. A. S. [Antonio Salamanca], "Algeri," [Rome], 1541. Photo Courtesy of the Newberry Library, Chicago, Novacco 2F 237.

Maps such as this one, even when detached from their written contexts, are inextricably linked to an enormous corpus of literature.[47] They flow naturally from texts and bend the visual conceptualizations of place to replicate the lines and distortions of narrative. Thus Algiers may be approximated to Sicily; or Vienna and Istanbul may be placed in the same horizontal plane so that viewers can better imagine the journey. Each map reveals the avenues by which European publics grasped and 'consumed' the Ottomans and their empire. The readers' universe of knowledge might stand unmentioned in the background of the map or it might take the form of elaborate textual explanations: for example, the transcriptions with iconographic and allegorical commentary that Coronelli produced for the six hundred textual cartouches on his terrestrial globe, or the "instructions and rationales" for their maps that Claude (1644–1720) and Guillaume (1675–1726) de l'Isle put forth in the *Journal des Sçavans*, a publication of the French Académie Royale des Sciences.[48] Even if the text on the body of the map was limited to a handful of place names, a whole universe of text and subtext was close at hand.[49] The image could not escape it.

Space Classified: Historical Space, Travel Space,

War Space, Sacred Space

Whether maps were inscribed with texts, embedded in texts, or detached from texts, they routinely conveyed impressions of history, travel, war, and the sacred. Those four categories were the primary and entangled prisms through which observers portrayed Ottoman space. History, as we have seen, served as an organizing principle for the reader's vision of the world. It was layered on the map like a set of transparencies placed one on top of the other. Travel was also a narrative mode that translated very directly onto the map. Although many maps presented space as static, many others indicated movement, the stages by which a traveler traced his or her way from one place to another. Many map legends cited the tales of individual travelers (ranging from the classical to the contemporary) as witnesses to the conditions, peoples, and geographies of the places depicted. History and travel were thus so tightly intertwined with the project of mapping, so ubiquitous in their presence, that they cannot be treated separately. (I will address them directly in Chapters 2, 6, and 7.) War and the sacred were also important categories

---

47 Similarly, Johan Verberckmoes, "The Imaginative Recreation of Overseas Cultures in Western European Pageants in the Sixteenth to Seventeenth Centuries," 361–80, in *Cultural Exchange in Early Modern Europe*, v. 4, 364, points out that European "festive culture," pageants, and their representations of "overseas people and cultures" .... "closely followed models of textual descriptions, often taken from travel journals...."

48 See Cosgrove, "Global Illumination and Enlightenment," 48; and Mary Pedley, *The Commerce of Cartography: Making and Marketing Maps in Eighteenth-Century France and England* (Chicago: University of Chicago Press, 2005), 166.

49 Emanuela Casti, *Reality as Representation: The Semiotics of Cartography and the Generation of Meaning* (Bergamo: Bergamo University Press, 2000), 9–10, 62, has written of the process of designation on maps in terms of an "intellectual appropriation of territory."

for mapping Ottoman space. War was mapped to embody strategy, chart events, and foster celebration. It served to certify kingly claims and establish a hierarchy of warrior states. But sacred spaces and the paths to them competed with conflict for attention on the map. As monarchs legitimized themselves through the invocation of an Abrahamic god, a crucial element of their sovereignty was the identification, possession, and protection of sacred space.

War Space

War was an old and large category in 'traditional' interpretations of the Ottomans. Geographical accounts of all sorts interspersed descriptions of Ottoman territory with accounts of the battles that took place there. In the European imagination, Ottoman space was war space (*dar ul-harb* in Ottoman parlance), including the land spaces of the Greco-Balkan peninsula and the sea spaces of the Aegean and Adriatic. Maps portrayed these two sites of conflict, focusing on the military ferocity of the Ottomans, but also on the points (ports and fortresses) where the "Christian" encountered the "Turk." These were the critical spaces that could signify the triumph of the Ottomans and a diminution of Christendom.

Sebastian Münster (1488–1552), in his 1544 *Cosmographia*, explicitly admired the discipline and soldierly qualities of the Ottomans: "nothing is more marvelous," he wrote, than their "speed in action, constancy in danger and obedience towards their empire."[50] That textual description of marvelous order was mapped in images of the Ottomans at war. In some representations of battle space the site itself was secondary to the image of Ottoman power. Ottoman armies were thus shown marching in undesignated space, an exemplary and fearsome force. The message of such images is one of control and obedience, echoing narrative portrayals of Ottoman troops as armies of "slaves," who would do anything to please their commanders.

In one such undated map, Antonio Lafreri (d. 1577) depicted the Ottoman army as Sultan Süleyman led his men on his last campaign in 1566 (Fig. 1.7). The caption suggests that both Muslims on the Ottomans' eastern frontiers and Christians to the west are the potential targets of this formidable force.

> *Order with which the Turkish army presents itself in the field against the Christians or the Persians. So splendid and industrious is it, that it can quickly mobilize, if need be, three or four hundred thousand persons, mostly cavalry...*[51]

---

[50] Matthew McLean, *The Cosmographia of Sebastian Münster: Describing the World in the Reformation* (Houndmills: Ashgate, 2007), 254–5, argues that Münster's "ethnographic passages betray the sixteenth-century European's fear of certain conquering races," but "the Turks, a very real contemporary are investigated in a more dispassionate and inquiring fashion" than for example the Huns.

[51] Antonio Lafreri, "Ordine con il quale l'esercito Turchesco suole presentarsi in Campagna contro de Christiani, o Persiani," Rome, 1566. Lafreri emigrated to Rome from France and set up as an engraver and print seller in 1544. See R. V. Tooley, "Maps in Italian Atlases of the Sixteenth Century, Being a Comparative List of the Italian Maps Issued by Lafreri, Forlani, Duchetti, Bertelli, and Others, Found in Atlases," *Imago Mundi*, 3 (1939): 12–47, esp. 12; Karrow, *Mapmakers of the Sixteenth Century*,

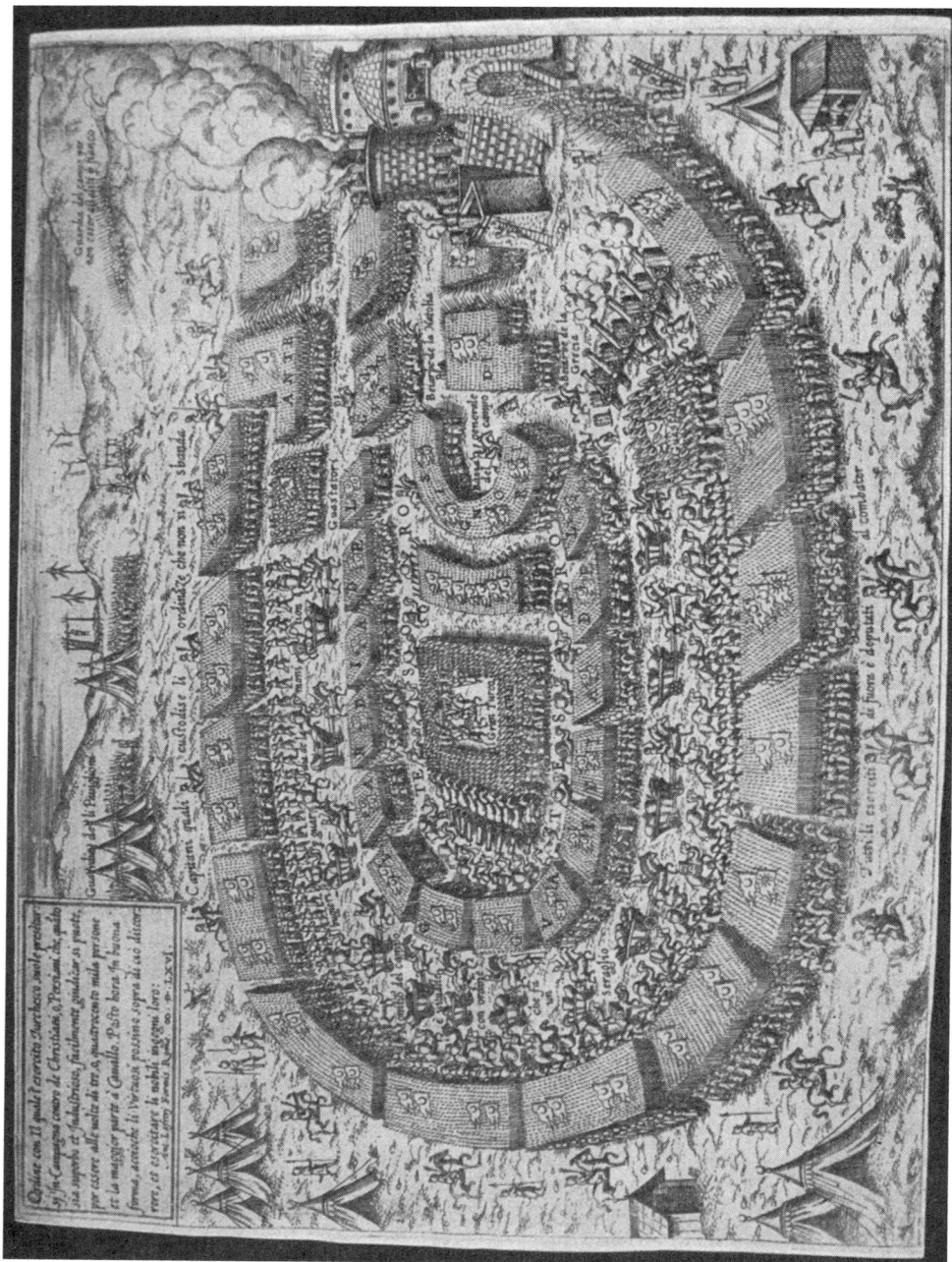

Figure 1.7. The Ottoman army. Antonio Lafreri, "Ordine con il quale l'esercito turchesco suole presentarsi in Campagna," Rome, 1566. Photo Courtesy of the Newberry Library, Chicago, Novacco 2F 48.

24

Christian observers, however, were primarily concerned with how far Ottoman armies might penetrate into Europe, and how many citadels they might attack on the way.[52] It was the mapmaker's task to show his audience that which it wished to "know and see," no matter the frisson of fear that such an image might generate.[53]

In other maps, specific place was critical to the viewer's vision of war. For example, the Ottoman siege of the Hungarian fortress of Sighetvar in 1566 galvanized the pens and brushes of Christendom. News maps invited the viewer to 'witness' the action. Thus the caption on another Lafreri map, printed in Rome (Fig. 1.8), reads

> *The true portrait of Zighet, with its castle, new fortress, marshes, lake, river, and bridge and other notable things indicated, [also] showing the "monte" (hill fortification) built by the Turks, and their assault.*[54]

This caption attempts to remind the viewer that he or she is receiving an up-to-date and "accurate" picture of the conflict with the "Turks" and its setting. Sighetvar was a centerpiece of this vision, one fortress in a chain of military installations that defined the borders between a Christian 'us' and a Muslim enemy (see Ch. 4). It was also central to the Ottomans' image of war space, the siege commemorated in multiple campaign miniatures to celebrate the glory of Ottoman arms (Fig. 1.9).[55]

Sea battles were also a favorite subject for the artists and mapmakers of Christian Europe.[56] The battle of Lepanto, which took place in the narrow channel connecting the Gulf of Patras to the Gulf of Corinth, on October 7, 1571, resulted in a victory for the combined fleets of Venice, the Holy League, and Don Juan of Austria, arrayed against the Ottoman fleet under Grand Admiral Müezzinzade Ali Pasha. Images of that victory spread swiftly to an audience eager for good news, with Venice, one of the major print capitals of Europe, spearheading the production of those images. The Venetian

230 n; and David Woodward, "The Italian Map Trade, 1480–1650," 773–803, in *HOC*, v. 3, pt. 1, 775–7.

[52] The legend on another map, "The Marvelous Order of the Grand Turkish Army," proposed that "for the delight of those who attempt to know and to see various and diverse things... no other thing supersedes the military order of the Grand Signor Turk:" "Il Meraviglioso Ordine de Gran Esercito Turchesco" [n.p., n.d.]. Rhoads Murphey, *Ottoman Warfare 1500–1700* (New Brunswick, NJ: Rutgers University Press, 1999), 6–7, has pointed out that Ottoman warfare could be "haphazard" as well as ordered.

[53] See David Buisseret, *The Mapmakers' Quest: Depicting New Worlds in Renaissance Europe* (Oxford: Oxford University Press, 2003), 47, 113–51.

[54] Antonio Lafreri, "La Vera ritratto de Zighet," Rome, 1566. M. Giulio Ballino, *De Disegnie delle Piu Illustri Città et Fortezze del Mondo* (Venetia: Bolognini Zaltieri, 1569), provides three different maps of Sighetvar. See also Jessica Maier, "A 'True Likeness': The Renaissance City Portrait," *Renaissance Quarterly* 65 (2012): 711–52, esp. 726, 730, 740, 748.

[55] On Ottoman commemorations of Sighetvar, see Emine Fetvacı, *Picturing History at the Ottoman Court* (Bloomington: Indiana University Press, 2013), 108–22, 136–7. See also Feridun Ahmet Bey, *Nüshet ül-Esrar ul-Ahbar fi Sefer-i Szigetvar*, Topkapı Saray-ı Müzesi [hereafter TKSM], H. 1339, fol. 40b–42a; and Géza Fehér, *Türkische Miniaturen aus den Chroniken der Ungarischen Feldzüge* (Budapest: Corvina Magyar Helikon, 1976), plates 38–42, which focuses on Ottoman frontiers. On Feridun Bey, who served on the Sighetvar campaign, see Feridun Ahmet, *Nüzhet-i Esrârü'l-Ahyâr Der-Ahbâr-ı Sefer-i Sigetvar: Sultan Süleyman'ın Son Seferi*, H. Ahmet Arslantürk and Günhan Börekçi, eds. (İstanbul: Zeytinburnu Belediyesi, 2012), 16–24, 54–5,72,116, 122–3.

[56] On the commemorations of Lepanto, see for example, Chew, *The Crescent and the Rose*, 125–33.

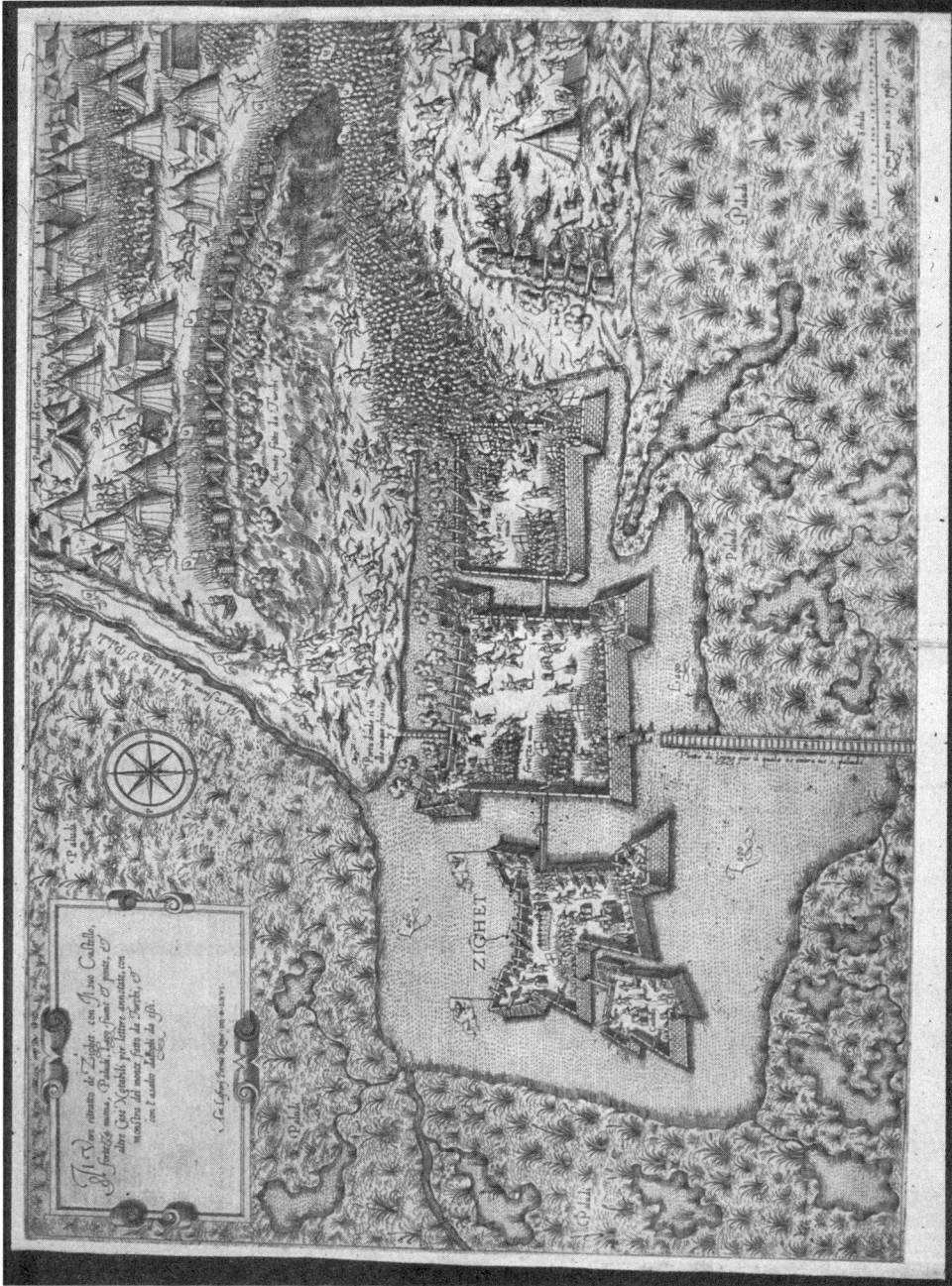

Figure 1.8. The Siege of Sighetvar. Antonio Lafreri, "Il Vero ritratto de Zighet," Rome, 1566. Photo Courtesy of the Newberry Library, Chicago, Novacco 4F 101.

Figure 1.9. Siege of Sighetvar. Seyyid Lokman, *Hünername (Book of Accomplishments)*, H. 1523, İstanbul, c. 1588. Topkapı Palace Museum, İstanbul. Photo Credit: Bridgeman-Giraudon/Art Resource, NY. (See color plate)

mapmaker Giovanni Camocio (c. 1501–75) captioned one image of Lepanto: "The true order of the two potent armadas, Christian and Turkish, as they approached to engage in battle" (Fig. 1.10).[57] Another image (not shown here) trumpeted "the success of the miraculous victory of the armada of the Christian Holy League against that of the most powerful and vainglorious prince of the Ottomans, Sultan Selim II" (r. 1566–74).[58] That characterization of arrogance was an elemental part of late sixteenth century images of the "Turk." His purported hubris fueled Christian hopes for his defeat, hopes that seemed to secure a divine answer in the Ottoman loss at Lepanto.[59]

These are conventional images: the Ottomans as a dominant military power threatening the kingdoms of the Christian kings and poised to wash over Christendom with a wave of unbelief that was temporarily turned aside by the victory at Lepanto. But images of battle and of armies on the march were only one of the multiple modes in which this enduring conflict was conceived. In both Ottoman and European mapping, war space might also be conveyed indirectly, as we shall see in later chapters, by allusion, by iconography, or via scenes of weapons, submission, and pageantry.

Sacred Space

From the point of view of Christian observers, Ottomans domains were littered with sacred sites: the birthplace of the Virgin Mary, the towns where Paul preached, and the peerless Jerusalem, center point of numerous medieval *mappaemundi*. The notion of a Holy Land (*Terra Sancta*) distorted the geographic construction of the edge of Europe and added a very particular historic layer to the mapping of Ottoman lands (see Ch. 3).[60] Some maps of Ottoman territory were produced specifically to adorn histories or geographies of ancient times. In other texts, however, temporal boundaries were purposefully blurred. The invocation of classical or Biblical space served to keep space timeless and recapture history for an early modern audience.[61]

---

[57] Giovanni Francesco Camocio, "Il vero ordine delle due potente armate...," Venice, 1571, map 38, in *Isole famose, porti, fortezze, e terre maritime, sotto poste alla Sigma Sig.ria di Venetia, ad altri Principi Christiani, et al Sig.or Turco, novamente poste in luce* (Venetia: Alla libraria des segno di S. Marco, [1574]).

[58] Camocio, "Il successo della mirabile vittoria della armata di la Santa Lega Christiana, contra la potentissima, et orgogliosa [di] Sultan Selim principe Ottomano...," [n.d.], map 39, *Isole famose*.

[59] The new treaty was confirmed in March 1573; see Alexander De Groot, "The Historical Development of the Capitulatory Regime in the Ottoman Middle East from the Fifteenth to the Nineteenth Centuries," *Oriente Moderno*, special edition, *The Ottoman Capitulations: Text and Context*, Maurits van den Boogert and Kate Fleet, eds., XXII (LXXXIII), n.s., 3 (2003): 575–604, esp. 593.

[60] Alessandro Scafi, *Mapping Paradise: A History of Heaven on Earth* (Chicago: University of Chicago Press, 2006), 285, and 105–6. "The division of human history into six world ages became a commonplace in the middle ages," as was the notion, extending into the sixteenth century at least, that man was at the end of the last of these ages (68–9). Paradise, in the fifteenth century, might be marked in the far east of Asia (where Gog and Magog were still often located on maps), or in Armenia as it appeared on Ortelius' 1601 map, *Geographia sacra,* in the Middle East, or in undesignated space among other locales (207, 254, 270–77, and plates 15–16 in Scafi). See also Ricardo Padrón, "Mapping Imaginary Worlds," 255–88, in *Maps: Place in the World,* James R. Ackerman and Robert Karrow, eds. (Chicago: University of Chicago Press, 2007), 261–5.

[61] Jean Baptiste d'Anville, "La Grece et les pays plus septentrionaux jusqu'au Danube: Pour l'Histoire Ancienne de Mr. Rollin," 1740. Charles Rollin (1661–1741) was a contemporary French historian

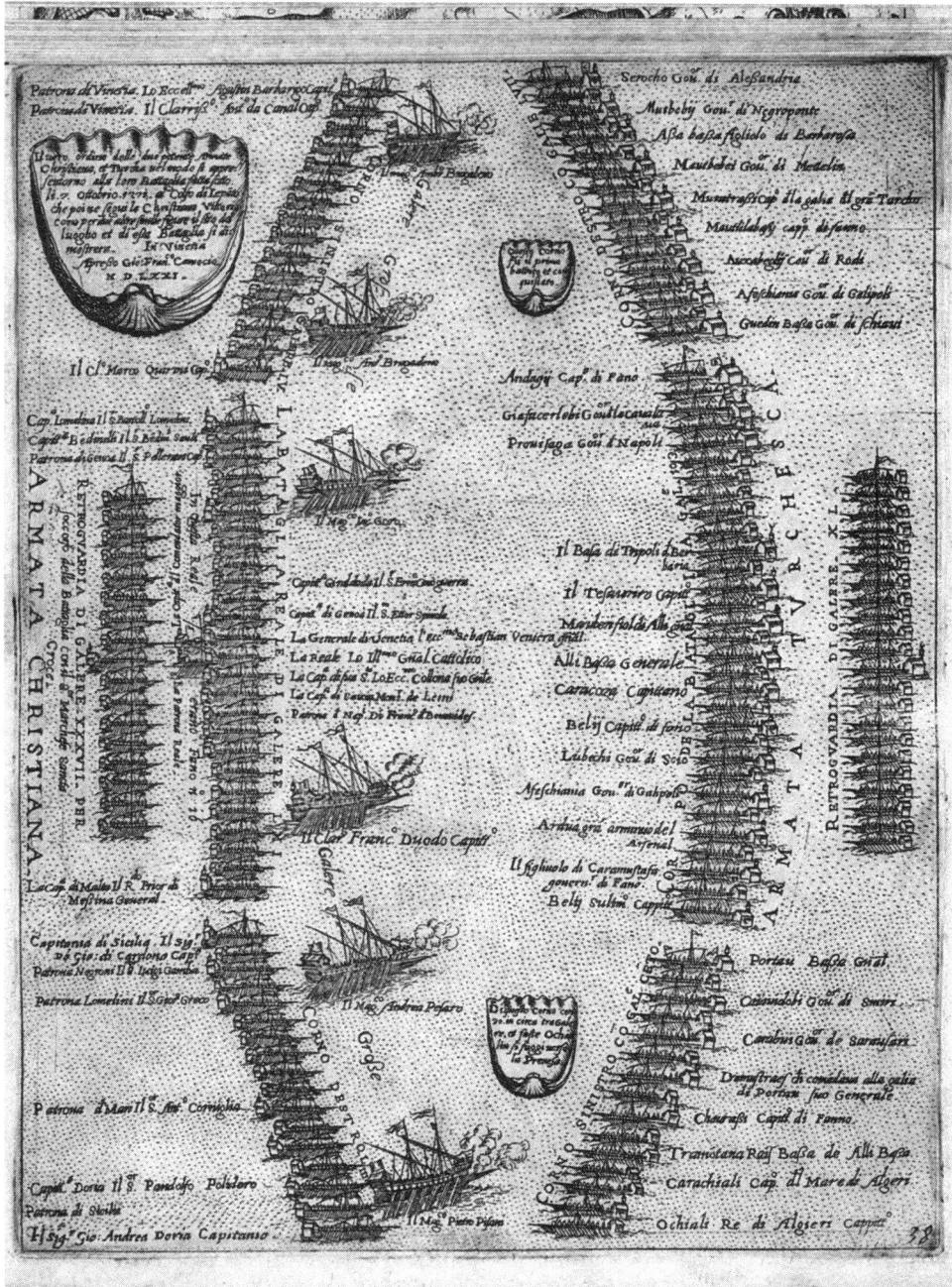

Figure 1.10. The Battle of Lepanto. Giovanni Camocio, "Il vero ordine delle due potente armate . . . (Christiana e Turchesca)," *Isole famose porti, fortezze, e terre maritime sottoposto all Ser.ma Sig.ria di Venetia*, map 38, Venetia [1574?]. By permission of the Folger Shakespeare Library, Shelfmark: G1015.C3 1574 Cage.

Thus, in Paolo Forlani's (fl. 1560s) map of "Europe," the sacred figures of Christian history, moving outward from Palestine, framed European space. The journeys of the apostles Paul and Peter were described, as were the travels of Christ.[62] The Christian savior and his acolytes would thus seem to draw the lands of Europe and the gaze of the viewer toward their eastern 'home.' Similarly, Abraham Ortelius' (1527–98) atlas, the *Theatrum Orbis Terrarum*, included a set of Biblical maps. Among them was a view of "Terra Chanaan" illustrating the life and travels of the patriarch Abraham, "Abrahami Patriarchae Peregrinatio et Vita."[63] The reader could experience the trials of the patriarch, depicted in twenty-two vignettes surrounding the map. Abraham thus walked Ottoman lands along with other father-travelers who served in Ortelius' atlas as witnesses to their Judeo-Christian identity.

Contemporary authors also pictured themselves as joining that historical parade of pilgrim travelers. For Thomas Fuller (1608–61), an outspoken Anglican preacher, prolific writer, and supporter of Charles I in the context of the English Civil War (1642–51), the "Holy Land" embodied the identity, history, and well-being of Christendom.[64] It transcended physical possession and sovereign claims; it was God's space.[65] In Fuller's *Historie of the Holy Warre*, published in Oxford in 1639, the whole Mediterranean was the site of a centuries-long battle between Christian kings and "Turks," for possession of the Holy Land. Saladin was thus a "Turk," and his seizing of Jerusalem in 1187 stood in a direct continuum with the Ottoman conquest of that city in 1516. Christendom, the churchman advised in his *Historie*, must not rest until the "Turks" were expelled from the Holy Land and the Christian pilgrims again in possession of their sacred sites.[66] The frontispiece of Fuller's book serves as a map (Fig. 1.11). It compresses the journey to the Holy Land onto a single page, moving from "Europe" (depicted as the "Church") to Jerusalem (embodied in the "Temple of the

whose *Histoire ancienne des Égyptiens...* was published in 1735–8 and reprinted many times. Or see the male and female "antients" of Judea and Babylon on the cartouche for Edward Wells, "A New Map of the Eastern Parts of Asia Minor, shewing their Antient Divisions, Countries or People, Chief Cities, Towns, Rivers, Mountains, &c," included in his *A Sett of Maps*, dated 1700.

[62] David Woodward, *The Maps and Prints of Paolo Forlani: A Descriptive Bibliography* (Chicago: Newberry Library, 1990), 52–3. Travelers also modeled their accounts on the journeys of Paul and other scriptural antecedents; see MacLean, *The Rise of Oriental Travel*, 73, 78, 85–7.

[63] Ariel Tishby, ed., *Holy Land in Maps* (Jerusalem: The Israel Museum, 2001), 94–5. Biblical segments in early modern atlases were not unusual; and maps such as Ortelius' on Abraham's Holy Land also circulated in single sheet and were inserted into historical texts.

[64] Norman Housley, "The Eschatological Imperative: Messianism and Holy War in Europe, 1260–1556," part III, 123–50, in *Crusading and Warfare in Medieval and Renaissance Europe* (Aldershot: Ashgate, Variorum Reprints, 2001), references Joseph Strayer who "illustrated how in the case of the French a similar transfer of the idea of the 'Holy Land' occurred, from a unique territory in Palestine to the patria of the Christian believer (148)."

[65] The notions of sacred space, pilgrimage, and forgiveness were shared by Muslims, Christians, and Jews. Abraham Balanzas, a Cretan Jew, drew up a will in 1626 when he was about sixty years old as a prelude to travel to Jerusalem, where he planned to end his days. See Chryssa Maltezou, "From Crete to Jerusalem: The Will of a Cretan Jew (1626)," 189–201, in *Intercultural Contacts in the Medieval Mediterranean: Studies in Honour of David Jacoby*, Benjamin Arbel, ed. (London: Frank Cass, 1996), 188.

[66] Thomas Fuller, *Historie of the Holy Warre* (Oxford: Thomas Buck, 1639). See W. B. Patterson, "Fuller, Thomas (1607/8–1661)," 159–63, in H. Matthew and Brian Harrison, eds., *Oxford Dictionary of National Biography*, v. 21 (Oxford: Oxford University Press, 2004).

Figure 1.11. Thomas Fuller, *Historie of the Holy Warre*, frontispiece, Oxford, 1639. By permission of the Folger Shakespeare Library, Shelfmark: STC11464, copy 2.

Sepulcher").[67] On the way, pilgrims face death in the form of Turks, disease, and an avenging angel. Fuller has thus violated the constraints of space, making Jerusalem proximate to Europe, or, more particularly, to Britain.

[67] This impressionistic "map" can be compared with Bernardo Salvioni's 1597 map of Venice, which commemorates, in an inset, the Corpus Christi procession in which Venetian senators had been accustomed to progress in the company of pilgrims en route to Jerusalem. Fuller's image is allegorical; Salvioni's is an impression of a past event. See Wilson, *The World in Venice*, 7, 163. See also Daniel

Inside Fuller's history, one also finds a map depicting Palestine and the eastern end of the Mediterranean (Fig. 1.12). The legend provides place names in
terms of four layers of time – Old Testament, Christ's Time, Saint Jerome's
Time, and "At This Day" – each layer crafted by the dictates of religion
that the clergyman thought most pertinent to his readers. That offering of
multiple time frames was echoed in other maps of the Holy Land as well.
Giuseppe Rosaccio (c. 1530–c. 1620), for example, offered his readers two
'time zones' in a map of Syria included in his 1598 travel book: "this plate is
the Antique Siria divided into twelve tribes, now called Soria and Holy Land
(*terra Santa*), [and] possessed by the Turk" (Fig. 1.13).[68]

Drawing sacred space, however, was not without its pitfalls. Under the
name-legend of his Palestine map, Fuller provides some insight on the logistics
of early modern mapping and the conflicted geographical visions of his own
time and place.

> *Of thirty maps and Descriptions of the Holy Land which I have perused,
> I never met with two in all considerables alike. Some sink valleys where
> others raise mountains; yea, end rivers where others begin them; and
> sometimes with a wanton dash of their pen, create a Stream in Land,
> a Creek in Sea, more than Nature ever owned. In these differences we
> have followed the Scripture as an unpartiall umpire. The Longitudes
> and Latitudes (wherein there be also unreconcileable discords) I have
> omitted, being advised that it will not quit cost in a map of so small
> extent.*

The preacher thus invoked truth claims of a rather different sort than
those employed in the news maps that reported the Ottoman–Hapsburg
or Ottoman–Venetian wars. His were based neither on claims of eyewitness
accuracy nor on the authority of scientific measurement. Rather "Scripture"
had the final word on the form and limits of Palestine. And where the science
of latitude and longitude was concerned, the purse of the publisher was the
determining factor, science giving way to the dictates of cost and demand
(not to mention the license of the king).

Like Jerusalem, Constantinople served as a sacred site, a royal capital sus-
pended between Europe and Asia in which the histories of empire and faith
were inextricably intertwined. This eastern "Rome" complicated Christian
efforts to form discrete dominions of the sacred and profane.[69] Thus the
front matter of the third edition of Henri Chatelain's (1684–1743), *Atlas
Historique, ou Nouvelle Introduction à l'Histoire*, traces sacred history from

---

Connolly, "Copying Maps by Matthew Paris: Itineraries Fit for a King," 159–204, in Palmira Brummett, ed., *The "Book" of Travels: Genre, Ethnology and Pilgrimage, 1250–1700* (Leiden: Brill, 2009),
for a medieval English example of collapsing space to map the journey from England to Jerusalem.

[68] Giuseppe Rosaccio, *Viaggio da Venetia a Costantinopoli* (Venetia: Giacomo Franco, 1598), 52 v. The
text for this work was provided by Rosaccio and the maps by the engraver and publisher Giacomo
Franco; see Leonora Navari, "Mapping the Mediterranean in the Gennadius Library," *New Griffon* 8
(2006): 8–21, see 15.

[69] See, for later American examples, "A Map of Assyria, Asia Minor, &c.," from *Sacred Geography*
(Philadelphia: American Sunday School Union, c. 1830); or Anon., "Map of Asia Minor Designed to
Illustrate the Third Volume of Union Questions," for *Union Questions, on select portions of Scripture
from the Old and New Testaments* (Philadelphia: American Sunday School Union, 1830).

Figure 1.12. Thomas Fuller, "A Table showing ye variety of Places names in Palestine," *Historie of the Holy Warre*, plate between pp. 38 and 39, Oxford, 1639. By permission of the Folger Shakespeare Library, Shelfmark: STC11464 copy 2.

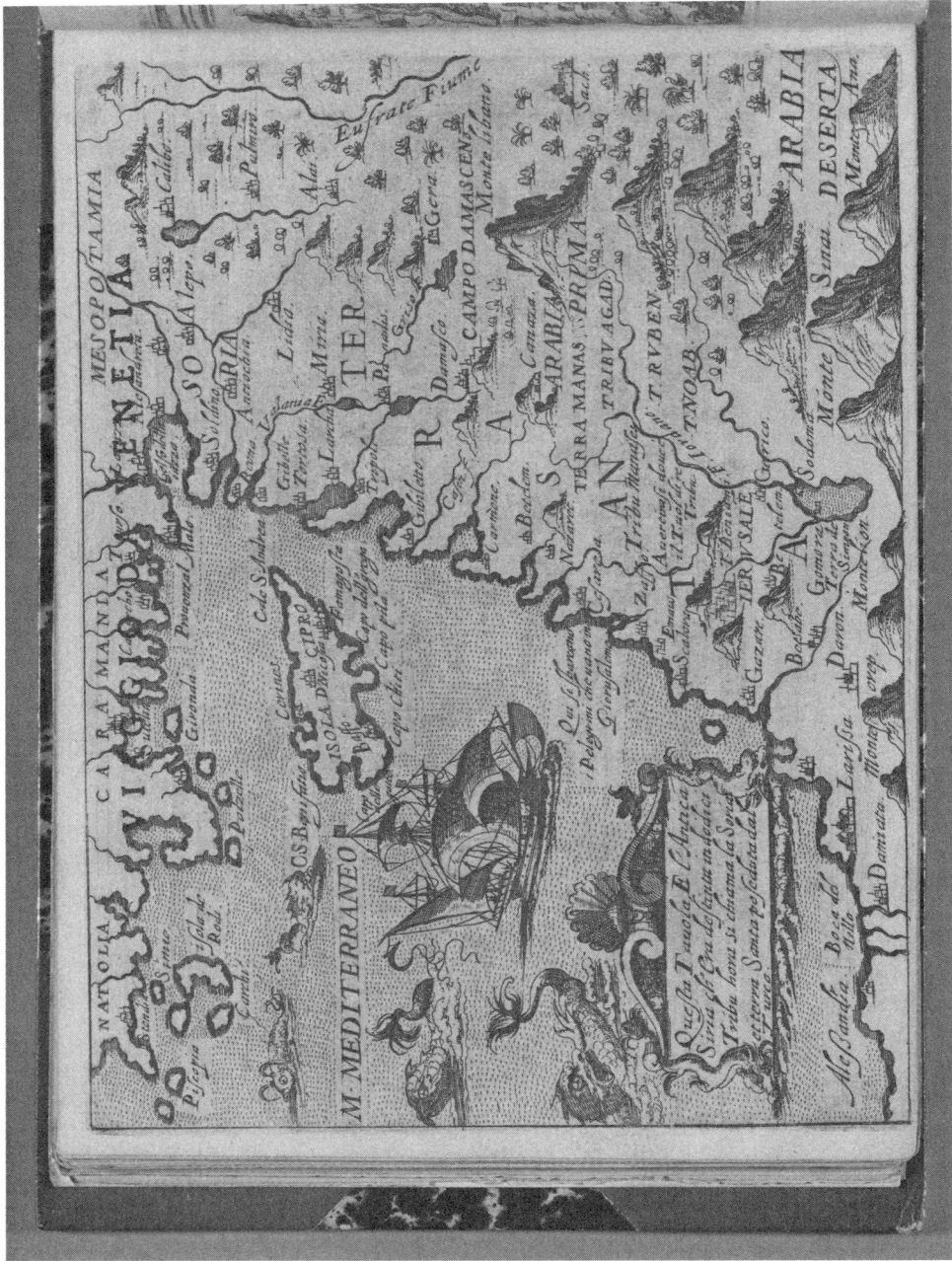

Figure 1.13. Giuseppe Rosaccio, "Antica Siria," *Viaggio da Venetia a Costantinopoli*, 52v, Venetia, 1598. Asia 9215.98.3, Houghton Library, Harvard University.

Adam and Eve, to Jesus Christ, to Clement XI, "245th Pontiff," in 1713 (Fig. 1.14).[70] Profane history begins with the first universal monarchy founded by the Assyrians and ends with two major imperial strands. The first (Oriental) strand traces through the Byzantines and Mehmet II (second r. 1451–1481), conqueror of Constantinople in 1453, to the contemporary Ottoman Sultan Ahmet III (r. 1703–30). The other (Occidental) strand traces through the Western Roman Emperor, Honorius, in 395, and Charlemagne (d. 814), and ends with the "German" empire under Charles V. The sacred and the profane (or imperial) are positioned side by side, but the East had to be separated from the West to preserve the strand of the "sacred" for Latin Christendom.

It was, however, difficult to extricate the Ottoman East from the Christian West. Vincenzo Coronelli marked his map of "Asia divided in its parts" as sacred space. The map was inscribed with a large cartouche bearing the Christogram "IHS." It described Asia as "the biggest part of the world with its vast kingdoms ... copiously fertilized by the sweat and the blood of the Religious of the Company of Jesuits." It was they who sought "the grand work of the conversion to the Faith of such a great land" (Fig. 1.15).[71] Asia was thus not simply an eastern space, or the site of the Holy Land, or a place of Muslim enemies and competitors. It was a space made sacred for Christendom by blood sacrifice and the weight of history.

Ottoman Self-Mapping

The Ottomans mapped themselves with many of the same intentions and devices employed by the authors and illustrators of the Christian kingdoms. History, travel, war, and the sacred were all prisms through which they conceptualized sovereign space. Istanbul had a long history of cosmopolitanism as an imperial center. It should therefore come as no surprise that its narrative, artistic, and technological influences were diverse and commingled, including the traditions of the East, the West, and everything in between.[72] As a center of learning and patronage, the city, with its notables and scholars, participated in an enduring and transcontinental process of cultural production and transmission. Geographic knowledge (derived from Arabic, Persian, Byzantine, and Italian traditions, among others) was part of

---

[70] Chatelain, *Atlas Historique,* 3rd ed. v. 1, part of the unpaginated front matter in two full-page tracings: "Chaine de l'Histoire Sacrée and Chaine de l'Histoire Prophane."

[71] Vincenzo Coronelli, "Asia, divisa nelle sue Parti," in *Atlante veneto, nel quale si contiene la descrittione geografica, storica, sacra, profana, e politica, degl'imperij, regni, provincie, e stati dell'universo ...,* v. 1 (Venetia: Appresso Domenico Padovani, 1690), plate after p. 40. See also the frontispiece for Nicolas Trigault (1577–1628), *De Christiana Expeditione apud Sinas* (Augsburg: 1615).

[72] Gottfried Hagen, "Afterword: Ottoman Understandings of the World in the Seventeenth Century," 215–56, in Robert Dankoff, *An Ottoman Mentality: The World of Evliya Çelebi* (Leiden: Brill, 2004), 249, points out the issue, not to mention the misunderstanding, of discerning "to what degree parallel developments occurred due to internal dynamics, and to what degree an exchange of ideas took place" between "East and West."

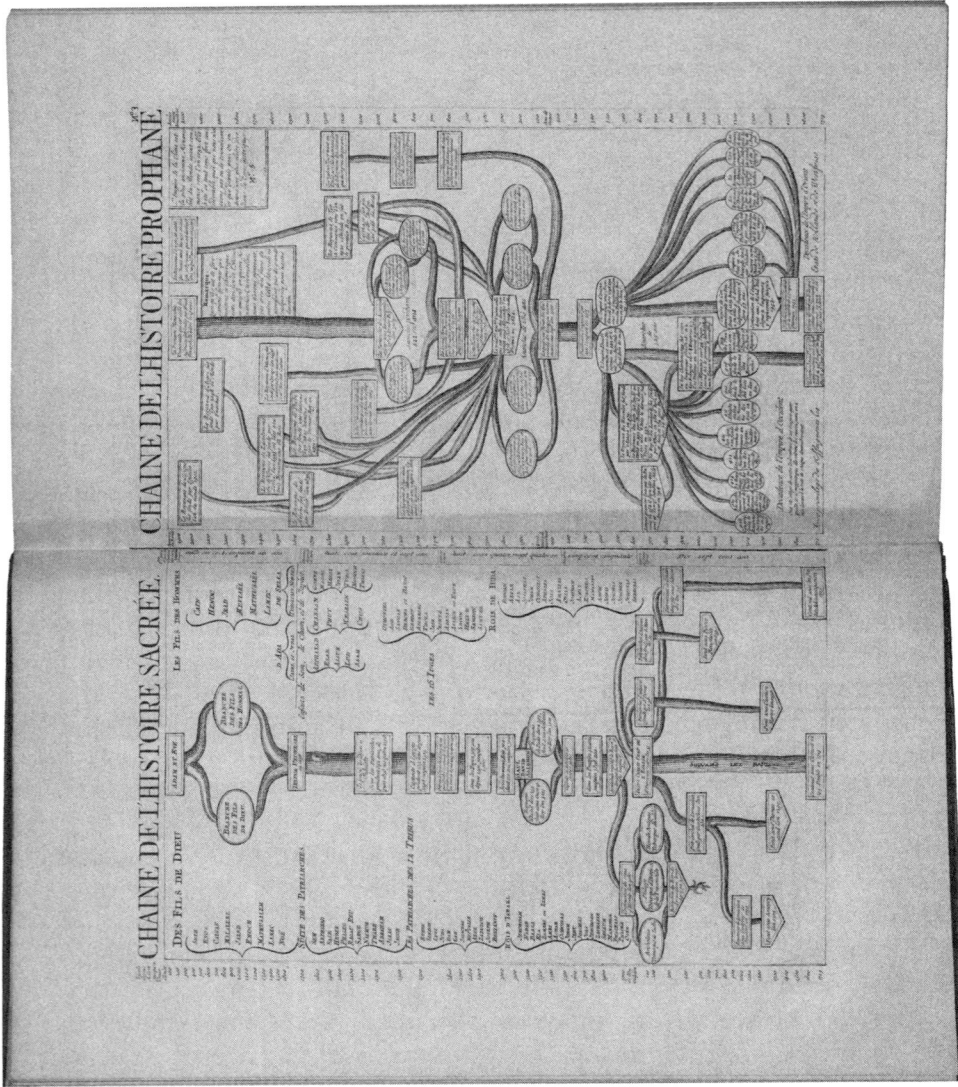

Figure 1.14. Henri Chatelain, "Chaine de l'Histoire Sacrée," "Chaine de l'Histoire Prophane," *Atlas Historique, ou Nouvelle Introduction à l'Histoire ...*, 3rd ed., v. 1, pl. 3, Amsterdam, 1739. By permission of the Folger Shakespeare Library, Shelfmark: D11.5 C6 v.1 Cage.

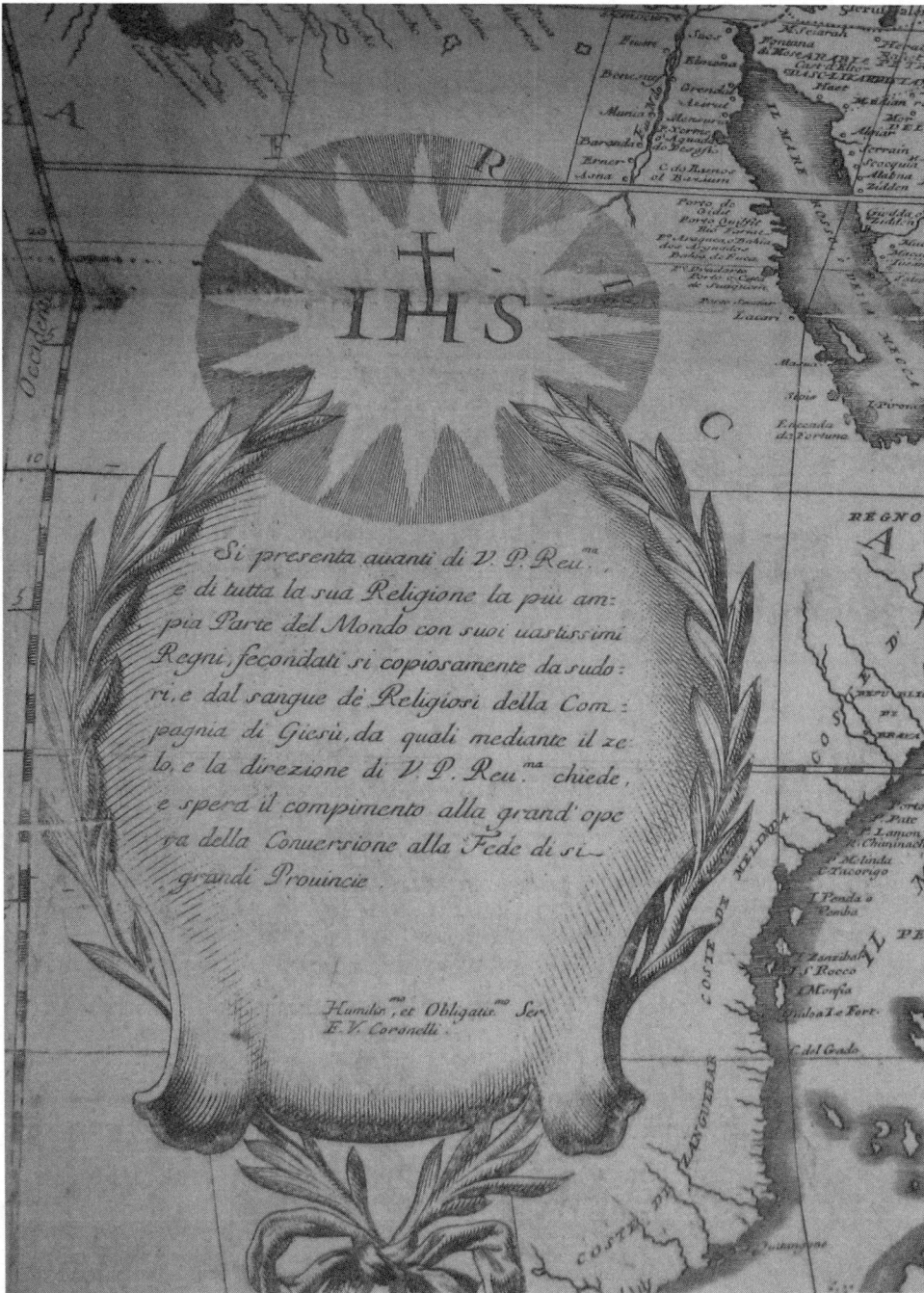

Figure 1.15. Vincenzo Coronelli, "Asia, divisa nelle sue Parti," cartouche, *Atlante Veneto*, v. 1, Venetia, 1690. Photo Courtesy of the Newberry Library, Chicago, Ayer 135 .C8 1690.

that process.[73] Mehmet the Conqueror's interest in geography is well known;
and geographic treatises are found in the libraries of the Ottoman military–
administrative (*askeri*) and clerical (*ulema*) classes.[74] The renowned world
map of Piri Reis (c. 1470–1554) and his *Book of the Sea* (*Kitab-ı Bahriye*)
are notable examples of Ottoman cartographic arts.[75] Evliya Çelebi (1611–
82), the famous Ottoman traveler, mentions in his *Book of Travels* (*Seyahatname*) that there were eight map ateliers in his time in Istanbul, whose
mapmakers were versed in multiple languages, including Latin, so that they
could read geographical works.[76] It is useful then to think of the Ottomans
as active participants in a cartographic European Republic of Letters (and
images).[77] We have only a limited number of Ottoman maps surviving (or
accessible) from the late fifteenth to the seventeenth century.[78] They do not
begin to approach the scale of mappings deriving from the print houses of
Christian Europe. Nonetheless, as Ahmet Karamustafa asserts, "the quality and diversity of extant premodern Ottoman maps certainly suggest that
there was a significant and continuous level of cartographic consciousness
in certain segments of premodern Ottoman high culture..."[79] Also, our
knowledge of Ottoman mapping in multiple formats is expanding all the

[73] Ekmeleddin İhsanoğlu, ed., *Osmanlı Coğrafya Literatürü (History of Geographical Literature During the Ottoman Period)* 2 vols. (İstanbul: IRCICA, 2000); Gottfried Hagen, "Some Considerations on the Study of Ottoman Geographical Writings," *Archivum Ottomanicum* 18 (2000): 183–93; Goodrich, *The Ottoman Turks and the New World*; J. M. Rogers, "Itineraries and Town Views in Ottoman Histories," 228–55, in *HOC*, v. 2, book 1. See also André Miquel, *La géographie humaine du monde musulman jusqu'au milieu du 11e siècle: Géographie arabe et représentation du monde: la terre et l'étranger* (Paris: Éditions de l'École des Hautes Études en Sciences Sociales, 2001) and Kemal Özdemir, *Ottoman Nautical Charts and the Atlas of Ali Macar Reis* (İstanbul: Creative Yayıncılık, 1992), which includes illustrations from a variety of Ottoman works.

[74] M. Pinar Emiralioğlu, "Cartography and Geographical Consciousness in the Ottoman Empire (1453–1730)," 97–107, in *European Cartographers and the Ottoman World*, 97. Jerry Brotton, *Trading Territories: Mapping the Early Modern World* (Ithaca, NY: Cornell University Press, 1998), 98–104. See also Benjamin Arbel, "Maps of the World for Ottoman Princes? Further Evidence and Questions Concerning 'The Mappamondo of Hajji Ahmed,'" *Imago Mundi* 54 (2002), 19–29, esp. 22–3, 26, on elite Ottoman demand for Venetian maps in the 1550s and 1560s, and the circulation of Venetian maps.

[75] On Piri Re'is, see Soucek, *Piri Reis and Turkish Mapmaking after Columbus: The Khalili Portolan Atlas* (London: Nour Foundation, 1996), 26–33, 36–105; Cengiz Orhonlu, "Hint Kaptanlığı ve Pîrî Reis," *Belleten* 34 (Türk Tarih Kurumu, 1970): 234–54; Thomas Goodrich, "Better Directions at Sea: The Pîrî Reis Innovation," Foundation for Science, Technology and Civilization, 2007, www.muslimheritage.com/uploads/The_Piri_Reis_Innovation11.pdf; Karen Pinto, "Searchin' His Eyes, Lookin' for Traces: Piri Reis' World Map of 1513 & Its Islamic Iconographic Connections (A Reading through Baghdat 334 and Proust)," *Osmanlı Araştırmaları/The Journal of Ottoman Studies*, 39 (2012): 63–94; Svat Soucek, "Islamic Charting in the Mediterranean," 265–87, in *HOC*, v. 2, book 1, 266–9.

[76] Soucek, "Islamic Charting in the Mediterranean," 284, on the *esnaf-ı haritaciyan* ateliers.

[77] Sonja Brentjes, "On the Relation between the Ottoman Empire and the West European Republic of Letters (17th–18th centuries)," section II, 121–48, in Brentjes, *Travellers from Europe in the Ottoman and Safavid Empires, 16th–17th Centuries: Seeking, Transforming, Discarding Knowledge* (Farnham, Surrey: Ashgate, Variorum Reprints, 2010), 122–3, 129.

[78] An excellent selection is provided by Kathryn Ebel, "City Views, Imperial Visions: Cartography and the Visual Cultural of Urban Space in the Ottoman Empire, 1453–1603," Ph.D. thesis, University of Texas, Department of Geography, 2002; and maps play a central role in M. Pinar Emiralioğlu, *Geographical Knowledge and Imperial Culture in the Early Modern Ottoman Empire* (Farnham, Surrey: Ashgate, 2014), 11, who argues for a unique Ottoman geographic consciousness.

[79] Ahmet Karamustafa, "Introduction to Ottoman Cartography," 206–8, esp. 206, in *HOC*, v. 2, book 1; and Karamustafa, "Military, Administrative, and Scholarly Maps and Plans," 209–27, in *HOC*, v. 2, book 1. Svat Soucek, "Islamic Charting in the Mediterranean," 263, has pointed out that the

time.[80] So our default assumption must be that the early modern Ottomans were (at least) cartographically opportunistic. As Gottfried Hagen puts it, the Ottoman "world-picture" was neither static, consistent, or "dogmatically exclusive."[81] Ottoman mapping cannot, therefore, be delineated as simply unique, "Oriental," or isolated from its surrounding cartographic contexts.[82]

There is no clear line between "European" mapping of the Ottomans and Ottoman self-mapping. Both emerge out of an older set of transnational, transimperial, and transcontinental cartographic, literary, historical, religious, and artistic precedents.[83] The self-image of Ottoman rulers, like those of other imperial entities, was referential, echoing and responding to the self-images of past and present hegemons in the pagan, Islamic, and Christian realms.[84] Mehmet the Conqueror was conscious of that array of options when he claimed the title "ruler of the two seas and the two continents" in an inscription on the gate of his new palace in Istanbul.[85] His gold *sultani* coins of 1477–8 called him "Striker of the glittering, Master of might and victorious on land and sea."[86] Mehmet and his successors saw themselves as participants in a long chain of powerful rulers and glorious events,

---

comparison of Ottoman and European charts "has tended to be somewhat nationalistic from both the Islamic and Western viewpoints."

[80] A double issue of the journal *Osmanlı Araştırmaları/Journal of Ottoman Studies* 39–40 (2012), *Essays in Honor of Thomas D. Goodrich*, Gottfried Hagen and Baki Tezcan, eds., has recently assembled a collection of new scholarship on Ottoman mapping, geography, and travel. See also Karen Pinto, "The Maps Are the Message: Mehmet II's Patronage of an 'Ottoman Cluster'," *Imago Mundi* 63. 2 (2011): 155–79.

[81] Hagen, "Afterword," 216. See also Rhoads Murphey, "Evolving Versus Static Elements in Ottoman Geographical Writing between 1598 and 1729, Perspectives and Real Life Experience of 'The Northern Lands' (*Taraf al-Shimali*) Over 130 Years," 73–82, in *Ottoman Bosnia: A History in Peril*, Markus Koller and Kemal Karpat, eds. (Madison: University of Wisconsin Press, 2004); and Jan Schmidt, "Franz Taeschner's Collection of Turkish Manuscripts in the Leiden University Library," 237–66, in *The Joys of Philology: Studies in Ottoman Literature, History and Orientalism (1500–1923)*, v. 2, *Studies in Ottoman Literature, History, and Orientalism*, Analecta Isisiana LX (İstanbul: Isis Press, 2002), 245, 249.

[82] The maps contained in the Istanbul naval museum give a sense of the intermingling of maps produced by the Ottomans with those (the majority) produced in Europe outside the empire: Şükrü Özpınar et al., eds. *Türk Deniz Müzesi, Harita Kataloğu/Chart and Map Catalogue of Turkish Naval Museum* (Ankara: Kültür Yayınları Tarih Dizisi, 2001). This catalog does not indicate date and mode of acquisition, but the Ottomans clearly consumed and utilized outside images of their domains and continued the long practice of "naturalizing," in this case Ottomanizing, maps produced in non-Ottoman languages.

[83] Serpil Bağci, "From Translated Word to Translated Image: The Illustrated Şehnâme-i Türkî Copies," *Muqarnas* 17 (2000): 162–76, see 162, has argued that "textual and visual cultures" were intimately entwined, and "freely circulated" throughout the Islamic world regardless of cultural differences. See also Emine Fetvacı, "The Production of the Şehnâme-i Selīm Hān," *Muqarnas* 26 (2009): 263–315.

[84] Câfer Iyânî, *Tevârîh-i Cedîd-i Vilâyet-i Üngürüs (Osmanlı-Macar Mücadelesi Tarihi, 1585–1595)*, Mehmet Kirişçioğlu, ed. (İstanbul: Kitabevi, 2001), 9, includes an imperial letter of Murad III (1574–95) to the Hapsburgs; and Rhoads Murphey, *Exploring Ottoman Sovereignty: Tradition, Image and Practice in the Ottoman Imperial Household, 1400–1800* (London: Continuum, 2008), 82–98, comments on Ottoman internal and external projection of power through titulature.

[85] Cemal Kafadar, *Between Two Worlds: The Construction of the Ottoman State* (Berkeley: University of California Press, 1995), 153. As Şevket Pamuk, *A Monetary History of the Ottoman Empire* (Cambridge: Cambridge University Press, 2000), 59, has noted: "Promoting trade and gaining control over trade routes, both overland and maritime, was an important part of the Ottoman strategy across the Mediterranean."

[86] Soon after the conquest the Ottomans began minting their own version of Venetian gold ducats (*frengi flori*). See Pamuk, *A Monetary History of the Ottoman Empire*, 61.

capitalizing on tradition when it served their ambitions, and setting it aside when it was expedient to do so.[87] Mapping, like palaces and coinage, served their rhetorics of legitimation and intimidation and demonstrated the expansive nature of Ottoman patronage.

As we examine the ways in which the print houses of Christian Europe depicted the Ottomans and their space, I will invoke Ottoman mappings (as available) by way of comparison, in particular those appearing in text and miniatures. One might object that a miniature does not constitute a map in the same way that many of the cartographic images in this volume do. But I will, throughout, employ the broad sense of mapping, articulated by J. B. Harley, that a map is a representation of space (and a visualization aid).[88] Hence the miniatures in a campaign account serve as 'real' maps just as readily as do the pages of a Mercator atlas (Fig. 1.16).

The Ottomans took the practice (already well developed in Iran and Central Asia) of "writing and illustrating world histories and manuscripts celebrating the victories of illustrious historical figures" to new heights after the mid-sixteenth century.[89] Murat III (r. 1574–95) was particularly known for his patronage of the arts of the book. And the sultans sponsored dynastic histories by the chroniclers Arifi Fethullah Çelebi (d. 1561–2), Seyyid Lokman (served 1569 to 1596–7), and others, placing fine copies of these often lavish manuscripts in the palace treasury and imperial library, or giving them as gifts.[90] Ottoman chroniclers cataloged victories and the acts of submission that accompanied them, consulting "first-hand witnesses of events" in the process.[91] And teams of painters in the sultan's *nakkaşhane* crafted the illustrations for commemorative campaign volumes that mapped out the stopping places on the way to the outposts of empire.[92] Their works certify sovereignty, but they also demonstrate the measuring out and envisioning of space. In the transimperial frontier linking Ottoman, Hapsburg, and Venetian powers, this counting out of victories and subordinates focuses on walled sites and the sieges and ceremonies that took place before them. There is much yet to be learned regarding the creation, patronage, and consumption of Ottoman images that depict space, borders, and imperial claims.

[87] Celalzade Mustafa, *Selim-Name*, Ahmet Uğur and Mustafa Çuhadar, eds. (Ankara: Kültür Bakanlığı, 1990), 22–3, on the invocation of Alexander, Hüsrev, and other glorious antecedents.

[88] Harley, *The New Nature of Maps*, 35–8, whose articulation of the "boundaries" of the meaning of "map" are rather broader than those found in sources like the *HOC*. See Buisseret, *The Mapmakers' Quest*, 29–48, on the "painterly origins of some European mapping."

[89] Serpil Bağcı and Zeren Tanındı, "The Ottomans: From Mehmed II to Murad III," 260–374, in *Turks: A Journey of a Thousand Years, 600–1600*, David Roxburgh, ed. (London: Royal Academy of Arts, 2005), 268–9.

[90] On the treasury, see Gülru Necipoğlu, *Architecture, Ceremonial, and Power: The Topkapı Palace in the Fifteenth and Sixteenth Centuries* (Cambridge: MIT Press, 1991), 133–140; and Cengiz Köseoğlu, *The Topkapı Saray Museum: The Treasury*, translated, expanded and edited by J. M. Rogers (Boston: Little, Brown and Co., 1987).

[91] Bağcı and Tanındı, "The Ottomans: From Mehmed II to Murad III," 269–71, 341. For the ways in which such manuscripts were patronized and produced, see Zeren Tanındı, "Bibliophile Aghas (Eunuchs) at Topkapı Palace," *Muqarnas* 21 *Essays in Honor of Michael Rogers* (2004): 333–43; and David Roxburgh, *Prefacing the Image: The Writing of Art History in Sixteenth-Century Iran* (Leiden: Brill, 2001), 52–72, 167–70, 179–200.

[92] See Esin Atıl, *The Age of Sultan Süleyman the Magnificent* (Washington, DC: The National Gallery of Art, 1987), 29–36, 78–97, 288, on palace art expenses.

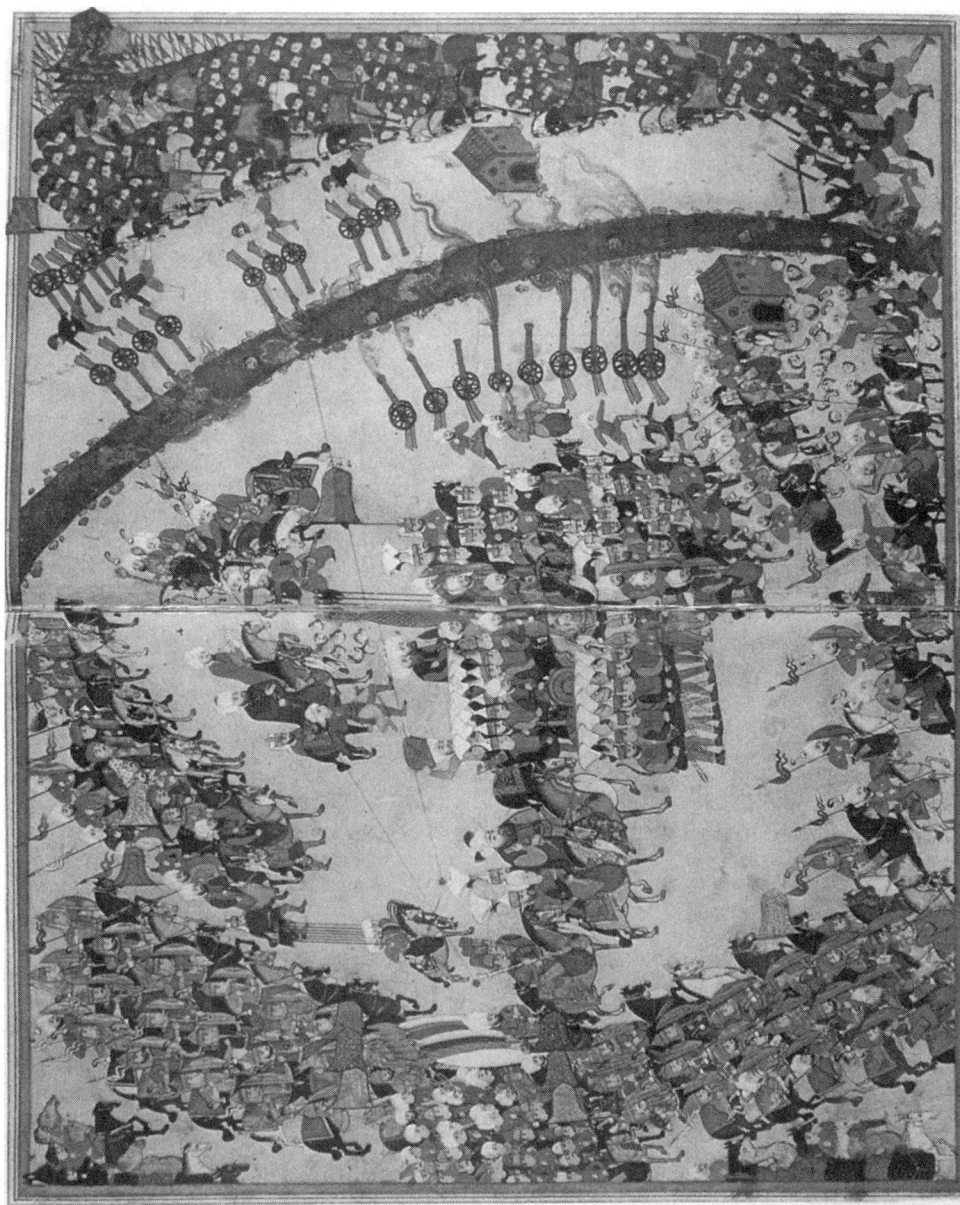

Figure 1.16. Battle of Keresztes, 1596. Talikizade Mehmet Subhi, *Şahname-i Sultan Mehmet III*, H. 1609, fol. 50b–51a, İstanbul [c. 1596–9]. Topkapı Palace Museum, İstanbul. (See color plate)

But Emine Fetvacı has argued for the end of the sixteenth and beginning of the seventeenth century, particularly the reign of Ahmet I (r. 1603–17), as a time in which imperial iconography shifted from an emphasis on "conquering castles" to depictions of processions, the administration of justice, and prayer.[93] These are processes that lend themselves to the arts of the map.

Like their Christian counterparts in Europe, the sultans and their artists envisioned space as both historical and sacred. No sultan ever made the pilgrimage to Mecca. But Mecca, like other sites of pilgrimage, was, for Ottoman publics including the sultan, a source of curiosity, worship, longing, and patronage. In the 1582 Ottoman version of the book *Jewels of Marvels: A Translation of the Sea of Wonders (Javahir-al-Gharaib Tarjomat Bahr al-Aja'ib)*, by Cennabi (d. 1590), one finds an image of the Ka'ba and its surrounding walls.[94] The same work depicts Murat III in his library in Istanbul, flanked on both sides by bookshelves, a consumer of the scholarly, the pious, and the exotic.[95] One can imagine him as an armchair traveler, like the consumers of so many maps, using the images to transport himself to distant lands: those he claimed, those he might conquer, and those he might only imagine.

[93] Emine Fetvacı, "Viziers to Eunuchs: Transitions in Ottoman Manuscript Patronage, 1566–1617," Ph.D. thesis, Harvard University, Department of History of Art and Architecture, 2005, esp. 309–10, 313, on the intersections of map production with other forms of image and text production and patronage. See also Ayşin Yoltar-Yıldırım, "A 1498–99 *Khusraw va Shīrīn*: Turning the Pages of an Ottoman Illustrated Manuscript," *Muqarnas* 22 (2005): 95–109.

[94] Edwin Binney, *Turkish Treasures From the Collection of Edwin Binney* (Portland, OR: Portland Art Museum, 1979), 33–4. Images of the Ka'ba served various purposes, including accompanying indices of the direction of prayer; but one cannot discount a more "secular" geographic and travel interest as well. See for another example of the mapping of sacred space in Mecca *Palace of Gold and Light: Treasures from the Topkapı, Istanbul* (Washington, DC: Palace Arts Foundation, 2000), 128, an image of *the haram al-şerif* from the *Futûh el-Harameyn* of Muhyi al-Din Lari (d. 1526–7).

[95] Binney, 3 *Turkish Treasures*, 6–37. The inscription notes that the illustrated volume was "Made for the Hazine (Treasury) of the Sultan [Murat III, 1574–95]."

2

Reading and Placing the "Turk"

But I feare my Reader will bee wearie of Turkie: from whence yet yee may not, shall not depart, till yee have beene made spectators of a Tragicall Comedie, and a Comicall Tragedie (Comicall, I hope to us, if the sinnes of Christendome prevent not, to the Turkes a Tragedie).

Samuel Purchas, *Hakluytus Posthumus,* 1625.[1]

The dreams of European dreamers were filled with magic carpets and Aladdin's lamps (albeit heavily disguised) long before Galland adapted the Thousand and One Nights [1704] to suit ears more accustomed to the Contes of Perrault, and before Irving and Doré translated the courtyards, gardens, and fountains of Granada into words and images that could be grasped by Western minds.

Franco Cardini, *Europe and Islam,* 1999.[2]

What exactly "Western minds" could grasp in the early modern era is a subject of long debate. But there is no doubt that Franco Cardini was right when he posited the familiarity of European audiences with images and stories of the Middle East. The figure of the "Turk" was everywhere in the imagery of sixteenth and seventeenth century Europe. He wields a hammer in the center of Tintoretto's *St. Mark Liberating a Slave* (1548), and casts the stones in Carpaccio's *Stoning of St. Stephen* (1520).[3] In the long line of windows from

[1] Samuel Purchas, *Hakluytus Posthumus, or Purchas His Pilgrimes,* v. 2 (London: 1625), 1360.
[2] Franco Cardini, *Europe and Islam,* Caroline Beamish trans. (Oxford: Blackwell, 1999), 185.
[3] Both paintings at the Academia in Venice. These are turbaned figures, not distinguishing "Turks" from "Moors." For a broad range of styles and materials of presentation, see *Im Lichte des Halbmonds: Das Abendland und der türkische Orient* (Leipzig: Edition Leipzig, 1995).

which spectators (almost all women) lean out to witness the festivities in
Matteo Pagan's *Procession of the Doge's Court in Piazza San Marco*, two
are occupied by turbaned "Turks."[4] Indeed the doge's palace in Venice was
filled with "Turks" looking out from canvases large and small on the proceedings of the Republic. Beyond the Signoria, the image of the Turk was also
ubiquitous. An edition of Pope Pius II's (d. 1464) *Epistola ad Morbisanum
Turcarum Principe[m]*, dated 1532, is decorated with the figure of a mounted
Turk, his face turned away from the viewer, his banner bearing a crescent
and star (Fig. 2.1).[5] But this turning away could not keep the visage of the
Ottoman and his empire from the forefront of the European Christian mind.
Samuel Purchas (c. 1575–1626), the English compiler of travel narratives,
knew well that the readers of Europe were spectators for "*Turquie*" and for
the showing and telling of the empire. Comedy and tragedy, however, were
only two of the options for its display. Instead, the process of translation and
familiarization could take multiple forms, which might draw the Ottomans
as irreparably foreign and enemy creatures, equate them with their European
Christian counterparts, or craft them as something in between.[6]

We need not rehearse here the elaborate literature that has emerged in
response to Edward Said's critique of constructions of the Oriental "other."[7]
It is quite clear by now that "difference" was only one possible topos. As the
people of the Christian kingdoms mapped the Ottomans and their territory,
they took that territory to be commensurate to their own in a variety of
ways. In fact, in many manifestations, the territory was imagined *as* their
"own," historically and by divine mandate. Thus the "West" did not simply
impose its image and geography on Ottoman lands, even though states and
mapmakers could and did inscribe the sovereignty of Western states or of
Christianity onto the territories of the sultan. Rather it reenvisioned familiar
spaces with the Ottomans (more or less) in them. That reenvisioning has
attracted a good deal of scholarly attention, particularly to travel literature.[8]

---

4   Matteo Pagan (fl. 1538–63), " La Processione del Corteo Ducale in Piazza San Marco, c. 1559," Museo
    Correr, n. 5933.
5   Pius II, Pope, *Epistola ad Morbisanum Turcarum Principe[m]* ... (Coloniae: Ex officina Eucharij
    Ceruicorni, 1532), title page verso.
6   Eric Dursteler, *Venetians in Constantinople: Nation, Identity, and Coexistence in the Early Modern
    Mediterranean* (Baltimore: Johns Hopkins University Press, 2006); and Soykut, *Image of the 'Turk' in
    Italy*. Linda Mc Jannet, *The Sultan Speaks: Dialogue in English Plays and Histories about the Ottoman
    Turks* (Houndmills: Palgrave, 2006), 91–121, *passim*, discusses the "eastern" sources available in
    English translation in the early modern era, particularly Johannes Leunclavius' (1533?-93), translation
    of the Ottoman chronicler Sadettin (1536–99), which was used by Richard Knolles and others. On
    European translation of the Ottomans, see Peter Burke, "Translations into Latin in Early Modern
    Europe," in *Cultural Translation in Early Modern Europe*, 65–80, esp. 75–80; and for one treatment
    of Ottoman translations of European cartographic texts, see Günergun, "Ottoman Encounters with
    European Science," 192–211, in the same volume. Matthew Dimmock, *New Turkes: Dramatizing
    Islam and the Ottomans in Early Modern England* (Houndmills: Ashgate, 2005), 66–7, uses an English
    account (dating to 1565) of the coronation of Prince Maximillian, attended by an Ottoman ambassador,
    to show how the Ottoman sultan's household was equated with those of other European royal houses.
7   Edward Said, *Orientalism* (New York: Vintage, 1979).
8   For some bibliographies, see Stephane Yerasimos, *Les voyageurs dans l'empire ottoman (XIVe–
    XVIe siècles* (Ankara: Société turque d'histoire, 1991); Carl Göllner, *Turcica: Die europäischen
    Türkendrucke des XVI. Jahrhunderts*, 3 vols. (Baden-Baden: Verlag Valentin Koerner, 1994); and
    Elisabetta Borromeo, *Voyageurs occidentaux dans l'empire ottoman (1600–1644)*, 2 vols. (Paris:
    Maisonneuve & Larose, 2007).

Figure 2.1. Mounted Turk. Pius II *[Epistola ad Mahomatem II]*, Pii Papae Secundi *Epistola ad Morbisanum Turcarum Principe[m]*, frontispiece, Coloniae, 1532. By permission of the Folger Shakespeare Library, Shelfmark: 192–847q.

What follows builds on that scholarship to suggest genre types, present an array of mappings, and discuss the ways in which the Ottomans were visualized and circulated.

Familiarity and Representation

First, however, it is important to understand the dichotomies that did and did not apply in the struggles that provided context for the early modern representation of the "Turk." The Ottomans, in the rhetorics of the Christian kingdoms, were crafted, as we have seen, as one "side" in a set of opposed pairs: Asia vs. Europe, Islam vs. Christendom, and the senselessly violent Oriental barbarian against the thoughtfully violent Western knight. But these juxtapositions were very consciously constructed, their authors inspired as much by particular political agendas as by religious pieties. Thus the enduring historiographic monolith of Christendom vs. Islam, which was deployed very consistently throughout the period under consideration, is insufficient to explain the situation.[9] The "Turks," after all, were part of a "world" imperial competition that transcended religion.[10] For some early modern observers, the Ottomans were a part of their picture of the world's peoples, places, and domains. They had an assigned place, determined by a set of evolving classificatory schemes, and deriving from a universe of knowledge, text, and experience. But, because Ottoman expansionist policies were so successful, the empire tested the limits of that assigned place. As both Asia and Europe, it demanded new knowledge and an amended map. European Christendom was long accustomed to a Holy Land ruled by Muslim kings; but the Ottomans had swallowed up the east, unifying the eastern Mediterranean under a single Muslim lord and, more to the point, taking giant steps into eastern Europe, settling, and becoming established. By the sixteenth century the Ottomans not only inhabited the Biblical and classical lands, but also had become next-door neighbors to the powers of Europe. That proximity was reflected in and enhanced by the texts and images through which the sultan and his servants were interpreted. The possibilities for representing the Ottomans were then stretched into an ever-burgeoning corpus on who the Turk was, how he acted, and what he looked like. Old tropes were preserved and new ones added.

---

[9] Lonnie Johnson, *Central Europe: Enemies, Neighbors, Friends* (New York: Oxford University Press, 1996), 96–7, notes for example that "The Turkish threat . . . was a godsend for denominational and dynastic opponents of the Hapsburgs."

[10] The expatriate Hungarian poet Parmenius (b. c. 1555–60), published in 1582 his *De navigatione*, thrilling at the "prospect of the Protestant Gilbert leading the English into a land not yet polluted by 'the Moslem wail' or 'the scheming hand of Spain,'" cited in Peter Mancall, *Hakluyt's Promise: An Elizabethan's Obsession for an English America* (New Haven, CT: Yale University Press, 2007), 123. Parmenius's friend Richard Hakluyt the Younger used the English translation of Bartolomé de las Casas' "scathing denunciation of Spanish actions towards the indigenous peoples of the Caribbean basin," published originally in Seville in 1552, to compare the Spanish, who had "exercised moste outrageous and more than Turkishe crueltes," unfavorably with the Ottomans (110, 151).

The Power of the Past

To understand the drawing of the Ottomans in the early modern era it is also useful to examine the medieval precedents by which the enemies of the crusaders were designated "Turks," along with other conventions of naming. For example, Peter Tudebode, a priest of Civray (in France), in his eyewitness account of the First Crusade, *Historia de Hierosolymitano Itinere*, gives some sense of the conventions. He notes that the Byzantine emperor Alexius Comnenus (r. 1081–1118) warned the crusaders at Constantinople in summer 1096 about the strength of the Seljuk "Turks."[11] Once the crusading army confronted that enemy, it found them arrogant and contemptuous of their Christian foes. Tudebode writes of the Seljukid "Kerbogha" (Berkyaruk, r. 1094–1105) of Mosul, who marched on Antioch to relieve it from a crusader siege in June 1098. He imagines a speech in which Berkyaruk, speaking to one of his lieutenants, says of the crusaders,

> *These are the warring and shining arms which the Christians bore to Asia. The Christians are originally from western lands, by that I mean Europe, which is a third part of the world. With these arms they think and are confident they can expel and chase us beyond the borders of Corozan [Khorasan in Persia] and blot out our names beyond the rivers of the Amazons. They have already driven out our kinsfolk in Romania and the region of Antioch, the renowned capital of all Syria.[12]*

This speech tells us more about Tudebode's vision of opposing peoples than it does about Seljuk ideology. It reflects a religious–continental divide, and the fears regarding whose "name" would survive and whose be obliterated. The name "Turk," as it turned out, would prove remarkably enduring as a catchall identity for those who would inhabit the expansive domains of the East (as were the designations "Frank" and the "West," for those who opposed them).

Tudebode went on to elaborate on this dichotomy, adding a taste for luxury and holy war to that for violence as qualities of the "Turk." Berkyaruk, he wrote, called a scribe to write to

> *Our Caliph, our pope, and to all the very wise knights of Corozan ... Let everyone indulge in lascivious luxury and again rejoice over siring many sons who will fight valiantly against the Christians ... Tell them that I have all the Franks hemmed in Antioch ... I hold them in my hand, and I shall either kill them or lead them into miserable captivity ... Henceforth, I swear by Mohammad and the names of all of the gods that I shall not return to your presence until I have captured with my mighty right hand the kingdom of Antioch and all*

---

[11] Peter Tudebode, *Historia de Hierosolymitano Itinere*, John Hill and Laurita Hill, ed. and trans. (Philadelphia: American Philosophical Society, 1974), 17, 19.
[12] Tudebode, *Historia*, 68.

*Syria, Bulgaria, yes, even as far as Apulia, to the honor of the gods, of
you, and all the offspring of the Turks.*[13]

In this passage we not only get a sense of the multifaceted characterization
of the Turk in the crusading era but also a prelude to the characterizations
found in Christian texts about the Ottomans a half millennium later. In them,
hubris goes hand in hand with a pronounced warrior ethos and an inclination
to invoke God. The supposed dream of a Muslim conquest of Apulia became
reality in the temporary conquest by the Ottomans of Otranto on the eastern
Italian coast in 1480. Their successes seemed a prophecy fulfilled.

For the authors of early modern Christendom, the tie that linked the
Ottomans to the heretical beliefs of Muhammad was coupled with one that
linked them to a chain of ferocious warrior peoples who had long plagued the
citadels of civilization, what Margaret Meserve has called the "barbarians at
the gates" phenomenon.[14] Thus Eneas Silvius Piccolomini, Pius II, along with
some of his humanist contemporaries, "insisted" on the "Scythian" origins
of the Turks.[15] In the narratives of Renaissance and Reform, the Ottomans,
for all their patronage of the arts and possession of the imperial capitals
of Eurasia and Africa, were not simply "Turks": they were Mongols, Tro-
jans, Scythians, and Gog and Magog, all rolled into one, a force destined
to overturn all obstacles. They were the most recent in a chain of "enemies
of Christian people," as Gabriele Paleotti (1522–97) wrote in his 1582 *Discourse on Sacred and Profane Imagery*; since ancient times they had been
"persecutors of our sacred religion."[16]

In the narratives of seventeenth century Europe, these "Turks" were rein-
carnated. Writers such as André Favyn picked up the identification of the
Ottomans with Scythian antecedents without question. Thus Favyn's 1620
French work on the insignia of knighthood, *The Theater of Honour and
Knight-Hood, or A Compendious Chronicle and Historie of the whole Christian World*, looks to the eleventh century for "the first knowledge of the cruell
and barbarous Turkes."[17] The "Turks," he wrote, emerged from the depths
of Scythia to confront the Saracens:

[13] Tudebode, *Historia*, 68.
[14] Margaret Meserve, *Empires of Islam in Renaissance Historical Thought* (Cambridge, MA: Harvard
University Press, 2008), 71–116, 149–55. Meserve notes the "operations" the humanists performed
on their medieval texts in order to achieve the objectives of being "authoritative, elegant, and plausible
all at the same time," while showing "the Turks in as poor a light as possible (115)." See also
Mary W. Helms, "Essay on Objects: Interpretations of Distance Made Tangible," 355–77, in *Implicit
Understandings: Observing, Reporting, and Reflecting on the Encounters between European and Other
Peoples in the Early Modern Era*, Stuart Schwartz, ed. (Cambridge: Cambridge University Press, 1994),
369; and Kenneth Gouwens, "Perceiving the Past: Renaissance Humanism after the 'Cognitive Turn,'"
American Historical Review 103.1 (February 1998): 55–82, see 57.
[15] Petkov, *Infidels, Turks, and Women*, 222.
[16] Gabriele Paleotti, *Discorso Intorno alle Immagini Sacre e Profane (1582)* (Vatican City: Libreria
Editrice Vaticana, 2002), 133. They followed in the footsteps of the "Roman emperors, Saracens,
Moors, Vandals, and Goths."
[17] André Favyn, *The Theater of Honor and Knight-Hood, or A Compendious Chronicle and Historie of
the whole Christian World Containing The originall of all Monarchies, Kingdomes, and Estates, with
their Emperours, Kings, Princes, and Governours, Their Beginnings, Continuance, and Successions, to
this present Time* [A.M., trans.?] (London: Printed by William Iaggard, 1623), 366.

> *For in the yeare of Grace, One thousand and twelve ... an accursed race of people, wilde salvage, and cruell, knowne by the name of Turkes, issued from forth the deepes of Scythia, after they had embraced the doctrine of impious Mahomet, making their fury and barbarous nature felt in Aegypt, Syria, Palestine, and other places of Asia, where they put all to fire and Sword, not meeting with any one that dared to make head against them: until such time as the Sarrazins ... made them retire into a corner of Asia, as it is recorded by Haitonius the Armenian, in his description of Tartaria.*

Favyn groups these Turks with (east) Indians and Jews, as sulliers of a Christianity that is embodied in the Church and gendered female, a pure, white dove, swooning and surrounded by malignant forces:

> *afflicted with torments and Martyrdomes, this dove behelde her selfe as dead and entranced, her heart transpierced with the Sword of bitternesse, among the Scullionly potts, spits, and dripping panns of Indian and Turkish Infidels, soyled in the Furnaces of persecutions, in the Synagogues of Heretiques, smoaked and darkened with infernall doctrine.*[18]

The Ottomans, here, were simply a contemporary version of those sulliers of captive Christendom.

By the mid seventeenth century, the tropes used to characterize the Ottomans had been formalized in various genres of literature. The *English Parnassus* (1654), a "rhyming dictionary for use in English schools," provided a "list of suitable synonyms and epithets for 'Turke' from a comprehensive survey of usages in 'the best authors'":

> *Unbelieving, misbelieving, thrifty, abstemious, cruel, unpitying, merciless, unrelenting, inexorable, warlike, circumcised, superstitious, bloody, wine-forbearing, turban'd, avaricious, covetous, erring.*[19]

Even when the subject was love, the "Turk" was characterized as violent and bloody. Thus, in the 1688 English translation of Du Vignau [Sieur des Joanots]'s *Le Secretaire Turc*, the translator explains to his readers the novelty of the work, which focused on "gallantries" rather than the customary: "Policy, Fire, and Sword ... "[20] He attributes the popularity of the work in France and Italy to its focus on love. But, for Du Vignau, even in love the Turks were violent creatures who did not have the "civilized"

---

[18] Favyn, *Theater of Honor*, 342. Chew, *The Crescent and the Rose*, 121, 145–6, notes the common English conflation of Turks and Saracens.

[19] Cited in Gerald MacLean, *Looking East: English Writing and the Ottoman Empire before 1800* (Houndmills, Basingstoke: Palgrave, 2007), 7.

[20] Du Vignau [Sieur des Joanots], *The Turkish Secretary, Containing The Art of Expressing ones Thoughts without Seeing, Speaking, or Writing to one another; With the Circumstances of a Turkish Adventure; As also A most Curious Relation of several particulars of the Serrail that have not before now ever been made publick*. Translated by the Author of the Monthly Account (London: 1688). Note that this is the same year that Giovanni Battista Donado's *Della letturatura de' Turchi* came out in Venice; see Mario Infelice, "The War, the News, and the Curious: Military Gazettes in Italy," 216–36, in Brendan Dooley and Sabrina Baron, eds., *The Politics of Information in Early Modern Europe* (London: Routledge, 2001), 228.

means of communicating emotions available to men and women in France or England:

> *They abandon themselves entirely to this Passion; they make it their Sovereign Pleasure; they push it even to fury.*
>
> *Nay, it has been averr'd to me that there are Turks, both Men and Women, who to prove their Love in their Extravagancies, run Daggers into their Arms, and cause burning Sulphur to be dropt into the Wound...*[21]

This image of ferocity and extravagance was transformed in H. Chatelain's *1739 Atlas Historique* into an engraving of the "*Turc Amoureux*," a lover cutting his arm before the watchful eyes of his beloved (Fig. 2.2).[22] That figure's appearance in an eighteenth-century atlas reminds us of the enduring nature of this particular characterization of Ottoman culture and space. The "Turks," it would seem, like their Scythian predecessors, would manage to draw blood one way or another, whether the targets of their violence were Christians, Saracens, occupants of the Holy Land, or their own love-besotted selves.[23]

Witnessing the Turk

Observers who experienced Ottoman lands first-hand did not depict the empire in any uniform way. But they did present the apparition of the Turk, at least in part, as either a direct political threat or an embodiment of divine punishment in the context of the Reformation. Both forms are apparent in the English translation, dated 1600, of Martin Fumée's (d. c. 1590) French history of the Ottoman wars in Hungary.[24] The English "Gentleman," R.C., who produced this translation provides us with an intriguing entry into the vision of the "Turk" that made its way from Hungary to France to England. First of all, the translator portrays Hungary as a distressed female pilgrim (rather like Favyn's dove), who has made her way, via his text, in ragged garments, "into our little Iland [sic.]... in the uttermost confines of Europe," having already petitioned the other "Princes of Christendome."[25] R.C. proposes that his patron, the powerful Robert Cecil (d. 1612), Secretary

---

[21] Du Vignau, *The Turkish Secretary*, 2.

[22] Chatelain, *Atlas Historique*, v. 5, 'ethnographic' images after page 41. Olga Nefedova, *A Journey into the World of the Ottomans: The Art of Jean-Baptiste Vanmour (1671–1737)* (Milan: Skira, 2009), traces this engraving (like other images in Chatelain) to a 1712 work by Vanmour.

[23] See Mary Pix, *Ibrahim, The Thirteenth Emperour of the Turks: A Tragedy As it is Acted By His Majesties Servants* (London: Printed for John Harding and Richard Wilkin, 1696). See also the play "Selimus," in Daniel Vitkus, ed., *Three Turk Plays from Early Modern England: Selimus, A Christian Turned Turk, and The Renegado* (New York: Columbia University Press, 2000). See also, on treachery and lasciviousness, Chew, *The Crescent and the Rose*, 142–5. These representations are rather different from the "rosy picture" view of Ottoman space as love space suggested in Alexander Bevilacqua and Helen Pfeifer, "Turquerie: Culture in Motion, 1650–1750," *Past and Present* 221 (November, 2013): 75–118, see 110.

[24] Mart. Fumée, *The Historie of the Troubles of Hungarie: Containing the Pitifull Losse and Ruine of that Kingdome, and the Warres Happened There, in That Time, betweene the Christians and Turkes*, trans. R.C. Gentleman (London: Felix Kyngston, 1600).

[25] Fumée, *The Historie of the Troubles*, first unnumbered page of dedication.

TURC AMOUREUX.

Il y en a d'assez fous pour se déchirer les bras en présence de leur Maîtresse afin de mieux prouver leur passion. Ceux qui se les déchirent davantage passent pour les plus amoureux.

Figure 2.2. Henri Chatelain, "Turc Amoureux," *Atlas Historique, ou Nouvelle Introduction a l'Histoire*, 3rd ed., v. 5, after p. 41, Amsterdam, 1739. By permission of the Folger Shakespeare Library, Shelfmark: D11.5 C6 v.5 Cage.

of State to "Her Majesty," Queen Elizabeth, receive this petitioner with his accustomed goodness, as he has received other "distressed strangers."[26]

Why should England take heed of the situation in Hungary, where the Ottomans had recently (1596) conquered the fortress of Egri? In his note "To the Reader," R.C. explains why word of the Ottomans must be translated and communicated to an English audience. First of all, he himself is a traveler, who has seen first-hand the miseries dealt to Hungary and her people by the Ottoman armies. Second, he judges the French work neither "fiction or fabulous," but a credible history as witnessed by the testimonials it contains from prominent men.[27] And third, despite England's location at the edges of Europe, he wishes to warn the English of their own peril. For those

> parts of Christendome that now thinke themselves as secure, as once the Hungars did, and they then as safe from the deluge of Infidels, as we doe now. But alas, such was their pride and dissention (unhappie people) that (through their owne misgovernment) God inflicted this punishment upon them, which now as remedilesse, and altogether in dispaire, they with wofull laments too late bewaile...[28]

The Ottomans, R.C. assures his readers, have men and military discipline far exceeding those of Christendom, leaving the possibility of Christians reconquering Hungary in great doubt. He then summons up the rhetorics of the crusading era, urging his readers to suffer the narration of the Turks' "horrible massacres" of Christian men, women, and children, maiden rape, burning, sacrilege, and "devastations of all manner of creatures" that is contained in the *History*, and to take it as a lesson (just as Fumée admonished his French readers to use the *History* as a "mirror").[29] Finally, the translator cautions the reader not to be fooled by the suggestion contained in the *History* itself that the Ottomans engage in friendly relations with their Christian neighbors:

> You may discerne their entercourse and temporizing with Christians, which indeed is nothing else, but only for their own commoditie to make use of them, until they finde fit oportunitie to advance their intended practices against them: and then adieu league and all societie of friendship.[30]

R.C. here suggests the complexity of the representational situation. He is aware that his readers may well be familiar with both the depredations of the Ottomans against Christians, and with tales of consorting, socializing, and even friendship, repeated in the very history he has translated. But he wants the reader to brook no illusions about who the "Turks" really are. The Ottomans may have relations with Christians, but what is important is that

---

[26] Fumée, *The Historie of the Troubles*, second unnumbered page of dedication.
[27] Fumée, *The Historie of the Troubles*, first unnumbered page of "To the Reader."
[28] Fumée, *The Historie of the Troubles*, second unnumbered page of "To the Reader."
[29] Fumée, *The Historie of the Troubles*, first unnumbered page of "The Authors Epistle to the people of France."
[30] Fumée, *The Historie of the Troubles*, second unnumbered page, "To the Reader."

God grant the extirpation of "these Mahometaines...who...Infringe the confines of Europe with their heathenish and barbarous proceedings."[31] The distraught female Hungary embodied in the text carries this message across the continent. Thus the distance between Hungary and England is bridged, and the English reader is led to a "proper" understanding that fraternity with the Turks is not an option.[32]

Consorting and fraternity, however, were most definitely an option, as various witnesses make clear. Another warning against fraternal behavior appears in the travel narrative of the Bohemian page Wenceslas Wratislaw, written just a year before R.C.'s translation.[33] Wratislaw traveled in 1591 from Vienna to Constantinople in the retinue of the Hapsburg ambassador Frederick Kregwitz, remaining in the empire for some years. There, as an energetic youth and later as a prisoner, Wratislaw became familiar with the "Turks," trying his hand at Turkish and even getting drunk on good Greek wine in Galata with two of the legation's janissaries, an escapade for which the ambassador punished him severely.[34] For Kregwitz, as for R.C., it was important for all Christians to remember their God and their identity and to make no mistake about the dangers (such as captivity and conversion) inherent in mixing with "Turks." Their admonitions, of course, simply reinforce the notion (as Wratislaw makes abundantly clear) that fraternization was a practice both common and longstanding. Indeed the intrepid young traveler's day book is shot through with references to intercourse between Christians and "Turks," from the jokes of the *beylerbey* (governor) of Sofia to the cheerful conversation and manly challenges of Hapsburg and Turk "hussars" who shared each other's company while Kregwitz dined with Ottoman hosts near the border at Gran (Esztergom).[35] For those experiencing the "Turk" close up rather than from the distance of R.C.'s "little Island," fraternization was both a distinct possibility and a perceived threat.[36]

Thanks to such encounters and the texts they engendered, "Europe" became familiar with the "Turk." Bernard Randolph (b. 1643), in his *The Present State of the Morea*, used the long Ottoman siege of Candia (on Crete) from 1648 to 1669 as a measure of the circulation of knowledge of the Ottomans.[37] "All Europe," he wrote, "has heard of this great Siege, how many thousand Bombs were cast into the City; How many Mines, and

---

[31] Fumée, *The Historie of the Troubles,* second unnumbered page, "To the Reader." On "anti-Muslim holy war jingoism," in England at the time, and James I's anti-Ottoman turn in 1603, see Nabil Matar, *Turks, Moors, and Englishmen in the Age of Discovery* (New York: Columbia University Press, 1999), 142–5.

[32] Adrian Johns, *The Nature of the Book: Print and Knowledge in the Making* (Chicago: University of Chicago Press, 1998), 158, on the relationship of "trust" between printer and reader.

[33] Václav Vratislav z Mitrovic, *Príhody*, Milada Nedvědová, ed. (Prague: M.F., 1976). The editor's note suggests the elaborate layers of translation, extraction, and editions taken from Wratislaw's account, which was not published until 1777 (217).

[34] Václav Vratislav, *Adventures of Baron Wenceslas Wratislaw* (n.p: Bibliobazar, n.d; reprint of London: Bell and Daldy, 1862 edition), 79–81.

[35] Vratislav, *Adventures*, 2, 35.

[36] See Matar, *Islam in Britain*, 1–72, on the fears and realities of captivity and conversion.

[37] Candia surrendered in September 1669, leaving Crete as a final and tardy prize in the long era of Ottoman expansion.

Fornellos were blown up; and how many bold assaults the Turks made . . ."[38]
With this assertion, Randolph imagined a consuming public that expected
a certain level of detail: reportage on military conflict that transcended the
impressionistic and fanciful and got down to brass tacks. If "all Europe"
was not familiar with the history of the Ottoman wars in the Mediterranean, Randolph assumed at any rate that his readers, certain members of
the English literate classes, were.[39] Their visions of the Ottoman realm were
based on a combination of classical constructions of the spaces the Ottomans
ruled (Ptolemy for example), histories such as Fumée's, second-hand images
from the Continent (Ortelius' maps, Venetian *relazioni*, and French tales of
courtly life), and accounts of the experiences of English merchants, adventurers and travelers. By Randolph's time, visualizing, producing, and staging
the Ottomans for European audiences was a well-established and thriving
business.

The siege of Candia went on for so long, decades, that its writers and
readers needed new episodes, rather like those in a Dickensian serial. Such
episodes might rely on the simple narration of battles and barbarisms, but
narratives such as Randolph's added detailed contexts, the frames on which
history is constructed: the character of the Turk, the types of weaponry and
tactics employed by both sides, and the associations of the Cretans with classical antecedents. As noted in the previous chapter, and as Ernest Gilman
has aptly argued, the "old" provided a comfortable foundation for the conceptualization of the "new," whether what was novel was a western continent, or just another incarnation of "Saracen" violence and expansionism.[40]
Randolph expected his audience to "know" the Ottomans. And for those like
him, who mapped Ottoman space, the "old" was in fact more than available;
it was a desirable and comfortable prism through which to familiarize, type,
and make accessible all the realms on which early modern European scholars,
notables, cartographers, and travelers cast their eyes. For the discriminating
reader then, history, eyewitness accounts, and the specificities of place and
action were required to flesh out the trite generalizations that might suffice
for sermon literature.[41] We can thus view the "progression" of early modern literature on the Ottomans in terms of the level of familiarity each text
assumes, the degree to which past knowledge and authorities are invoked,

[38] Bernard Randolph, *The Present State of the Morea, called anciently Peloponnesus: Together with a Description of the City of Athnes, Islands of Zant, Strafades, and Serrigo. With the Maps of Morea and Greece, and several Cities. Also a true Prospect of the Grand Serraglio, or Imperial Palace of Constantinople, as it appears from Galata: Curiously Engraved on Copper Plates*, Third Edition (London: Printed for Will. Notts, Tho. Basset; and Thomas Bennet, 1689), 70. Note that the first edition appeared in 1686, written after "several years of observation, from 1671–1679."

[39] See MacLean, *Looking East: English Writing and the Ottoman Empire*, 61; and P. J. Marshall and Glyndwr Williams, *The Great Map of Mankind: British Perceptions of the World in the Age of Enlightenment* (London: J.M. Dent & Sons, 1982), 13–18.

[40] Ernest Gilman, "Madagascar on My Mind: The Earl of Arundel and the Arts of Colonization," 284–314, in *Early Modern Visual Culture: Representation, Race, and Empire in Renaissance England*, Peter Erickson and Clark Hulse, eds. (Philadelphia: University of Pennsylvania Press, 2000), 285.

[41] Marshall and Williams, *The Great Map of Mankind*, note that François Bernier (1625–88), "who claimed that he had 'travelled through nearly every part of the empire,' reported that it was 'lamentably . . . ruined and depopulated' (16)."

and the extent to which the author claims (or does not claim) to be providing new or unique information, based on personal experience.[42]

Genre

The authors of Christian Europe approached the Ottomans through a combination of experience and story, fear and conversation, the logical outcomes of confronting a formidable foe in a known space already saturated with history and stamped with a set of enduring though mutable tropes of identity. They did so employing a variety of tones in a variety of genres.

Travel and History

Travel, in its variant forms, was perhaps *the* genre through which the audiences of Europe best experienced and came to "know" the Ottomans.[43] Travel comprised a continuum of narration that included the diplomatic report, campaign account, merchant itinerary, and captivity testimony, as well as the more leisurely journals and histories of a corps of sojourners who encountered the Ottoman empire voluntarily or involuntarily for a diverse set of stated and unstated reasons. In the early modern era such narratives evolved into "universal" histories of travel, compendia of knowledge, and atlases, among other genres.[44] It was through imagining travel that the reader at home "saw" Ottoman space. And by the eighteenth century, as one collection of narratives boasted, "travelling upon paper," by means of a literature of global exploits, had been made easy for the common man, and "knowledge" had been "made as familiar as possible."[45]

Travel itself was an opportunity, but also the necessary, tedious, and dangerous mode of getting from one space to another. Both of those factors (advantage and annoyance) were reflected in a burgeoning literature on the Ottoman empire that took inspiration from the tales of medieval travelers

---

[42] Jonathan Burton, *Traffic and Turning: Islam and English Drama, 1579–1624* (Newark: University of Delaware Press, 2005), 27, notes, "whatever version of the Turks was useful for English reasons was often presented as the essential truth about the Turks." Burton provides (257–8) a list of dramatic works with Muslim characters for the period treated.

[43] MacLean, *The Rise of Oriental Travel*, 130, points out that Bishop Henry King's dedication to Henry Blount's (1602–82) 1636 *Voyage* highlights his familiarity with things Ottoman as deriving from "looking over the maps of Ortelius and Mercator," and from reading travel accounts.

[44] Joachim Camerarius, *Symbolorum ac emblematum*, published in Nuremburg 1590–1604, which included four hundred etchings, and explanatory material, "derived from both classical and contemporary material," gives an indication of the state of the cosmographical and ethnographical arts, powered by travel literature, at the end of the sixteenth century. Donald Lach, *Asia in the Making of Europe*, v. II, *A Century of Wonder* (Chicago: University of Chicago Press, 1970), 86–7, notes the "geographical and cosmographical woodcuts printed by John Day in William Cunningham, *The Cosmographical Glasse* (London, 1550)" and the map emblems of the engravers of Antwerp, especially Phillippe Galle (1537–1612).

[45] *A New and Universal History of Voyages and Travels Collected from the most authentic Authors in all Languages...* (London: W. Owen, 1754), fourth and fifth unnumbered pages of "Introduction." Chatelain, *Atlas Historique*, v. 1, 3, in his 1739 introduction to universal history, notes that humankind's "ardor" for travel tales, the charms of learning about faraway people, and the opportunity to compare "their" customs with "ours" remained undiminished.

and from a genre of collected travels that both classified and allocated travel space. Narratives of travel brought tales of the "Turk" from the borders of the Ottoman empire to the bookstalls of London. In that process, Venice, with its maritime empire bumped up against the ambitions and turf of the sultan, and in its role as a primary center of print culture, was intimately engaged in the business of picturing the "Turk." It provided models in the forms of the pragmatic *relazioni* of the Signoria's envoys and resident bailos, and the "voyages" (*Delle navigationi et viaggi*, 1550–59) compiled by the Venetian civil servant Giovanni Battista Ramusio (1485–1557). Ramusio's collection not only assembled a hodgepodge group of voyagers, but also exemplified the layering of history so characteristic of the age, mingling the tales of fifteenth and sixteenth century travelers with excerpts from Hippocrates, Marco Polo, Haytham, and Arriano. Scythians heading west and medieval monks on their way to Tartary shared the pages of Ramusio's volumes with more contemporary travelers.[46]

Among the imitators of Ramusio were the English cleric Richard Hakluyt (c. 1552–1616) and his successor Samuel Purchas, who called Ramusio's *Navigationi* and Hakluyt's *Principal Navigations* (1598–1600) his "two libraries."[47] Hakluyt merged history and travel. He claimed that "Geographie and Chronologie . . . the right eye and left of all history" helped him place each account in its proper time and place.[48] Even the labor of his compiling, he wrote, with all its delays, expenses, frustrations, suffering, and seeking, was analogous to the arduous journeys of a traveler. Both travel and the assembling of travel narratives were "a way of properly ordering the world – subsuming both territorial property and literary propriety to the needs of the state."[49]

Hakluyt's England was the recipient, the reader, and the beneficiary of a varied set of representations, informations, and images that situated the two prospering entrepots of Venice and Constantinople in a landscape of history, literature, commerce, and communal conflict. Italian texts penetrated the English market in the mid sixteenth century, often through the vehicle of French. Benedetto Ramberti's (1503–46) *Libri tre delle cose de Turchi*, published in Venice in 1539, was translated into French and then into English, as

---

[46] Giovanni Battista Ramusio, *Delle Navigationi et Viaggi*, v. 2 (Venetia: i Giunti, 1583), unnumbered pages "*nomi de gli autori.*" See also Deborah Howard, "The Role of the Book in the Transfer of Culture between Venice and the Eastern Mediterranean," 97–107, in *The Renaissance and the Ottoman World*, esp. 105–6.

[47] Anthony Payne, " ' Strange, remote, and farre distant countreys': The Travel Books of Richard Hakluyt," 1–38, in *Journeys through the Market: Travel, Travellers, and the Book Trade*, Robin Myers and Michael Harris, eds. (Newcastle: Oak Knoll Press, 1999), 19; and David Harris Sacks, "Richard Hakluyt and his Publics, c. 1580–1620," 160–76, in *Making Publics in Early Modern Europe: People, Things, Forms of Knowledge*, Bronwen Wilson and Paul Yachnin, eds. (New York: Routledge, 2010), esp. 164–8. Archer, *Old Worlds*, 96, notes the Protestant objectives of Purchas, who "made use of the Tremellius–Junius Bible of 1590 with its maps and detailed notes on the location of Eden, which in turn depended on ancient geographical authorities."

[48] Richard Hakluyt, *Principal Navigations*, 1598 edition (1:19), cited in Kim F. Hall, *Things of Darkness: Economies of Race and Gender in Early Modern England* (Ithaca and New York: Cornell University Press, 1995), 45.

[49] Hall, *Things of Darkness*, 46.

The order of the greate Turckes court, in 1542.[50] Andrea Cambini's (d. 1527) *Della origine de Turchi et imperio della Casa ottomanna*, was translated into English is 1562.[51] From these "beginnings" the Ottomans moved firmly into the literatures and onto the stages of England.[52] The channels of translation thus moved from the most proximate and contested spaces, such as Venice and the Balkans, to the imperial, print, and cultural centers of Europe such as Prague, Augsburg, Nuremberg, Frankfort, Basel, Antwerp, Paris, Lisbon, Amsterdam, and London.

The genre of travel literature emerged with a vengeance in the sixteenth century in the domains of the Christian kings; and in that literature the articulation of the Turk played a pivotal role. French travelers made a significant contribution to the genres by which the Ottoman empire and points east were understood. Nicolas de Nicolay (1517–83), for example, served as an influential "pioneer" of the illustrated travel account,[53] while Jean-Baptiste Tavernier (1605–89), François Bernier (1625–88), and Jean Chardin (1643–1713) stood as a "great triumvirate" of travel, with Tavernier's *Voyages* (Paris, 1675) produced in "at least eighteen" reprints and reeditions by 1724.[54] And although this volume does not focus on Spain as a source for visions of Ottoman space, the Turk, in his various manifestations, looms large in its literature, and in the crafting of its strategic, religious, and commercial ambitions.[55] Muzaffar Alam and Sanjay Subrahmanyam, focusing

[50] Benedetto Ramberti, *Libri tre delle cose de Turchi* (Venetia: In casa de' figlioli di Aldo, 1539); Ramberti, *The order of the greate Turckes courte, of hys mene of warre, and of all hys conquests, with the summe of Mahumetes doctryne*. Translated out of the French ([London]: Ricardus Grafton, 1542). Paolo Giovio's *Commentario delle cose de' Turchi*, published in Venice in 1531, was translated into multiple languages, including English, and printed in twenty-one editions within fifteen years of its appearance. Matar, *Islam in Britain*, 12, has argued that in England knowledge of the Ottoman empire by 1603 "was becoming essential to the general reading public." He notes further the use of "theological polemic, drama and evangelism" to thwart the appeal of the Ottoman empire to Englishmen who might be tempted to convert (19).

[51] Andrea Cambini, *Two very notable commentaries [on the origins] of the Turcks and Empire of the house of Ottomanno,... and ... the warres of the Turcke against George Scanderbeg, prince of Epiro, and of the great victories obteyned by the sayd George as well against the Emperour of Turkie, as other princes* (London: Humphrey Toye, 1562), was translated out of French (from the 1541 original Italian).

[52] Lady Mary Wroth (1587–c. 1651) crafted a fictive eastern Europe and Asia Minor in *Urania* (1621). Sheila Cavanaugh, *Cherished Torment: The Emotional Geography of Lady Mary Wroth's Urania* (Pittsburgh: Duquesne University Press, 2001), 9–11, notes the influence of works such as Giovanni Botero's *The Travelers Breviat* (1601) and Nathanael Carpenter's *Geography Delineated* (1625) on Wroth's circle (13). "Readers of the complete *Urania*, therefore, are rewarded with a remarkable portrait of a diffusely interconnected world that reveals its origins in the writings of the ancients, in scripture, in roughly contemporary scientific and philosophical debates, in Greek and continental romance literature, and in maps and records produced in an era of prolific exploration (14)."

[53] Nicolas de Nicolay, *Les quatre premiers livres des navigations et peregrinations orientales de N. de Nicolay* (first published in Lyon in 1567), was rendered into Italian by 1576 and into English by 1585.

[54] Muzaffar Alam and Sanjay Subrahmanyam, *Indo Persian Travels in the Age of Discoveries, 1400–1800* (Cambridge: Cambridge University Press, 2007), 352. Tavernier's description of the sultan's seraglio also appeared in 1675.

[55] See Özlem Kumrular, *Las Relaciones entre el Imperio Otomano y la Monarquía Católica entre los años 1520–1535 y el papel de los Estados satélites* (İstanbul: Isis Press, 2003), 79, 141–55; and Barbara Fuchs, *Passing for Spain: Cervantes and the Fictions of Identity* (Urbana: University of Illinois Press, 2003), 66–79. María Judith Feliciano, "Picturing the Ottoman Threat in Sixteenth-Century New Spain," 243–66, in *The Turk and Islam in the Western Eye, 1450–1750: Visual Imagery before Orientalism*, James Harper, ed. (Farnham, Surrey: Ashgate, 2011), esp. 256–7, notes how news and

on Iberian sources, have argued that there was a growing market for travel accounts in Europe in the late sixteenth and early seventeenth centuries. On this "explosion" of travel literature and its periodization, they note: "For if, in the 1560s, chronicles, compendia, travel-texts, and other odd hybrid products ... all jostled for space on the reader's shelf, in the seventeenth century it was the European travel-account that swept all before it."[56]

Germany was also an important conduit for the channeling of information on the Turk. On its participation in choreographing the "East," Todd Kontje has noted that "throughout the sixteenth and seventeenth centuries German knowledge of Asia grew increasingly detailed as travelers published accounts of their experiences, and an 'Orientalizing cultural wave' [*orientalisierende Kulturwelle*] influenced many aspects of German culture," through goods such as coffee and porcelain as well as "Turkish costumes at parties and tournaments."[57] Fictional travelers also brought "news" of eastern spaces to the audiences of the Christian kingdoms. Thus, Hans Jakob Christoffel von Grimmelshausen (1621–176) made the hero of his 1669 novel *Der Abenteuerliche Simplicissimus Teutsch* (The Adventurous German Simplicissimus) a well-traveled man who, more or less like the story-spinning English Captain John Smith (of Virginia fame), was captured by "Tartars," victimized by Muslim pirates, and ended up in Constantinople.[58] Grimmelshausen "envisions global Christianity," achieved through military conquest, and makes Germany the "heir to Greco-Roman antiquity," thus putting it in direct competition with the Ottoman empire.[59]

There was a direct pipeline to Germany via Italy for texts about the Ottomans. Thus Johannes Piscatorius' *Herkommen, ursprung unnd auffgang des türkishen unnd ottomanischen Kayserthumms*, published in Augsburg in 1541, was based primarily on the Italian work of Paolo Giovio (1483–1552), bishop of Nocera, who was also responsible for the circulation of portraits of the Ottoman sultans.[60] The flow of images of the Turk was thus multiform and multidirectional. Indeed, the famous Ottoman court historiographer, Seyyid Lokman, noted that the portraits of the sultans in his own *Şemailname* (a work on the dress and physiognomy of the sultans, c. 1579) were modeled in part on a series of Italian portraits of the sultans brought to Istanbul by the Venetian bailo Daniele Barbarigo at the request of the

images of the Turk were channeled from the Iberian peninsula into "the consciousness of the viceregal world" and its theatrical performances.

[56] Alam and Subrahmanyam, *Indo Persian Travels*, 342, also 336, 357–61. See also Rubiés, *Travel and Ethnology*, and John Tolan, *Saint Francis and the Sultan: The Curious History of a Christian–Muslim Encounter* (Oxford: Oxford University Press, 2009), 221, on the translation and circulation of popular Iberian texts.

[57] Todd Kontje, *German Orientalisms* (Ann Arbor, MI: University of Michigan Press, 2007), 34; and Petkov, *Infidels, Turks, and Women*, 219–59.

[58] Kontje, *German Orientalisms*, 41–2. Unlike Smith, the hero does not end up glorifying his adventures.

[59] Kontje, *German Orientalisms*, 4, 47–8. Grimmelshausen's contemporary, Daniel Caspar von Lohenstein (1635–1683), produced dramas, *Ibrahim Bassa* (1653) and *Ibrahim Sultan* (1673), that also target the Ottomans, depicting, respectively, a "Christian" Ibrahim whom Sultan Süleyman has beheaded because he lusts after Ibrahim's wife, Isabella, and a monarchical Muslim, Ibrahim who is lewd, sexually insatiable, and bloodthirsty.

[60] Petkov, *Infidels, Turks, and Women*, 245; and Julian Raby, "From Europe to Istanbul," in *The Sultan's Portrait: Picturing the House of Osman* (İstanbul: İşbank, 2000), 136–63, esp. 141–4.

grand vezir Sokollu Mehmet Pasha.[61] Unlike their Christian counterparts, however, the Ottomans were not engulfed by the wave of travel writing that swept over the Christian kingdoms. The voyage literature of the Ottomans is quite limited, its central example the unique *Book of Travels* of Evliya Çelebi (1611–82), a contemporary of Grimmelshausen.[62] But the Ottomans participated in the same Afro-Eurasian universe of textual and visual exchange, of commerce, warfare, and pilgrimage.[63] What they did not write, they might very well have read. Travel, in that universe, crossed the boundaries of state as well as genre.

Sermons

Travel also crossed the boundaries of the sacred and profane; as such, it was an important source for sermons. Sermon literature took up the news coming from the Christian–Muslim frontiers and used it as a warning of apocalyptic doom or as a summons to believers to "clean house" and prepare for the coming of the Kingdom (see Ch. 3). Sermons reflected the persistent fear that the number of Christians converting to Islam might grow ever larger in the contexts of Reformation conflict and Ottoman prosperity. The sermon is a transitional genre that reached from orality to print, and on into various types of text that incorporated the ideologies and rhetorics of news, travel, and history. In England, "probably well over 2000 sermons were printed between 1590 and 1640, many of which passed through repeated editions and in larger print runs than before."[64] Once the sermon became pamphlet literature, it served as more than a model for preaching. It joined compendia of knowledge, histories, broadsheets, and other ephemera as a vehicle for

[61] See Filiz Çagman, "Portrait Series of Nakkaş Osman," in *The Sultan's Portrait*, 164–87, esp. 174. Barbarigo's *relazione* on his term as bailo dates to 1564. See also Emine Fetvacı, "From Print to Trace: An Ottoman Imperial Portrait Book and Its Western European Models," *Art Bulletin* 95.2 (June 2013): 243–68. Bronwen Wilson, "Foggie diverse di vestire de'Turchi: Turkish Costume Illustration and Cultural Translation," in Special Issue, *Mapping the Mediterranean*, Valeria Finucci, ed., *Journal of Medieval and Early Modern Studies*, 37.1 (Winter 2007): 97–140, documents the Venetian interest in portraits of the Ottoman sultans and argues that "The system of visual classification in Western costume books encouraged European viewers to compare themselves with the Ottoman Turks...(130)." See also Caroline Finkel, *Osman's Dream: The Story of the Ottoman Empire, 1300-1923* (New York: Basic Books, 2005), 194–5; and Julian Raby, "The Serenissima and the Sublime Porte," 107–9.
[62] As Suraiya Faroqhi has noted, it was only in the early eighteenth, century with the account of Yirmisekiz Mehmet Efendi's visit to Paris in 1720, that Ottoman "ambassadors begin to write in extenso about their experiences in foreign parts." Suraiya Faroqhi, *The Ottoman Empire and the World around It* (London: I.B. Tauris, 2004), 6–8.
[63] Costume manuals on both "sides" played a role in the enhanced perception of familiarity. Suraiya Faroqhi and Christoph Neumann, *Ottoman Costumes From Textile to Identity* (İstanbul: Eren, 2004), 110–11, note the issues involved when Muslims dressed like "foreigners," thus illustrating both the customs and the fears of dressing like a designated "other." See also Leslie Meral Schick, "Ottoman Costume Albums in a Cross-Cultural Context," *Art Turc/Turkish Art: 10th International Congress of Turkish Art, Geneva, 17–23 September 1995, Proceedings* (Geneva: Fondation Max Van Berchem, 1999), 625–8.
[64] Ian Green, "Orality, Script, and Print: The Case of the English Sermon c. 1530-1700," 236–55, in *Cultural Exchange in Early Modern Europe, v. 1, Religion and Cultural Exchange in Europe, 1400-1700*, 243, 250–52. Estimates for the period 1660–1783 range from 12,000 to more than 24,000. No scholar has published a systematic analysis of the vision of the "Turk" in the enormous body of sermon literature.

reinforcing the public's vision of various threats to Christendom. So the "Turk" served as an epic and convenient villain for the tracts of the pious as well as the stylish literary productions of intellectuals and playwrights. The sermon also easily bled into belles lettres. In the Dalmatian city states, such as Zadar, Split, and Trogir, for example, numerous "*Orationes contra Turcas*," speeches dedicated by intellectuals to prominent persons such as the pope, the emperor, or various aristocrats, can be found in manuscript and print form.[65] Thus, although I do not here address sermon literature directly, it is important to keep in mind the extent to which maps, travel literature, and other types of texts resonated with the warnings and admonitions found in religious invocations dating back to the medieval era. The sermon was yet one more avenue by which the "Turk" was mapped onto the consciousness of the subjects of the Christian kings.

Compendia of Knowledge

The literati of early modern Europe were compilers of knowledge in text and image, with no unmoving boundary between the world history and the atlas. Narrative both inspired and required maps, whereas collections of maps only became comprehensible when embedded in textual contexts. Thus Francesca Fiorani calls Sebastian Münster's *Cosmographia universalis* (Basel, 1544) the result of the ransacking of earlier authors, its "geographical narration" complemented by "an ample visual apparatus of maps, city views, portraits, coats of arms, genealogical trees, ancient inscriptions, coins and medals," among other things.[66] It was the

> tool of those who wished to learn about the world without the inconve-
> nience [or inspiration] of traveling, as well as the textbook of descriptive
> geography for young men and women who prepared for their political
> and social lives, and the desired travel companion of those who, like
> Michel de Montaigne [1533–1592], traveled in foreign lands.[67]

In his turn, Abraham Ortelius (1527–98), the Flemish cartographer, took Ptolemy's order of things and visualized his own theatre of the world through maps, "eliminating other kinds of images and limiting the verbal descrip-tions of places."[68] Maps were "visual aids to the recollection of events," whether the events were found in Exodus, Herodotus, or more contempo-rary narratives.[69] And the map provided a frame within which the viewer could see the layers of history and of action up to the present, choosing which layers might supersede the others.

   Into that early modern interplay of text, image, and commitment to the past marched the prophet Muhammad and then the "Turk," problematizing the

[65] Klemen Pust, "The Image of the 'Turk' in the Christian Countries of the Adriatic Basin in the Modern Age,"4 (English abstract), http://www.zrs.kp.si/konferenca/retorika_dev/avtorji/Klemen_P.html.
[66] Fiorani, *The Marvel of Maps*, 86–7.
[67] Fiorani, *The Marvel of Maps*, 85–6, notes that the *Cosmographia* went through more than 40 editions in German, Latin, French, Italian, and Bohemian in the century after its production.
[68] Fiorani, *The Marvel of Maps*, 87–8.
[69] Fiorani, *The Marvel of Maps*, 88.

comfortable flow of Christian history and Christian space. As the authors of sixteenth- and seventeenth-century Europe collected the world into histories and atlases that were more or less "universal," the Ottomans and their realms, in both Europe and Asia, played a prominent role. Jacques-Auguste de Thou's (1553–1617) monumental *Histoire Universelle*, running to more than ten thousand pages, devoted 900 pages to the Ottomans and their relations with Persia and the "*monde chrétien*," mapping the empire in an almost overwhelming body of text.[70]

By the later eighteenth century the Ottomans had been thoroughly synthesized and cataloged into the domains and peoples of the world. Indeed, by this later period "universal" histories proclaimed their ability to provide the short version of a globe compressed for a discriminating yet busy audience of readers. *The New Universal History of Voyages and Travels,* printed in London in 1754, boasted that it had "digested" the burdensome and voluminous travel literature for its readers, who could see the world "at one view," with "enough preserved of the lives, fortunes, and particular adventures of the most eminent persons, to gratify his curiosity; without leading him a wild-goose chase, after matters of little consequence . . . "[71] The reader imagined by the publishers was not confined to those "gentlemen" who had perused the classics, because "the far greater part of mankind are disabled from this accomplishment." As a result, aiming to edify this wider audience, the publishers had trimmed down world knowledge so that

> they who move in a lower orb, whose circumstances are cramped, and run counter to their inclinations, may improve in this sort of useful knowledge at a trifling expense, . . . and go . . . whither the fancy leads them, without the least difficulty, danger, or inconvenience; thro' all points of the world.[72]

In *The New Universal History's* radical abridgement (less than 500 pages) of that world, the Ottoman empire was reduced to a minor presence.

A later English compendium of voyages, published by John Moore, and claiming to describe "every place worthy of notice in Europe, Asia, Africa, and America" (see Ch. 7), also puts "Turkey" in its place.[73] In Moore's *New and Complete Collection of Voyages and Travels,* 1785, the Ottomans are again conflated with the "Saracens" who ended the "Eastern empire." Later they reappear as "Turks," taking on the role of foil to the expansion of the Portuguese empire in the East.[74] Indeed, for Moore the primary role of Ottoman territory is that it constitutes the object of European voyagers and their ambitions.[75] Beyond that, "Turkey in Europe" appears in volume two,

---

70 Claude Michaud, "Les Turcs dans l'Histoire universelle de Jacques-Auguste de Thou [1553–1617]," 241–4, in *Chrétiens et musulmans à la Renaissance*, Actes du 37e colloque international du CESR (1994), Bartolomé Bennassar and Robert Sauzet, eds. (Paris: Honoré Champion, 1998), 241.

71 *A New and Universal History of Voyages and Travels*, iii unnumbered page of "Introduction."

72 *A New and Universal History of Voyages and Travels*, iv unnumbered page of "Introduction."

73 John Hamilton Moore, *A New and Complete Collection of Voyages and Travels* . . . , 2 vols. (London: Printed for the Proprietors, [1785]).

74 Moore, *Voyages and Travels*, v. 1, vi, 284, 289, 292–4.

75 Moore, *Voyages and Travels*, v. 2, 677, Moore focuses on "modern" travelers to the East, like Pococke.

apparently (along with Iceland) one of the leftover spaces of the world.[76] This section includes a charming engraving of "the grand Seignior in an elegant Turkish habit, making a public appearance before his palace" (Fig. 2.3).[77] Thus the knowledge picture of the Turks has been condensed and made manageable. The sultan and the three men with him appear friendly and intelligent, associated neither with the classical nor the confrontational past. The author points out that the janissaries (once depicted as the scourge of Europe) seldom carry arms when not on duty and laugh at the "Franks" (Europeans) for wearing swords as they go about the streets.[78] The janissary corps is thus civilized and humanized at the same time. Turkey in Europe no longer seems to represent a bastion of imperial ambitions. And the Ottomans are a presence in the world, but not, seemingly, a threat.

Maps

The map was one of the most ubiquitous genres by which Europeans came to know the Turk. Maps were records of battle, conceptualizations of imperial space, indicators of networks of travel and of trade, and records of conventions of representation. They were the canvas on which knowledge and history were inscribed. They conveyed the temporal and spatial hot spots with which the "news" was consumed and traced the routes of travel and pilgrimage so that viewers could "see" the way from Vienna to Constantinople or from Venice to the Holy Land. Thus they served to direct the traveler, meet the "official representational needs" of the state, and familiarize a literate or semiliterate audience with the "look" of the Turk and the spaces that he controlled.[79]

Maps were an important element of the flourishing print industries of Europe in the period under consideration. They served as decorative items and as strategic and educational materials in courtly councils, audience halls, and palace schools. Maps were used to illustrate broadsheets, histories, travel accounts, and compendia of knowledge, as well as geographic literature. They embodied imperial competitions. They sold in single sheets, were bound into atlases, and were assembled into personalized groupings at the behest of well-heeled customers. They were hand-drawn, wood-block, engraved, painted, and lithographed. They were copied, altered, pirated, revised; and they functioned generally within a complex web of spatial exemplars and alternatives.[80]

It is noteworthy that two benchmarks for the transformation of the Mediterranean and the transformation of European mapping took place in

[76] Moore, *Voyages and Travels*, v. 2, 1157–9.

[77] Moore, *Voyages and Travels*, v. 2, 1159. Like many of the book's images, it is labeled "Engraved for Moore's New Complete Collections of Voyages and Travels," so that even if it is detached from the volume its provenance is clear.

[78] Moore, *Voyages and Travels*, v. 2, 1157.

[79] Wilson, *The World of Venice*, 163.

[80] Heleni Porfyriou, "The Cartography of Crete in the First Half of the 17th Century: A Collective Work of a Generation of Engineers," 65–92, in *Eastern Mediterranean Cartographies*, provides a neat set of alternative maps of Crete and its fortresses to illustrate one set of possibilities.

Figure 2.3. John Hamilton Moore, "The Grand Seignior," *A New and Complete Collection of Voyages and Travels*, v. 2, opp. p. 1159, London [1785]. By permission of the Folger Shakespeare Library, Shelfmark: G160.M8 v. 2 Cage.

1570: the Ottoman occupation of Cyprus (Nicosia fell September 9), and the publication of Abraham Ortelius' grand atlas, *Theatrum Orbis Terrarum*.[81] The fall of Cyprus cemented Ottoman dominance in the eastern Mediterranean. The *Theatrum* set the standard for the marriage of world map images with accompanying descriptive text, and of modern maps presented in the context of classical writers.[82] The Ottomans were an important presence in that global construction, one that Denis Cosgrove, writing of Gerardus Mercator (d. 1594), has called the "cosmographic mode:"

> *on his 1569 map, blank spaces of oceans and continental interiors are filled with detailed narrative descriptions of nature, ethnography, history, and other subjects... These pictorial elements should be seen not as decorative additions to a disinterested spatial description but as integral parts of a totalizing world picture, conveying to the eye a marvelously diverse world, exotic but ultimately ordered and intelligible, and perhaps therefore controllable.[83]*

In the aftermath of the Ottoman conquest of Cyprus, it was precisely that task of identifying, ordering, and controlling the Turk (in image and text) that consumed the map literatures of Europe.

But the cosmographic mode was not limited either to Europe or to the articulation of strategic interests. It moved through the circuits of trade that linked Europe and the Ottomans to both Atlantic and Pacific worlds.[84] Thus in a sumptuous pair of early seventeenth-century Japanese painted screens, dubbed the "World Map and Twenty-Eight Cities," one finds an ethnographic image of the warrior Turk adapted from "Pieter van der Keere's 1609 copy of Willem J. Blaeu's world map of 1606–1607."[85] Elite consumption linked the Japanese connoisseurs to their counterparts in the European centers of map production where the houses of notables displayed the Turk's place in the world on the walls of their domiciles. The Guardaroba Nova in one of Cosimo I de' Medici's (r. 1537–74) palaces in Florence, for example, was decorated with maps of the world, a counterpart to his Sala Grande, which displayed the iconography of kingship, including Cosimo's role as a warrior against the Turks.[86] Weapons and other "exotic Turkish" objects

---

[81] See C. [Cornelis] Koeman, *The History of Abraham Ortelius and his Theatrum Orbis Terrarum* (Lausanne: Sequoia, 1964); and Cornelis Koeman, Günter Schilder, Marco van Egmond, and Peter van der Krogt, "Commercial Cartography and Map Production in the Low Countries, 1500-ca. 1672," 1296–1383, in *HOC*, v. 3, pt. 2, 1318–21.

[82] Koeman, *The History of Abraham Ortelius*, 25–6, points out the importance of Ortelius' membership in the Guild of St. Luke from 1547 on, which provided or enhanced connections to a broad spectrum of practitioners of the engravers' art.

[83] Cosgrove, "Mapping the World," 65–116, in *Maps: Finding Our Place in the World*, 102–3.

[84] For just one example of the goods that characterized Ottoman trade with the Far East, see the blue and white porcelain flask, Ming 1575–1600, that was an emblem of the Ottoman palace's conspicuous consumption of luxury goods, in Bağcı and Tanındı, "The Ottomans: From Mehmed II to Murad III," 359.

[85] Miyoshi Tadayoshi, "Japanese Map Screens," 326–9, in *Encounters: The Meeting of Asia and Europe, 1500–1800*, Anna Jackson and Amin Jaffer, eds. (London: V & A Publications, [2004]), 326.

[86] Fiorani, *The Marvel of Maps*, 1–2, 21–3, 33–41, 61–3, 68, 85, 97, 105, assesses iconography, cosmography, maps, and sovereign claims in Cosimo's palace, where classes in cosmography were held for students including Cosimo's daughter Isabella Medici Orsini and some other "illustrious ladies" (45).

were included in the collections of the *guardaroba*, serving (along with the maps) to place the Ottomans materially in world space.[87]

The famous Elizabethan mathematician and statesman John Dee (1527–1608/9), a contemporary of Cosimo's, in his *Preface to Euclid* (1570), wrote that seeing a place, its adjoining regions, and "the distance from us" was one of the primary objectives of map consumption. Another was viewing "the large dominion of the Turk."[88] Short years later, Richard Hakluyt, the lawyer cousin of the more famous English publisher, advised the English explorers Arthur Pet and Charles Jackman in 1580 to take with them, should they undertake an expedition to China, a copy of Ortelius' atlas, along with a map of England "to make shew of your countrey and whence you come."[89] Maps were thus an important vehicle for discerning and marking out the places and identities of self and other. By the eighteenth century a more expansive group of Englishmen were writing of their travels with the expectation that their correspondents could follow their progress on their own maps back home. One thus sees a progression across the early modern era, from the idea of maps as necessities of exploration known to a mostly elite or professional group of consumers, to maps as popular broadsheets, to maps as a tool of the educated middle class household.[90]

"Translating" the Turks: The Circulation of Information

The authors and artists of Christendom thus employed a variety of genres to chart the Ottomans for European audiences eager for news, knowledge, and entertainment. Some narratives of the time proposed to present the "voices" and "words" of the Turk, once, twice, or more times removed from the actual protagonists.[91] Most, however, originated in one Western language and made their way into others depending on the popularity or strategic interest of the text. These ranged from the dramatic to the pragmatic.[92]

---

[87] Fiorani, *The Marvel of Maps*, 74–5. The author calls the *guardaroba* a "three-dimensional display of Gastaldi's edition of Ptolemy's *Geography* and Münster's *Cosmographia universalis* (89)," applying "the geographical order of Renaissance atlases and cosmography books," to the cabinet of curiosities (91). Much has been written on the collection of curiosities and the implications of those collections, for example Lach, *Asia in the Making of Europe*, v. II, *A Century of Wonder*, 25–54.

[88] E. G. R. Taylor, *Tudor Geography 1485–1583* (New York: Octagon Books, 1968), 283.

[89] Mancall, *Hakluyt's Promise*, 83–4. Mancall suggests that "during the sixteenth century the English public became adept at reading maps, so adept, in fact, that Shakespeare's characters in *Henry IV, Part I* could be seen by century's end using a map on stage (75)."

[90] E. A. Reitan, "Expanding Horizons: Maps in the *Gentleman's Magazine*, 1731–1754," *Imago Mundi* 37 (1985): 54–62, see 55, notes that "Publication of maps in the Gentleman's Magazine began in 1739, in connection with accounts of the victories of the Russian general, Münnich, in the war against the Turks.

[91] McJannet, *The Sultan Speaks*, 169, *passim.*, addresses the English translation of the Ottomans, including the first "direct translation of the Turkish historical text," in London in 1652, William Seaman's *The Reign of Sultan Orhan*.

[92] Andrew Pettegree, "Translation and Migration of Texts," 113–25, in *Borders and Travellers in Early Modern Europe*, Thomas Betteridge, ed. (Aldershot, Hampshire: Ashgate, 2007), 120: "More than four hundred texts [were] translated into French from Italian between 1570 and 1600." Pettegree traces the dissemination of the chivalric epic *Amadis de Gaule*, "one of the most popular and sought-after texts of the sixteenth century," from Spanish to French, German, and finally English editions (114).

François de Chassepol's lurid tale of sex, violence, and female plotters in the seraglio, *Histoire des grand viziers*, for example, published in Paris in 1676, quickly spawned an English edition in 1677, but also a Venetian one by 1683.[93] And after Paul Rycaut (b. c. 1628), English consul to Izmir from 1667 to 1678, published his *Present State of the Ottoman Empire* in London in 1668, it was translated into French in 1670, into Italian in 1672, and into Polish out of the French in 1678 as *Monarchia turecka*.[94] The frontispiece of the Polish edition with its spectacular woodcut depicting an Ottoman imperial submission ceremony suggests the empire of the Turks as both a familiar and an exotic place.

Such attempts to make the "Turk" accessible or capture his words also found expression on the map. Giovanni Camocio's Venetian atlas (on which more will be said later), published in the aftermath of the battle of Lepanto, included an image of a captured Ottoman military standard complete with an "interpretation of the Turkish letters" on the standard's finial.[95] That translation both certified the authority of the mapmaker and proved, seemingly, his familiarity with Ottoman letters. Another example is the travel account of the clergyman Salomon Schweigger (1551–1622). Narrating the journey of a Hapsburg embassy to Constantinople, and Schweigger's sojourn to Jerusalem, it included a full-page representation of a document written in the Ottoman script, complete with an impressionistic *tuğra* (sultan's signature).[96] Its intention was to show, in script, the formal, official "face" of the Ottoman hegemons. Schweigger thus translated the Ottomans by embedding their "own" words (unreadable to his audience) into his German text, whereas Camocio provided an Italian translation alongside the Ottoman words embedded in his atlas. Whether it was the traveler who went out in search of Ottoman texts, or the cartographer who stayed at home, the point was to put "real" Ottoman letters on the page.

The Information System

It did not suffice to reproduce the words and images of the Ottomans; they had to be told, shown, and read. Fortunately the possibilities for dissemination of word and image were expansive. The Afro-Eurasian oikumene of the early modern era was characterized by an intense and wide-reaching information order that relied on local, regional, and international circuits of exchange. Information followed the trade routes, capturing the imaginations of viewers and inflaming the demand for more descriptions and more images. Within this system of communication and exchange, there were keys

---

[93] François de Chassepol, *Histoire des grand viziers*... (Paris: E. Michalett, 1676).

[94] Paul Rycaut, *Istoria dello stato presente dell'imperio ottomano* (Venetia: Combi & La Noù, 1672), 62; and *War and Peace: Ottoman–Polish Relations in the 15th–19th Centuries* (İstanbul: MAS, 1999), 167, 254–5.

[95] Camocio, *Isole famose*, image 40: "On the part which one sees: God – Have no Other God – Muhammad is his nuncio. On the other part: To the faithful, divine, auspicious, and ornamented; in worthy military endeavors God favors Muhammad."

[96] Salomon Schweigger, *Ein newe reyssbeschreibung auss Teutschland nach Constantinopel und Jerusalem*..., Rudolf Neck, ed. (Nürnberg: Casper Fulden, 1619; reprint Graz: Akademische Druck v. Verlagsanstalt, 1964), 233.

points of diffusion through which visions of the Turk were circulated.[97] Venice and Ragusa were primary points for the direct dissemination of news about Ottoman affairs, which came in the form of written and oral reports, as well as manuscript and print newsletters.[98] The major emporia of print (Venice, Rome, Antwerp, Frankfort, Augsburg, Paris, Amsterdam, and London, among others) served as central nodes in the networks of both news and trade.[99] Wars might constitute an obstacle to the dissemination of knowledge, but they never managed to stop either news or goods from reaching their consumers. Indeed, news and war went hand in hand.[100]

Italian city-states, as we have seen, were key nodes in the circulation of both text and image. Nicholas Davidson writes, "Books from about 500 Venetian publishers in all have survived from the sixteenth century as a whole; . . . buyers came to the city from every part of western Europe to purchase books produced locally and elsewhere."[101] A catalog prepared for Francesco Rosselli, a cartographer and bookseller in Florence in the early sixteenth century, shows that he had "hundreds of printed maps in stock, including various maps of the world."[102] And David Woodward tells us that

---

[97] On the trading networks of Spain, for example, see Carla Rahn Phillips, *Spain's Golden Fleece: Wool Production and the Wool Trade from the Middle Ages to the Nineteenth Century* (Baltimore: Johns Hopkins University Press, 1997), 231–48; and on news networks, Cristina Borreguero Beltrán, "Philip of Spain: The Spider's Web of News and Information," 23–50, in *The Dissemination of News and the Emergence of Contemporaneity in Early Modern Europe*, Brendan Dooley, ed. (Farnham, Surrey: Ashgate, 2011), 26–7, 39, which discusses routes and times for land and sea post, as well as the critical role of Naples as a conduit for information from Constantinople and parts east (32–3).

[98] See Bariša Krekić, "Courier Traffic between Dubrovnik, Constantinople and Thessalonika in the First Half of the Fourteenth Century," XI, 1–8, in *Dubrovnik, Italy, and the Balkans in the Late Middle Ages* (London: Variorum Reprints, 1980), for the long history of this network. The overwhelming number of couriers at this time were "Slavs from the Balkan hinterland (5)." The "average one way trip to Constantinople from Dubrovnik was 24 days . . . (6)." On the flow of information from the frontiers, see Domagog Madunić, "Frontier Elites of the Ottoman Empire during the War for Crete (1645–1669): The Case of Ali-Pasha Čengić," 47–82, and Johann Petitjean, "On His Holiness' Secret Service: How Ragusa Became an Intelligence Agency after Lepanto," 83–106, both in *Europe and the "Ottoman World": Exchanges and Conflicts (Sixteenth to Seventeenth Centuries)*, Gábor Kármán and Radu Păun, eds. (İstanbul: Isis Press, 2013). Thomas Baker noted that the news of the Ottoman siege of Vienna that began July 14, 1683 arrived in Tripoli via a "French Barque" on September 25; see C. R. Pennell, ed. *Piracy and Diplomacy in Seventeenth-Century North Africa: The Journal of Thomas Baker, English Consul in Tripoli 1677–1685* (Rutherford, NJ: Fairleigh Dickinson University Press, 1989), 163. The Ottomans had already lost the battle for Vienna on September 12.

[99] Peter Burke, "Early Modern Venice as a Center of Information and Communication," 389–419, in *Venice Reconsidered: The History and Civilization of an Italian City-State, 1297–1797*, John Martin and Dennis Romano, eds. (Baltimore: Johns Hopkins University Press, 2000), 390, 405, counts Genoa, Antwerp, and Rome as the "closest rivals" of Venice as centers of information in fifteenth- and sixteenth-century Europe. Burke writes of the "geography" of news in Venice (396) and presents a portrait of its oral and print types, including a flourishing trade in translations (398–402).

[100] Mario Infelise, "News Networks between Italy and Europe," 51–68, in *The Dissemination of News*, 66, points out that in St. Mark's Square there "were 'uproarious scuffles' after every battle in Europe or the Mediterranean," as news-sheet readers came to blows over conflicting reports.

[101] Nicholas Davidson, "'As Much for its Culture as for its Arms,' The Cultural Relations of Venice and Its Dependent Cities, 1400–1700," 197–214, in *Mediterranean Urban Culture, 1400–1700*, Alexander Cowan, ed. (Exeter: University of Exeter Press, 2000), 205. On color prints, see Margaret Morgan Grasselli, "Color Printmaking before 1730," 1–8, in *Colorful Impressions: The Printmaking Revolution in Eighteenth-Century France*, Margaret Grasseli, ed. (Washington, DC: National Gallery of Art, 2003).

[102] Koeman, *The History of Abraham Ortelius*, 24; and Corradino Astengo, *La cartografia nautica mediterranea dei secoli XVI e XVII* (Genoa: Erga edizioni, 2000), 75.

"more map titles were printed in Venice in 1566 than in any other single year in any other city previously"; that year, "of the thirty-six *dated* plates issued . . . , eight were of subjects associated with the Turkish wars."[103] Rome, meanwhile, was a command center for the production of texts, news, maps, rumors, and prophecies about the Turks.[104] The larger, the more threatening, and the more dramatic the object of information, the wider the circulation. And who better than the "Turk" to capture the imagination of the audiences of Christian Europe?

An interesting snapshot of the circulation of information about the Turk at the turn of the seventeenth century may be found in the dedication of Lazzaro Soranzo's (fl. 1602) discourses "on the state of the Ottoman empire and true way to weaken it."[105] In the dedication to his treatise, *L'ottomano*, Soranzo indignantly notes that while he was in Venice for a few days his not yet published and still imperfect discourses were stolen and "by a furtive hand secretly disseminated [to many countries, in a form] all mangled and spoiled."[106] Resolving to finish and humbly offer a "true" version to His Holiness the pope, Soranzo retrieved the false copies that were full of errors and made an entirely new and correct version. In the process, however, he discovered that there were "many other bad copies" circulating. Soranzo's lament gives an indication of the demand and "curiosity," in Venice and beyond, for works on the Ottomans, their power, and their operations. Plagiarism and theft were rampant; and copies of works, stolen or otherwise, once available, might appear in a variety of forms, more or less faithful to their originals.[107] Soranzo describes his work as combining his reflections on what he himself had witnessed with information from "people of great experience and judgment who had come recently from those [Ottoman] regions," synthesized to produce a compendium designed to serve the Christian princes.[108] He proposed to advance scholarly work on the Turk as well as fostering Christian political objectives in this "circulatory system" of information.[109] But once Soranzo's work was pirated, he lost control of the

---

[103] David Woodward, *Maps as Prints in the Italian Renaissance: Makers, Distributors, and Consumers* (London: The British Library, 1997), 45; see also 42–53 on print shops.

[104] Brendan Dooley, *Morandi's Last Prophecy and the End of Renaissance Politics* (Princeton, NJ: Princeton University Press, 2002), 2.

[105] Lazzaro Soranzo, *L'ottomano*, 2nd edition (Ferrara: V. Baldini, 1607), 13th unnumbered page of dedication. A note by Angelo Benaducci, dated 8 May 1598 in Ferrara, "to the readers" in this volume, identifies Soranzo as "a very well-known gentleman, (both) in his patria Venice and in the Roman world where he served as *cammeriero d'honore* to the pope." There seem to have been at least four Italian editions of this work, the first dating to 1598. See Andrei Pippidi, *Visions of the Ottoman World in Renaissance Europe* (London: Hurst, 2012), 91.

[106] Soranzo, *L'ottomano*, 13th unnumbered page of dedication.

[107] Johns, *Piracy*, 49, referring to eighteenth-century London, has presented just such a "culture of piracy," although he would not apply the term in the same way to the sixteenth century. See also Catherine Hoffman, "Publishing and the Map Trade in France," 1569–88, in *HOC*, v. 3, pt. 2, 1577–8, who suggests that plagiarizing maps or prints did not "seem to have been dishonorable," in the seventeenth century. I suspect that very much depended on context, authorial relationships, and lack of enforcement of "privilege" to publish.

[108] Soranzo, 6th unnumbered page of "Proemio."

[109] See Claudia Römer, "An Ottoman Copyist Working for Sebastian Tengnagel, Librarian at the Vienna Hofbibliothek, 1608–1636," 331–50, in *Essays on Ottoman Civilization; Proceedings of the XIIth Congress of the Comité international d'études pré-ottomanes et ottomanes* (Prague: Essays

contents. Knowledge and news were simply not controllable, despite city, state, church, and artisanal attempts to keep them so.

By the first half of the seventeenth century, Paul Arblaster has argued, "The transmission of regular newsletters by the public posts so tightly interwove communication networks across Western Christendom that it is difficult not to speak of a single information community."[110] That same argument can be made regarding the circulation of maps in a system where the boundaries between reports, letters, and images as separate genres was often quite fluid. And of course the channels of communication did not end at the borders of Western Christendom (a spatial concept which in and of itself is quite problematic). They extended into Ottoman space, where the sultans in the sixteenth century had developed their own sophisticated systems of information gathering, specifically charging their administrators to "bring back news from European parts."[111] There existed, across this amorphous frontier, both state intelligence systems and the "overlapping groups of knowledge-rich communities" engaged in information exchange about which C. A. Bayly has written for a later era.[112] Information flowed more readily in some areas and along some routes than others. But certainly in the major urban areas there was the expectation of relatively swift transmission of news and of images, facilitated by the availability of translators and by the book fairs and other commercial exchanges of the day. News of the Ottomans was commingled with other news, embellished, and aggrandized as it moved from proximate centers of information to those at a greater distance.[113] Its transmission was active and passive, official and entrepreneurial, employing multiple types of intermediaries who crisscrossed the Eurasian world.[114]

---

on Ottoman Civilization, 1998): 331–2. See also István György Tóth, "Missionaries as Cultural Intermediaries in Religious Borderlands: Habsburg Hungary and Ottoman Hungary in the Seventeenth Century," 88–108, in *Cultural Exchange in Early Modern Europe*, v. 1, *Religion and Cultural Exchange*.

[110] Paul Arblaster, "Posts, Newsletters, Newspapers: England in a European System of Communication," 19–34, in *News Networks in Seventeenth Century Britain and Europe*, Joad Raymond, ed. (London: Routledge, 2006), 19. The author notes the sharing of "public news" across confessional and political boundaries. And he uses 1590 and Germany as a date and place from which there "was a constant improvement in the postal and carrier services available to the general public." Infelise, "News Networks between Italy and Europe," 53–7, illustrates the roles of Venice and Rome as production hubs for a network of "news-sheets which had customers throughout Europe."

[111] See Christine Philliou, "Communities on the Verge: Unraveling the Phanariot Ascendancy in Ottoman Governance," *Comparative Studies in Society and History* 51.1 (2009): 151–181, see 163; Gábor Ágoston, "Information, Ideology, and Limits of Imperial Policy: Ottoman Grand Strategy in the Context of Ottoman–Habsburg Rivalry," 75–103, in Aksan and Goffman, eds., *The Early Modern Ottomans*; Géza Dávid, "The Mühimme Defteri as a Source for Ottoman–Habsburg Rivalry in the Sixteenth Century," *Archivum Ottomanicum* 20 (2002): 167–209, on the demand for news (199). Giancarlo Casale, *The Ottoman Age of Exploration* (Oxford: Oxford University Press, 2010), 6–7, 9, has proposed an Ottoman grand strategy, comparable to that proposed by Ágoston for the Ottoman–Hapsburg zone, complete with networks of information for the Indian Ocean.

[112] C. A. Bayly, *Empire and Information: Intelligence Gathering and Social Communication in India, 1780–1870* (Cambridge: Cambridge University Press, 1996), 4–5, 13.

[113] See Kate Fleet, "Turks, Italians and intelligence in the fourteenth and fifteenth centuries," 98–112, in *The Balance of Truth: Essays in Honour of Geoffrey Lewis*, Çiğdem Balın-Harding and Colin Imber, eds. (İstanbul: Isis Press, 2000), 107–8.

[114] Natalie Rothman, "Self-Fashioning in the Mediterranean Contact Zone: Giovanni Battista Salvago and His *Africa Overo Barbaria* (1625)," 123–43, in *Renaissance Medievalisms*, Konrad Eisenbichler,

Among those intermediaries were communities active in both print and trade. Jewish diasporic and settled communities, for example, played an important role in the transfer of information to and from the Ottoman empire.[115] Nicolas de Nicolay, writing a narrative of the French embassy to Istanbul in 1551, noted the prosperous commercial position of the Jews of Constantinople and their role in publishing:

> they have established printing workshops which had never been seen before. They have published books in various languages, that is, Greek, Latin, Italian, Spanish, and also Hebrew... They are used to speak and understand all the other languages currently spoken in the Levant, which is quite useful for communicating and trading with foreign countries where they can function as interpreters.[116]

The reach of that Jewish information community was not new, of course; the Ottomans had inherited its possibilities just as they had inherited the Afro-Eurasian commercial networks of their imperial predecessors.[117]

Nicolay also described another important avenue of communication centered in Ragusa, the semiautonomous Adriatic port. There one found the "messengers," a special class of men who carried "the ordinary dispatches from Ragusa to Constantinople" and back, as well as the letters of Venetians, Florentines, and the ambassadors of France.[118] These same couriers brought the information that Giovanni Briccio in Venice used to certify the authenticity of his account of the janissaries' deposition and execution of Sultan Osman II (r. 1618–22), a cause célèbre in Christian Europe, as it suggested a fatal flaw in a monarchical system often viewed as absolute and inviolable. Briccio's pamphlet, published shortly after Osman's demise, employed "news brought by the courier dispatched from the Republic of the Ragusans to Venice... [ten days after the event]" and a subsequent corroborating report brought by another courier also sent from Ragusa.[119]

ed. (Toronto: Centre for Reformation and Renaissance Studies, 2009), 127, notes Salvago's "repeated trips between Istanbul and Venice."

[115] Donatella Calabi, "The Jews and the City in the Mediterranean Area," 56–68, in *Mediterranean Urban Culture*, 61, divides the Jews in Venice into three zones of residence in the seventeenth century comprising about 5,000 inhabitants: "People coming from every corner of Europe lived there together in a small area, distinguished by their attendance at synagogues using different rites (Italian, German, Spanish, Levantine), by their membership in different fraternities, and by the existence of different shops and services for people of distinct origins."

[116] Cited in Calabi, "The Jews and the City," 59.

[117] See Ágoston, "Information, Ideology, and Limits of Imperial Policy," 82–3, on the sultan's Jewish intermediaries (Joseph Nasi, an Ottoman advisor, and Don Alvaro Mendes/Solomon Abenaes, another resident of Istanbul who was the brother-in-law of Queen Elizabeth's physician). For more on Joseph Nasi and Mendes, see Claudia Römer, "A Firman of Süleyman the Magnificent to the King of France Preserved in an Exercise Book of the 'K.K. Akademie Orientalischer Sprachen' in Vienna, 1831," *Turcica* 31 (1999), 461–70, esp. 464–6. See also Finkel, *Osman's Dream*, 161–2; and Pál Fodor, "An Anti-Semite Grand Vezier? The Crisis in Ottoman–Jewish Relations in 1589–1591 and Its Consequences," 191–205 in *In Quest of the Golden Apple: Imperial Ideology, Politics, and Military Administrations in the Ottoman Empire, Analecta Isisiana XLV* (Istanbul: Isis Press, 2000).

[118] Nicolas de Nicolay, *The Nauigations, Peregrinations and Voyages Made into Turkie* (London: Thomas Dawson, 1585), 136r. Bariša Krekić, *Dubrovnik in the 14th and 15th Centuries: A City between East and West* (Norman: University of Oklahoma Press, 1972), 125, notes Dubrovnik as a nodal point for the circulation (and copying) of books as well as news.

[119] Giovanni Briccio, *Successo della sollevatione de Gianizzeri, contra il Gran Turco Sultan Osman...* (Bracciano and Rimino: Gio. Simbeni, 1622), first unnumbered page after title page, noted that his

Such letters and dispatches, in turn, were incorporated into the vast network of newsletters that channeled information in multiple directions. Filippo de Vivo notes that twice weekly the Venetian producers of manuscript newsletters "sent multiple copies of their *avvisi* to scores of subscribers – many of them news-writers too, who in turn added the information they received to their own newsletters for further subscribers," grist for the news mills of the rest of Europe.[120] In 1571 "*avvisi* on the overseas world printed in Portugal were sold on the streets of Rome."[121] Meanwhile, handwritten newsletters from Rome, as well as Venice, quickly conveyed reports on the battle of Lepanto to Germany, where the Fugger collection in Augsburg preserves them along with broadsheets on Lepanto published on the spot.[122] Further west, Antwerp was an important intermediary city for the distribution and redistribution of information, boasting two major international mail services by 1620.[123]

The demand for news and the willingness to respond to that demand are certified in this era by the poet Ben Jonson's (1572–1637) wicked satire that "lambastes the duplicitous nature of the 'weakly cheat' because it peddles fiction as fact and produces readers and readings as mistaken and ridiculous as the gossips with their disruptive tattle."[124] That satire illustrates the established nature of the news (and rumor) industry and the longstanding relationship among print, news, and the public, even in an area well distanced from the center of the action addressed here. Jonson's sentiments might be echoed with regard to the circulation of news in the letters and accounts of travelers. Thus Samuel Pepys, writing of his sojourn to Tangier in 1684, cited both the "jade at the Bagno" and officials in the English expatriate

publication had relied on the comparison of "diverse letters sent to (and by) the principle persons of Ragusa and Venice."

[120] Filippo de Vivo, "Paolo Sarpi and the Uses of Information in Seventeenth Century Venice," 35–49, in *News Networks in Seventeenth Century Britain and Europe*, 35, 38, 41–3.

[121] Lach, *Asia in the Making of Europe*, v. II, *A Century of Wonder*, 42–3, argues that Rome in the 1580s became a center for political and cartographic information that rivaled Lisbon and Venice. On the *avvisi*, see also Mario Infelice, "From Merchants' Letters to Handwritten Political *avvisi*: Notes on the Origin of Public Information," 33–52, in *Cultural Exchange in Early Modern Europe*, v. 3, *Correspondence and Cultural Exchange in Europe, 1400–1700*, Francisco Bethencourt and Florike Egmond, eds. (Cambridge: Cambridge University Press, 2006), 37–8, 41, 50. On German newsletters, see Johannes Weber, "The Early German Newspaper – A Medium of Contemporaneity," 69–79, in *The Dissemination of News*, 71; and Zsuzsa Barbarics-Hermanlik, "Handwritten Newsletters as Interregional Information Sources in Central and Southeastern Europe," 155–78, esp. 173–7, in the same volume.

[122] Zsuzsa Barbarics and Renate Pieper, "Handwritten Newsletters as a Means of Communication in Early Modern Europe," 53–79, in *Cultural Exchange in Early Modern Europe*, v. 3, *Correspondence and Cultural Exchange*, 65–74. "Four of the 93 broadsheets and pamphlets concerning Lepanto now preserved at Vienna's National Library were published in Augsburg and three in nearby Dillingen (71)."

[123] Arblaster, "Posts, Newsletters, Newspapers," 21, 25. See also Koeman et al., "Commercial Cartography and Map Production in the Low Countries," in *HOC*, v. 3, pt. 2, 1300–1305.

[124] Marcus Nevitt, "Ben Johnson and the Serial Publication of News," 51–66, in *News Networks in Seventeenth Century Britain and Europe,* 61. England, for Ottomans and Venetians and, for that matter, for the European mapmakers of the later sixteenth century, was itself on the frontier of the civilized world. Kathy Lavezzo, *Angels on the Edge of the World: Geography, Literature, and English Community, 1000–1534* (Ithaca, NY: Cornell University Press, 2006), 13, points out that earlier in the century the English priest and court poet John Skelton (c. 1465–1529) translated Poggio Bracciolini's Latin translation of Diodorus of Sicily's *Library of History* (ca. 36 B.C.), highlighting England as the "most alien" of frontier territories.

community as his sources for the goings-on in that city.[125] "Fact" and "fiction," of course, may not be the best operative categories for characterizing the information that circulated throughout the Afro-Eurasian world. Rather, travelers and other bearers of news synthesized a combination of what they witnessed themselves with what they heard from others, fabricated, or drew from the texts and stories circulating at the time.

News circulated within the Ottoman realm just as it did to the West. Christine Woodhead notes that Mustafa Selaniki (d. 1600), in his history of the Ottomans' 1595 campaign in Hungary, "was able to include detailed information on the campaign derived from [the commander] Sinan Pasha's own dispatches, or the reports of messengers and troops returning from the front."[126] The şehnameci (court historian) Talikizade Mehmet Subhi (d. 1599) thus ran the risk that his own official narrative would be "seen as little more than 'old news.'"[127] The sultans also took pains to disseminate news of their victories quickly, although (like other monarchs) they were less sanguine about circulating news of defeat.[128] In either case, news could not readily be suppressed, as Talikizade illustrates in his account of Sinan Pasha's unsuccessful attempt in 1594 to prevent word of Sultan Murat III's death from spreading to the troops in Belgrade. A Christian courier from Istanbul, on his way to Prague, passed the news to Christian inhabitants of the city and it was soon on everyone's lips.[129] News paid no heed to the rather arbitrary "borders" of empire and of faith; it sped from one city-node to another, there to satisfy the strategic interests of states, the commercial interests of merchants, and the demands of a curious citizenry. The bookshop, the trader, and the gossip, after all, sat cheek to jowl whether in the shadow of Aya Sofya, St. Mark's, or St. Paul's.[130]

News and the Map

News was thus a critical element of the early modern industry of print that churned out broadsheets, songs, rude verse, caricatures, tracts, maps, and "scandals" at the same time that it produced more weighty and more expensive volumes of history, literature, geography, and religion. The tools and plates of the cartographer's art, used to generate art maps and atlases, also stood ready to stamp out individual sheets of cities or regions, which could be adapted in order to tell of the battles, marvels, or encounters of the day.

---

[125] MacLean, *Looking East*, 92.

[126] Christine Woodhead, Ta'līkī-zāde's şehnāme-i hümāyūn: A History of the Ottoman Campaign into Hungary 1593–94, Islamkundliche Untersuchungen, band 82 (Berlin: Klaus Schwarz Verlag, 1983), 68–9; escaped prisoners also spread news (44–5).

[127] Woodhead, *Ta'līkī-zāde's şehnāme-i hümāyūn*, 68.

[128] Hakan Karateke, "Legitimizing the Ottoman Sultanate: A Framework for Historical Analysis," 13–52, in *Legitimizing the Order: The Ottoman Rhetoric of State Power*, Hakan Karateke and Maurus Reinkowski, eds. (Leiden: Brill, 2005), 42–5.

[129] Woodhead, *Ta'līkī-zāde's şehnāme-i hümāyūn*, 60.

[130] See Linda Levy Peck, *Consuming Splendor: Society and Culture in Seventeenth-Century England* (Cambridge: Cambridge University Press, 2005), 124–8, on St. Paul's, where the printer William Barrett was known for his "production of translations and works on travel, such as *Coryat's Crudities* (1610), and George Sandy's *Relation of a Journey ... containing a description of the Turkish Empire ...* (1615)."

The news map was a genre in and of itself, emanating in particular from Venice in the sixteenth century and depicting the frontier zones in which the armies of Christian kings battled the forces of the sultans (see Chapters 4–5). In Venice, where all were concerned with "the affairs of the Turks," as the scholar and civil servant Paolo Sarpi (1552–1623) put it, print shops rushed to disseminate "true and accurate" news maps, purporting to show the latest showdown between "*i Turchi*" and "*i Christiani*."[131] Such maps (following in the footsteps of oral and written reports) could be passed hand to hand in the city squares, posted in shop windows, or combined with others to produce bound volumes for the edification of discriminating and affluent customers.[132]

David Woodward cites the satirist Pietro Aretino's (1492–1556) *La Cortigiana* on the Roman *venditori ambulanti*, who sold maps and prints along with news stories:

> *Pretty stories, stories, stories, the war of the Turks in Hungary, the sermons [of] Father Martino, the Council, stories, stories, the facts of England, the festivities of the Pope and the Emperor, the circumcision of the Voivoda, the Sack of Rome, the Siege of Florence, the skirmish at Marseilles and its conclusion, stories, stories...*[133]

The prominent place given in this description to the Ottoman wars is not coincidental; nor is the juxtaposition of local interest and imperial contexts. Maps, in this presentation of local, regional, and foreign affairs, were not static items. As Woodward shows, maps were annotated to include recent events, older maps were juxtaposed to newer variants, and dramatic encounters such as the four-month-long Ottoman siege of Malta in 1565 generated "an extraordinary press," along with "step-by-step" documentation on the course of the siege, and a series of map engravings that added details after the fact.[134] News of the Turkish withdrawal from Malta took only six days to reach Rome, and only eleven more to reach Brussels.[135] The news was then

---

[131] De Vivo, "Paolo Sarpi and the Uses of Information in Seventeenth Century Venice," 37. See Brendan Dooley, "The Wages of War: Battles, Prints and Entrepreneurs in Late Seventeenth-Century Venice," *Word and Image* 17, nos. 1–2 (Jan–June 2001): 7–24; Fleet, "Turks, Italians and Intelligence," 99–112; and Infelice, "The War, the News, and the Curious," 216–17.

[132] Christopher Witcombe, *Copyright in the Renaissance: Prints and Privilegio in Sixteenth Century Venice and Rome* (Leiden: Brill, 2004), 244. A map, by Giovanni Battista de' Cavalieri, issued November 14 and entitled "Vero Retratto Del Armata Christiana et Turchesca...," showing the configuration of Turk and Christian fleets at Lepanto, October 7, 1571, was available on the streets of Rome within five weeks after the battle; others were probably available even sooner.

[133] Woodward, *Maps as Prints*, 93, reproduces a 1688 print by G.M. Mitelli that shows a street peddler hawking "a portrait of a Turk, a view of Buda, a map of central Europe (Allemania), portraits, and broadsides (93)." His prospective customers protest that they have more news than they want. See also, on nonprint circulation of information, in this case "gossip networks," Alexander Cowan, "Gossip and Street Culture in Early Modern Venice," *Journal of Early Modern History* 12 (2008): 313–33.

[134] Woodward, *Maps as Prints*, 93–9, traces Niccolo Nelli's map of the siege, which appeared only a month after the siege began, to an earlier drawing made for the Grand Master around 1558 by an Italian military engineer, Bartolomeo Genga. Woodward notes that "there were over 140 separate representations of the encounter over the next eighty years (99)," demonstrating both the popularity of such images and the demand for commemorations of Christian victories.

[135] Woodward, *Maps as Prints*, 94.

quickly translated into maps. Beyond Italy and the Mediterranean ports, C. Koemen tells us that Ortelius, like other sixteenth-century mapmakers, "carried on a lively exchange of letters with men of science from many European countries and constantly asked for information about maps, obviously for the purpose of enlarging his *Theatrum*."[136] That correspondence demonstrates that maps were embedded in a densely woven fabric of scholarly, cartographic, and antiquarian conversation (technical, commercial, and intellectual) that transcended the bounds of Europe. It was a conversation that reached Istanbul, where the Dutch ambassador in 1668 presented Mehmet IV (r. 1648–87) with an edition of the Dutch cartographers Willem (1571–1638) and Joan Blaeu's (1598–1673) *Atlas Maior*. The sultan thus became part of the "patrician audience" that could both "buy... and appreciate" such cartographic works.[137]

Genre, translation, and the routes and mechanisms of dissemination all affected familiarity with the "Turk." Given the tremendous volume of publications on the Ottomans, their mores, and their wars with the Christian kings, there can be little doubt that there was an avid market for images of Ottoman space. Those images appeared in histories, broadsheets, compendia of knowledge, and most particularly (for our purposes) in maps. These were consciously crafted and intimately associated with the overlapping genres of travel and of news. And although we have some conception of the nature and scope of this market for the Turk from the surviving products of the pens and presses of Christian Europe, we still do not have any comprehensive vision of the reception of this knowledge. One may argue, as Ben Jonson suggested, that the public is always gullible. Certainly the printmakers and newsmongers capitalized on that gullibility. But many readers of the Ottomans were both accomplished consumers and critical viewers, assembling bits and pieces of the Turk and formulating him into a picture of reality that resonated with their own reading and experience. The Ottoman empire remained embedded in the layers of the past and the predictions of the future. But it was becoming a three-dimensional empire in the sixteenth century, one whose space was increasingly bounded, and whose personnel and ambitions were increasingly familiar.

---

[136] Koeman, *The History of Abraham Ortelius*, 19–20. Ortelius and Mercator, "called each other's attention to the appearance of new maps and each lent the other material to complete or improve his work (20)." Koeman also notes that Ortelius "gratefully acknowledged Mercator's scientific superiority..."

[137] Hagen, "Afterward," 231; and Koeman, Schilder, van Egmond, and van der Krogt, "Commercial Cartography and Map Production in the Low Countries," 1325–30.

3

Borders

The Edge of Europe, the Ends of Empire, and the Redemption of Christendom

> *Know that in the past the ancients divided the world into four quarters,*
> *each with its own name. They gave the name of Europe to the interior*
> *part that is near the North Pole, from the Black Sea to the farthest end of*
> *al-Andalus. In this quarter is the world-famous and renowned city, the*
> *greatest of cities according to all knowledgeable peoples and religions:*
> *Constantinople, may God almighty protect it and preserve it for Islam*
> *as long as the world continues... Anything that is not inhabited by*
> *Muslims belongs to Christians...*

Ahmad ibn Qasim, *Description of the World*, 1642.[1]

With these words Ahmad ibn Qasim placed the city of Constantinople and its Ottoman lords squarely in Europe at the same time that he allocated to Christendom those spaces that did not belong by divine design to the Muslims. The world, at least in the "quarter" of Europe, was divided along communal lines. Ibn Qasim's designation was little different from those of his Christian contemporaries across the Mediterranean, although for many of them all of Europe fell 'naturally' into the category of Christian space. The notion of a world divided into the realms of Christendom and Islam remained a steadfast standard of the early modern era. But it coexisted with a set of more complicated visions of how the imperial spaces of Europe and Asia were bounded. The authors and artists of the Christian kingdoms knew, to a greater or lesser degree, that the Ottoman empire, physically and culturally, extended well into Europe, and that the frontiers of empire and of faith were wide, moveable, and difficult to control. Borders might divide one ethnocommunal group from another, but they were also places where states, residents, and transimperial subjects met, collected news, and

---

[1] Quoted in Nabil Matar, *Europe through Arab Eyes, 1578–1727* (New York: Columbia University Press, 2009), 201.

75

engaged in "intercourse of all sorts."² Maps reflected those characteristics and helped early modern readers to sort out the differences between Ottoman and non-Ottoman space.

In this chapter, in three sections, I address some of the modes by which text and image were employed in the Christian kingdoms of Europe to map the divisions of communal and sovereign space. First I examine the concept of the 'ends' of empire and their articulation in terms of the spaces of "Christians" and "Turks." This section begins with an examination of Ottoman conceptions of boundaries, proceeds to others from the Christian kingdoms, and then provides a case study on the Iranian frontier. Next, I look at the ways sovereignty was marked out in the transimperial zone between the Ottoman, Hapsburg, and Venetian polities, highlighting the role of the Danube.³ Finally, this chapter takes on a different conceptualization of borders, rooted in the idea of the Holy Land and the prophecies governing who was entitled to 'own' it. The Holy Land, as we shall see, despite its location in Asia, embedded in Ottoman domains, was considered to be a permanent appendage of Christian Europe, its ownership signaled by narratives of prophecy and redemption that were in turn reflected in maps.

Part 1. Envisioning Borders: The Ends of Empire and the

Christian–Turk Divide

Understanding the concept of the borders of the Ottoman empire is not simply a process of identifying the edge of Europe but one of assessing what the limits of Christendom and Islamdom were and, more to the point, what role those limits played in the spatial or imperial imaginations of the early modern world.⁴ That world shared with the twenty-first century a penchant for rhetorics of religious divide. Thus both the Ottomans and their rivals crafted the Ottoman realm and its neighbors in terms of communal difference.⁵ That convention was enduring and powerful, but it was not unilateral.

---

² See John Sanderson, *The Travels of John Sanderson in the Levant, 1584–1602*, William Foster, ed., Series 2, LXVII (London: Hakluyt Society, 1931), 265, Kitely to Sanderson, May 6, 1609. Rothman, *Brokering Empire,* who employs the term "transimperial subject," focuses on converts, dragomen, and commercial brokers, among others.

³ Michael Wintle, *The Image of Europe: Visualizing Europe in Cartography and Iconography throughout the Ages* (Cambridge: Cambridge University Press, 2009), 27, 280. Wintle has argued that maps functioned "to put distance between Europeans and their Others, and to reassure Europeans of their deserved ascendancy over other parts of the world . . ."

⁴ See Ariel Salzmann, *Tocqueville in the Ottoman Empire: Rival Paths to the Modern State* (Leiden: Brill, 2004), 38–51, on the "edges" of Europe.

⁵ Michel Balard, "The Genoese in the Aegean (1204–1566)," 158–74, in *Latins and Greeks in the Eastern Mediterranean after 1204*, Benjamin Arbel, Bernard Hamilton, and David Jacoby, eds. (London: Frank Cass, 1989), 158, 168–9, notes the "shift from ultra-violent hatred of the western invaders to resigned and even willing acceptance of their power."

Ottoman Self-Representation and the Marking of Boundaries

The Ottomans, we have often heard, employed the terms *dar ül-İslam* and *dar ul-harb* to mark the distinction between Muslim-governed space and war space. That dichotomy, however, fails to express the scope of Ottoman conceptualizations of space.[6] Operative 'borders' for the Ottomans included the distinctions between the spaces of believers and unbelievers, orthodox and heterodox, and loyal (tax-paying) and rebellious lords. The Ottoman eastern frontier was a broad zone of mutinous chieftains who used mountainous terrain and distance from the capital as leverage in the struggle to maintain their autonomy.[7] The Greco-Balkan frontier zone (which also housed such mutinous lords) traversed richer, more settled, and more accessible space. But the eastern frontier zone connected Istanbul to the classical centers of Islamic culture. Additionally and crucially, it also protected the "Holy Lands" (Jerusalem, Mecca, and Medina) from a rival in Safavid Iran that challenged Ottoman claims to hegemony in the Islamic world.[8] Beyond the limit towns (places that marked the far reaches of imperial power) such as Van or Erzurum in the east and Buda in the west were territories that remained uncontrollable by sultan, emperor, or shah. In the mental maps of the Ottoman regime the eastern and western ends of empire thus shared some similarities, though their foes and tributaries were on one side Muslim and on the other Christian.[9]

Like their counterparts in the Christian kingdoms, the Ottomans employed multiple measures for distinguishing the spaces of self and other. They did not eschew continental divisions when they conceptualized the territory they ruled. They were well aware of the Ptolemaic system. But their narratives of space focused on regions, relationships, and lands with sacred or imperial associations. In the *intitulatio* of Süleyman I's *ahdname* (grant of

---

[6] On some of the complexities of frontier zones, see Colin Heywood, "The Frontier in Ottoman History: Old Ideas and New Myths," 228–50, in Daniel Power and Naomi Standen, eds., *Frontiers in Question: Eurasian Borderlands 700–1700* (Houndmills, Basingstoke: Macmillan, 1999); and Colin Imber, Keiko Kiyotake, and Rhoads Murphey, eds., *Frontiers of Ottoman Studies: State, Province, and the West*, v. 2 (New York: I.B. Tauris, 2005).

[7] See Bekir Kütükoğlu, *Osmanlı-İran Siyâsî Münâsebetleri (1578–1612)* (İstanbul: İstanbul Fethi Cemiyeti, 1993), 43–6, 53–5. See also Matrakçı Nasuh, *Nasūhü's-Silāhī (Matrākçī), Beyān-ı Menāzil-i Sefer-i 'Irākeyn*, edited and commentary by H.G. Yurdaydın (Ankara: Türk Tarih Kurumu Basımevi, 1976), 235–8, 242, 250–51, 265, 272, 275 on the *kızılbaş* and the religionless enemy (*düşman*) shah.

[8] See M. Tayyip Gökbilgin, "Kanunî Sultan Süleiman'ın Macaristan ve Avrupa Siyasetinin Sebep ve Âmilleri Geçirdiği Safhalar," 5–40, in *Kanunî Armağanı* (Ankara: Türk Tarih Kurumu Basımevi, 1970), 33–5, on the Ottoman, French, and Hapsburg imperial contexts of the struggle for Hungary in the 1540s and 1550s.

[9] Ottoman historiography has its own foundational model of Muslim–Christian "borderlands," embodied in Wittek's 1930s *gazi* theory of frontier warriors and zones, which has recently been the subject of much revisionist critique. P. Wittek, *The Rise of the Ottoman Empire* (London, 1938); critiqued by Colin Imber, *The Ottoman Empire 1300–1481* (İstanbul: Isis Press, 1990), Introduction; and Kafadar, *Between Two Worlds*, 47–59. R. W. Brauer, "Boundaries and Frontiers in Medieval Muslim Geography," *Transactions of the American Philosophical Society*, v. 85, pt. 6 (1995): 1–73, has analyzed the development of Ottoman–Byzantine "border zones" (*tugūr*) between "Muslim and Infidel societies" that are similar to such zones elsewhere in the medieval world.

privilege) to Poland in 1525, the sultan claimed dominion in the following way:

> I who am the sultan of sultans, the proof of emperors, the distributor of the crowns of the Khusraws of the world, God's shadow on earth, the sultan and the padishah of the White [Mediterranean] Sea and the Black Sea, of Rumelia, Anatolia, Karaman, Rum, the provinces of Zulkadir, Diyarbakir, Kurdistan, Azerbaijan, Persia, Damascus, Haleb [Aleppo], Egypt, Mecca, Medina, Jerusalem, and all the lands of Arabia, of Yemen, and of the many lands conquered with the overwhelming power of my noble fathers... and also of the many countries that my glorious majesty has conquered with my flaming sword and victorious saber... [10]

This document defined the sultan as a ruler with a powerful lineage, managing frontier affairs through his vezirs, beylerbeys, sancakbeys, and border (or "edge") commanders (kenar sahibleri).[11] In this and similar treaties, territory was counted out in "provinces, reigns, and empires," as well as in "lands, fortresses, towns, and domains."[12] Frontiers (serhad) were the places where envoys and messengers approaching the Porte received an escort, merchants tried to smuggle goods and captives, and "beys... harbor masters... and tax collectors" were empowered to stop all those who were not properly authorized from moving in and out of the sultan's lands.[13] They were the places where the complex relationships among empires and their tributaries (the loyal and the not so loyal) were sorted out through legislation, negotiation, and battle, and where the miserable kafir (unbeliever) enemies were confronted.[14]

The titles employed by the Ottomans in their negotiations and treaty making recognized clear hierarchies of territory, authority, and status.[15] Like the Venetians, the Hapsburgs in the sixteenth century were obligated to pay

---

[10] Dariusz Kołodziejczyk, *Ottoman–Polish Diplomatic Relations (15th–18th Century): An Annotated Edition of 'Ahdnames and Other Documents* (Leiden: Brill, 2000), 14–17. An 'ahdname dated 1577 is more elaborate, including, among other conquests mentioned, Cyprus, Tunis, Algiers, La Goulette, Rumelia, Buda, Temesvar, Wallachia, Moldavia and Transylvania. The 1667 'ahdname also lists a series of cities and islands.

[11] Kołodziejczyk, *Ottoman–Polish Diplomatic Relations*, 223–5.

[12] Kołodziejczyk, *Ottoman–Polish Diplomatic Relations*, 228, 248, 363. Also see Géza Perjés, *The Fall of the Medieval Kingdome of Hungary: Mohács 1526–Buda 1541*, Márió Fenyö, trans. (Boulder, CO: Social Science Monographs, 1989), 142–5, on Süleyman's negotiations in 1533 for territorial sway in Hungary.

[13] Kołodziejczyk, *Ottoman–Polish Diplomatic Relations*, 241, 365.

[14] For a few references to *serhad* in the context of an Ottoman chronicler's campaign narratives, see Farıs Çerci, *Gelibolulu Mustafa Ali ve Künül-Ahbarında, II Selim, III Murat, ve III Mehmet Devrinleri* (Kayseri: Erciyes Üniversitesi, 2000), 247, 577, 584, 586, 591; Iyânî, *Tevârîh-i Cedîd-i Vilâyet-i Üngürüs*, 9, 12–13; and Kemal Paşazade, *Tevarih-i Âl-i Osman X. Defter*, Şefaettin Severcan, ed. (Ankara: Türk Tarih Kurumu, 1996), 86–7, 247, where rivers such as the Sava and Drava were counted as borders between the realms of the sultan and those of the unbelievers.

[15] Géza Dávid, "The Mühimme Defteri as a Source for Ottoman–Habsburg Rivalry in the Seventeenth Century," *Archivum Ottomanicum* 20 (2002): 167–209; see 192. The Hapsburg, French, and English kings were addressed through the letter (*name*) form, whereas vassals, such as the princes of Transylvania and the voyvodas of Wallachia, like Ottoman beylerbeys or sanjakbeys, were addressed through the form of an order (*hükm*).

"tributes" to the Ottomans; but neither formally admitted that the payments were tribute and the Ottomans refrained from characterizing the Hapsburgs as tribute-payers (*haraç-güzar*) "in contrast to Transylvania, Wallachia, Moldavia, and in the 1570s, Poland."[16] Thus borders were drawn between those with full sovereignty and those without. Viorel Panaite notes that in the trans-Danubian principalities, the Ottomans extended administrative autonomy while preserving their right to interfere in internal affairs.[17] Since the time of Süleyman I, the Ottomans had considered the Wallachian and Moldavian principalities part of the sultan's patrimony (*mülk-i mevrus*), the Abode of Islam (*dar ül-İslam*), and the Ottoman empire (*Devlet-i Aliye*). But they were also demarcated in terms of "*dar al-zimmet* (The Abode of Tributary Protection), *serbestiyet* (Freedom), and *eyalet-i mümtaze* (Privileged Provinces)."[18] This language suggests both inclusion and exclusion, a category of space that was "ours" but not quite "us."

Evliya Çelebi, the seventeenth century Ottoman courtier, in his *Seyahatname*, provides us with a different kind of narrative of Ottoman territory in the transimperial frontier zone. In his 1660 travel account of the region of Kosovo, Evliya describes the town of Zveçan near the fortress of Mitrovica as "at the utmost frontier (*ahirü'l-hudud*) . . . where the eyalet of Bosnia comes to an end."[19] That is, it was a limit town, a place where the notables from the surrounding territory of Rumelia were expected to gather to send off Evliya's master, the pasha, who represented the imperial center.[20] Evliya describes the province of Bosnia itself as a space that illustrated the limits of Ottoman authority. It was bordered by land and sea, with many "sides," counted in fortress points, towns, and governing units (*sanjaks*).[21]

Evliya's narrative maps were matched, in the Ottoman context, by schematic and material images of space. Despite the ambiguities of designating and controlling territory, the Ottomans and their rivals did make various efforts to pin down borders, in part to avoid the endless disputes that ensued in the aftermath of territory changing hands. In 1479–80, the Venetian *provveditore* Bartolomeo Minio reported that an agent of the Ottoman Porte had arrived in Nauplion (NE Peloponnesus) to assign boundaries to the area. Minio's dispatches mention that both the Ottoman *emin* (deputy) and the local notables drew up their own maps of the disputed territories.[22]

[16] Dávid, "The Mühimme Defteri as a Source," 193.
[17] Viorel Panaite, "Wallachia and Moldavia from the Ottoman Juridical and Political Viewpoint, 1774–1829," 21–44, in *Ottoman Rule and the Balkans, 1760–1850: Conflict, Transformation, Adaptation*, Proceedings of an International Conference Held in Rethymno, Greece, 13–14 December 2003, Antonis Anastasopoulos and Elias Kolovos, eds. (Rethymnon: University of Crete, 2007), 23. See also Murphey, *Exploring Ottoman Sovereignty*, 85–95 on internal and external deployment of titles and epithets.
[18] Panaite, "Wallachia and Moldavia," 31, 33, 35.
[19] Evliya Çelebi, *Evliya Çelebi in Albania and Adjacent Regions (Kosovo, Montenegro, Ohrid): The Relevant Sections of the Seyahatname*, Robert Dankoff and Robert Elsie, eds. and trans. (Brill: Leiden, 2000), 13.
[20] See also Kathryn Ebel, "Representations of the Frontier in Ottoman Town Views of the Sixteenth Century," *Imago Mundi* 60.1 (2008): 1–22.
[21] Evliya Çelebi, *Evliya Çelebi in Albania*, 13, 55. Evliya later calls Podgorica a fortress at the "extreme frontier," built by Mehmet the Conqueror in 1478 (47).
[22] Diana Gilliland Wright and John Melville-Jones, "Bartolomeo Minio: Dispacci 1479–1483 from Nauplion," online extracts, "Stato da Mar" section, 10 February 1479 and 14 August 1480, 4–14, in

The sultan's *emin* used documents, the testimony of "elderly witnesses," and tax records to help determine the "proper" boundaries. Familiarity with previous boundaries was a critical factor.[23] Then his commission marked off territory based on physical and social features such as coasts, mountains, wells, fortresses, and monasteries. As in Evliya's description (dated almost two centuries later), territory was described primarily in terms of castles (and the agricultural lands attached to them), the bases for defense and taxation. The documents employed were important not simply as a means of establishing boundaries; they were also part of the process of digesting territory by organizing, counting, registering, and taxing it. And the Ottomans were creative in negotiating that process whether they were demarcating space or determining the taxation and citizenship status of conquered peoples.[24]

In 1681, a joint commission of Ottomans and representatives of the Polish–Lithuanian Commonwealth delineated a set of borders using natural and built features such as those mentioned in Minio's account.[25] At the scene, Ottoman soldiers raised mounds to mark the border where natural features did not make it evident; and the mounds were then marked with crosses on the Polish side and "a wooden pile in the shape of a turbaned head" on the Ottoman side.[26] Ottoman documents of demarcation (*hududname* or *sınırname*) in the fifteenth through seventeenth centuries thus relied on physical features, established property boundaries, the testimony of reliable witnesses, and "old landmarks."[27] Finally, the Ottomans used various forms

The Greek Correspondence of Bartolomeo Minio, v. 1: Dispacci from Nauplion, 1479–83 (Padua: Unipress, 2008). See also Fariba Zarinebaf and Jack Davis, *A Historical and Economic Geography of Ottoman Greece* (Athens: American School of Classical Studies, 2004); and Tibor Halasi-Kun, "Ottoman Toponymic Data and Medieval Boundaries in Southeastern Hungary," 243–50, in János Bak and Béla Király, eds., *From Hunyadi to Rákóczi, War and Society in Late Medieval and Early Modern Hungary* (New York: Brooklyn College Press, 1982), 245, on the Ottoman retention of "boundaries of established local administration (245)." On a smaller scale, Ottomans employed title deeds called *sınırname* (line, or border documents) to define the limits of property.

[23] A Polish treaty document with the Porte in 1621, for example, concerning possession of Hotin, advised that "men of esteem," familiar with the territory, be appointed by both sides to sort out boundaries; see Kołodziejczyk, *Ottoman–Polish Diplomatic Relations*, 380; also 545, 555, and 626 for protocols of demarcation.

[24] As Machiel Kiel, *Art and Society of Bulgaria in the Turkish Period* (Assen/Maastricht, the Netherlands: Van Gorcum, 1985), 152–66, notes using Ottoman fermans and registers for monastic lands of the Peloponnese, Macedonia, and the Balkans. The monks were creative as well.

[25] The Commonwealth reached its greatest extent around 1630. Kolodziejczyk, *The Ottoman Survey Register of Podolia (ca. 1681): Defter-i Mufassal-ı Eyalet-i Kamaniçe* (Cambridge, MA: Harvard Ukrainian Research Institute, 2003), Introduction. I am not aware of such border markers on the Ottoman–Safavid frontier where fortresses and the allegiance of beys were the primary measure of territorial sovereignty; but that does not mean they did not exist. In 1699 the Hapsburgs established a border commission, including Count Marsigli, which mapped out part of the Ottoman–Hapsburg frontier. See John Stoye, *Marsigli's Europe 1680–1730: The Life and Time of Luigi Ferdinando Marsigli, Soldier and Virtuoso* (New Haven: Yale University Press, 1994), 164–215.

[26] Kołodziejczyk, *Ottoman–Polish Diplomatic Relations*, 61–2. Jan Sobieski was the Polish king 1674–96.

[27] Kołodziejczyk, *Ottoman–Polish Diplomatic Relations*, 58–61. See also Gilles Veinstein, "L'Occupation ottomane d'Očakov et le problème de la frontière lituano-tartare 1538–1544," 123–55, in *Passé Turco-Tatar présente soviétique: Études offertes à Alexandre Bennigsen* (Louvain-Paris: Éditions Peeters, 1986), esp. 137–41. Veinstein calls this the first such episode of proposed demarcation. See also

of imagery, from parades to miniatures to model castles, as Lucienne Thys-Şenocak has eloquently noted, that "pulled the vast frontiers of the Ottomans into the center of the empire and made victories visible to those who lived in the capital."[28]

Such efforts did not, however, obviate the fuzzy character of end-space zones or the reliance on city nodes and settlements to delineate territory. An Ottoman map for the district of Novigrad in Hungary, for example, "based on the settlement names of the detailed register (*defter-i mufassal*) of 1570, indicates a wide margin of no man's land instead of a clear frontier line between the Turks and the Habsburgs."[29] Sovereignty, after all, could prove elusive. In a copy of the document appended to the new Ottoman survey register for the province of Kamaniçe (Poldolia), a preamble has been added that begins by noting that "although the actual document deals with borders, one should not treat them too seriously since only God may hand out kingdoms to the rulers of this world."[30] That exalted sentiment was certainly representative of the rhetorics of the time. Nonetheless, the attention devoted to hammering out border agreements would suggest that men as well as gods were vested in the marking out of sovereign turf.

Once borders were demarcated, they could be used to negotiate treaties, levy taxes, address complaints, and make battle gains and sovereign claims concrete. And once negotiations had concluded, there was the expectation that decisions regarding the allocation of space and the behavior and movements of men would be enforced. Thus local janissaries in Vidin, after the Treaty of Passarowitz in 1718, alluded to the *kanun-ı serhad* (law of the frontier) in order to petition to have Christians banished from the fortified section of the city.[31] Such fortresses were commonly places of mixed religious identity; but the janissary demand is a reminder that communal affiliation was always implicit (if not explicit) when it came to dividing Ottoman and non-Ottoman space.

Mykhailo Hrushevsky, *History of the Ukraine–Rus*, v. 7, *The Cossack Age to 1625*, Bohdan Struminski, trans. (Edmonton: Canadian Institute of Ukrainian Studies Press, 1999), 7–16, on traditions of border demarcations. Hrushevsky notes that "ancient demarcations" of village and fortress territory, as well as "accounts of old people," were used by the representatives of sovereign powers to assess the location of borders (10). See also Dávid, "The Mühimme Defteri as a Source," 195 on a "committee for supervision of disputed localities near the [Hapsburg] frontier in 1571–2."

[28] Lucienne Thys-Şenocak, *Ottoman Women Builders: The Architectural Patronage of Hadice Turhan Sultan* (Aldershot: Ashgate, 2006), 123.

[29] Gustav Bayerle, *Ottoman Tributes in Hungary According to Sixteenth Century Tapu Registers of Novigrad* (The Hague: Mouton, 1973), 13. Bayerle suggests that frontiers could be marked with both lines and spaces in such maps. As Gabor Ágoston, "A Flexible Empire: Authority and Its Limits on the Ottoman Frontiers," 15–32, in *Ottoman Borderlands: Issues, Personalities, and Political Changes*, eds., Kemal Karpat with Robert Zens (Madison, WI: University of Wisconsin Press, 2003), esp. 23–7, has demonstrated, the Ottoman and Hapsburg sovereigns or their underlings could and did tax the same units of space in the frontier zone, causing significant complaints among the populace.

[30] Kołodziejczyk, *Ottoman–Polish Diplomatic Relations*, 62. See also Bruce McGowen, "Defter-i mufassal-ı liva-ı Sirem: An Ottoman Revenue Survey Dating from the Reign of Selim II," Ph.D. dissertation, Columbia University, 1967.

[31] Rossitsa Gradeva, "War and Peace Along the Danube," 107–32, in Rossitsa Gradeva, *Rumeli under the Ottomans, 15th–18th Centuries: Institutions and Communities* (İstanbul: Isis Press, 2004), 112.

The Christian Kingdoms and the Ends of Empire

The conundrum of identity, government, and space also posed a dilemma for the geographers and mapmakers of the Christian kingdoms of Europe. Abraham Ortelius glossed the entry 'Christians,' in his 1578 *Thesaurus Geographicus,* with 'see Europeans.'[32] Europe was thus made the primary space of Christianity, and the Christians outside that space were seemingly marginalized. But the Ottoman conquests had problematized that paradigm. Just as the Christian kings were re-establishing control in the west through the Spanish Reconquista, the Ottoman Turks had seized a substantial segment of eastern Europe. Geographers such as Ortelius, as Kiril Petkov points out,

> had to adjust to the situation . . . an alien entity, obviously confined only by natural limits and capable to expand over man-made hindrances had embedded itself into the European south east, rendering it Oriental.[33]

Such "Orientalizing" of territory complicated the designation of space within the map frame and the assignment of identity to the peoples of the Balkans.[34]

The Serbian Patriarch Arsenije III (r. 1674–91), for example, was confronted with the task of legitimizing Serbia as an enduring part of Christendom despite its long subordination to Ottoman rule. His chronicle celebrated the failed Ottoman siege of Vienna in 1683 as a divine sign:

> A great misfortune enveloped the Christians, as the Ottomans imposed large and unbearable taxes on the entire land. All the forces of the Islamic world that either sailed the seas or advanced on the land attacked, like winged serpents, the illustrious city of Vienna. But the Lord opposed the vain ones! The vain vizier returned empty handed, while his army was uniformly fed to the Hungarian swords. And the great terror began.[35]

The assault on Vienna, for the patriarch, was part of a big picture that pitted Christendom against the "Islamic world." The Serbs, a nation under the Christian God, thus owed no allegiance to their Ottoman masters, but required the protection of the Christian emperor to escape from "Ottoman slavery."[36] Ethnocommunal identity was presumed to transcend

---

[32] Noted in Petkov, *Infidels, Turks, and Women,* 199. Petkov suggests that "The massive loss of Christian territories during the fourteenth and fifteenth century brought about this equation of the terms Christian and European." And that equation sufficed for Matthias Dresser writing on the Turkish wars in 1595 as it did for Ortelius (256–7).

[33] Petkov, *Infidels, Turks, and Women,* 200. Petkov notes that Ortelius' two maps of "Europe" and "The Turkish Empire" both visually "claimed the Balkans as integral parts of their possession."

[34] Petkov, *Infidels, Turks, and Women,* 202.

[35] Quoted in Jelena Todorović, *An Orthodox Festival Book in the Habsburg Empire: Zaharija Orfelin's 'Festive Greeting to Mojsej Putnik' (1757)* (Aldershot, Hampshire: Ashgate, 2006), 1–2.

[36] In 1690, Leopold I offered the Serbs a protectorate of the Holy Roman empire to "save from Ottoman slavery all nations under our jurisdiction"; in return he expected loyalty and military support. Todorović, *An Orthodox Festival Book,* 4–5.

the frontier, despite the Serbs' day-to-day reality as residents in the sultan's domains.

That identity issue was resolved for the South Slavs, according to Petkov, by the German cartographer, Sebastian Münster, whose *Cosmographia* (1544) confirmed their Europeanness through their "origins, past and present affiliation, geographical locations, physical and social landscape, and political history."[37] The Serbs' positioning on the front lines against the "Turk," for Münster, reinforced the non-Ottoman nature of their identity.[38] But for other contemporary authors, the absorption of the peoples of the Greco-Balkan peninsula into the Ottoman military and administration created a crisis of identity. Georg Bömiche, for example, a scholar from Brandenburg, in his 1567 tract on Mehmet II's 1453 conquest of Constantinople, noted that the sultan drew his troops from "Greece, Wallachia, Bulgaria, Galatia, Cylicia, etc.," and, as a result, "the Turk rules over the Christian commonwealth [*Christen haus*] and fights us using the very people which are our relatives, which have our blood, and keep our beliefs . . ."[39] The narrators of Christendom might thereby claim Ottoman victories as the fruits of Christian "blood," but they were also wary of these "Orientalized" blood brothers. The discourse of shared origins and faith proved little comfort when it came to counting the expanding territories of the "Turk."

While the Ottomans became European, the mapmakers, historians, and statesmen of the Christian kingdoms were forced to scramble to define the limits of the sultan's empire and of Christendom. Broadly speaking, they laid out Ottoman space in three zones. The outermost zone of this spatial imaginary stretched as far as Central Asia and East Africa. The former, with its attendant notion of Gog and Magog (fabulous monsters who might break free and engulf the civilized world), was envisioned as the birthplace of the Turks. The latter was the home of Prester John, an imagined redeemer for Christendom who would march his armies out of Africa and put the Turk in his place.[40] Within this mythological frame, there was a whole universe of very real "neighbors," whose strategic and commercial interests were tied to the Ottoman state. Some neighbors (England, France, Holland, or the states of the South Asian littoral, for example) might encounter the Ottomans through war, commerce, or pilgrimage, but their borders were generally not directly threatened by Ottoman conquest.[41] They signed treaties and

[37] Petkov, *Infidels, Turks, and Women*, 236. Emphasis on the "ambiguity of Slavic nature," both European and Oriental, was a key trend (237). It is Münster that Nicolay cites as an authority in his narration of travels (beginning 1551) to the sultan's Porte; see Nicolay, *The Nauigations into Turkie*, 50r.

[38] Petkov, *Infidels, Turks, and Women*, 244. The historian Johannes Aventinus, in his *Bavarian Chronicle*, c. 1525, thus included both Constantinople and the peoples of the Balkans as neighbors and "next-door" nations.

[39] Petkov, *Infidels, Turks, and Women*, 257.

[40] See David Woodward, "Medieval Mappaemundi," 286–370, in *HOC*, v. 1, 332–3; and Miquel, *La géographie humaine*, v. 2, pt. 2 (Paris: Éditions de l'École des Hautes Études en Sciences Sociales, 2001), 503–11, on Arab geography and Gog and Magog.

[41] Emblematic of the individuals engaged in this transregional matrix of connections was Jacob Strycker (Stricher), from an immigrant Amsterdam merchant family in Venice, with a capital of 200,000 ducats

participated in far-flung and seaborne networks of trade and information.[42]
Those whose territories did abut the kingdom of the "Turk" constituted a
third, inner zone of intensive interaction. That zone was composed primarily
of the Hapsburg and Venetian territories to the northwest and the Safavid
lands to the east. These were war partners, intruding on the sovereignty of the
Turk and suffering his intrusions in return. They shared with the Ottomans
two broad, porous frontiers whose peoples confronted the hardships and
enjoyed the opportunities of that shared space. (A separate frontier zone
was constituted by coastal North Africa; but that sea space will be treated
elsewhere.)

Within this inner zone there existed a set of spaces that one might characterize as "end" territories, places where one empire flowed into (and out of)
another. On the European side of the empire, Bosnia, Hungary, Wallachia,
Moldavia, Transylvania, and the Adriatic littoral constituted such spaces,
ones in which wars were fought, garrisons built, and allegiances tested as
the Ottoman, Venetian, Hapsburg, Polish, and then Russian empires sought
to claim, conquer, or secure land, resources, entrepots, or tributaries.[43] The
ends of empire had their own special personnel and tactics.[44] Their residents
were forced by circumstances to maintain a certain degree of flexibility. Portrayals of such territories, in early modern narrative and image, often focus
attention on their status as imperial appendages, autonomous regions, or
objects of expansion. In Ottoman sources, as noted earlier, they were often
designated as places of either trouble or stability.[45] They were marked by
limit cities, where the management of frontiers was organized and where
troops were mobilized to invade enemy territory.[46]

in cash in 1652. His trading connections included Smyrna, Constantinople, Genoa, Livorno, Venice,
the Netherlands, England, and France; and in 1650 the Signoria required him to make available three
ships and "a long list of maritime provisions as part of the war effort against the Turks" at Candia.
See Alexander Cowan, "Foreigners and the City: The Case of the Immigrant Merchant," 45–55, in
Mediterranean Urban Culture, 48–53.

[42] Finbarr Flood, *Objects of Translation: Material Culture and Medieval 'Hindu–Muslim' Encounter*
(Princeton, NJ: Princeton University Press, 2009), 25, 133, has addressed those questions of circulation
and the translation of cultures and their objects for an earlier period. He differentiates between
the "cognitive regions" of the nation-state and the "functional regions" of the heterodox trading
communities of South Asia.

[43] For a summary and mapping of the attachment of Balkan territories (including the annexation of the
Black Sea littoral territories Jedisan, in 1526, and Budzhak, in 1538) to the Ottoman empire, see Paul
Robert Magocsi, *Historical Atlas of East Central Europe* (Seattle: University of Washington Press,
1993), 46–7. Wallachia and Moldavia were incorporated as vassal states early, by 1476 and 1512
respectively.

[44] Géza Pálffy, "The Origins and Development of the Border Defense System against the Ottoman Empire
in Hungary (up to the Early Eighteenth Century)," 3–70, in Géza Dávid and Pál Fodor, eds., *Ottomans,
Hungarians, and Habsburgs in Central Europe: The Military Confines in the Era of Ottoman Conquest*
(Leiden: Brill, 2000), 56–9.

[45] See also Johnson, *Central Europe*, 95.

[46] Gustav Bayerle, *Ottoman Diplomacy in Hungary: Letters from the Pashas of Buda 1590–1593* (Bloomington: Indiana University Press, 1972), 11, has called Buda Province (incorporated by the Ottomans
in 1541) a "permanent frontier zone." The Russian envoy Prince Repnin and the Ottoman envoy
Abdülkerim Pasha traveled, respectively, to Istanbul and Moscow in 1775, engaging in an exchange
near Hotin, at the Dniester, the middle ground; see *Mubadele: An Ottoman–Russian Exchange of
Ambassadors*, Norman Itzkowitz and Max Mote, eds. and trans. (Chicago: University of Chicago
Press, 1970).

The Example of the Ottoman–Iranian Frontier

When these spaces were inscribed on maps, the ends of empire might be precisely delineated or obscure. A most important end of empire was the contested space where Ottoman sovereign power met Safavid sovereign power in Iran and Iraq. This was the frontier where the Ottoman claim to the ancient east and its access to the holy cities of Arabia, Syria, and Iraq was threatened and challenged by Muslim rivals. For European mapmakers, those imperial borders were somewhat academic, whereas those where Ottoman lands bumped up against the Christian kingdoms of Europe were immediate and 'personal.' They drew the lands of the 'Great Turk' and the 'Great Sophy' (Sufi) in Safavid Iran on either side of a roughly vertical line that petered out somewhere between the Black and Caspian seas to the north and somewhere along the Euphrates and Tigris to the south.[47]

Nonetheless, Iran was a crucial space for classical antiquity: the seat of Darius and Xerxes, a land of Biblical villains, and a center of civilization that rivaled and outstripped that of the Greeks in its wealth, monuments, and military might. As such, in maps, it was often dressed in "classical" garb and labeled with the names of the ancients and the fires of Zoroaster.[48] Johann Baptist Homann's (1664–1724) early eighteenth-century map of the "Persian Empire" with all its provinces thus mingles the names of classical and contemporary places as it labels the spaces of the "*Imperii Turcici*" and "*Imperium Persicum*."[49] Its legend cartouche alludes to the "Armenian tigers" of Ovid's *Metamorphoses* (Fig. 3.1).[50] That classical identity merged for the authors of Christendom with other more contemporary identities. Persia was a neighbor and enemy of the Ottomans, a power that provided commercial opportunity along with a military diversion on the Ottoman eastern front that siphoned the sultan's troops away from Christian lands and wars.[51] Thus Iran was a potential Christian ally, whose Shi'ism seemed

[47] Brion de La Tour's, "Perse, Turquie Asiatique, et Arabie," Paris, 1766, provides a dotted line divider and also employs colored borders to mark Iranian or Ottoman space.

[48] Sonja Brentjes and Volkmar Schüller, "Pietro della Valle's Latin Geography of Safavid Iran (1624–1628): Introduction," *Journal of Early Modern History* 10.3 (2006): 169–219, trace the naming conventions on early modern European maps of Iran (182). They argue that della Valle distinguished himself by using knowledge of local geography, thus taking the approach of "cartographers and mapmakers" rather than that of contemporaries "who wrote on the history or geography of these regions [and who] often suppressed local knowledge, giving preference to terms from ancient Greek and Latin history and geography, enriched by reference to the Bible (172)."

[49] On the Homann family, see Tooley, *Maps and Mapmakers*, 27; and Markus Heinz, "The Homan Family in the Eighteenth Century," *Imago Mundi* 49 (1997): 104–15.

[50] Johann Baptist Homann, "Imperii Persici," Nuremberg, [c. 1720], refers to "Armenia Tygres iracundique leones." See Garth Tissol, *The Face of Nature: Wit, Narrative, and Cosmic Origins in Ovid's Metamorphoses* (Princeton, NJ: Princeton University Press, 1997), 152, n. 41. See Cyrus Alai, *General Maps of Persia 1477–1925* (Leiden: Brill, 2005); and Sonja Brentjes, "The Interests of the Republic of Letters in the Middle East (1550–1700)," Section I, 435–68, in Brentjes, *Travellers from Europe*, 453–4, on the evolution of Western mapping of Iran. In the same volume, Brentjes, "Pride and Prejudice: The Invention of a 'Historiography of Science' in the Ottoman and Safavid Empires by European Travellers and Writers in the Sixteenth and Seventeenth Centuries," Section VI, 229–54, see 245, notes the extensive, even "book-long" lists equating ancient and contemporary place names produced by European cartographers, geographers, and historians in the sixteenth and seventeenth centuries.

[51] See, Elio Brancaforte, *Visions of Persia: Mapping the Travels of Adam Olearius* (Cambridge, MA: Harvard University Press, 2003), 11–21. European mapping of Iran was also much influenced by the

Figure 3.1. Johann Baptist Homann, "Imperii Persici," Nuremberg [c. 1724]. The British Library Board, Maps K.Top. 114.96/C2491–04. (See color plate)

to Christian observers to be not the same thing at all as the Islam of the Ottomans.

The Ottoman–Safavid frontiers were a zone of great interest for such observers. George Abbot (1562–1633), Archbishop of Canterbury, in his *A Briefe Description of the Whole World* (London, 1599), compared the distinction between Turks and Persians to that between Catholics and Protestants, attributing their conflicts to communal hatred:

> *The Persians are all this day Saracens in religion, believing on Mahomet: but as Papistes and Protestants doe differ in opinion, concerning the same Christ: so doe the Turkes, and Persians about their Mahomet; the one pursuing the other as heretickes with most deadly hatred. Insomu[c]h, that there be in this respect, almost continuall warres betweene the Turkes and the Persians.*[52]

travel narrative of Sir John Chardin, *Travels in Persia 1673–1677*, N.M. Penzer and Sir Percy Sykes, Preface and Introduction (New York: Dover, 1988), 282–3, who commented on trade, travel, distance, and the cheap messenger service in 1660s and 1670s Iran. His *Journal du voyage du chevalier Chardin en Perse et aux Indes Oreintales* was issued in London in 1686.

[52] Relihan, *Cosmographical Glasses*, 59, citing George Abbot. See also Palmira Brummett, "The Myth of Shah Ismail Safavi: Political Rhetoric and 'Divine' Kingship," 331–59, in *Medieval Christian Perceptions of Islam*, John Tolan, ed. (New York: Garland Publishing, 1996).

If the Islam of the Persians did not correspond to that of the Turks, so much the better for Christendom. Abbot had little understanding of the range of Sunni–Shiʿa differences; but he was certainly correct when he suggested that the varieties of religious experience among Muslims were just as prone to promote conflict as were those among Christians. The Ottoman–Safavid frontier zone served as a refuge, a place of mystical and heterodox conjunction, where religious and political relations were never simple. The same could be said for parts of the transimperial Ottoman–Venetian–Hapsburg frontier.[53] There, Senj, for example, was a limit town on the Adriatic where, as Norman Housley has pointed out, "holy war and *convivencia* were both vigorously present."[54] Abbot's characterization thus reminds us that Colin Heywood is right when he proposes that Ottoman frontiers be compared to other early modern frontiers rather than viewed in isolation because of their Islamic character.[55]

For other early modern commentators, however, religiosity was not the primary source for identifying the dichotomies between Ottoman and non-Ottoman space. The young Venetian traveler Ambrosio Bembo (b. 1652), for example, who passed through Ottoman territory on his way to India in 1671, presented his readers with astute observations on the defining characteristics of the eastern borders. Physically the Ottoman empire was divided from the Persian by several days' journey through the mountains, a terrain where one could not count on recognition of Ottoman authority. That intermediate space was marked by limit towns such as Sumbar, on the Kangir river, "the last [or first] town of Persia."[56] "All" the inhabitants in Sumbar watched the Venetian and French travelers eat, noting their varied meals and their utensils, and asking if "all the Europeans ate like that."[57] For them, "Europe" was the remote, homogenized space lying west beyond the Ottoman empire. Both Persians and Turks, Bembo noted, shared an appreciation for coffee, which as a gift tended to transcend imperial boundaries. But he complained bitterly of the barely adequate food and the thievery, extortion, and "thousands of insolences, injuries, and discourtesies" that the traveler had to endure in the Ottoman frontier towns.[58] Once one crossed into Ottoman Iraq one had difficulty finding "even a miserable roof," whereas in Persia, Bembo wrote, he had found "delightful" lodging.[59]

[53] Norman Housley, " Frontier Societies and Crusading in the Later Middle Ages," 104–19, in *Intercultural Contacts in the Medieval Mediterranean*, 109. Housley characterizes both Transylvania and Albania as "mountainous regions, whose peoples needed little encouragement to settle into a pattern of belligerent raiding and rustling (109)."
[54] Housley, " Frontier Societies and Crusading," 111, draws comparisons between frontier life in Dalmatia, Prussia, and Granada. Transcommunal life styles were clearly in evidence when a 1579 synod had to bar Catholic priests from officiating "at blood brotherhood rites between Christians and Muslims (111)."
[55] Heywood, "The Frontier in Ottoman History," 242–4.
[56] Ambrosio Bembo, *The Travels and Journal of Ambrosio Bembo*, Clara Bargellini, trans., Anthony Welch, ed. (Berkeley: University of California Press, 2007), 388–9. For the Italian manuscript edition, see Ambrogio Bembo, *Il viaggio in Asia (1671-1675) nei manoscritti di Minneapolis e di Bergamo*, Antonio Invernizzi, ed. (Alessandria: Edizioni dell'Orso, 2012), 420–21.
[57] Bembo, *Travels*, 389.
[58] Bembo, *Travels*, 391.
[59] Bembo, *Travels*, 386–8.

The young Venetian thus defined borders in terms of the experience of satisfaction or deprivation and the vagaries of culture, as much as by communal difference or the claims of distant sovereign lords. For the Ottomans, however, Iraq was a territory to which they felt entitled. In his richly illustrated narrative of the stages of Sultan Süleyman's Baghdad campaign in the mid sixteenth century, the Ottoman commander Matrakçı Nasuh (d. 1564) only once noted a border (serhad).[60] A single map shows Mesopotamia divided into Irak-ı Arab and Irak-ı Acem (Arab and Persian Iraq) (Fig. 3.2).[61] Matrakçı, like Bembo, uses a limit town (along with a fortress and a palace) to mark this division; but he marks it as a regional rather than political border. This was the same border that Katib Çelebi (Haci Halifa, 1609–57) in his world atlas, the Cihannüma, would delineate more extensively in terms of territories at its borders (hudud), towns, and the history of who had owned them.[62] For Matrakçı, Iraq was the legitimate possession of his master, a land of sacred sites the possession of which helped certify Süleyman as paramount ruler in the Islamic world. Just as the kings of Europe claimed that the domain of Christendom extended well into Ottoman territory, so Matrakçı pushed the boundaries of the sultan well beyond the lands that his lord could actually control. What counted in such mapping was not simply physical possession but the mental maps of sovereign and religious legitimacy.

Part 2. Mapping Transimperial Space

On the European side of the empire, the competition for resources and faith pitted the Ottomans against a set of Christian rivals. To articulate that rivalry, the mapmakers of Christian Europe were faced with the task of transforming the unbounded ethnoregional spaces of the Ptolemaic world-vision into the imperial entities and bounded nation-states of the early modern era. The process, as we have seen, was neither simple nor strictly evolutionary. Throughout this period earlier traditions of mapmaking were enduring, representational objectives were complex, the edge of Europe was variable, and the fuzzy or unstamped frontier remained an option that existed side by side with the drawing of explicit state lines across contested frontier zones. Possession could be indicated through state and continental divisions but also

---

[60] Matrakçı Nasuh, Beyān-ı Menāzil-i Sefer-i 'Irākeyn-i Sultan Süleyman Hān. Matrakçı's campaign maps are often similar in their visualizations of space to the thirteenth-century world system model proposed by Janet Abu Lughod, Before European Hegemony: The World System A.D. 1250–1350 (New York: Oxford University Press, 1989), 34. They focus on city nodes and routes. See also Rudi Matthee, "The Safavid–Ottoman Frontier: Iraq-ı Arab as Seen by the Safavids," 157–73, in Ottoman Borderlands: Issues, Personalities, and Political Changes. Ottoman drawing of boundaries on the model of European maps was much more systematic by the nineteenth century. See Mehmed Hurşid [Paşa], Seyâhatnâme-i Hudûd, Alâattin Eser, ed. (İstanbul: Simurg, 1997).

[61] For the language of this frontier in the narratives of İdris-i Bidlisi (1457–1520) a scholar who wrote in Persian and served on both sides of the frontier, see Ebru Sönmez, İdris-i Bidlisi: Ottoman Kurdistan and Islamic Legitimacy (İstanbul: Libra Kitapçılık, 2012), 66–70.

[62] Kâtib Çelebi, Kitâb-ı Cihânnümâ, v. 1 (Ankara: Türk Tarih Kurumu, 2009), 289, 451; facsimile taken from the 1732 Müteferrika edition. See also Hagen, "Afterword," 227–33, on Katib Çelebi's organizational schema.

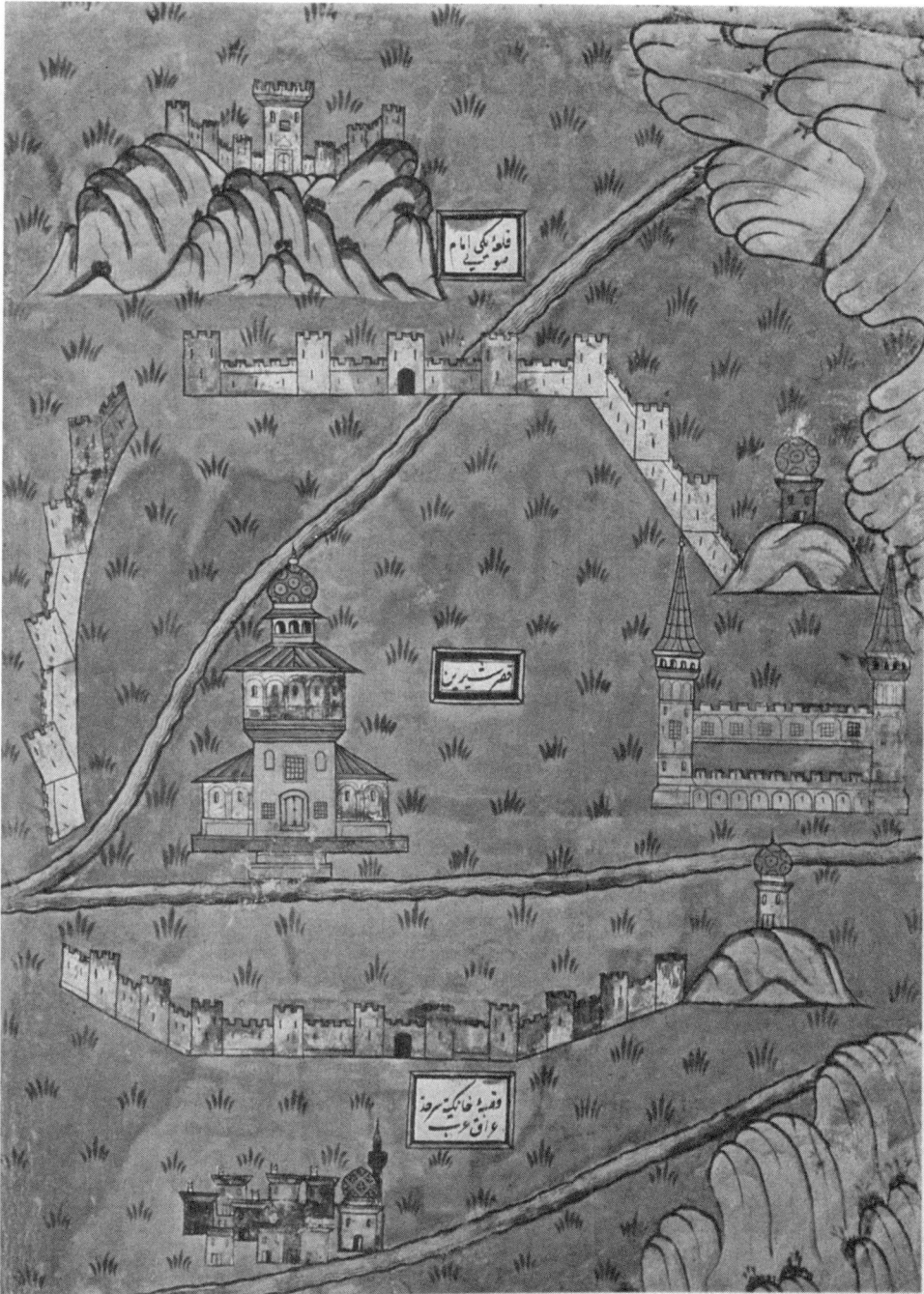

Figure 3.2. Arab and Persian Iraq. Matrakçı Nasuh, *Beyan-ı Menazil-i Sefer-i Irakeyn-i Sultan Süleyman,* fol. 42b, İstanbul, [c. 1537]. İstanbul University Library, 5967.

through iconographic alternatives that transcended the notion of the border 'line.'

The Danube

When it came to evaluating the borders between "Christendom" and the Ottomans, no dividing line was more visible than the Danube. On maps, because of its sheer size, this expansive river could not help but appear as a decisive physical marker. It stood out, demanding the attention of the viewer. Vienna was at one end and Istanbul (more or less) at the other. Beyond the barrier of the Danube there was no clear and consistent separation between the Europe of the Christian kings and the Europe of the Turk.[63]

Any sovereign (Christian or Muslim) wishing to extend his domains in the Balkan peninsula had to contend with that formidable physical barrier. Viorel Panaite, in his illuminating work, *The Ottoman Law of War and Peace*, has called the land beyond the Danube the "*gazi* river" zone, a place for the Ottomans of treaty people (*mu'ahidin*) and tribute payers, one of changeable status whose people the Ottoman empire had not fully secured.[64] Like other rivers, the Danube thus served as a place where the representatives of empires negotiated territory and status.[65] It was a primary impediment to the movement of troops, a primary line of defense for Hungarians and Ottomans, and a primary route of travel. Those who tried to possess the Danubian zone were forced to deal with water crossings and boat-riding brigands. The Danube had its own Ottoman "admiral," the "*Tuna kapudanı*," a counterpart to the *kapudan* pasha who was lord over the fleets and the beyliks of the Archipelago.[66]

In early modern maps the lands across the Danube could be characterized as the ends of empire, neither fully integrated nor truly detached from the empires on either side. Map makers depicted it surrounded with legends

---

[63] A German map by Gabriel Bodenehr (1673–1765), "Canal von Constantinople" or "Bosphorus," Augsburg, in [Gabriel Bodenehr], *A collection of plans and views of fortified towns in Europe* [Augsburg]: [c. 1730?], British Library, Maps, C24.aa.18, map 154, places the Ottomans squarely on the "edge" of Europe, with no indication of their ownership of "Asiae Pars" across the water. Only the lengthy legend gives us some notion of the history of the place. The map mirrors a 1688 map by Vincenzo Coronelli of "Bosforo Tracio," though the details and labels are different. Because this collected volume includes many city plans and fortress views, it gives a good sense of part of the state of map production at this time [ca. 1737].

[64] Viorel Panaite, *The Ottoman Law of War and Peace: The Ottoman Empire and Tribute Payers* (Boulder, CO: Columbia University Press, 2000), 385, 406, 416–29, 447–8.

[65] Kolodziejczyk, *Ottoman–Polish Diplomatic Relations*, 49. In October 1606 the Ottoman and Hapsburg representatives met on neutral ground at the point where the creek of Zsitva flows into the Danube; "the Hapsburg delegation prepared three copies of the final document in Hungarian, which was only later translated into Latin . . . the Ottoman documents were prepared in Turkish and Hungarian."

[66] Gilles Veinstein, "Some Views of Provisioning in the Hungarian Campaigns of Suleyman the Magnificent," in *Osmanistische Studien zur Wirschafts- und Sozialgeschichte: in memoriam Vančo Boškov*, H.S. Majer, ed. (Wiesbaden: 1986), 177–85, esp. 182. See also Gradeva, "War and Peace along the Danube," 120, on the escalating numbers of admirals and sea forces on the Danube; and Idris Bostan, "The establishment of the province of Cezayir-i Bahr-i Sefid," 241–52, in *The Kapudan Pasha: His Office and His Domains*, Elizabeth Zachariadou, ed. (Rethymnon: Crete University Press, 202).

Figure 3.3. Pieter van der Keere, "Nova et Recens Emendata Totius Regni Ungariae Una Cum Adiacentibus Et Finitimis Regionibus Delineatio," detail, [Amsterdam], 1620. Geography and Map Division, Library of Congress.

highlighting the victories and defeats of the Turks. In Kaerius' (Pieter van der Keere, c. 1571–1646?) "Nova et Recens Emendata Totius Regni Ungariae Una Cum Adiacentibus Et Finitimis Regionibus Delineatio," dated 1620, the Danube is a living thing, lined with castles and bearing vessels on its currents. Though the body of the map is stamped with the double-headed eagle, the legend across its bottom provides crescent and cross icons to guide the reader to those places "occupied" by "Turks" and "Christians" (Fig. 3.3).[67] A similar map was done by Jacob Sandrart (1630–1708) in Nuremburg in 1657: "Neue Land Tafel von Hungarn." Sandrart's map includes, at the top, a list of Hungarian kings and Turkish "Caesars," a form of counting kingly rivals also engaged in by Ottoman chroniclers (Fig. 3.4).[68] In both maps, the lands of the Danube seem to be counted in castle points, the potential sites for conflict, defense, occupation, and surrender. Opposing cavalry troops, armed with cross or crescent flags (devices used in multiple maps, including those of Sandrart and Kaerius) also appear on Nicolas Berey's (c. 1610–67) "Carte

---

[67] Pieter Kaerius, "Nova et Recens Emendata Totius Regni Ungariae Cum Adiacentibus Et Finitimis Regionibus Delineatio," [Amsterdam], 1620. The ribbon legend at the bottom of this map identifying icons for Turk and Christian space is repeated on D[ancker] Danckerts, "Nova et Recens Emendata Totius Regni Ungariae," 1663, which includes city vignettes of Buda and Presburg. There are no opposing cavalry on this map but there are small legends on the body of the map indicated Ottoman conquests. See also Catherine Delano-Smith, "Signs on Printed Topographical Maps, ca. 1470-ca. 1640," 529–90, in HOC, v. 3, pt. 1, 564–8; and Koeman et al., "Commercial Cartography and Map Production in the Low Countries," HOC, v. 3, pt. 2, 1313–14.

[68] Fetvacı, Picturing History, 139, notes the translation into Ottoman in 1572 of a French dynastic history.

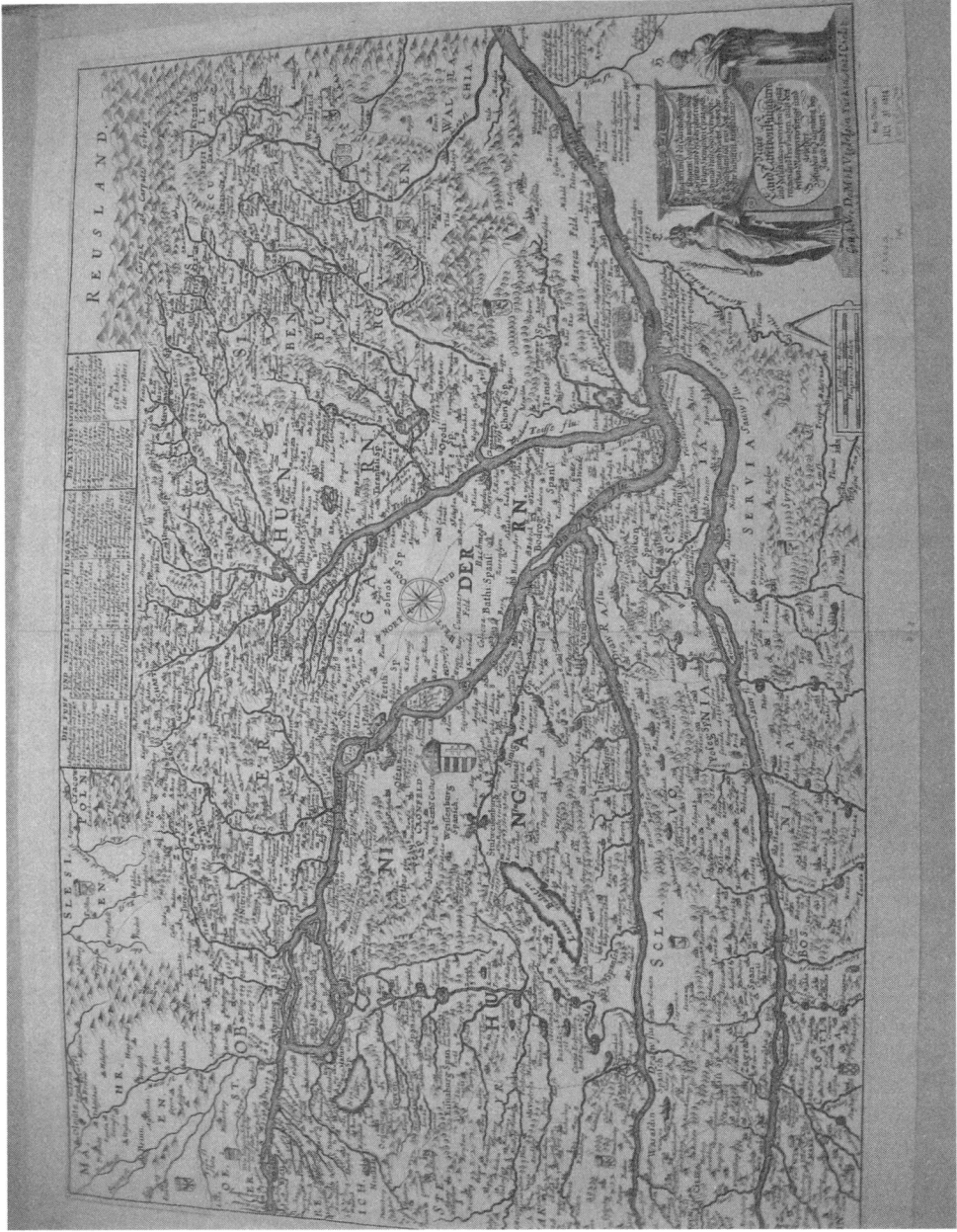

Figure 3.4. Jacob Sandrart, "Neue Land Tafel von Hungarn," Nuremberg, 1657. Geography and Map Division, Library of Congress.

de Haute et Basse Hongrie, Transylvanie, Sclavonie, Croatiae, et Dalmatie," produced in Paris in 1663.[69]

It is the Danube in each frame that defines the limits of Christian and Turk space, even though the river was so long it could not readily be constrained to a single map. Johann Baptist Homann, in Nuremberg, for example, mapped the *"Danubii Fluminis,"* across multiple map sheets as an expansive river system coursing through the bounded political units of the peninsula.[70] That multiframe image made visually clear that the Danube defied all borders except itself. It transcended empire, armies, and the will of men. It also transcended history, as Henri Chatelain's 1739 *Atlas Historique* demonstrated in a *"Carte Ancienne et Moderne des Differents Etats et Pais situez au Long du Danube, pour servir a L'Intelligence de L'Histoire."*[71] One of its many text boxes traces Danubian history beginning with Alexander, through Julius Caesar, Attila, the Lombards, and "Boleslaus King of Poland" [Bolesław V] in 1264, and on through to the "Turks."

Drawing Lines and Demarcating Land and Seascapes

Beyond the imposing boundary of the Danube, one of the simplest ways to designate the possession of space was to draw state lines and affix labels. But early modern mapping did not necessarily require that type of delineation. In an updated 1566 version of Ptolemy's "first part of Asia," Giacomo Gastaldi, for example, depicted the Asian core of Ottoman territory, Anatolia (see Fig. 1.1), as what J. B. Harley has called "socially empty space."[72] The map shows cities and physical regions, not sovereigns, states, or their peoples. The caption notes only that the map "represents the natural [limits] of the province of Anatolia and Caramania and part of Syria . . . "; it does not allude to the Ottoman empire at all. The legend in an earlier (1564) version, however, locates sovereignty in this place: "The design of the modern geography of the province of Anatolia, and Caramania, *'patria'* of the *'Signori Turchi'* of the House of Osman, its eastern boundaries at the Euphrates river and its western at the strait of Constantinople . . . "[73] That version acknowledged Ottoman rule in text if not in image, and suggested the reach of the sultan from the Straits to Iraq, providing a verbal bounding of Ottoman domains. Neither map employs lines to draw political boundaries.

Nevertheless, by the second half of the sixteenth century, it was becoming increasingly common to mark off the sovereign spaces of empires and

---

[69] N. Berey, "Carte de Haute et Basse Hongrie, Transylvanie, Sclavonie, Croatiae, et Dalmatie," Paris, 1663.

[70] Johann Baptist Homann (1633–1724), "Danubii Fluminis (hic ab urbe Belgrado, per Mare Negrum . . .)," Nuremberg, 1720.

[71] H. Chatelain, *Atlas Historique*, v. 2, map 40.

[72] See Karrow, *Mapmakers of the Sixteenth Century*, 246. For Ptolemaic Anatolia, see Claudius Ptolemy, *Géographie de Ptolémée*, Jacopo D'Angiolo, trans. (Paris: Catala Frères, [1926?], plates XXXI–XXXII, from Bibliothèque Nationale, mss. Latin 4802). See also Harley, *The New Nature of Maps*, 99–105.

[73] Fabio Licinio engraved a version of Gastaldi, "Il Disegno della prima Parte dell'Asia," 1559, which leaves the western edge of Anatolia off the map and extends to the east to the "Regno da Cabul (Kabul)." See also Karrow, *Mapmakers of the Sixteenth Century*, 232–3.

nations with lines as well as words. Mapmakers of the Italian peninsula thus employed more specific indicators of boundaries, or *confini*, to suggest Ottoman space. Giovanni Camocio, for example, in 1571, from his work-shop in Venice, issued many maps of the territory contested between the Porte and the Signoria. The eastern Adriatic in Camocio's time consisted of a mainland controlled primarily by the Ottomans and a coastal area divided among Venetian bases, Ottoman ports, and semiautonomous city states such as Ragusa or the piratic port of Senj. That division prompted the drawing of various kinds of line. One of the undated maps in Camocio's 1574 *isolario* (or island book) shows the island and harbor of Zara (Zadar) in the fore-ground fronted by Venetian ships as a marker of possession (Fig. 3.5). The rest of the map is a condensed inland space full of settlements and marching troops, many with crescent flags. In the background is a mountainous zone marked with the label "*confini di Crouatia*." The map thus shows a space divided into three tiers: the coastal space with its sea-based communication and defense; the middle space, near the sea and its inlets but the site of a set of land-based settlements and struggles; and the "borders," the mountainous terrain that separates regions and also divides Venetian sovereign space from the further inland "Croatian" and "Turk" lands.[74] The legend of the map reinforces this sense of division. It reads: "Zara and its countryside, principal city of Dalmatia located on the Adriatic Sea, a place of the Most Illustrious Venetians, at present molested by the Turks."[75] Borders thus separated the lands from the seas and the Venetians from the Turks, whose molestations, it was hoped, were only temporary.

Sea borders, of course, could not be marked in the same way that borders were marked on inland spaces, although mapmakers did draw lines across the watery segments of their maps. The Gulf of Lepanto, for example, constituted such a border. Just as the battle of Lepanto in 1571 was an imagined turning point in the historical narrative of Muslim vs. Christian ascendancy, the Gulf of Lepanto provided a space of seaborne encounter that divided the Adriatic and Ionian seas into Ottoman and Christian zones. The first fold-out map in Giuseppe Rosaccio's illustrated *Viaggio da Veneti a Costantinopoli*, published in Venice in 1598, claims to provide "The description of that which the Turks possess in Europe with the borders of the Christian princes."[76] On this map, Rosaccio harked back to the famous naval conflict as a boundary-defining moment in the establishment of Ottoman and non-Ottoman space. There, a line through the sea is labeled as follows: "Where this line finishes the Turkish armada was defeated by the armada of the Holy League on October 7, 1571." The line seems to suggest a simple dichotomy between "Turk"

[74] See Colin Heywood, "A Frontier without Archaeology? The Ottoman Maritime Frontier in the Western Mediterranean," Ch. XI, in Colin Heywood, *The Ottoman World, the Mediterranean and North Africa 1660–1760, Variorum Collected Studies* (Farnham, Surrey: Ashgate, 2013), 495, 500, 507, for commentary on the notion of Ottoman maritime frontiers in the North African context. Also, Daniel Panzac, *La Caravane maritime: marins européens et marchands ottomans en Méditerranée* (Paris: CNRS, 2004).

[75] "Zarra et contado città principale della Dalmatia posta sul mare Adriatico locho delli Ill.mi S.ri Venetiani al pr[ese]nte molestata da Turchi," in Camocio, *Isole famose*, map 7.

[76] Rosaccio, *Viaggio da Venetia*, first fold-out map.

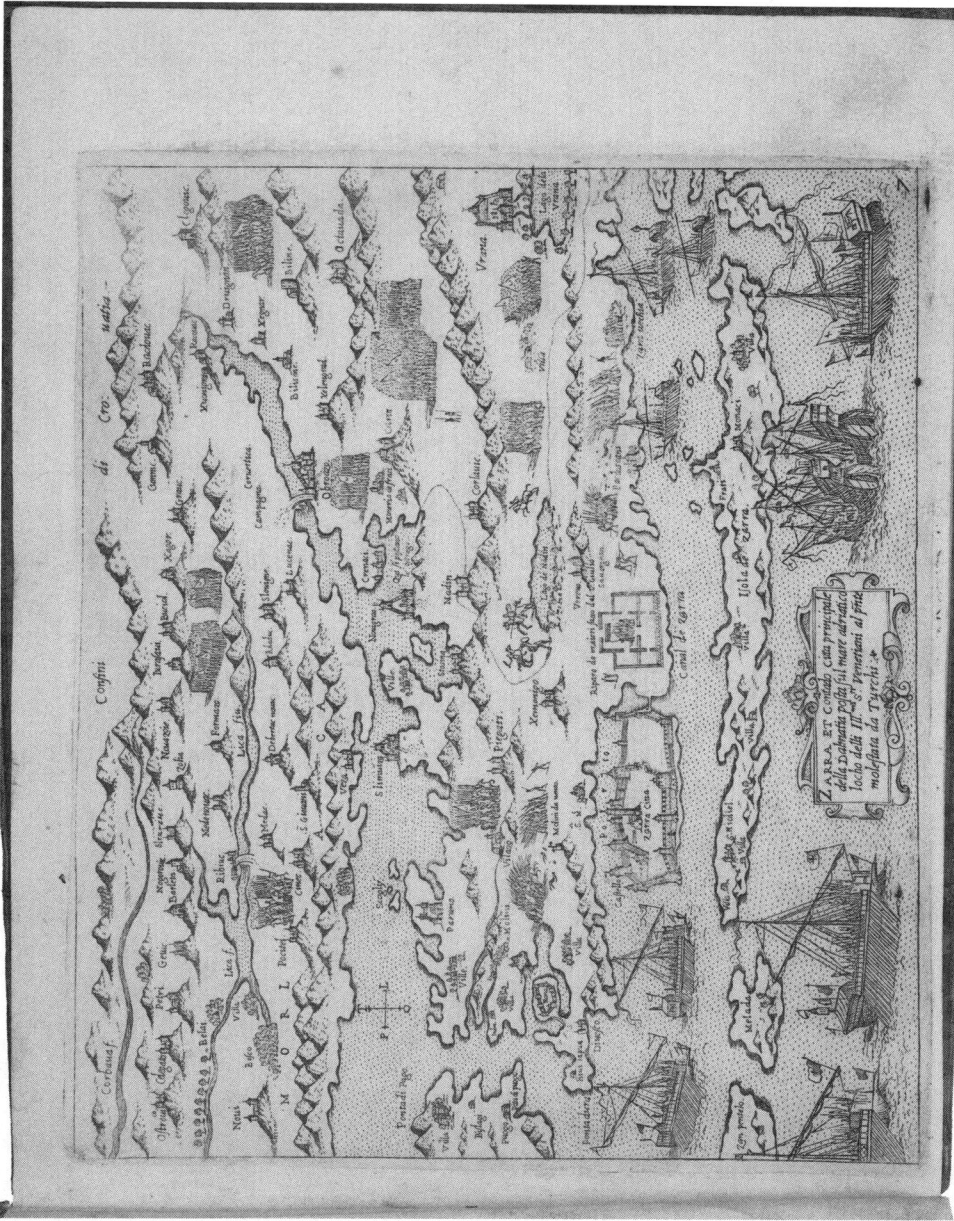

Figure 3.5. Giovanni Camocio, "Zarra et Contado," *Isole famose porti, fortezze, e terre maritime sottoposto all Ser.ma Sig.ria di Venetia*, map 7, Venetia, [1574?]. By permission of the Folger Shakespeare Library, Shelfmark: G1015.C3 1574 Cage.

Figure 3.6. Vincenzo Coronelli, "Contado di Zara. Parte della Dalmatia," inset, Venetia, 1688. Library Znanstvena knjižnica Zadar, ZKZD GK S-2.

and "Christian" space, one echoed by Abu Hasan 'Ali ibn Muhammad ibn 'Ali Muhammad al-Tamjruti, Moroccan ambassador to the Ottomans in 1590, as he commented on the fortresses on either side of the Dardanelles. "Thanks be to God," he wrote, "who has made that line a barrier against the entrance of Christians into the lands of the Muslims after the opposite had been the case."[77] Despite such rhetorics of division, Rosaccio's atlas as a whole served as both a guide for and a commemoration of the movement of people and goods between Christian and Muslim territory. Lines drawn across the sea might reinforce divided identities and claims of sovereignty; but they constituted no barrier to the elaborate intercommunal exchange that characterized the early modern Mediterranean.[78]

Other and later mapmakers, nonetheless, made Rosaccio's line in the sea more concrete. Vincenzo Coronelli (1650–1718), for example, in his 1688 map "Contado di Zara, Parte della Dalmatia," demarcated the sea space of the colony of Zara with a dotted line marking the limits of Venetian "territory" in the Adriatic (Fig. 3.6). And in John Fielding's 1783 map of "Turky in Europe," one finds a small dotted line reaching from the mouth of the Don River, through the Black Sea, the Bosporus, and the Aegean, ending in the Mediterranean Sea beneath Rhodes. This watery boundary line is labeled "Boundary of Europe" (Fig. 3.7).[79] One finds a similar line, labeled "Limite de l'Europe," drawn across the sea spaces of the 1788 "*Théâtre itinéraire de la Guerre actuelle entre les Turcs, d'une part, les Russes et les Impériaux*," by Louis Brion de la Tour (c. 1743–1803), geographer of the king of France. This was a map that suggested the imminent conquest of Ottoman territory. It showed a 'world' in which the bounded spaces of "*Turquie Européenne*" would inevitably be separated from the (here) unbounded spaces of "*Turquie Asiatique*" (Fig. 3.8). The drawing of lines on these maps was an attempt to confirm and advertise borders that were the subject of a longstanding and ongoing struggle in the transimperial space.[80] Those lines projected sovereign power, though no sovereign could effectively enforce his control over the spaces of the sea, no matter how many lines his cartographers might draw on the map.[81]

In any case, by the seventeenth century, the drawing of state lines had become the standard of European cartography. The solid or dotted line, showing the limits of kingly power and the perceived separations between

[77] Cited in Matar, *Europe Through Arab Eyes*, 152–3. Al-Tamjruti tells a fantastic story of the seventh century "creation" of the fortresses.

[78] Maria Pia Pedani, "Christiani e Musulmani nel Mediterraneo," 239–51, in *La mobilité des personnes en Méditerranée de l'antiquité à L'èpoque moderne*, Claudie Moatti ed., *Collection de l'Éçole Française de Rome* 341(2004), 243, 249, assesses the ambiguity of the sea frontiers most eloquently.

[79] J. Fielding, "Turky in Europe," [London], 1783. See Delano-Smith, "Signs on Printed Topographical Maps," 555–7.

[80] See Gökbilgin, "Yeni Belgelerin Işığı Altında Kanunî Sultan Süleyman," 175. Also on Venetian–Ottoman treaties, Hans Theunissen, *Ottoman–Venetian Diplomatics: The 'ahd-names: The Historical Background and the Development of a Category of Political–Commercial Instruments Together with an Annotated Edition of a Corpus of Relevant Documents*, in *Electronic Journal of Oriental Studies*, or reprint, 2 vols. (Utrecht: Universiteit Utrecht, 1998).

[81] Uriel Heyd, *Ottoman Documents on Palestine, 1552–1615: A Study of the Firman According to the Mühimme Defteri* (Oxford: Clarendon Press, 1960), 129–30, demonstrates how the Ottomans attempted to defend 'lines' in the sea surrounding their territories.

Figure 3.7. Boundary of Europe. John Fielding, "Turky in Europe," detail, London, 1783. Geography and Map Division, Library of Congress.

political entities, was associated with both sovereign claims and the science of measurement. In 1697, for example, Jacobus Hoffman presented a huge and elaborately decorated colored map of Hapsburg territory in four sheets (adapted from a 1669 wall map by Georg Matthäus Vischer): "Archiducatus Austria Inferioris Geographica et Noviter Emendata Accuratissima Descriptio."[82] He took pains to note that this work was newly updated. A cartouche at bottom center shows two surveyors on a promontory surrounded by an array of tools (Fig. 3.9). They hold a legend that shows the various icons employed on the map (for lakes, monasteries, markets, etc.) including the indications for borders: for *quad rantum* (a double dotted line) and for *fines provinicae* (a single dotted line). The borders of *"Pars Regni Ungariae"* are elaborately marked, and no "Turks" are to be seen. The clear message of this vignette is that border lines on the map are not impressionistic; they derive, rather, from careful and systematic measurement.[83]

But despite such insistence on 'accurate' and measured representation, the art of mapping continued to provide considerable scope for the imagination

[82] Jacobus Hoffman, "Archiducatus Austria Inferioris Geographicae et Noviter Emendata Accuratissima Descriptio," Vienna, 1697, adapted from Georg Vischer (1628–96). On the dotted line and the demarcation of sovereign space, see Biggs, "Putting the State on the Map," 393.

[83] Borders are also indicated with text on the map. Across the bottom parts of sheets 2 and 3 in very large green letters is written "*CONFINIA STYRIAE*," and written along the side of sheet four on the right in large green capital letters is "*PARS REGNI UNGARIAE*." Vienna is near the middle of sheet 3, fairly elaborately marked; and unlike so many of the maps depicting Hapsburg space, here there is no sign of Turks or things Ottoman.

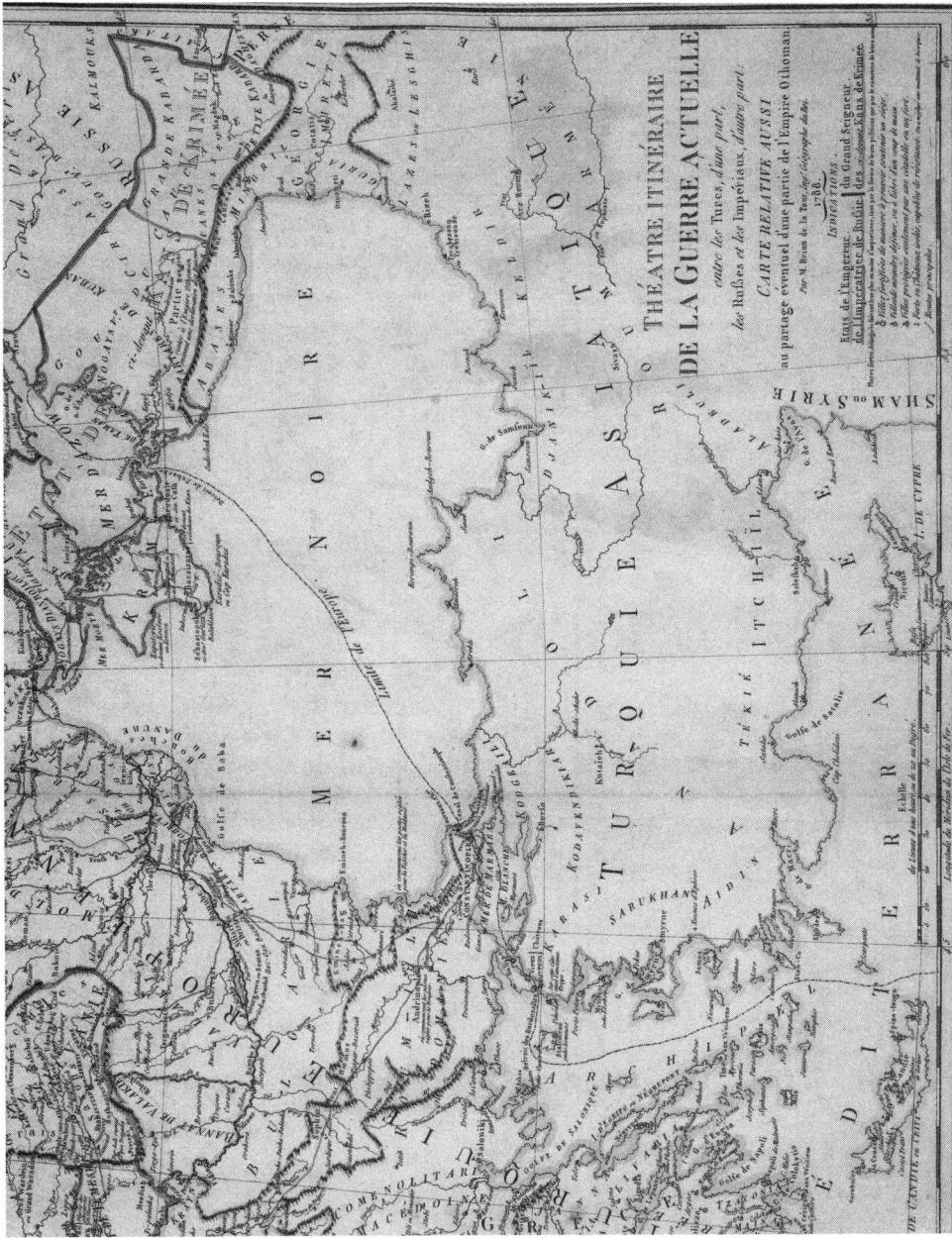

Figure 3.8. Louis Brion de la Tour, "Théâtre itinéraire de la Guerre actuelle entre les Turcs, d'une part, les Russes et les Impériaux," inset, Paris, 1788. The British Library Board, Maps K.Top. 113–18/C2490–05.

Figure 3.9. Surveyors. Jacob Hoffman, from Georg Matthäus Vischer, "Archiducatus Austria Inferioris Geographicae et Noviter Emendata Accuratissima Descriptio," cartouche [Vienna], 1697. Photo Courtesy of the Newberry Library, Chicago, Novacco 6F 21.

when it came to envisioning where Ottoman territory stopped and that of the Christian kings began. One year before Hoffman's map appeared, Nicolas de Fer (1646–1720), royal geographer of the French court, produced a wonderful illustrated "L'Asie" for the Dauphin, a large and beautiful colored map surrounded by a series of ethnographic vignettes.[84] The borders on this map are marked with dotted lines. One such line demarcates Ottoman territory from "Muscovie," and another separates Ottoman from Safavid territory in Iran.[85] But what is striking about this work is the large red designation "Frontières de l'Europe," in the upper left quadrant of the map, slashed from southwest to northeast across a large contrasting white space of eastern Europe (Figs. 3.10 and 3.11).[86] This is the cartographer's impressionistic

---

[84] Nicolas de Fer, "L'Asie, Ou tous les points Principaux sont placez sur les observations de Mrs. de l'Académie royale des sciences," Paris, 1696.

[85] Between Iran and Iraq there are places marked "Curdistan," and "Curdistan aux Turcs"; those territories, however, are not demarcated by boundaries.

[86] This labeling of the frontier occurs along a slanted line to the northwest of Ragusa and Albania and Cracow, which are among the furthest places to the northwest that are labeled on the map. "Turquie en Europe," "Bulgarie," "Macedonie," etc. are rather tenuous outliers to this contained "Asia."

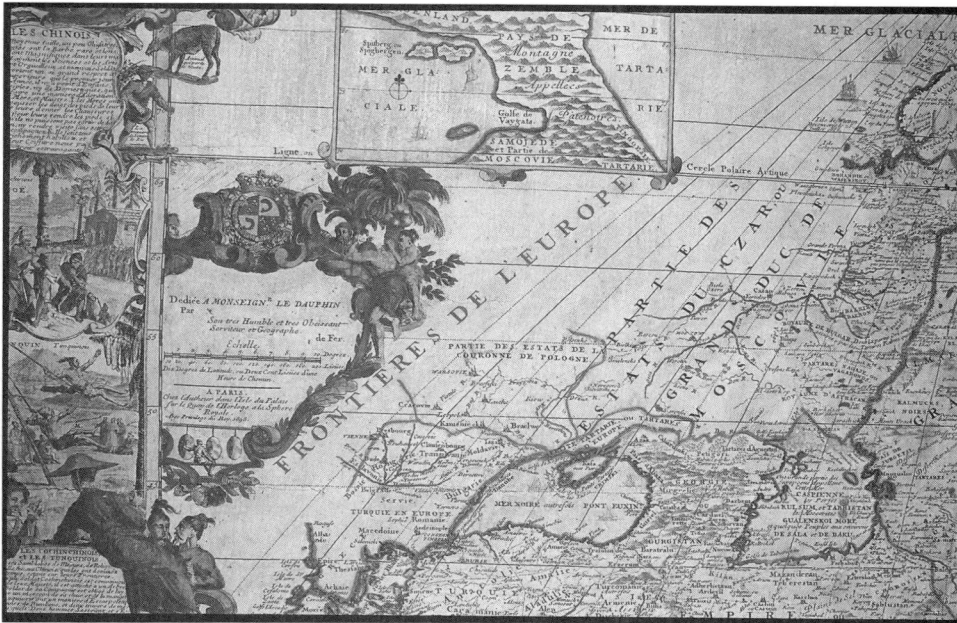

Figure 3.10. Frontiers of Europe. Nicolas de Fer, "L'Asie," inset, Paris, 1696. Photo Courtesy of the Newberry Library, Chicago, Novacco 8F 9. (See color plate)

vision of the dramatic division between the Ottoman empire and a Europe that is, in effect, mostly off the map.

Although this particular designation of 'frontier' is clear and bold, the space it occupies is empty, devoid of markings and of designations of people, cities, or states. Blank spaces were conventional parts of the design on some maps; and Asia in this map is surrounded by blank spaces. But such spaces also convey the message of ambiguous identity.[87] Iconographically, the designation "frontière" in de Fer's map reflects the ambiguities of power and possession in the areas between nations, peoples, and states. It also sets the boundary of Europe well west and north of the one Fielding drew through the sea.

The labels "Turkey in Europe" and "Turkey in Asia" on de Fer's map indicate the transcontinental reach of the Ottoman Porte.[88] And the elaborate illustrations around the edges of the map include another indicator of identity, an ethnographic vignette for the "Turcs Anatolienes." This vignette (employing Islamic judges, communal baths, a camel caravan, and veiled women) notes that these Anatolian Turks have the same religion as the Turks in Europe. De Fer's map, then, in its use of ethnographic material and its highly conscious demarcation of "frontiers" and states, approaches what

[87] Petkov, *Infidels, Turks, and Women*, 218, notes the blank space south of the Danube, and especially southeast of the Save, "covering the area of the central Balkan Slavic lands" in Ortelius' map of Hungary.

[88] For a discussion of the evolution of European designations for the Ottoman empire, and the division into Turkey in Europe and Turkey in Asia, see Manners, *European Cartographers and the Ottoman World*, 36, 39, 40–41, 50.

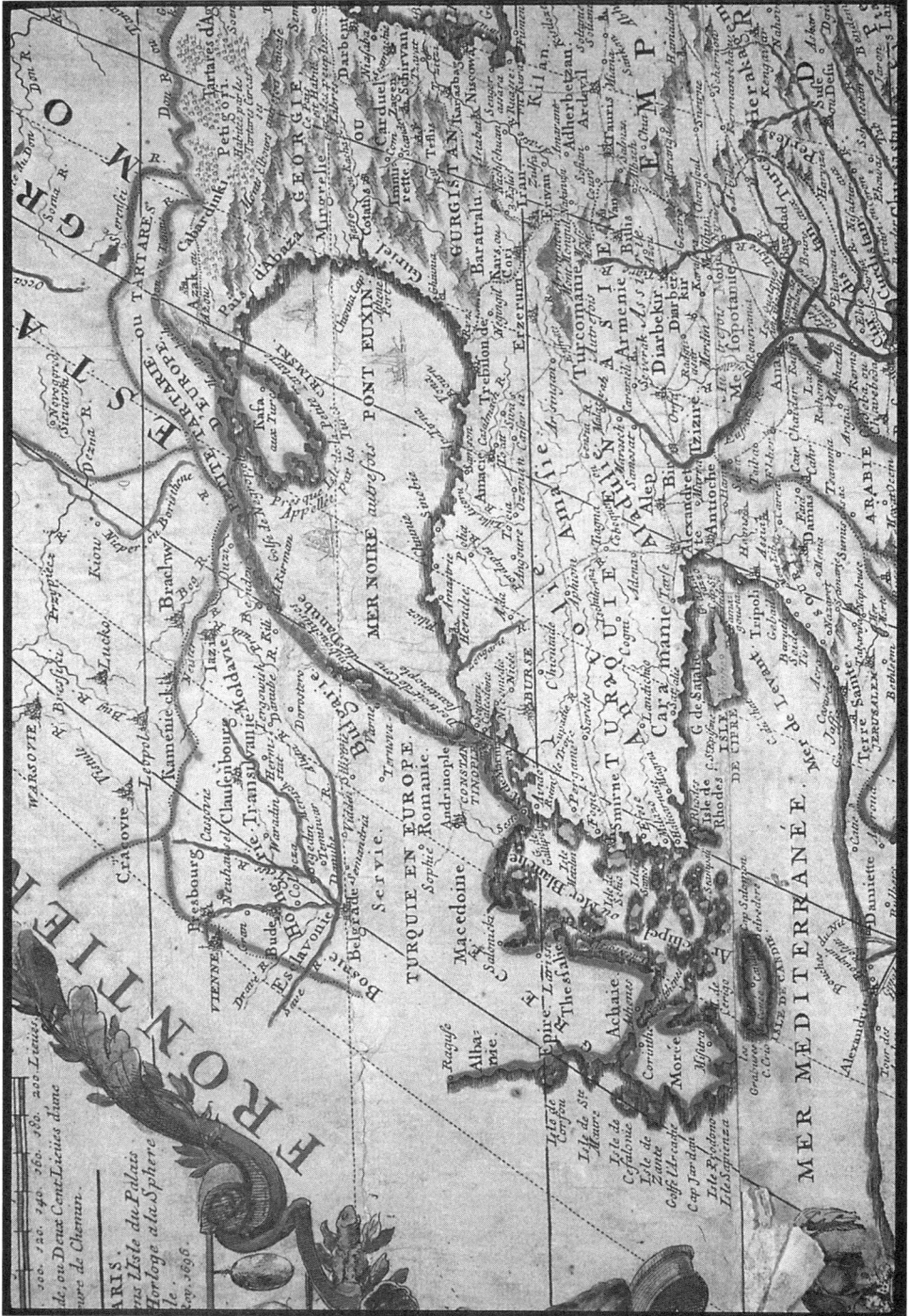

Figure 3.11. Nicolas de Fer, "L'Asie," detail, Paris, 1696. Photo Courtesy of the Newberry Library, Chicago, Novacco 8F 9.

we are accustomed to thinking of as a more "modern" representation.[89] Still, his striking image of the frontier makes clear the mobility of the edge of Europe from map to map and the utility of empty space as a means of indicating the divisions produced by Muslim possession of European space.

Even when continental space was highlighted and long after Ottoman sovereignty was recognized on the body of the map, the borders of Europe remained malleable. The work of a contemporary of de Fer's, Richard Blome (d. 1705), demonstrates further how problematic the division between Ottoman and European space could be. In his 1684 English *Cosmography and Geography*, Blome elaborated upon Bernhardus Varenius' (1622–50) *Geographia*, employing material cribbed from the French royal cartographer, Nicolas Sanson (1600–1667). He divided Europe into countries and their attendant religious affiliations, with some intermediate spaces in between:

> *Europe is one of the three parts of our Continent, of which Asia makes the most Eastern, Africa most Southern,... We will consider Europe in Nine... Principal parts: And of these, the first three shall be Spain, Italy, and the Estates of Turkey in Europe;.... Besides these 9 parts, there will remain some Estates and Lands between France, Germany, and Italy; likewise between Germany, Poland, and Turkey and Moscovia;... The Religions are the Protestant, which has spread itself where the Teutonick tongue is spoken; the Roman Catholick is almost everywhere with the Latin; Schism, alone and every where amongst the People speaking Sclavonian and Greek; the Mahumetan Religion is among the Natural Turks of Europe.*[90]

The importance of this description lies in its treatment of Ottoman Europe as one European "nation" among others and of Islam as one European religion among others. Also, the category employed by Blome, "Estates and Lands between," is noteworthy as it expresses the sense of areas (Croatia or "Barbaria" in North Africa for example) that did not cartographically fit the standard division of the empire into Asian and European "halves."

By the later seventeenth century, the recitation of formal Ottoman political divisions (*beyliks* and *sanjaks*) had become a commonplace. William Berry, freely using the work of Nicolas Sanson and claiming to amend it, produced an atlas in 1689 which included a large map labeled "Dominions or Empire of the Great Turke in Europe, Asia, and Africa, divided into all its Beglerbeglicz or Governments In which are also distinguished the States that are Tributary to him" (Fig. 3.12).[91] The tributary states are listed as "the Principalities

---

89 Other vignettes speak of the Arabs and their miserableness, calling them "Maures," "Vagabondes," and "Bedouins," but then going on to mention caravans, expertise in astrology and medicine, and the "famous" pilgrimage to Mecca. Elsewhere, "*Les femmes sont passables*" is said of the Tartars, and of the Georgians, "*Sont bien faites et leurs femmes tres belles.*" Wintle, *The Image of Europe*, 262–3, notes a frieze by Artus Quellinus on Amsterdam City Hall of 1648 which depicts the female continents (with Europe, of course at the center); Asia holds a camel's bridle and sports a turban headgear.

90 Richard Blome, *Cosmography and Geography* (London: S. Roycroft, 1684), pt. 2, 7, taken from the work of Nicolas Sanson.

91 It was a republication of Nicolas Sanson's (1600–1667) map of 1654. On the Sansons (and Jaillot) and their milieu, see Monique Pelletier, "National and Regional Mapping in France," 1480–1503, see 1497–1500; and Catherine Hoffmann, "Publishing and the Map Trade in France, 1470–1670,"

Figure 3.12. William Berry, from Nicolas Sanson, "Dominions or Empire of the Great Turke in Europe, Asia, and Africa, divided into all its Beglerbeglicz or Governments," cartouche, London, c. 1689. Geography and Map Division, Library of Congress.

of Little Tartary, Transilvania, Moldavia, Valachia, and the Republicks of Ragusa in Europe [and] ye Dominions of the Cherif of Mecca, and of the King of Arabia Deserta, in Asia; [and] the Kingdoms of Algier, Tunis and Tripoli, in Africa." Berry uses "Erak Atzem" (*Irak-ı Acem*, or Persian Iraq) to mark the frontier with Safavid Iran, the same designation employed by the Ottoman commander Matrakçı more than a century earlier. Another example is Hubert Jaillot's (1632–1712) "Estats del' Empire Du Grand Seigneur Des Turcs, en Europe, en Asie, et en Afrique, divisé en tous ses Beglerbeglicz, ou Gouvernements," also based on Sanson and published in multiple editions (Fig. 3.13).[92]

The empire was thus a complex set of regional and political entities extending across three continents and bounded by seas, other empires, states, and peoples, with "frontiers" separating one empire from another. It was a space with its own logics and designations of government. That complexity notwithstanding, for many seventeenth century cartographers, as we have seen with Nicolas de Fer, the titles "Turkey in Europe" and "Turkey in Asia" served to identify the major "estates" of the Ottomans while preserving the 'integrity' of continental Europe.[93] "Turkey in Asia" in this construction (echoing over two centuries of travel narratives) is part of the ancient world, whereas "Turkey in Europe" has been "ruined" by the occupation of the "Turk."[94] Both geographic and political designations, these titles survived until the end of World War I, when Christendom's hoped-for cleansing of the Turks from Europe was undertaken forcibly in the treaties that dismantled the empire (Fig. 3.14).[95]

1569–88, see 1584–8, both in *HOC*, v. 3, pt. 2. See also Vincenzo Coronelli, *Atlante veneto*, v. 1, 1690, second map after page 80.

[92] Hubert Jaillot, "Estats del' Empire Du Grand Seigneur Des Turcs, en Europe, en Asie, et en Afrique, divisé en tous ses Beglerbeglicz, ou Gouvernements," Paris, 1708; earlier editions were published in 1681, 1692 and 1696. See Manners, *European Cartographers*, 40–41. Robert Morden (d. 1703), *Geography Rectified; or, a description of the world, in all its kingdoms provinces, countries . . .* (London: R. Morden and T. Cockerill, 1680), 257–8, complements his maps with a narrative of the lands ruled by the sultan in Europe, Asia, and Africa, and a recitation of "*sanjaks*" (subprovinces) and their revenues, much as the Venetian bailos made a habit of including breakdowns of Ottoman revenues in their *relazioni*. In Nicolas Visscher's early seventeenth century map, "Magni Turcarum Domini Imperium in Europa, Asia, et Africa" [Amsterdam, c. 1680], Ottoman administrative divisions are marked as "*beglerbegliks*" and "*Praefectures general*."

[93] The ubiquity of that two-part designation is illustrated in the maps of the English cartographer Herman Moll (1654–1732), which were widely adapted and incorporated into atlases and encyclopedic works. Moll's maps provided the illustrations for Bowles's *Atlas minor*, London, c. 1781. See Alex Zukas, "The British Imperial Imagination in the Maps of Herman Moll, 1700–1730," *Proceedings of the American Historical Association*, 2009 (Ann Arbor: National Archive Publishing Company, 2009), Reference # 10485–2009.

[94] That trope was repeated in Herman Moll, *The Compleat Geographer of the Earth*, 4th ed. (London: J. Knapton, 1723), 5, which goes on to say that "Turkish Tyranny has rendered it almost Desart," so that English merchants who have "the Curiosity to visit the Antiquities of this once famous Country . . . see nothing but Ruins (6)."

[95] Herman Moll, "Turky in Asia," and accompanying text from unidentified work. This is one of multiple variants dating from the first half of the eighteenth century. For other eighteenth century map examples see the 1721 English version of G. de l'Isle, revised by John Senex (d. 1740), "A Map of Turky, Arabia, and Persia," which was "Corrected from the latest Travels and from ye observations of ye Royal Societys of London and Paris," London, c. 1721; and Brion de La Tour's "Perse, Turquie Asiatique, et Arabie," Paris, 1766. John Speed's "The Turkish Empire," London, 1626, does not employ the two-part division of Turkey, limiting itself, as in older maps, to the designation of cities and regions.

Figure 3.13 Hubert Jaillot, from Nicolas Sanson, "Estats de l'Empire du Grand Seigneur des Turcs," Paris, c. 1708. The British Library Board, Maps K.Top. 113.5.2.

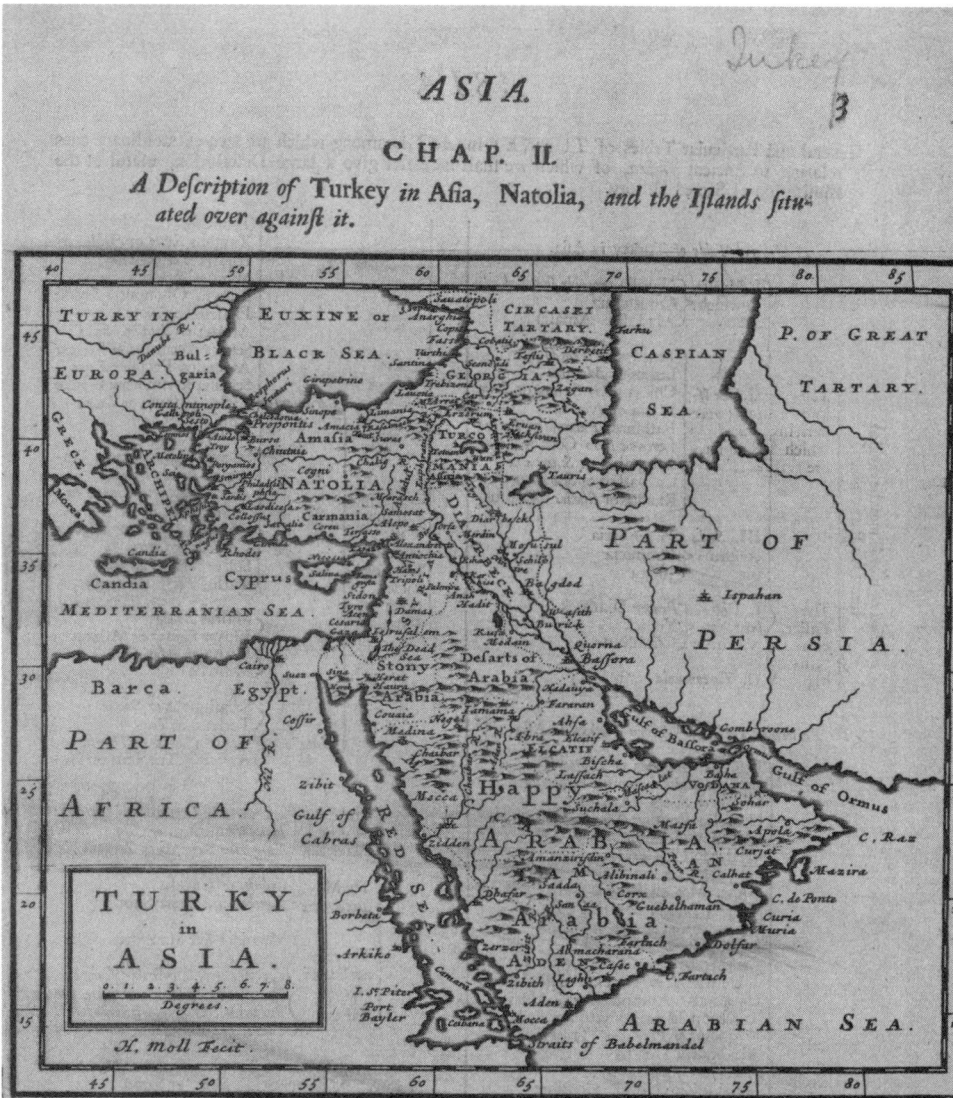

ASIA

CHAP. II.

A Description of Turkey *in* Asia, Natolia, *and the* Islands *situated over against it.*

I. AMONG the Parts of *Asia*, that subject to the Turk first offers it self to our View, as lying next to *Turkey in Europe* last described; and in regard that this Region constitutes the chiefest Part of the *Ottoman* Empire, even upon that account it ought not to be separated. The Bounds of *Turkey in Asia* on the North, are the *Euxine*, or Black Sea and *Georgia*; *Persia* on the East; *Arabia* on the South; and on the West *Egypt*, the Eastern Part of the Mediterranean Sea, the *Archipelago*, the Straight of *Gallipoli*, the *Propontis*, and the Straight of *Constantinople*. These Dominions thus bounded are situated between the 30th and the 43d Degr. of Northern Latitude, and the Soil produces every thing that is necessary for Humane Life; more especially Corn, Fruits, the best sort of Grapes, Saffron, Cotton, Silver, Copper, Iron, Crystal and Allum; but through the Severity of the Turkish Government it is not half Cultivated. The Division of the Countreys, with the chief Cities, is seen in the following Table.

Part 2   B 2   General

Figure 3.14. Herman Moll, "Turky in Asia," London, c. 1736. Geography and Map Division, Library of Congress.

Finally, the place of the empire in the world and its association with Europe
is certified in the 1788 Viennese map grouping showing the clash of empires
by François I. Maire (noted in Ch. 1). This map historicizes the portrayal
of Brion's "Théâtre itinéraire de la Guerre" (mentioned earlier), which was
produced in the same year. Maire's "Carte general des limites entre les trois
Empires, et leurs Variations successives dépuis l'année 1718 jusqu'à ce jour"
presents a vision of the Ottoman empire trampled under the imperial boots of
more formidable European foes.[96] The borders (*limites*) of empire are clearly
changing and the mapmakers could envision new 'owners' in the Ottoman
capital (Fig. 3.15). Separate lines mark "actual," "ancient," and "provincial"
boundaries as well as routes of travel. This map was produced as the Russian–
Austrian war against the Ottomans began to produce territorial results.[97] It
signaled a new world order.

Philip Eckebrecht in 1630 had crafted a world map that depicted the
double-headed Hapsburg eagle enfolding the entire world within its wings.[98]
That assertion of world hegemony was equally potent in 1788, by which
time the Ottomans and Hapsburgs had been rivals for more than two centuries. But by the end of the eighteenth century the configuration of imperial
combatants had changed; Russia had become a primary contender for world
power and joined a new transimperial confrontation, what Virginia Aksan
has called the "Austrian–Russian–Ottoman Danube waltz."[99] Meanwhile,
in the France of the 1780s and 1790s, one could see, as Aksan has pointed
out, "the early appearance of a particular blend of enthusiasm for the exotic
combined with a rising sense of mission to save the Ottoman empire from
itself, and an urge to territorial power which would become the familiar and
well-documented ideology of the nineteenth century empires."[100] The limits
of Ottoman space were being defined in ways that the empire itself could no
longer resist; and the 'edge' of Europe was closing in.

[96] F. I. Maire, "Carte générale des Limites entre les trois Empires," 1788. This roll map extends from
Vienna to the eastern edge of the Black Sea, and provides an elaborate recitation of authorities in a
note at bottom right: "*Cette Carte étant tirée en partie de celle de M.r de Janoni, de celles de M.rs
Kauffer et Fougeroh, Islenich Sulzer, Bauer et Kinsbergen, et rédigée sur les observations de S. Ex.ce.
M.r le Compte de Choiseul Gouffier, du Colonel Werrnon, sur les memoires du Baron Tot et sure
ceuse de M.r Peysonnel . . .*" Those authorities are cartographic, diplomatic, military, and historical;
but it is the treaties, "*traites respectifs de ces puissances,*" that provide a basis for the "actual" lines
of demarcation.

[97] See Stanford Shaw, *History of the Ottoman Empire and Modern Turkey*, v. 1, *Empire of the Gazis:
The Rise and Decline of the Ottoman Empire 1280–1808* (Cambridge: Cambridge University Press,
1976), 258–9; and Aksan, *Ottoman Wars 1700–1870*, 163–5.

[98] Wintle, *The Image of Europe*, 23: "the hemisphere-and-two-halves are assembled in such a way that,
when the eagle folds its wings, the world too will fold in on itself like an altar triptych or display
cupboard."

[99] Aksan, *Ottoman Wars*, 129–79. Aksan, "The One-Eyed Fighting the Blind: Mobilization, Supply,
and Command in the Russo-Turkish War of 1768–1774," 173–90, in *Ottomans and Europeans:
Contacts and Conflicts*, Analecta Isisiana LXXV (İstanbul: Isis Press, 2004), 188, 190, has argued
that the leadership of Field Marshal Rumiantsev, combined with the Ottomans' "lack of any semblance
of a command structure," was the decisive factor in the Russo–Ottoman war of 1768–74.

[100] Virginia Aksan, "Choiseul-Gouffier at the Sublime Porte 1784–1792," 59–65, in *Ottomans and
Europeans*, 59. The author notes that in 1783 the French ambassador in Istanbul, Saint' Priest, had
an announcement published in the *Gazette de France* "to the effect that the Sultan was not accepting
Christian officers in his service (59)." There was already a glut of applicants.

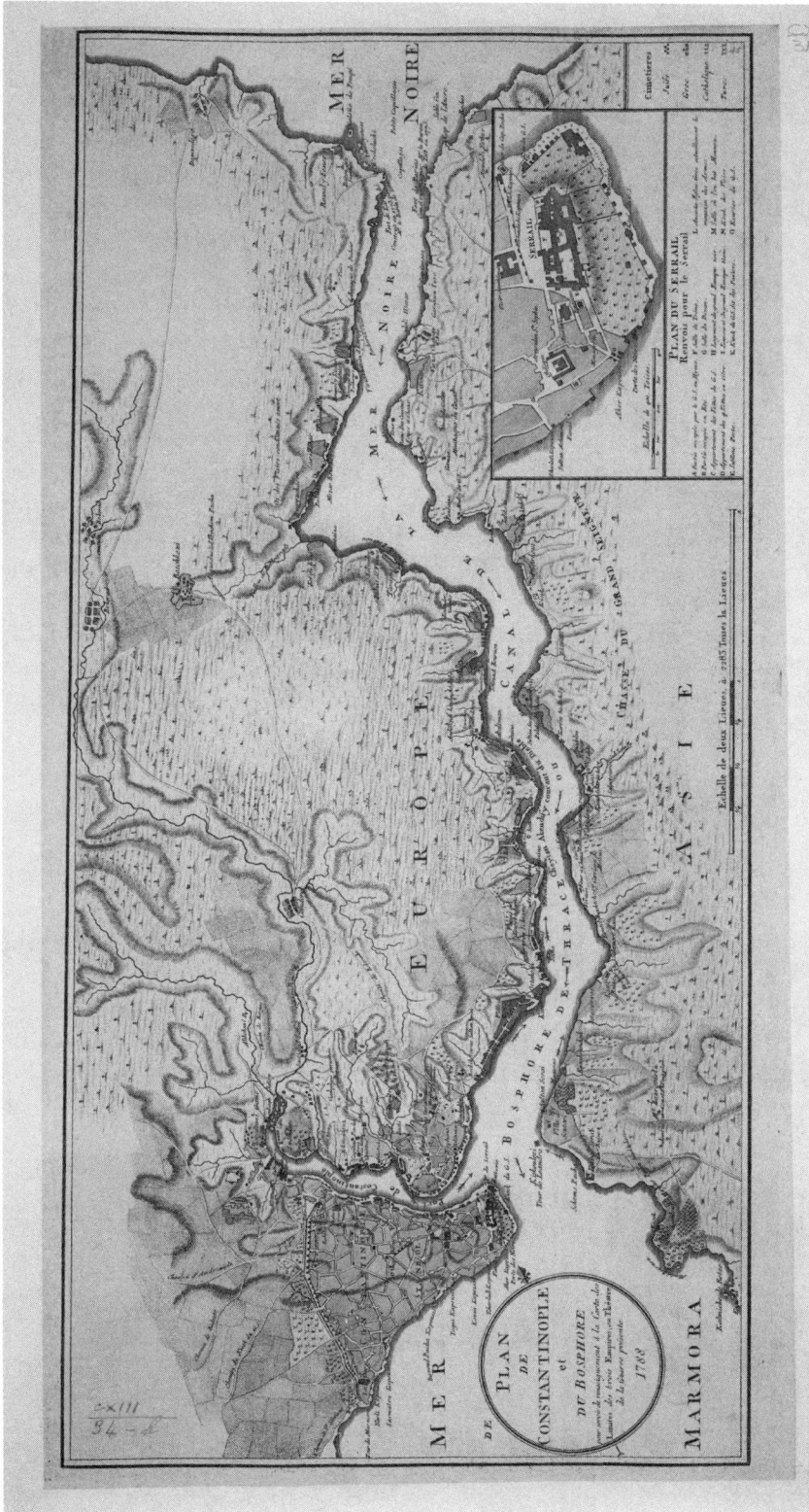

Figure 3.15. F. I. Maire, "Plan de Constantinople," supplement to "Carte générale des Limites entre les trois Empires et leurs variations successives depuis l'année 1718 jusqu'à ce jour, ou Théâtre de la Guerre présente," Vienna, 1788. The British Library Board, Maps K.Top. 34b/C2490–08.

Part 3. The Holy Land Writ Large and the Power of Prophecy

Before we abandon the question of boundaries, there remains another kind
of boundary, one that provided a rather different edge of Europe than those
found in the maps of Sanson or Coronelli. This was the boundary between
sacred and heretical space, one that posited the "Holy Land" as an annex
of Europe, a noncontiguous space that embodied the identity, history, and
well-being of Christendom.[101] The Holy Land was God's space and a place
of forgiveness for all the Abrahamic believers. As such, it problematized the
construction of the borders of Europe and the relationship of the lands of
the Christian kings to those of the Ottoman Empire. This was a realm of
devotion, martyrs, apostates, and miracles. It bent, distorted, or transformed
other sorts of cartographic measures. As Alessandro Scafi has pointed out,
"The Reformation and the spread of printing gave a new impulse to the
creation of maps of biblical history" and to "interest in sacred geography – the
use of contemporary geographical knowledge to identify and describe lands
and countries mentioned in the Bible ... "[102] Within that frame of reform and
counterreform, the concept of the Holy Land projected the authority of the
papacy and Protestant preachers onto the lands and peoples of the sultan,
anchored a complex hodgepodge of nations that were to remain indelibly
Christian regardless of how Ottoman they became or how "eastern" they
might be, and served as a focal point for a reanimated demand for Christian
redemption.

The "Holy Land": Annex of Europe

Jerusalem

Jerusalem was the "center" of Christendom in medieval maps.[103] It was the
promised land of the Jews and their Abrahamic successors, a pilgrimage
site longed for, imagined, achieved, and reported on. It was claimed by
Christian kings but controlled by the Ottomans. For Muslim readers and
travelers Jerusalem was a center point in the history of the life of the Prophet
Muhammad. The Ottoman author, Evliya Çelebi, cited that history and
called Jerusalem "the object of desire of the kings of all nations, especially
the Christians who, ever since Jesus was born ... have waged all their wars

[101] Housley, *Crusading and Warfare in Medieval and Renaissance Europe*, pt. III, "The Eschatological Imperative," 148, references Joseph Strayer who "illustrated how in the case of the French a similar transfer of the idea of the 'Holy Land' occurred, from a unique territory in Palestine to the patria of the Christian believer."
[102] Scafi, *Mapping Paradise*, 289, 343. As the author notes, "early European explorers would never have dreamt of trying to get past the flaming sword of the Cherubin to penetrate the mystery of the Garden of Eden ... the changed attitude towards the mapping of paradise in the Renaissance was a reflection of profound changes in theological and philosophical thinking that had been taking place since the thirteenth century" (254).
[103] See Tishby, ed., *Holy Land in Maps*, 72–105.

over Jerusalem."[104] Like other rulers before him, the Ottoman sultan also utilized Jerusalem to legitimize his rule and certify his authority. Jerusalem was neither a major commercial entrepot nor a provincial capital (Damascus played that role). But the city and its surrounding territories in Palestine were "holy land" (*arazi-i mukaddes*) that had to be protected from disorder, brigandage, oppression, and abuse of travelers.[105]

Having conquered Jerusalem in 1516, the Ottomans recognized its identity as a special transcommunal space. They invoked "ancient custom" to acknowledge the claims of "infidel" Christians to administer various sites in Jerusalem, such as the shrine of "the sacred footprint of the Lord Jesus," where "sacred law" and imperial decree confirmed the privileges of Armenian Christians in 1613 against the incursions of Muslims.[106] In 1609, a sultanic decree warned the chief judge (*kadı*) of Jerusalem to exercise due diligence in policing the sacred birthplace of Jesus in Bethlehem, which was administered by "Frankish monks." Those monks, the decree advised, must not interfere with anyone, Muslim or non-Muslim, who wanted to "hang up lamps and perform a pious act" in the shrine of the Nazarene.[107] In May 1552 the Ottoman government sent an imperial order to the beylerbey of Damascus noting that the "Franks" who "land at the port of Jaffa in order to make a pilgrimage to the Church of the Holy Sepulcher" should not be subjected to extortions in the form of tolls or protection fees, which threatened the lawful revenues of the empire.[108] Ideally, neither Muslim nor Christian officials were to abuse the pious; but neither were they to compromise the prerogatives of the state.

The Porte thus confirmed Jerusalem as a center of Christendom. But transcending the requirements of custom and history, the Ottomans were quite clear that this "sanctuary" had been given to Islam and to the sultan by divine intent. Thus, in a decree sent to the *kadı* of Jerusalem in 1589, the Porte traced its claim of possession to the "sixteenth year of the hijra" and the caliph Umar's (r. 634–44) taking of the city "by the grace of God."[109] So Jerusalem, in one set of early modern rhetorics (like those of the Reverend Fuller seen in Ch. 1) an indelible hearthstone of Christendom, was in another set of rhetorics a sacred part of the well-protected Ottoman domains, its possession justified by conquest and by history. And therein lay the rub, when it came to mapping the Holy Land.

[104] Evliya Çelebi, *An Ottoman Traveller: Selections from the* Book of Travels *of Evliya Çelebi*, Robert Dankoff and Sooyong Kim, ed. and trans. (London: Eland, 2010), 316. See also Samer Akkach, "The Poetics of Concealment: Al-Nabulusi's Encounter with the Dome of the Rock," *Muqarnas* 22 (2005): 110–27; and

[105] Heyd, *Ottoman Documents on Palestine*, 50–56. The Ottomans administered a large imperial pious endowment (*waqf*) for tending Jerusalem's poor (58–9). See also Amy Singer, *Constructing Ottoman Beneficence: An Imperial Soup Kitchen in Jerusalem* (Albany: State University of New York Press, 2002); and Amnon Cohen, *Economic Life in Ottoman Jerusalem* (Cambridge: Cambridge University Press, 2002).

[106] Heyd, *Ottoman Documents*, 180–81.

[107] Heyd, *Ottoman Documents*, 184.

[108] Heyd, *Ottoman Documents*, 182–3 and 180.

[109] Heyd, *Ottoman Documents*, 169–70.

Cyprus

For the cartographers of the Christian kingdoms, Jerusalem was indelibly Christian space; and Cyprus was a stepping stone on the journey.[110] Whereas Jerusalem had been part of the Muslim domains for centuries, Cyprus, until it was taken from Venice in 1571, had provided European Christians with a substantial pilgrimage and commercial base practically within sight of the Holy Land. Even after the Ottoman conquest, Cyprus was too big and too close to Jerusalem for the mapmakers of the Christian kingdoms willingly to mark it as Muslim territory. Instead, like Palestine, it played the role of an appendage of Europe groaning under the Ottoman "yoke" and in need of redemption.[111]

Cyprus had always been a place in between. Before the fall of the Levantine Crusader states, it served as "an annex of the more important Frankish settlements on the mainland, particularly . . . Jerusalem . . . a supply base and a stopover between Christianity and *outremer*."[112] That relationship persisted for Christian pilgrims and travelers. So the association of Cyprus and Jerusalem was one of long standing, as revealed in Benjamin Arbel's elegant treatment of the island under Venetian rule (1489–1571). Arbel writes of the "much richer and nuanced relationship" of Cyprus and its Muslim neighbors, "characterized by strong economic interdependence and intensive human contacts."[113] Under the Serenissima, Cyprus served as a base for pirates, a shelter for Ottoman repairs and provisioning, a pilgrim way station, and a crucial center for the transcommunal trade in grain (legal and illegal). It was a major entrepot in a commercial network that was both regional and international and "an ideal communication and information centre."[114]

Venice was determined to retain control of the island in the face of Ottoman expansion; it was a bridgehead for their commercial position in the Levant. The caption on a map of the eastern Mediterranean produced in 1570 by Antonio Lafreri makes the point. The map highlights a Venetian fleet headed toward Cyprus and informs the reader that it visualizes the island's "situation and the distance to many ports and maritime places: Karamania, Syria, Judea, and Egypt, Tripoli of Syria, Jaffa, and Alexandria" (Fig. 3.16).[115] What is crucial here is the approximation of Cyprus to "Judea" and the rest of the Levantine coastal zone. As long as Venice possessed Cyprus, it

---

[110] Laura Balletto, "Ethnic Groups, Cross-Social and Cross-Cultural Contacts on Fifteenth Century Cyprus," 35–48, *Intercultural Contacts in the Medieval Mediterranean*, 42, notes that the island in the fifteenth century had "a large contingent of families originating from the Holy Land."

[111] See S. Antonis Hadjikyriacou, "Society and Economy on an Ottoman Island: Cyprus in the Eighteenth Century," Ph.D. thesis, University of London, School of African and Oriental Studies, Department of History, 2011, 99–121, on the Ottomanization of Cyprus.

[112] Benjamin Arbel, "Venetian Cyprus and the Muslim Levant, 1473–1570," Section XII, in *Cyprus, the Franks, and Venice, 13th to 16th Centuries*, Variorum Collected Studies Series (Aldershot: Ashgate, 2000), 159.

[113] Arbel, "Venetian Cyprus," 167, 178.

[114] Arbel, "Venetian Cyprus," 165–6, 168–71.

[115] See Wilson, *The World in Venice*, 153–4. One of the earliest printed maps of Lepanto, by Lafreri in Rome, was dated 16 September 1571 and drawn in anticipation of the battle, explaining, "We presume the Turkish fleet will come at us in this way." See also John J. Norwich, *Venice: The Greatness and the Fall* (London: Penguin Books, 1981), 209–22.

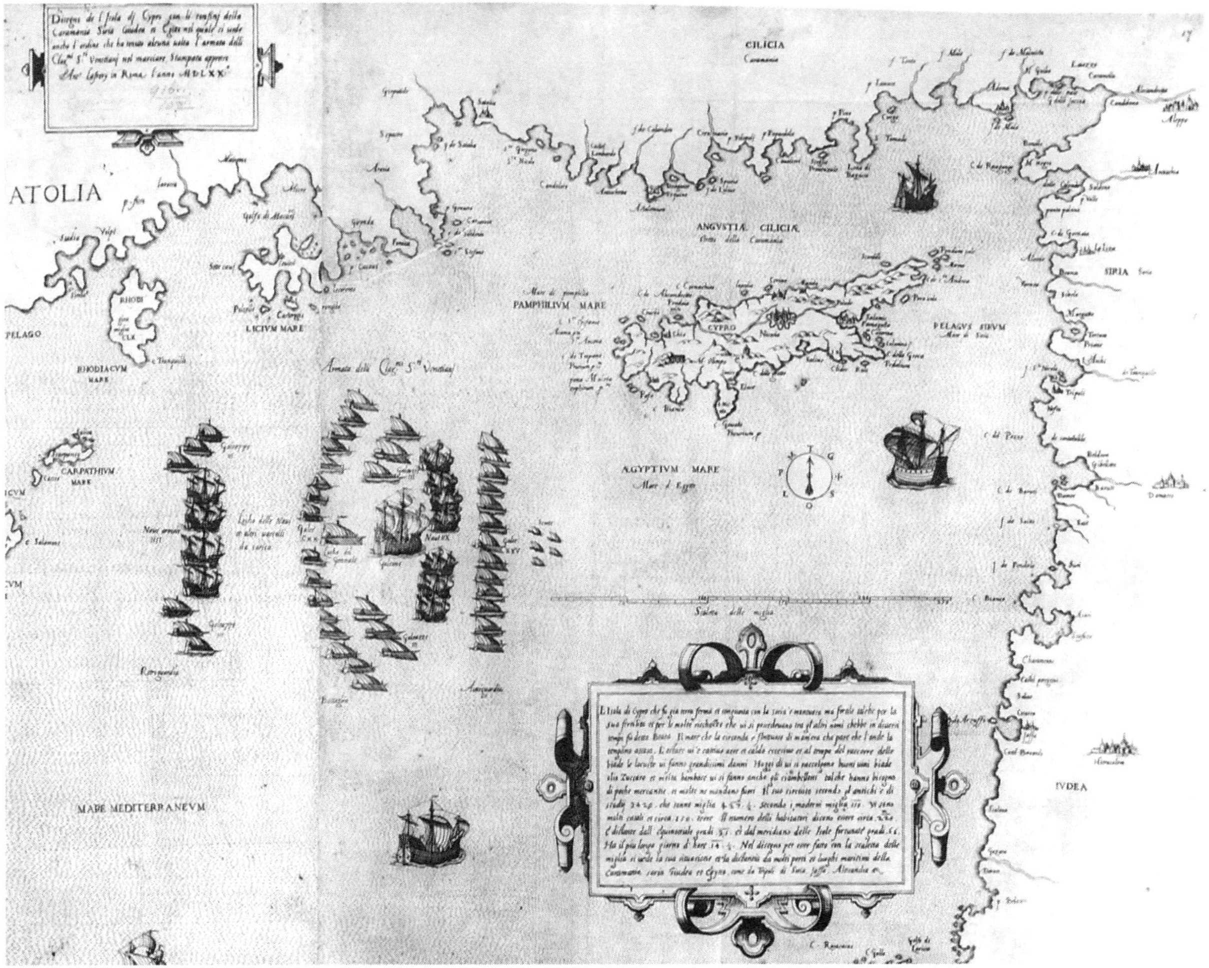

Figure 3.16. Antonio Lafreri, "Disegno de l'Isola di Cypro con li confini della Caramania, Siria, Giudea et Egitta," inset, Rome, 1570. The British Library Board, Maps C.7.e.2.(17).

remained a stepping stone to the Levant. Once the island became Ottoman space, the whole eastern Mediterranean seemed more decisively lost, Cyprus joining Constantinople, Rhodes, and Jerusalem in the litany of Ottoman conquests.[116] Those losses did not eliminate the claims of the Christian kings to the sacred spaces of the East; rather, they transformed the conquered territories into emblems of national honor and objects of prophecy.

The Ottomans, in turn, were determined to consolidate their own control over these contested spaces. Once they had taken Cyprus from Venice (Famagosta fell on 1 August, 1571), they acted swiftly to attach it to the Anatolian mainland. By the time the sultan, who was in Edirne, got the news of the defeat of the Ottoman fleet at Lepanto on 7 October 1571, about two weeks after the actual battle, the province of Cyprus (Kıbrıs) had already been created. It included the Anatolian mainland provinces of İçel, Tarsus, Alaiye, and Teke. Shocked by the defeat at Lepanto, the Porte promptly sent the governors (beys) of these mainland provinces, along with the beylerbey of Karaman (in southern Anatolia) "with all the forces under their command" to secure the island.[117] The Ottomans thus mapped Cyprus, physically and administratively, onto the core Ottoman province of Anatolia, effectively drawing a line out into the sea to encompass the island. Ottoman chroniclers, İnalcık notes, proposed that Lepanto "was God's scheme to warn the Muslim believers of their sins."[118] That rationalization approximates the Ottomans to their European Christian counterparts who employed the same rhetorics and rationale to explain their own losses.

Visions of Constantinople

Once Constantinople, after a long period of isolation, had fallen to the Ottomans in 1453, it immediately became a symbol of Christian endurance, divine intent, and apocalyptic speculation. The Christian rhetorics generated in response to Ottoman successes of the time mirrored those of the seventh and eighth century responses to the early Arab conquests.[119] Monks concealed in the walls of Santa Sofia would emerge again once a Christian ruler reclaimed the city. Churches converted to mosques or desecrated by the hands of unbelievers would retain their sanctity until Christian rituals once again purified their premises.[120] The German poet Hans Sachs (1494–1576),

---

[116] Jennifer Goodman, *Chivalry and Exploration, 1298–1630* (Woodbridge, Suffolk: Boydell Press, 1998), 61, notes the interest of authors of romances in Cyprus and Rhodes.

[117] İnalcık, "Lepanto in the Ottoman Documents," 192. "The captains of Paphos and Kyrenia were also ordered to return to Cyprus with their ships" and security was beefed up elsewhere in the Archipelago: "On October 24 new orders were sent to all the cadis (judges) on the coasts of the Mediterranean to place watchmen at dangerous points, to take the local populations up to heights difficult to reach, to complete or increase the garrisons in the fortresses. Special orders were dispatched to the wardens of the castles at the Straits, Rhodes, and Modon to be armed and on the alert."

[118] İnalcık, "Lepanto in the Ottoman Documents," 191.

[119] See Kaegi, "Initial Byzantine Reactions to the Arab Conquest," 139–49.

[120] Benjamin Lellouch and Stéphane Yerasimos, eds., *Les Traditions apocalyptiques au tournant de la chute de Constantinople, Actes de la Table Ronde d'Istanbul (13–14 avril 1996)* (Paris and Montreal: l'Harmattan, 1999). This volume goes beyond the predictions accompanying the fall of Constantinople to include earlier and late apocalyptic; see Yerasimos, "De l'arbre à la pomme: la généalogie d'un thème apocalyptique," 153–92. See also Kenneth Setton, *Western Hostility to Islam and Prophecies of*

in the aftermath of the failed Ottoman siege of Vienna in 1529, wrote a 'complaint to God,' demanding "how it had come to pass that the perfidious Turk, who originated in Asia, the land where Christianity was born, now holds that whole land under his sway . . . ?"[121] Sachs was asking a question that concerned all Christendom: How had these 'infidels' come to seize Constantinople and Jerusalem and march to the gates of Vienna, and where and how could they be stopped?

After the victory at Lepanto raised the hopes of many Christians that Constantinople would soon be redeemed, the chronic whispers of miraculous events became shouts, and accounts of portents echoed across Europe.[122] A commemorative atlas produced by Giovanni Camocio in Venice included a cartoonish image of Ottoman defenders futilely resisting the hand, or in this case the fire, of God descending on the imperial city.[123] A split frame in this 'map' of sacred territory shows "the Mosque of Piale Pasha in Constantinople" and "the first church built in Constantinople called [The Church of] the Madonna, now a mosque" (Fig. 3.17).[124] Perched at the top of the minaret on each edifice is a flaming or luminous cross surmounting the crescent that Christian imagery used to represent Islam.[125] Turbaned Ottomans (on the ground and scaling the roofs and minarets of these converted churches) aim their bows and firearms at the "miraculous apparition" to no avail, thus suggesting that the Ottoman regime, in turn, would be unable to resist the armies of the Christian kings.[126] Constantinople and the Holy Land after

<hr>

Turkish Doom, Memoirs, v. 201 (Philadelphia: America Philosophical Society, 1992), 9–10, 15–27, 37–40; Housley, "The Eschatological Imperative," 123–50; and Abbas Amanat, *Imagining the End: Visions of Apocalypse from the Ancient Middle East to Modern America* (London: I.B. Tauris, 2001), 23–184.

[121] Petkov, *Infidels, Turks, and Women*, 242; and also Machiel Kiel, *Art and Society of Bulgaria* (Assen/Maastricht, the Netherlands: Van Gorcum, 1985), 33, on the reach of the "catastrophe theory" of Ottoman conquest into modern Bulgarian historiography.

[122] Benjamin Paul, "'And the moon has started to bleed': Apocalypticism and Religious Reform in Venetian Art at the Time of the Battle of Lepanto," 67–94, in *The Turk and Islam in the Western Eye, 1450–1750*, James G. Harper, ed. (Farnham, Surrey: Ashgate, 2011), esp. 68, 74–5, 83, 87.

[123] Camocio, "Miracolo Apparso in Costantinopoli," in *Isole famose*, map 67. See also Özlem Kumrular, *The Ottoman World, Europe and the Mediterranean*, Analecta Isisiana CXVI (İstanbul, Isis Press, 2012), 5, for some prodigy narratives.

[124] The caption reads: Left: "*Moschea di Piali Bassa in Constantinopoli.*" Right: "*Prima Chiesa Fabricata in Constantinopoli Detta La Madona Et Hora Moschea.*" Legend: "*Questa miraculosa apparicione fu prima sopra le punte mochee dipoi tre giorni continui andorno ad un altra sopra S.to Sophia dove trei altri giorni vi stete poi seń andorno ad un altra appresso il Patriarcato et ivi stetero trei altri giorni finalmente redutto in Gallata cioe Pera sopra la chiesa di Christiani detta S.to Andrea et ivi sta.*"

[125] One cross enclosed in a fiery disk is reminiscent of both the sun and the host. The other is surrounded by tongues of flame suggesting Pentecost imagery (Acts 2:3), which was very popular in Byzantine and medieval iconography. For treatments of such motif precedents, see Robert Kaske, *Medieval Christian Literary Imagery: A Guide to Interpretation* (Toronto: University of Toronto, 1988); Stith Thompson, *Motif-Index of Folk Literature: A Classification of Narrative Elements in Folktales, Fables, Mediaeval Romances, Exempla, Fabliaux, Jest-Books, and Local Legends*, 6 vols., v. 6 (Bloomington, IN.: University of Indiana Press, 1956–8), 178, 286–7, 713–14; and Frederic Tubach, *Index Exemplorum: A Handbook of Medieval Religious Tales* (Helsinki: Suomalainen Tiedeakatemia, 1981.) I thank Thomas Heffernan for these references.

[126] Perhaps the Church of St. Andrew in Krisei, dedicated ca. 1284. See John Freely, *Istanbul, the Imperial City* (London: Penguin Books, 1998), 337. Certainly such imagery was intended to invoke other miracles of holy fire associated with hostile contexts, such as that accompanying Easter festivities

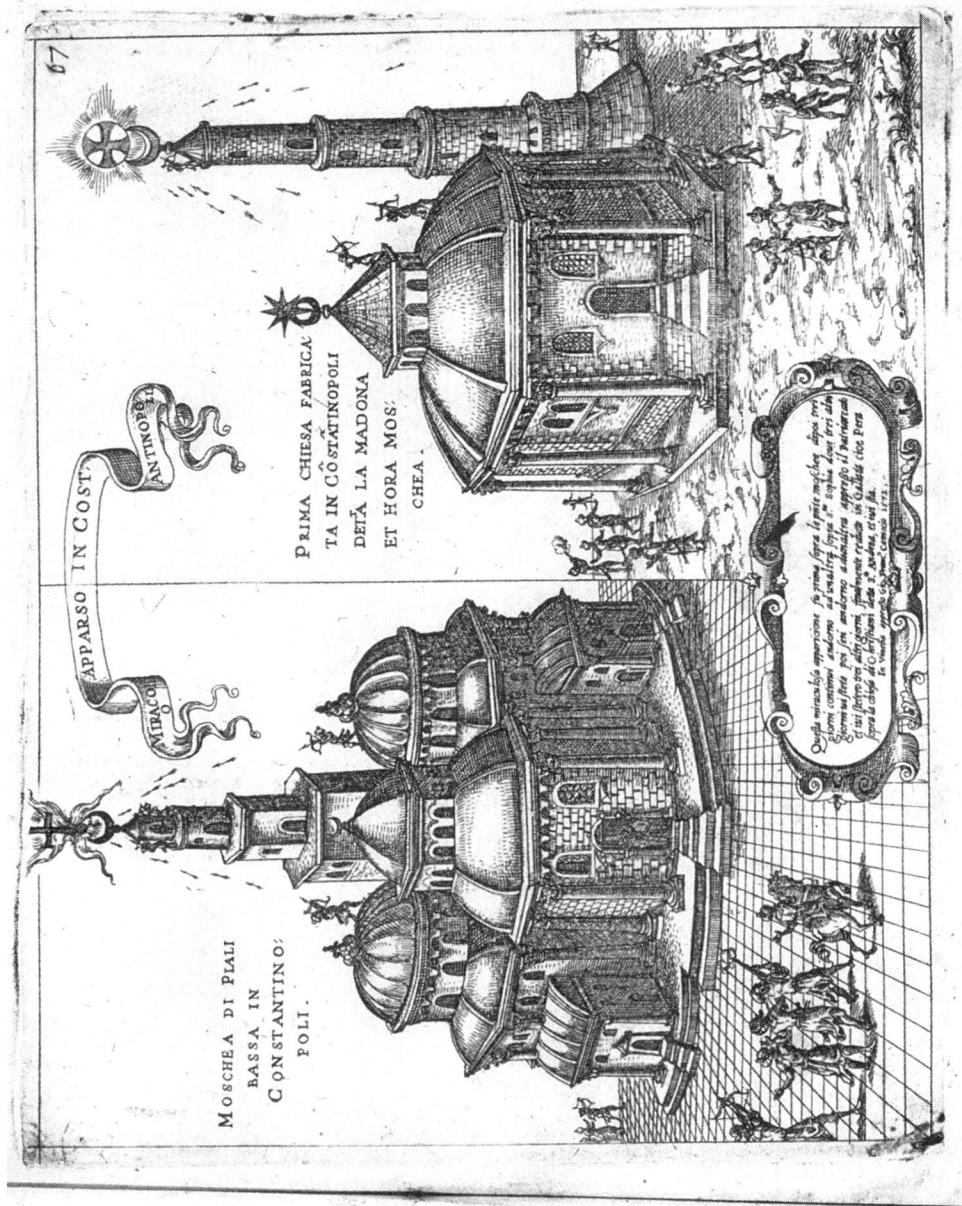

Figure 3.17. Giovanni Camocio, "Miracolo Apparso in Costantinopoli," *Isole famose porti, fortezze, e terre maritime sottoposto all Ser.ma Sig.ria di Venetia*, map 67, Venetia, [1574?]. By permission of the Folger Shakespeare Library, Shelfmark: G1015.C3 1574 Cage.

Lepanto would become "known again," visually, geographically, and icono-graphically, in the print output of the Christian kingdoms.[127] Readers were shown Constantinople as an ancient and familiar place, one link in a chain of Christian spaces.[128] It was part of their history. The "Turks" might claim it, but their occupation was only temporary.[129] The battle for Christian turf would thus be fought out street by street and church by church. Map and narrative echoed the message of space redeemed.

That message was repeated over and over throughout the early modern era. So Richard Chandler (1738–1810), a scholar travelling at the behest of the English Society of Diletanti in 1764, reported from Athens:

> *In the first year of our residence in the Levant, a rumour was current, that a cross of shining light had been seen at Constantinople, pen-dant in the air over the grand mosque, once a church dedicated to St. Sophia; and that the Turks were in consternation at the prodigy, and had endeavored in vain to dissipate the vapour. The sign was interpreted to portend the exaltation of the Christians above the Mahometans, and this many surmised was speedily to be effected . . .* [130]

Miraculous salvation was an enduring trope in the imagery of European Christendom long after the Ottomans were presumed to have been domesti-cated and put in their place by a resurgent Europe. It was applied to actual events as well as to hopes for the future such as those expressed by Chandler.

Thus, in 1704, the Polish artist and engraver, Nikodem Zubrzycki, produced a commemorative image showing the defense of the Poczajów

---

in Jerusalem; see Christopher MacEvitt, *The Crusades and the Christian World of the East: Rough Tolerance* (Philadelphia: University of Pennsylvania Press, 2008), 115–21.

[127] In the meantime, cities still under the sway of Christian rulers, such as Venice, would preserve the mon-uments, relics, and "sacred topography" of Jerusalem and Constantinople until they were redeemed. See Elisabeth Crouzet-Pavan, "Venice between Jerusalem, Byzantium, and Divine Retribution: the Origins of the Ghetto," 163–9, in *Jews, Christians, and Muslims in the Mediterranean World after 1492*, Alisa Meyuhas Ginio, ed. (London: Frank Cass, 1992),166.

[128] I have not found any illustrations that have this same 'Marvel Comics' quality, but that is not to say they do not exist. One can compare the images in England of divine intervention and salvation from popery associated with the Gunpowder Plot of 1605; see Anthony Griffiths, *The Print in Stuart Britain 1603–1689* (London: The British Museum, 1998), 152–6; and a broadside by Jan Barra entitled "To the Glory of God in thankfull Remembrance of our three great Deliverances," showing England's deliverance (indicated by signs in the sky) from three great threats (the Spanish Armada in 1588, the 1605 Gunpowder Plot, and the 1625 Plague), in Margery Corbett and Michael Norton, *Engraving in England In the Sixteenth and Seventeenth Centuries: A Descriptive Catalogue with Introductions*, Part III, *The Reign of Charles I* (Cambridge: Cambridge University Press, 1964), plate 51, 101. The less-than-palm-sized book of prayers, M. Sparke, *Crumms of Comfort And godly Prayers with Thankful Remembrance of Gods wonderful deliverances of this Land* ([[London]: Printed for Charles Brome [1708]), includes a series of pull-out illustrations that are similar to those of Barra. Divine intervention is pictured as a radiant eye in the sky or as a hand emerging from the clouds. In Sparke's "remembrances," the papists are designated "infidels."

[129] Just so the Ottomans had celebrated their own victories with churches turned into mosques. See, for example, Mehmed Neşri, *Kitâb-ı Cihan-nümâ: Neşri Tarihi*, Faik Reşit Unat and Mehmed Köymen, eds., v. 2 (Ankara: Türk Tarih Kurumu, 1995), 737, 759–61.

[130] Richard Chandler, D.D., *Travels in Asia Minor and Greece*, new edition, Nicholas Revett, ed., 2 vols., v. 2 (Oxford: Clarendon Press, 1825), 172–3. See also Kiel, *Art and Society of Bulgaria*, 174–7, on Ottoman millenarianism and the conversion of churches into mosques.

monastery against a 1675 Ottoman attack.[131] In this engraving a luminous
Virgin Mary stands poised in the clouds immediately above the Church
of St. Basil.[132] Turbaned attackers (like those in Camocio's map) fire their
guns at the monastery's buildings; but in the foreground Ottoman forces
give ground, confronted by an irresistible troop of mounted angels led by
the sword-wielding archangel Michael. Here crosses surmount the multiple
domed structures of the monastery, conveying the message that Virgin and
angels will not allow this church to be converted into a mosque. Whether
the images laid before Christian audiences showed fiery crosses descending on mosques, sectarian warriors clashing in the clouds, or legions of
angels routing the Turks, the message of miraculous redemption was the
same.[133]

But predictions of victory were not the sole preserve of the Christian kingdoms. In the context of the struggle for preeminence on both sides of the
Muslim–Christian divide, the Ottomans had their own highly developed system of prophecies, impassioned utterance, and interpretation of signs and
dreams, all of which figure prominently in narrative literature.[134] Fortresses
might be saved by the miraculous skills of their commanders.[135] And the
Ottomans also looked to the skies for indications of divine favor. Thus, the

---

[131] The image, from the National Library in Warsaw, is reproduced in the exhibition catalog, *War and Peace: Ottoman–Polish Relations*, 150.

[132] Cardini, *Europe and Islam*, 160, notes the common apocalyptic imagery of the Virgin standing on the moon, or in the iconography of Christian defeat of the Ottomans, trampling on the moon. See also Astango, *La cartografia nautical mediterranea*, 62–3, for cartographic images of the Virgin and Christ. Alexandra Walsham, "Miracles and the Counter-Reformation Mission to England," *The Historical Journal* 46, 4 (2003): 779–815, notes the Counter-Reformation's defense of miracles, and its cultivation and harnessing of "the culture of the miraculous" (779) in England, including Marian miracles (788–9).

[133] For other examples of the use of angels, aerial phenomena, and allegory to represent the triumph over the Ottomans see *Im Lichte des Halbmonds*, 126–7, 179. See also Andrew Cunningham and Ole Grell, *The Four Horsemen of the Apocalypse: Religion, War, Famine, and Death in Reformation Europe* (Cambridge: Cambridge University Press, 2004), 80–85.

[134] On this phenomenon in the time of Sultan Süleyman, see Cornell Fleischer, "Shadows of Shadows: Prophecy in Politics in 1530s Istanbul," *International Journal of Turkish Studies*, 13.1–2 (2007): 51–62, focusing on the circulation of apocalyptic literature as part of "prophetic traffic" (57), and on Süleyman as the embodiment of possibilities for millennial empire. Ottoman sources imagined Venetian texts predicting the victory of the Ottoman empire, just as Venetian sources imagined Ottoman texts or astrologers (53, 61). See Marcel Bataillon, "Mythe et connaissance de la Turquie en Occident au milieu du XVIe siècle," 451–70, in *Venezia e l'Oriente fra tardo Medioevo e Rinascimento* ([Firenze]: Sansoni, 1966), 458–63, on predicting their empire's fall. See also Fleischer, "The Lawgiver as Messiah: The Making of the Imperial Image in the Reign of Süleiman," 159–77, in *Soliman le Magnifique et son temps: Actes du Colloque de Paris*, Galeries Nationales du Grand Palais, 7–10 mars 1990, Gilles Veinstein, ed. (Paris: Ecole du Louvre, 1992). Fleischer has argued that territorialization coincides with sanctification of the dynasty in the later 16th century and makes an argument for a new prophetic dispensation as seen in Shah Ismail under the Safavids. On those Safavid rhetorics of apocalyptic violence, see Colin Mitchell, *The Practice of Politics in Safavid Iran: Power, Religion and Rhetoric* (London: I.B. Tauris, 2009), 30–45. See also Tülay Artan, "Arts and Architecture," 408–80, in *The Cambridge History of Turkey*, v. 3, *The Later Ottoman Empire, 1603–1839*, Suraiya Faroqhi, ed. (Cambridge: Cambridge University Press, 2006), 455, for one example of a prediction of doomsday in 1591.

[135] Claire Norton, "Smack-Head Hasan: Why Are All Turkic Superheroes Intemperate, Treacherous, or Stupid?," 263–74, in *Super/heroes: From Hercules to Superman*, Wendy Haslem, Angela Ndalianis, and C. J. Mackie, eds. (Washington: New Academia Press, 2007), 268–9.

lavish illustrated manuscripts, Lokman's *Şehinşehname* (Book of the King of Kings, 1581) and Mustafa Ali's (1541–1600) *Nusretname* (Book of Victory, 1584), both provide, early in the text, images of the sighting of a great comet shooting through the heavens over Istanbul, an auspicious manifestation read at the time as a promise of further Ottoman victories.[136]

Christendom Redeemed and the Borders of the Turk

The prophecies and portents surrounding the conquest of Constantinople and the battle of Lepanto fit into a larger context of narrative and visual imagery emerging out of the Reformation in Europe. There Jerusalem, Constantinople, and Rome were linked in ways that blurred the boundaries between past, present, and future.[137] Christian victories elsewhere raised hopes for the liberation of sacred space. Thus Charles V's victory over Francis I (r. 1515–47) at Pavia in 1525 was seen, at least by Charles' secretary Alfonso de Valdés, as clearing the way for an onslaught against the Ottomans. Valdés proposed, "It seems that God, by a miracle, has granted the emperor this victory so that he may not only defend Christendom and resist the power of the Turk . . . but that . . . he may also seek out the Turks and Moors on their own lands and . . . recover the empire of Constantinople and the holy mansion of Jerusalem."[138] This statement expresses the ambivalence over Ottoman space that prevailed in sixteenth century Europe; the land to be taken was both the Turks' and Moors' "own," and a Christian domain that had to be "recovered." Later the Capuchin Father Joseph, François Leclerc du Tremblay (d. 1638), in his famous Latin epic poem, *La Turciade*, written between 1617 and 1625, envisioned a Christian coalition inspired by Jesus and under the leadership of France ousting the "Turks" from Europe and going on to the salvation of Constantinople and Jerusalem.[139] And Jean Coppin (c. 1615–90), voyageur and French consul in Damietta (Egypt), in his late seventeenth century essay and travel narrative, *Le Bouclier de l'Europe ou la Guerre sainte . . .*, urged the Christian kings to take the offensive and oust the Ottomans from the territory they had "usurped."[140] Coppin envisioned a reconfigured Holy Land and western Asia in which the French would have the

---

[136] Ebel, "City Views, Imperial Visions: Cartography and the Visual Culture of Urban Space in the Ottoman Empire, 1453–1603," 294, 296, figs. 38, 40. See also Massumeh Farhad with Serpil Bağcı, *Falnama: The Book of Omens* (London: Thames and Hudson, 2010); and Cunningham and Grell, *The Four Horsemen of the Apocalypse*, 72–5, 182–3.

[137] See, for example, Guillaume Postel (1510–81), *Le thresor des prophéties de l'univers*, Manuscrit publié avec une introduction et des notes par François Secret (La Haye: Martinus Nijhoff, 1969), 101–6, 173–81, 186; and David Cook, *Studies in Muslim Apocalyptic* (Princeton: Darwin Press, 2002), 54–62, also 66–80 on Christian–Muslim counterattacks, and 182–8 on Gog and Magog. Goodman, *Chivalry and Exploration*, 58–9, notes that romance geography juxtaposed Jerusalem, Rome, and Constantinople "with less famous places, to offer the illusion of a real journey . . . By scrambling these geographic possibilities the creator of a romance could devise scenic effects ranging from the believable to the spectacularly weird."

[138] Quoted by Housley, *Crusading and Warfare*, 128. The redemption of the Holy Land, Housley notes, was also prophesied in the aftermath of the 1527 sack of Rome (134–5).

[139] Faruk Bilici, *XIV Louis ve İstanbul'u Fetih Tasarısı* (Ankara: Türk Tarih Kurumu, 2004), 66–7.

[140] Bilici, *XIV Louis ve İstanbul'u Fetih Tasarısı*, 90, 98–101.

lion's share of the spoils, although granting the emperor, Venice, England, and Poland their due portions. The pope in this imagined scenario would occupy Palestine.

But the successes of the "Turks" bore an alternative message in the Age of Reformation; they were viewed as evidence of divine disfavor and the need for repentance. Text and image filled the skies with portents to reinforce the message; and believers were warned that their very lives depended on the outcome. The Ottoman sultan, in Protestant iconography, was grouped with the pope as an Antichrist whose actions and heresies were designed to test the resolve of "true" Christians.[141] For Latin Christendom, on the other hand, the successes of the sultan served to certify the authority of pope, Church, and Christian kings, bastions from which the defense of Christendom and the redemption of Christian lands must be mobilized.[142] The Ottomans thus became part of a much more expansive disordering of the world, which was embodied in monstrous births, the clash of spirit armies in the sky, fiery manifestations, and the aberrant behavior of heavenly bodies, among other phenomena.[143] Rumors and fantasies labeled as "news" met the public's ravenous appetite for miracles and played a powerful role in visions of the Ottomans, their potential, and the frontier places where "Turks" met "Christians."[144] Thus a pamphlet published in Lyon and Paris in 1623, purportedly bearing "news" transmitted by the French ambassador to the Porte, announced the birth of the Antichrist in Ottoman territory to a beautiful but "public" woman.[145] By the eighth day of his birth this strange creature could walk and speak; the birth itself was attended by "great signs," the sun obscured, and flying serpents, "frightening and hideous."

Another pamphlet issued in London in 1606 drew the borders of the struggle for Christian space through the frontier territory of Croatia. Entitled *Strange Newes*, it purported to be a translation from the "Dutch," printed in Vienna, regarding fearful portents, seen in "the Kingdome of Croatia in

---

[141] Walter Strauss, *The German Single-Leaf Woodcut 1550–1600*, v. 1: *A–J* (New York: Abaris Books, 1975), 289, 305, 308. See also Kenneth Setton, "Lutheranism and the Turkish Peril," *Balkan Studies* 3 (1962): 133–68; Cardini, *Europe and Islam*, 149–51; Stephen Fischer-Galati, *Ottoman Imperialism and German Protestantism* (Cambridge, MA: Harvard University Press, 1959); and Cunningham and Grell, *The Four Horsemen of the Apocalypse*, 30–31, 141–5.

[142] On prophecy, the medieval eschatology of Islam vs. Christendom, and the "Turk," see John V. Tolan, *Saracens: Islam in the Medieval European Imagination* (New York: Columbia University Press, 2002), 194–217. See also Cardini, *Europe and Islam*, 112–14, 134, 149–50; Norman Daniel, *Islam and the West: The Making of an Image* (Oxford: Reprint, Oneworld Publications, 2000); and Ottavia Niccoli, *Prophecy and People in Renaissance Italy*, Lydia Cochrane, trans. (Princeton, NJ: Princeton University Press, 1990), 126–8.

[143] For celestial disturbances, see for example, Lucas Mayer, "Apparition in the Sky Seen at Nuremberg on the Night of 7 November 1605," in Strauss, *The German Single Leaf Woodcut 1550–1600*, v. 3, *S–Z*, 1391.

[144] Bataillon, "Mythe et connaissance," has pointed out this taste for "false news" and miracle tales in his treatment of two pamphlets printed in Venice earlier in the sixteenth century in 1538 and 1542. Bataillon, importantly, notes the course of the latter pamphlet, its translation into Latin, and German, and its adaptation into other sources (464–7). He also argues for the functioning of these pamphlets as part of a genre of "turquerie" produced in Venice at the time (468). See also Housley, *Crusading and Warfare*, 147.

[145] *La Naissance De L'Antechrist en Babillonee* (Paris: Laurent Lacquehay, 1623).

Germanie." The "news" had thus made its way from Croatia to Vienna and on to parts west. The title-page read,

> STRANGE *fearful & true newes, which happened at CARLSTADT, in the kingdome of CROATIA. DECLARING HOW THE Sunne did shine like Bloude nine dayes together, and how two Armies were seene in the Ayre, the one encountering the other. And how also a Woman was delivered of three prodigious sonnes, which Prophisied many strange & fearefull thinges, which should shortly come to passe, All which happened the twelfth of Iune, last, 1605...*[146]

The pamphlet began with a woodcut showing the sun with a crescent on either side (Fig. 3.18). Above it were two armies (one with star and crescent flags, the other with its banner emblazoned with a cross) riding at each other through the clouds. Below the sun were three figures (one black, one a skeleton, and one naked with four heads). This opening image is followed by an epistle "To The Reader" that argues for the authenticity of this "news" based in part on its simplicity of style and on the likelihood of such portents given celestial phenomenon such as "The Earth and Moones late and horrible obscurations, etc." The author warns his readers that they ignore such prodigious happenings, and those to come, at their peril.

The "translation" that followed also began with a warning that God intended to punish rich and poor alike for "our most foule and wicked sins."[147] It ended with the admonition, "Let us pray to God for grace, and call upon his holy name, both early and late, that we abstaine from sinne, and amend our lives, for the day of the Lord is at hand."[148] In between, the tale of two prodigious happenings focused on the threat of the Ottomans.

The first apparition left the good citizens of Carlstadt "mightily afraid"; "great and small" wrung their hands as the sounds of battle descended to the earth. And the "Turkish hostes did run up to the knees in the Christians' blood." The author urged his readers to "beholde the wonderful workes of Almighty God," for after the battle lasted from evening to morning, "the Moone did lose her light and the Mozlemen vanished quite away."[149] The

---

[146] STRANGE *fearful & true newes...* Translated out of the Dutch Coppie, Printed at VIENNA in Austria (London: Printed by R.B. for G. Vincent and W. Blackwall, [1606]), 2nd unnumbered page of "Epistle." Note that dating is somewhat problematic here, as the opening epistle, signed "Ed. Gresham," is dated February 11, 1605.

[147] *Strange Newes*, page labeled B2. This message fits well with the model of monstrous portents presented in Lorraine Daston and Katherine Park, *Wonders and the Order of Nature* (New York: Zone Books, 2001), 50–59, 177–89. The authors note that individual monsters, as opposed to the marvelous races that were "a phenomenon of the margins, an embellishment and completion of the natural order," instead "erupted in the Christian center, brought on by its corruption and sin...(189)." On margins and monsters, see also Asa Mittman, *Maps and Monsters in Medieval England* (New York: Routledge, 2006), 89.

[148] *Strange Newes*, fourth unnumbered page.

[149] *Strange Newes*, B2 verso, unnumbered page. In William Seaman's 'translation' of the Ottoman historian Hoca Sadettin (1536/37–99), miraculous "unseen armies strong and powerful" who appeared "in the likeness of men" came to the aid of the Ottoman forces and helped them defeat their enemies "the unbelievers." See Sadettin, *The Reign of sultan Orchan Second King of the Turks, Translated out of Hojah Effendi, an eminent Turkish Historian*, William Seaman, trans. (London: 1652), 91–2.

Figure 3.18. *Strange Newes*, title page, London, 1606. The British Library Board, Rare Book Room, C.143.a.19.

second prodigious happening, "marke what happened more...," was not an airy vision but a monstrous birth. After nine days of labor, a woman in Carlstadt bore three sons:

> *The Child with foure heads, began to cry aloud, and many women ran to heare it. One of the heads said with high voice: There shall shortly many Hungarians be slayne by the Turkes.*

> *The second head said: All the wonders of the Turks which you have seene in the Ayre: Shall all come to passe. The Turk with many Tartars, shall overcome all Hungarie, even to Austria and Moravia.*

The third head said. The Emperour, Kings Earles and Lords, shall then arise, and shall put the Turke to flight.

The fourth head said, before that come to pass, strange wonders shall appeare.

The black Child began to cry aloud, a time of dearth is at hand, both here and in other places, which shall not escape you, men shall perish for hunger, and great want shall be of corn and grain.

The third Child began to cry, repent and amend your lives, before death do catch hold on you, this Child was like unto Death to see, and said for certaine great death and mortality shall come over poor and Rich.

Having thus uttered their prophecies, the three children died; and "every man wondered, and the people were altogether astonished and moved to the heart, with the strangeness of this Prophecy."[150] These apparitions were both a warning and call to arms. With war would come want and death, not only for the citizens of Carlstadt but for those "in other places"; hence the message for the pamphlet's English readers struck close to home. And for those who did not repent before the Day of the Lord, a more fearful fate even than the Turks awaited. Martin Luther, after all, had characterized the "Turk" as both the rod of a wrathful God, the devil's servant, and the "schoolmaster" of Christian believers, teaching them to fear God and to pray.[151] Those who viewed the images or purchased the pamphlets might perceive the threat as a distant tragedy or as a suggestion of imminent doom. But a shiver of apprehension must have coursed through each reader, as he or she pondered the successes of the Turk and the contingent peril to the reader's immortal soul.

That these prodigies were said to be witnessed in Croatia is not coincidental. Carlstadt was a fortress built to retard the systematic advance of the Ottomans; and the whole Croatian region was on the frontlines of the transimperial conflict. While the English readers of *Strange Newes* imagined the Ottoman threat from the comfort of their parlors, the citizens of Carlstadt were in a zone where direct experience (and even collusion) with the enemy was taken for granted. There, the question of salvation was not just a spiritual matter; it was physical. The city could continue as an outpost of Christendom or be lost to the ravages of the unbelievers, its fate as yet undetermined. The pamphlet, thus, was "translating" not only the purported language of the

---

[150] *Strange Newes*, B3verso, unnumbered page. On the genres depicting monstrous births, see Julie Crawford, *Marvelous Protestantism: Monstrous Births in Post-Reformation England* (Baltimore: Johns Hopkins University Press, 2005). Three, of course, was a significant number, as Crawford illustrates on the cover of another pamphlet dated 1608 (57).

[151] Martin Luther, "On War against the Turk, 1529" (*Vom Kriege wider die Türken*), Charles Jacobs, trans. (Libronix Digital Library, http://www.libronix.com), 5; Martin Luther, "Appeal for Prayer Against the Turks, 1541" (*Vermahnung zum Gebet wider den Türcken*), Paul Moessner, trans. (Libronix Digital Library, http://www.libronix.com), 4. Crouzet-Pavan, "Venice between Jerusalem, Byzantium, and Divine Retribution," 168–9, has argued that the period from 1480 to the early 1500s is a time in which the perception of Venice as divinely protected was transformed into one of "eschatological anguish," aided by the circulation of handbills and poems, prophecies, disasters (like the arsenal fire), and "drastically increased outbreaks of miracles."

report, but also the experience of confronting the "Turk," mapping England into a chain of territories enmeshed in a struggle both earthly and divine.

Prophecies came in different forms: word of mouth, pamphlet literature, sermons, and scholarly tomes. Some had the feel of packaged and repackaged warnings whose longevity dated to the early centuries of Islam; others smacked of the new and the recent. Many were linked directly or indirectly to early modern predictions of the imminence of the end times. Thus Richard Knolles's (c. 1550–1610) *Generall Historie of the Turkes* included "The Prophesie of A Turk: concerning the Downfall of Mahometism And of the Setting up the Kingdom and Glory of Christ," which claimed to have been "taken out" of the *Turkish History* at Constantinople.[152] As in the pamphlet *Strange Newes*, the reader is here confronted with the issue of translation, not via Vienna and out of German, but purportedly via Istanbul and out of Ottoman Turkish (once or twice removed). In both cases the assertion of physical and linguistic proximity is meant to lend authenticity to the prophecy. Who better to utter the will of God than monstrous sons; who better to prophecy the downfall of the Ottomans than a "Turk?"

Knolles's polemical prophecy-narrative begins: "A Vision was seen at Medina Tilnaby in Arabia, where Mahomet their Prophet was Buryed; the apparition appeared three Weeks together, and terrified the whole Country, for that none could tell the Signification thereof."[153] Like Camocio's apparition, the validity of the "vision" is certified by its longevity. There was plenty of time for everyone to see it. Like the citizens of Carlstad in *Strange Newes*, the 'witnesses' here were also terrified. Knolles's rendering provides the details of time, space, and reaction.

> *About the twelfth of September One Thousand Six Hundred and Twenty there fell so great a Tempest and such fearful Thunder, about midnight, as that the Heavens were Darkness, and those that were awake almost Distracted; but the Vapours being dispersed, the People might Read, in the Firmament, in Arabian Caracters, these Words following, Oh! Why will you believe in Lies? Between two and three in the Morning there was seen a Woman in White, compassed with the Sun, having a very cheerful Countenance, holding in her Hand a*

[152] Richard Knolles, "The Prophesie of A Turk: concerning the Downfall of Mahometism And of the Setting up the Kingdom and Glory of Christ: For which he was Condemned, and put to Death, by diverse Cruel and Inhumane Tortures. Truly Related, as it was taken out of the *Turkish History* at Constantinople," in *Generall Historie of the Turkes* [first published in 1603] (London: Printed by Andrew Sowle, 1687), 1384. On Knolles' use of Ottoman sources, particularly Sadettin, as filtered through the 1588 *Annales sultanorum Othmanidarum* of Joannes Leunclavius, see McJannet, *The Sultan Speaks*, 96–7, 120–21, 132–40.

[153] Knolles, "The Prophesie of A Turk," 3. Visitors to the Ottoman capital also told of Ottoman prophecies that predicted a fall from grace and the loss of their empire. The Swedish envoy, Claes Rålamb, whose embassy took place in 1657–68, reports a superstition that the Ottomans would be defeated by a "northern nation" and that when a sultan named Mehmet was in power, "the Turks shall be reduced to so few in number that fifty Turkish women shall have but one husband between them." See Sten Westerberg, "Claes Rålamb: Statesman, Scholar and Ambassador," 26–57, in *The Sultan's Procession: The Swedish Embassy to Sultan Mehmed IV in 1657–1658*, Karin Ådahl, ed. (İstanbul: Swedish Research Institute in Istanbul, 2006), 41, 45.

Book, coming from the North-West, opposite against her were great Armies of Turkes, Persians, Arabians, and other Mahometans, ranging in order of Battel, to charge her; but she kept her standing. and only opened the Book, at the sight whereof those Armies fled, and presently all the Lamps about Mahomets Tomb went out; for as soon as the Vision vanished, which was commonly an hour before the Suns rising, a murmuring Wind was heard, to which they imputed the extinguishing of the Lamps, but could not conceive the meaning of the Vision; but at last one of the Dervishes (... a strict Religious Order amongst the Turks) Living in Contemplation, stood up very boldly and made a Speech to the People ... [154]

Apparitions thus dotted the narrative map of Ottoman space, marking the borders of victory and faith, and highlighting sacred turf. Here Arabia was drawn into the map of confrontation with the Ottomans. The dervish's speech rebuked the people, noting that God had grown weary of both Jews and Christians, dispossessing them of Jerusalem and Constantinople and raising up a new prophet, Muhammad. But the Muslims in their turn had "erred in every point" and God had provided signs of his anger. The current apparition, the dervish predicted, signified either a falling away from the law, or "some other Book in which we have not yet Read, and against which no Power shall prevail; so as I fear our Religion will prove Corrupt, and our Prophet an Imposter ... then that Christ they talk of shall shine as a Sun, and set up his Name Everlastingly." [155] Recovering from their stunned silence at this speech, the people charged the dervish with blasphemy, condemned him, and put him to death.

This account predicted the ultimate triumph of Christendom, but only when the believers were awakened to their errors and strove to please God. The resonances with the Crucifixion are not coincidental. Confronted with the signs of the Divine Master, whether tongues of flame, phantom armies, or women in white bearing mysterious books, even a "Turkish" holy man was supposedly forced to witness to that which was invariably true, the triumph of Christendom over Ottoman space. The fact that the "truth" of Christ's ultimate triumph is certified through a celestial message written in Arabic characters makes it clear that the message is more readily received when it appears in one's own tongue.

The testimony contained in Knolles's narrative was echoed in a 'news' pamphlet, published in London in 1620 and claiming to be a translation out of Italian. Titled *Good News to Christendom*, the pamphlet bears a woodcut showing another phantom Muslim army (Fig. 3.19). This troop of soldiers, bearing a crescent flag, rides across the clouds, retreating, apparently, from a female figure surrounded by a blazing sun. She bears a book in one hand and a sword in the other. Turbaned figures witness the miracle from below. On the

---

[154] Knolles, "The Prophesie of A Turk," 3–4.
[155] Knolles, "The Prophesie of A Turk," 5–6. The dervish noted apocalyptic sensibilities, saying that the predicted time of Muhammad's return had already passed.

Figure 3.19. [Ludovico Cortano], *Good Newes to Christendome*, title page, London, 1620. By permission of the Folger Shakespeare Library, Shelfmark: STC 5796.

woodcut, a caption provides the chain of authority for transmission of this news: "Sent to a Venetian in Ligorne, from a Merchant in Alexandria."[156]

---

[156] [Ludovico Cortano], "Good Newes to Christendome" (London: Printed [by G. Purslowe] for Nathanial Butter, 1620), reproduced in Chris Kyle and Jason Peacey, *Breaking News: Renaissance Journalism and the Birth of the Newspaper* (Washington, DC: Folger Shakespeare Library, 2008), 42, plate 9. The woodcut has a split frame, the bottom showing another apparition of blood raining from the clouds in Rome.

And it repeats the story of an apparition similar to that reported by Knolles:

> *Discouering a wonderfull and strange Apparition, visibly seene for many dayes together in Arabia, over the place, where the supposed Tombe of Mahomet (the Turkish Prophet) is inclosed: By which the learned Arabians prognosticate the Reducing & Calling of the great Turcke to Christianitie . . .*

No dervish is sacrificed in this version of the tale, but to the triumph of Christendom is added the fiat of the sultan's conversion. Whether such apparitions appeared at the tops of mosques or in the sky, place was important, from the transimperial frontier, to the capital of the eastern empire, to the tomb of Muhammad. War space and sacred space were thus conflated; and the desire to expand the borders of Christendom became a prediction of the redemption of Ottoman domains.

4

Sovereign Space

The Fortress as Marker of Possession

[To defeat the Turk] seize the fortresses, maintain them; take them one by one, not many at a time and in haste, and go into places where the necessities of provisioning will not constrain you to flight or disorder as has happened in the past...

Gherardo Borgogni, *Le Discordie christiane*, 1590.[1]

The fortress of Vlora [Avlonya, a port in southern Albania]... is octagonal in shape and very strong and solid, a veritable great wall of Sultan Süleyman. People say the Ottomans do not know how to build fortresses, but anyone who has not seen the fortress of Szeged on the frontier of Erlau, the fortress of Bender on the banks of the Dneister... and this fortress of Vlora, cannot understand how masterful Ottoman construction work can be. The walls... are 20 ells high and 10 ells thick... [and] At the 8 corners... are 8 large bastions each like the wall of Gog and Magog.

Evliya Çelebi, *Seyahatname*, 1670.[2]

The fortress, in the broad frontier zone separating the Ottoman empire from its Christian rivals, was the emblem of possession par excellence. It was an enduring presence in the narratives, imagery, and maps of the early modern era, standing in for states, rulers, and peoples. Also, as the preceding quotations make abundantly clear, the fortress was an edifice that prompted observers to invoke the past and contemplate the future. This chapter,

---

[1] Borgogni, *Le Discordie christiane*, 27.
[2] Evliya Çelebi, *Evliya Çelebi in Albania*, 135, also 25 for a description of the fortress of Kaçanik in Kosovo.

accordingly, examines the way the frontier fortress, in its inland, coastal, and island forms, was deployed in (visual) rhetorics of possession. It provides case studies ranging from Dalmatian Clissa to Barbary. And it addresses the juxtaposition of fortresses and rulers' portraits on maps as an assertive mode by which both the fortress and its surrounding spaces were claimed by contending empires.

The Fortress and Rhetorics of Possession

Among the holdings in the Dresden State Art Collection is a stunning engraving, by Giuseppe Mitelli, dated 1687 (in Bologna) and dedicated to Kaiser Leopold I, Holy Roman Emperor from 1658 to 1705 (Fig. 4.1). In this frame the benign-visaged emperor sits under a loggia. To his right and left stand allegorical warrior figures representing ingenuity, valor, and other unnamed virtues. But the bulk of the frame is full of "Turk" figures, decked out in turbans and a hodgepodge of hybrid hats.[3] These stand-ins for the Ottoman sultan and his Balkan tributaries are being driven into Leopold's audience hall by armed soldiers, there to bow before the Hapsburg lord and surrender their flags, each emblazoned with the name of a stronghold and the date it fell (Nayahysel 1685, Strigonia 1683, Patak 1684, and the infamous "Rout before Vienna 1683," among others). This mass of banners represents the crucial points of territory by which sovereignty and submission were truly measured, territory that had fallen first to one hegemon and now to another.[4] The nature of the conquests is made quite explicit. Buda is a "city and fortress," Patak a "castle and fortress," Nayahysel a "fortress," and so on. The human figures that represent them, "barbarians and rebels" in Mitelli's commemorative caption, unwillingly "bow their arrogant heads" in defeat.

This engraving is reminiscent of many audience scenes produced at the time. It melds the staging of the ambassadorial audience with the content of a military surrender.[5] But the inscribing of the names of conquered fortresses

[3] Giuseppe Mitelli, "Allegorie auf die Größe Kaiser Leopold I," Bologna, 1687. The loggia is inscribed with the legend "*Leopoldo Ignatio Austriaco Anagramma El'Ungaro ti dà poi Olocausti.*" See also *Im Lichte des Halbmonds*, 168. All sides in the transimperial conflict enjoyed consuming images of their rivals, or even their allies, bowing to their own sovereigns and lords. See Westerberg, "Claes Rålamb," 31, for a striking engraving of the Ottoman delegation of Hasan Ağa to the Swedish king Carl X Gustaf in 1656, taken from S. von Pufendorf, *De rebus a Carolo Gustavo Sveciae vege gestis commentatiorium*, Nürnberg, 1696. Frans Franken II provides an analogous image, "Allegory on the Abdication of Charles V," done in 1620, of Charles seated in a loggia surrounded by his "possessions," including female figures bearing the standards with the emblems of his lands, and turbaned male and female "Turk" figures; see Annemarie Vels, ed., *Rijksmuseum Amsterdam: Highlights from the Collection* (Amsterdam: Rijksmuseum, 1995), 131.

[4] Bayerle, *Ottoman Tributes in Hungary*, 11, noting the use of real banners to symbolize possession during Ottoman conquests of these territories, points out that Ali Pasha (governor-general of Buda) sent Süleyman Sultan forty captured banners after defeating the Hapsburg general Castaldo at Segedin in 1552.

[5] The posture of submission is echoed in later representations of the Ottomans, for example an engraving, after Mather Brown (1761–1831), dated 1793, "His Majesty and the Officers of State Receiving the Turkish Ambassador," which shows a bearded, turbaned Ottoman bowing down before Britain's George III (r. 1760–1820). See Charles Newton, *Images of the Ottoman Empire* (London: V and A

Figure 4.1. Giuseppe Mitelli, "Allegorie auf die Größe Kaiser Leopold I," [Bologna], 1687. Kupferstich-Kabinett, Staatliche Kunstsammlungen Dresden; photo: Herbert Boswank, A109075.

on the massed flags of those submitting is an ingenious take on the audience scene. Both legend and dedication suggest that this parade of conquests is a sign of things to come, more losses and more humiliation for the Ottomans and those who throw in their lot with them. Some of the figures bear broken shackles at wrist or ankle, suggesting that this is also a scene of redemption. Those Christian territories that had heretofore been forced to submit to the "Turk" and even don the turban (convert) were now, once again, bent beneath the scepter of a Christian monarch. And what Leopold has attained is more than territory; it is the right to determine the fates of the lands, peoples, symbols, and identity of that territory. It is perhaps not surprising then that a prominent figure in the right foreground, his turban fallen to the ground and a chain trailing from the same wrist that holds his flag, bears a look of shock and bewilderment.

The story of the ebb and flow of Ottoman expansion in European territory is not a simple one; but Mitelli's predictions were borne out in the eighteenth century and echoed in cartographic expression.[6] Matthäus Seutter (d. 1757), for example, a protégé of Homann who established himself in Augsburg, duplicated the image of kneeling, bare-headed petitioners presenting their territorial offerings to a noble and stern Hapsburg emperor. In his undated "Nova et Accurata Hungariae cum Adiacentib. Regni," Seutter showed the "vassal" figures of Dalmatia, Croatia, Hungary, Transylvania, Serbia, and Sclavonia offering their shields (instead of banners) to Charles VI (r. 1711–40), who stands astride an eagle and extends his scepter in proprietary fashion over what is still contested space (Fig. 4.2).[7]

These images by Mitelli and Seutter confirm the notion that territory was counted in fortresses (and the administrative districts they represented). That counting was not simply a phenomenon of early modern frontiers. It was an old, ongoing, and transcultural convention intimately attached to the interpretation of the status of kings and tributaries.[8] Thus the historian Mehmet Neşri (d. 1520) described Ottoman expansion in Europe under Mehmet II (second reign, 1451–81) in terms of the "conquest," "seizure," "entry," and "taking in hand" of one fortress after another.[9]

The fortress marked boundaries, sovereignty, and authority in the lands radiating out from its walls. Thus, in treaty negotiations, contending sides

---

Publications, 2007); also Ian Fenlon, *The Ceremonial City: History, Memory and Myth in Renaissance Venice* (New Haven, CT: Yale University Press, 2007), 329–30, for Tintoretto's 1580 painting of the Venetian Senate and doge receiving the submission of the provinces.

[6] Palmira Brummett, "Ottoman Expansion in Europe, 1453–1606," 44–73 in *Cambridge History of Turkey*, v. 2, *The Ottoman Empire as a World Power, 1453–1603*, Kate Fleet and Suraiya Faroqhi, eds. (Cambridge: Cambridge University Press, 2012).

[7] Georg Matthäus Seutter, Johann Baptist Homann [et al.], "Nova et Accurata Hungariae cum Adiacentib. Regni," [Weltatlas], [17–], map 98. Seutter's map celebrating the Treaty of Passarowitz, July 21, 1718, includes a similar image of submission to the emperor.

[8] For earlier examples, see Robert I. Burns and Paul Chevedden, with Míkel de Epalza, *Negotiating Cultures: Bilingual Surrender Treaties in Muslim–Crusader Spain under James the Conqueror* (Leiden: Brill, 1999), 15–59, on the al-Azraq treaty of 1245; and Asa Eger, *The Spaces between the Teeth: A Gazetteer of Towns on the Islamic–Byzantine Frontier* (İstanbul: Isis, 2012). Fortresses were also the sites for struggle among Ottoman lords and households jockeying for power in the frontier zones. See Pál Fodor, "Who Should Obtain the Castle of Pankota (1565)?" *Turcica* 31 (1999): 67–86.

[9] Mehmed Neşri, *Kitâb-ı Cihan-nümâ*, v. 2, 763–7.

Figure 4.2. Georg Matthäus Seutter, from Johann Baptist Homann [et al.], "Nova et Accurata Hungariae cum Adiacentib. Regn.," [*Weltatlas*], map 98, cartouche, [n.p.], [17–], Library Znanstvena knjižnica Zadar, ZKZD GA 10421-A. (See color plate)

routinely demanded the leveling of fortresses (or protested the building of new ones) to confirm exactly where borders lay. In 1640, for example, the Polish ambassador Wojciech Miaskowski was sent to Istanbul bearing the Ottoman *ahdname* (treaty-grant) of 1634 and requesting a new one. Negotiating with the grand vezir, Kara Mustafa Kemankeş, Miaskowski was confronted with the accusation that the Commonwealth had constructed "the new Dnieper fortress," Kudak, on Ottoman lands. He insisted, however that the fortress was on the Polish side of the border, having been built to discourage Cossack raids against Ottoman territory. "Having no map at his disposal, he proved his arguments by tracing the Polish–Ottoman border in sand with a staff."[10] Similarly, when the treaty of Carlowitz was negotiated in 1698–9, the Ottomans proposed to demolish the fortress of Kamieniec before withdrawing from the surrounding lands, whereas their rivals demanded that it be returned intact to Poland.[11] These examples suggest the crucial role that

[10] Kołodziejczyk, *Ottoman–Polish Diplomatic Relations*, 139–40. The two men used an interpreter of Hungarian origin (Zulfikar Ağa). "Fortress" was a category of space under *sanjak*. See Pál Fodor, "Making a Living on the Frontiers: Volunteers in the Sixteenth Century Ottoman Army," 229–63, in Dávid and Fodor, eds., *Ottomans, Hungarians, and Habsburgs in Central Europe*, 259.

[11] Kołodziejczyk, *Ottoman–Polish Diplomatic Relations*, 155, 157. Similar demands were made in Ottoman–Hapsburg negotiations. See Roider, *Austria's Eastern Question*, 26; also 29 on border commissions.

fortresses, critical points in a sovereign's lines of defense, played in the early modern conceptualization of space.[12] Fortresses also secured the roads; and roads were the means by which imperial powers and local lords ensured the prosperity of their lands.[13]

The centrality of the fortress is clearly illustrated by the Swedish diplomat Claes Rålamb, whose sojourn to Istanbul is preserved in several narratives. Rålamb reported that three days after his arrival in the Ottoman capital on May 14, 1657, he was received by the grand vezir Köprülü Mehmet (c. 1575–1661). After the usual formalities and having received the Swedish king's letter, Köprülü posed a series of questions. "How is his Majesty doing, Where is he? ... What does he plan to do now? Which towns and fortresses does he possess?"[14] The last of these questions is especially revealing; its answer would demonstrate how the Swedes were faring against their own enemies and suggest the scope of their ruler's power. More to the point, by placing these words in the mouth of the grand vezir, Rålamb suggests that counting space in fortresses is a concept that all men could understand. The narratives and imagery emerging out of both Muslim and Christian kingdoms bear out that assumption. The fortress appeared repeatedly, as the visible unit by which sovereignty was counted in forms that ranged from the allegorical to attempted verisimilitude. In Nuremberg, for example, seventeenth century commemorative medallions included images of cities and fortresses that were besieged, conquered, or redeemed: Gran, Neuhäusel, Buda, and Vienna.[15] In Istanbul, fortresses marched across the pages of royal presentation volumes and served as centerpieces for commemorative reports and poetry.[16] Seyyid Lokman's (d. 1601–2), *Book of Accomplishments* (*Hünername*) showed Süleyman I (r. 1520–66), and some of his forebears, parading through the broad Hungarian frontier from one fortress to another (Fig. 4.3).[17] So too Matrakçı Nasuh's account of Süleyman's

[12] Despite the dearth of surviving Ottoman maps, it is clear that the Ottomans drew strategic maps for treaty and military purposes and did systematic "mapping" for tax purposes in land/revenue surveys (*tahrir*). Ágoston, "Information, Ideology, and Limits of Imperial Policy," 75–103, has noted that Üveys Pasha, governor of Buda from 1578 to 1580, "prepared a detailed and surprisingly accurate map of the region [around Kanizsa in Transdanubia], which indicated all the fortresses and the major river crossings (89)." An illustrated map of the siege of Buda printed in 1684, with the victory going to the Hapsburgs, also indicates the nature of possession: see Klára Hegyi, *The Ottoman Empire in Europe* (Corvina, Budapest: Franklin Printing, 1989), 30–31.

[13] See Heyd, *Ottoman Documents on Palestine*, 102–16, 185–6, for a series of Ottoman communiqués regarding the building, staffing, and maintenance of fortresses to protect the roads and the borderlands of Palestine in the later sixteenth century.

[14] Westerberg, "Claes Rålamb," 26–57, 40.

[15] *Im Lichte des Halbmonds*, 203–6; and Jerry Brotton and Lisa Jardine, *Global Interests: Renaissance Art between East and West* (Ithaca, NY: Cornell University Press, 2000), 25–42, 172–83.

[16] Fetvacı, *Picturing History*, depicts a variety of fortresses (e.g., Figure 46 Sighetvar and Figure 96 Haçova). Also Binney, *Turkish Treasures*, 60–62.

[17] Gábor Ágoston, *Guns for the Sultan: Military Power and the Weapons Industry in the Ottoman Empire* (Cambridge: Cambridge University Press, 2005), 194, notes that "Until well into the seventeenth century, but especially in the fifteenth and sixteenth centuries, Ottoman artillery proved to be superior against European fortifications.... Between 1521 and 1566 only thirteen Hungarian forts were able to resist Ottoman firepower for more than ten days, merely nine castles for more than twenty days, and altogether four fortresses were able fully to withstand Ottoman assaults."

Figure 4.3. Mehmet II's Siege of Belgrade. Seyyid Lokman, *Hünername (Book of Accomplishments)*, H. 1523, 165a, İstanbul, c. 1588. Topkapı Palace Museum, İstanbul.

Figure 4.4 Matrakçı Nasuh, "Tata Fortress," *Tarih-i Feth-i Şikloş ve Estergon ve Estolnibelgrad (History of the Conquest of Siklós, Esztérgom, and Székesfehérvar)*, H. 1608, 113b, İstanbul, c. 1545. Topkapı Palace Museum, İstanbul. (See color plate)

Hungarian campaigns of 1542–3 marked space in terms of towns, fortresses, and stopping points (Fig. 4.4).[18] Those images highlighted strength and weakness, trumpeting both the sultan's glory and that of his ancestors.[19] On these frontiers hegemony was asserted, and local lords vied for the favor of

---

[18] Matrakçı Nasuh, *Tarih-i feth-i Şikloş ve Estergon ve Estolnibelgrad* [History of the Conquest of Siklós, Esztérgom and Székesfehérvar], c. 1545, Topkapı Sarayı Müzesi Kütüphanesi, H. 1608, 113b.

[19] Seyyid Lokman, *Hünername* (İstanbul: c. 1588), Topkapı Sarayı Müzesi Kütüphanesi, Hazine 1523, 165a. See, on Lokman, H. Sohrweide, "Lukman b. Sayyid Husayn," in *Encyclopedia of Islam*, CD-ROM ed., v.1.0. (Leiden: Brill, 1999). On the *Hünername*, see Metin And, *Turkish Miniature Painting: The Ottoman Period* (İstanbul: Dost, 1987), 32, 105–10, 114. See also Esin Atıl, "The Image of Süleymân in Ottoman Art," 333–41, in İnalcık and Kafadar, eds., *Süleymân the Second and His Time* (İstanbul: Isis Press, 1993).

Hapsburg or Ottoman king.[20] Their disputes remind us of Köprülü's query, to know of the Swedish king "Which towns and fortresses does he possess?" It was not an idle question.

One can also see the significance of the fortress expressed in Ottoman sources, using the example of the siege of Egri (Erlau, Agria, Eger) in Hungary northeast of Budapest in 1596.[21] After an eighteen-day siege, beginning September 21, Egri's garrison surrendered to the Ottoman army under Mehmet III (r. 1595–1603). But despite a written safe conduct from the sultan, "when they opened the gates most of the men were massacred by the janissaries in revenge for the murder of the Ottoman garrison" at Hatvan on September 3.[22] Shortly thereafter, the Hapsburg army under Archduke Maximilian III (r. c. 1595–1618) arrived and engaged the Ottomans at the nearby plain of Keresztes. Maximilian's forces overwhelmed the Ottomans and began to loot their camp. The English ambassador to the Porte at the time, Edward Barton (d. 1597), an eyewitness to the siege and battle at Keresztes, wrote that when the "terrified Turks" fled, "the Christians without resistance, approached even nigh the Pavilions of the Grand Signior."[23] Or, as the Ottoman historian Mustafa Naima (1655–1716), citing his predecessor Ibrahim Peçevi (c. 1574–1650), put it, the greedy attackers "charged the [tent holding] the Imperial treasury, and scattered the sipahis and janissaries who were its protectors. They dragged out the treasure chests, planted their cross-emblazoned flags, and began to dance."[24] A rout seemed imminent; but that near disaster was averted when Çigalzade Sinan Pasha (c. 1545–1605) arrived with relief forces. "Panic broke out among the

---

[20] See on the ambiguity of possession and multiplicity of identities in fortress life Klára Hegyi, "Freed Slaves as Soldiers in the Ottoman Fortresses in Hungary," 85–92, in *Ransom Slavery along the Ottoman Borders (Early Fifteenth–Early Eighteenth Centuries)*, Géza Dávid and Pál Fodor, eds. (Brill: Leiden, 2007), 85; Ferenc Szakály, "The Ransom of Ali Bey of Koppány: The Impact of Capturing Slaves on Trade in Ottoman Hungary," 93–114, in *Ransom Slavery along the Ottoman Borders*, 93–4; and Mark Stein, *Guarding the Frontier: Ottoman Border Forts and Garrisons in Europe* (London: I.B. Tauris, 2007).

[21] See Fetvacı, *Picturing History*, 47. For a tranquil view of the fortress, dated 1617, see Hegyi, *The Ottoman Empire in Europe*, 122. On Ottoman warfare and fortress architecture, see Murphey, *Ottoman Warfare*, 111–15. See also multiple contributions in Andrew Peacock, ed., *The Frontiers of the Ottoman World*, Proceedings of the British Academy (Oxford: Oxford University Press, 2009) and Ibolya Gerelyes and Gyöngyi Kovács, eds., *Archaeology of the Ottoman Period in Hungary* (Budapest: Hungarian National Museum, 2003).

[22] Jan Schmidt, "The Egri Campaign of 1596: Military History and the Problem of Sources," 107–21, in *The Joys of Philology*, v. 1, *Poetry, Historiography, Biography and Autobiography*, Analecta Isisiana LX (İstanbul: Isis Press, 2002), 109. The Ottoman historian Naima blames "the men of the borders and the Tatar military for the massacre"; see Mustafa Naima, *Annals of the Turkish Empire from 1591 to 1659 of the Christian Era*, Charles Fraser, trans., v. 1 (London: Oriental Translation Fund, 1832; reprint Arno Press, 1973), 77; or Mustafa Naima, *Tarih-i Na'ima*, Mehmet İpşirli, ed., v. 1 (Ankara: T.T.K., 2007), 109.

[23] For Barton's account, see, Samuel Purchas, *Hakluytus Posthumus*, 1625, v. 2, 1358–9; and Schmidt, "The Egri Campaign," 107–8. After the victory, Barton notes that the sultan "rested in his Pauilions there for three days (1360)." See Caroline Finkel, *The Administration of Warfare: The Ottoman Military Campaigns in Hungary, 1593–1606* (Wien: VWGÖ, 1988), 15; and Kelenik, "The Military Revolution in Hungary," 117–59, in Dávid and Fodor, eds., *Ottomans, Hungarians, and Habsburgs in Central Europe*, 151.

[24] Naima, *Tarih-i Na'ima*, v. 1, 117–18.

plunderers" and a "chaotic massacre followed," in which many of the Hapsburg troops were killed and the apparently triumphant Maximilian had to retreat.[25]

The theatrical nature of this reversal of fortune (the pathos and heroism of trapped citizens, the valor and determination of attackers, the earthworks and tunnels, the captives, the rituals of surrender, and the ever present suggestion of treachery) captivated observers near and far.[26] The siege and its aftermath were documented in verse by the Ottoman şehnameci Talikizade (d. 1599), the historian Hoca Sadettin, the poet Emini Çelebi, and Derviş Ağa (father of Evliya Çelebi), all in the retinue of the sultan. Ottoman historians such as Selaniki (d. c. 1600), Peçevi (1574–1650), and Naima recounted the unlikely victory. For the Ottomans, Egri was a place captured from an imperial rival, but also a space of redemption. It was one in a chain of "infidel fortresses" that had been converted into Muslim space.[27] Naima wrote that in the aftermath of Keresztes, the sultan (padişah) "was declared conqueror . . . his righteous cause triumphed, and the fame of Islam and that of the Ottoman empire was raised to the highest renown."[28] Another "possible witness," one Abülkadir Efendi, attributed the ultimate Ottoman victory to divine assistance, noting that "God sent 'holy spirits'" to help defeat the unbelievers.[29] Jan Schmidt rightly argues that reconstructing the exact sequence of events in such conflicts is most difficult, and that patronage relations and myth-making may have as much to do with the dramatic portrayal of the Ottoman escape from disaster as do the actual course of events for October 26.[30] But clearly the fortress was central to the myth.

Once the battles were fought, narrators and artists could choose which view of events they wished to present, thus compounding the mythmaking. The Ottoman historian Peçevi, for example, in his account of the siege, describes a painting by an Austrian artist that he saw a year later. It depicted the scene of the Hapsburg plunderers, "the shocked sultan on his

---

[25] Schmidt, "The Egri Campaign," 110–11. Schmidt deconstructs the sources on the siege and subsequent battle, examining their rhetorics and variations, including Barton's letters, which do not accuse the sultan of fleeing (118).

[26] Colin Imber, *The Ottoman Empire, 1300–1650: The Structure of Power* (Houndmills: Palgrave Macmillan, 2002), 279.

[27] Talikizade's *Fethname-i Eğri* begins its narration of this seizure of infidel space by invoking the conquests of glorious pre-Islamic and Ottoman heroes: Feridun, Şahriyar, Selim I, and Süleyman I; see Woodhead, *Ta'līkī-zāde's şehnāme-i hümāyūn*, translation, 2a–3a. For a contemporary history of the region that also counts space and time in terms of the conquest of fortresses, see Iyânî, *Tevârîh-i Cedîd-i Vilâyet-i Üngürüs*.

[28] Naima, *Annals*, 87–8; Naima, *Tarih-i Na'ima*, v. 1, 116–17.

[29] Schmidt, "The Egri Campaign," 114.

[30] Schmidt, "The Egri Campaign," 119–20. The drama was little diminished by the passage of time, as one sees, for example, in Rossini's 1820 opera *Mehmet II*, on the siege of Negroponte in 1470. The opera, reissued in French in 1826, transferred the site of the siege to Corinth, but the villain remained the Great Turk. A dramatic painting from 1842 by Cherubino Cornienti "commemorates" an imagined scene in which the Venetian commander Paolo Erizzo bids farewell to his daughter, who is being handed over to the lustful "Turk," a central theme in Rossini's *Mehmet II*. See also Margaret Meserve, "News from Negroponte," *Renaissance Quarterly* 59.2 (Summer 2006): 440–80.

horse and the *hoca* [Sadettin] next to him at his stirrup, his arms raised in supplication."³¹ A casual viewer might have assumed that the Hapsburg forces had been the victors. In art, defeat was thus transformed into victory; and European artists, statesmen, and the public, who evinced "a certain resistance to register as definitive the discomfiture of Christianity," were mollified.³² Thus the fortress served not only as a site of military combat, but also as a site of rhetorical contestation. And the rhetorics of possession were translated directly (or indirectly) onto contemporaneous maps.

The Fortress on the Map

The Hungarian soldier-poet Bálint Balassi, who died in 1594 of wounds suffered in the battle of Esztergom, invokes the multiple identities of the fortress on the Ottoman–Hapsburg frontier, calling it a "school of valour," a location for military training, and a setting in nature.³³ That construction dovetails neatly with the image of the fortress on the early modern map. On the broader stage, the fortress might serve as the setting for an epic struggle between empires and faiths, a context of which the mapmaker and his audience were highly conscious. More specifically though, the fortress was a concrete thing, its walls, gates, and towers the ideal vehicle for mapping changes in sovereignty.

Maps for the early modern viewer were a special form of knowledge and communication. Mapped fortresses could be collected and bound into assemblages of cities or ports, allowing the viewer to compare representations of edifices in different places or to hop along a coast from one landing point to another. Such fortress-viewing can be found, for example, in Giulio Ballino's collection of the "most illustrious cities and fortresses of the world" (1569), or in Benedetto Bordone's *Island Book* (1534), both produced in Venice.³⁴ Fortress imagery varies from the architecturally "correct," to the highly impressionistic, to the simply iconic.³⁵ But the fortress on the map was an

---

³¹ Schmidt, "The Egri Campaign," 114, citing *Peçevi Tarihi*, v. 2, 200–201. Other Ottoman sources do not mention the sultan's fear or the hoca's supposedly decisive role; and Selaniki gives special credit to Gazanfar Ağa.

³² Astango, *La cartografia nautica mediterranea*, 67. On Genoese maps, Rhodes after 1522 retained the gold cross of the Knights of St. John of Jerusalem, and Chios, after 1566, retained Genoa's red cross on a white ground.

³³ Mike Pincombe, "Life and Death on the Hapsburg–Ottoman Frontier: Bálint Balassi's 'In Laudem Confiniorum' and Other Soldier-Songs," 74–86, in *Borders and Travellers in Early Modern Europe*, Thomas Betteridge, ed. (Aldershot, Hampshire: Ashgate, 2007), 75, 78. Kelenik, "The Military Revolution in Hungary," 148, notes that the Vienna Kriegsarchiv includes drawings of Christian siege-relief forces engaged during the long war.

³⁴ Giulio Ballino, *De' disegni delle piu illustri città, et fortezze del Mondo* (Venetia: Bolognino Zaltieri, 1569); and Benedetto Bordone, *Isolario* (Venetia: Nicolo d'Aristoile, 1534).

³⁵ See for example two early eighteenth century maps of Corfu by G. Bodenehr, one a strategic overhead view of fortifications and the other a pleasing scene of town, castle, and harbor, in [Gabriel Bodenehr, *A collection of plans and views of fortified towns in Europe* ([Augsburg: c. 1730?], maps 158–9, British Library, Maps, C24.aa.18; also two similar images of Coron from Vincenzo Coronelli, *An historical and geographical account of the Morea, Negropont, and the maritime places*, R.W. Gent. trans. (London: Matth. Gillyflower, 1687). For Venetian maps of Corfu see Concina and Molteni,

owned space that could be taken, occupied, defended, and exploited. The discussion that follows illustrates that identity, presenting a set of inland, coastal, and island fortresses on the transimperial frontier.[36] These maps illustrate the ways in which the fortress served to define Ottoman frontiers, stamp sovereignty onto contested regional space, and homogenize, differentiate, or ignore the peoples who occupied the spaces depicted.

The fortress might be mapped in serene landscapes, devoid of action. But often enough the mapped fortress was war space, the site of confrontation in the transimperial struggle for hegemony. Fortresses were limit points, the places where land met sea, administrative districts ended, or imperial forces reached a standoff. There the "Christian warrior" encountered the "Turk," and the ungrateful tributary (or robber) encountered his vengeful or forgiving lord (as suggested in Mitelli's engraving). News maps depicting battle scenes, especially sieges, at these limit points were quite popular in the second half of the sixteenth century, for example, particularly in the aftermath of the land battle of Sighetvar in 1566, the sea battle of Lepanto in 1571,[37] and during the Ottoman–Hapsburg war of 1593–1606.[38]

Even when maps of city forts were not intended as reports from the 'front,' they still tended to highlight fortifications as a crucial element of the built space. Walls and bastions suggested military intent; they bore the flags and emblems of those who claimed them. Two Italian maps of Egri, an impressive fortress praised by Ottoman chroniclers, for example, demonstrate change of possession without depicting the battles themselves.[39] One, dated 1568, shows the bastioned town and its central tower surmounted by a cross and the double-eagle flag of the Hapsburgs.[40] This is a place of "great importance,"

La fabrica della fortezza, 119, 150–51, 174–5, 270–79. See also Astango, *La cartografia nautica mediterranea*, 66, on "realistic" city views.

[36] For an earlier version of this evaluation of the mapping of fortresses, see Palmira Brummett, "The Fortress: Defining & Mapping the Ottoman Frontier in the 16th–17th Centuries," 31–55, in *The Frontiers of the Ottoman World*.

[37] Dooley, "The Wages of War," and Infelice, "The War, the News, and the Curious." Also on the function and dissemination of maps, see George Tolias, "Nikolaos Sophiano's *Totius Graeciae Descriptio*: The Resources, Diffusion, and Function of a Sixteenth Century Antiquarian Map of Greece," *Imago Mundi*, 58. 2 (2006): 150–82.

[38] On the Ottoman–Hapsburg wars, see Finkel, *The Administration of Warfare*; and Ferenc Szakály, "The Early Ottoman Period, Including Royal Hungary, 1526–1606," 83–99, in Peter Sugar et al., eds., *A History of Hungary* (Bloomington: Indiana University Press, 1994), 96. Kelenik, "The Military Revolution in Hungary," 154–5, estimates the "effective fighting force of palace troops in this period" (1593–1606) as about 50,000 infantry and cavalry. For Venetian victories at Candia in 1649 and Lepanto in 1571, see Concina and Molteni, *La fabrica della fortezza*, 244; and for a vision of Lepanto printed in Nuremburg in 1571 see Gereon Sievernich and Hendrik Budde, eds., *Europa und der Orient 800–1900* (Berlin: Bertelsmann Lexikon Verlag, 1989), 721–2. See also Brancaforte, *Visions of Persia*, 49–50, on a Geran broadsheet depicting a Safavid victory over the Ottomans in 1578.

[39] Naima, *Tarih-i Na'ima*, v. 1, 107, enhances the dramas of the conquest by noting that Egri, from a distance, looked "like a mountain," with its strong walls and expansive ditch. On the design and depiction of fortresses, see Martha Pollak, "Military Architecture and Cartography in the Design of the Early Modern City," 109–24, in *Envisioning the City: Six Studies in Urban Cartography*, David Buisseret, ed. (Chicago: University of Chicago Press, 1998), 110, 118, and 113–14, figures 4.5a and 4.5b for Jacques Callot, "Plan of La Rochelle under siege 1630" and the pentagonal fortress. Pollack argues that there was "no systematic method for drawing parts or entire fortifications" until the seventeenth century (116).

[40] L. P., "Agria, Fortezza nel paese di Ongheria nel modo che al presente si trova" [Venetia?], 1568. Defenders had fought off an Ottoman siege in 1552. In a rather partisan description, Christopher Duffy,

the legend tells the reader (Fig. 4.5). A century later, another map provided a more fulsome vision of the city and illustrated a shift in identity (Fig. 4.6).[41] Tall buildings (including the cathedral and castle) sport crescents, informing the viewer that this is Ottoman space (the Ottomans held Egri from 1596 to 1687). Turbaned figures ride in the countryside, as if to reaffirm that Ottoman identity. Each map, in its own time, fixes the sovereignty of this significant frontier place. And as long as each map endured, it claimed the fortress for either emperor or sultan.

For European publics and officials, such maps served to notify, to inflame, to educate, to commemorate, and possibly to enhance Christian solidarity, even though that was a difficult task in the context of the Reformation era's complex political–religious struggles. War space could be construed in terms of land-based or seaborne conflict (or potential). It might be represented across broad swaths of the transimperial frontier zone; or it might zero in on a single point of settlement. For example, the Venetian cartographer Vincenzo Coronelli's 1688 map of Istria and Dalmatia included a large legend box commemorating the "victories reported" during the dogeship of Marc Antonio Giustiniani, from 1684 to 1688 (Fig. 4.7).[42] That list was an essential part of the counting of space. Dalmatia was not simply a place; it was a site of struggle. Even when a map was published in an atlas ten years after the battle, mapping victories made both place and victory 'real' for the viewer.

Inland, the reader could envision Christian triumph at fortress points all along the Ottoman–Hapsburg frontier. A German map of Hatvan, northeast of Buda, for example, shows the fortress besieged by Christian forces, identified as such in both key and legend (Fig. 4.8).[43] Crosses on their banners reinforce that identity, whereas the fortress itself is marked by a crescent.[44] The reader can see inside the fortress, where a building explodes into flame, and the smoke ascends to encompass the crescent flag hanging from the tallest tower of the town. He thus joins the anonymous eyewitness whose narrative of firing cannon and charging horses has made the map of the 1596 siege come alive.

A similar map by Heinrich Ullrich of the 1597 siege of Raab (Iavarino, Yanık, Györ) also presents a lively scene of an Ottoman fortress

---

Siege Warfare: The Fortress in the Early Modern World (New York: Barnes and Noble, 1979), 202, notes that Erlau "fell through the treachery of its mercenary garrison in 1596, though Grosswardein bravely repulsed the Turks two years later . . . "

[41] "Agria" [Rome?], [1683?].

[42] Vincenzo Coronelli, "Dalmatia and Istria" (Venetia, c. 1688), in *Isolario* [dell' *Atlante Veneto*], v. 1, c. 1696.

[43] J. S., "Abris Der Vöstung Hadtwan, Von den Christen Belegert und Eröbert. Den. 2 Septemb: A: 1596," [Vienna,] [1596]. The key marks the encampments of the general and commanders; rivers, roads, moat and entrenchments, and the attackers' gun emplacements with cannon and mortars. See Finkel, *The Administration of Warfare*, 14–15; Kelenik, "The Military Revolution in Hungary," 152; and Larry Silver, "East is East: Images of the Turkish Nemesis in the Hapsburg World," 185–215, in *The Turk and Islam in the Western Eye*, esp. 207–8, on siege imagery and German prints.

[44] See Palmira Brummett, "'Turks' and 'Christians': The Iconography of Possession in the Depiction of the Ottoman–Venetian–Hapsburg Frontiers, 1550–1689," 110–39, in *The Religions of the Book: Co-existence and Conflict, 1400–1660*, Matthew Dimmock and Andrew Hadfield, eds. (Houndmills, Basingstoke: Palgrave, 2008).

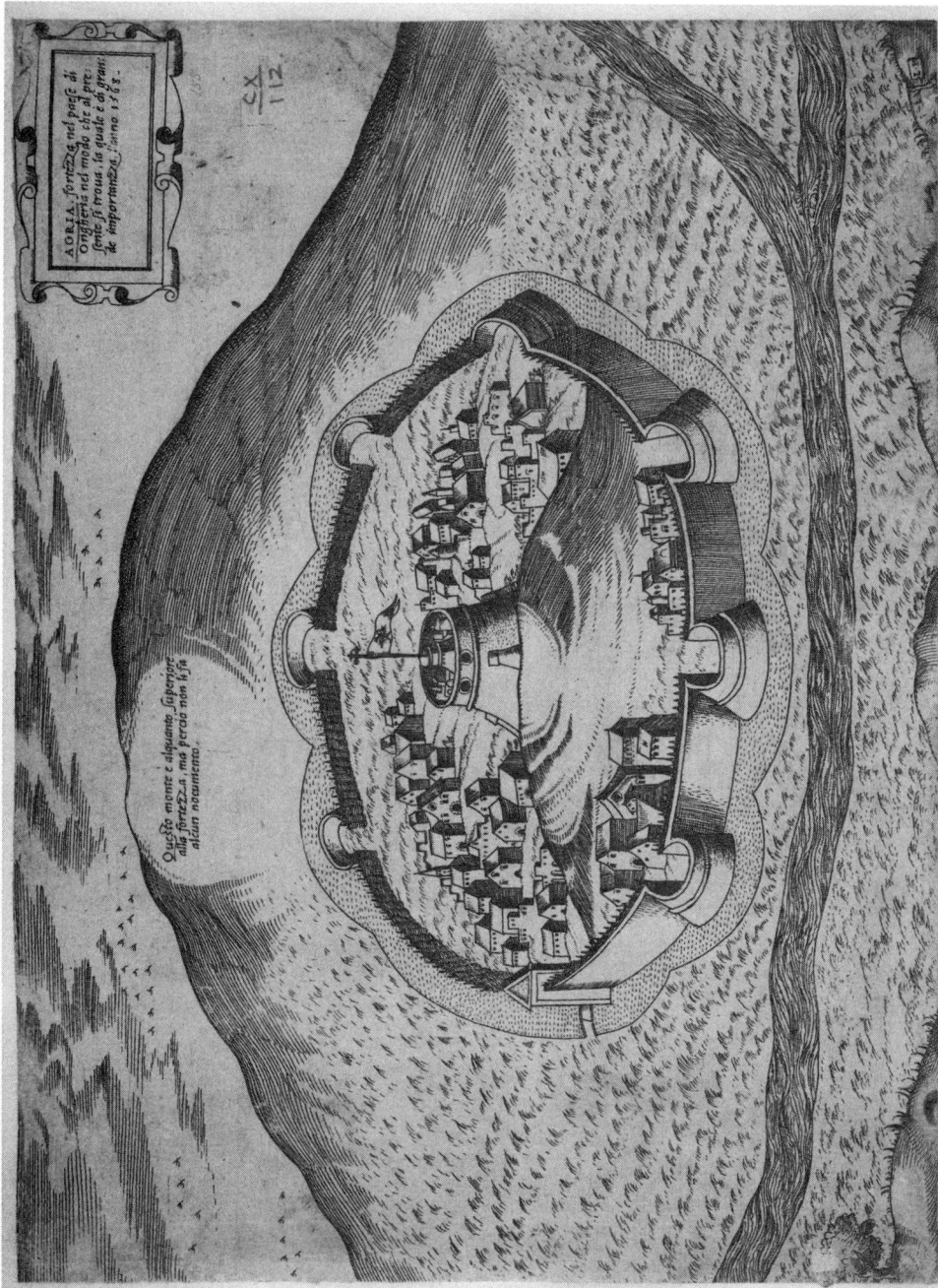

Figure 4.5. L.P., "Agria, fortezza nel paese di Ongheria nel modo che al presente si trova," [Venetia], 1568. The British Library Board, Maps K.Top. 110.112.

Figure 4.6. "Agria, Eger, O Erla," [Rome?], [1683?]. The British Library Board, Maps K.Top. 110.113.

1 Il Castello, o Fortezza . 2 Agria fiume . 3 La Citta . 4 La Catredale . 5 Palazzo del Magistrato .

AGRIA EGER. O ERLA

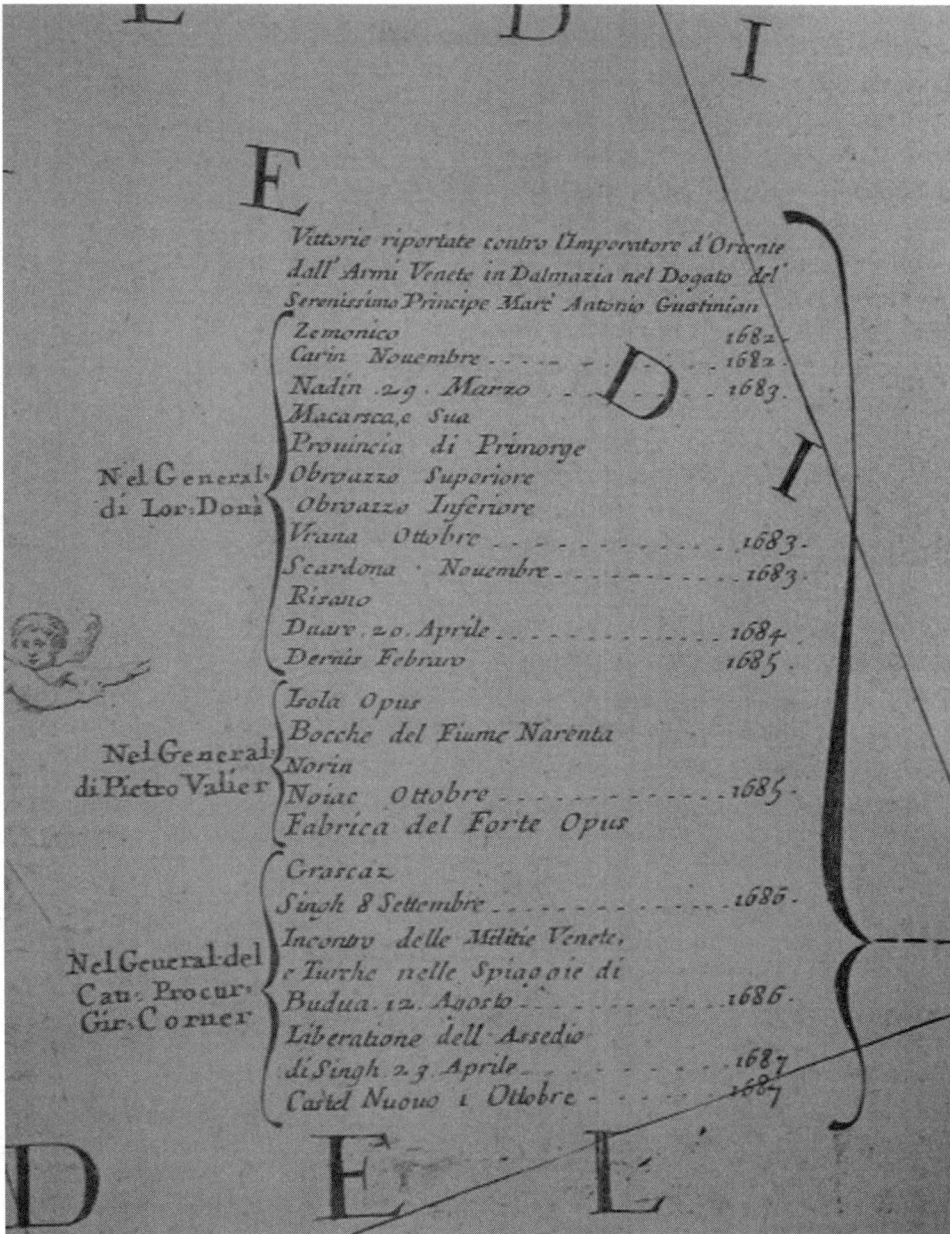

Figure 4.7. List of Victories. Vincenzo Coronelli, "Dalmatia and Istria," detail, *Isolario [dell' Atlante Veneto]*, v. 1, Venetia, c. 1696. Photo Courtesy of the Newberry Library, Chicago, Ayer 135 .C8 1696.

besieged (Fig. 4.9).[45] This densely packed map illustrates the various units (infantry and cavalry) involved in the attack, their weapons, and their

---

[45] Heinrich Ullrich, "Der Christen Belägerung Der Vesten Raab: in dem 1597 iar" [Nuremberg?], [1600?]. This map looks quite different from the inset of Raab in John Speed, "The Turkish Empire" [London], 1626, which sports a church with steeple; but the fortresses in both maps have seven bastions and two bridges. Raab was taken by the Ottomans in 1594 and besieged unsuccessfully by the Hapsburgs in 1597, and then taken by the generals Palffy and Schwarzenberg in March of 1598. See Finkel, *The*

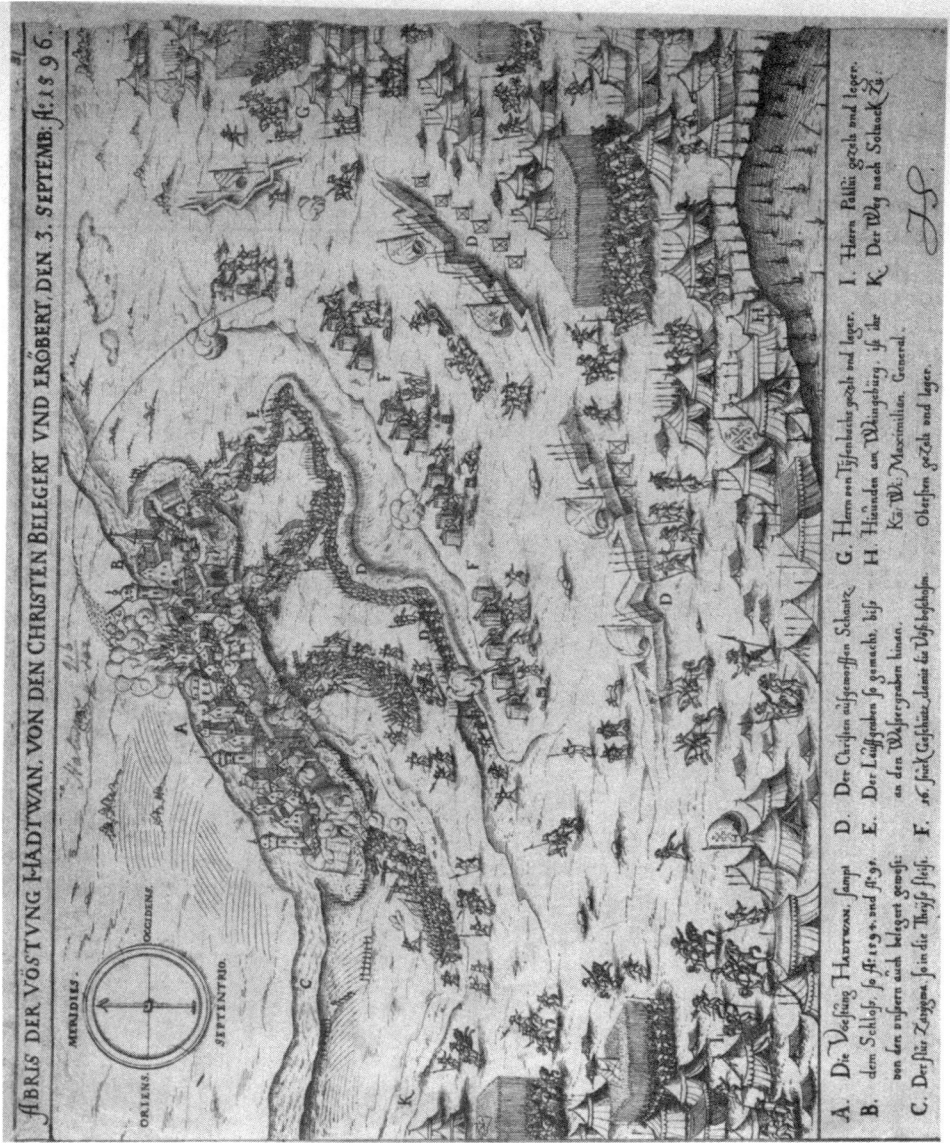

Figure 4.8. Siege of Hatvan. J. S., "Abris Der Vöstung Hadtwan," [n.p.], c. 1596. The British Library Board, Maps C.7.e.2.(.31).

Figure 4.9. Siege of Raab. Heinrich Ullrich, "Der Christen Belägerung Der Vesten Raab," [n.p.], c. 1597. The British Library Board, Maps 28225.

positions.[46] A large building in the center of the fortress sports a crescented dome and two large crescent flags. The bastioned walls are packed with defenders. Outside, attackers surround the walls, firing from behind their own fortifications, as a troop of "Italian cavalry" proceeds across a bridge on the Danube. In the right foreground, Austrian claims to sovereignty are embodied in the person of Maximilian III, who sits in a tent crested by flags bearing a cross, a single-headed eagle, and a double-headed eagle. Although Maximilian's determined look and the map's battle action suggest that the fortress cannot stand in the face of such formidable firepower, the siege was actually unsuccessful. The reader would have to wait for 1598 and another German map, published in Augsburg by Alexander Maier, to see Raab taken and the Ottomans defeated (see Ch. 5).[47] In that image, a fire also burns, presumably from gunpowder stores blowing up, a fairly common figural device that appeared in both European and Ottoman imagery and lent further immediacy to the map's portrayal.[48] Of course, many such representations are formulaic or iconic rather than expressive of the individual fortress's actual lines. Generic models were often used for fortresses and any given map image might or might not reflect a sense of that fortress's actual site, geographic context, and fortifications.

Nonetheless, though the modes of artistic representation are different, these three siege maps of Hatvan and Raab, taken together, suggest some standard options for the envisioning of contested space on the Ottoman–Hapsburg frontier at the end of the sixteenth century. Their focus on the individual fortress emphasizes the notion that frontiers are measured in the points where armies meet, not in blocks of territory. One does not see a system of defensive sites or a line of military advance; rather one sees sovereign power condensed into a set of walls, towers, and flags. Raab itself was thus emblematic of the advancing Ottoman frontier and the Hapsburg determination to stay that advance. In the early eighteenth century, Henri Chatelain's *Atlas Historique*, published in Amsterdam in seven volumes, would incorporate this same sense of struggle and counting of space into its historical narrative of the inconclusive war of 1593–1606. Chatelain's narrative counts the successes of Hapsburgs and Ottomans as their generals make themselves "master" of this fortress or that. It emphasizes both the "deliverance" of fortresses, towns, and countries from subordination to the "infidels" and the "drawing out from slavery of an infinite number of Christians."[49] Ottoman narratives

---

Administration of Warfare, 12–16; and Pálffy, "The Origins and Development of the Border Defense System," 55–7.

[46] Szakály, "The Early Ottoman Period," 97, gives the date of the conquest as 19 March, whereas the map legend says 29 March.

[47] Alexander Maire, "Iavarinum sive Raab a Christianis captum 29 die Martij Anno Christi 1598" [Augsburg?], [1598?]. Almost a hundred years later, Vincenzo Coronelli's map of the segments of the Danube portrayed it as a river marked by fortresses, including Iavarinum, whose history of conquest was charted in a small legend: Vincenzo Coronelli, "Corso del Danubio," *Atlante Veneto*, 1690, after page 110.

[48] Feridun Ahmed Bey, *Nüzhet-i Esrârü'l-Ahyâr Der-Ahbâr-ı Sefer-i Sigetvar*, 69, includes such a scene from the *Zafername* of Seyyid Lokman, dated 1579.

[49] Chatelain, *Atlas Historique*, v. 2, 81. See also Aksan, *Ottoman Wars*, 335, on fortresses and the role of "regional armies commanded by local strongmen who participated at will and abandoned the battlefront equally willfully."

did the same thing, focusing on the "grandeur and might of the Ottoman army" and the concomitant "infidel panic."[50]

Like the siege illustrations of European maps, Ottoman miniatures embodied the struggle for possession in the forms of marching soldiers, tents, and booming cannons. Costume was used to distinguish Muslim besieger from Christian besieged. One such miniature, from a şehname (book of kings) of Arifi (court chronicler 1540–61), shows the walls and towers of Belgrade during the siege of 1521, its fearful citizens watching through the window as one of those towers is consumed by fire (Fig. 4.10).[51] Armed soldiers man the bastions while the armies of the attackers, in this frame, remain 'off-screen.' Other miniatures might highlight the encampment of the Ottoman army, showing the commander and his subordinates, while figures in "Christian" garb appear in the form of captives or deputations coming to surrender (see Fig. 5.6). They move from inside to outside the walls, which have now been transferred to the Ottoman domain. Thus the miniature, like the news map, is both a battle report and a celebration of additions to Ottoman sovereign space.

Maps embodied news but also commemoration. The 1683 siege of Vienna, for example, was the subject of an enormous outpouring of pictorial representation. For the Christian kingdoms, this final Ottoman assault on a key bastion of Christendom was a source of agonized apprehension followed by ecstatic celebration. The sense of relief and vindication on the Christian side and the notion that the Ottoman tide had been turned meant that Vienna 1683 was the subject of both immediate and enduring interest.[52] A contemporary map by Giovanni Giacomo Rossi (1627–91), for example, shows "Vienna besieged by the Turk in the month of July, 1683" (Fig. 4.11).[53] The city is arrayed in its surrounding countryside, while cannons fire and forces inside and outside the city scramble to their posts. A huge flag is mounted in front of St. Stephan's cathedral, the only building depicted inside the city walls. Prominently featured in the lower right corner of the map is the elaborate "pavilion of the grand vezir," embroidered with multiple crescents. The Polish king, John Sobieski (r. 1674–1696), as in many other such images, is

[50] See Woodhead, Ta'līkī-zāde's şehnāme-i hümāyūn, 39–40, 53, which addresses some of the Ottoman conventions of narrating sieges.

[51] Arifi Fethullah Çelebi, Süleymanname, İstanbul, 1558, Topkapı Sarayı Müzesi Kütüphanesi, Hazine 1517. Other examples of miniatures are found in the hybrid seventeenth century source designated Memorie turchesche in the Correr Museum in Venice; see Carlo Pirovano, ed., Venezia e i Turchi: Scontri e confronti di due civiltà (Milan: Electa Editrice, 1985), 18–19.

[52] Günter Düriegl, "Geschichte der Belagerung Wiens," 131–50, in Die Türken vor Wien: Europea und die Entscheidung an der Donau, 1683 (Salzburg and Vienna: Residenz, 1982), esp. 137, 142–4; paintings by Franz Geffels and Jan Wyck feature the taking of the grand vezir's tent in the midst of chaotic scenes of combat. The same volume includes an Ottoman siege plan of Vienna (245). The 1529 siege was also the subject of multiple maps and other images, see Peter W. Schienerl, "Süleyman der Prächtige (1520–1566)," 62–7, in Im Lichte des Halbmonds, 63, for Niklas Meldemann's round map, done in Nuremberg in 1530.

[53] M. G. Rossi, "Dimostratione de confini delle principale Città dell' Austria et Ungaria" ("Vienna assediata dal Turco nel mese di Luglio, 1683"), Bayerische Staatsbibliothek, Abteilung Karten & Bilder There is a map in the British Library with the same title, also depicting the siege, but the images are quite different: British Library, Maps K.Top.90.31.2.

Figure 4.10. Siege of Belgrade. Arifi Fethullah Çelebi, *Süleymanname*, H. 1517, 108b, İstanbul, c. 1558. Topkapı Palace Museum, İstanbul.

prominently featured in the foreground, signaling his key role in the relief of the city and the eventual rout of the Ottoman forces on September 12.[54] He

---

[54] Martin Brice, *A Chronicle History of Forts and Fortresses* (New York: Barnes and Noble, 2006), 86, 93. The author also includes an elaborate image of the 1529 siege of Vienna featuring Sultan Süleyman in his imperial tent in the foreground with the besieged city in the background. Full bibliographic data

Figure 4.11. Siege of Vienna. M. G. [Giovanni Giacomo] Rossi, "[Dimostratione de confini delle principale Città dell' Austria et Ungaria]" or "Vienna assediata dalle Armii Ottomane...," detail, [Rome], [c. 1683]. Courtesy of the Bayerische Staatsbibliothek, Map Department.

is posed on a prancing charger, a banner clutched in one hand and a sword in the other. The vezir flees his tent and Sobieski's forces are free to plunder the booty piled inside.[55] But, occupied or not, the commander's tent, just as seen in Ullrich's 1597 map of Raab (see Fig. 4.9) and Barton's account of the aftermath of Egri, was an important symbol of imperial claims.[56] The taking of that tent was a signal token of supremacy and honor, readily understood across cultural lines.

The attempt on Vienna, for sultan and Porte, had been an act designed to consolidate control over the major city center at the western end of the transimperial frontier zone, a means of reducing their Hapsburg foe, gaining resources, and establishing more consistent control over the remainder of fractious Hungary. The grand vezir, Kara Mustafa Pasha, had "commissioned an excerpt" of the relevant segment of Willem Janszoon Blaeu's *Atlas Maior* in preparation for the campaign, an attempt, apparently, to solidify his knowledge of the terrain to be conquered.[57] There is also a hand-drawn and colored Ottoman plan of the siege (not shown here), which provides us with a distinctive Ottoman conceptualization of the attack.[58] This plan highlights both the Danube as a defensive barrier and the cannon of the various commanders arrayed outside the city walls. Although the defenders' flags are marked with crosses, the mapmaker did not mark the attackers' flags with crescents, illustrating the fact that it was European, not Ottoman, artistry that chose the crescent as the quintessential emblem of the "Turk."[59] Once the campaign ended, the Ottomans faced the long march back to Istanbul and the mapmakers of the Christian kings were free to commemorate their triumph for years to come.

---

are not provided. For another engraving showing the Ottoman trenches outside the city bastions and the relieving forces of Sobieski and the German prince Karl von Lothringen, see Inge Lehne and Lonnie Johnson, *Vienna: The Past in the Present, A Historical Survey,* 2nd ed. (Vienna: Österreichischer Bundesverlag, 1995), 33. See also Emiralioğlu, *Geographical Knowledge and Imperial Culture,* 85, on an Ottoman description of the imperial tent.

[55] Zdzisław Żygulski, *Ottoman Art in the Service of Empire* (New York: New York University, 1992), 153–76. See also Beata Biedrońska-Słota, "The history of Turkish textiles," 63–9, in *War and Peace: Ottoman–Polish Relations in the 15th–19th Centuries* (İstanbul: MAS, 1999), 63; and Magdalena Piwocka, "Turkish tents in Poland," 52–61, in *War and Peace: Ottoman–Polish Relations,* 53–4.

[56] A German map of the 1595 siege of Tergoviste highlights the attackers' tents in the foreground and incorporates two huge tents labeled "Sinan Basa" for the grand vezir directly into the city space, as if they were part of the city's defenses. See Szalai Béla, "A tizenöt éves háború metszetábrázolásai a frankfurti vásári tudósításokban (1593–1606)," *Cartograhica Hungarica* 8 (May 2004): 18–39, esp. 30. See also Klaus Schwarz, "Vom Krieg zum Frieden: Berlin, das Kurfürstentum Brandenburg, das Reich und die Türken," 245–78, in *Europa und der Orient 800–1900,* 266–7, 727, and 251, for a fifteenth century French image of the "Bacha's" tent at the siege of Rhodes.

[57] Hagen, "Afterword," 233. A translation of the *Atlas Maior* was completed in 1685, attributed to Ebu Bekr el-Dimişki, who died in 1691 (231). The circulation of maps may also be demonstrated by the presence of European maps in the Turkish Naval Museum, such as H. Jaillot's 1684 version of the map "Estats De L'Empire Des Turqs En Europe." See Özpınar et al., eds., *Türk Deniz Müzesi Harita Kataloğu,* 409, 415.

[58] See Ahmet Karamustafa, "Military, Administrative, and Scholarly Maps and Plans," 209–27, in *HOC,* v. 2, pt. 2, 213.

[59] On the Ottoman use of the crescent, see Nurhan Atasoy and Lale Uluç, *Impressions of Ottoman Culture in Europe: 1453–1699* (İstanbul: Turkish Cultural Foundation, 2012), 369–75, esp. 375, citing Pedani.

Sea Space, Coastal Space, Island Space – The Adriatic

and Barbary Zones

Coastal fortresses were a special subset of the depiction of fortresses on the map. They served the same purpose and took on the same forms as inland fortresses: standing for imperial, regional, and religious sovereignty; projecting power into the surrounding space; and functioning as points of conflict. But, because of their location, coastal fortresses were special points of diffusion for authority, personnel, goods, information, and culture (also serving as natural and necessary conduits to island bases). Sea space had its own logics of identity, transport, and access, a difference that was foundational for those who set out to describe it.[60]

One of Venice's strengths in its struggle against the Ottomans was its ability quickly to mobilize forces from its various port bases in the Adriatic. Egidio Scardassa, writing in 1647 of Venetian maritime strategies, demonstrates the use of Adriatic port fortresses as mobilizing points. His *Relation of the Happy Successes, Day by Day . . . Against the Turks in Dalmatia* proposes to provide a "distinct relation of all the cities, fortresses, and lands occupied" by Venice.[61] He details how the Venetian commander used the ports of Sebenico (Šibenik) and Zara (Zadar) to mount assaults on Ottoman fortresses and "sack the towns" round about, so that the "Turks" would be distracted.[62] In this endeavor, coastal bases allowed Venice to project its power inland, harassing enemy fortifications that were on or near the sea, and leaving inland territories to their Ottoman masters.

That imperial struggle and its distinctions of space were echoed by the Ottoman raconteur Evliya Çelebi, describing his sojourn through Albania in 1670. Evliya tells his journey in terms of movement from one fortress to another. At each of these fortified points he notes coastal or inland features, Muslim and Christian populations, commerce and resources, and scholars and shrines. And although he is traveling in a period of relative peace, he tells the histories of these spaces in terms of transfers of power from one lord to another. Qanye (Kanina) "on the border of the sanjak of Vlora [Avlonya]," he writes, was "initially constructed by the king of Spain" and subsequently conquered by the Ottomans, then the Venetians, and then the Ottomans again during the reign of Bayezid II (r. 1481–1512).[63] It is a fortress with a maritime orientation, exposed to seaborne conquerors. Evliya notes, "It

---

[60] On launching attacks against fortresses from ships, see John Guilmartin, *Gunpowder and Galleys: Changing Technology and Mediterranean Warfare at Sea in the 16th Century* (New York: Cambridge University Press, 1974). Although seaborne attacks on fortresses generally involved the offloading of forces onto the land, the mapping of sea sieges can be counted as a separate though overlapping category of narration and imagery.

[61] Egidio Scardassa, *Relatione delle felici successi giorno per giorno dopò la mossa dell'armi della Seréniss. Republica di Venetia contro Turchi nella Dalmatia* (Rome: Franco Moneta, 1647), 2, prefaces his account by telling his readers that he is late reporting the progress of the Republic because he wanted "to bring forth all the particulars with certainty (1)."

[62] Scardassa, *Relatione delli felici successi*, 2.

[63] Evliya Çelebi, *Evliya Çelebi in Albania*, 131, also 71, 161.

is said that Sultan Süleyman built the fortress of Vlora in order to protect the ships anchored in this harbor. Later he anchored the imperial fleet here, and it was from here that he attacked the Venetian island of Corfu."[64] The coastal fortress thus served both an offensive and defensive function. It was an end point on the overland route across Albania and a mobilizing point (as Zara was for Venice) for assaults on the spaces of the surrounding seas.[65]

Similar descriptive parameters are employed in geographic accounts. Richard Blome's 1684 English *Cosmography and Geography* (see Ch. 3) describes "the chief places of the Turks" and Venetians in Dalmatia in the following terms:

> 1. *Marenza, seated on the Sea-shoar; 2. Mostar, an Inland Town towards Bosnia; 3. Stagno, and 4. Sibioncello, both Maritime Towns; and nigh unto which is the Isle of MELEDA, which also belongs to the Grand Signior. The chief Towns in the possession of the Venetians, are 1. Rhaguse, seated on the Adriatick Sea, a City of great Traffick and Riches . . . 2. Spalato, a Maritime Town on the Adriatick, . . . This Town is kept by the Venetians as their only Emporium, plyed successively with two Gallies, which carry between this place and Venice such Merchandize as are Transported into Turkey, or from thence brought in. 3. Zara, a strong Fortress, seated on the Adriatick within the Gulph, which by reason of its commodious situation, is most apt to command the whole Adriatick, and is strong fortified and well Mann'd . . .* [66]

The province is thus assessed in terms of imperial possession, commerce, fortification, and location inland or on the sea.

Ports and News

Like their inland counterparts, sea fortresses were the centerpieces of news maps detailing transimperial conflict. An anonymous sheet map of Navarino (Pylos) and Modon (Methoni) on the west coast of the Peloponnese neatly illustrates that role (Fig. 4.12).[67] The distance between the two fortresses is collapsed to show the scope of the seaborne conflict and the relationship between inland and coastal bases (as suggested in the narratives of Scardassa and Evliya). The legend of the map, telegraphing the news, reads as follows:

> *Rome, 15 October, 1572: News from Corfu of the 29 of September, 1572, that the Armada of the Holy League [is] at the port and fortress of Navarino. That it has encountered the armada of the Turks under the walls of Modon, as one sees from this rendering. One can find the*

---

[64] Evliya Çelebi, *Evliya Çelebi in Albania*, 143.

[65] See for another example, Arnold Cassola, *The 1565 Ottoman Malta Campaign Register* (Malta: Publishers Enterprises Group, 1998), 347–55.

[66] Blome, *Cosmography and Geography*, pt. 2, 38–9. For a schematic of Zara dated c. 1564, see Concina and Molteni, *La fabrica della fortezza*, 114.

[67] [Anonymous], "Nova di Corfu . . . ," Rome, 1572. On Modon and its expansion under Venetian and Ottoman rule, see Ruth Gertwagen, "Venetian Modon and Its Port, 1358–1500," 15–148, in *Mediterranean Urban Culture*, esp. 140–41, 143–8. For a map of Modon, apparently a work of Matrakçı Nasuh, from the Topkapı Saray, see Concina and Molteni, *La fabrica della fortezza*, 18–19.

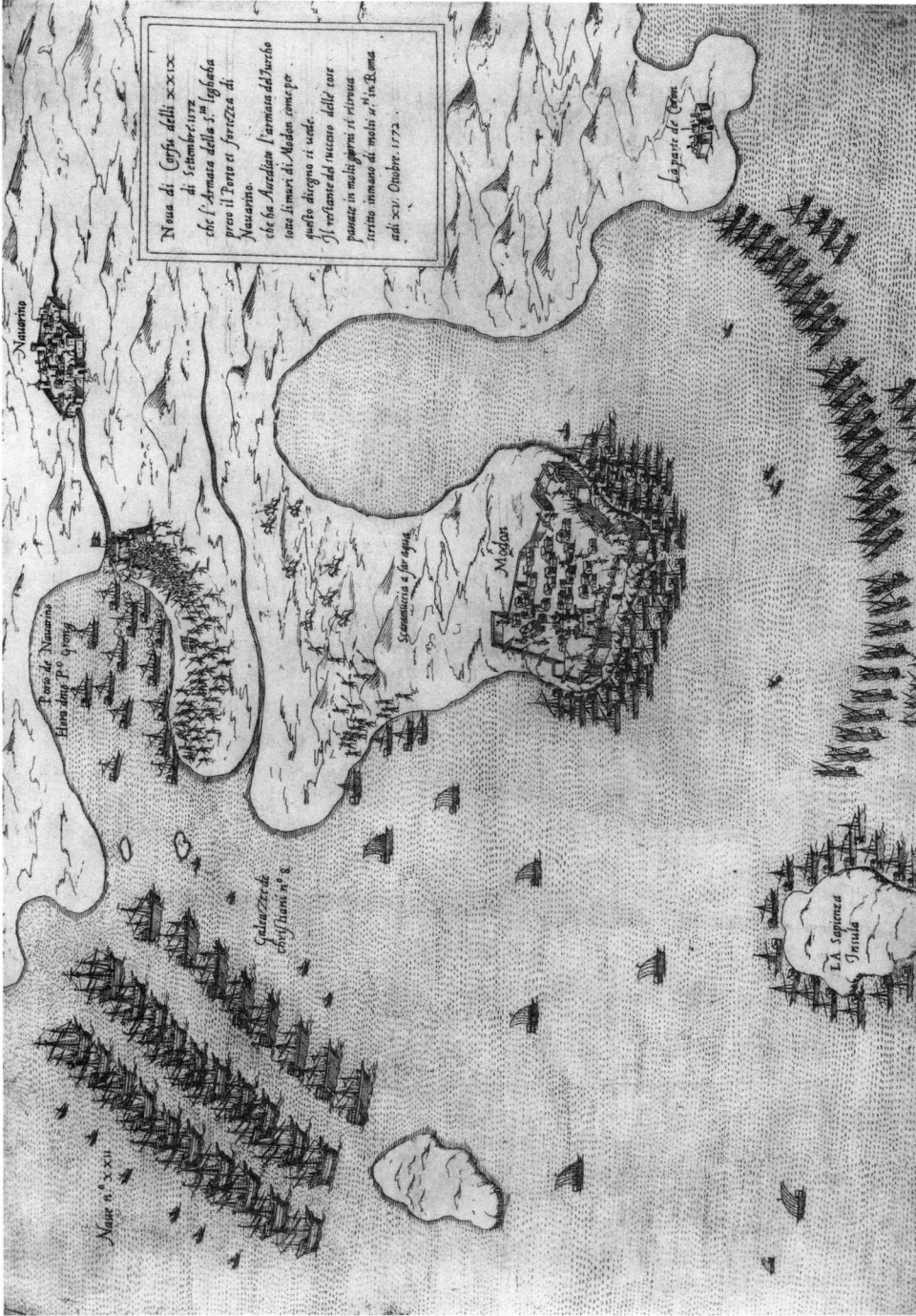

Figure 4.12. Navarino and Modon. [Anonymous], "Nova di Corfu…," Rome, 1572. The British Library Board, Maps C.7.e.2 1572.

remaining [news] of the success of things in the intervening days hand written in many [other sources].

This legend illustrates the speed with which news reached Rome, there to be turned into maps. It also illustrates the multiplicity of sources opportunistically detailing the Ottoman–Venetian conflict and the role of island bases in the transmission of news.[68]

Despite expectations raised by the image of Christian landing forces and a large Christian fleet on the map of Navarino, the assault on Modon was not successful. The Ottoman fleet retreated to safe harbor; Don Juan (1547–78), bastard son of Charles V, acting on orders from Spain, withdrew precipitously; and the Venetian commander Giacomo Foscarini was left with too few ships to pursue the fight.[69] The fortress thus stayed in Ottoman hands; and the "crescent" (at least in the map frame) remained perched atop the mapped battlements of Navarino.

Ships on the map, like crescents, were also indicators of possession. In a Venetian map from Giovanni Camocio's *isolario*, dating to the same era, one sees the ships of the Venetian fleet in the harbor of Sopoto on the Albanian coast (Fig. 4.13). The battle is personalized, each ship labeled with the name of a Venetian officer or patron, thus approximating the site of conflict to the imperial center from which the ship and its financing emerged. The troops of the attackers occupy the midground, on land, highlighted by the large tent of the Venetian *provveditore generale*. In the background, the fortress flies two crescent flags marking it as Ottoman space, drawing (without words) the connection between this fortress and Istanbul. Interestingly, the legend tells the reader that this is "a Turkish place, taken by the Illustrious Sebastian Venier, *provveditore generale* of the [nearby] island of Corfu, together with the Illustrious Zelfi, on June 10, 1570."[70] Sopoto thus seems to retain its association with Ottoman identity despite the conquest. And Corfu emerges in the text of the map as a distribution point for the deploying of ships, just as it was identified in the legend of the map of Navarino as a transmission point for the movement of news between Italy and points east.[71]

This map of Sopoto was also a type of news map, one that took pains to tell who was who and what was going on. But a news map did not necessarily remain a news map. Alternative images of the same siege are provided

---

[68] "La vera descrittione del sita della città de Tunisi," [1574], for example, narrates an attack by the "Turks" on Tunis, saying that news of the attack was received from Palermo August 3, 1574, brought by one "Trapani Ernando Gomes" who had left Goletta on July 29.

[69] Norwich, *Venice: The Greatness and the Fall*, 231.

[70] Camocio, "Soppoto fortezza," in *Isole famose* (Venetia, 1574).

[71] One sees similar constructions of islands in maps such as that of the attack on the fortress at the Brazzo de Maina by Nicolo Nelli in Simon Pinargenti, *Isole che son da Venetia nella Dalmatia, et per tutto l'Archipelago, fino a Costantinopoli* (Venetia: 1573). The caption notes that this "fortress of the Grand Turk in the Morea, [was] taken by the illustrious Captain of the Gulf, the Magnificent Marco Querini with the armada of Candia." It reminds the reader that Candia is a Venetian base, a mobilizing point for assaults on Ottoman territory. A more primitive, unsigned map adds the information that this place is at the borders of Greece (*nella confini della grecia*), thus situating it in its territorial context: "Brazo De Maina," Newberry Library, Novacco 2F32. See Concina and Molteni, *La fabrica della fortezza*, 214, 225–7, 234–48. See Pirovano, ed., *Venezia e i Turchi*, 244, for two sixteenth century schematics of Candia fortress; and Bilici, *XIV Louis ve İstanbul'u Fetih Tasarısı*, 22, for a 1686–7 French rendition after the conquest.

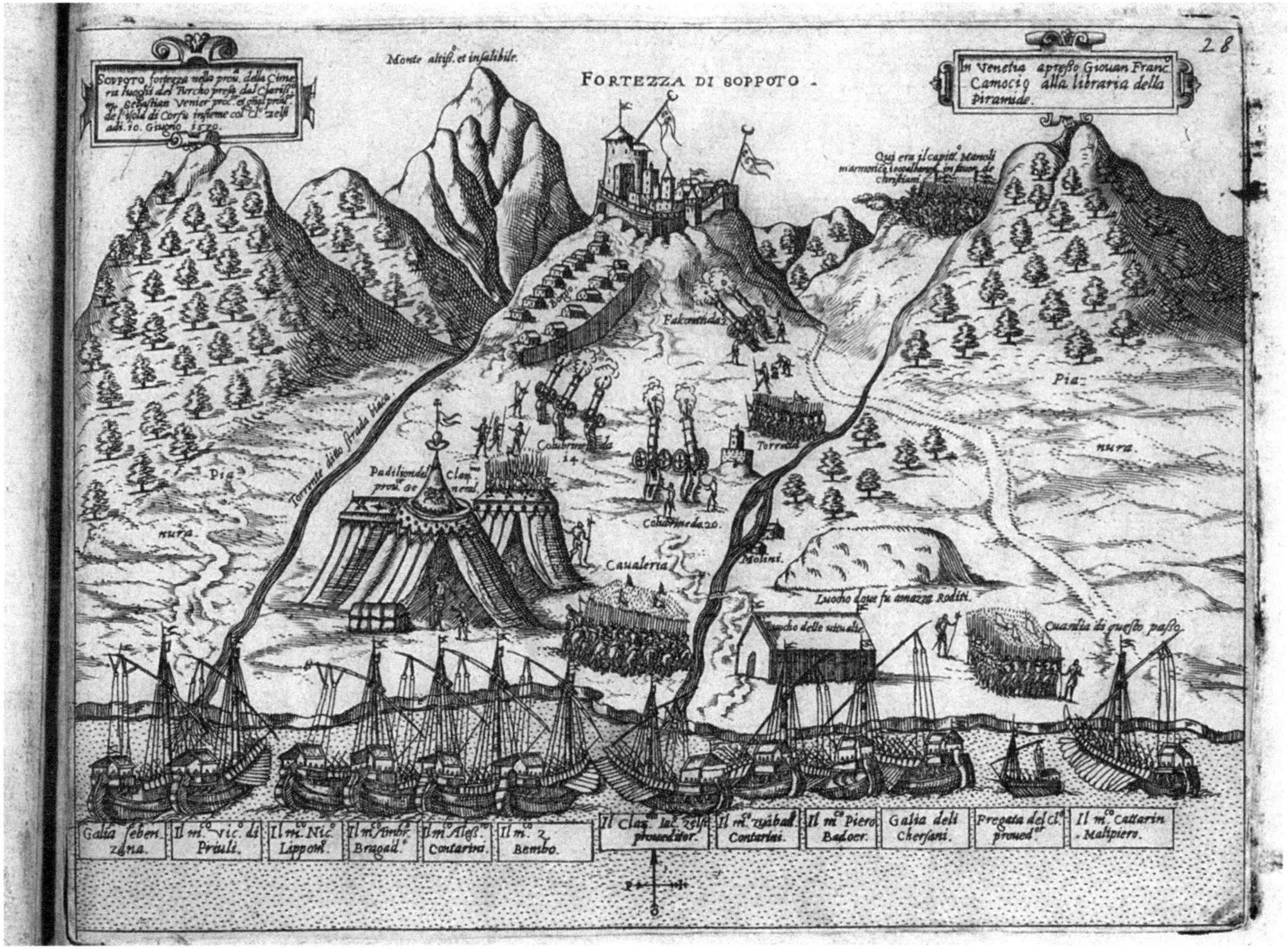

Figure 4.13. Giovanni Camocio, "Soppoto fortezza," *Isole famose porti, fortezze, e terre maritime sottoposto all Ser.ma Sig.ria di Venetia*, map 28, Venetia, [1574?]. By permission of the Folger Shakespeare Library, Shelfmark: G101.5.C3 1574 Cage.

in Giuseppe Rosaccio's 1598 travel book, *Viaggio da Venetia a Costanti-nopoli*. One of the maps in this itinerary places Sopoto, besieged and in flames, in the background, whereas the fortress of Margaritino surrounded by Christian attackers is in the foreground (Fig. 4.14). Here too one finds the iconography of divided space: tents in the foreground are topped with crosses, and a bedraggled crescent falls from the highest point of the belea-guered fortress.[72] Crescents thus turned into crosses. News maps were recy-cled after they no longer served as reports of current events. And mapmakers and publishers continued to use and adapt their maps as need and market permitted. Rosaccio's work was charting the stages of sea-based travel rather than current events. But he was also invoking the history of maritime places and the attendant memories of Venetian successes and failures. Maps thus intertwined: past, present, and future, war space, travel space, and historical space.

The Case of Clissa

As the mapmakers of the Christian kingdoms deployed frontier fortresses on maps, they were conscious of intersecting and serial identities, and of the juxtaposition of fortresses on the coast to those near the coast. Sometimes they expressed a sense of shared space ("Turk" and "Christian"); at others they suggested an implacable divide. Those options are illustrated in the mapping of the fortress of Clissa.

Although the Ottomans controlled the bulk of the Greco–Balkan peninsula, that did not guarantee their control over the coast.[73] Location near the sea made fortresses, even those not immediately on the coast, vulnerable to enemy fleets. Such was the case in the years 1645–8, when the Venetian commander, Leonardo Foscolo, was engaged in attacking bases on the Adriatic.[74] In the course of that campaign, Clissa (Klis), a few miles southeast of Spalato (Split) and a focal point of the Ottoman–Venetian rivalry, was seized by the Signoria. An image of the siege operation appears in a series of colored maps of fortresses, now in the British Library (Fig. 4.15).[75] Venetian forces in the foreground of the map fire on the fortress, which is marked by the crescents

---

[72] See Eugenio Turri, "Gli isolario ovvero l'idealizzazione cartografica," 19–36, in *Navigare e descrivere: Isolari e portolani del Museo Correr di Venezia XV–XVIII secolo*, Camillo Tonini and Piero Lucchi, eds. (Venice: Marsilio, 2001), 28.

[73] One could say that one of the ways that Ottomans "mapped" space was through a counting of garrison troops, the personnel whereby fortresses were defended and maintained. For one such example of a "roll-call" register, see Asparuch Velkov and Evgeniy Radushev, *Ottoman Garrisons on the Middle Danube: Based on Austrian National Library MS MXT 562 of 956/1549–1550* (Budapest: Akadémiai Kiadó, 1996), esp. 12–27. Such registers were a counterpart of the land counting (*tahrir*) surveys for tax purposes, both avenues for managing conquered space.

[74] Norwich, *Venice*, 300.

[75] "Clissa," *The Molina Family Atlas* [mid-17th c.], British Library, Maps K.Top. 78.31.b (Table 6, no. 5). The map bears a coat of arms that is repeated elsewhere in the atlas. I suspect this may be the Molin family that served Venice in Dalmatia as *Commissario* (Marco) in the 1640s and *Provveditore Generale* (Alessandro) in the 1680s; see Tea Mayhew, *Dalmatia between Ottoman and Venetian Rule: Contado di Zara 1645–1718* (Rome: Viella, 2008), 153–4, 169, 208–12, 257. But I have no further information on the assembling of this collection. It includes maps of many different styles but most focused on fortresses.

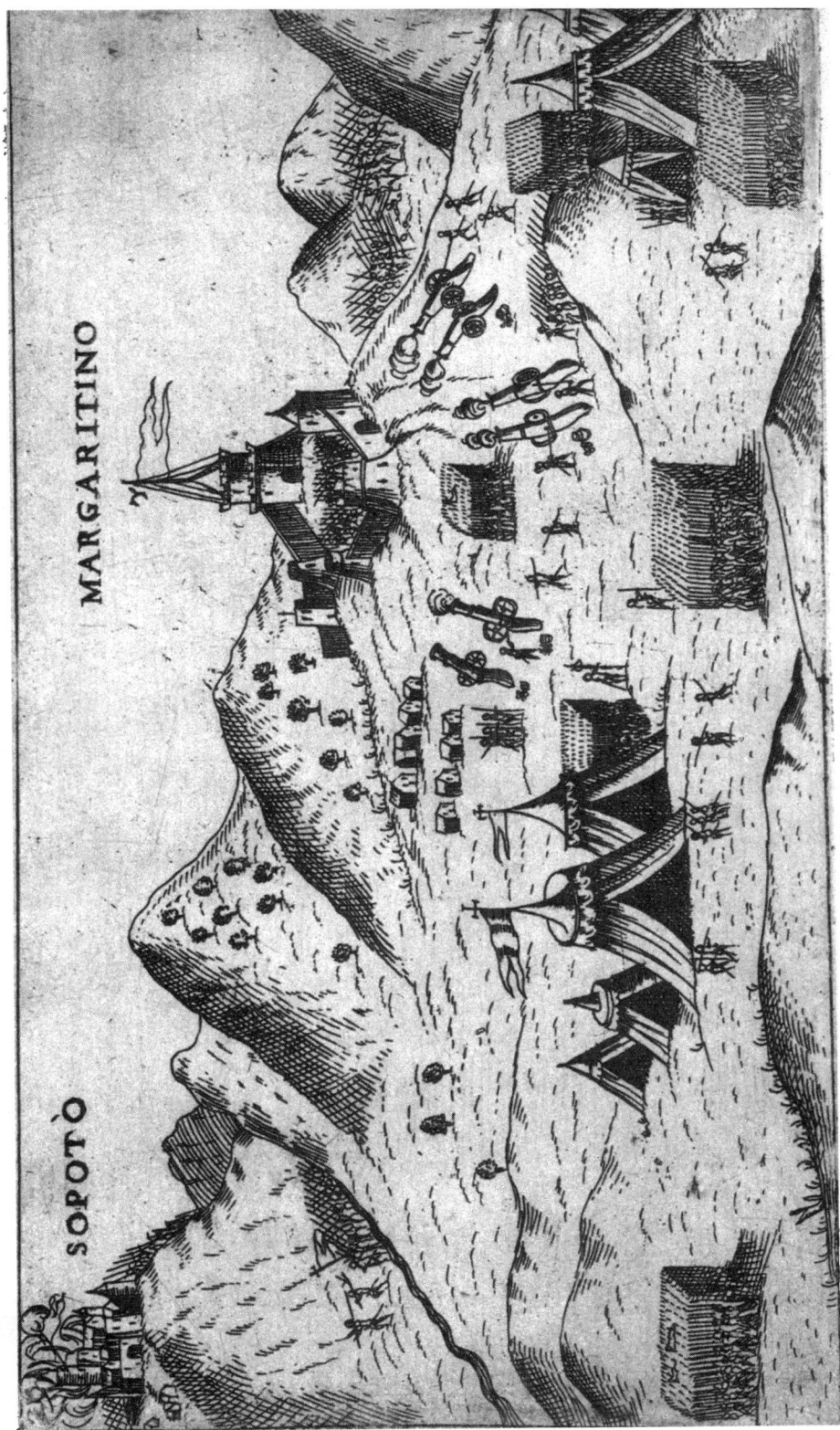

Figure 4.14. Margaritino and Sopoto. Giuseppe Rosaccio, *Viaggio da Venetia a Costantinopoli*, 32r, Venetia, c. 1598. The British Library Board, Maps C.27.b.26(.32).

Figure 4.15. "Clissa," *Molina Atlas*, table 6, no. 5 [n.p., mid 17th century]. The British Library Board, Maps K.Top. 78.31.b.

signifying Ottoman rule. The map key highlights various sites, including the location of the mosque. And on the ground directly in front of the advancing forces are two receptacles with crescents on top that may represent a Muslim cemetery.[76] The crescents mark them as artifacts of both Muslim faith and Ottoman rule. In this way, the map designates this assault not simply as a victory, but as a victory over Islam, its peoples, and its things. Once taken, Clissa was garrisoned by its conquerors, who could then withdraw back to their ships. But on the map Clissa is frozen in time, the sight lines for the attackers' artillery showing how the towers and walls would be breached.[77]

A quite different image of Clissa is found in a small series of beautiful pen and ink maps drawn in July 1605, when the fortress was still Ottoman territory. They were produced or sponsored by an adventurer and soldier of fortune named Christaforo Tarnowski, who was associated with various Christian plans to retake territory from the Ottomans.[78] Each of his drawings features a fortress in situ on the Adriatic littoral; and each frames its enlarged subject in terms of spatial relationships to surrounding sites. The confrontation between Christian and Turk is implicit, although Tarnowski's maps do not depict conflict; indeed, the maps are visions of tranquility. The map of Clissa is inscribed on the back, "Clissa, Chief Fortress of the Turk in Dalmatia and Key to the Kingdom of Bosnia, 5 miles distant from Spalato" (Fig. 4.16). It juxtaposes Clissa, sitting high in the hills and decorated with crescent flag and tower-tops, to Spalato on the coast. Unlike many such maps, this one clearly shows the two fortresses to be linked by a network of roads.[79] Spalato, with its cross-topped towers, thus sits in close proximity to its Muslim neighbor, peaceful but also full of potential as a base for reclaiming what had been Christian lands.[80] Spalato and Clissa shared goods, people, and a system of relationships and communications between the representatives of the Porte and the Signoria. This was a conversational space, a place

[76] These objects are marked in the key with the letter "G," which may read "sepulcher."

[77] The map, and others in this atlas, give the impression of sketches from an eyewitness artist. That impression, however, may be an illusion. Clissa (Klis), like some other border fortresses, had changed hands several times. In 1577 the Ottoman sancakbey of Clissa complained to his superior in Buda about the violations of Hapsburg subordinates in his territory; see Dávid, "The Mühimme Defteri," 197–8. For other visions of sight lines in siege operations, see Concina and Molteni, *La fabrica della fortezza*, 211, an illustration from Francesco Maria della Rovere, *Discorsi militari*, printed in 1583; and a German map of the siege of Buda, in Klaus Schwarz, "Vom Krieg zum Frieden: Berlin, das Kurfürstentum Brandenburg, das Reich und die Türken," 245–78, in *Europa und der Orient*, 269.

[78] Christaforo Tarnowski, "Clissa," [n.p.], 1605. See James Krokar, "The Ottoman Presence in Southeastern Europe, 16th–19th Centuries: A View in Maps," slide set text (Chicago: Newberry Library, 1997). Clissa, like other coastal towns on the frontier, was a focal point of complaints over treaty violations, whether the current rulers were Ottoman or Venetian.

[79] One wonders if Tarnowski had seen Camocio's early 1570s maps of Clissa (see Camocio, *Isole famose*, British Library, Maps C.22.a.3, map 12), or Spalato (which also include a network of roads). The fortress bears some similarity to that in an anonymous map of "Clissa, Praecipuum Turcarum in Dalmatia popugnaculum...," dated to about 1596, which does not, however, include Spalato.

[80] As is Spalato in Giuseppe Rosaccio, *Viaggio da Venetia, a Costantinopoli* (Venetia: Giacomo Franco, 1598), 16r; see Tonini and Lucchi, eds., *Navigare e descrivere*, 110. For a later description, see Jacob Spon, *Voyage d'Italie, de Dalmatie, de Grèce et du Levant, 1678* (Paris: Honoré Champion, 2004), 106–7, who notes that the "caravans of Turkey" deposit their goods there for shipment to Venice.

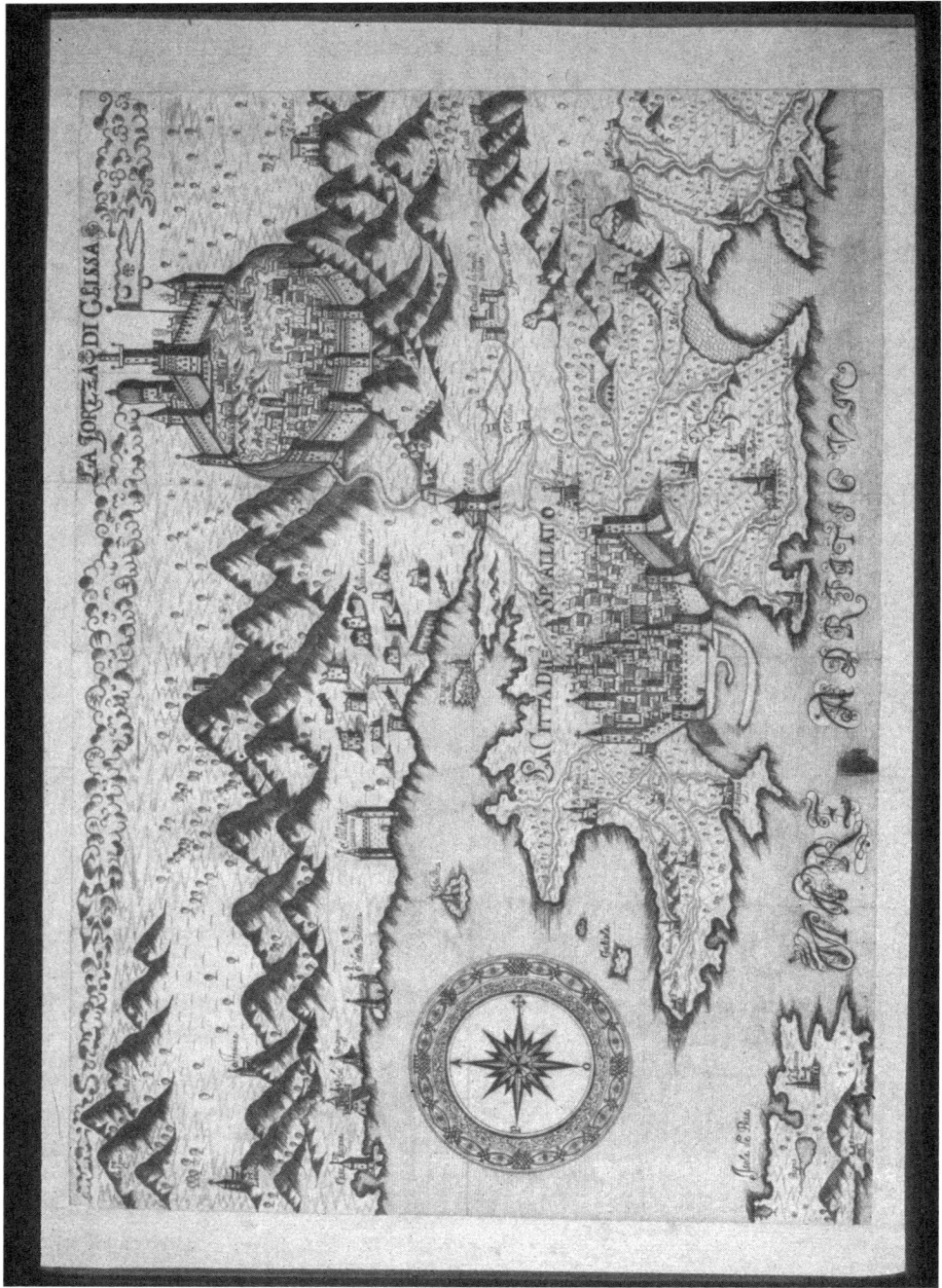

Figure 4.16. Christaforo Tarnowski, "Clissa" [n.p.], c. 1605. Photo Courtesy of the Newberry Library, Chicago, Novacco 2F 208.

of "strategic syncretism."[81] Tarnowski's roads hint at that complex identity, one that transcends the simple dichotomies of crescent and cross.

Another Tarnowski map reinforces the idea of shared but contested space. It depicts the fortresses of Castelnovo (Herceg Novi) and Risano, with their markers of Ottoman possession, cheek to jowl with Cattaro (on the Bay of Kotor), a fortress flying the banner of St. Mark, emblem of Venice.[82] In the lower right, the smaller Venetian fortress of Budua flies a flag inscribed with a cross. The inscription on the back of the map notes that it shows "Castelnovo on the border of Albania" (Fig. 4.17). Again the scene is tranquil, even idyllic, suggesting the potential for peaceable coexistence. Muslim houses sit next to a church representing "Old Ragusa (*Ragusi vecchia*)"; and the "salt works of Castelnovo" sit 'next to' Turk and Christian towns. Space here is decidedly collapsed to facilitate the message of the map; but the impression of a very mixed frontier zone, and of city-fortresses as the primary spaces in such zones, is unavoidable.

Tarnowski's representation of Castelnovo may in turn be compared to two maps in Camocio's 1574 *isolario*, one of which shows the Muslim fortress besieged by a Christian army and the other the fortress aligned peaceably along the coast with Ragusa and Cataro (Figs. 4.18 and 4.19).[83] Tranquility was in fact advantageous for both sides. Indeed, in the interests of promoting trade and peace, the Ottoman government attempted to keep a tight rein on its officials to prevent them from violating treaties forged with the encircled Venetian settlements in this Adriatic zone.[84] For the early modern cartographer faced with presenting frontier space, the context, the frame, or the map itself might focus on confrontation. But war was an intermittent and troublesome, however dramatic, thing; and mapmakers were cognizant of that fact. Thus they continued the traditions of presenting tranquil regional and city space, sometimes with prominent icons of possession and sometimes without.

Islands, Possession, and Connectivity

Islands were a special subset of the mapping of sea space.[85] They were drawn individually on single sheet maps, presented sequentially in island-books, or

[81] See Natalie Rothman, "Conversion, Convergence, and Commensuration in the Venetian–Ottoman Borderlands," *Journal of Medieval and Early Modern Studies* 41.3 (Fall, 2011): 601–33, on a female Muslim runaway from Klis; and Eric Dursteler, *Renegade Women: Gender, Identity, and Boundaries in the Early Modern Mediterranean* (Baltimore: Johns Hopkins University Press, 2011), 39–40, 63–4.

[82] Christaforo Tarnowski, "Castelnovo," 1605. The third of Tarnowski's drawings is of Scutari with its entire landscape appearing as Muslim space.

[83] Camocio, "Castelnovo," and "Golfo di Venetia," in *Isole famose*, maps 3, 20. For a later version of the same space, see F. I. Maire, "Carte. De la partie d'Albanie occupée par le Bacha de Scutari. le District des Montenegrins, et partie des Territoires des Rep.ques de Venise, et de Raguse," Vienna, 1788, which highlights the various "owners" of Albania. Part of the map assembly "Carte générale des Limites entre les trois Empires" it retains the iconography of crescent and cross.

[84] Suraiya Faroqhi, "The Venetian Presence in the Ottoman Empire (1600–1630)," *Journal of European Economic History* 15.2 (Fall 1986): 345–83; see 360.

[85] P. D. A. Harvey, "Local and Regional Cartography in Medieval Europe," 464–501, in *HOC*, v. 1, 484; and George Tolias,"*Isolarii*, Fifteenth to Seventeenth Centuries," 263–84, in *HOC*, v. 3, pt. 1, *Cartography in the European Renaissance*, David Woodward, ed. (Chicago: University of Chicago Press, 2007). See on Ottoman constructions of Aegean insularity Gilles Veinstein, "Le législateur

Figure 4.17. Christaforo Tarnowski, "Castelnovo" [n.p.], c. 1605. Photo Courtesy of the Newberry Library, Chicago, Novacco 2F 208.

Figure 4.18. Giovanni Camocio, "Castel novo," *Isole famose porti, fortezze, e terre maritime sottoposto all Ser.ma Sig.ria di Venetia*, map 20, Venetia, [1574?]. By permission of the Folger Shakespeare Library, Shelfmark: G1015.C3 1574 Cage.

Figure 4.19. Giovanni Camocio, "Golfo di Venetia," *Isole famose porti, fortezze, e terre maritime sottoposto all Ser.ma Sig.ria di Venetia*, map 12, Venetia [Alla libraria del segno di S. Marco] [1574?]. Photo Courtesy of the Newberry Library, Chicago, Baskes G1955.C3.

mapped as assemblages of like spaces, as if they had no relation to larger landmasses.[86] But, critically, they were also linking places that connected coasts, ports, empires, and peoples. Maps thus reflected the need to connect these sea-surrounded spaces with their attendant coasts or mainlands, the places on which they depended for supplies, defense, and communication. The fortress of the island of Tine (Tinos), in Camocio's *isolario*, for example, appears detached, perched on its mountain next to the sea, with ships in the foreground (Fig. 4.20). Its caption, however, tells the viewer its orientation in space and in time.

> *Tine, antique island and city, situated in the Archipelago where in ancient times there was the temple of Neptune. Distant 15 miles from Delos and Micone, [it is] a beautiful island of the most illustrious Venetian Signori. It is about 50 miles around.*[87]

The island thus had a size, a past, and a sovereign power. It also had a context of islands and adversaries as explained in the 1614 *relazione* of Pompeo Ferrari, a soldier and "gentleman" of Piacenza:

> *The island of Tine, called in antiquity Hidrussa either for the abundance of water or for the plentiful serpents it has, is situated almost in the middle of the Archipelago, surrounded by the other most famous [islands] of the Aegean. On the east is Samo, toward the side of Greece, Scio, to the west... and just as there is little distance from one island to another among them, so Tine has two nearby continents, Natolia distant a hundred miles and the Morea sixty, countries all subject to the Ottoman Empire. Whence one can truly say that it is little short of a miracle to see this little island maintained [by Venice] in the midst of [the possessions] of such a potent enemy.*[88]

For Ferrari, islands were framed in terms of their owners and their surrounding landmasses. Those factors had a bearing on questions of conflict and defense, a soldier's concerns. Islands might be close to the mainland or distant, as he points out, and that location affected their treatment in maps. Tine appeared enmeshed in a web of islands and surrounded by hostile seas.[89]

ottoman face à l'insularité. L'enseignement des kânûnnâme," 91–110, esp. 99, 105; and Colin Heywood, "Ottoman Territoriality versus Maritime Usage. The Ottoman Islands and English Privateering in the Wars with France (1689–1714)," 145–76, esp. 157–8; both in *Insularités ottomanes*, Nicolas Vatin and Gilles Veinstein, eds. (Paris: Maisonneuve & Larose, n.d.).

[86] Ortelius, "Archipelagi Insularum Aliquot Descrip," in *Theatrum Orbis Terrarum*, for example, frames each island in a grouping. Similar groupings are found in Vincenzo Coronelli's *Specchio del Mare* (Venetia: 1664).

[87] "Tine," in Camocio, *Isole famose*, map 56.

[88] Ermanno Armao, *Venezia in Oriente: La "Relatione dell'Isola et Città di Tine" di Pompeo Ferrari Gentil'huomo piacentino* (Rome: Dott. G. Bardi, 1938), 27. He went on to elaborate on the island's fortress, forces, and prospects for resisting attack. Anthony Luttrell, "The Latins and Life on the Smaller Aegean Islands, 1204–1453," 146–57, in *Latins and Greeks in the Eastern Mediterranean after 1204*, Benjamin Arbel, Bernard Hamilton, and David Jacoby, eds. (London: Frank Cass, 1989), 146, employs the term "miniature continents" for the Aegean islands.

[89] As O[lfert] Dapper (c. 1635–89), a Dutch scholar and physician, noted of the Ottoman castle on Tenedos (Bozcaada), it was designed to ward off pirates and protect the coastal towns. See O. Dapper, *Description exacte des isles de l'archipel, et de quelques autres adjacentes... Traduit du Flamand d'O.*

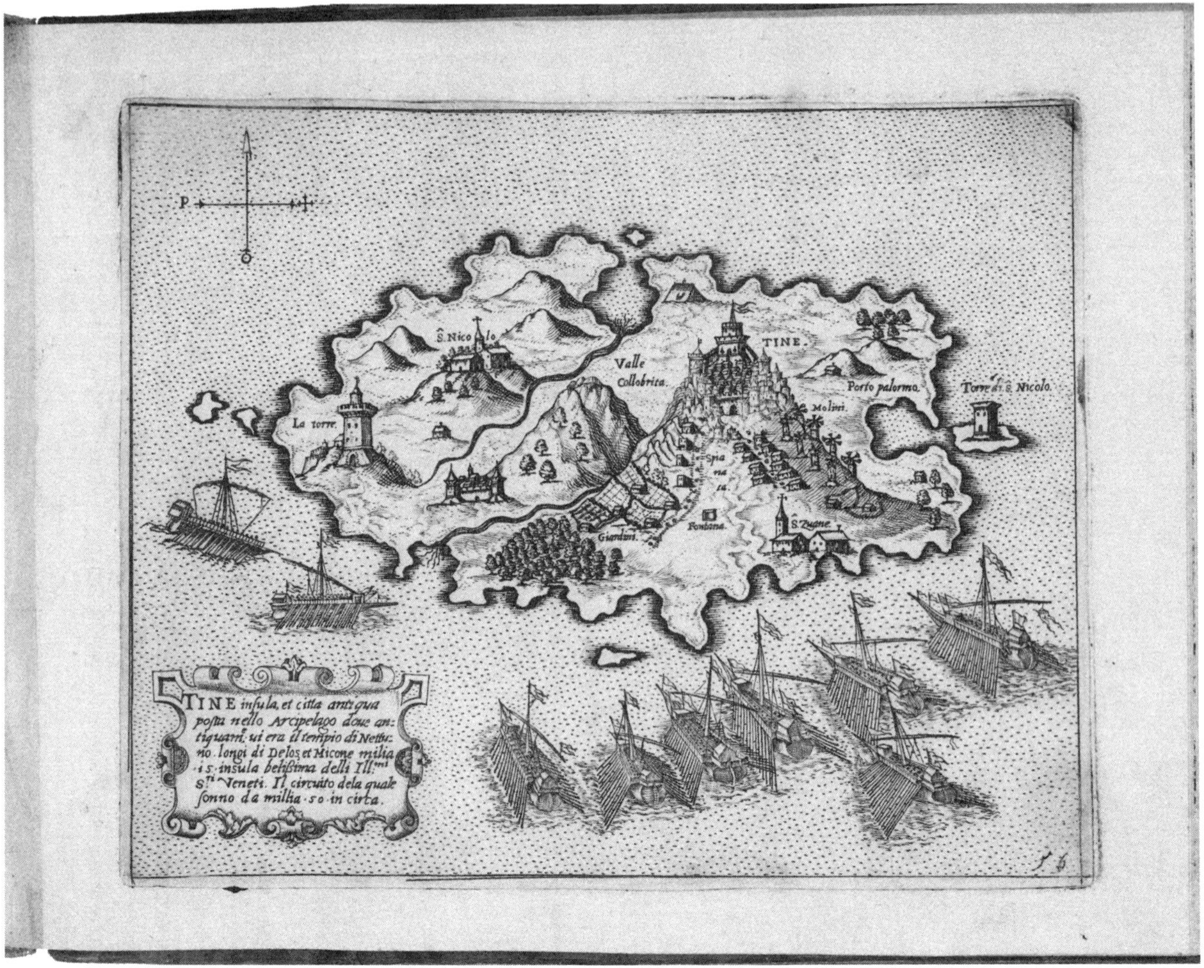

Figure 4.20. Giovanni Camocio, "Tine, insula et citta," *Isole famose porti, fortezze, e terre maritime sottoposto all Ser.ma Sig.ria di Venetia*, map 56, Venetia, [1574?]. By permission of the Folger Shakespeare Library, Shelfmark: G1015.C3 1574 Cage.

The Ottomans attempted to take Tine several times in the seventeenth century, without success. But Katib Çelebi (1609–57), in his history of the Ottoman maritime campaigns, *Tuhfet ül-kibar fi esfar ül-bihar,* makes clear what exactly "hostile seas" might mean. He describes an assault on Tine (İnebahtı) by Ahmet Pasha, whose ships approach the shore:

> *They besieged the area surrounding the fortress, sacked and burned the towns, and for two days and two nights they wrought such devastation that the lands were laid waste (şenlikden eser kalmadı). Most of the people were shut up in the fortress. On the third day the soldiers went back to their ships and sailed away.*[90]

This account illustrates a further division of space, that between the protected interior of the castle and the exposed areas outside its walls.

Like Tine, Cyprus's strategic location and connections to the mainland made it contested space. Mapping Cyprus became particularly important to the Christian kingdoms after the Ottomans gained control of the eastern Mediterranean littoral in 1516–17. But by 1570 the prosperous island had clearly become the object of Ottoman ambitions. Famagosta, for example, Cyprus's major port, is thus shown as a center-point of Mediterranean contention in Camocio's 1571 news map, which depicts it embedded in its surrounding land and seascapes (Fig. 4.21).[91] In the sea, ships sail, decked out in flags bearing either crescents or the lion of St. Mark. On the land side of the fortress, units of Ottoman infantry and some cavalry seem poised to overwhelm the city. The reader sees the Ottoman encampment in the background and is directed to note the inlet where the armada of Mustafa Pasha has landed.[92] This is a seaside battleground where the struggle for sovereignty appears front and center. The battle links Famagosta to other sites of confrontation on the transimperial frontiers; and for the moment the location of the fortress is not so critical as is the question of who will be winner and who loser.[93] Famagosta ultimately surrendered on September 1, 1571. Nicosia, Cyprus's other major fortress, had fallen even earlier, on September 9, 1570, after a forty-five-day siege.[94]

Dapper, M.D. (Amsterdam: Chez George Gallet, 1703), 237. The Dutch original of this text was published in 1688.

[90] Katib Çelebi, *Tuhfet ül-kibar fi esfar ül-bihar* ([İstanbul]: Matbaa-ı Bahriye, 1911), 131. No date is given; and the text suggests that the pasha had been in pursuit of a corsair.

[91] Camocio, *Isole famose,* map 71. For a range of contemporary maps of Cyprus island and its fortresses, see Sotheby's "Natural History, Travel, Atlases and Maps," London, Thursday 18 November, 2004, 110–23.

[92] John Speed, "The Turkish Empire," London, 1626, features the fortress of Famagosta on the top tier of its vignettes.

[93] On the Ottoman–Venetian sea frontiers, see Maria Pia Pedani, *Dalla frontiera al confine, Quaderni di studi Arabi, Studi e testi* 5 (Venice: Università Ca' Foscari di Venezia, Herder Editrice, 2002), esp. 39–51, on fortresses. See also, for details on coastal fortifications in North Africa, Neji Djelloul, *Les fortifications côtieres ottomanes de la régence de Tunis (XVIe–XIXe siècles)* (Zaghouan: Fondation Temimi pour la receherche scientifique et l'information, 1995).

[94] Norwich, *Venice,* 215–17. A colored woodcut shows Nicosia surrounded by Ottoman forces, some of them breaching the bastions on September 9, 1570; see [Anonymous], "Nicosia Regal Cita.d.Cipro Combatvta da Turchi," Sotheby's, "Natural History, Travel, Atlases and Maps," 122, plate 210.

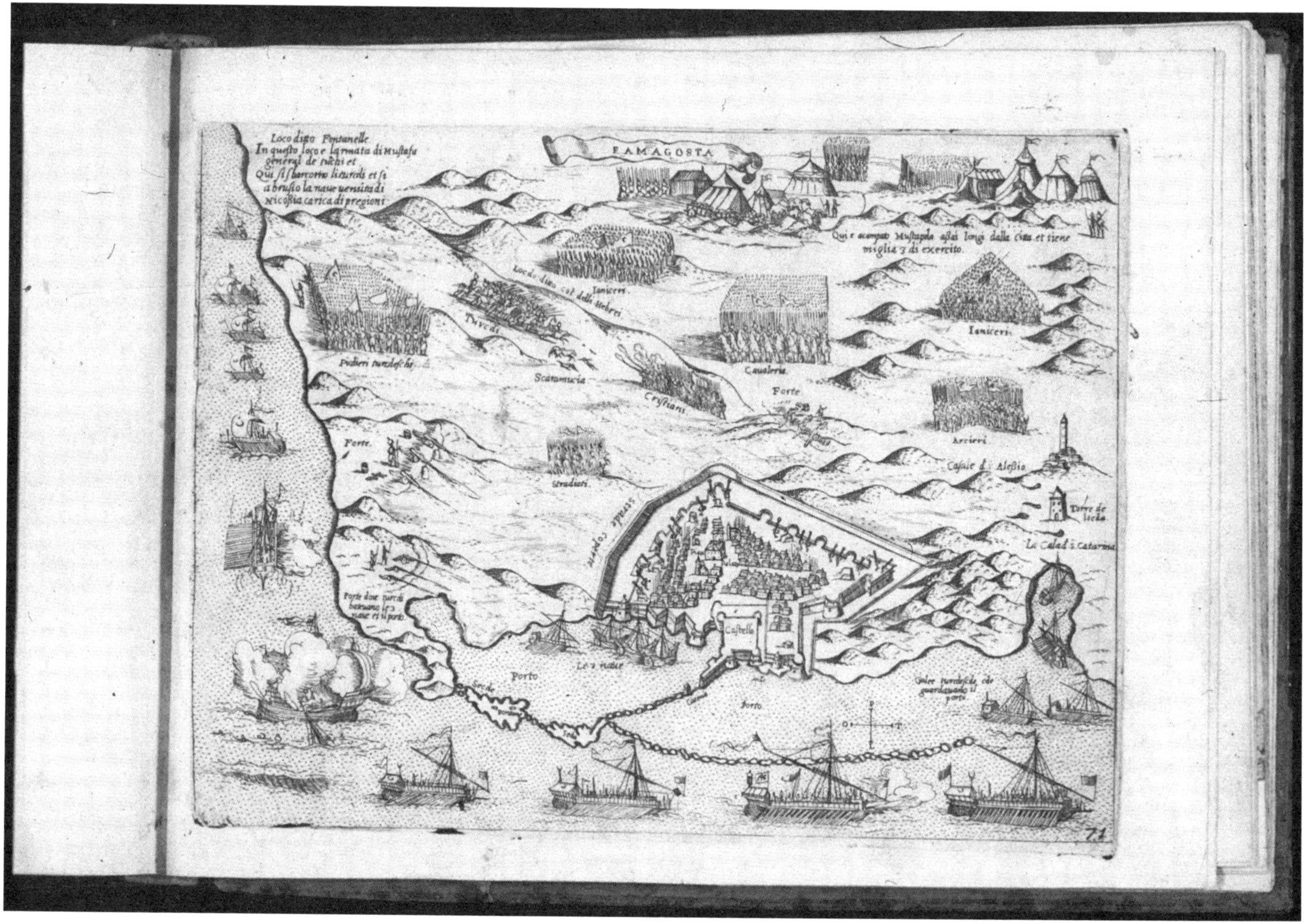

Figure 4.21. Giovanni Camocio, "Famagosta," *Isole famose porti, fortezze, e terre maritime sottoposto all Ser.ma Sig.ria di Venetia*, map 71, Venetia, [1574?]. By permission of the Folger Shakespeare Library, Shelfmark: G1015.C3 1574 Cage.

When Simon Pinargenti published his 1573 Venetian *isolario*, he resurrected a narrower vision of the city besieged (Fig. 4.22).[95] His focus was on the fortress of Nicosia itself as an island of walled, interior, urban space juxtaposed to a chaotic exterior full of the tents, cannon, and troops of Ottoman attackers. The tent complex of "General Pialj" (Piale Pasha, the Ottoman fleet commander) is labeled, as are the various units of the Ottoman army (archers, cavalry, etc.), providing, like the labels in Ullrich's siege map of Raab, a sense of authenticity. "Turchi" and "Christiani" face each other beneath the formidable walls. Thus the map returns its readers to 1570 and to the notion of religious confrontation. The viewer does not see the contexts of land and sea, but the message is clear. If the Turks succeed, one more point of Christendom and of Venetian empire will be lost. Of course the real ethno-religious identities of the participants in such struggles along the long Ottoman frontiers were quite complex. Conversions and intermarriage were common, and those living in frontier areas were often cited as people of questionable loyalties.[96]

Barbary Space

The Christian kings encountered the Turks in two Mediterranean realms of sea space, one as we have seen in the broader archipelago stretching from the Adriatic to the shores of the eastern Mediterranean, and the other in "Barbary" along the coast of North Africa.[97] The nature of Ottoman administration in these two zones varied substantially. But in the imagery of Christian Europe the zones were equated as realms subject to an ongoing struggle for hegemony with the Ottomans, and as places where Christians, willing or not, "turned Turk." These realms were mapped accordingly, predominantly as war space, but also as shared spaces, and intensely commercial spaces of mixed ethno-national identity.

In mapping the connectivity of Istanbul and Barbary, the relationship of contested islands to the shore could be made eminently clear.[98] Thus Domenico Zenoi's (fl. ca. 1560–70) 1565 map of Malta shows the outsized island squeezed into collapsed space between Sicily to the north and the coast of Africa to the south, as if to link the island confrontations of the middle Mediterranean with the coastal confrontations of Barbary

---

[95] Simon Pinargenti, *Isole che son da Venetia nella Dalmatia* (Venetia: 1573), map 42. See Eugenia Bevilacqua, *Le Immagini dell'Isola di Creta nella Cartografia Storica* (Venezia: Istituto Veneto di Scienze, Lettere ed Arti, 1997).

[96] See Evliya Çelebi, *Evliya Çelebi in Albania*, 85, 93, 191.

[97] Andrew Hess, *The Forgotten Frontier: A History of the Sixteenth Century Ibero-African Frontier* (Chicago: University of Chicago Press, 1978), 3, argues for a "separation of the Mediterranean world into different, well-defined cultural spheres" in the sixteenth century. Just how separate remains a contested question.

[98] See the 1565 map, or siege (*kuşatma*) plan, of Mustafa Pasha for Malta and an illustration of the siege of İnebahtı from Katib Çelebi's *Tuhfet ül-kibar fi esfar ül-bihar*, Topkapı Sarayı Müzesi, R. 1192, v17a, in Idris Bostan, *Kürekli ve Yelkenli Osmanlı Gemileri* (İstanbul: Bilge, 2005), 78–9, 88–9.

Figure 4.22. Simon Pinargenti, "Nicosia," *Isole che son da Venetia nella Dalmatia, et per tutto l'Archipelago*, Venetia, 1573. The British Library Board, Maps C.24.g.10(.42).

(Fig. 4.23).[99] Two fleets, one marked with crescent sails and one marked with crosses, maneuver to the north of the island and the major port of Valletta. Meanwhile the body of the island contains a dramatic action scene of hand-to-hand combat, cannon dragged into place, and provisions being unloaded. Men flee, surrender, and lie wounded on the ground.[100] Small legends chart the action. The famous siege of 1565 was a victory for the Christian defenders, and this map depicts the Ottoman fleet withdrawing from the scene of battle. The conflict seems to sketch a western limit to Ottoman reach (even though the Ottoman ships are shown sailing westward), a point beyond which the forces of Christendom may feel confident in their hold over the Middle Sea. Malta, as an island space, thus serves as a link between the imperial centers of Ottoman and Christian kings and the southern shores of the Mediterranean. It is an intermediate step on the way to Barbary, just as Cyprus is an intermediate step on the way to the Levant.

That sense of attachment is echoed in other types of representation as well. The frescoes in the Vatican's Gallery of Maps, painted around 1580–81, include depictions of Corfu, Malta, and Elba as part of the "Italian regions and the papal properties at the time of Pope Gregory XIII (r. 1572–85)."[101] The defense of Malta and defeat of the Ottoman fleet were events of recent memory. And the fresco captures the glory of those events in a representation of city and siege, at the same time reinforcing papal claims through the juxtaposition of islands to terra firma, in other words the proximity of Valletta to Rome.

Further away, in Britain, the assault of the Ottomans on Malta generated prayers and anxiety. The diocese of Salisbury, as Samuel Chew shows us, admonished its parishioners, "it is our part, which for distance of place cannot succour them with temporal relief, to assist them with spiritual aid ... [therefore] implore God to deliver Christians from the rage and violence of enemies whose purpose is to root out the very name and memory of Christ."[102] Once the Ottomans were repulsed, the Archbishop of Canterbury issued a "*Form of Thanksgiving* to be used thrice weekly for six weeks."[103] In these ways, Malta was anticipated and commemorated in image and word,

---

[99] Domenico Zenoi, "L'Ultimo disegno de l'isola di Malta" (Venetia, 1565). Another fascinating map of Malta (not shown here), which defies insistence on a single spatial "norm," was produced by Giovanni Giacomo Rossi in Rome in 1686. The map shows Malta and the next-door island of Gozzo upended with the "Mare di Barbaria" on the top of the map and the "Mare Ionio" underneath the islands, which are placed in the upper register of the frame. Beneath the islands is an "annotated" schema of the "old and new fortifications of Malta." See Sotheby's, "Natural History, Travel, Atlases and Maps," No. 410, 233. See also Albert Ganado, *A Study in Depth of 143 Maps Representing the Great Siege of Malta of 1566*, v. 1 (Valetta, Malta: Bank of Valetta, 1994), 110, 237, 241.

[100] Katib Çelebi, *Tuhfet ül-kibar fi esfar ül-bihar*, 78–81, describes the action from its initial "happy" successes to Ottoman retreat. See also Hess, *The Forgotten Frontier*, 84; and Kate Fleet, "Ottoman Expansion in the Mediterranean," 141–72, in *The Cambridge History of Turkey*, v. 2, *The Ottoman Empire as a World Power, 1453–1603*, Suraiya Faroqhi and Kate Fleet, eds. (Cambridge: Cambridge University Press, 2013), 164–5.

[101] http://www.vaticanstate.va/EN/Monuments/The_Vatican_Museums/Gallery_of_Maps.htm. See on the gallery and Malta, Lucio Gambi, et al., *La Galleria delle Carte geographiche in Vaticano*, v. 1 (Modena: Franco Cosimo Panini, 1994), 198–201.

[102] Chew, *The Crescent and the Rose*, 123.

[103] Chew, *The Crescent and the Rose*, 124.

Figure 4.23. Domenico Zenoi, "L'Ultimo disegno de l'isola di Malta" [Venetia], 1565. The British Library Board, Maps C.7.e.1(.119).

sprawled across the walls of the Vatican and passed hand to hand through the pews of London. The navy of the "Turks" had collapsed the space between northern and southern Europe and breached the boundaries between Latin and Protestant Christendom.

From Malta, the northern coasts of Africa with their Ottoman adjuncts were close at hand. Algiers, Tunis, Tripoli, and Jerba were objects of the European mapmakers' attention, both for their association with pirates and for their location in contested sea space.[104] The struggle to connect "Barbaria" to either the domains of the Christian kings or those of the sultan is neatly expressed in an Italian map of Jerba (Djerba), an appendage of Tunisia, that was crafted prior to the Ottoman seizure of the fortress in 1560. The image shows an island covered in palm trees interspersed with marching units of Christian infantry (Fig. 4.24). To the north lies the fortress, looking out (as in Zenoi's map of Malta) onto a seascape filled with the sails of "Christian" and "Turkish" armadas. The caption reads:

> Design of the Island of Jerba... site of the fortress made by the Christians in defense of which 5000 valiant soldiers were left, along with a good supply of provisions and munitions that, with the help of God, will suffice to defend it from the insults of the Turkish armada.[105]

Jerba, like Malta, was thus an intermediate island space, caught between north and south and, more particularly, the sites from which the armadas of contending lords were launched (a point also emphasized by the Ottoman historian Katib Çelebi in his narrative of the Ottoman naval campaigns of the time).[106] The island's fate depended on its fortifications, the will and equipment of its defenders, and, from the point of view of the mapmakers, the favor of its God.

Though such maps routinely depicted siege activities, they might also demonstrate the situation of shared space in the aftermath of conquest.[107] A detailed map of "Algeri," for example, dating to the end of the sixteenth century, does not present a scene of conflict; it shows Algiers in its coastal contexts, with mosques, palaces, and cemeteries noted in the key (Fig. 4.25). At the edge of the water, however, along the eastern end of the sheltering bay, one finds inscribed a historical notation of the confrontation between Christian and Turk: "Shore where by the fortune of the north winds the

[104] C. Koemen, *The Sea on Paper: The Story of the Van Keulens and Their "Sea-Torch"* (Amsterdam: Theatrum Orbis Terrarum, 1972), 4th plate after page 20, from University Library of Leiden, port. 283, no. 75, for a Van Keulen map of the port fortress of Tripoli. See also on maps of North Africa, Carla Kayvanian, "Maps and Wars: Charting the Mediterranean in the Sixteenth Century," 38–60, in *Cities of the Mediterranean from the Ottomans to the Present Day*, Biray Kolluoğlu and Meltem Toksöz, eds. (London: I.B. Tauris, 2010).

[105] "Disegno dell'Isola de Gerbi," [c. 1560]. Newberry Library, Novacco 2F 240.

[106] Katib Çelebi, *Tuhfet ül-kibar fi esfar ül-bihar*, 74, demonstrates the lines of connection between Jerba, Tripoli, Tunis, Malta, and the further bases at Avlonya and Istanbul.

[107] For an Italian map with key, see "Tripoli Citta di Barberia," c. 1570, Newberry Library, Novacco 4F 404, illustrating a land- and sea-based attack by Christian forces. The map shows the fortress as Muslim, with the ships and soldiers of the attackers bearing flags with crosses and double (and single) headed eagles.

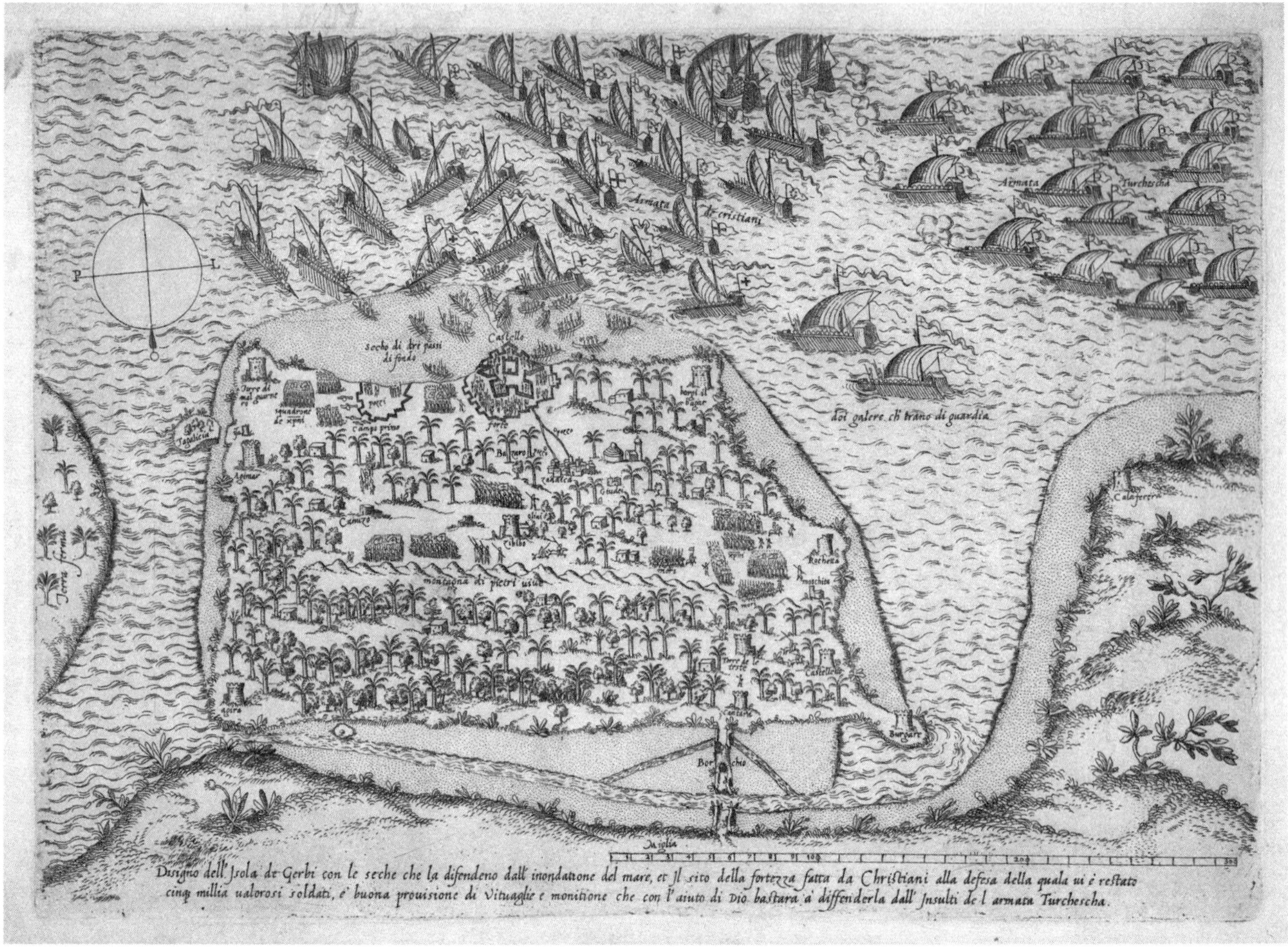

Figure 4.24. Jerba. "Disegno dell' Isola de Gerbi" [n.p., n.d.]. Photo Courtesy of the Newberry Library, Chicago, Novacco 2F 240.

Plate 1.2. F.I. Maire, "Carte générale des Limites entre les trois Empires et leurs variations successives depuis l'année 1718 jusqu'à ce jour, ou Théâtre de la Guerre présente," cartouche, Vienna, 1788. The British Library Board, Maps K.Top. 113.34.a.11.

Plate 1.9. Siege of Sighetvar. Seyyid Lokman, *Hünername (Book of Accomplishments)*, H. 1523, İstanbul, c. 1588. Topkapı Palace Museum, İstanbul. Photo Credit: Bridgeman-Giraudon/Art Resource, NY.

Plate 1.16. Battle of Keresztes, 1596. Talikizade Mehmet Subhi, *Şahname-i Sultan Mehmet III*, H. 1609, fol. 50b–51a, İstanbul, [c. 1596–9]. Topkapı Palace Museum, İstanbul.

Plate 3.1. Johann Baptist Homann, "Imperii Persici," Nuremberg, [c. 1724]. The British Library Board, Maps K.Top. 114.96/C2491-04.

Plate 3.10. Frontiers of Europe. Nicolas de Fer, "L'Asie," inset, Paris, 1696. Photo Courtesy of the Newberry Library, Chicago, Novacco 8F 9.

Plate 4.2. Georg Matthäus Seutter, from Johann Baptist Homann [et al.], "Nova et Accurata Hungariae cum Adiacentib. Regn.," [*Weltatlas*], map 98, cartouche, [n.p.], [17–], Library Znanstvena knjižnica Zadar, ZKZD GA 10421-A.

Plate 4.4. Matrakçı Nasuh, "Tata Fortress," *Tarih-i Feth-i Şikloş ve Estergon ve Estolnibelgrad (History of the Conquest of Siklós, Esztérgom, and Székesfehérvar)*, H. 1608, 113b, İstanbul, c. 1545. Topkapı Palace Museum, İstanbul.

Plate 4.29. Ioannes van Deutecum and Lucas van Deutecum, after Matthias Zündt, ["Hungariae totius"], inset, [Antwerp], [1593]. Harvard Map Library, Harvard University, G6500_1593_28.

Plate 5.2. [Du Vignau, Sieur des Joanots] Person of Quality, "Soliman ye III. d," [*Secrétaire turc*. English] *A New Account of the Present Condition of Turkish Affairs*, frontispiece, London, 1688. By permission of the Folger Shakespeare Library, Shelfmark: D2922.

Plate 5.5. Sighetvar Campaign, Heads Presented to Grand Vezir Sokollu Mehmet. Ahmet Feridun Bey, *Nüshet ül-Esrar ul-Ahbar fi Sefer-i Szigetvar*, H. 1339, fol. 41b, İstanbul, [n.d.]. Topkapı Palace Museum, İstanbul.

Plate 5.11. John Capistrano Pulpit, mounted on Stephansdom, Vienna, exterior wall, with blue tarp. Photograph: Palmira Brummett.

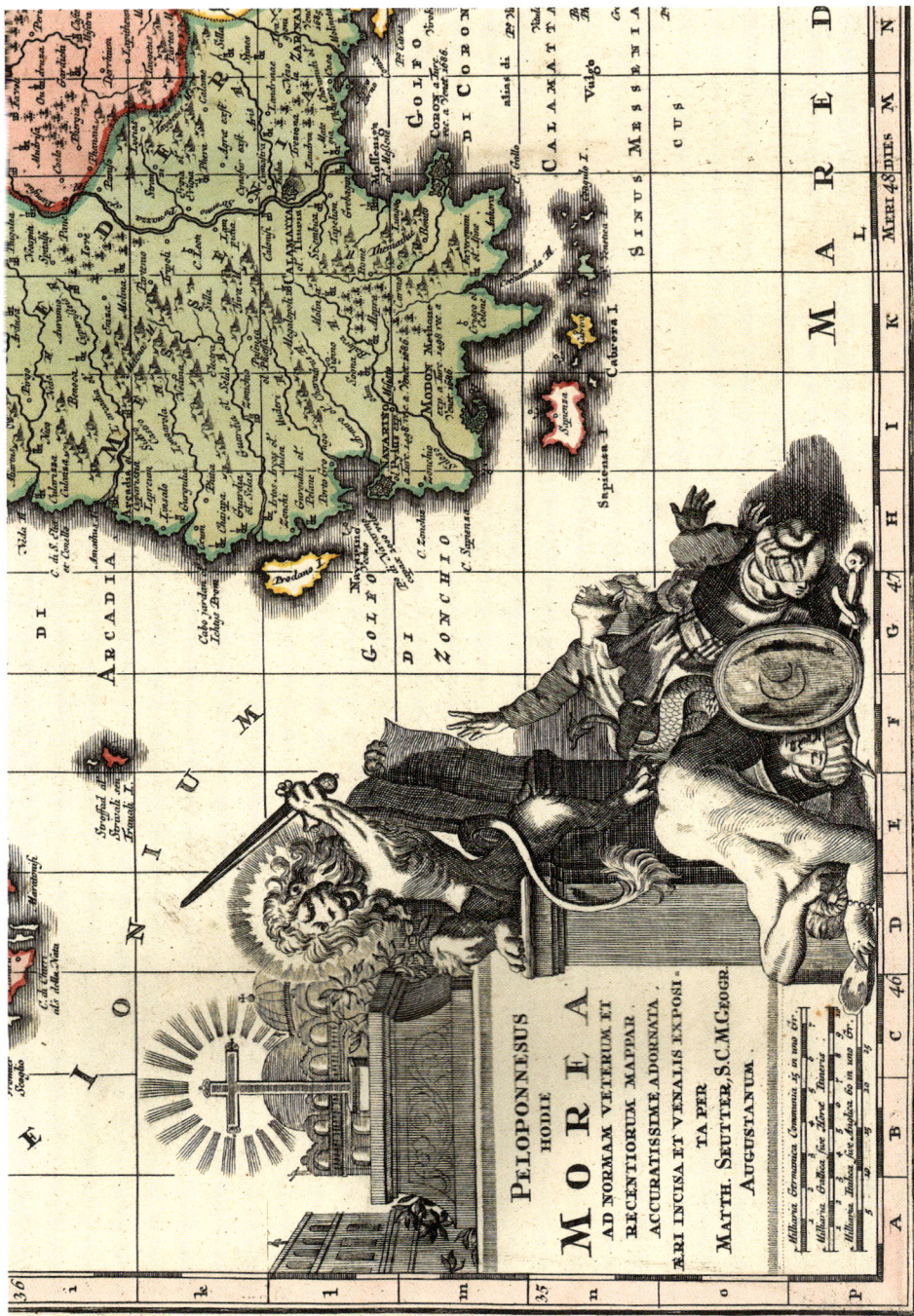

Plate 5.17. Georg Matthäus Seutter, Johann Baptist Homann [et al.], "Peloponnesus hodie Morea," map 102, cartouche [Weltatlas]. [n.p.] [17–]. Library Znanstvena knjižnica Zadar, ZKZD GA 10421-A.

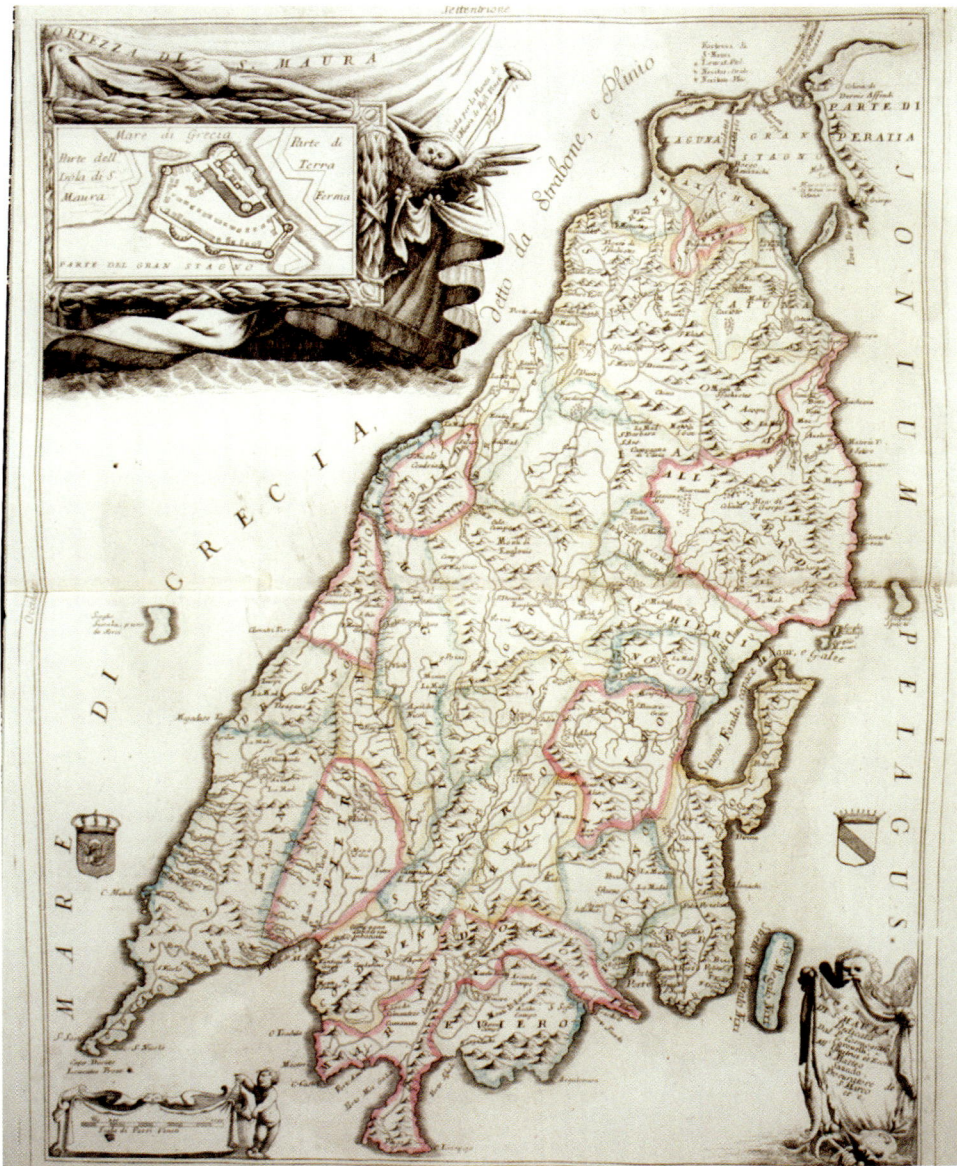

Plate 5.18. Vincenzo Coronelli, "Fortezza di Santa Maura," Venetia, [c. 1685]. The British Library Board, Maps C.27.g.16(.61).

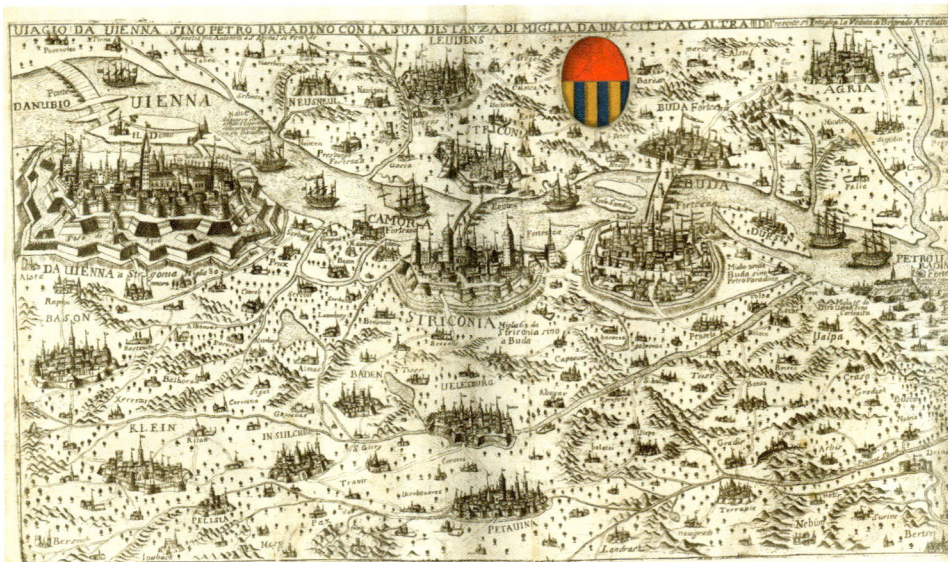

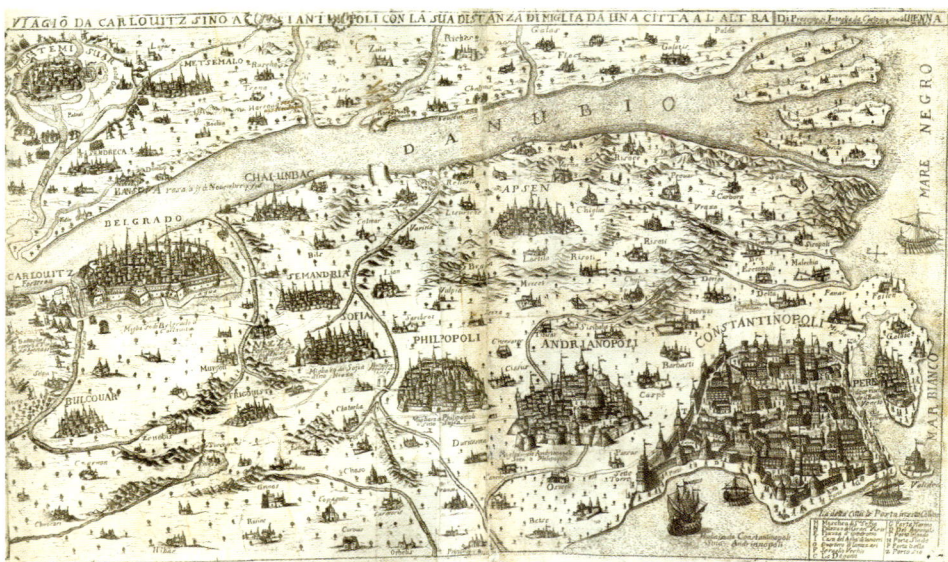

Plate 6.4. Vienna to Constantinople. Stefano Scolari, "Viagio Da Vienna Sino Petro Varadino, Con La Distanza Di Miglia Da Una Citta Al Altra. Viagio Da Carlovitz Sino A Costantinopoli . . . " [Venetia?], [c. 1717, from 1590 original]. Map divided into two parts. Photo Courtesy of the Newberry Library, Chicago, Novacco 2 F 184.

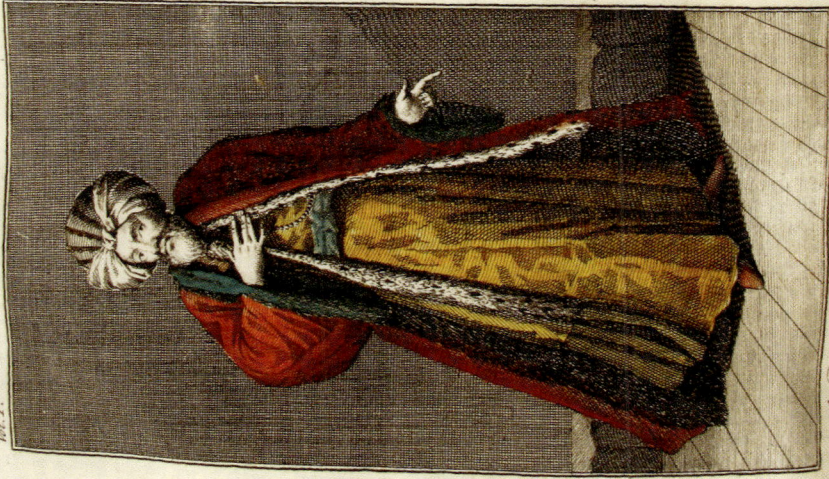

Plate 7.2. Thomas Salmon, Herman Moll, "A Turkish Gentleman, A Turkish Gentlewoman," *Modern History or the Present State of All Nations*, v. 1, after p. 414, London, 1744. Photo Courtesy of the Newberry Library, Chicago, Baskes folio G114.S17.

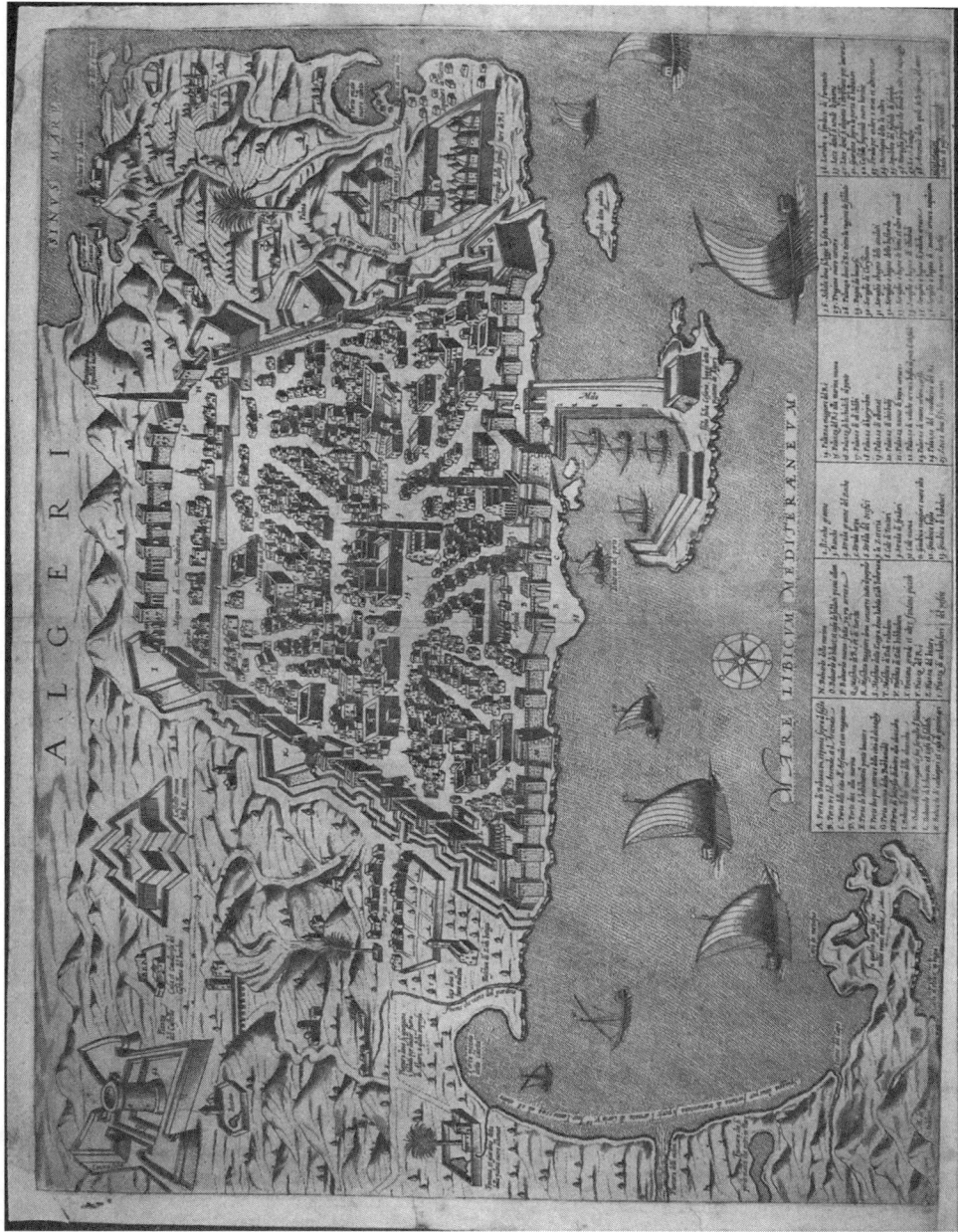

Figure 4.25. "Algeri" [n.p.], c. 1590. Photo Courtesy of the Newberry Library, Chicago, Novacco 4F 398.

armada of Emperor Charles V was lost, the 28th of October, 1541."[108] The map thus functioned as a memorial to the fortunes of seafaring and war, and the opportunity Charles lost to turn a "Turk" space into a "Christian" one.

A map printed by Bolognini Zaltieri (fl. 1560s) in Venice in 1566 takes a different tack, suggesting the social organization of such frontier ports and their hybrid identities (Fig. 4.26). Zaltieri's map envisioned the city of Tunis 'attached' to Europe, with Christian ships in the harbor and Christian forces on its land. His legend describes the city and surroundings: its old silted-in harbor of Carthage, its fruitful and barren hills, and its weak walls. Within those walls, "Christian soldiers" inhabit the Nifet quarter and "Arabs" occupy the Rabat quarter; the trade in cattle goes on in the piazza near the mosque. Although the city was at that time under the rule of the Hafsid dynasty (1228–1574), clients of Spain, it would change hands three times in the subsequent eight years, ending up a subordinate of the Ottoman sultan. In each case, conquest did not replace the population of the town, nor eliminate its trading activities; rather it altered the order (and sometimes the allegiance) of its communally mixed occupants.

That changing of hands, sharing of space, and counting of fortresses as sites of possession was echoed in the miniatures of the Ottoman *şehname* of Selim II, dating to 1581, which depicts the Ottoman conquests in 1569 and 1574.[109] It was also was echoed in the Arabic travel account of al-Tamjruti (d. 1594), the Moroccan ambassador to Istanbul in 1590, who included a short history of Tunis in his embassy narrative:

> *The Turks seized it [Tunis] from the last Hafsides [in 1533], but then the Christians conquered it with the help of the Hafsides who had remained there. The Christians divided the city in half between them and the remaining Muslims... [and] built a magnificent and strong fort... that the Turks were unable to raze when they seized the city. They filled it with provisions, equipment, men, and cannons to the point where they believed they had come to possess the land and that none could ever dislodge them. But the Turks attacked them with 450 ships from Constantinople and the rest of Africa... they laid siege to the Halq al-Wadi [one of the city's three ports], after which they seized it. They then took the other two forts and the city fort and spread out into the rest of the land... That happened in the year 982 [August 1574].*[110]

---

[108] "Algeri," c. 1590, Newberry Library, Novacco 4F 398. See also a map of "De stad Algiers," by Hendrik de Leth (1692–1759), in Amsterdam, British Library, Maps C.2491.02, which shows a panorama of the port from the sea as an inset to a broader map of the coast of "Barbarie" and the sea leading up to a segment of the Spanish peninsula. Two other insets show the "Baye D'Alger, and the fortress of "Cercelli," complete with crescents but no conflict. See also Mehmet Tütüncü, *Cezair'de Osmanlı İzleri (1516–1830)* (İstanbul: Çamlıca Basım, 2013), 58–77, 258–9, for some early modern Ottoman and French imagery of the Barbarossas and Algiers.

[109] Emine Fetvacı, "Others and Other Geographies in the Şehnāme-i Selīm Hān," *Osmanlı Araştırmaları/Journal of Ottoman Studies* 40, (2012): 81–100, see 89–93.

[110] Quoted in Nabil Matar, *Europe Through Arab Eyes, 1578–1727*, 149, 151. On the effects of Charles V's temporary capture of Tunis and its contexts in Hungary, see Perjés, *The Fall of the Medieval Kingdom of Hungary*, 147.

Figure 4.26. Bolognini Zaltieri ["Tunis and Goletta"], Venetia, 1566. Photo Courtesy of the Newberry Library, Chicago, Novacco 2F 243.

Tunis, for the ambassador, was connected to Istanbul, its conquest symbolizing the sultan's imperial reach. And when al-Tamjruti counted that Turk "territory" in miles he included both land spaces and the sea spaces in between.[111]

Jerba, Malta, and other island and coastal territories of the Mediterranean were linked in the spatial imagination of early modern observers by the confrontations of Christian and Muslim armadas but also by the activities of pirates.[112] Thus the corsairing initiatives of the Knights of Malta and of the petty governors of North Africa transcended the sovereign claims of empires (and the simple dichotomies of maps). Witnesses from both sides of the Mediterranean described the piratical sea and the crucial role that Malta, like Rhodes before it, played. Al-Tamjruti described his voyage to Istanbul as fraught with danger from lurking corsairs of all sorts, "Christian and Muslim mariners."[113] Piracy was also a primary concern for Ibn Abi Dinar, who wrote a history of Tunis in the later seventeenth century, as Nabil Matar tells us. "Maltese galleons," he wrote, served as both predator and prey for the deys of Tunis. The "city celebrated their seizure" in 1625 and suffered their depredations at other times.[114]

Another witness, J.P. Laugier de Tassy, in his 1725 history of Algiers, suggested that such brigandage, whether by sea or by land, was a universal human characteristic:

> It is said that the Arabs and the Moors of Barbary are brigands, thieves, and miscreants who ruin Christian travelers, kill or enslave them, and pillage the ships, including those of the Turks, that founder near their shores... The Arabs and the Moors in their turn are subjugated by the Christians and by the Turks, losing all they have... and held in abject misery... Should one then be astonished [by the actions of the Barbary pirates] since in the most well ordered states one does not lack for thieves and assassins [even though they] face the most hideous punishments? Have the Pyrenees no more Miquelets, the Alps no more Montagnards? Is there a shortage in Sardinia and Corsica of office-holding bandits and assassins, protected by the Seigneurs of the Lands and Forests? In that regard, one must acknowledge that the Christians more or less resemble the Barbarians.[115]

---

[111] Matar, *Europe through Arab Eyes*, 158. Thus the journey from Morocco to Istanbul covered "3,200 miles. Seven hundred miles were in the territory of the Turks, from Constantinople to Modon..."

[112] See Molly Greene, *Catholic Pirates and Greek Merchants: A Maritime History of the Mediterranean* (Princeton, NJ: Princeton University Press, 2010), 7, 133–5, 146, which focuses on Malta, legal actions, and the struggle to establish identity and ownership in the transcommunal spaces of the Mediterranean.

[113] Matar, *Europe through Arab Eyes*, 148.

[114] Matar, *Europe through Arab Eyes*, 222, 224. Julia Clancy-Smith, *Mediterraneans: North Africa and Europe in an Age of Migration, c. 1800–1900* (Berkeley: University of California Press, 2012), has traced the elaborate connectivity of Malta, Tunis, and Algiers for a later period.

[115] [Jacques Philippe] Laugier de Tassy, *Histoire du royaume d'Alger, Avec l'etat de son gouvernement de ses forces de terre & de mer, de ses revenus, police, justice politique, & commerce* (Amsterdam: Chez Henri du Sauzet, 1725; reprint N.P.: Elibron Classics, 2007), 311–12.

De Tassy thus not only points out the transcommunal, transimperial operations of the piratic class, but also suggests the relationships between the predators of mountains and coasts and their seigniorial patrons. These diverse competitors problematized simple dichotomies of Christian vs. "Turk." The homogenizing categories of a cartographic "us" and "them," seldom did them justice. But the strongholds of mountain and coast sheltered both "seigneur" and "bandit," one reason, perhaps, that the fortress was such a focus of both government policy and cartographic representation.

Portraits and Possession

Although the fortress thus measured out the spaces of both land and sea and marked them as Ottoman, Christian, or something in between, there were other options for stamping possession onto the map. Portraits served this function, using the kingly visage like a flag, a tugh (horsetail standard), a crescent, or a coat of arms, to claim territory. Portraits did not necessarily depict the warrior Turk, or the infidel Turk; sometimes they represented the benign, the sovereign, or the imperial Turk, a monarch like any other.[116] One finds such portraits of the sultan, the vezir, or the Ottoman admiral, for example, in G. Franco's book of "major princes and valiant captains," published in Venice in 1596, or in George de la Chapelle's *Recueil de divers portraits des principales dames de la Porte du Grand Turc*, published in Paris in 1648.[117] As these images multiplied and circulated, they logically found their way onto the body of the map. The same year that Franco's work appeared, Johan Bussemecher (fl. 1580–1613), in Cologne, published a map of Sclavonia on which one finds a portrait of Kaiser Rudolph II (Holy Roman Emperor 1576–1612) looking out over what is apparently his territory: Sclavonia, Croatia, Bosnia, and Dalmatia (Fig. 4.27).[118]

[116] See Selmin Kangal, ed., *The Sultan's Portrait: Picturing the House of Osman* (İstanbul: İşbank, 1999); Hans Geog Majer, "Europäische und osmanische Sultansporträts," 37–42, in *Im Lichte des Halbmonds*; Alastair Hamilton, *Arab Culture and Ottoman Magnificence in Antwerp's Golden Age* (Oxford: Arcadian Library and Oxford University Press, 2001), 27, 45, 47; and Gerald MacLean and William Dalrymple, eds., *Re-Orienting the Renaissance: Cultural Exchange with the East* (London: Palgrave, 2005).

[117] Pirovano, ed., *Venezia e i Turchi*, 104; the work is G. Franco, *Effiggie naturali dei maggior prencipi et più valorosi capitani di questa età con l'arme loro*. For the frontispiece of Chapelle's work, see Nurhan Atasoy and Lale Uluç, *Impressions of Ottoman Culture in Europe: 1453–1699* (İstanbul: Turkish Cultural Foundation, 2012), 356. Portraits might include queenly Turks. See Hegyi, *The Ottoman Empire in Europe*, 40, for a portrait of Roxelana, Hurrem Sultan, wife of Süleyman II; and *Im Lichte des Halbmonds*, 165, 196, catalog nos. 196–7, for mournful and bold images of Kara Mustafa Pasha done in Vienna and Amsterdam.

[118] Ioani Bussemechers [Johan Bussemacher], "Sclavonia, Croatia, Bosnia & Dalmatiae Pars Maior," [Köln], 1596, British Library, Maps C.39.c.1. In a rather different type of portrait image, "Rudolphus II Romanorum Imperator Augustus Rex," lord of Hungary, Bohemia, and other lands, a 1603 commemorative scene, the Flemish engraver Aegidius Sadeler II (c. 1570–1629) embeds the "Roman" emperor's triumphant portrait medallion in a monument; and crouched before that monument are two bare-chested battle captives, one (clearly a "Turk") leaning on what appears to be a turban, and the other (possibly an Ottoman vassal) kneeling beside his own displaced hat. Elsewhere, Maurice Bouguereau, "*Le Théâtre françois*," 1594, depicts Henry IV smiling contentedly over a map of France, as shown in Tom Conley, *The Self-Made Map*, 215.

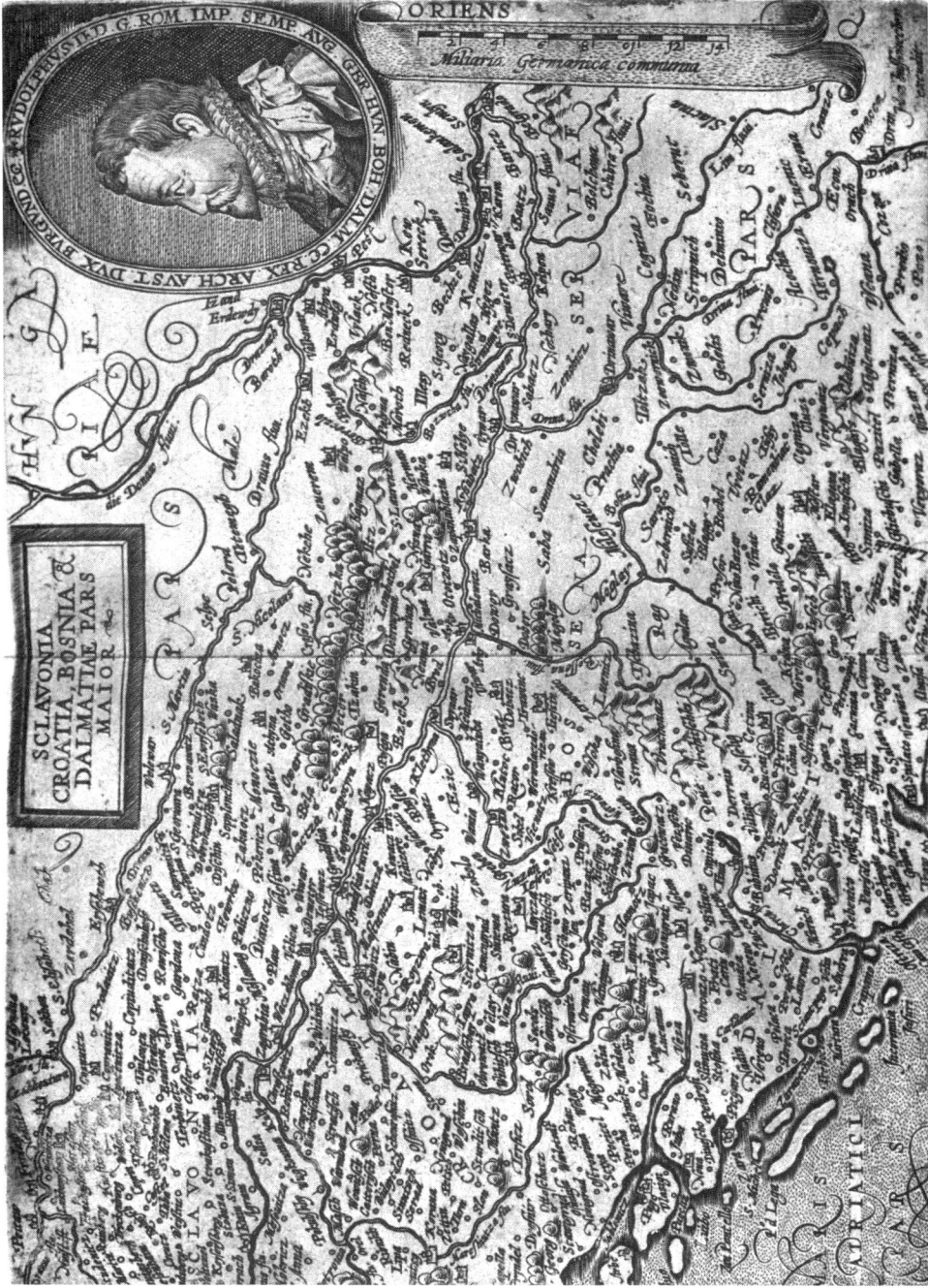

Figure 4.27. Johan Bussemecher, "Sclavonia, Croatia, Bosnia & Dalmatiae Pars Maior," Cologne, 1596. The British Library Board, Maps C.39. c.1 (.70).

There is no evidence of Ottoman claims or penetration on the map of Sclavonia. But on a partner map of the same vintage, Bussemecher shows Thrace, Bulgaria, and surrounding lands portrayed as Ottoman space, identified as such by the proprietorial gaze of the sultan, Mehmet III (r. 1595–1603), whose portrait appears in the lower left corner (Fig. 4.28).[119] The sultan here is an exact counterpart to the kaiser. His portrait links the western reaches of Ottoman domains (real and claimed) to the imperial Ottoman capital, Istanbul. The Balkan outlands look back to their "hinterland" just as islands like Malta or Tenedos were made to "look back" to the mainlands that claimed them. In such cartographic assertions, two sovereigns could occupy the same landmass or sea space. Another, earlier map of "All Hungary," originally done in 1567 by the Nuremberg mapmaker Matthias Zündt (from whom Bussemecher may have drawn his inspiration), shows Rudolph sharing the Balkan space with Mehmet's predecessor, Murat III (r. 1574–95) (Fig. 4.29).[120] Framed by the Danube and its tributaries, portraits of both monarchs occupy a contested territory that is neither east nor west. In this juxtaposition, however, the kings gaze off into the distance; they do not appear to challenge each other.

Sometimes the fortress itself, rather than the human masters of land and sea, was encircled in portrait form. Thus, for example, on the English historian and mapmaker John Speed's (1552–1629) well-known 1626 map, "The Turkish Empire," the representation of the sultan's domains is surrounded by a series of ethnographic vignettes and portrait medallions of fortresses (Fig. 4.30).[121] These represent major inland and coastal fortifications, such as Constantinople, Famagosta, and Jerusalem, lost possessions of Christendom.[122] The map itself labels rivers, seas, cities, and regions; but the surrounding portraits give the empire its identity through built and fortified spaces and ethnic types. There is no ethnic "Turk," however; rather the "armes of Turkie" are represented in the map's cartouche by the face of a

[119] Ioani Bussemechers [Johan Bussemacher], "Thracia Et Bulgaria Cum Viciniis" [Köln], 1596. He is mistakenly designated as Mehmet II, although the year of his accession is indicated correctly. For other portrait medallions of sultans on fortress map imagery, see Béla, "A tizenöt éves háború metszetábrázolásai a frankfurti vásári tudósításokban (1593–1606)," 26, 32, 38, in conjunction with some stunning German siege maps.

[120] Ioannes van Deutecum and Lucas van Deutecum, Matthias Zündt, "Hungariae Totius", [Nuremberg, c. 1567]. Karrow, *Mapmakers of the Sixteenth Century*, 618–19, notes that Gerard de Jode in Antwerp "made a reduced copy" for his *Speculum orbis terrarum* in 1578. This particular version may have been done by de Jode's son Cornelis. The original by Zündt, done in Nuremberg in 1567, did not contain the portrait medallions. See also Hegyi, *The Ottoman Empire in Europe*, 28, for a portrait map of the siege of Vienna. In 1708 the emperor's representative in Istanbul, Michael von Talman, claimed to have deflected Ottoman war aspirations by showing the chief black eunuch and master of the hunt a portrait of the blond emperor Joseph and citing a prophecy that a blond ruler would take Constantinople from Islam. See Roider, *Austria's Eastern Question*, 30.

[121] Speed's map is similar in this regard to Willem Blaeu's, "Asia Noviter Delineata," c. 1635, based on his 1608 wall map. See Koeman et al., "Commercial Cartography and Map Production in the Low Countries," *HOC*, v.3, pt. 2, 1350–52. On Speed, see Peter Barber, "Mapmaking in England, ca. 1470–1650," 1589–1669, in *HOC*, v. 3, pt. 2, 1635–6; and Laurence Worms, "The London Map Trade to 1640," 1693–1721, in *HOC*, v. 3, pt. 2, 1710–11.

[122] Speed, "The Turkish Empire" [London], 1626. Astango, *La cartografia nautica mediterranea*, 64–6, treats of the use of edge vignettes of fortresses and cities as well as issues of "accuracy" in Italian nautical charts.

Figure 4.28. Johan Bussemecher, "Thracia et Bulgaria Cum Viciniis," Cologne, 1596. The British Library Board, Maps C.39. c.1(.67).

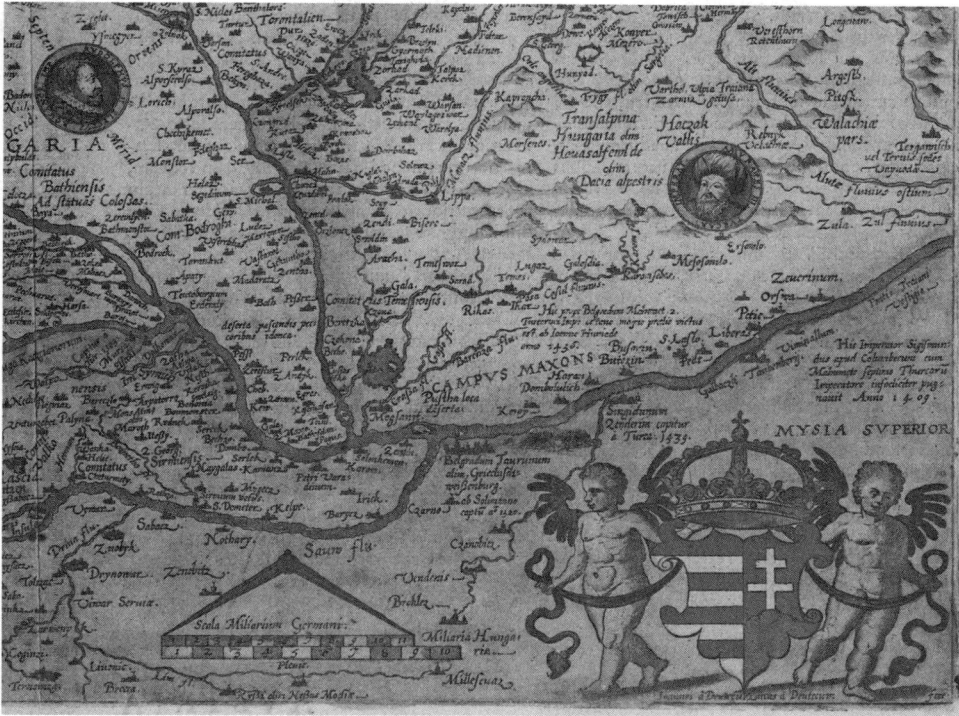

Figure 4.29. Ioannes van Deutecum and Lucas van Deutecum, after Matthias Zündt ["Hungariae totius"], inset [Antwerp], [1593]. Harvard Map Library, Harvard University, G6500_1593_28. (See color plate)

crescent moon, and on the body of the map by historical legends of Ottoman conquest. In Speed's narrative "Description of the Turkish Empire," the emphasis on expansion and ethnography continues. He declares that "The Turke is admired for nothing more, than his sodaine aduancement to so great an Empire"; and he lists the provinces of the empire in Europe, Africa, and Asia, noting which ones "run" along the seacoast.[123] Text and image thus present the empire in terms of place and people, cities and provinces, maritime and inland space. The fortress vignettes on his map are the concrete embodiment of those places, now occupied by the Ottomans, that Speed's countrymen hoped to recapture.

Another mapmaker who employed the fortress-portrait to decorate his maps was Vincenzo Coronelli, the seventeenth century monk and cartographer, whose works were widely copied across Europe.[124] In his Venetian *Isolario* of 1696, Coronelli placed fortress medallions all around a map commemorating Doge Francesco Morosini's (r. 1688–94) conquest of Corinth (Fig. 4.31).[125] Each vignette (including Modon and Lepanto) provides a

[123] John Speed, *Prospect of the Most Famous Parts of the World* (London: By M.F. for W. Humble, 1646), 35–6, contains the map of the empire but without the ethnographic and fortress vignettes.

[124] See Armao, *Vincenzo Coronelli: cenni sull'uomo*; and Midhat Kozličić, *Kartografski Spomenici Hrvatskoga Jadrana: Izbor karata, planova i veduta do kraja 17 stoljeća* (Zagreb: AGM, 1995), 258–75, for more of Coronelli's fortress images.

Figure 4.30. John Speed, "The Turkish Empire," *Prospect of the Most Famous Parts of the World*, pl. 18, inset, London, 1627. Geography and Map Division, Library of Congress, G1015 .S73 Vault.

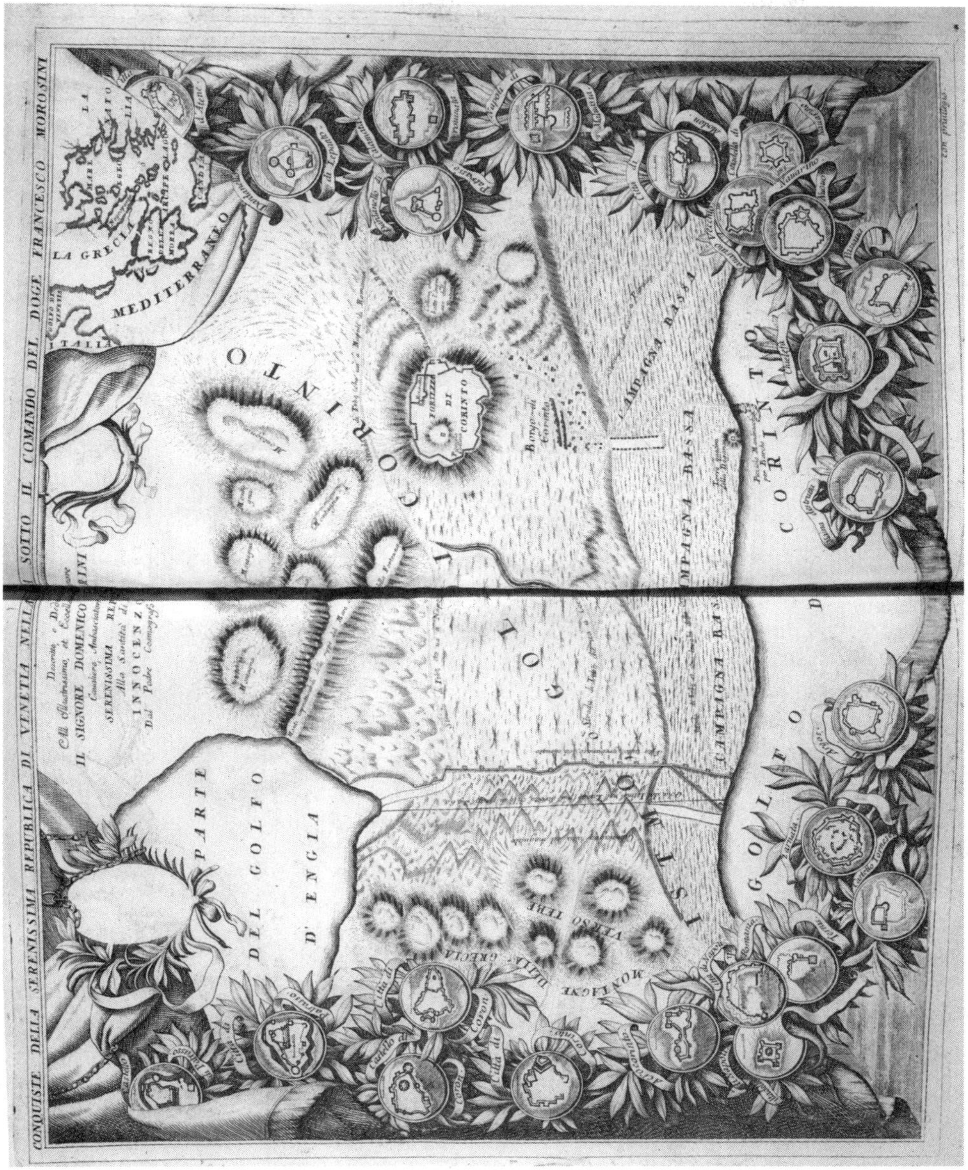

Figure 4.31. Vincenzo Coronelli, "Golfo di Corinto," *Isolario [dell'Atlante Veneto]*, v. 1, map 14, Venetia, c. 1696. Photo Courtesy of the Newberry Library, Chicago, Ayer 135.C8 1696.

schematic of the fortress depicted. The real message, however, is not the nature of fortifications but the advancement of Venetian objectives, a poke in the eye to the territorial ambitions of the Ottomans.

Portraits, whether of monarchs or of fortresses, thus embodied the ownership of space in the transimperial zone.[126] Maps and other texts allowed ownership to be "maintained" even when it had been lost, or asserted when it had not been won. And even when ownership had been achieved through conquest, it was never easy to expunge the portraits of past owners, as Evliya Çelebi tells us. Describing the Albanian fortress of Gjirokastër, held by the Ottomans in 1670, he wrote

> Its initial founder was the son of Philip, one of the Greek kings. It later fell into the hands of various rulers and finally . . . was seized from Albanian rebels by Sultan Bayezid II (r. 1481–1512) the Saint in person. Many buildings in Gjirokastër appear to have been built by the Venetian infidels because you can see portraits of Saint Mark on them, which is the symbol of Venice.[127]

The portraits of St. Mark thus preserved the "face" of Venice in the fortress, long after it had passed into Ottoman hands. Evliya did not seem to mind. The images of St. Mark simply represented one stage in the history of Gjirokastër. The current stage belonged to the sultan.

[125] Coronelli, *Isolario* [*dell'Atlante Veneto*], 1696, plate after page 181; also the map of Corfu, located after page 167 in this atlas. Coronelli used such fortress vignettes elsewhere as in his map of the Gulf of Arta with an inset, "Golfo Della Prevesa," plate 13 in Coronelli, *Atlante Veneto*, v. 1 (Venetia: 1690). In the same year Hubert Jaillot published in Paris a map based on Coronelli's (*dressé sur les Memoires les plus Nouveaux du P. Coronelli & autres*) map of the Gulf of Venice complete with fortress vignettes. See also S. de Beaulieu's 1674 and F. de Witt's 1680 maps of Crete, with fortress insets, in Sphyroeras, Avramea, and Asdrahas, *Maps and Map-Makers*, 128–9, 134–5, plates 84 and 88. In Beaulieu's map, "Candie" is framed by both fortresses and smaller islands.

[126] On the notion of city portraits, see Renzo Dubbini, *Geography of the Gaze in Early Modern Europe*, Lydia Cochrane, trans. (Chicago: University of Chicago Press, 2002), 50.

[127] Evliya Çelebi, *Evliya Çelebi in Albania*, 71.

5

Heads and Skins

Mapping the Fallen Turk

> [The Ottomans] are most certainly, very able to make a great Noise,
> to express themselves in their Discourses and Writings, with emphatick
> and swelling Terms, big with Vanity and Ostentation, extending them-
> selves in campaigns, to appear more numerous than they are, and in
> shewing themselves desperate on Breaches, the Scimitar in their Hands,
> themselves half-naked, bawling and roaring like posses'd People, to
> imprint Terror, and cut off mens Heads when they have first struck
> them with this foolish Fear. But those who are concerned and inter-
> ested, should know how to deal with them . . .'

> [Du Vignau, Sieur des Joanots] Person of Quality, *A New Account of the
> Present Condition of Turkish Affairs*, 1688.[1]

For the French author who wrote this description, the Ottoman in the
"breach," scimitar in hand, was indelibly linked to the Ottoman in text. He
was a familiar character in early modern European literatures, with 'known'
characteristics such as an inclination toward head cutting and noisy attempts
to impress and terrorize. Readers had the testimony, for example, of the
Polish captive Albertus Bobovius (1610–75), an instructor of music in the
Ottoman palace for nineteen years in the mid-seventeenth century, who wrote
of the grand vezir Köprülü Mehmet Pasha, "He had no other expedient for
maintaining his power than to cut off the heads of the most elevated and
of those exercising feelings of jealousy."[2] Similarly, English "Turk" plays
(e.g., *Selimus Emperour of the Turks*, 1594) illustrate the fascination with

---

[1] [Du Vignau, Sieur des Joanots], Person of Quality, *A New Account of the Present Condition of Turkish
Affairs* (London: Randall Taylor, 1688), 117–18.

[2] C. G. Fisher and A. Fisher, "Topkapı Sarayı in the Mid-Seventeenth Century: Bobovi's Description,"
5–81, *Archivum ottomanicum* (1985–1987): 57. The authors provide an English translation from a
1686 manuscript translation of Bobovi's c. 1657 work.

Ottoman decapitations on the battlefield and with punishments such as the formal strangulation of members of the Ottoman elite who had fallen from favor.[3] Capital punishments seemed in these literatures to be a particular Ottoman preserve.

A brief survey of world history, however, clearly demonstrates that the taking of heads was hardly restricted to Ottoman courts or lands. How then, do we account for the prominence of such brutalities in visualizations of the Ottoman polity? First of all, in the hard-fought struggles for sovereignty over the sprawling frontier zone between Muslim and Christian lords, the taking of enemy heads was a universally understood symbol of dominance and humiliation, a declaration of possession of that which the enemy held most dear, and a customary mode of enacting vengeance. Once heads were taken they needed to be displayed, in fact, in word, and in image. That display was more than a declaration of victory, power, and prestige. It was a public gift that could be witnessed and enjoyed by king, army, and public alike. Early modern audiences demanded the display of enemy heads and the narration of the shedding of blood. Hence the various works of the time took pains to enhance their tales of combat with pictures of enemy heads, either attached in the case of captives destined to be sold into slavery, or detached in the case of those slain in battle or its aftermath.[4] Within this violent frame, the Ottomans were pictured losing or taking heads, as a means of both associating them with barbarism and putting them in their place.

Where Chapter 4 addressed the rhetorics of place, situating the Ottomans in their fortress strongholds, this chapter addresses the rhetorics of people and how they might best be controlled. As Du Vignau proposes in the opening quote, those who paid attention would know how to deal with the Turks. And there was no better way to silence the "noise" of the Ottoman enemy than to show him (in stories, histories, broadsheets, or maps) losing his head. The arrogant Turk could thereby be turned into the fallen Turk.

The Ottomans, as we have seen, were the subject of a complex representational system motivated by fear, curiosity, and the desire for knowledge. The "Turk," in that system, was often ferocious and militant, though sometimes benign, noble, or convivial. Thus a primary and reassuring element of this matrix of narrative and pictorial representation was the fallen Turk, an iconic figure representing the accomplishments and aspirations of the Christian kings and their publics.[5] The fallen Turk signified that the Ottoman empire could be beaten, lost territories recovered, and the glory of state and

---

3   See Vitkus, *Three Turk Plays*; and Dimmock, *New Turks: Dramatizing Islam*.

4   See Salomon Schweigger, *Ein newe reyssbeschreibung auss Teutschland nach Constantinople und Jerusalem . . .*, Rudolf Neck, ed. (Nürnberg: Casper Fulden, 1619; reprint Graz: Akademische Druck v. Verlagsanstalt, 1964), 94, for a woodcut depicting Ottoman-held Christian captives and heads; or Wratislaw, *Adventures*, 101, which depicts captives bearing heads being marched into Istanbul. The display of enemy heads is a phenomenon that survived into the modern era in East and West, although the public taste for such emblems has diminished.

5   Female "Turks" also appeared but with nowhere near the frequency of male. On the gendered body in early modern European cartouches, see Valerie Traub, "Mapping the Global Body," 43–97 in *Early Modern Visual Culture: Representation, Race, and Empire in Renaissance England*, Peter Erickson and Clark Hulse, eds. (Philadelphia: University of Pennsylvania Press, 2000).

faith resurrected. His head was a grisly souvenir marking the boundaries of both territory and masculine honor.

Accordingly, I propose here to zero in on the imagery of the fallen Turk. But by way of introduction, the first section of this chapter will present a historiography of sorts of the taking and display of heads in a broader temporal, spatial, and cultural context. I hope thereby to set the stage for a presentation of the ways in which the Ottomans, their heads, and their territory were mapped in the lands of the Christian kings. The second section will juxtapose representations of the taking of heads and of captives in the texts and imagery of the Ottoman empire and its European Christian rivals. And the third section will transition from the broader rhetorics of the fallen Turk to those produced particularly for the cartographic space and the audiences of European Christendom.

In early modern imagery, the head (and body) of the Turk appeared in various forms (Figs. 5.1–5.3).[6] Portraits of Ottomans, particularly the visage of the sultan, decorated histories and broadsheets. Ethnographic "Turks" appeared in the stock images of costume manuals, or as artistic supplements to diplomatic reports and travel literature.[7] "Turks" also sauntered, swaggered, and pranced across the stages and streets of Europe.[8] Not surprisingly, then, the image of the Turk and his head also made its way into the cartographic space (Fig. 5.4).[9] Sometimes, the head of a turbaned Turk provided part of the decorative flourishes on the map cartouche. In other cases the Turk's head served a more particular function, suggesting the location of the edge of Europe, and the conflictual relations of the transimperial frontier. Displaying the enemy head was emblematic of the restoration, however

---

[6] See, for example, Arthur Hind and Margery Corbett, *Engraving in England in the Sixteenth and Seventeenth Centuries: A Descriptive Catalogue*, v. 2 (Cambridge: Cambridge University Press, 1964), plates 136a, 144c, v. 3, plate 27b; and *Colorful Impressions*, 75. In 1737 Carle Vanloo produced a painting entitled "The Grand Turk giving a Concert to His Mistress", which later served as a model for individual images of Turks' heads, including "Head of a Man Wearing Plumed Turban," from the atelier of Billes Demarteau the Elder, 1772.

[7] On Ottoman costume and representations thereof see, for example, Cesare Vecellio, *Vecellio's Renaissance Costume Book* (New York: Dover, 1977, reprint of *Degli habiti antiche, et moderni di tutto il mondo* (Venetia: Giovanni Bernardo Sessa, 1598), 110–18; this was the second edition of Vecellio's much copied costume book. See Bronwen Wilson, "Foggi diverse di vestire de' Turchi," 125, on Venetian–Ottoman portrait sharing. Leslie Meral Schick, "The Place of Dress in Pre-modern Costume Albums," 93–101, in Faroqhi and Neuman, eds., *Ottoman Costumes*, argues that the Ottoman costume manual was "meant to be no less than a portrait of society, conveniently packaged for the consumption of the European and later also the upper-class Ottoman public (93)."

[8] The head of a defeated "Turk" graces the entryway to the riding school at Versailles, while a beautiful colored "Carte du canal des Dardanelles," produced in Paris in 1686, is embellished with a cartouche of chained, kneeling, and bare-chested Turks. See Bilici, *XIV Louis ve İstanbul'u Fetih Tasarısı*, 61, 133–7, 145–6, 150. And a 1543 inventory of the Ducal Palace at Nancy in Lorraine lists among the objects in its *Kunstkammer* "Le portrait en pappier de la teste du grand Turque; Plusieurs acoustremens de Turquie de differentes façons, le tout fait de plumes de perroquetz et de paon; Le portrait d'une teste de turcque en cuyr"; see Paulette Choné, "Le portrait du Turc: Les artistes devant le rêve héroïque de la maison de Lorraine (XVIe-XVIIe siècles)," 61–74, in *Chrétiens et musulmans à la Renaissance*, Actes du 37e colloque international du CESR (1994), Bartolomé Bennassar and Robert Sauzet, eds. (Paris: Honoré Champion, 1998), 61–2.

[9] For example, John Senex (1678–1740), from G. de l'Isle, "A Map of Turky, Arabia, and Persia: Corrected from the latest Travels and from ye Observations of ye Royal Society's [sic.] of London and Paris," London, [c. 1721].

Figure 5.1. Wenceslaus Hollar (1607–77) ["Turk's Head"], Antwerp, 1645. By permission of the Folger Shakespeare Library, Shelfmark: ART 254–213 (size S).

temporary, of "proper" order in an imagined or hoped-for hierarchy of possession and prestige.

History in Heads

Historically, depicting the taking of fortress walls has not sufficed to convey the glory of conquerors. That glory was contingent upon the image of a land's populace, soldiers, and lords being made to submit. And a prominent signifier of that submission has been the severed head; it possesses a timeless ability to

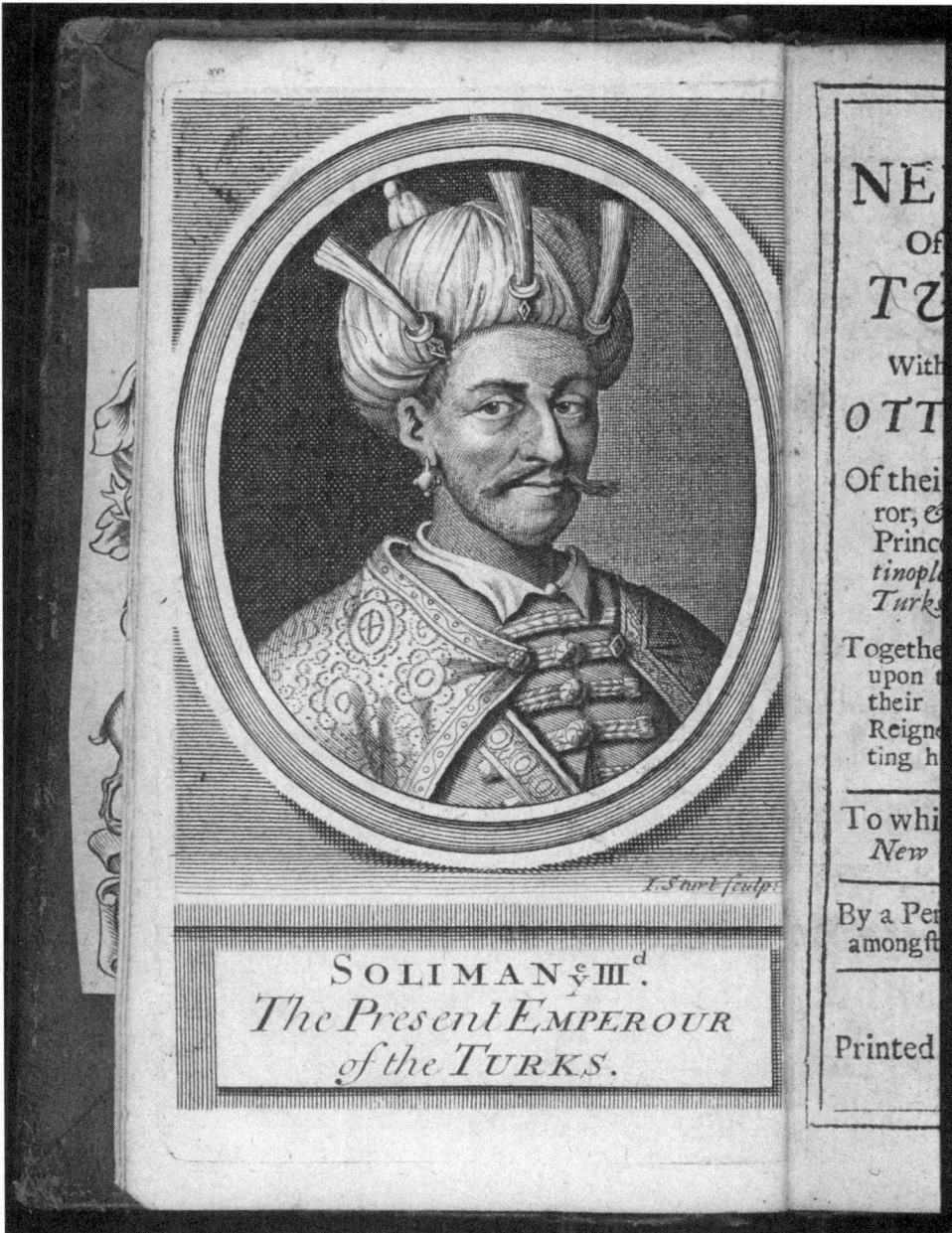

Figure 5.2. [Du Vignau, Sieur des Joanots] Person of Quality, "Soliman ye III.d" [*Secrétaire turc*. English] *A New Account of the Present Condition of Turkish Affairs*, frontispiece, London, 1688. By permission of the Folger Shakespeare Library, Shelfmark: D2922. (See color plate)

awe and disturb the viewer.[10] As a symbol of victory, justice, and masculine honor, it transcends the boundaries of time, ethnicity, region, and religion. For example, in the history of the Grand Historian of China, Sima Qian

[10] Richard Onians, *The Origins of European Thought: About the Body, the Mind, the Soul, the World, Time, and Fate* (Cambridge: Cambridge University Press, 1954), 93–109, 129–67.

Figure 5.3. Janissary. Nicolas de Nicolay, "Ianissaire allant à la guerre," *Les navigations peregrinations et voyages*, fol. 137, Antwerp, 1576. *64–730, Houghton Library, Harvard University.

(c. 145–86 B.C.E.), concerning the era of Emperor Wu (r. 141–87 B.C.E.), one finds the following cross-cultural observations on the wars between the Chinese and their Central Asian foes the Xiongnu:

> Whenever the Hsiung-nu [Xiongnu] begin some undertaking, they
> observe the stars and the moon. They attack when the moon is full

Figure 5.4. John Senex, from G. de l'Isle, "A Map of Turky, Arabia and Persia," cartouche, London, 1721. Geography and Map Division, Library of Congress, G7420 1721. M3 TIL Vault.

and withdraw their troops when it wanes. After a battle those who have cut off the heads of the enemy or taken prisoners are presented with a cup of wine and allowed to keep the spoils they have captured. Any prisoners that are taken are made slaves. Therefore, when they fight, each man strives for his own gain . . . When they catch sight of the enemy, they swoop down like a flock of birds, eager for booty, but

*when they find themselves hard pressed and beaten, they scatter and
vanish like the mist.*[11]

Although illustrating the Central Asian warriors' use of the enemy head as
booty, the same source acknowledges the Chinese use of the enemy head as
public spectacle and mode of intimidation:

> *At this time the emperor was making a tour of the border [c. 111
> B.C.] . . . [he dispatched] a man named Kuo Chi to the Shan-yü [leader
> of the Xiongnu] to make sure that [they] were fully informed of the
> event. When Kuo Chi . . . was shown before the Shan-yü he said, 'The
> head of the king of Southern Yüeh hangs above the northern gate of the
> Han capital. Now, if you are able, advance and engage the Han forces
> in battle! The Son of Heaven has led his troops in person and is waiting
> on the border. But if you are not able, then turn your face to the south
> and acknowledge yourself a subject of the Han! . . .'*[12]

Thus Kuo Chi aggressively confronted the Han's own particular brand of
'Turks.' The Shan-yü responded to this diplomatic nicety with rage; he had
his master-of-guests cut down on the spot, and detained Kuo Chi. But he was
not baited into attacking the Chinese. This episode provides an object lesson
in the universal message of the severed head in a context in which the Han
emissary had no doubt concerning who exactly constituted the "civilized"
and who the "barbarian."

Moving westward, and to a later, Muslim context, the protocols of submission and of heads are depicted in the unusual and personal memoir of
the Mughul emperor Zahiruddin Muhammad Babur (r. 1526–30) as he too
relates his dealings with conquered foes and contested territories. Babur was
a contemporary of the Ottoman sultans Selim I (r. 1512–20) and Süleyman I
(r. 1520–66). His *Baburnama* reveals the crucial nature of contests for power
and ceremonies of submission and their role in defining the boundaries of
territory and status.[13] The conjunction of these elements is perhaps best
expressed during Babur's conquest and pacification of the territory around
Bhera, northwest of Lahore. There Babur relates that one of his new subordinates, Muhammad Ali Jang-Jang, was anxious to stay in Bhera. That region,
however, had already been given to Hindu Beg; so Muhammad Ali Jang-Jang
was awarded the territories between Bhera and the Indus. Editorializing on
that distribution of governed space, Babur comments:

> *Let him who bows his head in submission act like a subject,
> but any place and any territory that does not bow its head –*

---

[11] Burton Watson, ed. and trans, *Record of the Grand Historian of China, Translated from the Shih chi
of Ssu-ma Ch'ien* [became grand historian in 108 B.C.], v. 2, *The Age of Emperor Wu, 140 to circa
100 B.C.* (New York: Columbia University Press, 1961), 164–5, 184, 190.

[12] Watson, *Record of the Grand Historian,* 184–5. In another episode from the same text, the author
refers to another of the uses of decapitation, the punishment of the ruler of a kingdom who refused to
submit to the Chinese (190).

[13] Babur, *The Baburnama: Memoirs of Babur, Prince and Emperor*, Wheeler Thackston, ed. and trans,
(Washington, DC: Freer Gallery of Art, 1996). A descendent of Timur, Babur managed to establish
himself in Kabul in 1504. He invaded the Punjab several times between 1519 and 1524 before finally
successfully taking Delhi in 1526.

Whoever does not bow his head, strike him, strip him, and make him obey.[14]

The personification of territories as bowing their heads (as we saw in Ch. 4) and the juxtaposition of those territories with chieftains enacting rituals of submission is telling. That same personification is found in early modern maps on which the land is decorated with vignettes of conquered foes: bowing their heads, stripped of their skins, deprived of their heads, their emblems trampled underfoot. Both the land and its defenders are thus labeled as conquered and submissive. There is a constant threat of force behind Babur's distribution of lands and acts of magnanimity. Because Muhammad Ali Jang-Jang was willing to accept the territories and authority Babur offered, he was additionally awarded "royal black velvet headgear and royal Qalmaqi armor," indicators of both status and wealth.[15] But those who did not bow their heads were deprived of their goods and their honor, even if they retained their heads. It is little wonder, then, that in narrative and image one routinely finds an equating of body, territory, and submission.

In the space occupied by Ottoman lords and coveted by the Christian kings of Europe, the history of the taking of heads long predated the rule of the Ottoman sultans. Stories abound in the literature. As Sergio Bertelli has pointed out in his wonderful study of "the king's body," the formal Byzantine triumph was often marked by ritual insulting of the conquered foe. In 1042, "when the eunuch Stephanus Pergamenus defeated usurper Georgios Maniakes, he sent the head to the Christian emperor Constantine IX who had it carried in procession through the streets of Constantinople."[16] Medieval Muslim lords are also shown demanding heads. In his 1264 *Legenda Maior* the Franciscan philosopher Bonaventure (1221–74), writing of St. Francis's journey to Egypt during the Fifth Crusade and his attempt to preach before the Ayyubid sultan al-Malik al-Kamil I (r. 1218–38), could not resist the urge to embellish the story with grisly highlights. To heighten the sense of danger in Francis' encounter with the sultan, Bonaventure claimed "that the Sultan had decreed a reward of a Byzantine gold piece for every Christian head brought to him . . . "[17] Such tales served to enhance the power of intimidation exercised by Christian and Muslim monarchs alike.[18]

---

[14] Babur, *Baburnama*, 284. On Safavid ritual violence, use of decapitation, and its Central Asian precedents, see Mitchell, *The Practice of Politics in Safavid Iran*, 20–25, 38; see also Babak Rahimi, "The Rebound Theater State: The Politics of the Safavid Camel Sacrifice Rituals, 1598–1695 C.E.," 1–28, *Iranian Studies* 37.3 (September 2004), 15–16, 22–5. Beheading was also immortalized in the epic *şehname* literature. For a miniature of Afrasiyab beheading Naudar after Turan defeated Iran, see Oleg Grabar and Sheila Blair, *Epic Images and Contemporary History: The Illustrations of the Great Mongol Shahnama* (Chicago: University of Chicago Press, 1980), 82–3.

[15] Babur, *Baburnama*, 284.

[16] Sergio Bertelli, *The King's Body* (University Park: Pennsylvania State University Press, 1995), 235.

[17] Adnan Husain, "Mission and Imagination: Franciscan William Rubruck and Interreligious Encounters in the Mongol East," unpublished mss., 199.

[18] Khaled Abou El Fadl, *Rebellion and Violence in Islamic Law* (Cambridge: Cambridge University Press, 2001), 53. Muslim rulers from very early on in the history of the Islamic state took the heads of enemies and rebels.

The Ottoman Display of Heads (Captives, Booty, and Women)

The Ottomans, in their turn, took, counted, and displayed heads taken in battle for purposes of reward, punishment, and intimidation.[19] Jakob von Betzek, an imperial scribe in a Hapsburg delegation to Constantinople, was a witness to the mobilization of the famous 1565 Ottoman campaign against Malta. He recorded the use of Christian captives on Muslim warships and the disposition of eighty enemy heads.[20] His account is echoed in an Ottoman register of the same campaign that includes a list of troops who distinguished themselves, such as "Mehmet b. Mustafa . . . [who] captured the enemy banner in the battle of the Santarma fortress [and] entered the enemy bastion and chopped off some heads in the battle of the Malta fortress."[21] Such documentary claims were reproduced in Ottoman miniatures that show commanders laying enemy heads at the feet of a sultan or vezir, an emblematic act illustrating their participation and successes in battle. In such illustrations, a court official may be seen noting down individual accomplishments, creating a record of heads, territory won, and those deserving of promotion, much like the reward ceremonies depicted for the Xiongnu in the Chinese history cited earlier.

In Ahmet Feridun Bey's (d. 1583) illustrated chronicle of the 1566 Sighetvar campaign in Hungary, commanders are shown presenting heads to the grand vezir, Sokollu Mehmet Pasha, seated in front of his tent. The heads of the defeated serve both as a form of tribute and as a request for recognition (Fig. 5.5).[22] Similarly, an anonymous chronicle shows commanders bearing severed heads and paying homage to Sokollu Mehmet after the conquest of Lipova on the Hapsburg frontier (Fig. 5.6).[23] Captives in European dress are paraded in the middle ground of the miniature, witnesses to the Ottoman triumph and the grisly spectacle of the heads of the fallen. The message of the frame is that loyal troops will be rewarded and that the residents of the frontier zone would be well advised to surrender and submit. Borders are thus marked with the bodies of the living and the heads of the dead.[24]

---

[19] Indeed, heads were taken in battle as late as World War I, and photos of these "prizes" were published in official yearbooks.

[20] Jakob von Betzek, *Gesandtschaftsreise nach Ungarn und die Türkei im Jahre 1564/5*, Karl Nehring, ed. (Munich: Veröffentlichungen des Finnisch-Ugrischen Seminars an der Universität München, 1979), 36–8. I thank Michael McConnell for this reference.

[21] Cassola, *The 1565 Ottoman Malta Campaign Register*, 369.

[22] See Fehér, *Türkische Miniaturen*, tafel XLIV. The miniature is taken from Ahmed Feridun, *Nüshet ül-Esrar ul-Ahbar fi Sefer-i Szigetvar*, Topkapı Saray-ı Müzesi Kütüphanesi, Hazine 1339, fol. 41b.

[23] Fehér, *Türkische Miniaturen*, tafel XXXIII, Anonymous, *Fütuhat-ı Cemile*, Topkapı Saray-ı Kütüphanesi, Hazine 1592, fol. 9a; and Fetvacı, *Picturing History at the Ottoman Court*, Figure 75, from Mustafa Ali, *Nusretname*, for a similar presentation on the Ottomans' eastern frontier.

[24] Iveta Todorova-Pirgova, "Cultural Images of the Ethnic Groups and Ethnic Interrelations in the Balkans," *Ethnologies* 21. 2 (1999): 147–75, see 156, illustrates the equating of heads, bones, and space in the shared memories of late twentieth century peoples in the Balkans. One such Serbian lyric, among her recordings of songs, notes: "There are towers of skulls beyond count/ All over the land of heroes . . . Wherever the bones of our ancestors lie/ there are the borders of the land of the Serbs."

Figure 5.5. Sighetvar Campaign, Heads Presented to Grand Vezir Sokollu Mehmet. Ahmet Feridun Bey, *Nüshet ül-Esrar ul-Ahbar fi Sefer-i Szigetvar*, H. 1339, fol. 41b, İstanbul, [n.d.]. Topkapı Palace Museum, İstanbul. (See color plate)

Figure 5.6. Conquest of Lipova, Heads Presented to Sokollu Mehmet. Anonymous, *Fütuhat-ı Cemile*, H. 1592, fol. 9a, İstanbul, 1556. Topkapı Palace Museum, İstanbul.

Counterparts to such Ottoman artistry in the Christian West also used the image of the grand vezir's tent to send a message of triumphant conquest.[25] The Dutch artist Romeyn de Hooghe (1645–1708), for example, chose the grand vezir's tent as the centerpiece for his 1684 commemoration of the Hapsburg victory over Kara Mustafa Pasha at the 1683 siege of Vienna.[26] His engraving used the sumptuous folds of *"de Tent des Grooten Vizirs"* to enclose an imagined scene in which the victorious emperor and his men enter Ottoman space to lay hands upon the possessions of the defeated vezir (Fig. 5.7). One soldier reaches out to touch the shoulder of a bashful-looking maiden, while a kneeling male figure in high conical hat bows low to the beplumed victor.[27] Outside the tent, a tattered crescent flag still hangs in the breeze, but bare-chested Ottoman prisoners crouch next to their fallen *tughs* (horsetail standards) on the ground. Although there are no heads in this frame, the message is the same as that of the Ottoman miniatures: to the victor go the spoils and a sense of satisfaction from seeing the enemy brought low.[28]

De Hooghe's engraving served as an act of pictorial vengeance because the enslavement of Christian men, women, and children by "Turks" was a constant trope in the imagery of the early modern Christian kingdoms. A travel album dated 1590, for example, commissioned by Bartholomäus Schachman (1559–1614), who journeyed from Danzig through the Ottoman empire in 1588–9, includes an image of chained "Christians taken prisoner in the border wars," and another of "Christian captives being inspected," including a woman whose breasts are exposed, in the Istanbul slave market.[29] Shortly thereafter, the English ambassador Edward Barton, describing the pathetic scene after the capitulation of Egri to the Ottomans in October 1596, reported seeing janissaries who had purchased women and children captives, including one girl of "five yeeres, and the other sucking the mother's breast."[30] His description joined a long litany of Christian captivity narratives, like that of Cyriac of Ancona (1391–1452) who claimed personally to have seen long lines of Christian boys, unmarried girls, "and masses of married women,"

[25] Fetvacı, *Picturing History*, 115, 136. See also Baki Tezcan, "The Frank in the Ottoman Eye of 1583," 267–96, in *The Turk and Islam in the Western Eye*.

[26] *Im Lichte des Halbmonds*, 202. Later, the supposed skull of Kara Mustafa was eventually taken from a tomb in Belgrade and displayed in the Vienna Municipal Historical Museum; see Thomas Barker, *Double Eagle and Crescent: Vienna's Second Turkish Siege and Its Historical Setting* (Albany: SUNY Press, 1967), 69, 363–4. On the symbolism of the vezir's tent and decapitation in European artistry, see Karen Barzman, "Gregorio Lazzarini's Judith and Holofernes: Decapitation, Islam, and the Venetian State," 445–76, in *Gifts in Return: Essays in Honour of Charles Dempsey*, Melinda Wilcox Schlitt, ed. (Toronto: Centre for Reformation and Renaissance Studies, 2012).

[27] Romeyn de Hooghe ["The Defeat of Kara Mustafa Pasha,"], Amsterdam, 1684. Ottoman miniatures did not depict women in the vezir's tent in such campaign scenes.

[28] Nurhan Atasoy, *Otağ-ı Hümayun: The Ottoman Imperial Tent Complex* (İstanbul: MEPA, 2000), 238–87. Captured tents figured prominently in the booty taken in such battles.

[29] Olga Nefedova, Sara Al Mana, and Farhad Al Faihani, "The Travel Album of Bartholomäus Schachman," 63–90, in *Bartholomäus Schachman (1559–1614), The Art of Travel* (Milan: Skira, 2012), 63–5, and 181 (26v), 189 (29v).

[30] Purchas, *Hakluytus Posthumus*, 1625, v. 2, 1359. Barton notes that the Polish ambassador purchased the five-year-old from the janissaries for "ten Chekines." See on the Ottoman campaign Finkel, *The Administration of Warfare*, 15. Matar, *Islam in Britain*, provides a nuanced and detailed description of the use of the ideas of captives and converts to Islam in Britain.

Figure 5.7. Triumph in the Tent of the Grand Vezir. Romeyn de Hooghe, Nicolas Visscher, "Over-wonnen Turken knielen voor Leopold I," Amsterdam, 1684. Rijksmuseum, Amsterdam, RP-P-OB-55-142.

chained, whipped, and "put up for sale" by the "thoroughly execrable tribe of Turks."[31] Barton does not comment on whether the Egri captives were more or less fortunate than their dead co-religionists, "heaped up together close to the [castle] wall, about two fathome high, all naked, frying in the Sunne..."[32] But he clearly intends to inspire a sense of outrage and compassion among the folks back home.

Ottoman narrators might wax just as poetic as Barton when describing the humiliation that ensued from making their women vulnerable to the enemy. Their miniatures did not, to my knowledge, show captive women in their framing of victory and defeat, but the idea of female captives inflamed the minds of Ottoman audiences just as it did the minds of European Christian audiences. The chronicler Mustafa Selaniki (d. c. 1600), pointing out the power of rumor in Istanbul, noted that Ottoman officials had to heed the "complaints of mosque-goers, fired up by members of the ulema," who were distressed that the sultan did not plan to go on campaign, thus "allowing Muslim women to be enslaved by infidels."[33]

The Ottoman 'crowd' much preferred the public display of the humiliated enemy, a constant subject in narrative and miniatures. The flamboyant raconteur, Evliya Çelebi (1611–1682), for example, provides a characteristically dramatic and fulsome tale of heads in the aftermath of a siege. Evliya writes about the victories of his patron, Malek Ahmet Pasha, and the Ottoman relief of Özu fortress, east of Moldavia, on the Black Sea, in 1656–7. He tells his readers that he had been put in "charge of the booty and the prisoners (who had been given the task of skinning and salting the heads of the defeated foe)."[34] These heads were sent to Istanbul; and Evliya proceeded to the capital to proclaim Malek's victory:

> God be praised, eight days later all the carts arrived with the heads and trotters and the munitions. They were stowed in [Malek Pasha's wife] Kaya Sultan's palace at Topçular outside the Edirne gate. I immediately went with the pasha's court agent (Zühdi Efendi) to the deputy grand

[31] Cyriac of Ancona, *Later Travels*, Edward Bodnar, ed. and trans. (London: Harvard University Press, 2003), 13; and for an account from 1565, see von Betzek, *Gesandtschaftsreise nach Ungarn*, 48–52, who marks the space from Constantinople to the Hapsburg border through the vision of Christian captives, especially women, being transported to the Ottoman capital. See also Bartolomé Bennassar, "Malte, le traffic d'esclaves et l'inquisition," 375–81, in *Hommage à Alain Ducellier: Byzance et ses périphéries*, Bernard Doumerc and Christophe Picard, eds. (Toulouse: CNRS, 2004); and Pippidi, *Visions of the Ottoman World*, 19, 71, 144–5.

[32] Purchas, *Hakluytus Posthumus*, 1625, v. 2, 1359. Barton's deputy in Istanbul, Sanderson, in *The Travels of John Sanderson*, 60, notes receiving Barton's letter describing the conquest of Egri. See also Michaud, "Les Turcs Dans L'Histoire Universelle," 246–7, on the narrative litany of such Christian tragedies.

[33] Ebru Boyar and Kate Fleet, *A Social History of Ottoman Istanbul* (Cambridge: Cambridge University Press, 2010), 45. Emine Fetvacı, "Others and Other Geographies," 85–6, suggests that a woman with child shown in an unusual Ottoman miniature of a rebel leader being led to execution in Basra is the man's wife. In that sense she could be seen as a captive. On the question of Ottoman women and slavery more generally, see Madeline Zilfi, *Women and Slavery in the Late Ottoman Empire* (Cambridge: Cambridge University Press, 2010).

[34] Robert Dankoff, ed. and trans. *The Intimate Life of an Ottoman Statesman: Melek Ahmed Pasha (1588–1662) as Portrayed in Evliya Çelebi's Book of Travels* (Albany: State University of New York Press, 1991), 218.

vizier to inform him . . . "Quickly," he ordered, "inform the captain of the guard, the chief of police and the viceroy of the arsenal. Have all the armorers and the gunners with their colonels go to Topçular, outside the Edirne gate, and proceed from there with the multitude of heads and captives, parading them through Istanbul and before the felicitous Padishah . . . [35]

Not only were these trophies of war to be publicly displayed to the Istanbul masses, but also Evliya portrays Kaya Sultan herself as actively participating in the preparations. "Kaya Sultan had already arrived, with forty or fifty carts of hay and had ordered her gardeners and her halberdiers and all the poor people to Topçular quarter to stuff the salted heads with hay. The heads were piled up like mountains."[36]

This description is not designed to illustrate an Ottoman fascination with severed heads, nor, indeed, to illustrate the participation of elite Ottoman women such as Kaya Sultan in spectacles of power. Rather, it is designed to provide a context for the presentation of severed heads in maps and other public imagery of the early modern era. Evliya is well known for his tendency to exaggerate and his love of drama. But his classification of war booty into heads, captives, and munitions rings true. All three were important elements of the presentation of victory, a spectacle that demonstrated military prowess, presented evidence of the subordination of enemies, and consolidated power at home for the sultan and his victorious commanders (all before an audience in the imperial capital that consisted not solely of citizens and members of the military–bureaucratic class, but also of foreign diplomats, merchants, and visitors from the far-flung Ottoman provinces).[37] Those audiences also witnessed punishments in Istanbul, where the sultans "used the city as a canvas for the graphic illustration" of their power.[38] Both triumph and punishment were commemorated afterward in the narratives and miniatures of chroniclers such as Evliya, not to mention the letters, travel accounts, and reports of foreign witnesses. We do not know if Kaya actually mobilized the labor forces of household and neighborhood to stuff the enemy heads. But it would not be so surprising if she did, thus helping to magnify the reputation of her pasha husband. This vignette of the female as conqueror-by-association provides an interesting contrast to Romeyn de Hooghe's vignette of the Ottoman female as captive booty in the grand vezir's tent.

Displaying Heads in the Christian Kingdoms of Europe

Lest the previous examples seem to suggest that the Ottomans had any monopoly on the taking of early modern heads, it is common knowledge

[35] Dankoff, *The Intimate Life*, 218–19. For an earlier era, there are Ottoman stories of the head of King Wladlislaw III of Poland and Hungary, who was killed at the Battle of Varna in 1444 and his head supposedly sent to Bursa for display.

[36] Ibid., 219.

[37] Wratislaw, *Adventures*, 101–2, provides a dramatic description of the triumph of Hasan Pasha returning from Croatia at the end of the sixteenth century, and the parade of booty, heads, and captives.

[38] Boyar and Fleet, *A Social History*, 111–12, 119. There, the heads of rebels were mounted on an "'example stone' situated in front the Orta Kapı, the middle gate within Topkapı palace."

that there were numerous instances in Christian Europe of the separation of head from body.[39] Those instances were portrayed in narrative and image whether decapitation was employed against enemies, rebels, or subjects who offended their kings. European visitors to Muslim lands commented on the cultural and moral hierarchies of modes of killing. Thus the French traveler Jean Chardin (1643–1713), sojourning in Persia in the 1670s, noted that the Persian approach to punishment, cutting open the belly, was "not of so quick a Dispatch" as the French mode of beheading.[40] And John Sanderson, who made several visits to Istanbul around the turn of the seventeenth century, used the customs of his native England, to make comparisons with those of the Ottoman capital. He called the Ottomans "most cruel" in their practices of punishment; but he narrated them, like Chardin, in a rather matter-of-fact fashion. Thus he wrote disparagingly of the parading through the streets of the head of a wealthy Jewess, agent of the valide sultan, calling her execution a political "act of spite" on the part of the *sipahis* (Ottoman fief-holding cavalry).[41] It was not, however, the beheading per se that prompted Sanderson's condemnation, but its unwarranted use unjustly to secure wealth and political advantage.

Of course political objectives prompted many of the capital punishments commemorated in the lands of the Christian kings.[42] When Spanish ships, remnants of the great armada of 1588, washed up on the shores of Ireland, English commanders, fearing the survivors might join the "always simmering resistance of local Catholics . . . ordered two hundred of them decapitated."[43] Witnessing such decapitations was no rarity for audiences in England, whether the victims were enemies, rebels, or secret Catholics.[44] Once complete, these spectacles were commemorated in print. "A pamphlet published in London in 1581 contained an image of English soldiers marching through Ireland with heads mounted on the ends of their pikes above a poem celebrating the 'wonder' of decapitation."[45] The pamphlet was designed not only to titillate, but also to demonstrate the reach of imperial power.

Nonetheless, for audiences in the Christian kingdoms, the Turk's head was a special kind of trophy, illustrating as it did not only the triumph of a

---

[39] K. M. Matthew, *History of the Portuguese Navigations in India* (Delhi: Mittal Publications, 1988), 202. Writing of the Portuguese on the west coast of India in the late sixteenth century, Matthew notes that "George de Menezes Barocha surrounded the enemy by sea with five ships and Pedro de Castro by land with two hundred men and forced them to surrender. The Portuguese slaughtered their enemy and returned to the city with their vessels filled with the heads of the defeated Muslims."

[40] Sir John Chardin, *Travels in Persia 1673–1677*, N.M. Penzer and Sir Percy Sykes, preface and introduction (New York: Dover, 1988), 53–4.

[41] Sanderson, *The Travels*, 85–6. This account is told during his sojourn in 1599–1600. The envoy Thomas Glover used the same matter-of-fact tone in letters to Sanderson from Istanbul, dated March 17 and April 5, 1609, referring to the hundreds of heads of "rebels that were scattered in the woods and mountaynes," sent into the divan, "and those that bringe them to the port have a chequine per head" (261–2).

[42] Johnson, *Central Europe*, 89. After the Battle of White Mountain in 1620, for example, Ferdinand II had twenty-seven leaders of the Bohemian uprising beheaded in the square outside Prague's town hall.

[43] Mancall, *Hakluyt's Promise*, 182.

[44] Knolles, *Generall Historie of the Turkes*, 1603, 913, cites a staged execution of the warlord "Ioan," voyvoda of Moldavia at the hands of an Ottoman pasha and his janissaries. See also Palmira Brummett, "The Early Modern Ottoman Campaign: Containing Violence, Commemorating Allegiance, and Securing Submission," *Eurasian Studies* III/I (2004): 1–19, esp. 19.

[45] Mancall, *Hakluyt's Promise*, 103, also 151, 206.

sovereign state but also the legitimation of Christianity over Islam. That was particularly the case on the imperial frontiers closer to Ottoman domains. One can look, for example, to the account of Egidio Scardassa, writing of a Venetian assault on Zemonico, near the Adriatic port of Zara. The Venetian campaign was successful and "Durach Beg," Ottoman commander of the city, was killed. Afterward, Scardassa tells his audience,

> *His head was taken by a soldier . . . to the superintendent of cavalry (provveditor de cavalli) who received it with joy, as that of the fiercest enemy of the Republic in those parts, who, along with his father, had for long been stirring up the [local] populace . . . [Durach] was a fine-looking man (huomo d'assai bell'aspetto) and even in death his countenance gave indication of his pride and ferocity.[46]*

The killing of an enemy did not preclude his being viewed with respect, even if he was a "Turk." But the narration of vengeance was customary and expected. Once Zemonico was taken, Scardassa tells us, Christian captives were freed, many Ottomans were made slaves, and the surrounding territories were sacked. All of these satisfying outcomes, along with a sense of ethnocommunal pride, were conveyed to the reader in the tale of the Ottoman commander's head. The more fierce the foe, the greater the pride.

Captain John Smith, Imagining the Turk's Head

Italian narrators, such as Scardassa, and their readers, felt close to the frontiers on which the battle with the "Turk" was fought. But even in the remote realms of the North Atlantic, Christian audiences thrilled to visions of the Turk's head. Among the most famous of these trophies are those inscribed on the coat of arms purportedly awarded to the English Captain John Smith (1580–1631), a soldier of fortune on the Ottoman–Hapsburg frontiers (Fig. 5.8).[47] Smith became a cultural icon of the New World: warrior, colonizer, and grizzled leading man to the youthful Pocahontas. But before he ever set foot in Virginia, the illustrious Captain Smith claimed to have been the beneficiary of the salvation and affections provided by an Ottoman lady while he was enslaved by the "Turks."

Smith's story, set forth in a 1630 edition entitled *The True Travels, Adventures, and Observations of Captain John Smith in Europe, Affrica, and America, from Anno Domini 1593 to 1629*, combines a travel-romance reminiscent of the tales of Sindbad with a campaign account of the Ottoman–Hungarian wars.[48] It reveals contemporary English notions of masculine honor and

---

[46] Scardassa, *Relatione delle felici successi giorno per giorno*, 4.

[47] John Smith, *The True Travels, Adventures, and Observations of Captain John Smith in Europe, Affrica, and America, from Anno Domini 1593 to 1629* (London: Printed by I[ohn]. H[aviland] for Thomas Slater, 1630), title page verso. All quotes used here are taken from this version.

[48] Goodman, *Chivalry and Exploration*, 47–8, writing on late medieval and Renaissance romance as an imaginative literature of travel, suggests that "three geographical registers recur throughout this literature": Arthurian romances whose heroes are deployed "across a fictionalized British Isles and France . . . "; romances that "look to the East, sending European heroes out on the trails of Alexander

Figure 5.8. Coat of Arms. John Smith, *The True Travels, Adventures, and Obser-vations*, frontispiece verso, London, 1630. By permission of the Folger Shakespeare Library, Shelfmark: STC 22796 copy 2, bound with STC 22790 copy 2.

cross-cultural gender relations, as well as constructions of the Ottoman frontiers. The story of the lady and the knight was an old one.[49] Taken in its
entirety, and especially combined with his other works, such as *The General
Historie of Virginia*, Smith's story serves to map Old World and New into a
single terrain upon which the deeds of adventurous men are enacted (before
the admiring eyes of courageous women). The Ottomans, in this scenario, are
one set of barbarians, sharing the space of incivility with pirates and Native
Americans, yet distinguished by the broad sweep and long history of their
sovereign lands and by the power of their armies. That same juxtaposition
may be found in *The Indies, Oriental and Occidental*, an exotic ethnography of engravings by Romeyn de Hooghe, published in Amsterdam, c. 1685,
which includes images of Ottoman slavers and capital punishments, as well as
a rather lascivious vignette of Smith and Pocahontas called "Ceremonies de
Virginie."[50] In Smith's version of the Turks, we find the seventeenth century
imperative to take "back" the Old World lands that the "infidel" had seized,
along with assurances (similar to Du Vignau's) that the Turk, although a
formidable enemy, was still vulnerable, especially to the arms and wiles of
the European knight.[51]

I take for granted that the travel narrative, by definition and by demand,
contains an artful melding of myth, history, and experience. It is not my
objective here to sort out the balance of fantasy and reality in Smith's account
(he is a raconteur, much like the Ottoman Evliya Çelebi.) Rather, Smith's text
here is employed to lay out a popular English vision of Ottoman space, with
particular attention to the ways in which the severed enemy head served as an
emblem marking the frontiers between empires, cultures, and men.[52] Smith,

and the crusaders"; and narratives that "unroll themselves against a factual map of the world," whose
"knights have their feet planted firmly on the same ground that their readers tread." Goodman argues
that "Where the Greek prose romances depict the heterogeneous religious landscape of the ancient
Mediterranean, the latter medieval and Renaissance texts focus almost exclusively on the confrontation
of Christianity and Islam (47)."

[49] Goodman, *Chivalry and Exploration*, 61, 66–7, notes that Constantinople had become "a particular
obsession" of European romance authors after its fall to the Ottomans in 1453. According to Goodman,
"two great fantasies of the late medieval knight" were "acquiring a fairy mistress" and "winning
Constantinople (71)." European men getting into Ottoman harems was a staple of early modern
literature on the "Turks." See for example, Giovanni Battista Chiarello, *Historia degl' avvenimenti
dell' armi imperiali contro a' ribelli, et Ottomani* (Venetia: 1687), 5–6.

[50] Romeyn de Hooghe, *Les Indes Orientales et Occidentales, et autres lieux* (Amsterdam: Van Hoeve,
reprint of c. 1685 Leiden edition), figures 7, 22, 29.

[51] For a recent scholarly edition of Smith's work, see Philip L. Barbour, ed., *The Complete Works
of Captain John Smith (1580–1631) in Three Volumes* (Chapel Hill and London: University of
North Carolina Press, 1986). Any consideration of Smith's account of the Ottoman–Hungarian wars
should be supplemented with a consultation of Finkel, *The Administration of Warfare*, an analysis
of Ottoman sources. See also on Smith's narratives J. A. Leo Lemay, *Did Pocahontas Save Captain
John Smith?* (Athens, GA: University of Georgia Press, 1992); Alden T. Vaughan, "John Smith Satirized: The Legend of Captaine Iones," *William and Mary Quarterly*, 3rd series, 45.4 (Oct. 1988):
712–32, esp. 715, for a satirical image of a Smith-like figure and heads as the "spoils of war"; and
Pompa Banerjee, "The White Othello: Turkey and Virginia in John Smith's True Travels," 135–51,
in *Envisioning the English Empire: Jamestown and the Emergence of the North Atlantic World*,
Robert Applebaum and John Wood Sweet, eds. (Philadelphia: University of Pennsylvania Press, 2005).
Zilfi, *Women and Slavery in the Late Ottoman Empire*, 17–18, comments on issues of gender and
power.

[52] Smith, *The True Travels, Adventures, and Observations*, 21–3, is wounded and taken captive, and
then nursed to health in the hope of ransom and brought to a slave market at "Axapolis." Later

in his own telling, is warrior, captive, and observer. Memory, audience, and the heroic sensibilities of the age all played a role in his crafting of Ottoman space.

In 1601 Smith journeyed to Graz, proposing unsuccessfully to join the Hapsburg forces in Hungary under the Duke of Mercoeur. He ended up instead (by his own account) serving with a Hungarian unit under Henry Volda, the Earl of Meldritch, who had joined forces with Sigismund Bathory, Prince of Transylvania (r. c. 1588–99, 1600–1602) in the chaotic struggle for control of that principality.[53] Smith described the situation as follows:

> Now the Noble Earle [Meldritch] was a Transylvanian borne, and his fathers Countrey yet inhabited by the Turkes . . . though the Prince [Bathory] had the hearts both of Country and people; yet the Frontiers had a Garrison amongst the unpassable mountaines, some for the [Hapsburg] Emperour, some for the Prince, and some for the Turke . . .[54]

In this passage Smith conveys a vivid picture of the mixed, mutable, and dangerous nature of the transimperial frontier. After a month-long confrontation at this fortified oasis in the plains of "Regall," Smith tells his readers that the "Turks" tired of awaiting the attack, and that the "ladies" inside the fortress apparently grew weary of the dearth of entertainment.[55] Thus, "to delight the Ladies, who did long to see some court-like pastime, the Lord Turbashaw" challenged the captains of the besieging army to "combate with him for his head."[56] Smith was chosen as champion and proceeded to dispatch not one but three "Turks" in sequential single combat. This feat supposedly thrilled his army and his commander. By way of reward, Smith tells his readers, he was promoted to sergeant major and was personally received at his general's tent accompanied by an honor guard of six thousand men and "three spare horses, before each a Turkes head upon a Lance" (Fig. 5.9).[57] With a patent purportedly dated December 1603, Bathory also granted Smith a coat of arms featuring the heads of the three Turks he had

he purportedly escaped captivity, slew the "Bashaw of Nalbrits in Cambia," and went on to Russia, Transylvania, the "middle of Europe," and Africa (31–3).

53 Laura Polanyi Striker, "Appendix I: Captain John Smith's Hungary and Transylvania," 311–42, in Bradford Smith, *Captain John Smith, His Life and Legend* (Philadelphia: J.B. Lippincott Co., 1953), 314–15, 323. See also Gábor Barta, "The First Period of the Principality of Transylvania (1526–1606)," 593–770, in Béla Köpeczi, ed., *History of Transylvania*, v. 1, *From the Beginnings to 1606* (Boulder: Social Science Monographs, 2001), 752–7.

54 Smith, *The True Travels*, 11.

55 Both Barbour and Polanyi-Striker are inclined to think that there is more of truth in Smith's account than earlier analyses may have suggested. On Smith's "heavily textualized" life and his constructions of "female benevolence and masculine violence," see Mary C. Fuller, *English Travel to America, 1576–1624* (Cambridge: Cambridge University Press, 2007), 131, 135.

56 Smith, *The True Travels*, 12. The taking of a rival's head in single combat is also immortalized in a Turkic epic, Islamized and recorded in the fourteenth century (or earlier); see *The Book of Dede Korkut: A Turkish Epic*, Faruk Sümer, Ahmet Uysal, and Warren Walker, eds. and trans. (Austin: University of Texas Press, 1972), 174–5.

57 Smith, *The True Travels*, 14, and fold-out image before 1.

Figure 5.9. John Smith, "Three Turks Heads," *The True Travels, Adventures, and Observations*, foldout map before p. 1, London, 1630. By permission of the Folger Shakespeare Library, Shelfmark: STC 22796 copy 2, bound with STC 22790 copy 2.

dispatched.[58] The legend in Latin reads *Vincere est Vivere*, with *Accordamus* inscribed underneath.

Smith's narration of recognition and reward recalls Babur's account of Muhammad Ali Jang-Jang. It also echoes an Ottoman account by Evliya Çelebi, who, as part of an official visit to Berat in Albania, presented the heads of outlaws to the governor Osman Pasha in 1670. Evliya noted that the governor was particularly pleased that he had made a public display of the heads when he presented his credentials and the sultan's imperial decrees: "For displaying the heads, I was awarded a plumed crest and dressed in a robe of honor."[59] Both the heads and the credentials served to legitimate Osman Pasha's authority. It is thus little wonder that Evliya's purported award, like Smith's, was a handsome one.[60] The "crest" in one form or another, along

---

[58] Smith, *The True Travels*, 15–18; the coat of arms appears on the unnumbered verso of the frontispiece. A fold-out image before page one contains a series of vignettes illustrating Smith's conquests, including an image of three Turks' heads on pikes.

[59] Evliya Çelebi, *Evliya Çelebi in Albania*, 111.

[60] Smith's mid-twentieth-century biographer comments rather wryly on English conventions of head taking when he recounts Miles Standish's display of an Indian head at Plymouth (and the appearance of London bridge which "bristled with pikes on which the heads of the executed were impaled"). See Bradford Smith, *Captain John Smith*, 52–3. Conversely, the frontispiece of Ortelius' *Theatrum Orbis Terrarum* (first published Antwerp, 1570) shows a naked and recumbent Lady America casually contemplating the severed head of a bearded European male. One also thinks of Nicolas Visscher's famous, c. 1652, map of London, which includes the piked heads on the London bridge.

with horses and robes of honor, seems thus to stand as a shared emblem of gratitude for the dispatch of enemies and outlaws. At the same time, the ritual presentation of heads cements the relationship between "heroic" deed and official recognition, whether the warrior's lord is Christian or Muslim.

Smith's story illustrates the day-to-day familiarity of the severed head, both for warriors and urban audiences. Those audiences ravenously consumed such imagery, familiar as it was. Richard Knolles, a contemporary of John Smith, capitalized upon that demand in his 1603 *General History of the Turkes*. For Knolles, the Turk's head was a symbol of Christian victory, a piece of booty seized on the Hapsburg–Ottoman frontiers and brought back to Vienna to serve a rhetorical purpose (just like Smith's coat of arms). Knolles thus repeated an account of Sultan Süleyman's Hungarian campaign in 1532. With the sultan's army arrayed outside the town of Gunza, two hundred Ottoman horsemen went off in search of booty. They were, Knolles tells his readers,

> *intercepted and all slaine or taken, whose heads the Hungarians brought to Vienna; and the more to encourage the soldiers which daily repaired thither, in token of good lucke set them up upon stakes upon the walls of the citie...* [61]

The Ottoman heads functioned rhetorically at two sites. On the battlefield they were the proof of Christian military prowess and a much needed sign of Ottoman vulnerability. In Vienna, set up on stakes for all to see, they served not only as a statement of the city's defiance, but also as a token of encouragement for troops preparing to take the field against the Ottoman foe.

The Fallen Turk, from Narrative and Image to Map

The display of heads was thus part of a much more expansive set of rhetorics and representations by which ceremonies of submission marked out both status and territory. [62] In that rhetorical scheme the fallen Turk played a prominent role. Lords and clerics used him (along with the threat of Ottoman advances) to rally the support of their followers. He (this figure was almost always gendered male) was also, as we have seen, a commemorative figure, reminding Christian audiences of their own victories and their fallen "brothers" and co-religionists. The allegorical frontispiece of Lazzaro Soranzo's 1598 *L'ottomano*, for example, features two dignified females who stand, almost casually, perched on the severed heads of two turbaned Turks (Fig. 5.10). [63] The Turk as trophy, forced to submit, soothed the fears and

[61] Knolles, *A General History of the Turkes*, 618. Knolles also notes a Hungarian ambush on the convoy of the "old pasha" of Temesvar who was slain and "whose head they sent for a present to the princess of Alba Iulia (1088–1089)."

[62] See Brummett, "The Early Modern Ottoman Campaign"; and "A Kiss Is Just a Kiss: Rituals of Submission Along the East–West Divide," 107–31, in *Cultural Encounters between East and West, 1453–1699*, Matthew Birchwood and Matthew Dimmock, eds. (Cambridge: Cambridge Scholars Press, 2005).

[63] Lazzaro Soranzo, *L'ottomano* (Ferrara: Vittorio Baldini, 1598), frontispiece.

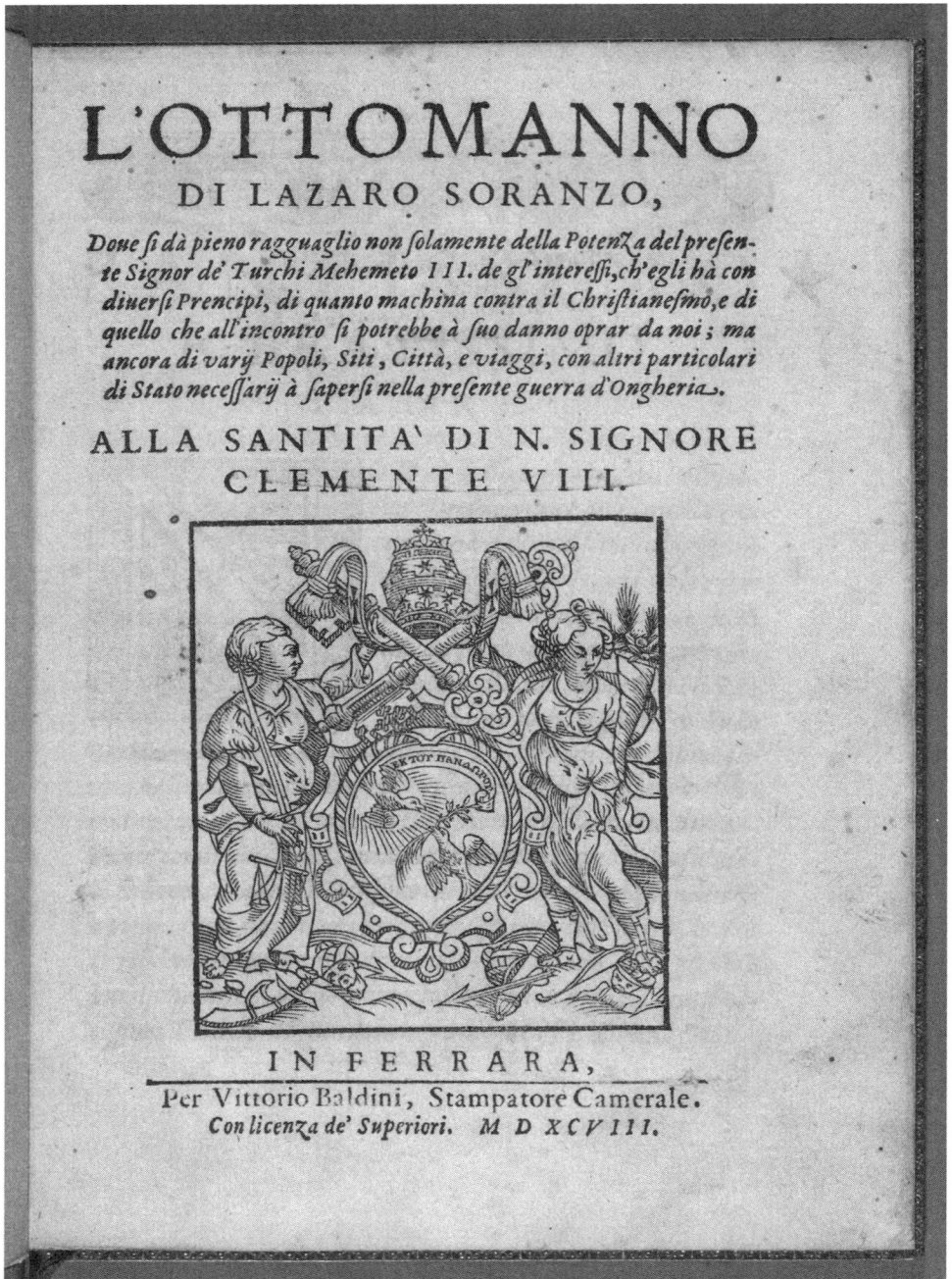

Figure 5.10. Lazzaro Soranzo, *L'ottomano*, frontispiece, Ferrara, 1598. *IC5 S0681 5980, Houghton Library, Harvard University.

enhanced the manhood of Christian viewers and asserted the legitimacy of their leaders.[64]

---

[64] See for example, *Die Türken vor Wien*, plates 72, 113, 116, 117 (among others) for the fallen Turk in seventeenth and eighteenth century statuary, in medallions, as a bedpost, and in a commemorative engraving.

The history of such representations traces back to the early Ottoman conquests in Europe. St. John Capistrano (1386–1456), for example, a papal nuncio, and a fiery preacher who at the age of seventy led an army to help raise the Ottoman siege of Belgrade in 1456, serves as an oft-represented father-figure embodying resistance against the Ottomans.[65] A large and dramatic statue now gracing the side of St. Stephan's Cathedral in Vienna depicts Capistrano in glory perched on the body of a bare-chested and top-knotted Ottoman warrior (Fig. 5.11).[66] It is the quintessential image of the sanctified against the "barbarian," the latter fallen across his cannon and surrounded by crescent-topped banners, arrows, and tughs while the saint, sporting Franciscan robes and halo, gazes heavenward. This image was kept 'fresh' before the eyes of its viewers. Indeed, a similar statue of much more recent vintage, but also depicting the monk with his foot resting on the back of a mostly naked Turk, graces the courtyard outside the military museum in Buda.[67]

It is worth noting here that depicting the defeated "Turk" without his hat was a sign of disrespect. The honorable Ottoman male wore a head covering that indicated his rank and station. In the illustrated *Surname*, for example, a presentation volume by Abdülcelil Levni (d. 1732) showing the 1720 circumcision festival for Sultan Ahmet III's sons, one can see an almost endless stream of Ottoman men of all backgrounds in their various headgear. Only the wrestlers are bare-chested and bare-headed (as would be men depicted in a bathhouse scene).[68] But European observers were fascinated by the shaved head and topknots of Ottoman *askeri*. Thomas Dallam (b. c. 1570), the English artisan sent by Queen Elizabeth in 1599 to present his marvelous mechanical organ as a gift to the Ottoman court, described the sultan's pageboys as wearing little caps of gold cloth beneath which their heads were "all shaven, saving that behind their ears did hang a lock of hair like a squirrel's tail."[69] The shaved head and topknot for such interpreters became symbols of "Turk" identity, whereas the absence of headgear became a purposeful marker of the humbled condition of the defeated Turk.

[65] Other monks continued the tradition of "crusade" rhetoric and imagery. See Nirit Ben-Aryeh Debby, "Crusade Propaganda in Word and Image in Early Modern Italy Niccolò Guidalotto's Panorama of Constantinople (1662)," *Renaissance Quarterly* (forthcoming, 2014).

[66] Stephansdom was begun in the 1230s. The statuary was added to an older pulpit which was relocated, c. 1738; see http://worldimages.sjsu.edu/Obj93589/sid=34552&x=8190289&port=1260. Capistrano was canonized in 1690, the date's proximity to the Battle of Vienna in 1683 perhaps not coincidental. I thank Cristelle Baskins for the reference. Vienna is still decorated with images of the Turk, for example on the frieze of the Spanish riding school, which shows warrior torsos with necks and head gear (no actual heads) one of which is a turbaned Turk with tughs.

[67] In this more modern incarnation, Capistrano looks more fanatical than saintly. Nenad Moačanin, *Town and Country on the Middle Danube, 1526–1690* (Leiden: Brill, 2006), 179, points out that Capistrano's tomb was a pilgrimage site and the saint became a European cult figure.

[68] Esin Atıl, *Levni and the Surname: The Story of an Eighteenth-Century Ottoman Festival* (İstanbul: Koçbank, 1999), 156–7, 226. Levni depicts a janissary with topknot revealed in one miniature; but he is shown scrambling for his hat which he has lost in a tumble.

[69] Mary C. Fuller, compiler, "Thomas Dallam's – Excerpts from his diary," 53–9, in *Travel Knowledge: European 'Discoveries' in the Early Modern Period*, Ivo Kamps and Jyotsna Singh, eds. (Houndmills: Palgrave, 2001), 55.

Figure 5.11. John Capistrano Pulpit, mounted on Stephansdom, Vienna, exterior wall, with blue tarp. Photograph: Palmira Brummett. (See color plate)

By Dallam's time there were various opportunities to celebrate Christian victories and to show the Turk without his hat. As we have seen, the victory of a Christian naval coalition at Lepanto in 1571 prompted a great outpouring of images of the fallen Turk as news flowed out in ever widening circles from the region of the battle. Venetian artisans produced carvings, paintings, maps, and broadsheets to commemorate the humiliation of the sultan's admirals. The Vatican, too, had its monumental celebrations of the victory, as witnessed by the 1572 paintings of Giorgio Vasari and his workshop.[70] One of these paintings (not shown here) depicts a woman bearing a large cross and a chalice with host. She is seated on a heap of bound Turks, a turban and crescent beneath her foot. Further west, King Philip II (1556–98) of Spain also commissioned large commemorative paintings, recording the triumph of Lepanto and attaching that victory to the proclamation of his own sovereign claims. Titian produced an *Allegory of Lepanto* for Philip showing the armored king raising up the naked figure of his newborn son to touch a winged angel of victory. In the foreground sits the chastened figure of a defeated Ottoman, nude save for sash and boots, his turban fallen to the floor.

On the Map: The Turk as News, the Turk as Trophy

The attributes of the statues of Capistrano or the paintings of Lepanto reappear routinely on early modern maps, cementing the relationship between sovereignty, legitimacy, and possessed space.[71] The map, particularly the cartouche, was often a visualization of identity. It served as a display case for the trophies of war. Map legends were surrounded by the emblems of battle, some generic and some representative of a particular friend or foe. In these displays of martial character or intent, ownership of space, as we have already seen, could be indicated through the placing of fortresses, the unfurling of flags, the stamping of coats of arms, or the inscribing of the names of leaders and states upon contested territory. But the image of the defeated enemy was a particularly effective space-claiming device: dead, bound, seated, kneeling, or sprawled beneath the feet of the triumphant self for the edification of an audience presumed to be part of the same "cherished community."[72]

News maps detailing the action and results of specific sieges might show the heads of "Turks" mounted on pikes, whereas other visions of frontier space adapted the fallen Turk as a more general representational convention. For example, an eight-sheet map of Europe printed by Christoph Zell in Nuremburg in 1536, and dedicated to Charles V, gives no direct indication of Ottoman rule in the Balkans. Nonetheless, "right next to the legend

---

[70] For other imagery of the captive and defeated Turk, see Benjamin Paul, "'And the moon has started to bleed,'" 67–94, in *The Turk and Islam in the Western Eye*, 78; and Christina Strunck, "The Barbarous and Noble Enemy: Pictorial Representations of the Battle of Lepanto," 217–42, in the same volume. See also Partridge and Starn, "Triumphalism and the Sala Regia in the Vatican," figs. 1–26, pp. 1–27. One of these depicts a woman bearing a large cross and a chalice with host, seated on a heap of bound Turks, a turban and crescent beneath her foot. An ivory statuette in the Rijksmuseum of Amsterdam, done by Matteus van Beveren (1630–90) in Antwerp, omits the captives but shows the blessed "Virgin of the apocalypse" perched on a crescent moon and a dragon (a figure used often to symbolize the "Turk").

[71] See Willem Janszoon and Joan Blaeu, "Transylvania Siebenburgen," in various editions of the Blaeu atlas *Theatrum orbis terrarum*, first published in 1635 in two volumes, in German, Dutch, Latin and French. The cartouche shows two bare-breasted women on either side of a three-clawed emblem of Transylvania. One holds a crucifix, and warring armies are seen marching across the landscape.

[72] Charles Press, *The Political Cartoon* (Rutherford, NJ: Fairleigh Dickinson University Press, 1981), 50–79, elaborates this notion of the "cherished community" in terms of the ways in which cartoons take for granted symbols of community affinity.

'Bosnia' there is a coat of arms displaying crossed sticks with impaled
'Moors" heads."[73] This iconic labeling is an early cartographic instance of
the inclination both to signal defeat of the Ottomans through the display
of "Turk" trophies, and to give back to the Ottomans for their displays of
conquered Christian heads.

   Over a century later, in his 1687 *History of the Actions of the Imperial
Army against Rebels and Ottomans*, Giovanni Battista Chiarello told the
story of the 1685–7 wars for the Morea, expressing his devout hope that the
Cross would soon return to the "Orient." In a note to his readers (*Cortese
Lettore*), Chiarello characterized the combatants in these wars: the Christian
potentates arrayed against the "universal enemy," the Ottoman sultan, in a
contest for the borderlands.[74] No ruler, Chiarello told his audience, could
control those lands without employing the power of violence: "the scepter
does not rest securely in the right hand of the monarch unless... he also
grips the sword."[75] As if to illustrate that point, Chiarello told a dramatic
and impressionistic story of the fall of the fortress of Nayahysel (Neuhäusel
or Uyvar on the River Neutra/Nitra in Royal Hungary). When the Turks
realize they have lost, they raise the white flag. But the victorious soldiers,
"hearing the possibility of a surrender agreement began shouting at the top of
their voices, 'Kill them, Kill them, they'll throw bombs [on us].'"[76] Some of
the Ottoman defenders then threw themselves from the wall. Others, trying
to escape, were cut to pieces:

> the cries, the screams, the tears of the women and children, were enough
> to prompt pity and despair. But one could not stay the hostility of
> the attackers, who, giving no heed to the pleas for salvation... at the
> first rush took four hundred heads, including those of women and
> children... until ultimately, the human impulse won out and they held
> their swords, sparing the women...[77]

This tale is reminiscent of Barton's account of the surrender of Egri, although
in this case it is Muslim defenders who are slaughtered rather than Christians.
   To complement his text, Chiarello included visuals of the relevant spaces:
one map of Hungary, one plan of Vienna, and five battle maps showing the
sites of military action. The cartouche on the map of Nayahysel is decorated
with the piked heads of defeated Ottomans (Fig. 5.12).[78] This map imagery is
rather iconic, whereas the narrative image prompts the reader to sympathy or
satisfaction. Both, however, suggest the endemic fear of losing one's head on

[73] Petkov, *Infidels, Turks, and Women*, 217. See also Mária Ivanics, "The March of the Imperial Relief
   Forces to Kanizsa in Contemporary Illustrations," 351–8, in Hasan Güzel, et al., eds., *The Turks*, v. 3
   (Ankara: Yeni Türkiye, 2002), 354.
[74] Chiarello, *Historia degl' avvenimenti*, second dedication.
[75] Chiarello, *Historia degl' avvenimenti*, unnumbered section entitled "Notitie Historiche e Geografiche
   del Regno dell'Hungaria, Schiavonia, e Croatia," which is located after the first map, "Hungaria
   Millitaria," in the front matter.
[76] Chiarello, *Historia degl' avvenimenti*, 345.
[77] Chiarello, *Historia degl' avvenimenti*, 344–6.
[78] Chiarello, *Historia degl' avvenimenti*, map after page 346. The key says, "Spiegatione Dell'Assedio di
   Nayhay sel Seguito l'Anno MDCLXXXV."

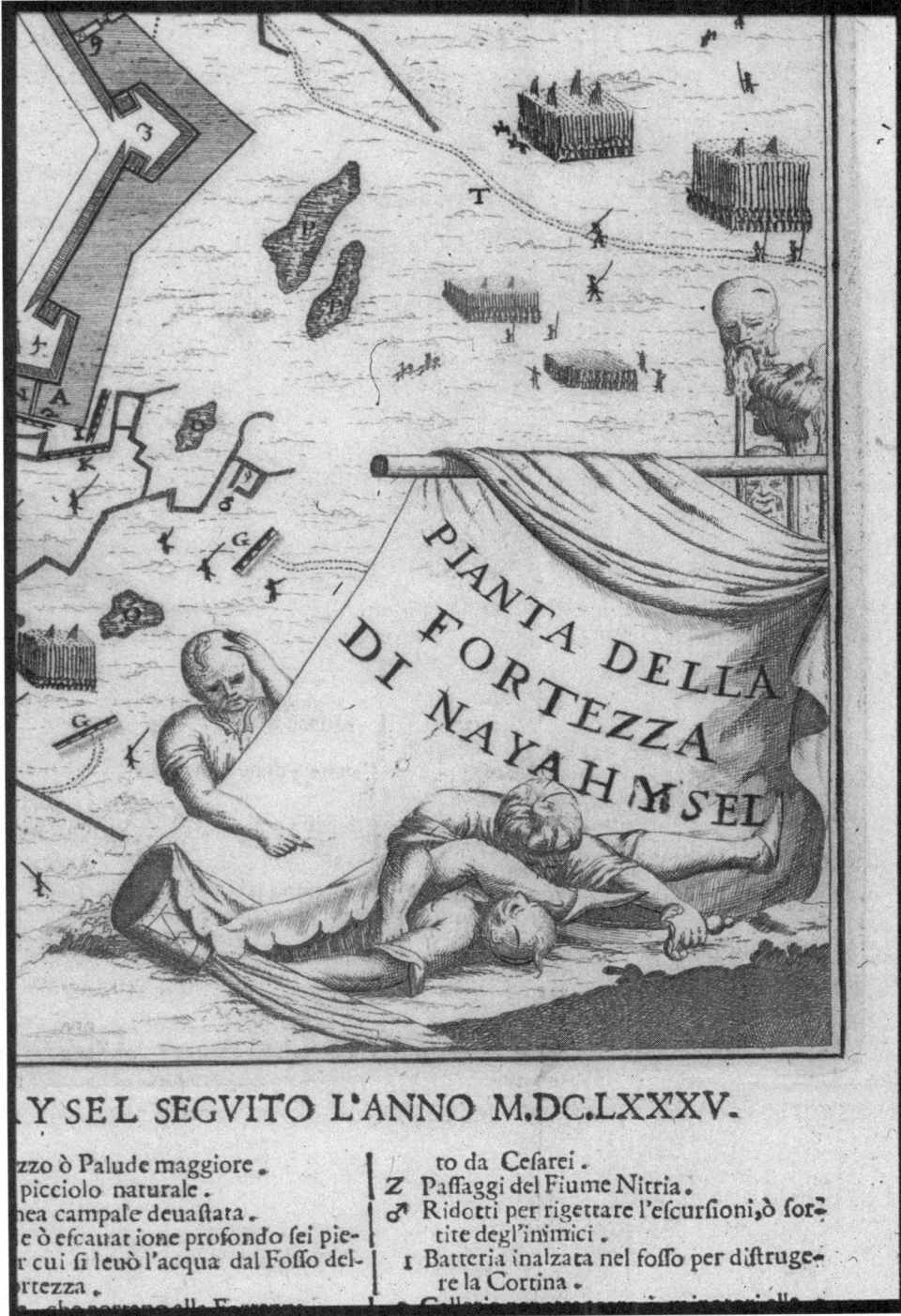

Figure 5.12. Giovanni Battista Chiarello, "Pianta Della Fortezza Di Nayahysel," cartouche, *Historia degl' avvenimenti dell' armi imperiali contro a' ribelli, et Ottomani*, map following p. 346, Venetia, 1687. By permission of the Folger Shakespeare Library, Shelfmark: 246080.

the transimperial frontier. Surrender was no guarantee of survival, regardless of the faith of the victors.

Such scenarios of dominance and submission appear on map after map. Theodor de Bry's (1528–98) 1596 map of Hungary, for example, bears a cartouche showing European knights dispatching fallen, turbaned Turks with sword and lance (Fig. 5.13).[79] De Bry's knights are perched upon a legend box attributing victory to Jesus Christ. Indicators of military violence were, of course, commonly accompanied by invocations of the divine. Thus when Justus Danckerts (1635–1701) produced a map of Hungary, Greece, and the Morea, he employed a Christlike figure bearing a cross to point at those territories that "once were Christian regions" (Fig. 5.14).[80] There is no fallen Turk in Danckerts's frame, but a battle rages in the foreground, suggesting an enduring struggle for Greco-Balkan space. Half a century later F. De Wit's (1630–1706) 1680 English map of the same region featured one putto wielding a cross and standing astride a fallen Turk and another holding a crown, both little angels suggesting the advancing fortunes of the Christian kings (Fig. 5.15).[81] Finally, the allegorical frontispiece of Henri Abraham Chatelain's monumental *Atlas Historique*, volume four, published in Amsterdam in 1739, shows a robust, noble, crowned female (one of several representing European Christian accomplishments) posed with her right foot resting on the neck of a supine Turk (Fig. 5.16).[82] His shaved head and bulging muscles glisten; his turban and arrows lie by his side. A shield bearing the double-headed eagle and an image of St. George posed astride the dragon are propped behind the turban, mirroring the juxtaposition of 'madonna' and Turk.[83]

That juxtaposition finds a new configuration in a particularly extravagant cartouche on the Augsburg cartographer Matthäus Seutter's early eighteenth century map of the Morea (Fig. 5.17).[84] Against a backdrop of a radiant cross perched in front of a domed cityscape, a ferocious, joyous lion of San Marco wields his sword against the Turk. Before him are three turbaned men flung backward off their feet, their crescent shield on the ground. But a fourth figure also lies under the lion's sword. Directly beneath his outstretched claw are the buttocks of a female figure, naked, her back to the viewer. But this is no madonna. Her torso ends not in two legs but in a snaky dragon's tail. The vanquished dragon thus served as a stand-in for the Ottomans, a violent or tempting, but always insidious, foe of Christendom.

---

[79] Workshop of Theodor de Bry (1528–98), "Vetutissimi, Potentissimique Hungariae Regni . . . ," Frankfort, 1596.

[80] Justinum Danckerum, "Regni Hungariae, Graeciae, et Moreae," [Amsterdam], [c. 1688?]. British Library, Maps 28195(.31). The cartouche includes the same "national" Hungarian emblem and crown with cross that de Bry's cartouche includes.

[81] F. De Wit, "Regnum Hungaria in Omnes suos Comitatus" [Amsterdam], [1680].

[82] Chatelain, *Atlas Historique,* v. 4, frontispiece.

[83] For an armored female victory with double-headed eagle shield see the cartouche for Joannes de Ram, "Regnum Hungariae in Omnes suos Comitatutus," c. 1680, Amsterdam, shown in an advertisement in *Cartographica Hungarica* 8 (May 2004): 83.

[84] Georg Matthäus Seutter, Johann Baptist Homann [et al.], "Peloponnesus hodie Morea" [Weltatlas], [17–], ([Augsburg], no date), map 102, Knanstvena knjižnica Zadar, GA10421A. The atelier of Nicolas Visscher, in Amsterdam, produced a map sometime between 1690 and 1720 that seems to be the model for Seutter's map.

Figure 5.13. Theodor de Bry, "Vertutissimi, Potentissimique Hungariae Regni," cartouche, Frankfurt, 1596. The British Library Board, Maps 28195(.91).

Figure 5.14. Justus Danckerts /Danckerum, "Regni Hungariae, Graeciae, et Moreae," cartouche [Amsterdam] [c. 1688]. The British Library Board, Maps 28195(.31).

Figure 5.15. Frederick de Wit, "Regnum Hungaria," cartouche [Amsterdam] [c. 1680]. The British Library Board, Maps C.27.g.6.(86).

Figure 5.16. Henri Chatelain, *Atlas Historique, ou Nouvelle Introduction à l'Histoire...*, 3rd ed., v. 4, frontispiece, Amsterdam, 1739. By permission of the Folger Shakespeare Library, Shelfmark: D11.5 C6 v.4 Cage.

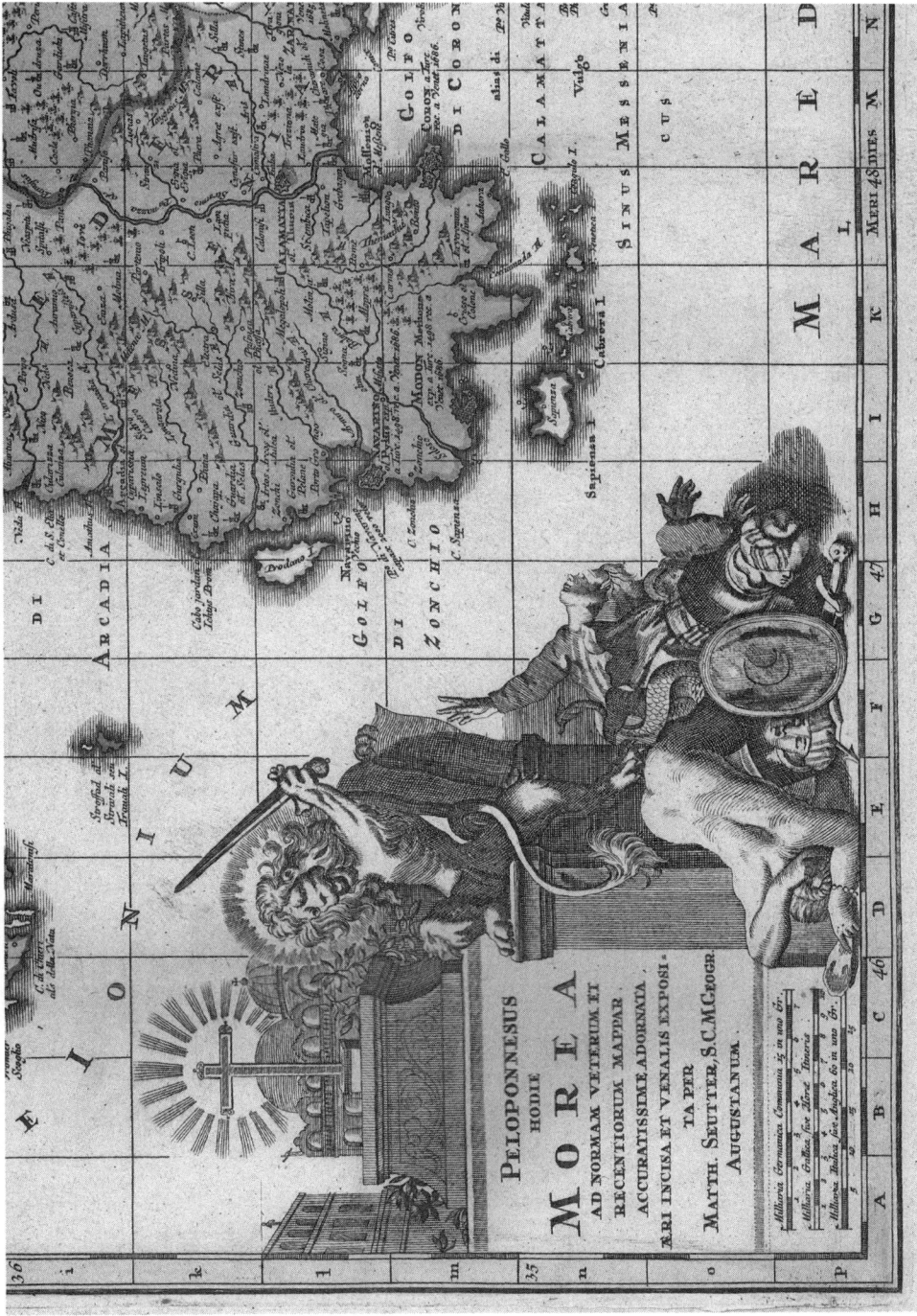

Figure 5.17. Georg Matthäus Seutter, Johann Baptist Homann [et al.], "Peloponnesus hodie Morea," map 102, cartouche [*Weltatlas*] [n.p.] [17–]. Library Znanstvena knjižnica Zadar, ZKZD GA 10421-A. (See color plate)

Vincenzo Coronelli, Mapping Memory

The Venetian lion was a widespread icon of the struggle against the Turk, even though Venice negotiated with the Ottomans as readily as it fought them. On the map, Venice militant was a potent and recognizable symbol of the confrontation with the Turk. And nowhere was that role demonstrated more clearly than in the work of the Venetian cosmographer Vincenzo Coronelli (1650–1718).

Coronelli's map of the fortress of Santa Maura (on the Ionian island of Levkas) embodies the history and memory of Venice's rivalry with the Ottoman empire. Though undated, the map was apparently produced to celebrate the taking of Santa Maura in 1684 (Figs. 5.18 and 5.19). The island fills most of the map frame, whereas an elaborate cartouche, in the upper left hand corner, presents the fortress itself.[85] In the lower right hand corner, however, one finds a different sort of cartouche. There the lion of San Marco grips in his teeth a parchment on which the map legend is inscribed. But this 'parchment' is the skinned body of a Turk, his top-knotted head dangling on the ground.[86] Beneath the lion's feet rest a crescent and the broken sword of his Ottoman foe. Coronelli dedicated this map to Matteo Sanuto, *procuratore* of Venice. But no doubt he also had in mind Marcantonio Bragadino, the commander of Famagosta on Cyprus when it was forced to surrender to the Ottomans in 1571. At that time, the victorious Lala Mustafa Pasha had Bragadino flayed alive and his skin sent to the sultan.[87] One hundred years later the humiliation of Venice and its commander still rankled. Like similar early modern map images, Coronelli's cartouche framed the conquest of Santa Maura in the context of a 'universal' struggle between the representatives of Christian and Muslim kings. Thus, the title page of the Dutch *Hollandsche Mercurius* for 1684 featured an image by Romeyn de Hooghe showing a Christian knight and a turbaned Ottoman matching swords over a map of the fortresses of Buda and Pest. Looking on is a helmeted female whose shield bears an image of the lion of San Marco rampant and whose banner reads "S. Maura."[88] But Coronelli's sly and vicious 'parchment' was personal.[89] By inscribing Santa Maura's conquest on the skin of a Turk the cartographer gained a bit of vengeance for his history-conscious Venetian audience. And for those with an even longer memory, vengeance was also served for the Christian "martyrs" of Otranto, the Apulian port seized by the Ottomans in 1480.

[85] Vincenzo Coronelli, "Fortezza di S. Maura," Venetia, [c. 1695], British Library, Maps, C.27.g.16(.61). The map is undated but presumably was produced in the aftermath of the conquest. It includes a fine little schematic of the walls and fortifications and a decorative owl bearing a scale of "passi Veneti" to indicate the size of the fortress in paces or "Venetian steps."

[86] This mascot, with tughs but without the skinned Turk, was used on other maps; for example, N. Sanson's "Le Golfe de Venise," Paris, [1696].

[87] Norwich, *Venice*, 220–21. Bragadino's death served as a horrific and heartrending moment in the literatures of European Christendom for many years. See Michaud, "Les Turcs dans l'histoire universelle," 244. The image of Bragadino's skin also found its way into Ottoman texts and imagery. See Emine Fetvacı, "Others and Other Geographies in the Şehnāme-i Selīm Hān," 95–8.

[88] *Hollandsche Mercurius*, Haarlem, 1684, title page.

[89] For Cervantes, who began his *Novela del amante liberal* with a lament over the valiant and ill-fortuned defenders of Nicosia on Cyprus, it was personal in a much more immediate way: Miguel de Cervantes, *Novelas ejemplares I*, Harry Sieber, ed. (Madrid: Ediciones Cátedra, 1980), 137.

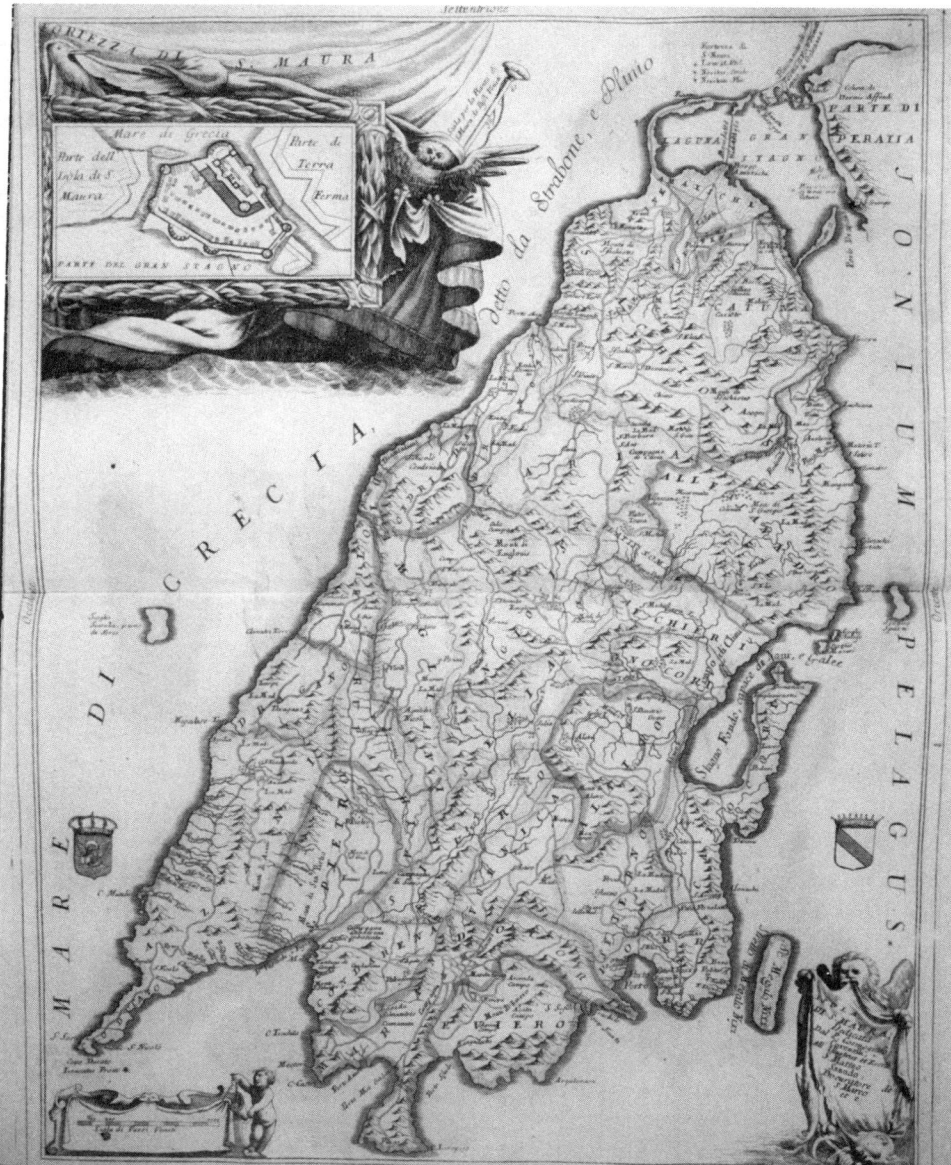

Figure 5.18. Vincenzo Coronelli, "Fortezza di Santa Maura," Venetia [c. 1685]. The British Library Board, Maps C.27.g.16(.61). (See color plate)

Stories of Ottoman atrocities, especially beheadings, during the Otranto episode had reached mythic proportions long before Coronelli's time, contributing to a collective consciousness of injury and insult at the hand of the Turk.[90]

[90] And the commemorations continued in various forms from dramatic paintings to the preserved heads of the "eight-hundred martyrs" in an Otranto reliquary chapel. See Angelo Maria Monaco, " 'Qui sunt et unde venerunt?' Topoi iconografici per il consenso agiografico nel culto degli ottocento Martiri di Otranto," 157–95, in *La conquista turca di Otranto (1480) tra storia e mito, Atti del convegno internazionale di studio Otranto-Muro Leccese, 28–31 marzo 2007*, Hubert Houben, ed., v. 2 (Galatina:

Figure 5.19. Vincenzo Coronelli, "Fortezza di Santa Maura," detail, Venetia [c. 1685]. The British Library Board, Maps C.27.g.16(.61).

Coronelli readily made the transition from narrative to map and back. His 1686 description of the siege of Coron (on the southwest tip of the Morea) collapses the events of several weeks into a dramatic recitation of

Congedo Editor, 2008). See also Özlem Kumrular, *The Ottoman World, Europe and the Mediterranean* (İstanbul, Isis Press, 2012), 30, on the long Catalan memory for the 1558 Ottoman sacking of Ciutadella on Minorca, 30, on the long Catalan memory for the 1558 Ottoman sacking of Ciutadella on Minorca.

Venetian triumph.[91] Coron had been commemorated by the Ottoman chronicler, Kemalpaşazade (İbn Kemal, 1468–1536), as "a famous fortress at the edge of the sea (and the border with Venice) . . . its walls as strong as the wall of Alexander and as high as the spheres."[92] Coronelli's account of Coron is illustrated (rather like Chiarello's history) with five images: three maps of the fortress and its surroundings, an engraving of a captured Ottoman battle flag, and another of two captured *tughs*.[93] The author writes that this booty was obtained in the course of a ferocious encounter:

> [the Venetian general] . . . poured upon them [the Ottomans] a Body of Foot and Dragoons, and . . . in the end . . . there were left 400 of them dead upon the place, and as many wounded: Our [men] got by this Action several worthy Spoils, amongst the rest seventeen Standards; and at their return into their Trenches, they exposed to the view of the Besieged 130 Turks Heads, as a frightful dismaying Spectacle.[94]

The one hundred thirty Turks' heads, like the broken lines separating territories on maps, defined a new boundary; they shifted Coron from war space to Venetian space.[95] Victory was commemorated in situ by the erection of heads on walls or pikes. And victory was carried home to Venice in the form of Ottoman standards and other captured booty, to be recycled for Venetian military endeavors, or to be displayed in churches and other public places.

Civic ritual and military morale thus demanded enemy heads. That demand was transimperial and cross-communal. Coronelli's description of the siege of Coron can be paired with one by the Ottoman official court chronicler Talikizade describing the late sixteenth century siege of Yanık (Györ or Iavarinum) on the Danube and Raab rivers. Talikizade tells his readers that the Ottoman troops had been surprised by an enemy sortie; but they regrouped and repulsed their attackers. Then the Ottomans loaded the enemy heads on carts, set them up on poles and rolled them up to a high point confronting the castle where they could be seen by those inside the fortress. When the "accursed infidels beheld" this dispiriting sight, according to the author,

[91] I am using here the English translation, P.M. Coronelli, *An Historical and Geographical Account of the Morea, Negropont, and the Maritime Places, as Far As Thessalonica; Illustrated with 42 Maps of the Countries, Plains, and Draughts of the Cities, Towns and Fortifications.* Englished by R.W. Gent (London: Printed for Matth. Gillyflower and W. Canning, 1687), 74–84. The Italian original was swiftly translated into French, and then into English, and reproduced in another Italian edition in 1688. See also Alessandro Locatelli, *Racconto historico della Veneta guerra in Levante* (Venetia: Girolamo Albrizzi, 1691), fortress image insert after p. 44.

[92] İbn Kemâl [Kemalpaşazade], *Tevârîh-i Âl-i Osmân, VIII Defter*, Ahmet Uğur, ed. (Ankara: Türk Tarih Kurumu, 1997), 205–6.

[93] Coron was taken in August 1685 by Francesco Morosini, beginning a successful set of campaigns by Venice and its allies (German, papal, Tuscan, and the Knights of St. John) to retake the Morea. Coronelli, *An Historical and Geographical Account*, 81. See, for a Venetian representation (dating from 1687) of an Ottoman banner and tughs (which are juxtaposed with a cross), Alberto Tenenti, "Profilo di un conflitto secolare," in *Venezia e i Turchi: Scontri e confronti di due civiltà*, ed. Carlo Pirovano (Milan: Electa Editrice, 1985), figure 28, p. 32.

[94] Coronelli, *An Historical and Geographical Account*, 75–6.

[95] Coronelli, *An Historical and Geographical Account*, 79–81. On Ottoman insignia, see Murphey, *Exploring Ottoman Sovereignty*, 71–2; and Żygulski, *Ottoman Art in the Service of Empire*, 18, 34, 47, who provides images of Ottoman standards, and addresses the symbols, fabrics, and meanings of Ottoman ritual.

"they trembled like autumn leaves," but still refused to surrender.[96] Talik-izade, like Coronelli and other history writers before him, combined the tasks of recording, instructing, and bragging for his audience. He wanted to share with his readers the heroism of "their" soldiers and the frisson of fear and horror imposed upon the enemy by the display of the dead.[97] Victory itself was believed to signify righteousness and the favor of God. As Coronelli told his readers, the "sign" of the Christians would one day triumph over that of the "perfidious Ottomans... when we shall have made our selves worthy of this Favor from Heaven by our constant prayers."[98]

Captives and Refugees

The triumph over space was signified by captives and refugees as well as by corpses. Battles and sieges created captives who might remain in place, incorporated into the households of their conquerors, or be transported else-where for sale and display as symbols of military prowess. They also created refugees, who might elect (or be forced) to flee space that had changed hands.[99] The captive was a powerful and ubiquitous figure in the imagery of the Eurasian world, as elsewhere. He or she played a part, as we have seen, in triumphal processions at the site of conquest or back in the impe-rial capital. Such displays were witnessed by conquered and conqueror alike, narrated along the routes taken by returning armies, translated into text and image for a diverse set of audiences, and reproduced on maps for purposes of incitement and commemoration.

Captives could represent group identity or, less often, named indi-viduals.[100] On the map they were more likely to represent the former; and in maps deriving from the Christian kingdoms of Europe, captives might sig-nify either "us" or "them." Thus, for example, the title cartouche of Nicolas Visscher's (1649–1702) late seventeenth century map of the "Turkish Empire in Europe, Asia, and Africa" shows, among other stock images, Ottoman warriors bearing a crescent flag, tugh, firebrands and lances posed behind a bare-chested and presumably Christian captive (Fig. 5.20).[101] Another kneel-ing figure offers money and goods to the sultan, mingling imagery of human

---

[96] Woodhead, *Ta'līkī-zāde's şehnāme-i hümāyūn*, 48, 262. The author notes that a register of those who had distinguished themselves, as in other campaigns, was drawn up (51). See also Fetvacı, *Picturing History*, 67–8.

[97] Siege imagery was so popular that Jacque-Auguste de Thou's monumental *Histoire Universelle* devoted "36 pages to the siege of Malta in 1565, 55 to that of Cyprus in 1570, 36 more to the attack on Famagosta, 40 to Szighetvar in 1566, and 17 to Esztergom in 1595"; Michaud, "Les Turcs dans l'histoire universelle," 243–4.

[98] Coronelli, *An Historical and Geographical Account*, 84.

[99] See David Abulafia, *The Great Sea: A Human History of the Mediterranean* (Oxford: Oxford Uni-versity Press, 2011), 470–87, on the Mediterranean region as a place of reshaped communities and identities.

[100] Vincenzo Coronelli, *Isolario: [dell'Atlante Veneto]*, v. 1, 241, juxtaposes an engraving of a Venetian naval battle in 1668 with a text that names and gives the ranks of the Ottoman beys taken captive, and claims a total of 900 anonymous "Turk" prisoners. Some were chained, some drowned, and some put to the sword.

[101] Nicolaum Visscher, "Magni Turcarum Domini Imperium in Europa, Asia, et Africa," Amsterdam, no date. Nicholas Visscher the father died in 1679.

Figure 5.20. Nicolas Visscher, "Magni Turcarum Domini Imperium in Europa, Asia, et Africa," cartouche, Amsterdam [1680?]. The British Library Board, Maps K.Top.113.9.

bondage with that of the exploitation of the fruits of the land. And by way of provoking a response from the faithful viewers, the Ottoman side of the cartouche depicts the sultan standing on a cross, a counterpart to Christian figures shown standing on the crescent. Another group of Christian captives (men, woman, and children) appears in the title cartouche for Johannes van Keulen's (1654–c.1715) 1680 sea chart of the Aegean archipelago and western Anatolia (not shown here). The setting seems to be the slave market rather than the aftermath of battle. The captives kneel at the foot of a dominant "Turk" figure, equipped with turban and stick, who seems to be scrutinizing them for their economic potential.[102] In both cartographic frames the captive is associated with the riches deriving (directly or indirectly) from conquest and with a message of warning or admonition to the Christian audience.

Elsewhere it was the Turk who embodied captivity on the map. In 1598 Alexander Maier published at Augsburg a map showing "Christian" forces capturing Iavarinum (Györ or Yanık) (Fig. 5.21).[103] A flag with a large cross floats over the wall, signifying the new Christian identity of the fortress. The Hapsburg double-headed eagle and the coat of arms of Hungary are displayed prominently on other banners. In the foreground one finds a cartouche in the form of a monument dedicated to the Hapsburg general Count Adolph Schwarzenberg (1547–1600), one of the "liberators" of the citadel.[104] An angel raises two victory wreaths over two "classically" inspired obelisks. She is perched on two tied and captive Turks who have in this instance retained their headgear (a turban and the peaked hat of a janissary).[105] Iavarinum had been seized by Sinan Pasha in September 1594; and the forces of royal Hungary had failed to recapture it in 1597.[106] Its reconquest in 1598 was thus viewed as a salutary sign. To seal that message the mapmaker employed a Latin passage from the Vulgate as a legend across the bottom of the map:

> *Just like the fire which burns down the forest, and just like a flame burning up the mountains, thus will you destroy them in your fury, and scatter them utterly in your rage. [Sicut ignis qui comburit silvam, et sicut flamma comburens montes; ita persequêris illos in tempestate tua, et in ira tua turbabis eos.]*[107]

---

[102] Ioannes van Keulen, "Paskaerte Vande Archipel en de Eylanden..." Amsterdam [1680]. University of Melbourne Library, Map Collection, 10187/3016.

[103] Alexander Maier, "Iavarinum sive Raab à Christianis captum 29 die Martij Anno Christi 1598," [Augsburg], [1598]. British Library, Maps 28335.(.5).

[104] In the upper left, a smaller legend offers the map to "Mariae Fuggerae," possibly a patron of the mapmaker. It invokes the name of the Hapsburg Rudolph II (Holy Roman emperor, 1576–1612).

[105] For a later map cartouche of female victory and chained Turk, see M.A. Baudrand, "La Grece," Paris, 1716, in Sphyroeras, Avramea, and Asdrahas, *Maps and Map-Makers of the Aegean*, 178–9, plate 129. See also Jutta Kappel, "Die Türkennot des Kaisers: Zu einigen Aspekten der Darstellung des Türkenkrieges (1593–1606) in der Hofkunst Rudolfs II," 124–33, in *Im Lichte des Halbmonds*. A liberating angel, standing on a crescent and flanked by half-naked prisoners (of indeterminate identity), also decorates the cartouche of the map, Homann heirs, "Bosniae Regnum," no date, British Library K.Top.113.54.

[106] Wratislaw, *Adventures*, 163–4, a captive himself at the time, describes being confronted with the news of Sinan's victory in 1594 and "Turk" boasting of the "artillery, booty, and provisions" taken from the fortress.

[107] *Vulgate*, Psalms, 82:15–16. Another legend ribbon at the top of the map, the relevance of which is more obscure, cites a passage from 1 Samuel 3:11. Thanks to my colleague Michael Kulikowski for this translation. See Brummett, "The Fortress: Defining & Mapping the Ottoman Frontier," 37.

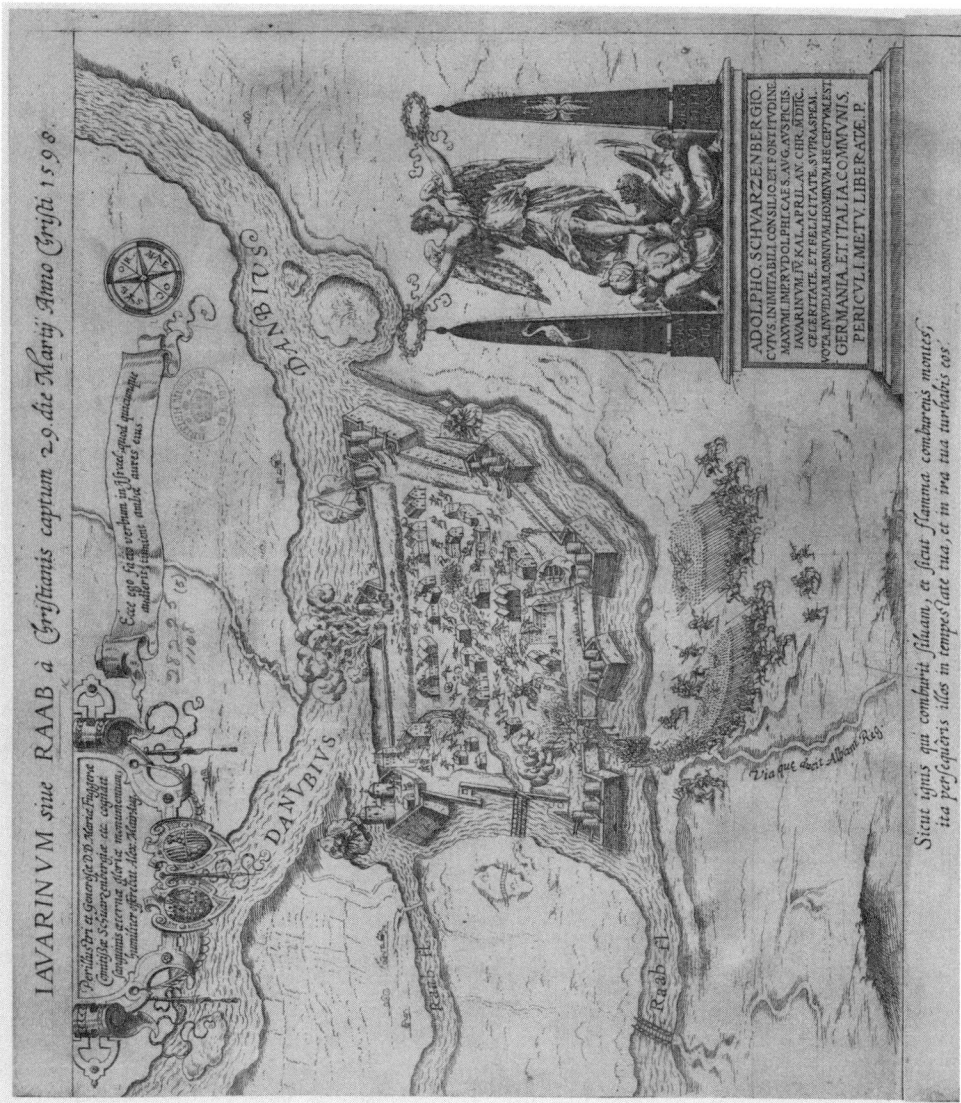

Figure 5.21. Siege of Raab. Alexander Maier, "Iavarinum sive Raab à Christianis captum 29 die Martij Anno Christi 1598" [Augsburg] [1598]. The British Library Board, Maps 28225·(·5).

The Ottoman captives embodied that destruction and "scattering." Where Coronelli, writing of the Venetian conquest of Coron, had invoked the ruin of the Sabines by Rome, Maier invoked the Psalms and their calling forth divine wrath upon the "enemies" of God and of Israel. Both men used the power of the Latin caption embedded in vernacular surrounding text (Italian and German respectively) to show the historical continuity of the struggle against the Ottomans with earlier endeavors against the "infidel."

Although captives were thus common figures in early modern cartography, the figure of the refugee was less likely to appear on the body of the map. Vincenzo Coronelli, however, in his 1696 chart of the Archipelago, produced a highly impressionistic image of the Turk as refugee (Fig. 5.22). In this representation, he provides an unusual gendered 'take' on the defeated Ottoman. For although narratives of piracy or the victories of Christian kings might include descriptions of the Ottoman female, it was relatively uncommon for her to appear on the map except as an ethnographic type. Here, instead, Coronelli includes her in an unbounded cartouche splashed directly across the land of "Romania."[108]

The image shows the winged lion of St. Mark. He rears up on what appear to be the building blocks of a devastated city. The legend of the map is inscribed on the broken wall of a large edifice; and the lion, a flaming brand in one hand, appears to be driving a fearful group of residents out of the building. Emerging through an archway, carrying their possessions, their faces gripped by anxiety and woe, three men, a woman, two naked children, and even a dog flee to the east toward the Sea of Marmara and Anatolia.[109] The men wear turbans and the woman wears the high beribboned hat frequently seen in ethnographic imagery of the "Turk." The building from which they are escaping is engulfed in flames. In the background other figures flee with their livestock. Exactly whom these people represent we do not know, but they seem clearly to represent Muslim inhabitants being driven back to 'where they belong.' Interestingly, the hodgepodge cartouche of Pieter van der Aa's (1659–1733) 1729 map of the Archipelago (not shown here), published in Leiden, also features "Turk" refugees (father, son, and grandfather) fleeing from a burning city. They do not have a female companion; but the Ottoman female is suggested by a fallen statue of a bare-breasted woman with a crescent as her headdress.[110]

In any case, Coronelli seems to have found the image of the refugee an affecting one, perhaps a sign of God's divine 'justice.' The message of the cartouche on his map of the Archipelago is mirrored in his chronicle of the Venetian victories in the Adriatic in 1684–5. There he provides another

---

[108] Coronelli, *Isolario: [dell'Atlante Veneto]*, v. 1, 1696, map after 182. Note that the dedication here is dated 1697.

[109] A similar image in words is included in Ahmad ibn Khaled al-Nasiri's description of the French bombardment of Tripoli in 1685: "The people in the city became terrified and had no clear idea of what to do. They started removing their possessions to the countryside, and transporting their women and families to Al-Manchia." Cited in Matar, *Europe through Arab Eyes*, 211.

[110] P. Van der Aa, "Archipel Septentrional ou Mer Egée," Leiden, 1729, plate 133, in Sphyroeras, Avramea, and Asdrahas, *Maps and Map-Makers of the Aegean*, 184–185. There may be two female figures posed on the shore in the cartouche image, but they are difficult to make out.

Figure 5.22. Vincenzo Coronelli, "Parallello Geographico Dell'Antico Col Moderno Archipelago," cartouche, *Isolario* [*dell' Atlante Veneto*], v. 1, Venetia, 1696. Photo Courtesy of the Newberry Library, Chicago, Ayer 135.C8 Vault.

scenario of burning and desolation in his narrative of Venetian raids on
Ottoman villages near Lepanto:

> *After a while the Venetian troop entered five Turkish villages, enslaving*
> *some of the inhabitants while others fled. They burned all the houses*
> *and villas of the infidels in which there was a great quantity of grain and*
> *other crops. After five days of destruction . . . they sailed away toward*
> *Santa Maura.*[111]

A clue to Coronelli's point of view may also be found in the dedication to
volume one of the atlas in which the map of the Archipelago appeared. Coronelli dedicated that volume to the "Emperor of the Romans," Leopold I (Holy
Roman Emperor 1658–1705), lauding his efforts against both the Ottomans
and the ungrateful Christian "rebels" who allied with them. The Ottomans,
he noted, "had already despoiled the vast provinces of Asia and Africa, not
to mention Europe . . . with a formidable army of three hundred thousand
warriors . . . reducing the Occident to a bloody desolation and threatening to
trample to the very threshold of the Vatican."[112] It is only through Leopold's
intercession, the author suggests, that the Ottomans and their allies can be
destroyed. The refugees in Coronelli's paean to imperial power would thus be
the lucky ones, survivors of the combined onslaught of the forces of doge and
emperor.[113] The message of driving out the Turk and celebrating his demise
thus echoed among the histories, maps and atlas texts of the early modern
Christian world. The mapmaker, whether he plied his trade in Venice, Augsburg, or Amsterdam, could count on finding an appreciative audience when
he inscribed his works with images of the fallen Turk.

De Jode and Circulating the Image of the Turk's Head

It did not suffice that the image of the Turk's head be published. It also had to
circulate; and the mapmaker was always on the lookout for embellishments
that might be used to refresh stock images already to hand. That seems to have
been the case when Cornelis de Jode in Antwerp, published a map of Croatia,
one part of the contested Ottoman–Hapsburg frontier. De Jode had already
produced such a map in 1593 in his *Speculum Orbis Terrae.* Entitled "Croatia
& circumiacentium Regionum versus Turcam nova delineatio," the map
included the stock device of small massed armies marching across contested

---

[111] Vincenzo Coronelli, *Conquiste della Serenissima Republica di Venezia nella Damazia, Epiro, e Morea durante la guerra intrapresa contro Meemet IV Imperr: De Turchi* ([Venetia]: Nel Laboratorio del P.M. Coronelli Cosmografo Publica, 1686), second section, last part on Patrasso. Pages of volume are unnumbered, Correr D. 520. See also, on raiding for captives, Mayhew, *Dalmatia between Ottoman and Venetian Rule*, 263–5.

[112] Coronelli, *Isolario*, v. 1, second unnumbered page of dedication.

[113] Describing the conquest of Prevesa in 1684, Coronelli, *Conquiste della Serenissima Republica di Venezia nella Dalmazia, Epiro, e Morea*, part 2: "Dalmazia, Prevesa," second unnumbered page of section, wrote, "Questa finalmente cadde sotto il Dominio della Serenissima Republica li 29 Settembre 1684 . . . ; e consegnate dagl'Assediati nelle mani del Generrale Strasoldo le munizioni da bocca, e da fuoco, e tutte le bandiere, uscirono solo trenta di loro principali, e gli altri colle loro Donne solamente vestiti, furono assicurati di passo per Quattro miglia sopra la marina, & inviati all'Arta."

space (Fig. 5.23).[114] This was not an unusual map. Yet, some time later, de Jode amended the map in response to events on the Ottoman–Hapsburg war front, providing two titillating vignettes designed to delight and inform his audience. This amended map, entitled "Croatia versus Turcam," suggests the ways in which both news and imagery of the Ottomans were assembled and circulated in the Christian realms (Fig. 5.24).[115] It also conveys the ways in which the male head and the female body were employed in early modern iconography to suggest the boundaries of human identity and the options for dominance and submission.

In the two lower corners, directly on the body of the amended map, de Jode has posed images of masculine and feminine submission. In the lower right corner is a couple representing Sultan Murad III (r. 1574–95), the "Turkish Kaiser" (labeled *T. K. Contrafatiur*), and a female figure of his "sister" (*T. K. Swester*).[116] The latter represents the Ottoman harem but also, by allusion, territories like Croatia that the Ottomans proposed to subordinate. Dressed in courtly gown and elaborate headgear, this woman kneels like a petitioner at the sultan's feet. Holding a piece of script in one hand, Murad uses the other to extend his scepter out over her head. He appears as the benevolent father, his face serene. In the left-side vignette, the couple is male. The Ban of Croatia kneels before Kaiser Rudolph (d. 1612), the Hapsburg emperor, in the classic position of a warrior submitting to his lord. The Ban salutes the crowned Rudolph with his saber; and a grateful Rudolph holds his own scepter off to the side. But there is another head in this scenario. Pierced by a tall stake, the mustachioed severed head of Telli Hasan Pasha, bey of Bosnia, occupies the space between the governor and his liege.[117] His eyes are closed in death and his head, ingloriously, devoid of covering.

These cartouches are a commemorative device. Croatia was a critical frontier zone in the long Ottoman–Hapsburg war of 1593–1606.[118] Hasan Pasha,

[114] Cornelius de Iudaeis [Cornelis de Jode] (1568–1600), "Croatiae & circumiacentiu[m] Regionu[m] versus Turcam nova delineatio," undated map, in Cornelis de Jode, *Speculum Orbis Terrae* (Antwerp, 1593). This is an edition of the 1578 atlas by his father, Gerard de Jode (c. 1509–91), entitled *Speculum Orbis Terrarum*. See Cornelis Koeman, *Atlantes Neerlandici*, v. 2 (Amsterdam: Theatrum Orbis Terrarum, 1967), 205–12.

[115] Maria Pia Pedani, "Venetians in the Levant in the Age of Selim I," 99–112, in *Conquête ottomane de l'Égypte (1517)*, Benjamin Lellouch and Nicolas Michel, eds. (Leiden: Brill, 2013), 108, shows for an earlier period how Matteo Pagan's roughly 1549 map of Cairo employed material probably dating back at least to 1497, and layered on an image of Sultan Selim's 1517 conquest of the city.

[116] Cornelius de Iudaeis [Cornelis de Jode] (1568–1600), "Croatiae & circumiacentiu[m] Regionu[m] versus Turcam nova delineatio," undated map, published in Harrie Teunissen and John Steegh, *Balkan in kaart: Vijf eeuwen strijd om identiteit*. Catalogus bij een tentoonstelling in de Universiteitsbibliotheek Leiden, 4 September–16 Oktober 2003 (Leiden: Universiteitsbibliotheek, 2003), plate 14. The authors identify this image as dating from approximately 1598.

[117] The COPAC online map catalog, wrongly I think, identifies the figures on the British Library's copy of this map as Ferdinand I, King of the Romans (standing), his general Jean Baptiste Gastaldi (kneeling), and Friar George Martinuzzi (head). Martinuzzi, treasurer of John Zapolyi, as power behind the throne for Zapolya's son, submitted personally to the Ottomans at Buda in 1541. He died in 1551, and Ferdinand's rule ended in 1564.

[118] See Finkel, *The Administration of Warfare*, 7–20, 36–7; Gustav Bayerle, *Ottoman Diplomacy in Hungary*, 9–10, which notes the accounts of Ottoman historians; and Szakály, "The Early Ottoman Period, Including Royal Hungary, 1526–1606," in *A History of Hungary*, 83–99, esp. 96. See also Gunther Erich Rothenberg, *The Austrian Military Border in Croatia, 1522–1747* (Urbana, IL: University of Illinois Press, 1960), 52–63; and Colin Heywood, "Bosnia under Ottoman Rule, 1463–1800,"

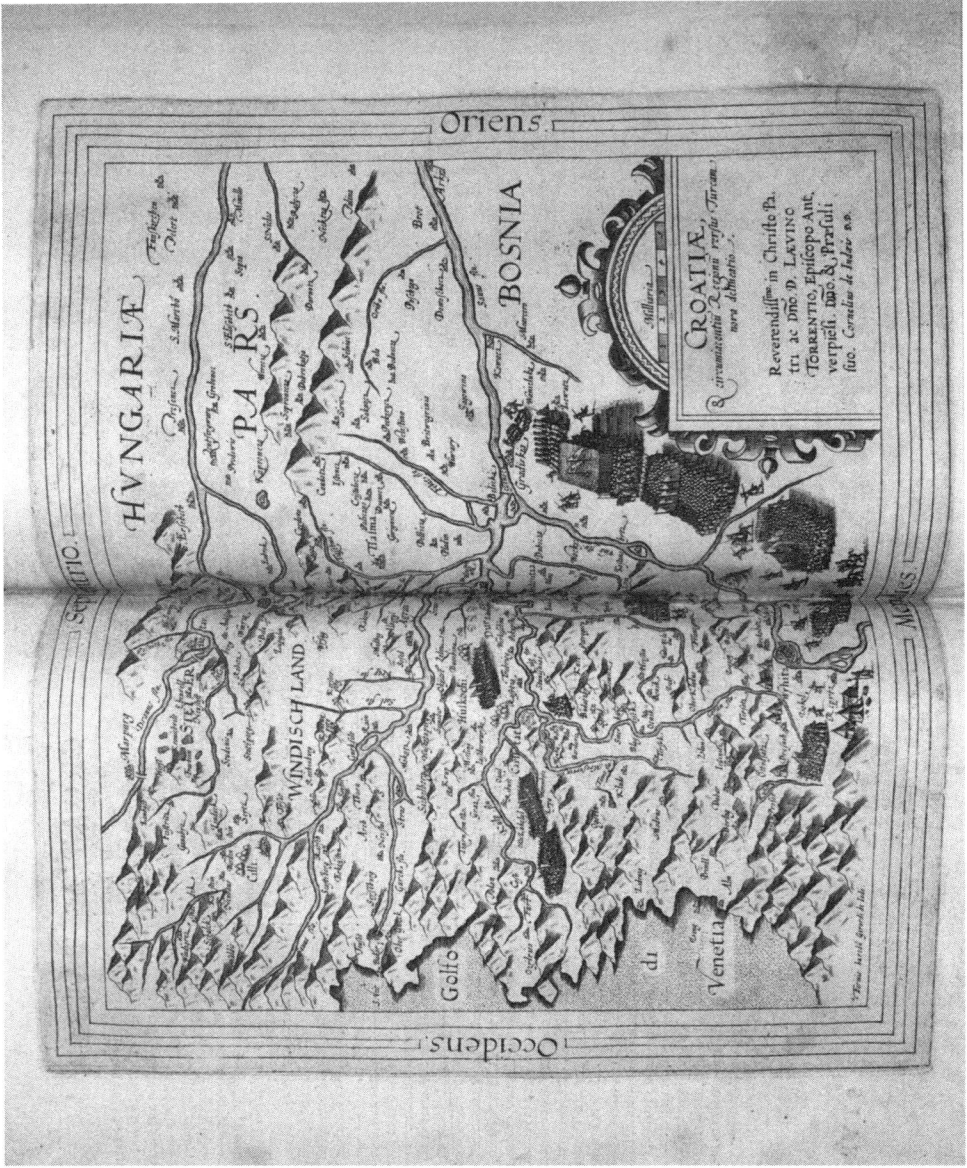

Figure 5.23. Cornelis de Jode, "Croatia & circumiacentium Regionum versus Turcam nova delineatio," from *Speculum Orbis Terrae*, Antwerp, 1593. The British Library Board, Maps C.7.c.13.

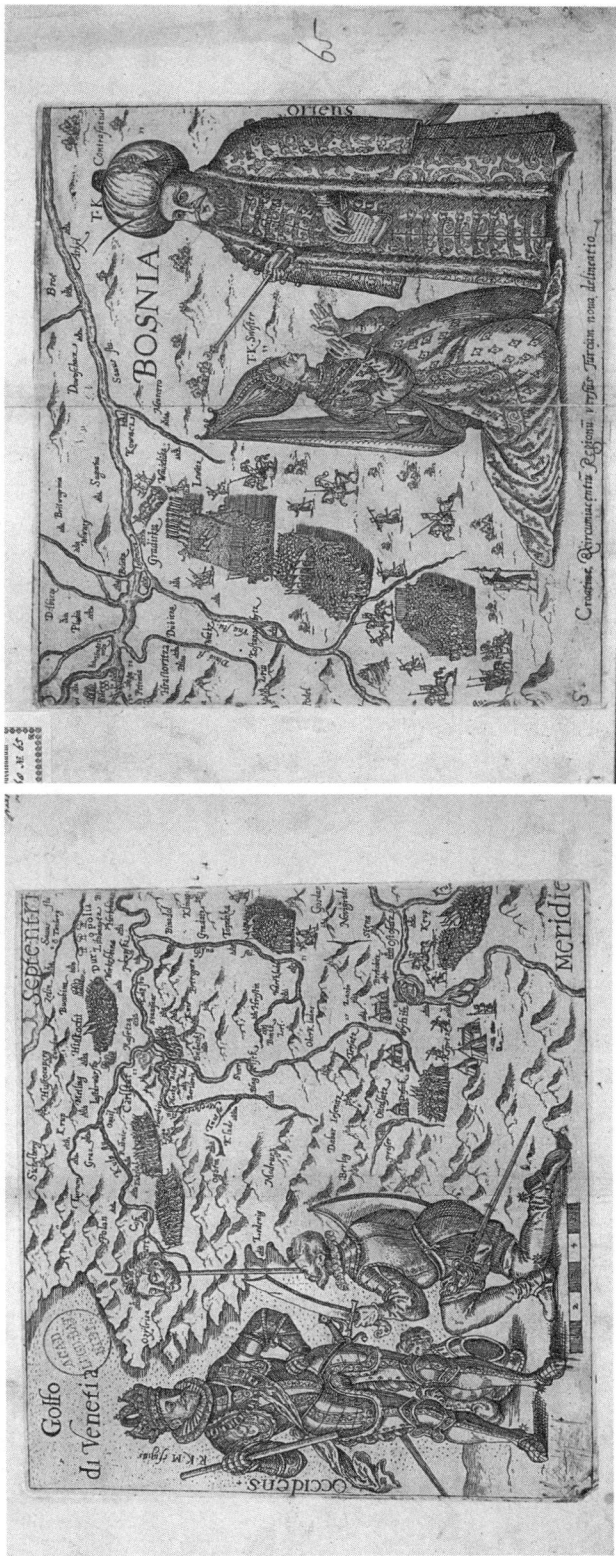

Figure 5.24. Cornelis de Jode, "Croatia & circumiacentium Regionum versus Turcam nova delineatio," insets, Antwerp, [c. 1594]. Leiden University Library, Special Collections, COLLBN Port 123 N 138 and Port 168 N 65.

according to the Ottoman chronicle of Mustafa Naima, had won a decisive victory on the Croatian frontiers in spring of 1592, taking "limitless slaves and booty (*esir u emval*)." He purportedly sent "two thousand heads and two hundred captives in chains" to the Porte.[119] On June 22, 1593, the pasha was besieging the town of Siska, on the Sava River. But his Ottoman force was stunned by a hastily mobilized counter attack that left its commander dead and his army decimated. This "dreadful news," Naima writes, reached Istanbul by courier, and ultimately provoked a full-scale retaliatory Ottoman campaign.[120] The same news was cause for celebration in the realms of the Christian kings; and word of it apparently spread widely, if de Jode's map is any indication. I suspect, however, that de Jode was not the originator of the images that graced his new map. Rather, news accompanied goods and intelligence traveling along the land and sea routes linking Antwerp and the Ottoman military frontier, generating images along the way. De Jode's atelier sent agents to the German book fairs and his map vignettes echo those in a German broadsheet dated 1594.[121] Regardless of the direct source for de Jode's vignettes, they are evidence for the circulation of victory stories and their attendant imagery, and for the opportunistic nature of the map trade. Antwerp was in no danger of assault by the Turk, but the image of Telli Hasan's head, like the victory commemorations of Lepanto, signified the unity of Christendom, at least superficially, when it came to opposition to the expansion of Muslim empires. Iconographically, the juxtaposition of Ottoman and Hapsburg lords to their male and female underlings put the two sovereigns on an equal footing, both with the power to command. But Rudolph bears a sword whereas Murad holds a text. And the insertion of Telli Hasan's head, at least for the moment, makes the message of Hapsburg martial superiority clear.

One sees the female body and the male head deployed again in the cartouche of Nicolas Sanson's 1654 map, "Estats De L'Empire Du Grand Seigneur des Turqs" (Fig. 5.25).[122] Two female figures in 'characteristic' headgear flank the sultan's "estates" in "Asia, Africa, and Europe," and what may be the head of the Grand Seigneur himself, turbaned, bodiless, and bearing a rather quizzical expression, is perched beneath the map's legend. This is not a martial image like that on de Jode's map. There are no invocations of the Christian God. The crescent, rather than trodden under the feet of an avenging angel, is posed decoratively at the top of the legend.

22–53, in Mark Pinson, ed. *The Muslims of Bosnia-Herzegovina: Their Historic Development from the Middle Ages to the Dissolution of Yugoslavia* (Cambridge, MA: Harvard University Press, 1993).

[119] Naima, *Tarih-i Na'ima*, v. 1, 53. Or, for an English version, see Naima, *Annals of the Turkish Empire*, 5.

[120] Naima, *Tarih-i Na'ima*, v. 1, 62.

[121] See the advertisement for Hartung and Hartung in *Geographica Hungarica*, 8 (May 2004): 122. The broadsheet is approximately 2/3 text and the map territory less expansive than that seen in de Jode's map. We need to know more before the chain of imitation can be properly identified. Koeman, Schilder, Egmond, and van der Krogt, "Commercial Cartography and Map Production in the Low Countries," *HOC*, v. 3, pt. 2, 300–302, points out the de Jode atelier's use of the Frankfurt Book Fair as a means of both selling and acquiring images.

[122] Nicolas Sanson d'Abbeville, "Estats De L'Empire Du Grand Seigneur des Turqs ou Sultan des Ottomans En Asie, en Afrique, et en Europe," Paris, 1654.

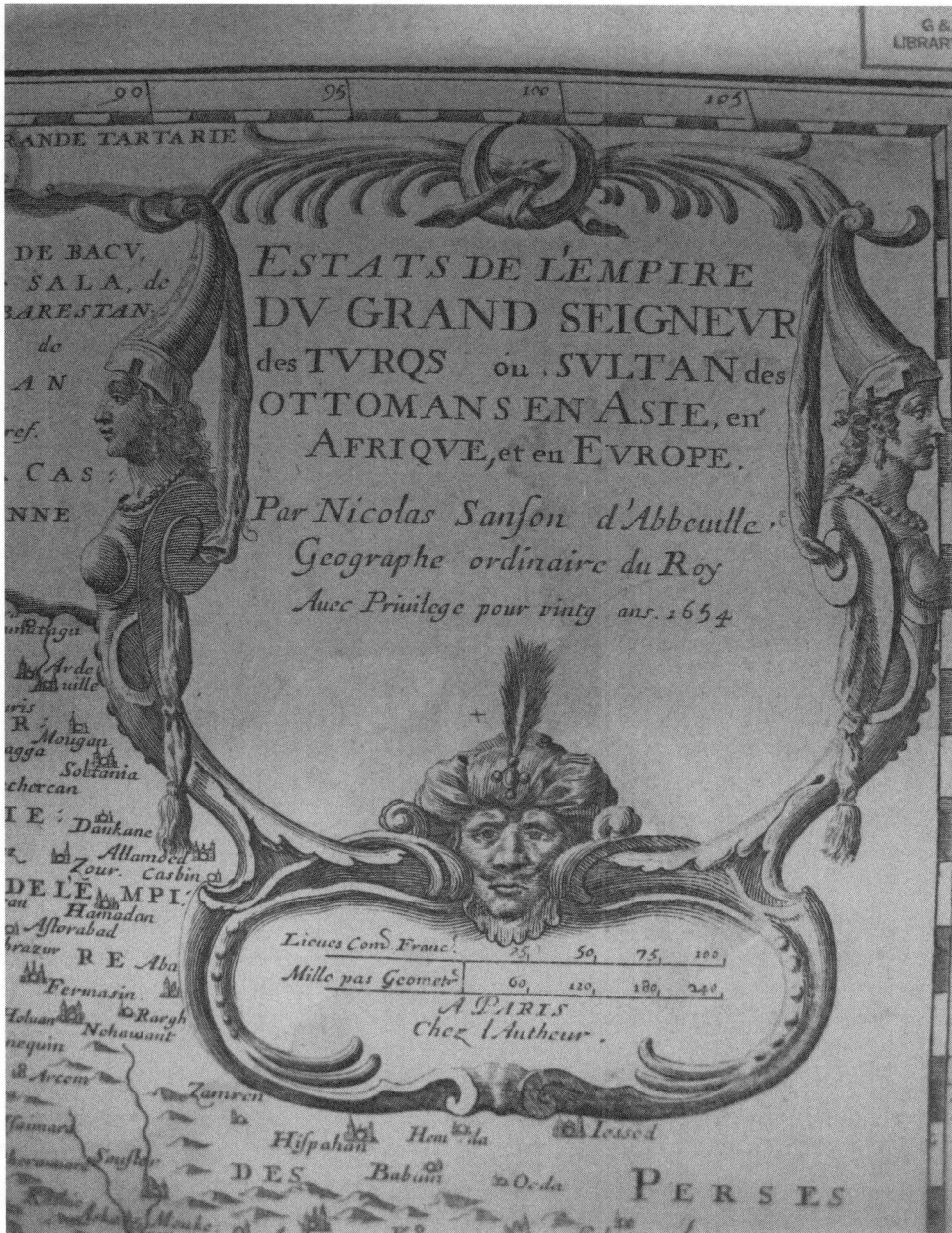

Figure 5.25. Nicolas Sanson, "Estats De L'Empire Du Grand Seigneur des Turqs," cartouche, Paris, 1654. Geography and Map Division, Library of Congress.

In this cartouche, the empire is normalized, its lord a king like any other, though with transcontinental territories. He keeps his turban and aigrette to show who he is. The females too, beyond their peaked hats, are homogenized rather than demonized; they would not seem out of place in allegories of Europe.

Thus the head of the Turk moved from narrative to image and back as the lords and printers of Christian Europe confronted Ottoman expansion into Europe. On the map, the image of the Turk complemented cartographic legends and surrounding texts; or it served as an already understood icon of victory, defeat, and allegiance. The severed head of this formidable enemy was emblematic of the fears and exultations of Ottoman rivals. But the head and body of the Turk were also used to express familiarity, interest, and contempt. They were displayed in various configurations and situated in multiple sites on the map: sovereign, onlooker, soldier, captive, thug, and refugee, intruding on Christian space, fleeing reclaimed space, and strewn or heaped on conquered space. They embodied a complex set of emotions and a complex hierarchy of political and cultural space. But often enough the message was simple: we have conquered (or hope to conquer) this man, his possessions and his lands; we have thrown down his headgear, and made him submit.

6

From Venice and Vienna to Istanbul

The Travel Space between Christendom and Islam

> *The general aim of Nasuh, known as Matrakçı, who seeks forgiveness of God, being the poorest and the meanest of the soldiers, was that this book should serve as a guide for travelers as well as for those who join in Royal expeditions.*

Matrakçı Nasuh, *Fethname-i Karabuğdan*, [c. 1538].[1]

So wrote the Ottoman official Matrakçı Nasuh, in his illustrated chronicle of Sultan Süleyman I's exploits, suggesting the intimate associations of travel and military endeavor. All sojourners (soldiers, merchants, pilgrims, or adventurers), he presumed, needed narrative and visual guides to help them navigate the stages of travel between one point and another. Some of those guides and stages constitute the subject matter of this chapter, which highlights the ways that the travel spaces between Ottoman domains and the lands of the Christian kings were charted in narratives and maps. In particular, I will focus on the major avenues linking those domains, the land and sea routes connecting Vienna and Venice to Istanbul, and the critical place they held in the mental maps of European observers.

For Matrakçı, as for his Christian counterparts, the movement of troops and the movement of travelers took place over the same routes, linking the same urban centers. Those routes and cities were embedded in spatial contexts that could be imagined, described, and illustrated in certain familiar ways.[2] The modes of describing space found in such early modern texts and imagery are for the most part habits of long standing. Mapped spaces were

---

[1] See Matrakçı, *Beyān-ı Menāzil-i Sefer-i 'Irākeyn*, 130. The quotation used here is from a continuation of Matrakçı's account of the reign of Süleyman I: *Fethname-i Karabuğdan*, İstanbul [c. 1538]. See also Emiralioğlu, *Geographical Knowledge and Imperial Culture*, 84–5.

[2] Catherine Delano-Smith, "Milieus of Mobility: Itineraries, Route Maps, and Road Maps," 16–68, in *Cartographies of Travel and Navigation*, James R. Akerman, ed. (Chicago: University of Chicago Press, 2006), 22, writes of a Spanish army commander named Don Lope de Acuña who in 1572 "provided

articulated as both place (current and historical) and passage. There were land and sea spaces in the seven climes, proximate to or distant from the narrator, relatively known or relatively unknown, and relatively full or relatively empty (the "inhabited lands" and the "uninhabited lands," as the tenth century Persian work *Borders of the World* puts it).[3] These places were characterized by their physical geography, goods, urban centers, "nations," and lords and the character, looks, language, and customs of their people (warlike or timid, archers or monks, idol-worshippers or monotheists, "sociable" or "quarrelsome," modest or lascivious).[4] But they were characterized further by the ease or difficulty and delights or hazards of travel. Artists and narrators might lay out parts of the world simply as objects for observation and edification (pieces of the cosmographical and geographic divisions of the world). Often, however, they approached them more directly through envisioned stages of travel and the witnesses who made that envisioning possible. The world, as Matrakçı suggests, was understood as the object of a journey (setting off, arriving, staying, and departing) not to mention an object of conquest, pilgrimage, and commercial endeavor.[5] The mapping of Ottoman space (from within or without) was thus a story of what it was like to go to and be in Ottoman realms. That story required authoritative witnesses, celebrations of sovereignty, and historically layered descriptions of places, routes, peoples, and things.

Ottoman Stages

Ottoman modes of conceptualizing space were in many ways analogous to those of their neighbors on either side. The Ottoman elite described the sultan as master of the two lands and two seas (Black and Mediterranean), lord of the Holy Places, and provider of justice to Muslim and non-Muslim (*zimmi*) subjects in his vast domains. Within that broad and ecumenical space, the Ottomans counted travel in terms of distance and time, which constituted the *menazil*, or stages, of a journey.[6] Those stages were further elaborated in

---

himself with simple but effective sketch maps showing everything an army on the march needed to know: the route, major rivers and forests, alternative itineraries, and the nearest towns."

3   Anonymous, *Hudud al-'Alam* (982–3 C.E.), cited in Scott Levi and Ron Sela, eds., *Islamic Central Asia: An Anthology of Historical Sources* (Bloomington: Indiana University Press, 2010), 28, 30, 32, of which the authors say, "Although written in Persian, the work falls into the category of Arab geographies, a genre that emerged from the earlier Greek tradition and developed in sophistication from the early years of the Abbasid caliphate (750–1258)."

4   Anonymous, *Hudud al-'Alam*, 31. See also John Wansborough, *Lingua Franca in the Mediterranean* (Richmond, Surrey: Curzon Press, 1996), 1–2, on "orbital" routes, diplomacy, and contact.

5   Bayly, *Empire and Information*, 21, notes the "Mughul accumulation of large archives of route maps and strip-maps." Brotton, *Trading Territories*, 115, comments on Matrakci's "visual rhetorics."

6   Matrakçı, *Beyān-ı Menāzil-i Sefer-i 'Irākeyn*, 134, 173. Matrakçı's account of the first Persian campaign suggested the time (dates of departure) required to complete each stage; his account of the second Persian campaign gave distances in miles. This Ottoman officer's description of stages is not unlike those found in other Ottoman narratives and, for that matter, in Italian narratives of the same era. For example, see Giovanni Tommaso Minadoi da Rovigo, *Historia della Guerra fra Turchi et Persiani* (Venetia: Andrea Muschio & Barezzo Barezzi, 1588), 375–6 on getting to Tabriz; and Casale, *The Ottoman Age of Exploration*, 188, on an Arabic work produced in Süleyman's reign showing the distances between one hundred cities and Istanbul.

terms of stopping places (cities, fortresses, camps, sufi *tekkes*, palaces, rivers, and mountain passes), acquiescent or recalcitrant lords, and confirmed or ambiguous possession. Matrakçı's manuscript, *The Description of the Stages of Sultan Süleyman Han's Campaign in the Two Iraqs*, is often called simply *The Stages* (*Menazil*).[7] Describing the nature of this work, Matrakçı notes that he is explaining, "one by one in writing and with illustrations in a well-ordered, well-arranged, gilded and detailed way,"

> *the captured fortresses, provinces, towns, and places and countries situated between them, caravanserais built for rest; worn out fortresses, ruined places, well-known mountains, difficult straits, renowned rivers, and barren lands, tulips in their meadows, the names, pictures and true realities...*[8]

The idea of *menazil* here includes not just the "true realities" of a march or a campaign but also a vision of the ordered nature of the world in a literary and artistic tapestry arrayed before the eyes of the armchair traveler.[9] Matrakçı made a point especially of listing saints' tombs in Iraq and carefully depicting the shrines of Imam Husein (martyred grandson of the Prophet) and other prominent religious figures (Fig. 6.1). Thus, his text and images not only document a series of military victories, they also act as a travel guide to sacred space and as a legitimation of Süleyman by means of his "redemption" of sacred sites.[10]

As the Ottomans celebrated their lordship, they also recorded space in campaign narratives as a progression (and procession) of places and of acts of submission.[11] But that progression might take different visual forms. Lokman, the Ottoman court panegyrist, for example, in recording the victories of Süleyman in Europe, depicted the sultan, vezirs, janissaries, other soldiery, and local inhabitants in elaborate miniatures.[12] The images of Matrakçı's *Menazil*, however, were devoid of people.[13] Visually the book emphasized

---

[7] It was a presentation volume for the sultan. Although historians differ on the level of his participation in painting the maps in this work, he was clearly a participant in the Iraq campaign. See Matrakçı, *Beyān-ı Menāzil-i Sefer-i 'Irākeyn*, 132, 151; and Rogers, "Itineraries and Town Views," in *HOC*, v. 2, 229–30, 239–40. The two Iraqs are Persian Iraq and Arabian Iraq. Matrakçı's own title for the work seems to have been simply *Mecmu'-i Menazil*. Yurdaydın notes, 153, that the topographical information, dates, and place names in the text of this account are very similar to those found in the earlier work (*Mecmua-ı Münşeat*) of Feridun Bey. See Suraiya Faroqhi, *Subjects of the Sultan: Culture and Daily Life in the Ottoman Empire* (London: I.B. Tauris, 2007), 71, on the "campaign itinerary of Sultan Süleyman from the years 1533 to 1536" included in Feridun Bey.

[8] Matrakçı, *Beyān-ı Menāzil-i Sefer-i 'Irākeyn*, 131–2. Yurdaydın translates "whole world" here from seven climes (*akalim seb'a*).

[9] Emiralioğlu, *Geographical Knowledge and Imperial Culture*, 38, 80, notes Mustafa ibn Ali al-Muvakkit's 1525 book, *Public Instructions for the Distances of Countries*.

[10] On a seventeenth century Damascene scholar's modes of seeing on a pilgrimage from Damascus to Jerusalem see Akkach, "The Poetics of concealment," 119.

[11] The illustrations from Feridun Ahmed's chronicle of the siege of Sighetvar show Süleyman (both dead and alive) receiving the obeisance of his subordinates: *Nüzhet ül-Esrar ül-Ahbar der Sefer-i Szigetvar*, Topkapı Sarayı Müzesi Kütüphanesi, Hazine 1339. See Atıl, *The Age of Sultan Süleiman*, 91–6; and Fehér, *Türkische Miniaturen*, plates 37, 44–47, and Lokman, *Hünername*, plates 38–39, 41, 43.

[12] Lokman, *Hünername*, Topkapı Sarayı Müzesi Kütüphanesi, Hazine 1524.

[13] See Halil Sahillioğlu, "Dördüncü Muradın Bağdat Seferi Menzilnamesi," *Belgeler* 2. 3–4 (1965): 1–36; and Hedda Reindl, "Zu einigen Miniaturen und Karten aus Handschriften Matraqçı Nasuh's"

Figure 6.1. Imam Husein Mosque, Karbala. Matrakçı Nasuh, *Beyan-ı Menazil-i Sefer-i Irakeyn-i Sultan Süleyman*, fol. 62b, İstanbul, [c. 1537]. İstanbul University Library, 5967.

the succession of Asian territories through which Süleyman's army marched to Iraq. Specific claims to Ottoman glory and hegemony in the Islamic world

Islamkundliche Abhandlungen, Beiträge zur Kenntnis Südosteuropas und des Nahen Orients, XVII band (Munich: Institut für Geschichte und Kultur des Nahen Orients, Universität München, 1974), 146–71.

were relegated to the text. Nonetheless, the submission of places and people along the routes shown was implicit in his visuals.[14] The procession through various stages of territory represented the certification of authority and its public persona, part of what Sergio Bertelli has called the "grand theatre of state," in its multiple forms.[15] In this form of mapping the Ottomans were not alone; their visions mirrored those of the Christian kingdoms of Europe and those of their predecessors, Islamic or otherwise, in the Afro-Eurasian oikumene. As stages of travel were crafted, the rituals of power and the rivalries of state and commune were always part of the narrative and visual terrain.

The Travel Narrative as a Model for the Map: Counting Stages

Travel narratives emerging out of the kingdoms of the Christian kings served to measure out Ottoman domains in terms of typologies of space that also took such rituals and rivalries for granted. It is those typologies and their translation onto maps with which the remainder of this chapter is concerned.[16] European travelers moving into Ottoman lands measured space in terms of distance and time, but also history, routes, and stopping places. As Dr. John Covel (1638–1722) noted in his seventeenth century travel narrative, "You must note that in Turkey travaylers reckon their way by houres, not by miles; however, I have made an estimate of every dayes journey both wayes, reckoning 3 miles to the hour, and truely I believe our pace in generall did come pretty just to that proportion."[17] Days were a better unit of measure for the actual traveler concerned with time, weather, provisions, and expenses. Miles were easier to mark on a map. But waystations were the primary embodiments of the stages of travel whether on the map, in travel narratives, or in the miniatures of Ottoman campaign accounts. These were the known places (linked by roads that ensured the greatest ease of travel), the sites of memory, and the sites of arrival or departure that provided resources and safe haven from the places (and peoples) in between.[18]

An anonymous merchant traveling in the early sixteenth century before the Ottoman conquest of Syria thus counted his journey from Aleppo to Persia in terms of walled cities, castles, and number of days journey between

---

[14] On the rhetorics of such acts of submission, see Rhoads Murphey, "The Cultural and Political Meaning of Ottoman Rituals of Welcome: A Text-Linked Analysis Based on Accounts by Three Key Ottoman Historians," 247–55, in Markus Köhback, Gisela Procházka-Eisl, and Claudia Römer, *Acta Viennensis Ottomanica, Akten des 13 CIEPO – Symposiums (Comité international des études pré-ottomanes et ottomanes), vom 21 bis 25 September, 1998* (Vienna: Selbstverlag des Instituts für Orientalistik, 1999).

[15] Bertelli, *The King's Body*, 37, 62–96; and Hakan Karateke, "Legitimizing the Ottoman Sultanate: A Framework for Historical Analysis," 13–52, in *Legitimizing the Order*, esp. 46–50.

[16] One cannot assume the necessity of maps in travel texts. As Anthony Payne has pointed out, Richard Hakluyt (b. 1552) felt no particular imperative to include maps in his three collections of voyages; Payne, "'Strange, remote, and farre distant countreys,'" 15.

[17] Dr. John Covel, *Voyages en Turquie 1675–1677*, Jean-Piere Grélois, trans., series *Réalités Byzantines* 6 (Paris: Éditions P. Lethielleux, 1998), 264. Covel held a chair in theology at Cambridge and was named chaplain of the English Levant Company in 1669 (7–8).

[18] Delano-Smith, "Milieus of Mobility," 31–32, distinguishes between roads (physical features, with implied passability), and routes (directions and imaginary lines linking departure points and destinations).

cities.[19] Although the Euphrates was the major physical divider between
Ottoman and Safavid space in the east, the ancient city of "Orfa" (Urfa), for
our traveler, was "the first city of the domains of Sultan Shah Ismail [Safavi,
r. 1501–1524]."[20] It served as a limit point of empires and the gateway "to
Bagdad, to Persia, to Turkey, and to Syria." It was also a reference point for
memory. There the merchant encountered the remnants of Biblical history,
in a place "encircled with walls by Nimrod," where "our father Abraham
wished to sacrifice his son Isaac to God."[21]

Beyond the conventions (and logistics) of counting time and space, travel
was divided into segments in terms of peoples and cultures. The conventions
of narrating space demanded attention to language, ethnicity, religious affiliation, rituals, entertainments, housing styles, and dress (particularly women's
dress) as indicators of where one was. These complemented references to
notables, political space, physical boundaries, and measures of comfort such
as post stations, conveyances, food and drink, furnishings, and the availability of other consumer goods. For some observers, the primary category
marking any stage of travel was convenience: whether the 'locals' were a
help or a hindrance. Could they provide wine or vermin-free beds? Did local
headmen or bandits harass and detain the 'innocent' traveler, or could he be
assured of adequate protection and security? For others, peoples and places
had to be scrutinized more carefully to address scholarly, strategic, or literary
objectives. The realms of Islam and Christendom were primary categories of
division, but they did not suffice to characterize the multiple and overlapping
identities of the inhabitants of the broad frontier zones through which the
sojourner had to pass. Some European travelers routinely invoked the trope
of Greco-Balkan space ruined by the advent of the "Turks," a trope that
endured throughout the period under consideration here (Fig. 6.2).[22] Others
commented on the economic opportunities provided by Ottoman rule. Some
were preoccupied with the conditions of their own countrymen resident in
Ottoman lands.[23] Others were preoccupied with the inevitable connections
of Ottoman realms to the past. Thus, mythical and historical sites were given
their Latin or Greek names, classical edifices and inscriptions were noted,
and visions of the heroes and heroines of ancient times were conjured up, so
the traveler might see beyond what was actually in front of his eyes.

[19] Anonymous Merchant, "Viaggio d'un mercante che fu nella Persia," 78–91, in *Navigationi et viaggi*,
Gian. Battista Ramusio, ed., v. 2 (Venetia: I Giunti, 1583; reprint, Amsterdam: Theatrum Orbis
Terrarum, 1968), 78v.
[20] Merchant, "Viaggio," 78v–79r. Later, an anonymous Venetian relazione from 1553 would pinpoint
the Tigris as constituting the boundary between the Ottoman and Safavid domains. But the author
noted that in the mountains there were various lords who vacillated between the sides of "sufi" and
"Turk." See Eugenio Alberi, *Relazioni degli Ambasciatori Veneti al Senato*, series III, v. 1 (Firenze:
Tipografia all' Insegna di Clio, 1840; reprint, University of Michigan Library, n.d.), 197.
[21] Merchant, "Viaggio," 78v–79r.
[22] See, for example, Marie-Gabriel-Florent-Auguste de Choiseul-Gouffier, *Voyage Pittoresque*, 2 vols.,
v. 1 (Paris: 1782), frontispiece and explication.
[23] Thus Samuel Pepys, sojourning to Tangier in 1684, commented upon how "mightily altered" both
his brother in law and an acquaintance, Lady Mary Howard, wife of the governor, were since leaving
London; MacLean, *Looking East*, 91–2. Apparently Pepys was also suggesting that the governor and
his wife had acculturated to the lascivious lifestyle of Tangier. Pepys complained of Tangier as a place
of bedbugs, whores, wanton behavior on the part of acclimatized Englishmen, and general corruption.

A PARIS,

Figure 6.2. Marie-Gabriel-Auguste-Florent Choiseul-Gouffier, *Voyage Pittoresque de la Grèce*, v. 1, frontispiece, detail, Paris, 1824. John Hay Library, Brown University Library.

George Sandys (1578–1644), for example, an English traveler approaching Ottoman lands, noted that Eastern places had to be shown both "in their present condition and in their former states."[24] Travel had to be narrated in terms of classical history and that of former Christian rulers, as well as in terms of adventure and the logistics of travel. The reader of travel literature (and maps), as he read, was thus expected to process through layers of text and time just as surely as through physical space. Where the Apostle Paul had walked, there too would the reader walk; where Alexander had conquered, there too did Süleyman conquer. Seldom does one find an author who arrayed Ottoman space before his audience without a clear sense that

[24] George Sandys, *A Relation of a Journey begun An: Dom: 1610. Containing a Description of the Turkish Empire of Aegypt, of the Holy Land, of the Remote parts of Italy and Llands ad ioyning,* 2nd ed. (Amsterdam: Theatrum Orbis Terrarum, 1973; reprint of London: W. Barren, 1615 edition), "dedication."

his work took its place among other and earlier texts that the reader had already consumed.[25]

Relazioni

Beyond classical exemplars, such as Herodotus or Pausanias, the model par excellence for the travel narrative in the sixteenth century was the *relazione* of Venetian envoys. These narratives marked the stages of the journey from Signoria to Porte and fleshed out the Ottoman, his domains, and his court. Combinations of diplomatic report and literary exercise, the *relazioni* were widely translated and circulated throughout Europe. They did not all devote attention to the journey, as opposed to the sites of negotiation and conflict; but they did include stages of travel as part of the official narration of how an envoy spent his time. Marino Cavalli, for example, a Venetian bailo writing in 1560, appended to his narrative an itinerary of his journey from Dulcigno (Ulcinj) on the Adriatic coast to Constantinople, providing the distance in miles from one stopping point to another.[26] Other considerations were principal cities, "pleasant or prosperous locales," the locations of mineral baths, and the places where horses could be changed or shod. In sum, Cavalli focused on distance and convenience.[27] Beyond those measures, he assessed the space between empires in terms of ethnicity, religion, environments, and relationships. First of all, he framed the intervening territory as either Christian-Ottoman space or Muslim-Ottoman space. Then he assessed its peoples (both Christian and Muslim) in terms of their ethnicity. Cavalli's primary concern was whether or not borders were sources of conflict. His intent, like that of the authors of all the *relazioni*, was to convey to his readers or listeners the nature and scope of Ottoman sovereignty and power. But he did not forget that they would also be interested in ways to get through Ottoman territory and back again.

Nicolay

Other narrators traveled further, were less familiar with Ottoman space, and were more concerned with mapping out borders for their readers. One such official sojourner to Ottoman lands was Nicolas de Nicolay (1517–83), a scholar, artist, and geographer attached to the embassy of Gabriel

[25] Purchas, *Hakluytus Postumus*, v. 2, 873, "The Reader may, if he please, certifie and satisfie himself in Master Edens, and Master Hackluyt Voyages. English Nauigations are now advanced to so great Adventure, and new or remote Discoveries, that I rather haste to them..." On Purchas, see Joan-Pau Rubiés, *Travel and Ethnology*, 349–52. The array of stories and texts employed by the travel author is also illustrated by John-Paul Ghobrial, "The Secret Life of Elias of Babylon and the Uses of Global Microhistory," *Past and Present* 222.1 (2014): 51–93.
[26] Alberi, *Relazioni*, series III, v. 1, 297–8.
[27] Alberi, *Relazioni*, series III, v. 1, 277–9. See also Rothman, "Self-Fashioning in the Mediterranean Contact Zone," 130–31, for a *relazione* on Ottoman Barbary; Yerasimos, *Les Voyageurs dans l'empire ottoman*, which contains an elaborate list of travel accounts along with routes of travel; and Borromeo, *Voyageurs occidentaux*.

d'Aramon, sent by Henri II (r. 1547–59) of France to the Porte in May of 1551. Nicolay charted the seventy-eight day journey from Marseilles to Istanbul (with preliminary stops on the North African coast) by describing the stopping places of his vessel along with historical insights, cultural observations, and commentary on the fruits of the land. His elaborate account, here cited in its English translation, provides a wealth of detail as well as a narration of the stages by which an ambassador approached the Ottoman king. As in Ottoman miniatures, or procession narratives, Nicolay took pains to represent the joy and reverence with which his lord was received at each stage of his journey. Like other travelers, he also made a point of noting the point at which he traversed a boundary (physical but also psychological) between "Christian" and "Turk" space. For Nicolay, Algiers seems to be the initiation point of the sojourn in the Ottoman realm. He thus links the coast of North Africa to the political core of the empire in Anatolia and the Balkans. In Algiers, Nicolay's master was presented with a "fayre horse of Turkie" and visited by "a great number of Turks, and Moores."[28] At Tripoli, they entered solidly "Turk" space, where the ambassador was received into the "royal galley" and began negotiations with the Ottoman pasha to desist from the siege of Tripoli. The French ship was visited all day by "divers Turkes and [renegade] Christians."[29] Nicolay traces Tripoli's lineage as a city "of Barbarie, situated on the maine lande up on the coast of the Sea Mediterrane ... first built by the Romans, and afterwards subdued by the Gothes which possessed the same unto the time of Homer [Umar] the second [Muslim] Calife ... "[30] He then lists subsequent kings up to the emperor Charles V. Tripoli was a place embedded in history and the object of a chain of imperial conquests that continued to Nicolay's own day.

After a stop in Malta, Nicolay's French expedition sailed for Istanbul, passing Cephalonia (in the Ionian Sea) and Zante. Both, he noted, were "subject unto the Venetians and contributory unto the Turke."[31] This characterization of Cephalonia and Zante is an interesting one because it expresses the dual identity of these frontier places caught between empires and their competing demands. That ambiguity of identity was reinforced when, in those same waters, Nicolay's party encountered "a great ship of Candia laden with malmsies, muscadels, and other marchandises, being bound for Venice."[32] The Candian ship, expecting corsairs, prepared to engage Nicolay's vessel, despite the "shot of assurance" given by the French. But its captain was soon reassured as d'Aramon

> *made them believe that he was of Sicilia [whereupon they struck their sails] ... and the maister with his barke came to salute the Ambassador, whom he straightwaies knew, for that he had oftentimes furnished him*

[28] Nicolay, *The Nauigations into Turkie*, 4. Although "Turk" was a default designation for Muslim in this era, the author refers to the "Turks and Moors" collectively as a "nation" characterized by "theft and covetousness (5)." On Nicolay's contribution to English cartographic knowledge, see Taylor, *Tudor Geography 1485–1583*, 59–60.

[29] Nicolay, *The Nauigations*, 18–20.

[30] Nicolay, *The Nauigations*, 20.

[31] Nicolay, *The Nauigations*, 31r.

[32] Nicolay, *The Nauigations*, 31r.

*of wines at Constantinople, and therefore presented him with a great
barrel of muscadel, a mutton & divers other pouncils, citrons, and
oranges, desiring him [d'Aramon] to helpe him with a barrel of fresh
water, for theirs began to stinke: which forthwith was delivered unto
him.*[33]

Nicolay's galley was also approached in these frontier waters by "an Italian
slave" who had escaped Constantinople and who swam out to the French-
men's vessel, seeing it as an embodiment of Christian space. For both captive
and ship captain, Nicolay's ship thus represented a welcoming space in a
potentially hostile and hybrid environment.[34] These vignettes of encounter
illustrate the inclination to distrust identities at sea; the affinities produced by
wine and water; the role of the Ottoman Archipelago as a meeting ground for
"foreigners"; and the role played by ships plying that sea zone in transferring
the goods and personnel of nations from one imperial space to another.

As the French delegation continued on its course for Constantinople, Nicolay found other opportunities to comment on the nature of boundaries and
identity. Passing Chios (an island off the Anatolian coast) prompted a long
disquisition. When Nicolay first saw the island it was still nominally Genoese,
though an Ottoman tributary. Its women embodied for Nicolay both the
enduring presence of Christian beauties in the "East" and the enduring connection of such places to classical history. Hence the Chian women had no
equal in "all the East," in terms of beauty, accomplishment, "good grace and
amorous courtesy." They "attire[d] themselves finely" and had "so modest
countenance and grace, that men would judge them rather to be Nymphs
or Goddesses than women or mortal maidens."[35] Such was the language
in which European travelers were inclined to describe at least some of the
women of the Archipelago. The ladies of Chios were "of the East," but
decidedly not "Turks," despite their proximity to Istanbul.[36] Like Nicolay's
ship, these Christian women constituted a reliable 'haven' of sorts in "Turk"
territory; they kept the space from being entirely Ottoman. But the Ottomans
conquered Chios in 1566 before the *Navigations* were published; and
although the Christian women remained an ongoing object of attention for
male narrators (see Ch. 7 on women's dress), there was no longer any illusion of the island itself being sovereign Christian space. Nicolay thus used

[33] Nicolay, *The Nauigations*, 31 r.
[34] It is in these very spaces between Western Europe, North Africa, and the Archipelago that the vagaries
of identity between Muslim and Christian space are illustrated in the works of Cervantes and other
contemporary authors. See Barbara Fuchs, *Passing for Spain: Cervantes and the Fictions of Identity*
(Urbana: University of Illinois Press, 2003), 62.
[35] Nicolay, *The Nauigations*, 37–8.
[36] For Nicolay, in *The Nauigations*, the operative categories seem to be woman or maiden, although he
does identify women using ethnic designators. He illustrates these distinctions in drawings of women
and their costumes. Later illustrations draw distinctions among "woman," "maiden," "gentlewoman,"
"Turk woman," and "great lady" (52–68). In his long commentary on the baths in Istabul, the author
notes that "Turk" and "Grecian" women go to the baths together; later he writes "Turks" and
"Christians" (60r). In Pera, he distinguishes the Grecian women from both the Turks and the "*Peratin
Franques*" (Latin Christians) (65v–88r). See Stephan Gerlach, *Türkiye Günlüğü 1573–1576*, Kemal
Beydilli, ed., Türkis Noyan, trans., v. 1 (İstanbul: Kitap Yayınevi, 2006), 74, for designations of Serbian
women and Turkish women on the journey from Vienna to Constantinople.

his description of Chios to meditate on the vagaries of empire, the power of the past, and the long and ultimately fruitless defense by the Genoese against "the fury and rage of the Turkes."[37]

The magnetic attraction of the past became more powerful as Nicolay approached the fabled city of Constantine. Passing the isle of St. Stephano and sailing near the shore, Nicolay's ship stopped at the port of Segre and then at Metelin (Lesbos) before arriving at Tenedos, each stopping place suggesting the histories and personalities of Greek and Roman lore. Having had "presents" extorted from them at ancient Abyde, the castle on the Asian side of the straits, they stopped at the village of Maiton and the city of Gallipoli before arriving at the Constantinople side of the horn. There the delegation was received "with great countenance of friendship" by Rüstem Pasha (d. 1561), the grand vezir.[38] The last stage of Nicolay's journey thus provided both a cautionary tale of extortion, and a narrative of celebration as the travelers were welcomed into the womb of Islamic Byzantium. It was a place swathed in the garments of its past; there, the delegation both expected diplomatic gain and looked with some trepidation to dealings with the vainglorious "Turk."

Busbecq

Another traveler who charted the stages of entry into the empire was Ogier Ghiselin de Busbecq (1522–92), a Hapsburg ambassador, who traveled at roughly the same time as Nicolay. Remaining in the empire from 1554 to 1562, Busbecq became well acquainted with Ottoman affairs, and his narrative has often served as a benchmark for representation of sultanic domains. Busbecq's journey to Istanbul was over land from Vienna. Thus he witnessed Balkan lands directly, commenting on mountain passes, stopping places, cities, fortresses, and the safety of boat travel down the Danube. Like Nicolay, at each stage of his journey the envoy called up classical imagery to describe Ottoman space. He kept an eye out for the presence of Roman antiquities. But Busbecq was also closely attuned to the present. He divided territory into lands that the Ottomans had seized and those that they might seize, always conscious of the ongoing Ottoman threats to Hapsburg sovereignty.

Belgrade was the dividing line, the first major city where Busbecq felt he had truly entered Ottoman space, and the first place where he found merchants offering "ancient (Roman) coins."[39] Ottoman territory, Busbecq wryly noted in an oft repeated trope, was barred to foreigners except those willing to disburse money freely:

> In fact, a man who intends to go among the Turks must be prepared, as soon as he has crossed the frontier, to open his purse and never close it till he leaves the country... Money acts as a charm to sooth

37 Nicolay, *The Nauigations*, 36v–37r.
38 Nicolay, *The Nauigations*, 46.
39 Ogier Ghiselin de Busbecq, *The Turkish Letters of Ogier Ghiselin de Busbecq: Imperial Ambassador at Constantinople 1554–1562*, Edward Forster, trans. (Oxford: Clarendon Press, 1968), 14–15.

their otherwise intractable minds. Were it not for this expedient, their
country would be as inaccessible to foreigners as those lands which are
supposed to be condemned to perpetual solitude by excessive heat or
cold.[40]

Like other travelers, Busbecq was concerned with how much he had to spend
and who might extort money from him or impede his progress. But his eth-
nocentric rhetoric also reveals categories of marking stages of travel. Travel
space was accessible or inaccessible; and it was not Ottoman armies but lack
of resources that might impede travelers wishing to traverse the lands of the
"Turks."

   Like Nicolay, Busbecq was also concerned to narrate the comforts and
discomforts of travel and the categories of people found in the course of his
journey. It was not just the availability of antique coins that set Ottoman
space apart. Inside Ottoman realms the availability of wine differentiated
"Christian" from "Turk" space. Once in Ottoman territory, Busbecq tells
his readers that the barriers of rivers, cities, and money are not the only
boundaries to be negotiated:

> *It will perhaps occur to you to ask how I consoled my followers for*
> *such bad lodging . . . Wine, it is true, is not to be found in every village,*
> *especially where the inhabitants are not Christians . . . Whenever [my*
> *Ottoman escort] saw that we were approaching a wineless district,*
> *they would warn us that no wine would be obtainable; and then our*
> *steward was sent a day ahead, accompanied by a Turk, to seek a supply*
> *from the nearest Christian villages. Thus my people were never without*
> *this alleviation of their hardships.*[41]

In this passage Busbecq suggests a rather singular vision of the "road" to
Constantinople. Rather than a set of fortress points linking Vienna and Istanbul, Busbecq's route is an archipelago of Christian space embedded in a sea
of apparently teetotaling Muslim space. On the way, "Turks" facilitate the
movement of imbibing Christians, making sure that their supply of the fruits
of the vine does not run short. Of course we know that many Muslims
routinely consumed wine and other spirits. That inclination is illustrated in
John Covel's narrative of a village that "lived" by the wine trade, drawing
"hundreds" of people out from Edirne every day, and lining the pockets of
the janissary ağa with taxes from the trade. "I must tell you that the Turkes
love wine, and drink as much as other people; I am assur'd not one person in five (throughout all this part that I have traveled) refuseth it . . . "[42]
Wine could thus readily fuel the fires of commonality and conviviality. Nevertheless, Busbecq felt his course had to be plotted with an eye to securing
the alcoholic necessities. The wine-selling Christian village was another safe
haven, providing relief at each stage of an arduous journey.

[40] Busbecq, *The Turkish Letters*, 25.
[41] Busbecq, *The Turkish Letters*, 19. The author notes that he himself "had in my carriage bottles of a
    better brand of wine, and was thus well supplied."
[42] Covel, *Voyages*, 88–90.

Busbecq also counted space and the limits of Christendom through descriptions of local women. But the women of Bulgaria, where even the daughters of great houses were now married to "ploughmen and shepherds," simply reminded him of the low state to which the Christian nobility under Ottoman rule had been reduced. Even the descendants of imperial families, according to the Hapsburg envoy, were brought to "a humbler position than Dionysius at Corinth."[43] Conquest for Busbecq, as for Nicolay, had transformed this 'classical' space; but where Nicolay's Chian women had retained their appeal; Busbecq's Bulgarians were degraded (perhaps a result in his mind of their peasant status, perhaps of the length of time they had been subject to Ottoman rule).

Many of Busbecq's categories of marking space are echoed in the account of Jakob von Betzek, a Hapsburg scribe who narrated his own journey to Ottoman lands in 1564–5. For Betzek the fortress of Gran (Esztergon, north of Buda) and the crossing of the River Danube were the portals into and out of Ottoman space.[44] But, between Gran and Istanbul, territory was characterized by the availability of wine, the vigor of the inhabitants, their relative prosperity, the presence of Christians living as Turks (converts), and a progression of women's dress styles, culminating in Macedonia, where according to Betzek one was hard put to distinguish between the styles of "Greek" and of "Turk."[45]

Wratislaw

Gran was a critical border marker for another traveler, Wenceslas Wratislaw, an ebullient adolescent traveling in the entourage of Rudolph II's ambassador to Murat III, Frederick Kregwitz, in 1591. Wratislaw charted the group's stages of progress down the Danube, noting the stopping points and the cities and villages on either side of the great river. From Comorn, the Hapsburg legation sent a message to the bey of Gran to announce their impending arrival. Notified that the "Turks" were ready to receive them, they marched to the Danube and sailed down it until they encountered ten Ottoman boats and, on land, a troop of "fine-looking and well-appointed Turkish horsemen."[46] This assemblage constituted what in modern times might be considered the "welcome wagon" to Ottoman space. It served as a mechanism of both protection and surveillance. After a preliminary meal the "Turkish" boatmen lashed the Hapsburg vessels to their own and towed them down river to Gran. Only there was official business conducted between bey and ambassador (much as official business for Nicolay's embassy was first conducted at Tripoli). But Wratislaw's account suggests the expansive

---

43 Busbecq, *The Turkish Letters*, 23.
44 Jakob von Betzek, *Gesandtschaftsreise nach Ungarn*, 58–9.
45 Von Betzek, *Gesandtschaftsreise nach Ungarn*, 3–20. Even Jewish traders might dress as Turks. See also Gerlach, *Türkiye Günlüğü*, v. 1, 55–6, on his arrival at Gran Castle in 1573.
46 Vratislav, *Adventures*, 2–4. See also, James Naughton, University Lecturer at Oxford, "Czech and Slovak Literature Resources: Renaissance and Humanism," http://users.ox.ac.uk/~tayloo10/lit_renais.htm.

nature of the border zone, a stage of travel that began with the exchange of messages at Comorn, continued over land, river, and land again to Gran, and was marked by procession, the display of arms, the presentation of gifts, and the sharing of meals. Once the ambassador's party had toured Gran, it returned to its boats on the Danube for the next stage of travel, to Buda where the ceremonies of encounter were magnified, a prelude to the antici-pated audience at Istanbul.[47]

Like Busbecq, Wratislaw paid attention to the availability of wine, and marked his journey by commenting on history, the relative prosperity of town and countryside, local customs, the dress of the women, and the style and comfort of accommodations.[48] He noted that the ambassador preferred Christian cottages to the inns of "Turkey" (by which he meant those along the route from Gran to Istanbul), because "no small stench proceeded from both human beings and cattle" at the inns, and "all the Turks... stared at us when we ate."[49] Despite those discomforts, Wratislaw was rather more open-minded about the local peoples, and rather less snide in his commentary on their women.

For Busbecq, the 'classical' carriage of Bulgarian women was due not to their innate grace but a necessity due to their "towering" hats. These were covered "from top to bottom... with little coins and figures and pieces of glass...; and anything else which glitters, however worthless, is hung on as an ornament."[50] Busbecq thought little better of the women's dresses and their "clumsy and ridiculous embroidery."[51] Wratislaw, though his narrative echoed that of his predecessor, seemed more interested and less judgmental:

> They go in white shirts or smocks, which are of coreded linen, not very thin, and of all colours, embroidered with turkey yarn made of plain silk upon the seams, round the hem and waist, and almost everywhere. In these they are extremely well satisfied with themselves, and despise our plain thin shirts. Their head-dresses are tower-shaped, very comical, and covered with hats of platted straw and lined with linen... The part which with us is broad below, and meets the head, they wear wide above, and top-shaped, in a manner more suitable for catching the sun and rain than for any other purpose... They have also glass beads round the neck and in the ears, and ear-rings hanging from the ears to the shoulders, like a variegated rosary; and in these they are just as satisfied with themselves as if they were queens of Bulgaria, and walk as grandly amongst strange people.[52]

---

[47] Vratislav, *Adventures*, 9. Wratislaw writes of "splendidly caparisoned" horses, soldiers lining the way as the legation processed to the pasha's palace, massed janissaries at the entrance, and the pasha seated on a divan surrounded by "handsome carpets."
[48] Vratislav, *Adventures*, 21–2, 25, 29, 36–7.
[49] Vratislav, *Adventures*, 29.
[50] Busbecq, *The Turkish Letters*, 22.
[51] Busbecq, *The Turkish Letters*, 21.
[52] Vratislav, *Adventures*, 37.

Although Wratislaw writes of familiar intercourse with the Ottomans, he also repeats the notion of that nation as avaricious and argues that the entry into Ottoman lands coincides with a continuous outflow of cash:

> in truth, whoever wishes to dwell amongst the Turks cannot help himself, but as soon as he enters into their territories, must immediately open his purse and not shut it till he leaves them again, and must constantly be sowing money as a kind of seed, since for money he can procure himself favour, love, and everything that he wants... the Turks allow themselves to be calmed by money... otherwise it would be impossible to have any dealings or transact any business with them.[53]

Thus Wratislaw shared in a set of ethnographic tropes by which the movement into Ottoman space was commemorated for the readers of European Christian kingdoms.[54]

The publication of accounts such as Busbecq's (or the Venetian *relazioni*), which appeared in many editions, educated an elite public in the ways by which Ottoman space might be read and told. That is not to say that personality, occupation, and experience were not important factors in the shaping of each individual travel narrative. But the traveler had (more or less) at his fingertips a set of contexts, characterizations, and histories by which to understand Ottoman space. He could then choose to repeat, update, or reject those authorities as he made sense of Ottoman domains on his own and in the company of others.

The English Traveler

For an English audience, knowledge of the Ottomans tended to come from sources south and east of their island: translations of dispatches, narratives, and histories arising in Italy, Hungary, Germany, France, or Spain.[55] But increasingly, as the early modern era unfolded, English readers had the eyewitness accounts of fellow Englishmen such as George Sandys to guide them in their appreciation of the empire of the sultans. By the eighteenth century, the English had placed their own characteristic stamp on knowledge of the "Turk," and the sojourn to his kingdom. The Cambridge scholar and clergyman Richard Chandler (d. 1810), for example, who journeyed

[53] Vratislav, *Adventures*, 43.
[54] In fact Wratislaw could possibly have read Busbecq's published letters which first appeared in their entirety in Paris in 1589. The first letter was published in Antwerp in 1581; see Vratislav, *Príhody*, second to fifth unnumbered pages of biographical note, by Milada Nedvědová, which notes that Czech readers by the end of the 16th century had ten published versions of John Mandeville, as well as editions of Johannes Leunclavius' *History of the Ottomans* and Busbecq's work. See also Hamilton, *Arab Culture and Ottoman Magnificence in Antwerp's Golden Age*, 40–41, 45, on both Nicolay and Busbecq.
[55] See Barbara Fuchs, *The Poetics of Piracy: Emulating Spain in English Literature* (Philadelphia: University of Pennsylvania Press, 2013), Ch. 1, "Forcible Translation," on the influences of Spanish narratives on England.

into Ottoman lands in 1764 and published his observations in *Travels in Greece and Asia Minor* (1775–6), provides a late eighteenth century model for charting Ottoman space.[56] As he plotted excursions to view antiquities, Chandler commented on counting distance in time: "[The Ottoman] mode of computing by time prevails universally in these countries, and is taken from the caravans, which move [at] a uniform pace, about three or four miles in an hour."[57] Such calculation was practical in the face of bandits, floods, and other factors that changed the "distance" a traveler must go through, thus changing the duration of the trip. But for Chandler, as for Covel before him, it also served rhetorically to mark the cultural differences between the European traveler and his hosts.

Chandler also saw Ottoman space in terms of its historical pasts. Indeed his journey was motivated expressly by the prospect of seeing those pasts. When he narrated Alexander's conquests in what had become Ottoman territory, for example, Chandler lauded the Macedonian's mode of passing through space:

> *Alexander the Great, instead of marking his progress by devastations, wisely provided more lasting and honourable monuments of his passage through the countries which he subdued; causing cities and temples to be erected, and forming plans for their improvement and future prosperity.*[58]

Cities and monuments were standard markers of travel space. But for Chandler they also provided the opportunity to draw unfavorable comparisons between the Ottomans and their illustrious predecessor, whose devastations the author considered more acceptable than those of his imperial Muslim successors.

Chandler draws several kinds of line between Ottoman and Christian space, those of faith, nation, and culture. Faith served as a unifying force once the traveler moved into Muslim domains, linking him to any Christian he found there. But nation (Englishness) was also a critical category of identity. Then there was the line crafted by the sea. Chandler saw his ship, the *Anglicana*, as bearing a form of English space into Ottoman territorial waters. It was only when he left the ship that he felt immersed in both Ottoman and classical space. As we have seen, the land-based borders of "Christendom" ranged over Balkan territory and even stretched as far as Jerusalem. But for Chandler, Christian space was confirmed by the availability of Christian compatriots and institutions in the port cities of the Mediterranean. He used Izmir (Smyrna) as a base for his labors, a primary center for English trade in the Levant. It was a 'safe' haven from which he could venture forth with

---

[56] Chandler, D.D., *Travels in Asia Minor and Greece*, new edition, Nicholas Revett, ed., 2 vols., v. 1 (Oxford: Clarendon Press, 1825), iii–xiv.

[57] Chandler, *Travels*, v. 1, 38; v. 2, 244. Chandler, conversely, was tasked by the English Society of Dilettanti with marking distance and direction as accurately as possible, using "watches and pocket compasses" among other instruments (v. 1, ix).

[58] Chandler, *Travels*, v. 1, 28.

confidence to interact with the populace, knowing that representatives of his own nation were not far away.[59]

Similarly, Chandler's formal return from Ottoman lands to "Christendom" occurred in July 1766 when his ship arrived in the harbor at Zante, the same city in the Ionian Sea that Nicolay in 1551 characterized as "both subiect unto the Venetians and contributory unto the Turke." There a Venetian fleet lay at anchor; there Chandler's ship was hailed by the British consul, "John Sargint, esq."; and there he and his companions were quarantined at the port's lazaretto. Their stay was rendered as pleasurable as possible: "The civility of the prior of the lazaretto, and of the good fathers of the Latin convent adjoining, with the attention of our countrymen, rendered our confinement very tolerable."[60] Once released from quarantine, Chandler relished the sight of the prosperous harbor and the "dress and manners of Italy." The transition, he wrote, "from misery and desolation" was as striking as it had been sudden. "We drew a most favorable contrast, and rejoiced on our safe arrival in the happier regions of Christendom," those, that is, that were not occupied by the "Turk" and rendered, as a result, only partially recognizable to the eyewitness more interested in classical pasts than in present conditions.[61]

The rhetoric of happy relief in the transition from the lands of Islam to the lands of Christendom was a standard of the literature. But Chandler's description should not be taken as the sole option for the English traveler's vision of entering and quitting Ottoman realms. Just over a century earlier, the diary of the English merchant Robert Bargrave both echoed and dismissed Chandler's simple dichotomy of happy and miserable space. Bargrave traveled to Istanbul by sea in 1647, where, as Daniel Goffman has noted, he threw himself wholeheartedly into a new life.[62] But in 1652 he undertook to make the journey home by land. Passing over the Danube at the fortress of "Ibraïl" (Brăila') in Wallachia, Bargrave engaged in the standard tropes of farewell, bidding "Adieu to Turkey" and to "Sultan Mahmet and all his cursed Crew."[63] In this more or less Christian space, Bargrave and his companions "found very good beere and excellent Mede, liquors strange to our Palates; & with them we endeavored to drowne the care & Vexation we had passed in the Turkish Quarters." That endeavor, in the realms of easily accessible "liquor," must have been successful. For Bargrave then waxed nostalgic; and his very next sentiment was not a tribute to

[59] See Daniel Goffman, *Izmir and the Levantine World, 1556–1650* (Seattle: University of Washington Press, 1990), 37, 94, 99–102, for the establishment of the English at Izmir.

[60] Chandler, *Travels*, v. 2, 362–3.

[61] Chandler, *Travels*, v. 2, 263.

[62] Daniel Goffman, *Britons in the Ottoman Empire, 1642–1660* (Seattle: University of Washington Press, 1998), 25, has clarified the position of the English communities of the time in Ottoman domains. He notes that such men were "a far cry from the stereotypical English imperialists of a later time"; instead they were "more nearly marginal men, even cultural hybrids, who prospered by learning to live with, rather than trying to recast, the civilization with which they had to treat (24)."

[63] Robert Bargrave, *The Travel Diary of Robert Bargrave Levant Merchant (1647–1656)*, Michael Brennan, ed. (London: Hakluyt Society, 1999), 133.

Christendom but one to the lands of "Turkey," where as far as the traveler
was concerned:

> *the Aire is so good, the weather so Temperat, provisions so cheap,*
> *& Travellers by Custome so Charitable, as scarce any Country can*
> *equall; nay such as whosoever has but a complacent humour, & his*
> *health: cannot be so poore but he may range in it, almost whither he*
> *will.*[64]

Bargrave here does not echo the sentiments of Busbecq and others regarding
the necessity of a large purse for gaining access to Ottoman domains. Indeed
he suggests that the traveler may find hospitality as well as extortion, and
enjoy the fair lands of the present day rather than dwelling simply on the
relics (or monuments) of a classical past.[65] Ottoman domains were a rich
destination for the merchant traveler; and in Bargrave's narrative we get the
impression that convenience, comraderie, and profit were more compelling
measures of the stages of travel than was access to Chian "nymphs" or Latin
"convents."

The Ottoman Traveler, Evliya Çelebi

Ottoman courtiers and their lieutenants, like their counterparts in the lands
of the Christian kings, also traveled across the Afro-Eurasian oikumene bearing messages, engaging in trade, and observing the countryside, resources,
built space, administrative and military personnel, and cultural conventions.
Where the latter were concerned, Christian travelers had no monopoly on
ethnographic typologies of space. Unfortunately we do not have the wealth
of travel narratives for these Ottoman observers that we have for the min-
ions of the Christian kings.[66] As Gottfried Hagen has pointed out, "many
members of Ottoman officialdom . . . spent a lot of time on the road, but we
know next to nothing of how they experienced these travels."[67] There are,
however, intriguing glimpses of that experience, for example the cosmography, *Menazır ül-avalim*, of the well-traveled Ottoman scribe Mehmet Aşık,
completed in 1598.[68] Aşık portrayed "geographical space" as separate points
on the map (e. g., towns and lakes) rather than characterizing regions; and
he described in detail the built space of the cities he visited.[69] His experience

---

[64] Bargrave, *The Travel Diary*, 133–4.

[65] John B. S. Morritt, *The Letters of John B. S. Morritt of Rokeby, Descriptive of Journeys in Europe and Asia Minor in the Years 1794–1796*, G.E. Marindin, ed. (London: John Murray, 1914), 64–5, another Englishman, traveling in 1794, shared Bargrave's sense of the beauty of the land on the "Turkish" side of the Danube. And unlike Chandler, he felt no remorse when he "bid adieu to Christianity."

[66] Hagen, "Afterword," 254, points out the narrative of Osman Ağa of Temesvar, whose "account of his adventures in German captivity," is relatively unknown.

[67] Gottfried Hagen, "The Traveller Mehmed Aşık," 145–54, in *Essays on Ottoman Civilization: Proceedings of the XIIth Congress of the Comité international d'études pré-ottomanes et ottomanes* (Prague: Academy of Sciences of the Czech Republic, 1998), 149.

[68] Hagen, "The Traveller," 145–54, esp. 148.

[69] Hagen, "The Traveller," 149–51.

transcended nation and commune. And, like travelers elsewhere, he was pre-occupied with the factors that contributed to "physical well-being," such as food.[70] Much more familiar than this obscure scribe, however, is the extraordinary example of the seventeenth century Ottoman sojourner, Evliya Çelebi (1611–82), whom we have already met. Evliya has been made to stand for the Ottoman all-traveler because of both the dearth of alternative narratives and the elaborate and expansive nature of his multivolume *Book of Travels* (*Seyahatname*).

Evliya's disquisitions on people and spaces have been set in their literary contexts (description, storytelling, reportage, entertainment, ethnography), by Robert Dankoff, thus putting him on a plane with his English, French, or German contemporaries as a traveler with a diverse set of personal, political, and cultural agendas.[71] For Evliya, in his travels to the western and Christian reaches of the empire, the "natives" were both fascinating and never quite a part of his own elite, metropolitan, Ottoman "us." In this regard, Evliya was like Busbecq, a cosmopolitan representative of the imperial center who cast a rather jaundiced eye on the mores of those on the outskirts of civilization. He was not so much interested in antiquities; but he was interested in the layers of history by which a place might be characterized. And he was a highly conscious observer (like the youthful Wratislaw) of cultural habits and political machinations.

Unsurprisingly, like the travelers we have already considered, Evliya related the journey in his *Book of Travels* in terms of stages of time, distance, and stopping places. As he moved from the inland fortress of Berat in Albania to the port fortress of Avlonya (Vlore) he told the direction of travel and how many hours (or days) it took to move from village to village. He noted river crossings and other physical features as well as local governors and modes of travel "at times on horseback and at times on foot."[72] Tales of the cultural proclivities of the inhabitants, the hospitality found at each stopping point, and the luxuries and conveniences available to a traveler lend flesh to the bones of Evliya's stages.[73] He also addressed questions of relative prosperity, detailing notable features of the places he saw along the way, such as a mine of black pitch where "thousands of people make their living."[74] The world atlas of Katib Çelebi (1609–57), a contemporary of Evliya's, does not elaborate on cultural phenomena in the same ways that the flamboyant traveler does,

[70] Hagen, "The Traveller," 153.
[71] On Evliya's veracity, see Dankoff, *An Ottoman Mentality*, 153–84, 196; and Snježana Buzov, "Ottoman Perceptions of Bosnia as Reflected in the World of Ottoman Authors who Visited or Lived in Bosnia," 83–91, in *Ottoman Bosnia: A History in Peril*, Markus Koller and Kemal Karpat, eds. (Madison: University of Wisconsin Press, 2004), 8.
[72] Evliya Çelebi, *Evliya Çelebi in Albania*, 135.
[73] Evliya Çelebi, *An Ottoman Traveller*, 163, 198–9.
[74] Evliya Çelebi, *Evliya Çelebi in Albania*, 129. Like Evliya, an earlier traveler, Naser-e Khosraw, a Seljuk administrator and poet who went on pilgrimage to Mecca from Marv in 1045, particularly noted schools, bazaars, and learned men becoming much more expansive in the larger cities such as Cairo and pilgrimage cites such as Mecca. He counted the distance between cities in terms of both parasangs and companions. He marked his journey, sometimes, by noting major physical features, events such as a lunar eclipse, novelties such as an ammonia extraction works, and availability of provisions and water. See Nasir-i Khusraw, *Nāser-e Khosraw's Book of Travels (Safarnāma)*, W.M. Thackston, trans. (New York: Bibliotheca Persica, 1986), 1–3.

but it also marks space using the conventions of borders (*hudud*), stages (*menazil*), and days' journeys (*merhale*).[75]

Evliya made a point of distinguishing the nature of frontiers. He noted the imperial competition between Venice and the Porte for the coastal and interior spaces of the Adriatic, and the ambivalent religious identities engendered in that transimperial zone. In the town of Gjirokastër in Albania, "even the most fragile old men brazenly gird on arms and ride or hike up into the Kurvelesh mountains to put down Albanian rebels or to fight the Venetian infidels."[76] The ritual practice of the Muslims in these places was frontier practice, caught between the habits of Balkan Christendom and associations with the Muslim East. They mourned their dead for "decades" so that the "noise and uproar" made being in the town on Sunday intolerable.[77] And although their women were "chaste and virtuous," the men "shamelessly" drank wine as they celebrated weddings, and at both the feasts of Christian saints and the Muslim *bayram* festivals:

> *they put on their finery and drink various alcoholic beverages. Lovers go hand in hand with their pretty boys and embrace them and dance about in the manner of the Christians. This is quite shameful behavior, characteristic of the infidels; but it is their custom, so we cannot censure it.*[78]

Albania was thus neither Ottoman nor Venetian, rather like Nicolay's characterization of Cephalonia and Zante. Its frontier people mixed the wine of Christendom with the devotions of Islam, behaving in ways that Evliya found reprehensible. Their identities were layered and sometimes incomprehensible, so that not even the distinctions Busbecq cited between Muslim and Christian villages could be counted on. These were the same people, in the "heart of Albania," that the Benedictine Casimiro Freschot, writing in 1687, lauded for their "freedom." Despite being in the hands of "the Turk," he wrote, "they do not recognize the dominion of the Porte with any tribute unless they are constrained to do so by the open threat of violence."[79] That description would certainly have resonated with Evliya. Like many Christian authors narrating frontier identities, the Muslim Evliya was defined by his class, his urbanity, and his status as a traveler as much as by his faith. He wanted to discern the differences between familiar space and the spaces in between empires. He wanted to be comfortable, satisfy his curiosity, and entertain his readers.

Unlike some of his European counterparts, however, Evliya did not use commentary on the women of the Greco-Balkan peninsula to bemoan the lost territories of Christian empires or the degeneration of civilization. He routinely commented on the "darling boys and lovely girls," of the places

---

[75] For example, for Azerbaijan, Kâtib Çelebi, *Kitâb-ı Cihânnümâ*, v. 1 (Ankara: Türk Tarih Kurumu, 2009), 389, which also employs *fersah* (league or parasang) to count distances.

[76] Evliya Çelebi, *Evliya Çelebi in Albania*, 81.

[77] Evliya Çelebi, *Evliya Çelebi in Albania*, 83.

[78] Evliya Çelebi, *Evliya Çelebi in Albania*, 85, 87.

[79] Casimiro Freschot, *Memorie Historiche, e Geografiche della Dalmazia Raccolte da D. Casimiro Freschot Benedettino* (Bologna: Giacomo Monti, 1687), 343.

he visited and was fond of a bawdy story; but he was not so inclined as some of our narrators to comment at length on the local women.[80] Like Wenceslas Wratislaw, though, he did find some of the Balkan country girls quite appealing. Describing a mountain picnic outside of Sofia for example, Evliya first described the food, the feasting, and the huts of the shepherds. Then he turned to the shepherds' daughters, "Bulgarian mountain beauties,... the plump and ruddy girls of the Yörüks and Çıtaks and the other country bumpkins win the beauty prize of the Franks."[81] Here nation and rural residence trumped faith as markers of identity, although Evliya did occasionally use women as embodiments of the borders between Christendom and Islam. He noted in Dubrovnik (Ragusa), for example, that "matrons and lovely maiden girls" openly displayed their wares in the marketplace; but as this was the territory of "Christendom," he said, such behavior could not be "considered shameful."[82]

And so we see some of the alternatives for narrating space as expressed in the early modern travel tale. The itinerary, with its counting of stopping places and stages of travel from point of origin to point of destination, formed a baseline for the travel account.[83] The stages themselves were counted in distance, time, empire, nation, faith, logistics, and ethnographies. Beyond the urgency of securing transport, food, and accommodation, the ethnography of place determined whether the traveler would have hospitality, entertainment, and a sense of ease, or tension, boredom, and discomfort. It determined whether women would be absent or present, seen or unseen; and whether the "natives" would be comprehensible or incomprehensible. And beneath these exigencies lay a sense of place that often had more to do with books and memories than with what the sojourner actually saw, a vision of space counted in myths, monuments, tropes, and the identities of the past (those things, that is, that made even the unfamiliar familiar).

Travel on the Map

The travel narrative in its visions of space and imaginings of peoples and pasts was the model for the map, which reflected, repeated, and invoked the authority of the traveler and his texts. The map, after all, was not an isolated depiction of space. It accompanied the texts of war, history, pilgrimage, and travel that served to establish and transmit the categories by which space

80 Evliya Çelebi, An Ottoman Traveller, 231.
81 Evliya Çelebi, An Ottoman Traveller, 106.
82 Evliya Çelebi, An Ottoman Traveller, 210; also 167, 207 on Split (Spalato) and Dubrovnik. Evliya might also indicate the Christian "Franks" as either Catholic or Protestant. Bembo, The Travels and Journal of Ambrosio Bembo, 43–4, describing the Druse, made similar statements about this particular brand of infidel, made fierce by life in the mountains and adhering to neither Christian nor Muslim orthodoxy in their habits and beliefs. Like the residents of Evliya's Albania, these frontier peoples scoffed at the idea of Ottoman hegemony.
83 Delano-Smith, "Milieus of Mobility," 38, has characterized itineraries as basically "functional route descriptions that were recycled over and over again." After the first half of the sixteenth century, "road books," including itineraries, often with "historical anecdotes" or other comments "were issued with impressive frequency (39). These could be supplemented with distance tables (56–7).

should be counted. It captured the mental maps of its viewers by reprising and highlighting the ways in which they were accustomed to hearing and reading territory. Maps revealed the distinctions between imperial centers and the outposts of empire so important to travelers like Evliya and Busbecq. They traced the journey from Venice and Vienna to Istanbul; they showed whose territory was whose.

In 1566, Paolo Forlani published a variant of a 1559 map by Giacomo Gastaldi entitled "Particular scheme of the kingdoms and regions from Venice to Constantinople and from Constantinople to Vienna in Austria, and from Vienna to Prague, royal city of Bohemia, and [on] to the royal city of Polonia, and other countries outside of these travel-routes, as one can distinctly see in the design" (Fig. 6.3).[84] The title of this set of three maps is instructive. The key structure organizing these kingdoms and regions is a network of *viaggi* (journeys) from one principal urban node to another. There are other places "outside these travel-routes," but they are of secondary importance. Critical space was space that could be accessed and witnessed. And it was through an understanding of travel that the viewer comprehended this space and its various parts. Placing the three sheets of the map together, one sees an elemental association, that of Venice on the first sheet, Ragusa on the second, and Constantinople on the third (each one tucked into a corner of its map, an anchor for the broad expanse of transimperial space). The Ottoman capital is a final destination or the limit point of southeastern Europe. Ragusa (Dubrovnik) is the link between the two imperial centers, a midpoint of communication, trade, and cultural and political exchange that suggests the significance of interchange on an east–west axis.[85] Or, as Evliya put it (commenting on the lazaretto of Ragusa): merchants and diplomats, "whether from India or Yemen or Samarkand, Arabia or Persia, or from the Ottoman sultan or the vizir of Bosnia or the Pasha of Herzegovina," meet here in preparation for their encounters with "the infidel."[86]

Travel thus provided a logic for the portrayal of space and a set of authoritative narratives by which cartographic authenticity could be claimed (see Ch. 7). And on the map, as in the narrative, travel shared the stage with war, history, and the sacred as delimiters of space and the ways in which it could be understood. The journey from Vienna to Constantinople and the voyage from Venice to Constantinople provided a core around which Ottoman space could be elaborated. These were the routes taken by envoys, traders, scholars, and armies while the Ottoman, Venetian, and Hapsburg polities (among

---

[84] Paolo Forlani, "Disegno particolare di Regni e Regioni che son da Venetia a Costantinopoli e da Costantinopoli a Vienna d'Austria, et da Vienna a Praga Citta regal di Boemia, et alla Citta regal di Polonia, et altri paesi fuori di detti viaggi, come si vede distintamente nel disegno," [Venetia], [1566], Newberry Novacco 4F 119. See Karrow, *Mapmakers of the Sixteenth Century*, 233–4. Forlani made additions and divided Gastaldi's two-part map into three parts.

[85] Krekić, *Dubrovnik in the 14th and 15th Centuries*, 116, 121, notes the well advanced Slavicization of Ragusa by the fifteenth century, though Latin remained the language of governance and the city drew in teachers, physicians, priests, and other experts from Italy who participated in the dissemination of Latin knowledge and education. Ragusan youths also traveled across the Adriatic to be educated, especially in Padua (121–2). See also on roads Zdenko Zlatar, *Dubrovnik's Merchants and Capital in the Ottoman Empire (1520–1620): A Quantitative Study* (İstanbul: Isis Press, 2010), 173–83.

[86] Evliya Çelebi, *An Ottoman Traveller*, 204.

Figure 6.3. Paolo Forlani (fl. 1560–71), derived from Giacomo Gastaldi, "Disegno particolare di Regni e Regioni che son da Venetia a Costantinopoli e da Costantinopoli a Vienna d'Austria...," Venice segment, cropped, Venetia, 1566. Photo Courtesy of the Newberry Library, Chicago, Novacco 4 F 119, sheet 1.

others) strove for dominance in the broad transimperial frontier. Although each route comprised variations, the general trajectories and their major stopping points were well known. These were the routes of historic and contemporary travelers, as we have seen, the most famous and well publicized of whom were routinely cited in map legends.

Vienna to Constantinople

Vienna was notable among the critical limit points on the early modern map, an imperial center but also a last bastion of Christendom's sovereign sway and a starting point on the long journey along the Danube to places east, those places in Europe, that is, where imperial and communal identities were not always easy to sort out. One could not envision the intermediate space along the Danube without also acknowledging the two imperial centers that framed it: Vienna at one "end," and Istanbul at the other. Vienna is at 48.12 N latitude (and 16.22 E longitude), whereas Istanbul is at 41.01 N latitude (and 28.58 E longitude). Yet a map dated 1590, printed in Venice, and reproduced or amended around 1717, depicts the route between those two cities on an almost horizontal plane, flattening the seven intervening degrees of latitude (Fig. 6.4).[87] For the mapmaker and his audience, the relative position on the globe of the Ottoman and Austrian capitals was not particularly the point; rather the journey and its envisioning was at issue. Thus the Danube, the quintessential dividing line between the Ottoman and the European Christian selves, traces the length of this map, which is broader than it is high. And the mighty river seems to empty into the Black Sea mere miles north of Constantinople, thus conveying some of the ways in which proximity was distorted. Along its course one sees the cities and fortresses that a wayfarer might encounter, and the stages of travel that he or she might undertake (or that an armchair traveler might imagine), as he or she moved from the Hapsburg lands to the domains of the sultan.

On this map, the sovereign space governed by any given monarch is not the primary concern, even though the sites of a few strategic battles are indicated along the way. There is no line or city that marks clearly the place where the lands of the emperor give way to the lands of the "Great Turk." And although Gran (here labelled "Strigonia"), the point of crossing so critical to various of our travelers as the gateway to Ottoman space, is prominently depicted, its bridge and fortress produce no hint that here the Danube divides one imperial entity from another. Instead, the viewer regards a landscape composed of routes, impediments, and safe havens, along with the names of towns and the

---

[87] Stefano Scolari, "Viagio Da Vienna Sino Petro Varadino, Con La Distanza Di Miglia Da Una Citta Al Altra. Viagio Da Carlovitz Sino A Costantinopoli Con La Sua Distanza Di Miglia Da Una Citta Al Altra," Venetia, 1590, Newberry Library, Novacco 2F 184. The area between the fortresses of Petro Varadino and Carlowitz has cannon and fighting forces, labeled "battaglia siguite contro il Turco a 5 Agusto 1716." This map can be contrasted with another early eighteenth century map by Gabriel Bodenehr, in Augsburg, which depicts the land and sea routes linking Belgrade, Petrovaradin, and points west into Hungary highlighting the fortress positions on the river: British Library, Maps C.24.22.18.

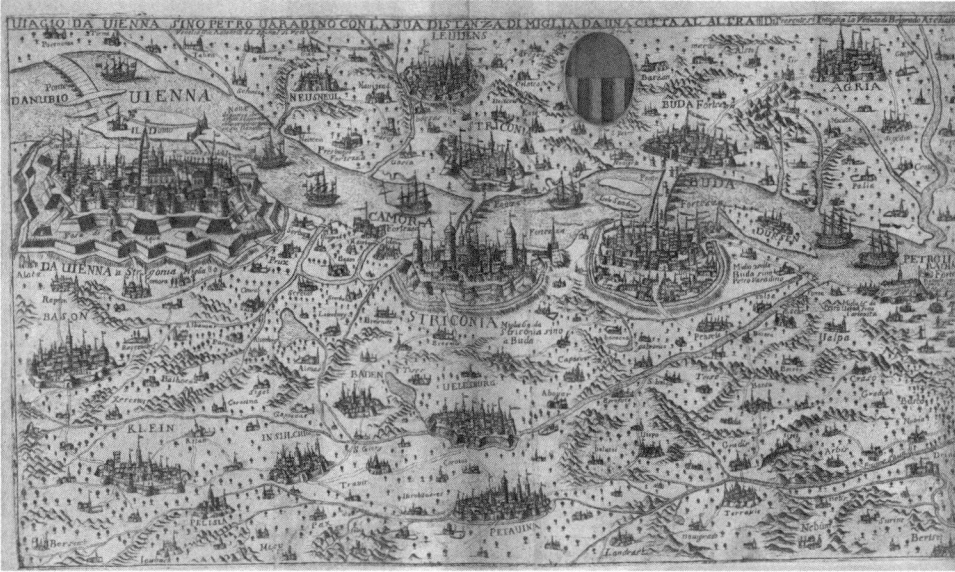

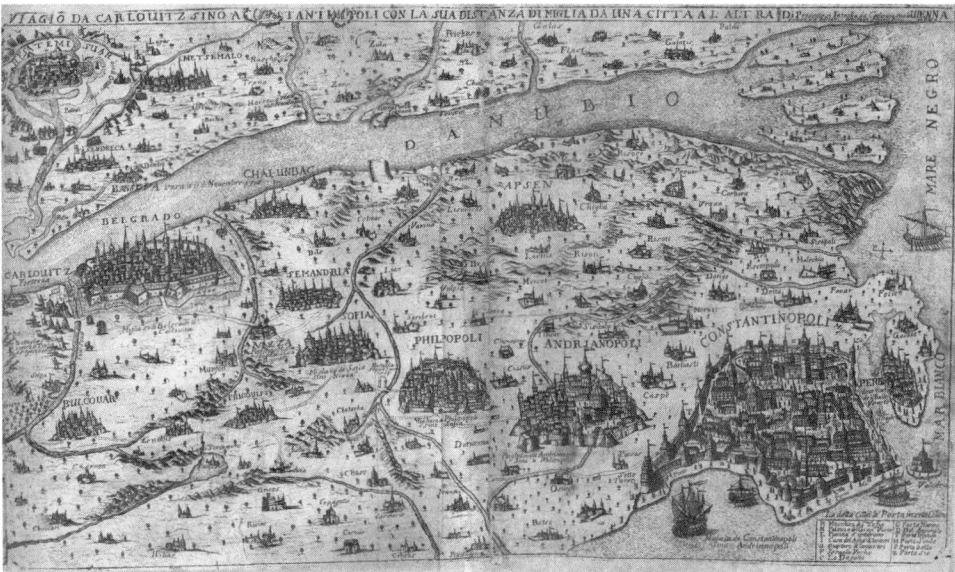

Figure 6.4. Vienna to Constantinople. Stefano Scolari, "Viagio Da Vienna Sino Petro Varadino, Con La Distanza Di Miglia Da Una Citta Al Altra. Viagio Da Carlovitz Sino A Costantinopoli . . . " [Venetia?] [c. 1717, from 1590 original]. Map divided into two parts. Photo Courtesy of the Newberry Library, Chicago, Novacco 2F 184. (See color plate)

distances in miles between them. Space is collapsed, so that stopping places seem relatively close together; and Adrianople (Edirne) seems visible from the walls of Constantinople, a comforting thought for the weary traveler. The imagined journey seems relatively easy, each major way station just a stone's throw from the next, although men and cannon arrayed outside the fortresses of Temesvar (Timişoara, Romania) and Belgrade illustrate the potential for a landscape wracked by military conflict. The condition of war space was, after all, a primary emphasis in maps of the frontier zone. Nonetheless, large ships sail the Danube around Vienna, Budapest, and the straits around Constantinople, suggesting the identity of these places as centers of free-flowing trade.

Despite the impression of proximity of one city to the next, the map's title, "Journey from Vienna as far as Petro Varadino with the distance in miles from one city to another [and] Journey from Carlowitz as far as Constantinople with its distance in miles from one city to another," highlights the realities of covering the terrain from Vienna to Istanbul, and intrudes on the vision of easily traversed space.[88] This was a map deriving not so much from the accomplishments of eighteenth century science as from the textual compounding of measurement, observation, and experience. It provided its viewers with the journey from Vienna to Constantinople in a single frame, anchored at each end by a magnificent, walled, imperial fortress and trading emporium. Vienna, twice besieged and twice redeemed from Ottoman assault, seems impregnable with its multiple layers of defenses. Constantinople seems more benign, with small figures walking its streets and strolling or laboring along its esplanade. The legend at the top of this map is interrupted by two inserts advertising engravings in preparation, "the panorama of Belgrade besieged," and "the space from Carlowitz to Vienna." These notices to prospective purchasers remind us that maps also functioned as visual news, reporting sieges such as that of Belgrade, which was occupied by Hapsburg troops in 1717.

There is nothing coincidental about the collapsing of space on this Vienna-to-Istanbul map. Mapmakers were well aware of the route of the Danube and of the distance between its mouth at the Black Sea and the Ottoman capital.[89] The map's horizontal presentation was purposeful, tailored to match a particular vision of travel space. As such, it may be contrasted with an engraving by Paulus Fürst, "Image of Royal Hungary to Turkey as far as Constantinople," which directed the viewer's attention to political and military space (Fig. 6.5). That map, dating from the second half of the seventeenth century, places Vienna at the upper left and Constantinople at the lower right of the frame, highlighting the various tributaries of the Danube.[90] The distance and difficulty of the terrain between Constantinople and Belgrade, or Belgrade and Buda, is apparent.[91] The message is one of sovereignty rather than travel. Both conflict and history are crucial elements of the map, which

[88] On the riverine *menzils* (both way stations and stages of travel) see Rossitsa Gradeva, "War and Peace along the Danube," 107–32, in Gradeva, *Rumeli under the Ottomans*, 125–6.
[89] Louis Szántai, "The riddle of de l'Isle's 1703 map of Hungary," *Cartograhica Hungarica* 8 (May 2004): 79, suggests that de l' Isle's 1703 map for the first time showed the "more or less correct line of the Danube."
[90] Paulus Fürst, "Abbildung Des Königreich Ungarn Durch Türckey Bis Nach Constantinopel," Nuremberg, [c. 1658], British Library, Maps 28195.34. Kaiser Leopold I, Holy Roman Emperor, is listed as the current king of Hungary hence the map dates between 1658 and 1705. This map can be compared to the map of Hungary of Jacob Sandrart (1630–1708), also produced in Nuremberg during Leopold's reign. Its depiction focuses on the territory from Vienna to Belgrade with Sophia at the eastern margins.
[91] Bayerle, *Ottoman Diplomacy in Hungary*, 11. Navigating the stages of travel was also complicated by a lack of security due to ambushes, kidnapping, and various forms of banditry.

Figure 6.5. Vienna to Constantinople. Paulus Fürst, "Abbildung Des Königreich Ungarn Durch Türckey Bis Nach Constantinople," Nuremberg [c. 1658]. The British Library Board, Maps 28195.34.

labels, in both German and Latin, the sites of Ottoman victories. Here (as in many maps, such as Forlani's "Particular Scheme") Constantinople is truly an end point of Europe and gateway to "Turkey" because the map cuts off the Asian half of the city and the Bosphorus. That corner of the map where Europe meets Asia is occupied instead by a scale of miles and four Ottoman soldiers, "Turks" with naked chests, mustaches, and topknots, surrounded by imagery of flags, arrows, and cannon.[92] Next to them is a presumably "Christian" captive identified by his long hair. These are the cartographic embodiment of the ethnographic types found in travel literature. Just as the traveler provided snapshots of local peoples, often without cultural context, to "represent" nations and his experience of place, so too representative figures were stamped onto the body or borders of the map to suggest the ethnicity, commune, character, and identity of a place.[93]

The cartographic juxtaposition of Christian and Turk might also include iconic females to designate the identity of Greco-Balkan space. Another map (not shown here) highlights the Danube itself as a vehicle for the transition from the territories of the Christian kings to the territories of the sultan. This large format map, done in Amsterdam in 1635 by Willem Blaeu, with a variant by Johannes Janssonius (Jan Jansson, 1588–1664) in 1636, was reproduced with slight changes by Cornelis Danckerts (1603–56) in 1647, also in Amsterdam.[94] It is not the stopping places that are emphasized here but the incredible reach of the mighty river. A cartouche at lower left shows an allegory of the river and its tributaries. But the large title cartouche juxtaposes the realms of the Ottomans with those of the Christian monarchs through two pairs of male and female characters. To the left of the "*Danubius*" legend box stands a figure representing the Holy Roman emperor, with globe and cross both held in his hand and gracing his crown. Leaning out from behind him and partially obscured by a large shield bearing the double-headed eagle is a rather angelic-looking female holding a crucifix. To the right of the legend, sword raised, stands another bearded monarch in a fur-lined robe, a turban with multiple aigrettes on his head. Behind him, but looking much less demure than her counterpart, is a saucy lady with one breast exposed. She holds an incense burner in one hand and with the other raises her skirt so that her bare foot, treading on a crucifix, is plainly visible.

Nobility and aggression, modesty and flirtation, religiosity and blasphemy thus confront each other across the Danube, while a gargoyle-like figure at the top of the legend box looks on. The ambiguous identity of Danubian space is thus highlighted on the map, caught between sovereigns and between 'ladies'

---

[92] Other maps conveyed segments of the journey, like that from Belgrade to Constantinople; see Johann Baptist Homann, "Danubii Fluminis (hic ab urbe Belgrado, per Mare Negrum . . . ," Nuremberg, 1720. This map is part of a series that depicts the course of the river.

[93] Those images are in some ways analogous to Pompa Banerjee's notion in " Postcards from the Harem: The Cultural Translation of Niccolao Manucci's Book of Travels," 242–82, in Brummett, ed, *The Book of Travels*, 244, of "postcards from the edge" to describe the vignettes of the foreign found in travel narratives.

[94] C. Dankerts (Danckerts), "Danubius Fluvius Europae Maximus, A Fontibus as Ostia, Cum omnibus Flumnibus ab utroque latere. In illum defluentibus," Amsterdam, 1647. This map is taken from a 1635 map by W. Blaeu in Amsterdam making minor changes and altering the colors. The title is the same except this version uses "defluentibus" instead of "fluentibus."

who either hold the crucifix aloft or tread it underfoot. It is these female figures rather than the Hapsburg and Ottoman potentates who remind us of the ways in which travelers such as Busbecq, Wratislaw, and Evliya counted frontier space. They are two sides of a coin, one inclined to Christendom and all that it implied, the other inclined to Islam and the shameful behaviors that the authors of Christian Europe often associated with it, particularly in those territories that had 'turned' to the Turk.

That confrontation is made explicit in other maps. Thus the Royal French Geographer Nicolas de Fer (1646–1720) depicts "*Hongrie*" and surrounding territories as the "Theatre of War on the Frontiers of Two Empires," in a map that shows the Danube as border, slashing across the land space between Vienna and Constantinople (Fig. 6.6).[95] The title legend tells the viewer what he or she is looking at, and notes that the depiction of space here is drawn from the accounts of "many voyages and embassies." The travel texts authenticate the map. In a list of regions referenced in the title, Ragusa, in addition to the terminus points of Vienna and Constantinople, is highlighted as a 'mid' point in the land- and sea-based journey to and from Ottoman domains. These cities, along with the narratives that describe them, frame the map and its depictions of war.

Travelers might plug into the route from Vienna or Venice to Constantinople at any stage of the journey; or they might travel from points further west. Pierre Duval (1619–83), another French royal cartographer, presented his "Itineraire de Paris à Constantinople" (one of a set of maps) in both text and map format, noting the options for travel both by land and by sea (Figs. 6.7 and 6.8).[96] Narrative and map were intimately intertwined. The map begins with an outlining (in words) of five routes to the Ottoman capital. That delineation is followed by a visual map, "Chemin de Constantinople, par la Servie, et par la Bosnie," of a segment of the overland journey, one that alerts the traveler to two alternate routes for reaching Nisse (Niš) either from Belgrade or Ragusa. The "four principal routes" and an alternate are described in the following terms:

(1) By sea, one embarks from Marseilles.
(2) From Germany and Hungary one may pass through Strasbourg to Vlone or take advantage of the option to travel via the Danube as far as Belgrade.
(3) From Sclavonia, one goes by the Sea of Venice to Ragusa and from there overland via Niš.
(4) From Italy and Greece one arrives at Otranto and passes [by sea] to Corfu. From there, one has two options, the first via Bastie, passing

95 N. de Fer, "Le Theatre De La Guerre Sur Les Frontieres Des Deux Empires de puis Vienne jusques à Constantinople," Paris, Chez l'Auteur, 1705.

96 Pierre Du Val, "Itineraire de Paris à Constantinople," in *Diverses Cartes et Tables pour la Géographie Ancienne, pour la Chronologie et pour les Itinéraires et voyages modernes* (Paris: 1665), British Library, Maps C.38.b.1 (.41). The maps are reminiscent of others by Vincenzo Coronelli, produced somewhat later – for example, "Viaggio Ragusi a Costantinopoli," Venetia, 1688; see Kozličić, *Kartografski Spomenici Hrvatskoga Jadrana*, 269. See also Delano-Smith, "Milieus of Mobility," 60, 64, on English and continental itineraries. For ancient and medieval precedents to horizontal and vertical mapping of itineraries, see *HOC*, v. 1, plates 3 and 38.

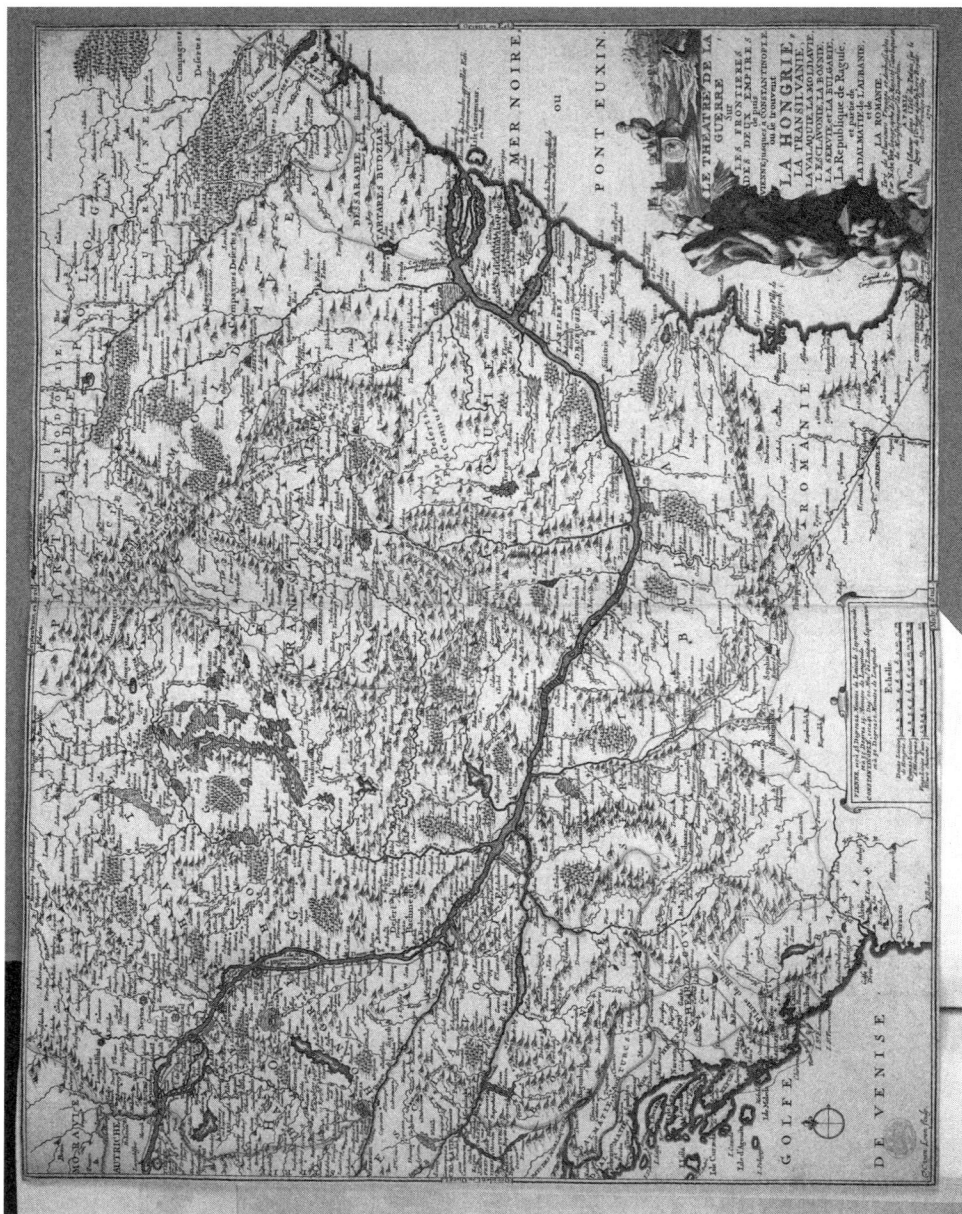

Figure 6.6. Nicolas de Fer, "Le Theatre De La Guerre Sur Les Frontieres Des Deux Empires de puis Vienne jusques à Constantinople," Paris, 1705. The British Library Board, Maps K.Top. 113.27, C2490-06.

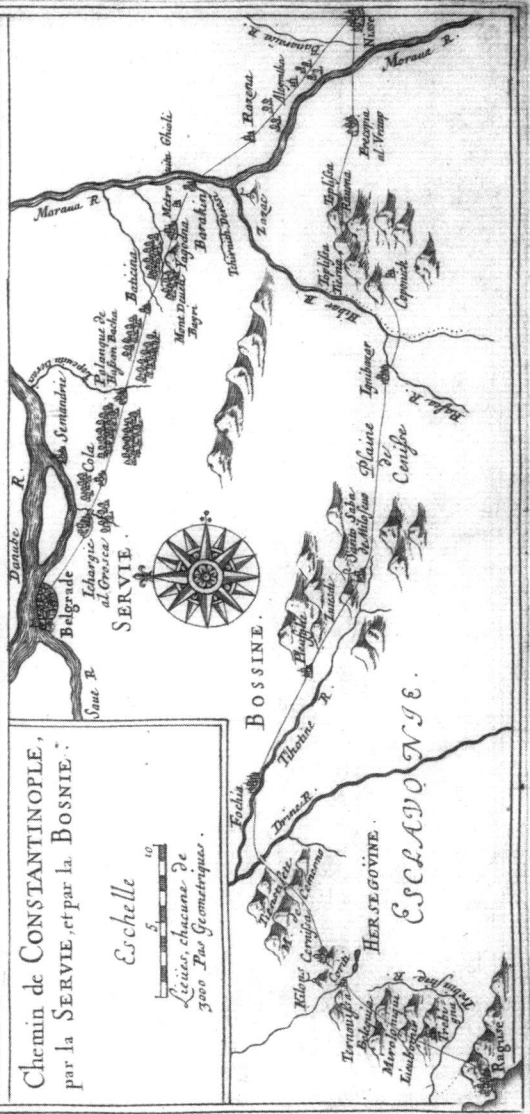

Figure 6.7. Pierre Du Val, "Itineraire de Paris à Constantinople," "Chemin de Constantinople par la Servie, et par la Bosnie," in *Diverses Cartes et Tables pour la Géographie Ancienne, pour la Chronologie et pour les Itinéraires et voyages modernes*, Paris [c. 1665]. The British Library Board, Maps C.38.b.1(41).

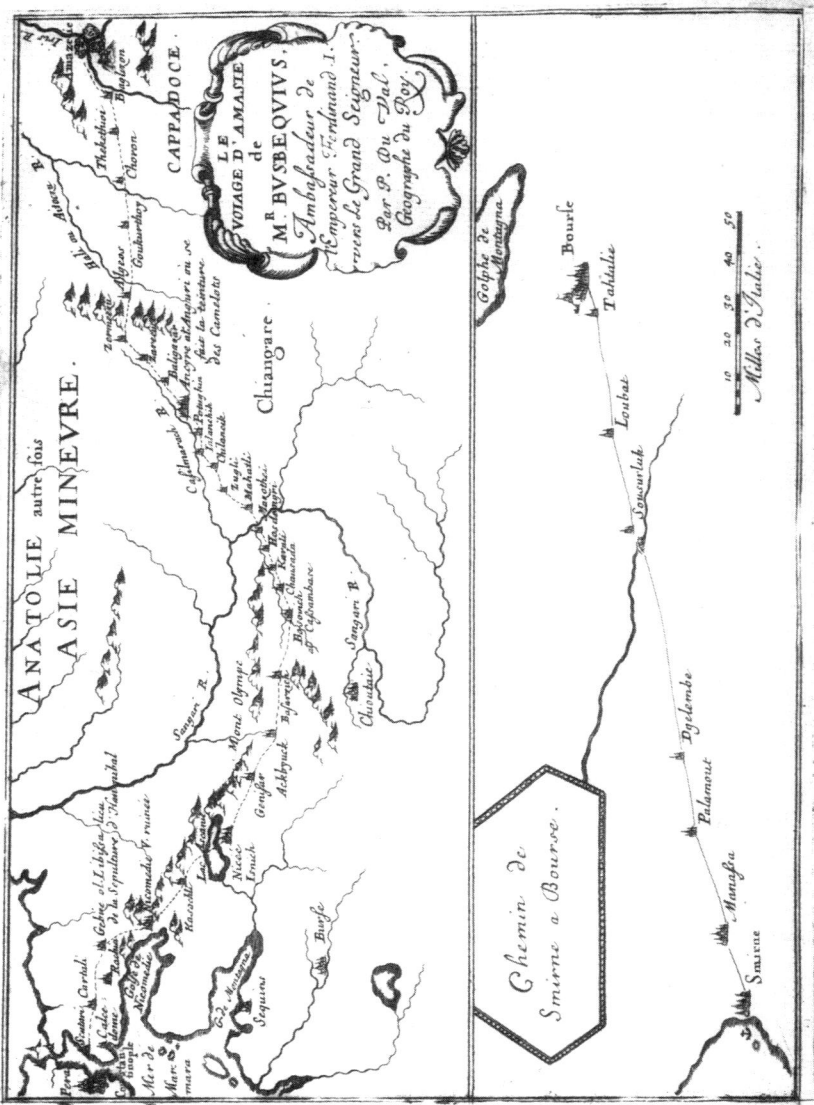

Figure 6.8. Pierre Du Val, "Le Voiage D'Amasie de Mr. Busbequius," "Chemin de Smirne a Bourse," in *Diverses Cartes et Tables pour la Géographie Ancienne, pour la Chronologie et pour les Itinéraires et voyages modernes*, Paris [c. 1665], The British Library Board, Maps C.38.b.1.(31).

from there on horseback for an eight day journey to Salonica and twelve days via carriage to Constantinople. The second option takes one by sea to Castel-Tornese [Peloponnese], and via land to Patras, Corinth, Setines, and again by sea to Constantinople.

After these major routes, Du Val provides another option: "There is a route from Valone, to Albasana, 10 Lieues [leagues], to Monastier, 10 Lieues, to Castel-Novo, 10 Lieues, to Paliocastro, to Heraclea, to Salonica 3 days, to Seiton, to Traianopoli, to Heraclea, to Seliuvreé, to Constantinople." These itineraries measure out travel in stopping places (the primary category), distance in leagues for certain stages, distance in days, and modes of transportation. There are no 'natives' or ethnographic scenes here to enhance the picture of local culture; no saucy, modest, or "ridiculous" females. But Du Val's maps are rooted in the travel narratives of the past; each one traces the route of a European traveler, from Pietro della Valle (1586–1652) and Busbecq to the more recent travelers Sr. Quiclet and "Mr. des Hayes," whose voyages were published in Paris in 1664.[97] They 'reproduce' the itineraries of travelers for the reader who wishes to see and perhaps undertake the journey.

Venice to Constantinople

Travelers could take advantage of a number of enduring land routes linking Constantinople to points north and west.[98] Famous among those avenues was the Via Egnatia, the original Roman road leading from Salonica to the Adriatic at Durazzo (Durres) or Avlonya (Vlore).[99] Along this route the Ottomans founded a large number of *evkaf* [pious endowments] to ensure urban prosperity, promote commerce, and establish a strong Ottoman presence.[100] This

---

[97] See, M. Quiclet, *Les voyages de M. Quiclet a Constantinople par terre* (Paris: Chez Pierre Prome, 1664); and Louis des Hayes [or Deshayes] de Courmenin, *Voyages* (Paris: Chez Pierre Promé, 1664). See also, on the Leiden sketchbook, which depicts the towns on a journey from Vienna to Istanbul, Luud'a Klusáková, *The Road to Constantinople: The Sixteenth-Century Ottoman Towns Through Christian Eyes* (Prague: ISV, 2002), 24, 215. The author dates the sketchbook to the period 1577–85 and discusses the Hapsburg traveler's sense of "terrible cultural loss" when confronting Ottoman Hungary.

[98] See Slavia Barlieva, "Two Venetians in Bulgaria in 1575," *Etudes Balkaniques* 2 (1996): 124–6. Among the available land routes were Trebine, Foca, Novi Pazar, and Niš, which joined the main route from Central Europe through Sofia, Plovdiv, and Adrianople; and the Skopje (Kosova) road which branched at Novi Pazar, linking Rogozina Mountain, Pristine, Skopje, Kumanovo, Kyustendil, Doupnitsa, and Sofia, or joining the road to Constantinople through Samokov, Kostenec, and Momin Prohod Pass.

[99] Elizabeth Zachariadou, ed., *The Via Egnatia under Ottoman Rule (1380–1699)* (Rethymnon: Crete University Press, 1996).

[100] Christine Woodhead, "Environment, Communications and Economy in the Ottoman Balkans and Eastern Mediterranean," *International Journal of Turkish Studies* 14, 1–2 (Fall, 2008):117–23, esp.121–2: "The eastern part of the road from Edirne to Selanik was particularly well served by imperial *evkaf*, founded by Murat II, Bayezid II, and Süleyman and by their chief associates and vezirs... Rebuilding the coastal town of Kavala in the 1530s... again reflects official encouragement of Jewish settlement to promote trade as well as an increase in the Muslim population from one- to two-thirds to seal the Ottomanization of the town." See also Yerasimos, *Les Voyageurs*, 33–57 who traces the various routes across the Balkans from the Adriatic and Vienna to Istanbul (as well as the route north through Moldavia) using ambassadorial and other travel accounts.

was the quickest route through the Ottoman Balkans; "Utilizing an extensive network of post-stations (*menzilhane*) for hire of horses, seventeenth century couriers could travel from Istanbul to Durazzo in fourteen days, as opposed to fifteen or twenty to Ragusa."[101] But land routes, as Du Val pointed out, were only part of the equation when it came to mapping approaches to Ottoman space.

The other part was the journey by sea. The sea, like the Danube, was a realm of space and experience that affected the map in very specific ways. Travelers and their readers clearly acknowledged that the sea was a different sort of space, one in which sovereignty was more ambiguous and travel less secure. The Dutch traveler and historian, Jan Huyghen van Linschoten (1563–1611), concluded in his *Voyages*, "No doubt it is very troublesome and laborious to journey by land . . . but . . . they [who travel by sea] are the most miserable Creatures of the worlde."[102] For the sea traveler, the port was the launching and reception place. It provided security, along with opportunities for the ethnographic scrutiny of inhabitants, and the designation of Ottoman and non-Ottoman space.[103]

Among the routes that proceeded by sea, the path from Venice to Constantinople looms large, embedded as it was in the minds and itineraries of merchants, diplomats, strategists, and mapmakers. A major path thus began in the lagoon and progressed via sea and land depending on whether the traveler sailed all the way to the Ottoman capital or disembarked at Ragusa or elsewhere along the Dalmatian coast and proceeded overland through Sofia and Edirne. The sea route, as Du Val's itineraries suggest, traversed the Adriatic and Aegean, sometimes continuing on to Alexandria, Syrian ports, or Cyprus, before turning toward Constantinople.[104] Venice to Istanbul was thus a well-practiced tangent among the routes radiating out from Venice, one with a baggage of history and diplomacy, a set of conventional stopping places, iconic markers of possessed space, and an aura of danger produced by the unpredictability of sea travel and the ready availability of predators.[105] It was a path of information and of profit, charted in a variety of ways including the characteristically Venetian form of the *isolario*, the illustrated itinerary

[101] Woodhead, "Environment, Communications and Economy," 122. Barlieva, "Two Venetians in Bulgaria in 1575," 126, notes that a Venetian envoy and bailo, Giacomo Soranzo and Giovanni Correr, on their way to Istanbul in 1575, mailed a letter from the midpoint of Doupnitsa back to the Signoria. The letter was posted on July 7 and reached the doge's chancery on July 22, the same day the travelers arrived in Constantinople.

[102] Jan Huyghen van Linschoten, *John Huighen Van Linschoten, his Discourse of Voyages into East and West Indies* (London: by John Wolfe Printer, [1598]), "To the Reader," second unnumbered page after "Dedication." Wolfe ntoes that Richard Hakluyt recommended to him this translation of Linschoten.

[103] For views from the sea in Jacob Aertsz Colon's *Colom de la mer Méditerranée*, Amsterdam, 1650, see Monica Viero and Yoo Omi Serena Campagnol, "Opera a Stampa," 84–152, in *Navigare e descrivere*, 114, also 132–5. See also Whitfield, *The Charting of the Oceans*, 77.

[104] Benjamin Arbel, "The Port Towns of the Levant in Sixteenth-Century Travel Literature," 151–64, in *Mediterranean Urban Culture*, provides a brief survey of late medieval (15th–16th C.) travel literature on Alexandria, Rosetta, Damietta, Beirut, and Tripoli, noting Western travelers' interest in classical and church history, water supply, trade, Western merchants, fortifications, produce, housing, and entertainments.

[105] Both of these dangers are well known, from the depredations of the Uskoks of Senj for example, to the toll taken by wind and rocks. On the latter risks, see for example, Marcello Berti, *Nel Mediterraneo ed Oltre: Temi di storia e storiografia marittima Toscana (Secoli XIII–XVIII)* (Pisa: ETS, 2000), 268.

that combined image with text, tracing the route from port to port and coast to coast.[106]

Tomaso Porcacchi (1530–85), in *The Most Famous Islands of the World*, published in 1572, spoke of the space between the Adriatic and the approaches to Istanbul as "the head, or prince of the seas, because of the many islands it has."[107] It was the same space that the Ottomans assigned to their admiral, the *kapudan* pasha, a critical zone of commerce and war, with its multiple landing places and dazzling array of goods, from wine to slaves to sailing boats. Here the Ottoman government established naval bases, collected taxes, and incorporated a complex network of local citizens into the operations of its bureaucracy. In the course of the intermittent warfare in the Mediterranean, the fortunes of such bases rose and fell. Piri Reis, the famous Ottoman captain, in his *Book of the Sea* (*Kitab-ı Bahriye*), thus pointed out the strategic importance of the port of Tenedos (Bozcaada) off the west Anatolian coast. From its high hill, ships could be seen at a distance of forty miles, and in its harbor small vessels could shelter from the wind.[108] Venice captured Tenedos from the Ottomans in July 1656, but the Ottomans forced Venice out on 31 August 1657.[109] At issue were both sovereignty and the security of the sea route into and out of the Archipelago. As Nicolas de Nicolay suggested, the Archipelago was a contested frontier, caught between the Porte and the Signoria, a condition of ultimate importance for the traveler.

For Giuseppe Rosaccio, in his 1598 *Viaggio da Venetia a Constantinopoli*, the Adriatic and Aegean composed a zone of places possessed by the "Turks" in Europe, little separated from the possessions of the Christian kings. Rosaccio's mapping of the route juxtaposed visual images (72 copper plate engravings "crafted with the utmost care") and texts as equal partners to show the way.[110] The words in his dedication are reminiscent of those of Matrakçı Nasuh used in the opening of this chapter; they tell his readers that the journey from Venice to Constantinople is worthy of everyone's notice:

> *I have deemed it both useful and entertaining to describe it and to represent it, beyond the expression of words, with these engravings and copper prints of all the cities, islands, and places of note, with the various notices required of such a journey, in such a way that one can*

[106] For collected views of islands and coasts, see Sphyroeras, Avramea, and Asdrahas, *Maps and Map-Makers of the Aegean*; Bevilacqua, *Le immagini dell'isola di Creta*. Portolans and isolarii tend to ignore the inland spaces or leave them blank, begging the question of sovereignty over land masses.

[107] Gerstenberg, *Thomaso Porcacchi's 'L'Isole piu famose del mondo*, 102–4, from the 1572 edition, 27 s. He compared it to the archipelago of the Gulf of Bengal and that of Malacca.

[108] Ersin Gülsoy, "Bozcaada (Tenedos) before and After its Capture by Venice in 1656," *II. National Aegean Islands Symposium, 2–3- July 2004, Gökçeada–Çanakkale*, İdris Bostan and Sertaç Başeren, eds. (İstanbul: Turkish Marine Research Foundation, 2004), 71–9, see 71.

[109] Afterward, the Ottomans drew up a register, *tahrir defter*, to identify and restore lands to those who held them prior to the Venetian invasion. Gülsoy, "Bozcaada (Tenedos)," 73–4, notes that the *tahrir* seems to have been drawn up by Mustafa Efendi the *kadı* of the army during the Ottoman campaign to retake the island. He also notes that Fazıl Ahmet Pasha, son of the grand vezir, and Mustafa Efendi, the *kadı* of Edirne, both invested in properties on the island after the reconquest (77).

[110] Rosaccio, *Viaggio da Venetia*, Venetia, 1598, unnumbered front matter, 1r. British Library, Maps 571.b.21.

not only learn by reading but virtually see in fact with ones own eyes [ma quasi vedere in fatto con gli occhi propri].[111]

As if to emphasize the stages of the journey, the author begins his work with a list giving the distance in miles between one stopping place and the next, beginning with Venice ("mirror" of the world) and ending with Constantinople (a city "unsurpassed in Europe in magnificence and wealth").[112] Rosaccio notes that his itineraries are useful for commercial travelers and for "those studying Geography." This is a voyage by land and by sea, he writes, in which one discovers the geography and chorography of the journey depicted in terms of cities, castles, ports, gulfs, islands, mountains, rivers, and seas.[113] At Ragusa (Dubrovnik), the reader can witness the place where the traveler chooses whether to complete his journey to Istanbul by land or by sea. But Rosaccio focuses on the sea route; and his itinerary does not proceed directly to the Ottoman capital. Instead it takes a detour, incorporating a pilgrimage to that outpost of Europe, Jerusalem, via Cyprus. On the map of Jerusalem, the Temple of Solomon sits to one side of the city, and towers topped by crescents appear on the other (Fig. 6.9). In his narrative, Rosaccio invokes Jesus, Paul, Adam, and the prophets of the Old Testament, reminding his readers that this Holy Land was chosen by God as "special above all others." Then he lists its conquerors, concluding with Selim II (r. 1566–74) and the "Turks," saying "now it is theirs."[114] The map of the route from Venice to Constantinople is thus a certification of both history and sovereignty, showing and telling the viewer whose territory is whose.[115]

Thus, the journeys from Venice and Vienna to Istanbul moved from narrative to map, synthesizing imperial claims and contemporary logistics with classical imagery and an antiquarian impulse. The past as reference point was a commonplace in these mappings of space, whether it was the past of the prophets and the Crusaders invoked in Rosaccio's narratives, or the classical

[111] Rosaccio, *Viaggio da Venetia*, unnumbered front matter. This dedication is to Marco Veniero, whom Rosaccio notes had served as bailo in Constantinopoli. This viaggio, he says, thus recreates the journey that Veniero himself "walked."

[112] Rosaccio, *Viaggio da Venetia*, 1r–2r, 4v, 76v.

[113] Precursors to Rosaccio's contribution to this genre include the *isolarii* of Bartolomeo dalli Sonetti in 1485, Giovanni Camocio in 1574, Tomaso Porcacchi in 1576, and Benedetto Bordone in 1528 (which appeared in several subsequent editions). See P. D. A. Harvey, "Local and Regional Cartography in Medieval Europe," 482–4; and Gerstenberg, *Thomaso Porcacchi's 'L'Isole piu famose*, 49–64. Chet Van Duzer, "From Odysseus to Robinson Crusoe: A Survey of Early Western Island Literature," *Island Studies Journal* 1.1 (2006): 143–62, glosses *isolario* as "island-book illustrated with maps (143)," a definition that leaves plenty of scope for the variations in the genre. Conley, *The Self-Made Map*, 187, writes of the enduring nature of the "island-city as a model for the world … "

[114] Rosaccio, *Viaggio da Venetia*, 53r–54r.

[115] In the same year that Rosaccio published his *Viaggio*, Marcus Welser published a version of the famous Peutinger "Tabula Itineraria," a horizontal map of the Roman road system dating to the twelfth century and from there back to Roman antecedents, a declaration of sovereignty, and an illustration of the historical linkage between the fourth and the sixteenth centuries in the mental maps of Renaissance readers. See Drago Novak, Miljenko Lapaine, and Dubravka Mlinarić, eds., *Five Centuries of Maps and Charts of Croatia/Pet stoljeća geografskih i pomorskih karata Hrvatske* (Zagreb: Školska Knjiga, 2005), 30–33, with the Adriatic displayed horizontally in sheet 2, segments 3 and 4. See also O. A. W. Dilke, "Itineraries and Geographical Maps in the Early and Late Roman Empires," 234–57, in *HOC*, v. 1, esp. 236–42.

Figure 6.9. Giuseppe Rosaccio, "Jerusalem," *Viaggio da Venetia a Costantinopoli*, 53r, Venetia, 1598. Asia 9215.98.3, Houghton Library, Harvard University.

past of Porcacchi's islands. And the past was complemented by an ethnographic present. Francesco Lupazzolo's *Isolario dell'Archipelago*, compiled
in 1638, advises its readers that they will see within "antique and modern
names, modes of life, the number of inhabitants, the costumes of the women,
and antiquities."[116] The work was itself an example of the recycling of the
past; it made extensive use of maps and texts from Benedetto Bordone's
(c. 1460–c. 1539) *Isolario*, first published more than a hundred years previously, in 1528.[117] And its particular emphasis on the costumes of the women
as a primary factor in the identification of space reminds us that female costume was a staple of the traveler's tale, a means by which he (and she) could
demonstrate mastery of the stages of travel and of foreign realms, as we shall
see in the following chapter.

[116] Colin Heywood, "Standing on Hasluck's Shoulders: Another Look at Francesco Lupazzolo and His
Aegean Isolario (1638)," 349–75, in *Archaeology Anthropology and Heritage in the Balkans and
Anatolia: The Life and Times of F. W. Hasluck, 1878–1920*, David Shankland ed., v. 1 (İstanbul: Isis
Press, 2013), 353. Also see Bronwen Wilson, "Francesco Lupazolo's Isolario and the Rewriting of
the Mediterranean," *Festschrift for Patricia Fortini Brown*, Blake de Maria and Tracy Cooper, eds.
(Milan: Five Continents, in press).
[117] Heywood, "Standing on Hasluck's Shoulders," 358–9.

7

Authority, Travel, and the Map

As we cannot better undeceive Mens Minds, and obliterate the strong Impressions which are had of a thing, than by Facts, and Instances of the contrary; I shall therefore . . . lay down nothing, but what shall be grounded in sensible proofs . . .

[Du Vignau, Sieur des Joanots] Person of Quality, *A New Account of the Present Condition of Turkish Affairs*, 1688.[1]

Mappings of Ottoman territory, whether focused on actual travel, imagined travel, or the depiction of sovereignty, conflict, and culture in geographic space, all required knowledge claims to legitimize the 'truth' of their depictions. That is, maps called on historical texts, eyewitness accounts, the reputations of mapmakers, and the expectations of their audiences in order to demonstrate that what they provided was an authoritative picture of the Ottomans and their realm. Some maps, as we have seen, claimed to show a "true and accurate" picture of events such as sieges. Others cited known travel narratives as sources for their knowledge.

In this chapter, I wish to focus on that question of authority, to suggest the range of ways in which narrative and image were employed in an effort to legitimize maps of Ottoman space. In Part 1, I suggest a typology of authority, address a set of eyewitness claims in narrative and map, and then scrutinize individual travelers' invocations of authority. Among other factors, I assess travelers' use of descriptions of female dress as a means of bolstering their claims to familiarity with cultural conventions and participation in Ottoman systems of sociability. Such descriptions illustrate both a specific form of ethnographic narration and a specific mode of authorial certification. In Part 2, I examine the evolution of the English traveler and the deployment of

---

[1] [Du Vignau, Sieur des Joanots] Person of Quality, *A New Account of the Present Condition of Turkish Affairs*, 117–18, second unnumbered page of Preface.

history and knowledge claims in the letters of John B. S. Morritt (who traveled
to Istanbul in 1794) and in an English atlas published in 1785 at the end of
the era under consideration here. Because invoking authority transcended the
borders of empire and of time, I will begin in a space removed in time and
place from the early modern Ottomans and their European frontiers.

Part 1. A Typology of Authority

Thomas Allsen has called Rashid al-Din (c. 1247–1318), the famed author
and statesman of the Mongol Ilkhans, "the first scholar to try to treat in a
systematic and comprehensive fashion the history of the known world."[2] His
Jāmi' al-tavārīkh (*Collected Chronicles*), completed around 1308, included

> *a history of the biblical prophets, Muhammad, and the emergence of
> Islam, the Caliphates and major sultanates, a history of the Mongolian
> and Turkic peoples, the rise of the Chinggisid dynasty, and separate
> accounts of the Chinese, Indians, Jews, and Franks, as well as an exten-
> sive genealogical supplement and a geographical compendium.*[3]

Rashid al-Din's world history was not simply a historical or geographical
text, but also a compendium of knowledge oriented around the dynastic
and religious centers of the Mongols. In this regard it is a counterpart to
early modern European compendia of knowledge, which shared some of
the same religious centers but placed their dynastic emphases further west.
Like other authors, Rashid al-Din took pains to legitimize his writings as
up-to-date and authoritative; he notes that the information contained in his
geographical compendium was "researched and authenticated," based on
what was known and found in the books of Iran and the "learned men of
India, South China, France, North China, etc...." Knowledge and texts are
thus the key categories of authority for his construction of geography. In
the later Arabic and Persian digests of this scholar's works, Rashid al-Din's
geography is said to include

> *a discussion of the borders of the seven climes, that is, the world, the
> extent and position of the major countries and states, their longitude
> and latitude, the mileposts placed along the great roads, and an enumer-
> ation of the postal relay stations (yāmhā) established throughout Eura-
> sia by order of the Mongolian rulers. All this we are told, was derived
> from literary sources and eyewitness testimony. Finally, all these data
> were depicted on maps according to a system devised by the author.*[4]

[2] Thomas Allsen, *Culture and Conquest in Mongol Eurasia* (Cambridge: Cambridge University Press, 2001), 83. Rashid al-Din was born a Jew in Hamadan; he converted to Islam at the age of thirty, and entered the service of the Mongol Ilkhans. See Rashīd al-Dīn, *The Successors of Genghis Khan*, trans. John Andrew Boyle (New York: Columbia University Press, 1971), 3–5.
[3] Allsen, *Culture and Conquest*, 83, also 75.
[4] Allsen, *Culture and Conquest*, 103–5. Allsen further comments on the contribution of the Mongols to the "promotion, creation, and circulation" of geographical knowledge (113).

In this description we find a third source of authority, eyewitness testimony. That three-part and overlapping foundation (knowledge, text, and personal experience) for geographic representation remained a characteristic of the early modern era, fine-tuned to suit specificities of space and situation.[5] Muzzafar Alam and Sanjay Subrahmanyam, for example, characterize the authority of the Indo-Persian travel-text narrator in the seventeenth century as "defined through an education, a set of proper references, received notions of honour, proper conduct and behaviour, and the capacity to respond to given situations (including hardship)... " They argue, further, that this form of authority is "not all that distant from the situation in seventeenth century Europe... "[6] Rashid al-Din counted space in terms of the categories noted in the previous chapter: stages of travel (mileposts and postal stations), geographic features, political units, and cities. Those categories (shared, if not universal) transcended divisions of "East and West."

The recitations of Rashid al-Din's foundations for authority resound throughout the late medieval and early modern periods. They are echoed, for example, in Thomas Salmon's (1679–1767) multivolume world history and atlas, published in London in 1744.[7] In the dedication Salmon addresses the contents of his volumes,

> *In which are comprehended not only such Voyages and Travels, as have been published already, but the Accounts and Observations of several judicious Travellers, who have lately visited the remotest parts of the Globe, and had great Opportunities of informing themselves of the present State of the respective Nations they describe: the Third Edition, with considerable Additions and Improvements, and an Abstract of the ancient History of most of the Countries described, frought down to the present Time. The whole adorned with Cuts of the various Inhabitants, and Maps of the several Countries, projected by Herman Moll, the most accurate and correct Geographer of this Age...*[8]

These are the categories by which "modern" history and nations were to be measured. In short, neither texts nor the accumulation of knowledge had been neglected. They are, however, complemented by the accounts of "judicious" eyewitnesses armed with up-to-date intelligence and familiar with inaccessible parts of the globe. Salmon elaborates upon these categories by specifying ancient history as a critical realm of knowledge. Text, knowledge, and eyewitness account are thus illuminated by ethnographic illustrations and maps, purportedly as accurate as they can be, so that the reader can

---

[5] Deborah Howard, *Venice and the East: The Impact of the Islamic World on Venetian Architecture 1100–1500* (New Haven: Yale University Press, 2000), 52, speaks of travelers as employing personal, cognitive, and habit memory to assess foreign spaces and cultures.

[6] Alam and Subrahmanyam, *Indo-Persian Travels*, 361.

[7] Thomas Salmon, *Modern History or the Present State of All Nations Describing their respective Situations, Persons, Habits, and Buildings; Manners, Laws and Customs, Religion, and Policy; Arts and Sciences, Trades, Manufactures, and Husbandry; Plants, Animals, and Minerals. By Mr. Salmon Illustrated with Cuts and Maps, accurately drawn according the Geographical part of this Work, By Herman Moll.*, 3rd ed., 3 vols., v. 1 (London: T. Longman, T. Osborne, J. Shuckburgh, C. Hitch, S. Austen, and J. Rivington [1744]).

[8] Salmon, *Modern History*, dedication.

see world space and know that what he or she is seeing is correct.[9] Salmon directly invokes his publics, those who have business in this visualized world and those who aspire simply to education and edification. In this regard, he echoes the claims of travel accounts such as that of Paul Lucas who sojourned through Ottoman lands in 1714. Lucas provided maps of his journey, noting that he had laid out the exact routes "pour faire un parallele des découvertes Modernes avec les observations des Anciens."[10] To satisfy his readers, ancient geography and characters were animated so that they could occupy the same universe as the traveler. Hence Lucas and his readers walk not in the footsteps of Alexander, Pompei, and St. Paul, but by their side.[11]

The Salmon atlas's coverage of the Ottoman empire begins with a geographic characterization:

> As the Turkish empire extends itself into three parts of the world, namely Asia, Africa, and Europe, I shall make three divisions of it; and having described their respective boundaries, and enumerated the provinces and chief towns each part contains, and taken notice of the principal seas and rivers, I shall enquire into the state of the empire in general, and then proceed to give an account of the several provinces in particular . . . [12]

That three-part empire is then illustrated with two maps, "agreeable to modern history," and a set of ethnographic plates.[13] The first map is "Turkey in Natolia"; the second shows "The Whole Turkish Empire with Countries and Territories bordering upon it" (Fig. 7.1).

As for who and what are contained in this empire, the reader is treated to views of Jerusalem and Constantinople, along with emblematic figures of some of the empire's inhabitants.[14] These figures are hardly representative but they are customary examples harking back to the ethnographic vignettes that decorated earlier maps such as those of Pieter van der Keere's "Nova totius orbis mappa ex optimus auctoribus desumpta [New Map of the Whole Earth . . .]," c. 1611, a spectacular world map, which touts in bold letters its reliance on the "best authorities."[15] In a 1744 version of Salmon's atlas, a "Turkish Gentleman" in an ermine-lined robe and turban is complemented by a "Turkish Gentlewoman" wearing a costume of overdress and under petticoats; embroidered, low-cut neckline; cloth head wrap; and ermine cape

---

[9] Herman Moll (c. 1654–1732) was a distinguished and prolific mapmaker, whose illustrations are found in various works of the time. By 1744, Moll was already deceased.

[10] Paul Lucas, *Troisième voyage du sieur Paul Lucas: fait en MDCCXIV . . . dans la Turquie, l'Asie, la Sourie, la Palestine, la Haute et la Basse Egypte, &c.*, v. 1 (Rouen: Chez Robert Machuel le jeune, 1719), 47. Johns, *Piracy*, 48, has characterized eighteenth century England as a time in which "People found themselves living amid countless experiments in authenticity."

[11] Lucas, *Troisième voyage*, preface, 11–15, 29.

[12] Salmon, *Modern History*, v. 1, 409.

[13] Salmon, *Modern History*, v. 1, unnumbered pages before 409 and between 556 and 557.

[14] Salmon, *Modern History*, v. 1, after pages 460 and 520 for the city views.

[15] Cosgrove, "Mapping the World," 103, 111–12, notes that "The ethnographic border [on seventeenth century world maps] continues the tradition of representing strangeness at the edges of the world maps, and is itself succeeded by world maps of 'races' in the nineteenth century," in which "physiognomy has replaced costume as a marker of human difference (110)."

Figure 7.1. Thomas Salmon, Herman Moll, "The Whole Turkish Empire," *Modern History or the Present State of All Nations*, v. 1, London, 1737. Photo Courtesy of the Newberry Library, Chicago, G 117.777.

(Fig. 7.2).[16] Next appear the "officiating habit of a Greek papa or Priest," shown front and back, and, as counterparts to the "Turkish" couple, the "Habit" of a Grecian man and woman "in the Islands of the Archipelago" (Fig. 7.3).[17] As if to complete this fragmentary picture of empire, the author presents an engraving of a marvelous touristic site that beckoned to the adventurous eighteenth century traveler: "The Marble Grotto in the Island of Antiparos" (among the Aegean Cyclades).[18]

---

[16] Salmon, *Modern History*, image after p. 414.

[17] Salmon, *Modern History*, v. 1, images after pages 544 and 575. See also Joseph Pitton de Tournefort, *Relation d'un voyage du Levant*, 2 vols., v. 1 (Paris: Imprimerie royale, 1717), plates before pp. 84, 87, 149.

[18] Salmon, *Modern History*, v. 1, after p. 576.

Figure 7.2. Thomas Salmon, Herman Moll, "A Turkish Gentleman, a Turkish Gentlewoman," *Modern History or the Present State of All Nations*, v. 1, after p. 414, London, 1744. Photo Courtesy of the Newberry Library, Chicago, Baskes folio G114.S17. (See color plate)

Salmon's assembled maps and illustrations do not really take the reader on a staged journey along the routes leading to and through the Ottoman realms. Rather, the Ottomans are among the assembled nations of the world, lords of an empire in which the reader can find famous cities, wonders, gentlemen and gentlewomen, and ethnonational diversity. The empire has been updated for the reader seeking knowledge and accuracy, presenting what its educated audience needs to know in order to situate this place and its inhabitants among the diverse peoples and kingdoms of the globe. Like Rashid al-Din, Salmon had his own vision of which empire was the most dominant and glorious of his era – self as world center – but the pursuit of knowledge, recognition, remuneration, and authority led both men to situate their own nations in the context of many present and historical others.[19]

Taking the overlapping foundations for geographic representation (knowledge, text, and eyewitness testimony) found in Rashid al-Din's history and Salmon's atlas, what follows now is a consideration of invocations of authority in early modern constructions of Ottoman space. Travelers from Italy and England will serve as our primary witnesses, revealing textual precedents, the scale of perceived wisdom, and the varieties of travel experience. Each

---

[19] For the invocations of authority used to justify fifteenth century humanist accounts of the Ottomans see Meserve, *Empires of Islam*, 169–202.

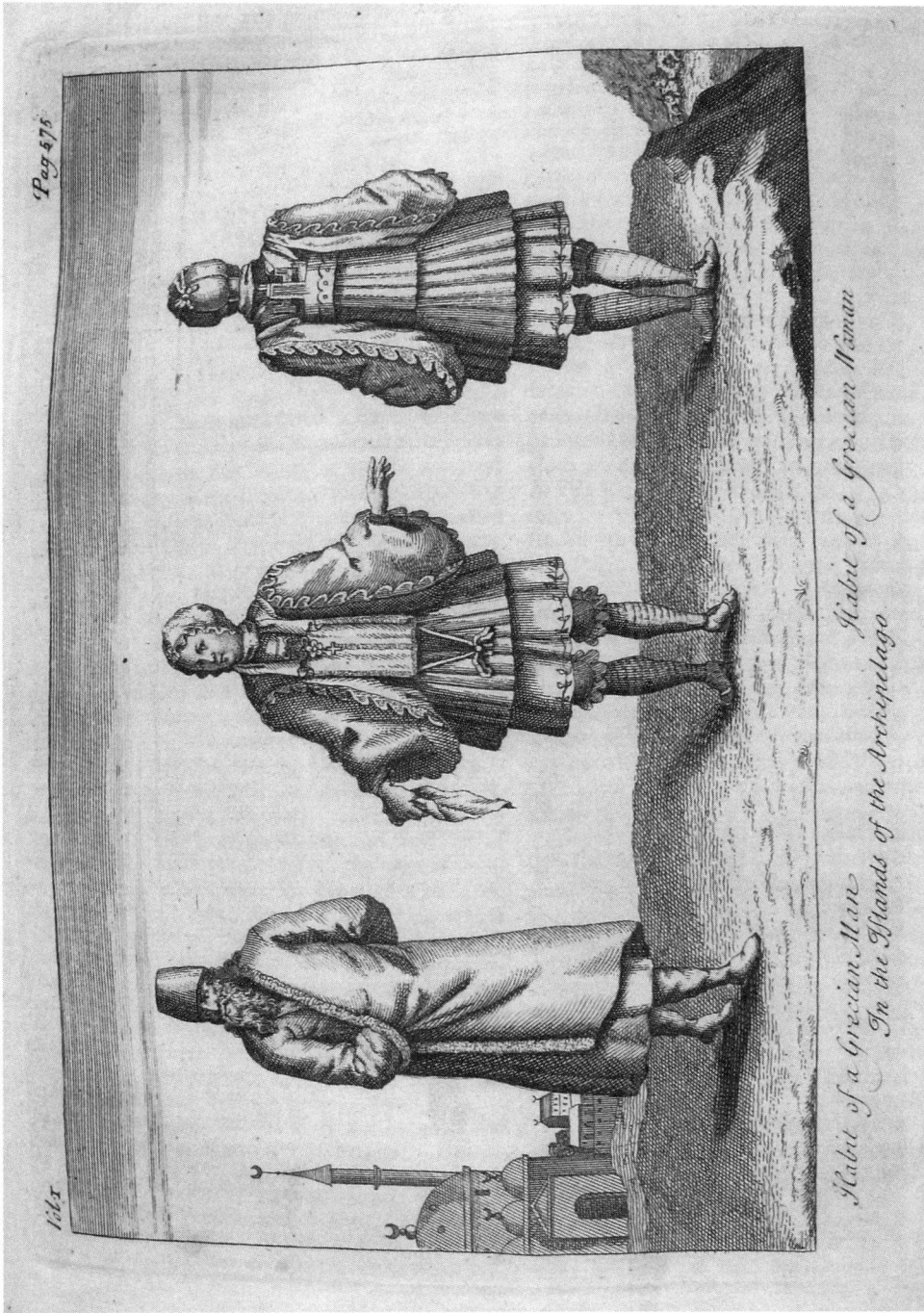

Habit of a Grecian Man
In the Islands of the Archipelago

Habit of a Grecian Woman

Figure 7.3 Thomas Salmon, Herman Moll, "Habit of a Grecian Man, [and] Habit of a Grecian Woman in the Islands of the Archipelago," *Modern History or the Present State of All Nations*, v. 1, after p. 575, London, 1744. Photo Courtesy of the Newberry Library, Chicago, Baskes folio G114.S17.

traveler (actual or armchair) is examined with an eye to discerning what types of authority he employs, and how that use of authority played upon notions of familiar or unfamiliar, ancient or modern.

The Eyewitness and the Limits of Authority

The early modern author allocated authority to himself (or herself, though female narrators are few and far between) by pointing out that he had actually "seen" people and their places rather than simply recounting the visions or tales of others. And because European audiences were especially curious about the "eastern" female, tales of access to local women further certified the narrator as someone with an enhanced knowledge base. Having seen Ottoman space and its peoples, the author could then employ images further to enhance the eyewitness experience. Itineraries showed where the authors had 'actually' been; illustrations penned 'on the spot' brought Ottoman space 'home' for the reader; and maps suggested the relationships between known and unknown space.[20] Such claims to authority cannot, of course, be construed as evidence that readers accepted everything they saw. Some were critical, as we shall see, and measured the truth claims of author or image against their own experiences or their 'archives' of assembled knowledge.

Translating eyewitness experience into cartographic form, mapmakers of the time placed travel authorities directly onto the body of the map via citations or routes marking the "footsteps" of travelers from the classical to the Biblical to the recently famous. A Genoese world map of 1457, for example, incorporated details "of the recently completed travels by the Venetian Nicolo Conti." The Venetian cartographer Fra Mauro employed Conti's travels along with those of Marco Polo in the world map he was drawing when he died in 1459.[21] André Thevet (1516–1592), the French Franciscan author of the *Cosmographie de Levant* (1554 and 1556), presented the classical and Biblical pasts as living, necessary frames through which his readers could comprehend the geography of the Mediterranean. He addressed mythical and historical figures (e. g. Odysseus and Xerxes) and praised the knowledge and writings of classical authors (Socrates, Plato, Aristotle) and Saint Jerome.[22] Similarly, the legend in Vincenzo Luchini's 1558 map, "Totius Graeciae Descriptio," cites Herodotus, Thucydides, Pausanias, Strabo,

---

[20] For example, "Carte du voyage du S. Daulier Deslandes en Perse 1665," with the itinerary marked with a dotted line, served to illustrate André Daulier Deslandes, *Les beautez de la Perse . . .* (Paris: Gervais Clouzier, 1673).

[21] J. R. S. Phillips, *The Medieval Expansion of Europe*, 2nd ed. (Oxford: Clarendon Press, 1998), 209. Philips characterizes the fifteenth century cartographers as caught in a "limbo" in which they knew the old ideas had to be modified or discarded but "could not yet decide on how they should be replaced (210)." On Fra Mauro, see also David Woodward, "Mapping the World," 14–31, in *Encounters: The Meeting of Asia and Europe, 1500–1800*, Anna Jackson and Amin Jaffer, eds. (London: V & A Publications, n.d. [2004]), 21–2.

[22] André Thevet, *Cosmographie de Levant*, Frank Lestringant, ed. (Geneva: Librairie Droz, 1985), 5–6, 13–14. On Thevet and his "ethnographic sensibility," see Conley, *The Self-Made Map*, 178, 192–3.

and Ptolemy as important authorities.[23] By the seventeenth century, such invocations of authority, along with ethnographic or pseudo-ethnographic depictions of the target cultures, were routinely deployed on maps or in compendia of knowledge to certify authorial legitimacy.

For other writers, however, the melding of drawn space and the recitation of a litany of precedents were not enough. Instead, they argued, the 'realities' of the Ottoman world could only be truly apprehended through personal experience. Thus James Howell (1594?–1666), in his 1650 treatise on *Instructions for forreine travell*, included an "Appendix of some directions for travelling into Turky and the Levant parts." Howell had already made clear on the first page of his book the relative validity of places seen vs. places read:

> *But to be a Sedentary Traveller only penn'd up between Walls, and to stand poring all day upon a Map, upon Artificiall Globes or Planisphares ... is like him who thought to come to be a Fencer, by looking on Agrippa's or Don Lius de Nervius' booke-postures only: As also to run over and traverse the world by Hearesay, and traditionall relation, with other mens eyes, and so take all things upon courtesie, is but a confused and imperfect kind of speculation, which leaveth weake and distrustfull notions behind it ...* [24]

He who wished to be knowledgeable must witness the place with his own eye, Howell argued, and not "through the mist of other men's breaths."[25] Having done so, he might then return "to his Mother soile ... " contented, and better able to evaluate the maps and narrations of others.[26]

That said, it was through the "mist of other men's breaths" that early modern authors and readers expected to 'see' and consume the Ottoman world, whether they themselves traveled or not. Narratives and maps combined the names and symbols of authorities present, recent, or distant in time, often feeling no particular compunction to differentiate among them. The Dutch traveler Jan Huyghen van Linschoten, for example, in the preface "To the Reader" of his *Voyages*, harks back to Roman times to begin the story of man's fascination with travel and ethnography:

> *Lucian in one of his Dialogues intituled Surveyers, writeth of Charon the old Ferrie-Man of Hell, that upon a great desire which he had conceived to view this world and the Actions of men therein, he begged leave of Pluto, that he might have a playing day, and be absent from*

[23] Vinceniij Luchini, "Totius Graeciae Descriptio," Rome, 1558. British Library, Maps. C.7.e.2.(.29). The map is copied from Nikolaos Sophianos' (b.c. 1500) 1540 original; see George Tolias, "Nikolaos Sophianos's *Totius Graeciae Descriptio*: The Resources, Diffusion, and Function of a Sixteenth Century Antiquarian Map of Greece," *Imago Mundi* 58.2 (July 2006): 150–82. Such assertions of authority were ubiquitous and ongoing. Thus, the legend of Brion de La Tour's "Perse, Turquie Asiatique, et Arabie," Paris, 1766, claims it is "Suivant les Rélations les plus éxactes"; and Nicolas de Fer's "Theatre de la Guerre Hongrie, Danube," Paris, 1705, legitimizes itself on the basis of the best information from travel and ambassadorial literature.
[24] James Howell, *Instructions and directions for forreine travell* (London: W.W. for Humphrey Moseley, 1650), 1–2.
[25] Howell, *Instructions and directions*, 139.
[26] Howell, *Instructions and directions*, 140.

his boat, to the end he might satisfie his thirsty humour, that troubled him so eagerly...

[Together with Mercury, who also conducted souls in Charon's barge, the gatekeeper to the netherworld piled Mts. Pelius, Ossa, Oeta, and Parnassus together, one upon the other.]

> *Upon the toppe wherof, having settled themselves, they did at leysure and pleasure take a view not onely of the Seas, and Mountaines, and Cities of the world: but also of the Inhabitants therof, together with their Speeches, Actions, and Manners.*[27]

From this base in Roman mythology, Linschoten then transitioned to the 'real' and the recent to provide a model for the accumulation and transcription of knowledge:

> *But to leave these Poeticall Fictions and vaine Fables, which do but declare the Nature of Man to be desirous of Novelties, and curious to know those things whereof he is ignorant; let us come to those that being neither conjured out of hell, nor rapt into the heavens, but of their owne honourable disposition and instinct of Nature, have not only compassed Sea and Land in their own persons to learne and beholde Nations, Realms, Peoples, and Countries unknowne for the augmentation of their owne private skill and cunning, but also have committed their knowledge and labours to writing for the propagation of the service and glorie of God in Pagan and Heathen places, and the great pleasure, profit and commodity of their Countrymen.*[28]

For Linschoten, and others, it was classical figures such as Homer and Strabo who began to build this 'mountain' of travel knowledge.[29] But, more particularly, it is scholars, travelers, and mapmakers of "our later times" such as Mercator, Thevet, and many others who have contributed the most. Indeed, it is Linschoten's own time that has made the most significant contribution, for, he writes,

> *the ancient Travellers had in deede a certain kind of knowledge... but it was very uncertaine and unperfect. Whereas we in our times are thoroughly learned and instructed by our owne experience, in the Provinces,*

---

[27] Linschoten, *John Huighen Van Linschoten, his Discourse of Voyages* [1598], "To the Reader," fourth unnumbered page after "Dedication."

[28] Linschoten, *John Huighen Van Linschoten, his Discourse of Voyages*, "To the Reader," first unnumbered page after "Dedication".

[29] Nicolay, *The Nauigations*, 117r, describing his discussion of Persia, wrote, "I am deliberated... to follow the most auncient, famous, and moderne Geographers & Historians, which are found to have thereof written." Nicolay made a habit in his travel narrative of invoking classical authorities, like Herodotus (42), Ptolemy, Pliny, and Strabo (139r–140r), and classical figures (e.g., 152r). Favyn, *The Theater of Honor and Knight-Hood*, 409–10, claimed, "I have read all the Authors, and seen the Maps or Tables of them... I have a great Manuscript in folio, and the Maps of the Holy Land... traced and figured by the hand and penne of my late Uncle..."

Cities, Rivers, Havens, and Trafficks of them all. So that now [the Indies] is become knowne to the whole world...[30]

'Seeing' the world, much as Charon and Mercury saw it, was the objective that Linschoten believed had been accomplished, through accumulated knowledge and especially the experiences of contemporary eyewitnesses.

Some contemporary writers echoed that sense of knowledge accomplished; others expressed less certainty regarding the exactitude of 'modern' mapping. Such was the case with two historians focusing on the frontiers of the Ottoman sultan and the Christian kings of Europe. Alessandro Vernino, in the dedication to his history of the Ottoman–Venetian wars in Dalmatia, published in 1648, made a point first and foremost of putting would-be critics in their places. He was writing, he argued, for "posterity" with a commitment to the "major triumph... of Christianity against its most fierce and potent enemies," the Ottomans.[31] In defense of that narrative, and against the "dogs" who would challenge it, he trumpets his eyewitness status, approximates himself to Demosthenes in his devotion to the truth (*verita*), and compares his work to the *Commentaries* of Julius Caesar.[32] For Vernino there is a clear hierarchy of classical and more contemporary authorities. Through invoking the proper range of authorities within that hierarchy, he cloaks himself in a garment of seriousness and authenticity, attempting to ward off those who would challenge his eyewitness vision of Ottoman space.

Conversely, the Benedictine Casimiro Freschot, writing a history of Dalmatia from Bologna in 1687, noted that knowledge of this frontier space was always compromised by a "diversity of accounts altered through the inclination, caprice, or ignorance of those who publish them to the world." Responding to criticism of some of his maps, he countered,

> *I must also protest that just as I do not make any claims without the authority of those geographers who seem to me most well regarded, so I do not pretend to assert the verity of my descriptions, recognizing in fact how difficult it is to disentangle that which is certain from that which is confused....*[33]

Maps, in Freschot's apologia, like narratives, were subject to false representations for a variety of reasons.[34] The chain of authority could thus cause the replication of error as well as truth. As proof he cited errors of naming and placement made by the famous Flemish and French mapmakers Ortelius and

---

[30] Linschoten, *John Huighen Van Linschoten, his Discourse of Voyages*, "To the Reader," second unnumbered page after "Dedication." The translator, John Wolfe, notes that Linschoten himself brought "rare inelligences from foreign parts." The interplay of recent and classical authorities is also quite evident in Jacob Spon, *Voyage d'Italie, de Dalmatie*, 103–9, when, for example, he describes Trau and the port of Spalatro (using contemporary French historians, Strabo, incriptions, and manuscript references, along with his own observations).

[31] Alessandro Vernino, *Della historia delle guerre di Dalmatia sotto il generalato di Leonardo Foscolo* (Venetia: G.G. Herz, 1648), unnumbered pages of dedication 3–4.

[32] Vernino, *Della historia*, unnumbered pages of note to readers (Lettore), 2–3, 5–6, 12.

[33] Casimiro Freschot, *Memorie historiche, e geografiche della Dalmazia* (Bologna: Per Giacomo Monti, 1687), 266.

[34] By way of example, he noted that in a recent map of Dalmatia, printed in Rome, Narenta (Neretva) was placed more than 40 miles away from its actual site. Freschot, *Memorie historiche*, 321.

Sanson.[35] Freschot, in other words, concurred with Du Vignau, the French author of *A New Account of the Present Condition of Turkish Affairs* (1688), who argued that it was both ingrained impressions and intentional misrepresentation that kept readers from grasping the nature of such foreign places.[36]

Despite these weaknesses, the map was routinely employed to reinforce and reaffirm the authorities invoked in historical, geographic, and travel texts. The narrative description for Porcacchi's 1572 map of the "Archipelago," for example, begins, "That sea, which Thucydides in his first book called 'Greek,' today, by our navigators is called 'Archipelago.'"[37] The reader is thus presented with a name, two types of authority, and a book, anchors by which the designations of the contemporary world could be connected to the respected geographic visions of the past. That tradition continued in the 1690 edition of Vincenzo Coronelli's *Isolario dell' Atlante Veneto*. There, Coronelli included a list of "antique and modern geographical authors," a common device in early modern atlases.[38] The first author listed among the pantheon of "moderns" is the Damascus-born "Arab" geographer Abu'l-Fida (1273–1331), confirming Europe's debt to medieval Arabic scholarship. Also included are various of the mapmakers we have already seen in earlier chapters: Giacomo Gastaldi (c. 1500–1566), Sebastian Münster (1488–1552), Gerardus Mercator (1512–1594), Abraham Ortelius (1527–1598), and Giovanni Botero (1544–1617), all mappers of Ottoman space in narrative and image who set the stage for Coronelli's own work. And Coronelli's texts, like his images, highlighted the weight of the classics in understanding and reading space. His history of Rhodes, published in 1702, calls up Eusebius, Glycas, Strabo, Homer, and Ptolemy, all in its first few pages.[39]

The weight of the classics, however, only went so far. Coronelli's map of the Bosporus, or the "Canal of Constantinople," as he called it, is taken from the work of two contemporary authors (Fig. 7.4).[40] First he employed the description of Count Luigi Ferdinando Marsigli (1658–1730), the Bolognese natural historian, Hapsburg officer, and onetime Ottoman captive, whose observations on the nature and organization of the Ottoman military influenced multiple generations of European observers.[41] He also utilized the "*relationi* of Monsieur Galland," a reference to the French Orientalist

---

[35] Freschot, *Memorie historiche*, 335–6. The importance of Ortelius as an authority is clear from such references, in which authors amend their readers' sense of place by making corrections to the mapmaker. See, for example, Covel, *Dr. John Covel Voyages*, 32–3, 70–71.

[36] [Du Vignau], Person of Quality, *A New Account of the Present Condition of Turkish Affairs*, unnumbered second page of "Preface to the Reader."

[37] See Gerstenberg, *Thomaso Porcacchi's L'Isole piu famose del mondo*, 86. Porcacchi in discussing the scope and designations of the sea also brings in Pliny and the Romans.

[38] Coronelli, *Atlante Veneto*, 1690, v. 1, unnumbered pages 8–9.

[39] Vincenzo Coronelli, *Isola di Rodi geografica-storica, antica e moderna: coll' altre adiacenti, gia possedute dà Cavalieri Hospitalieri di Giovanni di Gerusalemme* (Venetia: [n.p.] 1702), 4, 6, 15, 23, 25. See Sean Roberts, *Printing a Mediterranean World: Florence, Constantinople, and the Renaissance of Geography* (Cambridge: Harvard University Press, 2013), 67–84, 104, on Ptolemy as enduring authority.

[40] Vincenzo Coronelli, "Canal of Constantinople" (Venetia: 1690), *Atlante Veneto*, v. 1, plate 24, after p. 82, map 61.

[41] See Stoye, *Marsigli's Europe*. Coronelli's inset map of the Bosporus, presumably, was taken from Marsigli's *Osservazioni interne al Bosforo Tracio*, published in Rome in 1681.

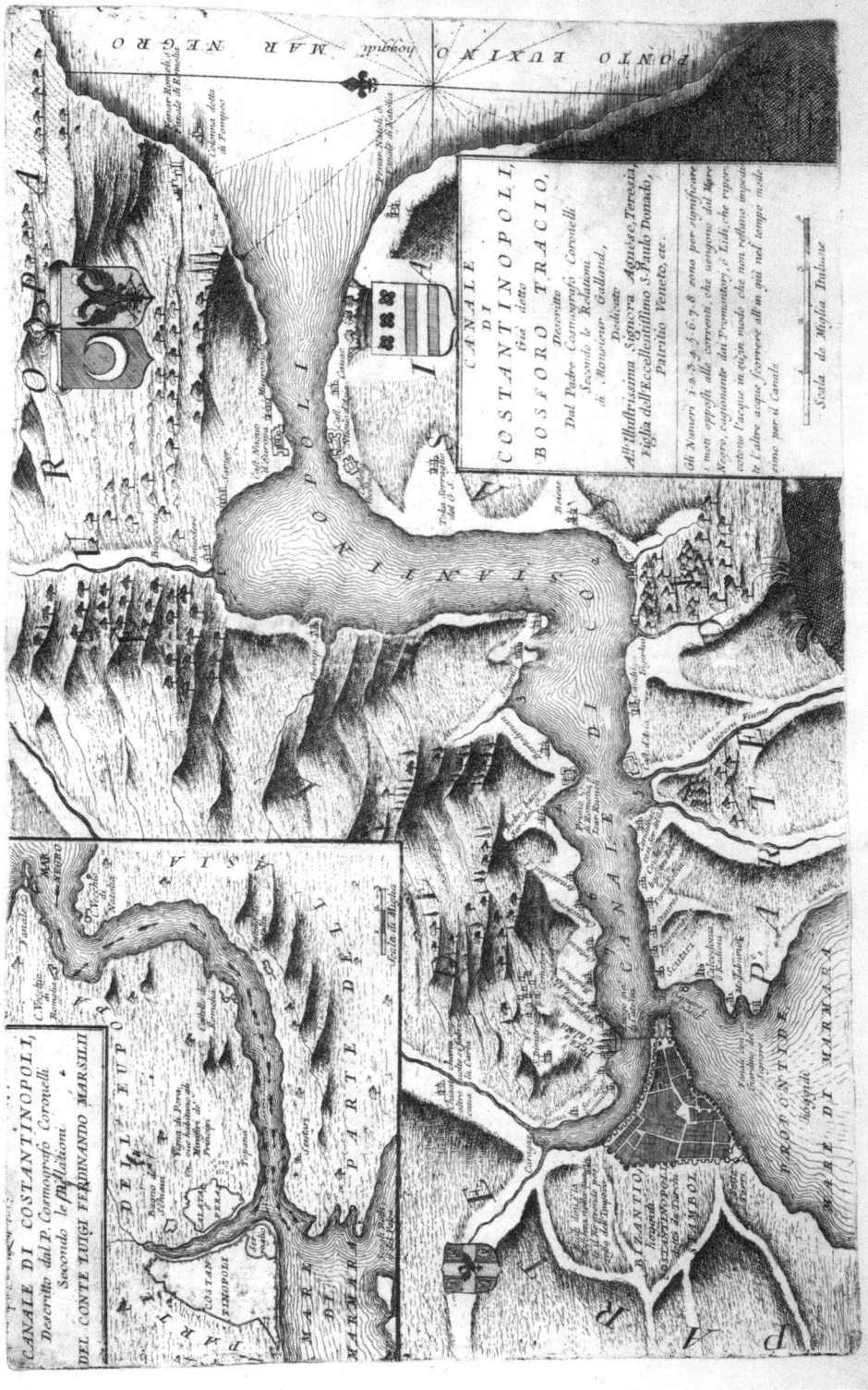

Figure 7.4. Vincenzo Coronelli, "Canale di Costantinopoli," *Atlante Veneto*, v. 1, pl. 24, Venetia, 1690. Photo Courtesy of the Newberry Library, Chicago, Ayer 135 C8 1690 Vault.

Antoine Galland (1646–1715) whose 1704 translation of the *Thousand and One Nights* would become a cause célèbre in Europe. Coronelli's assembly of map authorities thus reached from the geographers of the classical era, to the treatises of the medieval Arab world, to the popular texts of his own day. He was not an eyewitness like Marsigli and Galland; but such eyewitnesses (along with a diverse range of known and respected scholars) provided the lenses through which he and his readers could pin down Ottoman space.

The Italian Traveler and the Chain of Authority

We see then that the notion of a well-established system of authoritative referencing, based on scholarship and 'seeing,' was common in the early modern era for those who sought to depict the nature and boundaries of the "East." When travelers, authors, cartographers, and readers approached the Ottomans, they tended already to possess a series of associations by which to understand them. I turn now to a specific set of narrators and mapmakers to take a more elaborate look at how this system of authority was deployed in the mapping of early modern Ottoman space.

The emblematic narrators of the sixteenth century Ottoman world, as noted in Chapter 6, were the envoys, resident and temporary, of the Venetian Republic. Venice and the Ottoman empire were proximate, entangled, interested, and engaged in a fierce competition for space, reputation, and economic gain. And European Christendom looked to Venice (the "mirror of the familiar" in Deborah Howard's phrase), for its accumulated knowledge and its modes of framing, depicting, and telling the Ottomans, even after the role of the Signoria was overshadowed by the commercial inroads of the French, English, and Dutch.[42]

Marino Cavalli, who spent two years as Venetian bailo in Constantinople, began his *relazione* to the Signoria in 1560 by saying that the Spanish king (Philip II), having made the "inexcusable error" of engaging the Ottoman fleet off Djerba (Tunisia), to the great detriment of Christendom, must have been poorly informed of "things Turkish."[43] Venice, on the other hand, he congratulated his audience, "most wisely" saw to it that those who "had dealt with or seen things of any importance" kept the Signoria well informed. As a result, Cavalli noted that he would limit his remarks to particular commercial and diplomatic affairs because his listeners had already

> heard from my excellent predecessors, told with the utmost diligence
> and order, the origins of the Turk, the means by which he became so
> powerful, the ways of the court, the ranks and stipends of the sultan's

---

[42] See for example, Maria Pia Pedani Fabris, ed., *Relazioni di Ambasciatori Veneti al Senato, v. XIV, Costantinopoli Relazioni Inedite (1512–1789)* (Padova: Bottega d'Erasmo, 1996). The *relazione* format, including the place names of antiquity, was well established by the fourteenth century; see Howard, *Venice and the East*, 44–5. Venetian envoys were the practical-minded travelers of whom Rubiés, *Travel and Ethnology in the Renaissance*, 359, writes.
[43] Alberi, *Relazioni*, series III, v. 1, 273.

*'slaves,' Ottoman dress, income, expenses, and the countries that the
sultan rules. Nothing having changed [in those regards] it seems vain to
repeat them unless you so desire, especially since many of these particulars are also available in writing and in print (scritte ed in stampa).*[44]

Just as Rashid al-Din gathered up the accounts of knowledgeable men, so
too European publishers began to assemble the *relazioni* and other narratives
of travelers past and present and combine them. Such compendia aimed at
presenting a travel-knowledge picture of the world. When Giovanni Batista
Ramusio (1485–1557), Secretary of the Venetian Council of Ten, assembled
the texts of his three-volume *Delle navigationi et viaggi* (1550–56), he commissioned Giacomo Gastaldi, the illustrious mapmaker, to illustrate parts of
them. Those illustrations already lent authority to the *Navigations* as conveying an accurate picture of the world.[45] Indeed, Cavalli could have been
referring to Ramusio's work when he noted that the *relazioni* were available in print. But Ramusio also began the dedication of his second volume
with an invocation of "illustrious authors" beginning with Homer and pro-
ceeding through Ptolemy and the Portuguese navigators, who had outlined
the contours and contents of the world for previous generations.[46] In that
same volume, which was published after Ramusio's death, Tommaso Giunti
(the publisher) lauded Ramusio himself as an authority, a man who had
become an expert through his "singular intellect," his desire to share the
news of "so many and distant countries (including many unknown to the
ancients)," his judiciousness, and his knowledge of science, Latin, Greek,
French, Spanish, and geography (acquired through "diligent study" and
through personal experience traveling and translating in the service of the
Most Serene Republic).[47] Ramusio's *Navigations and Travels* became a much
copied representational standard, whereas half a century later, influenced by
Ramusio, so too did the compilation of travels by the English publisher
Samuel Purchas (1577?–1626), which purported to include "relations" dat-
ing from the Creation to the present.[48]

Individual travelers invoked authority in ways that varied by personality
and objective. They interacted with their destinations in ways ranging from
the highly self-conscious to the relatively unconscious. But all invoked some
kind of authority to bolster the truth claims of their narratives. Sonja Brentjes
and Volkmar Schüller have illustrated the process by which travel literature
could be carefully crafted and framed in their analysis of the famous Roman
traveler Pietro della Valle (1586–1652), who journeyed to Iran and South
Asia. Of his letters they note that "the traveler assured his addressee of his
continuous efforts at improving the quality of such [travel] knowledge by
studying local languages, buying local manuscripts, talking to local scholars

[44] Alberi, *Relazioni*, series III, v. 1, 274.
[45] See Woodward, "Mapping the World," 24–5. Ortelius acknowledged Gastaldi, along with other
mapmakers, in his *Theatrum*'s list of authors.
[46] Ramusio, *Delle navigationi et viaggi*, v. 2, dedication 3r.
[47] Ramusio, *Delle navigationi et viaggi*, v. 2, "to the readers," recto and verso of unnumbered page one.
[48] Samuel Purchas, *Purchas his pilgrimage, or Relations of the world and the religions obserued in all
ages and places discouered, from the Creation vnto this present* (London: William Stansby for Henry
Fetherstone, 1613).

and nobles, and undertaking excursions to verify that the local information that contradicted beliefs at home was indeed correct."[49] Della Valle and others, however, as these authors note, still operated in the context of a literary, historical, and pictorial tradition of knowledge, which their audiences relied on to achieve a sense of the familiar. Though anticipating being educated and amazed by the travel account, literate audiences could be critical. They had expectations of what they were supposed to hear and see. In order to join the chain of authoritative witnesses who laid out the places of the East for that expectant audience, della Valle needed to document his methods of assessing Ottoman space and subjects.

Adding to the authority of text and eyewitness experience, as della Valle suggested, were the opportunities to hear and converse directly with "the Turk." In a short late-sixteenth-century treatise providing advice on how to defeat the Ottomans, Gherardo Borgogni (1526–1608) invoked both textual and oral authorities as his sources of information. Not only had he employed the *Commentaries* of Anton Francesco Cirni (b. 1510), but also, he tells his readers, he had the benefit of conversations with "a Turk from Constantinople" named Hasan, a man very knowledgeable about the Ottoman Porte. This informant was "not well known," but Borgogni tells his readers that he "is a most judicious and intelligent person . . . well versed in Italian."[50] Taken prisoner at the battle of Lepanto in 1571, Hasan was a new "Turk," a convert to Islam. As such he was not only able to provide purportedly authoritative insights into the life of the Turk but also intelligible to the author and his readers. He served as an intermediary between the European Christian "self" and the "born Turk."[51] Borgogni concluded his treatise by urging King Phillip of Spain to heed the cries of suffering humanity and turn all his energies to stopping the Ottomans. In so doing, he proclaimed, "You, Oh benign, potent, and revered king will be an Alexander against Darius, a Themistocles against Xerxes, and a Judah Macabee against Antioch."[52] The transition from the classics to the present for Borgogni (as for Linschoten and Vernino) was as easy as it was natural. And Hasan provided him with an added source of authority, the next best thing to a 'real' Turk.

The chain of authority moved readily between text and map and across state boundaries. Marco Boschini, for example, in his 1658 *isolario* of the Archipelago, like Rosaccio before him, saw his task as describing islands,

---

[49] Brentjes and Schüller, "Pietro della Valle's Latin Geography of Safavid Iran," 182–3, 185. The authors note that della Valle reworked his letters for a print version "filled with hundreds of quotes from ancient secular and sacred books . . . (182–3).

[50] Borgogni, *Le Discordie christiane*, 29. Bibliotheca Correr, Cicogna 558.I8(816.17).

[51] Bargrave, *The Travel Diary*, 118, an English merchant traveling in Ottoman lands between 1647 and 1652, invoked descriptions of "Par [Parastaeis?], & others in manuscript, who turnd Turkes & served some years within the Seraglio," as his authorities for the goings on in the Ottoman palace. In Sadettin, *The Reign of Sultan Orchan Second King of the Turks*, 10th–11th unnumbered pages of preface, William Seaman notes that he used Richard Knolles as an authority on place names in Ottoman lands, because "we have no Geographie that giveth any certain light to the knowledge of most of those places mentioned here . . . " But he also critiques Knolles as having followed "the tradition of the Arabians," because his place names are not coincident with "the Grecian" ones.

[52] Borgogni, *Le Discordie christiane*, 29.

coasts, ports, seas and castles, "in the form in which one sees them at the present time," and providing their names, stories, and history, both antique and modern.[53] That task served to link antique history to the on-going struggle against the Turk. But for Boschini, a Venetian, the depiction of Ottoman territory was also personal. He dedicated his work to Alessandro Farnese, "General of the Cavalry in the fight against the Ottomans." His first image was a fold-out map of Venetian Candia (Crete), where the Ottomans were engaged in a siege operation that lasted off and on from 1648 to 1669.[54]

Boschini, in turn, became one of the authoritative sources for the Dutch scholar Olfert Dapper's (c. 1636–89) 1688 description of the Archipelago (Fig. 7.5). Indeed, Dapper overwhelms the reader with his citations of authority. In his preface he notes the numerous Italian authors who have written about these islands (Buondelmonti in 1440, Bordoni in 1547, Porcacchi in 1610, and Boschini in 1658). Besides these, he notes ancient descriptions (Strabo, Virgil, Ptolemy, Mela, Pliny, Solon), and modern geographers. Dapper writes that he has employed Dutch maritime narratives and multinational voyagers' accounts such as those of Belon, della Valle, Du Loir, Spon, Wheler, Sandys, and Stokhove. He advises his readers that he has perused all these materials and more in order to hone his information about the Archipelago.[55] In the text, he cites these sources in the marginal notes, adding others such as Tavernier and Rycaut.[56] Dapper even called up the 'voice' of the Turk to make his atlas more authoritative. On the siege of Rhodes, for example, he 'cites' Mustafa Pasha and Sultan Süleyman, though he does not indicate the histories from which these supposed "quotes" were derived.[57] Nor does he provide the provenance for the many maps that "enrich" his text.[58] The Archipelago for Dapper is a part of Europe "that directs its gaze most closely towards the Orient."[59] It has a rich history of rule under the Greeks, Romans, Byzantines, and Venetians, has produced numerous illustrious men, and has a reputation for good wines. But at present it is desolate and deserted, weighed down under the "heavy yoke of the Empire of the Turks," a condition that Dapper hoped would be ameliorated by a return to Christian rule.

[53] Marco Boschini, *L'Archipelago Con tutte le Isole, Scogli Secche, e Bassi Fondi, Con i Mari, Golfi, Seni, Porti, Citt', e Castelli; Nella Forma, Che si Vedono al Tempo Presente. Con una succinta narrativa de i loro nomi, Favole, & Historie, tanto antiche quanto moderne. Non meno utile alli Studiosi di Cosmografia, che dilettevole all'universale* (Venetia: Per Francesco Nicolini, 1658), has three fold-out maps and forty-six full-page engraved maps and charts.

[54] See Maria Georgopoulou, *Venice's Mediterranean Colonies: Architecture and Urbanism* (Cambridge: Cambridge University Press, 2001), 36, 142, 263, for maps and a standard commemorating the struggle.

[55] I am using the 1703 French edition: O. Dapper, *Description exacte des Isles de l'Archipel* (Amsterdam: Chez George Gallet, 1703), Preface, fourth page of front matter, "*L'on verra que nous avons eu soin de mettre par tout le sentiment des Anciens & ceux des Modernes immédiatement l'un après l'autre, & que nous avons laissé presque toûjours la liberté au Lecteur d'en juger comme il le trouveroit à propos.*"

[56] About the same time, c. 1720, Tavernier's account also appeared, grouped with Olearius and other "authors" as sources for the map by Johann Baptist Homann, "Imperii Persici in Omnes Suas Provincias," Nuremberg, [c. 1720].

[57] Dapper, *Description*, 112, 119.

[58] Dapper, *Description*, 88–159, on Rhodes.

[59] Dapper, *Description*, Preface, fourth page of front matter.

Figure 7.5. Olfert Dapper, *Description exacte des isles de l'archipel*, frontispiece, Amsterdam, 1703. fMG 1070.1.2, Houghton Library, Harvard University.

Authority, Ethnography, and Costume

Mapmakers and compilers of geographic and travel texts, along with
adventurers, merchants, and envoys, thus replicated the tropes of classical,
medieval, and early modern models, embellishing them as they sorted the
peoples of the Ottoman domains into various categories of identity. They
defended themselves preemptively against the anticipated criticism of skepti-
cal readers. And as they asserted their authority beyond the citation of texts,
the presentation of costume (especially the dress of the Ottoman female)
served as a special category of eyewitness knowledge.

Bembo

A contemporary of Boschini's was the young Venetian nobleman Ambrosio Bembo, who noted a variety of authorities, beyond his own experience
and observations, for his *Travels and Journal through Part of Asia*, beginning in 1671.[60] Venetian diplomatic and commercial personnel, such as the
consul of Aleppo, joined with the monks of an elaborate network of mission houses to provide Bembo with experienced informers on the lands
of the sultan and shah.[61] To these advisors he added his reading of texts
such as della Valle's *Viaggi*, the itinerary of a fellow Venetian, Marco Polo,
and his face-to-face encounters with more seasoned travelers such as the
Anglo-French author and merchant Jean Chardin (1643–1713).[62] Bembo
met the French artist Guillaume Joseph Grélot, who became his traveling
companion and produced fifty-one of the fifty-two drawings that illustrate
the *Travels*.[63] He hired Grélot away from Chardin, seizing on the importance of expert visual documentation of "landscape, buildings, ships and
rafts, rock reliefs, ruins, and costume" as a means of showing the 'real'
East.[64] Bembo carefully supervised the production of Grélot's drawings, so
that they might map out what he called his "truthful account"; and he hoped
that his long wanderings might "bring pleasure to all those who, during the
leisure of domestic tranquility, may want to spend only a little time in reading
them..."[65]

Bembo was a keen observer of technical processes; he also provided elaborate commentary on the mores and dress of the people he encountered.[66]

---

[60] Bembo, *Travels*, 3.

[61] Bembo, *Travels*, 19, 39–40.

[62] Bembo, *Travels*, 35. See Rubiés, *Travel and Ethnology in the Renaissance*, 384–5, on Chardin and the
"critical mass of independent travelers whose accounts after 1650 contributed so much to the crystal-
lization of notions of oriental despotism, natural religion, and the relativity of human customs..."

[63] Bembo, *Travels*, 10, 14, 21, 26–8, 84.

[64] Bembo, *Travels*, 28–9.

[65] Bembo, *Travels*, 35–6.

[66] For the costume "mapping" of the day, see, for example, Abraham de Bruyn (1540–87), *Omnium
pene Europae, Asiae, Aphricae atque Americae gentium habitus* (Antwerp: Michel Colijn [1581]);
Hamilton, *Arab Culture and Ottoman Magnificence in Antwerp's Golden Age*, 26–7, 41–4; Lach, *Asia
in the Making of Europe*, v. 2, 90–92; Rachel Doggett, ed., *New World of Wonders: European Images
of the Americas 1492–1700* (Seattle: University of Washington Press, 1992), 89–90; Julian Raby,
Venice, Dürer, and the Oriental Mode (Totawa, NJ: Islamic Art Publications, 1982); Leslie Luebbers,
"Documenting the Invisible: European Images of Ottoman Women, 1567–1867," *The Print Collector's*

In his description, some of the inhabitants of Ottoman lands had their own distinctive dress and some wore the dress of other "nations," for example, the Greeks of Cyprus who wore "Venetian" dress, or the Druze in Syria who wore "Turkish" costume. Women's dress required special attention in Bembo's discourse. It possessed an element of the sexual that transcended ethnographic curiosity and the "science" of costume; and it augmented the authority of his narrative by highlighting both his descriptive talents and his access to the native population.[67]

Like Nicolas de Nicolay before him, Bembo thus mapped Ottoman terrain and his own authority in terms of female dress. Commenting on the distinctive costume of the locals, Bembo notes that the women of Aleppo wear pants and their dress resembles that of the men, except for female headgear "shaped like a bowl . . . of gold, silver, tin, or cardboard covered with silk, depending on the rank and wealth of the wearer."[68] Their hair, he noted, was plaited with ribbons that reached their feet, some with silver bells attached. Bembo included figure drawings of inside and outside garb, dividing his subjects into Turk, Christian, Syrian, and "Bedouin."[69] All the women are veiled when they venture out except the Bedouin, whom Bembo calls "the peasants." His designations thus range from the religious and gendered to the regional and ethno-rural. He describes the dress of Muslim, Christian, and Jewish women as similar, with some variations. Jewish women, for example, "wear for whimsy a little ring or pendant in their nose, which is pierced, as are the ears of our women. Others pierce their upper lip on one side, where they put a gold rosette that looks like a mole and gives them great charm."[70] Although Bembo clearly enjoys these piercings, he is less sanguine about the conventions of makeup that females in "the greater part of the Orient," share, which he says do not "satisfy the eye." We are not always sure which women Bembo is seeing, or where; but he does point up his own authority by noting that he has gained the confidence of many Christians and some Jews in Ottoman lands, and been invited to their houses "many times."[71] It was customary, of course, for travelers to include commentary on the Ottoman harem, its ranks, and its intrigues (a subject of great interest to European audiences), as part of the discussion of Ottoman space; but the description of Ottoman women 'actually' seen lent the author's narrative greater immediacy.[72]

Newsletter 24.1 (March–April 1993): 2–7; Günsel Renda, "The Ottoman Empire and Europe in the 17th Century: Changing Images," 44–55, in *Image of the Turks in the 17th Century Europe* (Istanbul: Sabancı University, 2005); Amanda Wunder, "Western Travelers, Eastern Antiquities, and the Image of the Turk in Early Modern Europe," *Journal of Early Modern History*, v. 7, 1–2 (2003): 90–119.

[67] See Wilson, "Foggi diverse," 102, 110–23.
[68] Bembo, *Travels*, 61–2.
[69] Bembo, *Travels*, 62–3. The term 'Syrian,' or 'Soriane,' here probably denotes Syrian Christian, rather than the more modern ethnonational meaning.
[70] Bembo, *Travels*, 79.
[71] Ibid.
[72] See for example Michael Austin, trans., Geoffrey Lewis, ed. *Domenico's Istanbul* (London: Gibb Memorial Trust, 2001), i–ii, vi, on Domenico Hierosolimitano (c. 1552–1622), a Jew from Safed in Palestine, who served as court physician to Sultan Murat III (r. 1574–95) from approximately 1578/9

Costume, of course, not only identified the local representatives of a given culture, but also served as a disguise for those crossing boundaries and attempting to blend in and gain more intimate knowledge. When he left Ottoman Aleppo for Iraq and Iran, Bembo took on a "foreign" costume, growing his beard, dressing *alla Turca*, and securing "Turkish" eating utensils and equipment. As a witness he attempted to acquire authority by 'becoming' a Turk, though he did smuggle some pork into his provisions without letting his traveling companions know.[73] But long before Bembo left Venice in 1671, Michele Membré, a Venetian on a mission to Persia from 1539 to 1542, and traveling through Ottomans lands, had also adopted a disguise in the "Turkish fashion."[74] Membré's *relazione*, written when he returned to Venice, illustrates the ways in which a foreign Christian, posing as a merchant, could be readily integrated (however briefly) into networks of Muslim commercial exchange. That apparent integration made the narrator a more 'authoritative' witness.[75] When he returned home, Membré was celebrated as an authority on the "East," and that notoriety prompted a joint proposal, with the mapmaker Giacomo Gastaldi, in 1550, to produce a map tracing the places from the Mediterranean, through the realms of sultan and shah, and on to South Asia and Cathay.[76]

It is clear from that proposed collaboration that travel was viewed as translating naturally into projects of representation, so that knowledge could be shared and map images paraded before a demanding public. Eyewitness testimony, in a very immediate way, could thus be made to serve the interests of empire, commerce, and ethnography. And the notion of a Christian disguised as a "Turk" served not only to certify Membré's intercultural skills but also to titillate his intended audience with visions of the unsuspecting Turk.[77] The question of masquerade, after all, has intrigued readers of the "Orient" for a very long time; witness the responses to Richard Burton and Lawrence of Arabia. Thus, although it is important to differentiate the reasons for which both viewers and impersonators of the empire donned "Eastern" or "Turk" dress, it is also critical to note the ways in which dressing up transcended era and occupation. If travelers such as Ambrosio Bembo and Michel Membré

---

to 1588/9. Domenico remarks on the differential tax applied to Turkish, Jewish, and Christian maidens who were married in the city, thus suggesting some intimacy with the details of Ottoman law (12). See also Ebru Boyar and Kate Fleet, "Introduction," in *Ottoman Women in Public Space*, Kate Fleet and Ebru Boyar, eds. (Leiden: Brill, in preparation), on the question of public visibility of women in the 16th–19th century Ottoman empire.

73 Bembo, *Travels*, 78, 82.

74 See Michele Membré, *Mission to the Lord Sophy of Persia*, A.H. Morton, ed. and trans. (London: School of Oriental and African Studies, 1993), 5.

75 Membré, *Mission*, 8, notes that he loaded his merchandise at Candia, "together with other Turkish merchants."

76 See also Karrow, *Mapmakers of the Sixteenth Century*, 225, on the proposal of Membré and Giacomo Gastaldi to produce a map of Asia, beginning at the Mediterranean and on to Cathay and South Asia. The map was apparently not published.

77 Similarly, Claes Rålamb, Karl X Gustaf's envoy to the Ottoman court in 1657, "was equipped with all kinds of disguises and while in enemy territory posed variously as a merchant, a student, a stablemaster trading in horses, and a musician." See Westerberg, "Claes Rålamb: Statesman, Scholar and Ambassador," 32.

dressed *alla Turca* it was not simply for convenience or espionage; it reflected their personalities, their testing of ethnocouturial limits, and their assessment of audience demands.[78]

Busbecq and Nicolay

Ambassadors and members of their entourages were often perceived as expert witnesses, and they set the tone for other sorts of travelers, especially when they were able to spend some significant time in the empire. Thus (as we have seen in Ch. 6), the courtiers Ogier Ghislen de Busbecq, the Hapsburg envoy to the Porte from 1554 to 1562, and Nicolas de Nicolay, the geographer who accompanied a French embassy to Istanbul in 1551, both produced travel narratives that were widely read, translated, and emulated. And, as with previous writers, both used 'knowledge' of local mores as evidence of their eyewitness status and testimony to their penchant for brushing up against the local peoples. Busbecq was more concerned with strategic interests and a comparison of Hapsburg to Ottoman might than with the dress of Ottoman subjects. But he did not neglect commentary on public mores. He complimented the simple costume of Ottoman courtiers and conjured up the Trojan Wars to describe women's dress in Bulgaria.[79] Those details enlivened his narrative and presumably enhanced its appeal to a wide readership.

When it came to details, however, Nicolas de Nicolay had the advantage of linking his narrative to images. Nicolay made the depiction of women's dress central to his volume; and its visual ethnography became a celebrated model of Ottoman modes. He thus claimed authority on Ottoman women based not simply on eyewitness experience but on apparent careful observation. The English translation of his work, done originally in French, for example, provides this elaborate description of the maidens and matrons of Chios.

> *The women of reputation weare their gownes or coates of velvet, satten, damask, or other rich silkes, white, or of other seemlie colour, which they gard about with broad bands of velvet, and doe fasten their sleeves above with silk ryband lace of divers colours . . . and attire their head with a coyfe of white satten or other colour embroidered with gold and peareles, and close the same about the head with long fringes & other ribands of lyke silke . . . & before their forehead they weare a yeallow Cypresse wrought upon gold folie, which they shut and knit fast behind their coyfe: but the married women differing from the maidens in steed*

---

[78] See Kader Konuk, "Ethnomasquerade in Ottoman–European Encounters: Reenacting Lady Mary Wortley Montagu," *Criticism* 46.3 (Summer, 2004): 393–414. The author is dealing with a later period, but his emphasis on the "historically specific ways in which ethnomasquerade operates as a literary strategy (394)" is important.

[79] Ogier Ghiselin de Busbecq, *The Turkish Letters of Ogier Ghiselin de Busbecq: Imperial Ambassador at Constantinople 1554–1562*, trans. Edward Forster (Oxford: Clarendon Press, 1968), 21–2, 26. Anton Vrančić, the Bosnian bishop of Peć, also took a diplomatic mission to Constantinople in 1553 on behalf of the Hapsburg Ferdinand. His diary, as Todorova, *Imagining the Balkans*, 23, 67, notes, provides a full-page description of the hairstyle and "unique headgear of Bulgarian women of the Pirot district, their rings and bracelets." These "objects which cost nothing" he compared favorably to the costly extravagance of those he referred to as "our women."

*of a cypresse, weare on their shoulders a fair raile white as the snow
and generally their hosen and pattins are of colour white. Briefly there
is nothing to be seen upon them which is not proper & pleasant, but
that they make their bodies short, & have their brests hanging, because
of the continuous frequentation of the bathes, but about their neck and
upon their stomacke, they wear many chaines, tablets, & other trinkets
of gold, pearles, or other fine stones of great value, every one according
to her qualitie and degree, so that all their pleasure and studie is to
attire and set out themselves to make them the more acceptable unto
men aswel private as strangers.[80]*

No doubt the women of Chios might have construed their objectives a
bit differently; but Nicolay's narrative descriptions of women are effectively
juxtaposed to his illustrations of the Ottoman female. He discusses women
going to the baths and visiting the cemeteries, drawing attention to his supposed intimacy with the layout of the city, his knowledge of social mores,
and his ability to 'watch' what women were doing, at least up to a point.
He also highlights the conventional relegation of women to a separate space,
one divided into categories based on ethnicity, class, matrimonial status, and
rural or urban identity (Figs. 7.6 and 7.7). On his return to France, he turned
that knowledge of the Ottoman female into a text that achieved transnational
appeal.

Evliya: An Ottoman Vision

Another emblem of his age was Evliya Çelebi (1611–84): Muslim, servant
of the sultan, raconteur, and (older) contemporary of Ambrosio Bembo. His
Seyahatname, as already noted, is a unique Ottoman source, composed by a
member of the Ottoman elite class who used his wit and ingenuity to craft
an autonomous role for himself within that class, and who defied customary categories of genre to compose a noisy, nosey, people-oriented vision of
Ottoman realms and relationships.[81] Thus, Evliya has become the default
Ottoman authority, a conjurer of Ottoman space, expansive in his attention to ethnographic detail. Though Evliya was clearly an unusual man, his
training, companions, and intellectual milieu mirrored those of his fellows,
a group of what one might call military–literary elites. That cadre of elites
spills out over the boundaries of Ottoman space, and its literary and historical points of reference span the Mediterranean.[82] As he described his
milieu and his travels, Evliya shared many of the modes and sources of

---

[80] Nicolay, *The Nauigations*, 37–8, 51–68, 119. For comparison, the album of Bartholomäus Schachman,
the mayor of Danzig, who traveled through the empire in 1588–9, *Bartholomäus Schachman (1559–
1614), The Art of Travel*, 231, fig. 46r, depicts a "Greek woman from Chios" rather differently, in
an elaborate red gown but without sash or jewelry. Schachman's album includes many of the stock
Ottoman figures, but it also includes images of "Christian" and "Jewish" women (both shown with
long blonde hair) mourning their dead (155, 313).

[81] Alam and Subrahmanyam, *Indo-Persian Travels*, 6–10, 243–95; Tezcan, "The Frank in the Ottoman
Eye," 267–96; and Nurhan Tezcan and Semih Tezcan, eds., *Evliyâ Çelebi: Doğumunun 40. Yılında*
(Ankara: T.C. Kültür ve Turizm Bakanlığı, 2011).

[82] Andrews and Kalpaklı, *Age of Beloveds*; Evliya Çelebi, *Evliya Çelebi in Albania*, 193.

Figure 7.6. Nicolas de Nicolay, "Femme de l'isle de Chio," *Les navigations peregri-nations et voyages*, fol. 71, Antwerp, 1576. *64–730, Houghton Library, Harvard University.

authority employed by his travel counterparts coming from the lands of the Christian kings.[83] Travel was, after all, a transimperial genre. Like that of Busbecq, in the various outposts of Ottoman civilization (whether in eastern

[83] For an evaluation of Evliya's citation of authorities, see Dankoff, *An Ottoman Mentality*, 194–6; and Hagen, "Afterword" to that volume, "Ottoman Understandings of the World in the Seventeenth Century," 215–56.

Figure 7.7. Nicolas de Nicolay, "Fille de l'isle de Chio," *Les navigations peregrinations et voyages*, fol. 72, Antwerp, 1576. *64–730, Houghton Library, Harvard University.

Anatolia or Albania) Evliya's cosmopolitan identity colored his assessments of the provincial, the rude, and the unruly whose mores, religious practice, and sense of civility did not match his own. Yet he was curious, open to new experience, and admiring of virtue wherever he found it.[84]

[84] Dankoff, *An Ottoman Mentality*, 197; and Evliya, *Evliya Çelebi in Albania*, 213, 217.

Evliya was not preoccupied with women or costume. He is much more likely to describe food and drink, funeral customs, or religious institutions than he is to provide the details of inhabitants' dress. He does, however, sometimes comment on the local females, describing Christian villagers in Albania as "all enchantresses," although such remarks seem to take the form of general ethnographic remarks rather than claims to particular familiarity.[85] In the town of Elbasan he notes that "most of the women and girls wear broadcloth robes and go about in flat headpieces which they cover with white muslin kerchiefs"; but he does not wax poetic about such headgear as did Busbecq or Wratislaw.

In fact, Evliya is rather more likely to describe male dress than he is to go into detail about that of women.[86] Thus he characterizes the uniforms of the good Muslim *gazis* of Podgorica fortress in Montenegro as "quite ridiculous," and their "tiny headpiece," as "funny looking... the size of a cup, to cover their kettle-sized cabbage-shaped heads."[87] Conversely, the people of Ohrid in Macedonia spoke "elegant Turkish" and appeared to be a much more civilized lot:

> *The young men wear sable and martin kalpaks lined with red broadcloth, and varicolored broadcloth jackets, and tight trousers fastened with hooks and eyes, and strut about with yellow kubadi slippers on their feet and scimitars at their waist... [They] bind round turbans on their flat heads and go for elegant strolls about the bazaars.*[88]

In these regards, Evliya's descriptions are certainly designed to display his eyewitness authority. But they seem equally calculated to amuse and to play on the ethnic stereotypes of his readers.[89]

Clearly, then, European Christians were not the only observers employing a context of ethnic and gendered typing to certify both their knowledge of texts and their eyewitness experience. The Ottomans had their stereotypes, just as did their neighbors, which were immortalized in sources from the Karagöz shadow theater to poetry to geographic and historical writing.[90] A late Ottoman example of such gendered (and sexualized) commentary is the work of Fazıl Enderuni (1759–1810), who wrote both a *Zenanname* (Book

[85] Evliya Çelebi, *Evliya Çelebi in Albania*, 27. On market fair days, "fair Albanian maidens also come in from the villages, each one with the face of a nymph and the form of an angel (175)."

[86] Evliya Çelebi, *Evliya Çelebi in Albania*, 179, also 35.

[87] Evliya Çelebi, *Evliya Çelebi in Albania*, 47–9.

[88] Evliya Çelebi, *Evliya Çelebi in Albania*, 217. Evliya's descriptions of ethnicity, language, and male and female dress and beauty in Diyarbakir in eastern Anatolia can be found in Evliya Çelebi, *Evliya Çelebi in Diyarbekir*, Martin Van Bruinessen and Hendrik Boeschoten, ed. and trans. (Brill: Leiden, 1988), 156–9, 160–61, 182–3.

[89] See, for a contemporary comparison, Richard Blome, *Cosmography and Geography* (London: S. Roycroft, 1684), pt. 2, 37, on the inhabitants of Hungary. Blome's work derives from that of the French cartographer Nicolas Sanson (1600–1667).

[90] See Murphey, "Evolving versus Static Elements in Ottoman Geographical Writing," 80; Buzov, "Ottoman Perceptions of Bosnia," 83–91, for the contrasting descriptions of Tursun Bey and Mustafa Ali in the fifteenth and sixteenth centuries, respectively; and Jan Schmidt, "Mustafā 'Ālī of Gallipoli, A Moralistic Littérateur on History and the Contemporary Ottoman World," 123–43, in *The Joys of Philology*, v. 1, 140–41.

of the Ladies) and a *Hubanname* (Book of Beauties), on men, in the late eighteenth century.[91] The latter begins with a map of the globe and then proceeds to illustrations of boys or young men of different ethnic and locational identities, each with his own particular accoutrements (e. g., a Dutch boy with a fur muff and a "New World" youth wearing skins).[92] Describing the dress and habits of ethnic groups in all their specificity was a standard mode of claiming authority in the narratives of early modern authors.[93] Claims to expertise on sexual practice served further both to titillate the reader and to suggest the author's "intimacy" with foreign cultures. Some travelers paid attention to ethnographic detail; others did not. But describing costume remained an easy way to certify the traveler's exposure to the "Turk" and her (or his) ways.

Part 2. Claims to Authority and the 'Evolution' of the English Traveler

There is a distinct continuity in the nature of claims to authority between the earlier and later parts of the early modern era. But by the eighteenth century the matrix of encounter had become more dense; that is, more subjects of the Christian kingdoms had the opportunity to experience Ottoman realms personally, and the literature of that experience was more voluminous and widespread. Within that matrix of encounter, the figure of the English traveler has become a three-dimensional one thanks to the expansive nature of the scholarship on English travel literature.[94] It is thus worth looking a bit further at several English travelers to the Ottoman realm to ascertain their use of claims to authority.

One of the most well-known among them is Fynes Moryson (1566–1630), the son of a member of Parliament who headed off to see the world in two long journeys spanning the years 1591–7. The story of his travels, *Itinerary... Containing His Ten Yeeres Travell through the Twelve Dominions of Germany, Bohmerland, Switzerland, Netherland, Denmarke, Poland, Italy, Turky, France, England, Scotland and Ireland*, was published in London in 1617. It recommended a set of behaviors for the traveller, including familiarizing himself with cosmography, dressing to blend in with the locals, and avoiding quick judgments about the behavior of foreign women.[95]

[91] J. M. Rogers, *Empire of the Sultans: Ottoman Art from the Khalili Collection* (London: The Nour Foundation, 2000), 245; and Fariba Zarinebaf, *Crime and Punishment in Istanbul 1700–1800* (Berkeley: University of California Press, 2010), 88.

[92] Binney, *Turkish Treasures*, 117–25.

[93] Although as Bronwen Wilson, *The World in Venice*, 181, points out, even Cesare Vecellio, the late-sixteenth-century authority on dress types and author of *De gli habiti antichi et moderni* (Venetia: 1590), complained that definitive characterizations of women's dress were not possible in any simple way, given the variability and change of styles.

[94] For a selection of that literature, see Kenneth Parker, ed. *Early Modern Tales of Orient*; MacLean, *The Rise of Oriental Travel*; MacLean, *Looking East*; Brotton, *Trading Territories*; Matar, *Islam in Britain*; Dimmock, *New Turkes: Dramatizing Islam and the Ottomans*; and Vitkus, *Turning Turk*.

[95] Peter Mancall, "Introduction: What Fynes Moryson Knew," *Journal of Early Modern History* 10.1–2 (2006): 1–9, esp. 1–3. Influential predecessors and contemporaries, who produced collections of travels, of which Moryson was presumably aware were: Giovanni Battista Ramusio (1485–1557), *Navigationi e Viaggi* (Venetia: 1550–59); Richard Hakluyt, *Principall Navigations...* (London, 1589, and fuller edition 1598–1600); Samuel Purchas, *Purchas his Pilgrimage* (London, 1613, 1614, 1617, 1625). See

Moryson, like other sojourners of his time, launched his travels after a
period of study at university (both Cambridge and Oxford), which provided a groundwork and a worldview on the basis of which travel could
be understood. After exploring Europe, Moryson had "a particular desire
to see 'Jerusalem, the fountaine of Religion, and Constantinople, of old the
seat of Christian Emperours, and now the seat of the Turkish Ottoman.'"[96]
That three-part spatial 'draw' for the educated Englishman linked Moryson
to the travelers who came before and after him. Ottoman turf comprised the
centers of Christendom and of imperial power. In its Roman, Byzantine, and
contemporary forms, it seized the imagination of the inquiring traveler.

  The later sixteenth century was a time of the flowering of English–Ottoman
relations. Queen Elizabeth I (r. 1558–1603) corresponded with the sultan;
and William Harborne became England's first ambassador to the Porte (arriving in Istanbul in 1583).[97] Contacts began to increase significantly; and
English dramatic, historical, and diplomatic literatures popularized images
of "the Turk" in the English imagination. Such visions were based on a
combination of classical literature, maps and translations from the Continent, accounts of the English "Turkey Company" (chartered in 1581), and
the experiences of English travelers. E. G. R. Taylor notes that in the mid
sixteenth century geographic knowledge had been enlarged by French cos-
mographers and navigators "with Huguenot sympathies" seeking service in
England, by the translation into English in 1546 by Peter Ashton of Paolo
Giovio's *Commentario de le cose de Turchi*, and by the translation of other
Italian works.[98] He suggests that the influence of Spain, via Englishmen trading in that country, was also significant, along with that of Antwerp and
the Low Countries, in forging the English geographical imagination.[99] By
the 1590s the tales and translations had multiplied. Thus Fynes Moryson
ventured into Ottoman lands at an exciting time for the English traveler, one
in which there would surely be a demand for his musings on Ottoman space,
sultanic power, and the Holy Land.

Greaves and Bargrave

Some Englishmen traveled for adventure and literary acclaim; others traveled
for more scholarly purposes. But in either case they traveled with an already

also Nicholas Dew, "'Toutes les Curiosités du Monde': The Geographic Projects of Melchisédech
Thévenot," chapter 2 in *Orientalism in Louis XIV's France* (Oxford: Oxford University Press, 2009),
on the French scholar and envoy (c. 1620–92) whose collection of voyages, *Relations de divers voyages
curieux* (Paris, 1663), including maps of Ottoman lands, later became quite influential.
[96] See Hadfield, ed. *Amazons, Savages, and Machiavels*, 81. Also on Moryson's biography, see Charles
Hughes, ed., *Shakespeare's Europe: A Survey of the Condition of Europe at the End of the 16th
century, Being unpublished chapters of Fynes Moryson's Itinerary (1617)* (New York: Benjamin Blom,
1967; reprint of 1903 edition), i–xlvi.
[97] Susan Skilliter, *William Harborne and the Trade with Turkey 1578–1582. A Documentary Study
of the First Anglo–Ottoman Relations* (Oxford: Oxford University Press, 1977), 45–54, 69–72, 77,
86–104; and MacLean, *The Rise of Oriental Travel*, 1–47.
[98] Taylor, *Tudor Geography*, 15–17. See McJannet, *The Sultan Speaks*, 39–50, on Ashton, Giovo, and
English translations of works on the Ottomans.
[99] Taylor, *Tudor Geography*, 10–11, 14; also Chaney, *The Evolution of the Grand Tour*, 58–142, on
Italy in the English travel imagination and the nascent Grand Tour.

constructed set of mental images of Ottoman space and peoples. Constantino-ple, in the early modern imagination, tied together the classical and the medieval. Thus when John Greaves (1602–52), an Oxford scholar and Pro-fessor of Geometry at Gresham College, London, came to Istanbul in 1638, he came in search of Greek and Latin texts, supposedly cajoling an Ottoman cavalry officer into stealing a copy of Ptolemy's *Almagest* for him out of the Topkapı Library.[100] Greaves traveled to Rome, Athens, Istanbul, and Egypt, collecting books and manuscripts, and armed with precise rulers for measur-ing monuments. After his return home he used the authority deriving from his travels to publish a description of the sultan's seraglio, plagiarized without acknowledgment and rendered into English from the *relazione* of Ottaviano Bon (1552–1623), Venetian bailo to Istanbul from 1605–7. Greaves was apparently not aware of the original author and thought the description to be the work of Robert Withers, a young client of Sir Paul Pindar, English ambassador to Istanbul from 1611 to 1620.[101] Thus his *Description of the Grand Seignor's Seraglio*, when laid before the eyes of an intrigued English public, was a narrative twice removed from its Italian original.

What is interesting for our purposes about Greaves's and Withers's *Description* of the sultan's palace is that it indicates both the degree to which the English had become invested in travel to Ottoman domains and the extent to which Greaves's English audience had been conditioned to con-sume insider information about Ottoman space. Writing of literacy in the Ottoman world, Withers (channeling Bon) wrote,

> *And among the Turks, he that can but read, and write, is held a very learned man, and esteemed far above others, by the common ignorant people; insomuch that when a crafty fellow hath got a book, which he knows will please their humours (they altogether delighting in books like Palmerin d'Oliva, the knight of the fun, Amadis de Gaule, and the like) he forthwith gets him with his book to some Cahve [coffee] house or other... and there, being set down in the middle of them, he falls to reading, the people evermore giving credit to whatsoever he says; and so having spent an hour, or two, he takes their benevolences, which is usually more than the price his book comes to; such is their simplicity, and such is their delight in hearing a man read fables.*[102]

Greaves's mid seventeenth century readers thus 'saw,' by means of a Vene-tian *relazione*, an audience of "common Turks" in Istanbul enjoying medieval Spanish or Portuguese romances, much like those translated into English by Anthony Mundy (1560–1633) in the late sixteenth century and available in London.[103] Those medieval tales, in turn, told of the amorous exploits of

[100] Ottaviano Bon, *The Sultan's Seraglio: An Intimate Portrait of Life at the Ottoman Court (from the Seventeenth-Century Edition of John Withers)*, Godfrey Goodwin, ed. (London: Saqi Books, 1996), 16–17. Greaves published (London, 1650) Ottaviano Bon's description of the sultan's seraglio taken from the 1625 English version by Withers, published in Purchas' *Pilgrims*, v. II.

[101] Bon, *The Sultan's Seraglio*, 14–17.

[102] Bon, *The Sultan's Seraglio*, 143–4.

[103] Tracey Hill, *Anthony Munday and Civic Culture: Theatre, History and Power in Early Modern London, 1580–1633* (Manchester: Manchester University Press, 2004), 44–5, 74–5, on the context

an imaginary emperor of Constantinople. Certainly an Istanbul audience of
Turkish, Greek, or Italian speakers, for example, might well have sat enthu-
siastically through readings of the *Palmerin*; and Bon or Withers may well
have witnessed such a reading. The text clearly intends to suggest that the
popularity of romances and the avariciousness of 'scholars' were universals,
things that Greaves's own audience would readily understand.[104] And its
insider tone made "the people" in the sultan's dominions that much more
believable (though our evidence on reception by English reading communities
is limited at best).

Greaves was not the only traveler whose imagery made the Ottomans
seems more familiar. The English merchant Robert Bargrave, introduced
in Ch. 6, also approximated the people of Ottoman domains to those in
Europe; but he did so using ethnicity, dress, customs, and acts of kindness.
Bargrave claimed authority based on personal contact with "Turks" of all
sorts. Traveling from Istanbul to England through Thrace and then Bulgaria
in 1652, Bargrave, unlike Greaves, looked on Ottoman lands in terms of
whether they made commercial exchange easy or difficult. He included in his
travel diary a series of engaging comments on dress and the ambiguities of
ethnic or religious identity. In Istanbul, speaking of Ottoman hostilities with
Venice, he noted that he and his fellow Englishmen were in constant danger
(as "Franks") of being mistaken for Venetians:

> *drunken sottish Turkes; who supposing all to be Venetians that wore
> our western habit, (as if all the world were divided between Venetians &
> Turkes) & . . . having lost in the war perhaps some near relations, were
> always apt to mischief [against] us, unless we could defend ourselves,
> or were relieved by some accidental passengers more civilized.*[105]

Clothes apparently did make the man for inebriated "Turks." But what
is interesting here is the merchant's observations that "Turks" were as
likely to homogenize their 'others' as Englishmen were to homogenize theirs,
and that Ottoman passersby could easily be divided, by their comportment,
into the civilized and the uncivilized. Among the civilized, Bargrave also
counted those Turks who were "so Christian" as to save him and his companions when the French were "so Turkish" as to try to have them deported.[106]
The simple designation, "Turk," was thus not adequate as a predictor of

---

and marketing for such books. Bon could well have been conversant with these romances. *Historia
di Palmerin d'Oliva*, translated from the Spanish by Mambrino Roseo, was published in Venice by
Domenico Farri in 1570. Amadis was published in Spanish in Venice in 1533. See Peter Burke, "Early
Modern Venice as a Center of Information and Communication," 389–419, in *Venice Reconsidered:
the History and Civilization of an Italian City-State, 1297–1797*, John Martin and Dennis Romano,
eds. (Baltimore: John's Hopkins University Press, 2000), 402.

[104] The story appears in the last part of this English edition, but it does not appear in a recently published
Italian rendering, Ottaviano Bon, *Il seraglio del Gransignore*, Bruno Basile, ed. (Rome: Salerno
Editrice, 2002), 116; so it may be Withers's invention, an embellishment, or a vignette that appeared
in one edition and not another. The English text varies from the Italian in multiple other ways.

[105] Bargrave, *The Travel Diary*, 87. Goffman, *Britons in the Ottoman Empire*, 172–6, delineates the
whole situation. See also Linda Darling, "Mediterranean Borderlands: Early English Merchants in the
Levant," 173–88, in *The Ottoman Empire: Myths, Realities and 'Black Holes,'* Eugenia Kermeli and
Oktay Özel, eds. (İstanbul: Isis Press, 2006).

[106] Bargrave, *The Travel Diary*, 106.

behavior. Ethnicity, nation, and dress all mattered; but what mattered more was the familiar division between those who treated one well and those who did not.

Bargrave also used commentary on women to help map out the ethnography of his travel space. He claimed that Bulgarian women did "almost all the work" and were suited to that task by their "masculine proportions."[107] His description of their dress reminds us of Busbecq:

> a kind of Gown without Sleeves wrought round at the bottom; as are also theyr smocks; so ordering the length of Either, that the works on both do appear: they wear Sylver Rings almost on every finger, Braceletts of black & white Beads or Shells upon theyr wrists, & great Collars of sylver Coines about theyr Necks.[108]

Presumably this is a composite image and the Bulgarian women did not wear all their finery while doing "all" the work. But their costume did seem to make an impression on Bargrave. Like Wratislaw and Evliya, he seemed to enjoy the vision of the "young Bulgar wenches, in theyr gay wrought" smocks and gowns, who enlivened the market place.[109] From drunken Turks, to gentlemanly janissaries, to Bulgar wenches, Bargrave's diary provides a certain immediacy, and a vision of himself as knowledgeable witness. Thanks to that knowledge, his audience could envision which peoples and spaces were analogous to their own. Thus they could read of Wallachia that "Mens Freedome with Women, & theyr Customes at the table, had so much of Christian in it, that it seemed a faint Reflexion of England."[110]

Chandler

Fynes Moryson's "seats" of Christendom and of imperial power remained the primary sites of interest for the English traveler, along with what might be called the 'nearer Ottoman empire,' that, is the sites of classical antiquity in Ottoman Europe, particularly Greece. One eighteenth century observer, Richard Chandler (1738–1810), whom we met in Ch. 6, is emblematic of both the accretion of English travel knowledge, and of the ways in which narratives fossilized Ottoman territory as the early modern era unfolded. Chandler embarked England for the sultan's domains, intending not so much to record the nature of Ottoman lives, government, and power, but to record and commemorate the classical foundations of Ottoman space. His *Travels in Greece and Asia Minor* (1775–6) became a model for the explorations of

---

[107] Bargrave, *The Travel Diary*, 128. Hall, *Things of Darkness*, 8–9, treating the language applied to race in early modern England, has pointed out the ways in which the language of designating people, "especially in connection to race, is highly gendered." That conflation or confusion of race and gender, as well as culture and ethnicity, is particularly poignant in transimperial and transethnic zones where the possibilities for designation span a whole range of color, ethnolinguistic, and cultural options.
[108] Bargrave, *The Travel Diary*, 128.
[109] Bargrave, *The Travel Diary*, 130.
[110] Bargrave, *The Travel Diary*, 134. Bargrave was from a prominent Kentish family and was educated at Cambridge and Oxford (1).

later Englishmen. A scholar and clergyman, Chandler was born in Hampshire and educated at Cambridge.[111] His travels were commissioned by the Society of Dilettanti: "to some parts of the East, in order to collect informations, and to make observations, relative to the ancient state of those countries, and to such monuments of antiquity as are still remaining..."[112]

Thus instructed, Chandler and company embarked on 17 June 1764. They were armed with texts and looking for more texts. Given his education, one can imagine that Chandler was prepared for a mode of seeing that stressed the "ancient state" of Ottoman lands, as the mandate of the Dilettanti put it (or the ancient history stressed in Salmon's atlas, which Chandler might well have seen). Everything was to be recorded in word and image. Chandler notes in the preface to his work on Asia Minor that he expected to improve the vision of Ottoman domains: "no labour has been spared; the geography of the country has been improved; many mistakes have been rectified; and difficulties obviated or removed."[113] This was the same claim made by Chandler's contemporary, Marie-Gabriel-Florent-Auguste de Choiseul-Gouffier (1752–1817), French ambassador to the Ottoman empire and also a scholar of Greece. In his own *Voyage Pittoresque*, Choiseul-Gouffier noted how maps of the Mediterranean from Ptolemy on had been revised, corrected, and perfected up to his own day through observation and measurement.[114] Both men saw themselves as joining a long line of historically oriented recorders, each one (hopefully) making the image of Ottoman space increasingly more clear and correct.

As he moved from "Christendom" to the Mediterranean port of Izmir, Chandler employed a series of classical names and references to frame his encounter with Ottoman territory: Hadrian, Xerxes, and Alexander appear along with Hector and the *Iliad*.[115] Herodotus, Strabo, and Pausanias are important authorities.[116] Of the places between Sicyon and Patrae, in Greece, Chandler wrote,

> *their order, their situation, their distances from the sea and from each other, are so exactly marked by Strabo and Pausanias, as not easily*

[111] Chandler, *Travels in Asia Minor and Greece*, v. 1, preface, iii–xiv.

[112] Chandler, *Travels*, vii. Chandler was to go armed with letters from "one of His Majesty's principal secretaries of state and from the Turkey company (viii–x)," and with 200 pounds initial expenses and a credit for 800 pounds a year for himself and his two companions, an architect and a painter. The fruits of this expedition, along with the drawings and travel narrative, were a volume on Ionian Antiquities, and a separate volume on inscriptions. "Collecting" inscriptions and monuments in Ottoman realms was not a new phenomenon, but one that gained momentum in the 18th century. See, for example, Jan Schmidt, "The Travel Notes of a Dutch Pastor in Anatolia 1717–1727," 279–300, in *The Joys of Philology*, v. 2, 281.

[113] Chandler, *Travels*, v. 1, xiii.

[114] Choiseul-Gouffier, *Voyage Pittoresque*, v. 2, 6–12, a member of the Académie française.

[115] Chandler, *Travels*, v. 1: 15–35. In the dedication to the 1585 English translation of Nicolas de Nicolay's *Navigations*, John Stell managed to invoke Aristotle, Solomon, Hannibal, Homer, and Mithridates in less than a page as he justified travel for old men and even women. See Nicolay, *The Nauigations*, unnumbered pages of dedication 3–4.

[116] Chandler, *Travels*, v. 1, 15; 2: 110, 183, 185, 195, 252. Chandler thus joins Pausanias in mapping memory and "classical" pasts. See Ada Cohen, "Art, Myth, and Travel in the Hellenistic World," 93–126, in *Pausanias: Travel, Myth and Memory in Roman Greece*, Susan Alcock, John Cherry, and Jaś Elsner, eds. (Oxford: Oxford University Press, 2001).

to be mistaken. It is a matter of regret, that travellers too commonly hasten along in the beaten road, uninformed of the objects on the way; when by consulting and following these invaluable guides, they might increase their own pleasure, and at the same time greatly advance the general knowledge of ancient geography.[117]

Classical histories, travel narratives, and maps were thus all-important guides, measuring out distances, what to see, and how to see it.

For more recent authorities, Chandler alludes to the observations of the Anglican bishop Richard Pococke (1704–65) and to "Mr. [Robert]Wood (1717–71)," the English classical scholar and traveler who had drawn up instructions for the expedition.[118] At the port of Troas he wrote,

A map belonging to Mr. Wood, and made, as we supposed, by a Frenchman, in 1726, served as a guide. The author, it is imagined, believed, as other travellers had done, that this was the site of Troy, or of a more recent city named Ilium, instead of Alexandria Troas.[119]

This map served as one element of the range of authoritative materials by which Chandler charted his trip and identified what he was seeing. But most particularly, at least for the Greek segment of his journey, Chandler references and juxtaposes his own travels to those of Sir George Wheler (1651–1724), tracing Wheler's steps, telling where he went, where he ate, and what he saw.[120] Wheler was Chandler's anchor to reading the past. Other authorities were flesh and blood and close at hand, such as European consular representatives and the renegade "Lombardi," a guide whose services Chandler employed, but whom he personally detested.[121]

As he charted the course plotted for him by the Dilettanti, Chandler (like Busbecq before him) kept an eye peeled for ancient coins, inscriptions that revealed the customs of the Greeks and Romans, and the "many scraps of Greek and Latin" that could be found in local cemeteries.[122] He had little respect for the illiterate and impoverished residents among whom he found these remnants of the past; and he bemoaned the condition into which they had fallen.[123] Of the "Tower of the Winds" of Andronicus Cyrrhestes in Athens, "mentioned by Varro and Vitruvius," he noted that it had been converted to a dervish *tekke* (convent). As Chandler witnessed the whirling

---

[117] Chandler, *Travels*, v. 2, 338–9.

[118] Chandler, *Travels*, v. 1, xii; 2: 297, 338. See also, Richard Pococke, *A Description of the East and Some Other Countries*, 2 vols. (London: 1743–5).

[119] Chandler, *Travels*, v. 1, 29–30.

[120] Chandler, *Travels*, v. 2: 185, 197–8, 203, 212, 215–16, 231, 304, 311, 338. See Sir George Wheler, *A journey into Greece, by George Wheler Esq; in company of Dr Spon of Lyons* (London: William Cademan, Robert Kettlewell, and Awnsham Churchill, 1682). Wheler was also the author of a journey to the Holy Land, using Eusebius as his foundation; see George Wheler, *An account of the churches, or places of assembly, of the primitive Christians; from the churches of Tyre, Jerusalem, and Constantinople. Described by Eusebius. And ocular observations of several very ancient edifices of churches yet extant in those parts* (London: S. Roycroft, for R. Clavell, 1689).

[121] Chandler, *Travels*, v. 2, 173–4.

[122] Chandler, *Travels*, v. 1, 39, 43, 45–6.

[123] Chandler, *Travels*, v. 1, 42–4, 49. Passing centuries to arrive at 1697–8, Chandler then related the Venetian (re)conquest of the Corinthian peninsula.

devotional rituals of the sufis there, he was amazed at the rapidity of their
revolutions, "the dome re-echoing the wild and loud music, and the noise as it
were of frantic Bacchanals."[124] Even the dervishes were comprehensible only
when seen in terms of their raucous classical antecedents. Unlike some of our
other travelers, Chandler's authority derived from 'rediscovering' the past,
not from illuminating the present. Indeed it is often only when he complains
about the degenerating state of ancient sites that the reader is reminded that
Chandler is moving through Ottoman space.[125] At Corinth, he began his
account with Neptune and Venus, proceeded to Julius Caesar, Caligula, and
Nero, citing Pausanias, and then turned to the wars of Murat II (r. 1421–
44; 1446–51) and Mehmet II (r. 1444–6; 1451–81) against the Byzantines.
Even the Ottomans were more important for their past glories than for their
present situation.[126]

The details of local customs or dress were of secondary concern. Chandler did make the requisite foray into descriptions of women, their culture,
and their costume, echoing earlier travelers. When his ship passed the Dardanelles, and dropped anchor along the Asiatic shore, Chandler described the
"Turkish" women walking on shore as "wrapped in a white sheet, shapeless
and stalking in boots"; the rest was left to the imagination of the reader.[127]
In Athens, he opined that "The liberty of the fair sex ... is almost equally
abridged by the Turks and Greeks."[128] In that particular Ottoman space,
commune and ethnicity were subordinated to patriarchy; and "houses are
secured with high walls, and the windows turned from the street, and latticed
or boarded up so as to preclude all intercourse even of the eyes." Neither was
there much consideration for female "improvement of mind and morals."[129]

Beyond those commonalities of protection and subservience there were
divisions of ethnoreligious identity and class, of "virgin" vs. "matron," and
inner vs. outer wear, much as one finds in Nicolay's *Navigations*. The intrepid
European male might be admitted by his Greek host to the women's quarters where a girl, "like Thetis, treading on a soft carpet, has her white and
delicate feet naked; the nails tinged with red."[130] Here we see Chandler as
a connoisseur of the 'Orient.' But often enough one wonders whether the
author is 'seeing' real women or imagining beauties taken off the pages of
classical history. Even when speaking of a rougher brand of female, Chandler
could not quite distance himself from a concern for antiquities. Describing
the work-worn Albanian women in their coarse shifts, he observed,

> *Their hair is platted in two divisions, and the ends fastened to a red
> silken string, which, with a tassel, is pendant to their heels, and fre-
> quently laden with pieces of silver coin, of various sizes, diminishing*

---

[124] Chandler, 2, 131–2. For the author's general description of "the Turk" see 2: 165–6.
[125] Chandler, *Travels*, v. 2, 173.
[126] Chandler, v. 2, 295–7.
[127] Chandler, v. 1, 14.
[128] Chandler, v. 2, 153.
[129] Chandler, v. 2, 156–7.
[130] Chandler, v. 2, 155–6.

gradually to the bottom. Among these, the antiquarian may often discover medals of value.[131]

The women whom he encounters in Ottoman space thus do not serve so much to cement the eyewitness authority of Chandler's text; rather, they serve to remind the reader of their connections to a present that is both romantic and barbaric, or to a mythical past.

The antiquarian impulse was, of course, not new. While Busbecq searched the markets for ancient coins, Melchior Lorichs (c. 1527–90?), the Danish engraver who accompanied Busbecq's Hapsburg mission to the Sublime Porte in 1555, saw his artistic objective as finding and examining the "true sources of classical Antiquity."[132] Almost a century later, the Reverend William Petty, laboring tirelessly on behalf of Thomas Howard Earl of Arundel (1585–1646), "scoured Italy, Greece, and Asia Minor..., acquiring marbles, old manuscripts, and a host of other antiquities, often in competition with agents dispatched by [Lord] Buckingham to the same territories."[133] This imperative, by Chandler's time, had passed to the educated young men of England. Coming out of Oxford and Cambridge and setting out for a course of eastern travel, they saw themselves as commissioned to explore, record, and retrieve (through polite or not so polite inquiry) the classical remains of the East in the territories of the Grand Signor.

Morritt

With the publication of his observations, Richard Chandler became an authority on the remains of the past, the stages of travel, and the ethnology of Ottoman territory. He joined the ranks of those read and cited by later-day travelers to chart their own way and measure the accuracy of their predecessors. One such follower was John B. S. Morritt of Rokeby, an Englishman whose postcollegiate journey took him from Vienna to Istanbul in 1794. Eloquent and enthusiastic, he was representative of a certain type of well-off, educated English traveler who crafted the Ottoman empire in discursive, conversational letters home (which were assembled and published only in 1914, long after his death).[134]

[131] Chandler, v. 2, 154.
[132] Lach, *Asia in the Making of Europe*, v. 2, 90. Lorichs returned to Vienna in 1560 with numerous sketches of things Ottoman, and in 1574 he was employed by the Antwerp publisher Christopher Plantin, and worked as an engraver with Phillipe Galle.
[133] Gilman, "Madagascar on My Mind: The Earl of Arundel and the Arts of Colonization," 299–300. Citing also Franciscus Junius the Younger's (1591–1677) "near-exhaustive survey of all references to the visual arts in the literature of the Greeks and Romans," Gilman argues for the opening up of the world of antiquity in the seventeenth century: "Arundel's agents follow the Homeric routes to return from the shores of Ilium with treasures that will now accrue to the glory of Britain (302)."
[134] The editor of his missives, tells us that Morritt was "a good scholar, well-read in Greek and Latin literature..." When he returned from his travels he "settled down as an influential country squire and admirable landlord in Yorkshire..." and "his taste for art and literature and antiquities remained with him throughout his long life." John B. S. Morritt, *The Letters of John B. S. Morritt of Rokeby,*

For Morritt, travel to the Ottoman empire was an opportunity to put his education to work, studying the artifacts of classical history, observing the peoples of eastern Europe and Anatolia, and practicing a way of seeing that was both erudite and engaged. Richard Chandler seems to occupy the role of primary and proximate authority for Morritt's meanderings, a scholar and traveler well suited to appeal to a sojourner with an interest in antiquities. Like Chandler, Morritt wanted pictorial evidence of the things he saw, and for that purpose, according to his editor, brought with him a "Viennese draughtsman" whose sketches, for the most part, did not survive in a condition suitable for reproduction.[135] But, also like Chandler, Morritt saw his task as revising and correcting earlier observations; thus he made a point of telling his readers where and how Chandler had gotten it wrong. Morritt was more ethnographically oriented than Chandler, not so constrained by a formal task and its requisite written forms. His letters are notable because his primary audience was female, his mother and his sister Anne. His travelog is thus conversational, conveying to that audience in familiar terms what moving through Ottoman space was like.

Morritt traveled overland from Vienna to Istanbul, repeating the stages of travel of his predecessors and many of the tropes of earlier narratives, including complaints about bedding and transport. Once in Ottoman space, however, he crafted what he saw in terms of both ancient empire and contemporary England. The comparison to home served as yet another vehicle for claiming authority. Thus, a day after crossing the Danube, Morritt advised his mother and sister that he was "approaching classic ground." He crossed from Bulgaria to Romania ("the ancient Thrace"), but not before comparing the countryside to a more familiar one in England: "those rich, varied countries we admired between Doncaster [South Yorkshire] and Rotherham."[136] Britain and the Greek classics remained points of reference as Morritt traveled on, from the Maritza River, "the Hebrus, so famous for the unfortunate story of Orpheus," to Adrianople (Edirne), where he juxtaposed the columns of the great mosque to "the Monument at London."[137] He compared the streets of Constantinople to those of York; and the floor of a dervish convent where they went to witness a *sema* ceremony as "railed in like the circus at Astley's."[138] Unlike Chandler, he found no echoes of the "bacchanal" in these sufi rites.

Morritt's narrative presumed a literate, map-using audience with a historical memory.[139] It employed the map as an authoritative measure of

Descriptive of Journeys in Europe and Asia Minor in the Years 1794–1796, G. E. Marindin, ed. (London: John Murray, 1914), v–vi.
[135] Morritt, *Letters*, viii, 68, 115.
[136] Morritt, *Letters*, 65.
[137] Morritt, *Letters*, 65–6.
[138] Morritt, *Letters*, 70, 96, and 66 on bacchanal.
[139] Morritt's letters coincide with the end of our rather arbitrary periodization based on the Ottoman–Hapsburg–Russian wars. They also coincide with what Reinhard Wittmann, "Was There a Reading Revolution at the End of the Eighteenth Century?" 284–312, in *A History of Reading in the West*, Guglielmo Cavallo and Roger Chartier, eds., Lydia Cochrane, trans. (Amherst: University of Massachusetts Press, 1997), 311, has called a "reading revolution" in Europe.

location.[140] The young scholar assumed his correspondents would have maps readily to hand to consult as they read his letters.[141]

> *You will see by your map that very soon afterwards we left Transylvania, and entered the Turkish dominions* ... [142]

> *Our road to Bucharest was through the towns of Arjis and Pitesti, which you will perhaps see marked on your map, though they are neither of them larger than Bowes [in England].*[143]

> *After sleeping there [on the island of Prinkipos] we proceeded in our boat to Nicomedia, which your maps will tell you is at the end of a long gulf of the Sea of Marmora.*[144]

The shared maps thus served to bolster the narrative authorities Morritt cited by which both he and his correspondents 'knew' the Ottoman space that he traversed. He describes Istanbul as a panorama so that his family can imagine themselves poised before the city, viewing it from right to left. But he also expects them to have a vision of Istanbul already in mind: "You will no doubt have read a great deal about the situation in Constantinople, and know the raptures in which it is generally described."[145] Morritt suggests that they are well aware of the organization and officers of the sultan's seraglio, "whose names and offices are sufficiently detailed in a thousand publications you have met with in England... "[146] These familiar readings include the *Turkish Letters* of Lady Mary Wortley Montagu (1689–1762), aristocrat, member of the English literati, and wife of the English ambassador to Istanbul in the early eighteenth century.[147]

Morritt combines references to more contemporary literature with references to classical literatures in order to present a multilayered image of

---

[140] According to Alam and Subrahmanyam, *Indo-Persian Travels*, 341–2, the English bookman, Richard Hakluyt, in his 1601 translation of António Galvão's 1563 *Tratado dos descobrimentos*, urged his patron "Sir Robert Cecil, Principal Secretary to Queen Elizabeth and Chancellor of the University of Cambridge," to read the narrative with the aid of "a sea card or mappe of the world and carie your eie upon the coast of Africa from Cape de Non... and follow the shore... " The difference in Morritt's account was that his audience was female, of a lesser class status than Cecil's, and one with (more common) maps close at hand for more common use.

[141] Jordana Dym, "The Familiar and the Strange: Western Travelers' Maps of Europe and Asia, ca. 1600–1800," *Philosophy and Geography* 7.2 (August 2004): 155–91. Dym argues that Grand Tour travelers in the seventeenth century were expected to "turn to abundant locally-produced guidebooks and itineraries," and hence Grand Tour travel accounts had little need of maps for the familiar territories of Europe, as opposed to the unfamiliar territories of South and East Asia (161). The Grand Tour traveler, she asserts, "presumed that any armchair travelers in his audience would also have maps (164)." Although I disagree with Dym's genre dichotomies, she does attempt a chronology based on assumed familiarity (170), which proposes an eighteenth century break marked by the use and kinds of map deployed in travel accounts (176, 185).

[142] Morritt, 61. Delano-Smith, "Milieus of Mobility," 42, notes that "Maps were only occasionally included in almanacs and road books and then only from the late seventeenth century onwards. In 1676, however, the publishers of a new edition of John Speed's *Theatre of the Empire of Great Britaine* added five itinerary or route maps."

[143] Morritt, *Letters*, 62.

[144] Morritt, *Letters*, 99, 109.

[145] Morritt, *Letters*, 68.

[146] Morritt, *Letters*, 74–5.

[147] Morritt, *Letters*, 94, 96.

the sultan's domains. Thus Herodotus, the French botanist Joseph Pitton de Tournefort (1656–1708), and a certain "Mr. Jacky Curious" (whose "elaborate work" included letters to his "mama"), all appear on the page on which Morritt describes the temple of Juno on Samos.[148] Tournefort's *Relation d'un voyage du Levant* was published in 1717. Letters from "Jacky Curious" form part of the work *Museum for Young Gentlemen and Ladies, or a Private Tutor for Little Masters and Misses*, printed in London in multiple editions from 1760 on. At Athens, describing the ruins, Morritt wrote, "I tell you what you may read in fifty books – however, I tell you what I see."[149] The vision of the eyewitness was still important, despite the plethora of literature on the "East." Indeed, Morritt himself read while looking, as he wrote to his mother, creating new memories as he called up the old:

> You see I am not tired of my tour; a more satisfactory one you cannot conceive. Every hill I see here is interesting, and seems an old friend after what one has read about them; . . . except when on horseback I am reading or writing all day long.[150]

At Miletus, to describe the beauties of the countryside, Morritt calls up Endymion and Diana as well as quoting from Barthélemy's *Anacharsis* (1787).[151] At the narrow point of the Bosporus, "we found from our books and remembered with pleasure" that this was the place "Darius marched across on a bridge of boats with 700000 men on his Scythian expedition, as a prelude to his Grecian one."[152] Mapping Ottoman space, for Morritt and the recipients of his letters, meant staging the events of the past on the terrain of the present. Beyond his textual authorities, Morritt made use of the services of a Greek interpreter, various acquaintances (such as the "knowledgeable" Mr. Dallaway, chaplain to Robert Liston, England's ambassador to the Porte), members of the "Corps Diplomatique," and the relations of merchants and locals whom he routinely interviewed.[153] On the situation of women in Ottoman lands, he claimed the authority of "Grecian and Frank ladies" who were acquainted with Turkish women.[154]

Like Robert Withers, in his translation of Bon's *relazione*, Morritt also knew a popular text that was sure to resonate with his audience when it came to invoking Ottoman space:

> Since we left Hermanstadt we have been traveling in a Greek country, and the whole scene is so new, so extraordinary that we are afraid we are dreaming out of the Arabian Nights Entertainments.[155]

---

[148] Morritt, *Letters*, 118. See *Museum for Young Gentlemen and Ladies, or a Private Tutor for Little Masters and Misses* (London: T. Carnan . . . B. Collins, 1782).

[149] Morritt, *Letters*, 178. Here Morritt also mentions Wheler's measurements of "Hadrian's Pillars."

[150] Morritt, *Letters*, 116.

[151] Morritt, *Letters*, 114. Jean-Jacques Barthélemy (1716–95), scholar of antiquities and numismatics, published his *Voyage du jeune Anacharsis en Grèce* in Paris in 1787.

[152] Morritt, *Letters*, 88, 107. Many of Morritt's classical allusions come without specific citations.

[153] Morritt, *Letters*, 75, 80, 96, 98–9, 100, 103.

[154] Morritt, *Letters*, 79.

[155] Morritt, *Letters*, 60.

The "Greek country" was thus transformed, losing its classical garb and taking its place firmly within the Orient. Literature, at least momentarily, trumped observation when it came to identifying the country through which Morritt was traveling. This is an eloquent example, among many in early modern imagery, of the difficulty involved in placing, or even locating, a discrete East or West. The space between Bucharest and Istanbul was not so much Christian or Muslim, European or Ottoman; rather it was a place of fantasy and excitement for the young scholar.[156] A traveler, such as Morritt, who was conversant with both the literature and the history of those lands thus found his experiences abundantly enriched.

Like Chandler before him, Morritt was interested in the ways in which the past was inscribed on the physical present. Greek and Roman inscriptions bore witness to the knowledge he had gained from a different sort of text at university; they made the emperors and their accomplishments "live" in the sultan's domains.[157] Approaching Smyrna, Morritt tells his readers that the remains of antiquity are even less than what Chandler recorded in his "very minute account."[158] Yet Chandler's appeal went only so far; and Morritt criticized his predecessor for the narrowness of his vision:

> *I own I always expected more pleasure from a country than from the ancient buildings in their present ruined state, and when an author gives me a long account of old stones and rubbish without containing one remark on a country interesting on account of great actions, and the birthplace of the first men of the world, I think him perhaps a good antiquarian, but certainly not a classical traveller.*[159]

"Classical" times, literature, "first men," and deeds provided a backdrop for his narration; but for Morritt they are no longer the primary frame of reference or the primary mode for denoting Ottoman space. Nonetheless, a "classical traveler" is what Morritt aspired to be; and he approached that task through an inquiring gaze directed at the "country," its sites, its history, and its inhabitants. In that regard, he found Chandler most wanting, in part because he was inclined to shy away from encounters with the "Turk." Assuring his mother when she inquired that "the walls of Tiryns near Argos . . . exist as much as ever . . . in the place the ancients assign them," he suggested that Chandler may have described things he did not see.

> *This will convince you, as many other circumstances have us, of the superficial manner Chandler saw this country in. He strikes me as a*

---

[156] Morritt, *Letters*, 64, suggests the boundary of Christendom is Sistova: "On entering Bulgaria at Sistova, we bid adieu to Christianity . . . " Morritt was traveling during the reign of Selim III (r. 1789–1807), who had signed a peace treaty with Austria in 1792 at Sistova. In 1774 the treaty of Küçük Kaynarca had fixed relations between Ottomans and Russians. Many maps of the era were generated to depict the newly crafted boundaries between the Ottoman, Russian, and Hapsburg empires. See Aksan, *An Ottoman Statesman in War and Peace*, 201–3; and Itzkowitz and Mote, ed. and trans., *Mubadele*.

[157] Morritt, *Letters*, 119, *passim*.

[158] Morritt, *Letters*, 110.

[159] Morritt, *Letters*, 110, 112. Morritt was responding here in part to his sister's desire for "views" of the country.

*college fellow turned fresh out of Magdalen to a difficult and somewhat
fatiguing voyage, for which he was as unfit as could be; and though
very good at an inscription, was sure to go in the beaten track, and be
bugbeared by every story of danger and every Turk that pleased to take
the trouble.*[160]

This uncharitable evaluation demonstrates that the competition for superiority in claims to personal experience continued to flourish in the later eighteenth century, as it had in the sixteenth.[161] And although Morritt cannot
be made to stand for an entire reading community back home, his map use,
commentary, and criticism of Chandler are all emblematic of the possibilities
for an elite, youthful, Oxbridge audience that had become accustomed to the
idea of the Grand Tour.

As Morritt set out to be a well-rounded "classical traveler," he made it
clear that he was not deterred from meeting the Turk. And he found much
to please and interest him in the habits of the people. His party, he asserts,
has "everywhere met with the greatest goodwill" from the "Turks." Even
when they were subjected to a bit of harassment, Morritt noted that it was
insignificant compared to what a foreign traveler might suffer in England.

> *Once or twice a child or two has saluted us with the gentle appellation,
> jawr [giaour/infidel], that is devil; but could any men in England travel
> in a Turkish or other foreign dress without ten times the insult?*[162]

Undeterred, Morritt visited mosques and sufi convents, conversed with people
from various classes and contexts, and made it his business to sample the
wine, the food, and the culture wherever he went (though most of his contacts
were elites). In this way he set out to establish his authority as a witness
employing a range of senses.

Morritt's "natives," as in Chandler's work, can be a source of amusement,
not because they are Muslim but because they are uncouth rurals who find
the elite, well-equipped Englishman a source of amazement.

> *I write to you in rather an extraordinary situation, being at this moment
> on the steps of a Turkish inn in a small town some way beyond Adri-
> anople [Edirne], surrounded by Turks and infidels, all astonished at my
> writing apparatus, and fingering every part of it. I have just rescued my
> pen from their paws...*[163]

Chandler had told a similar story of a young shepherd who "stared with a
face of wonder not to be described" at his pocket watch.[164] Making the young
man the butt of their amusement Chandler and his companions asked the

---

[160] Morritt, *Letters*, 191. See Wes Williams, "'A mirrour of mis-haps, / A Mappe of Miserie': Dangers,
Strangers, and Friends in Renaissance Pilgrimage," 205–41; and Pompa Banerjee, "Postcards from the
Harem," 241–82, both in Brummett, ed., *The 'Book' of Travels: Genre, Ethnology, and Pilgrimage*,
on confronting dangers and the competition of eyewitnesses.

[161] Morritt, *Letters*, 198; at Calamata in Greece, Morritt claimed, "We were the only English who had
been here in the memory of the oldest residents."

[162] Morritt, *Letters*, 67.

[163] Morritt, *Letters*, 61.

[164] Chandler, 2: 262.

man what he thought the watch was, and he "replied he could not tell unless it was a snuffbox." Morritt, on the other hand, without abandoning the conceits of his class, viewed the situation with humor rather than contempt.

Finally, Morritt, even more than our other travelers, was concerned to report on the appearance and mores of Ottoman women. This may be a function of his female correspondents, who he suggests are interested in women's affairs. But it may also be a function of Morritt's own apparent interest in the social scene. When his party visited "a noble Wallachian's country seat," people apparently of a similar class to his own, Morritt suggested they represented "the manners of the country." There he and his companions were most graciously treated, and Morritt's letter focused its ethnographic curiosity primarily on the dress of the lady of the house: "the first specimen I saw of the Greek dress of which you have heard so much." The lady entertained them sitting on a low sofa with her legs crossed "*à la Turque*":

> *Her gown was long-sleeved, coming up before no higher than her cestus, which was tied à la Campbell. It was gathered round her ankles and legs like trousers, and was made of a spotted light muslin. On her head she wore a flat-topped high cap with a gold tassel on the top, and a shawl handkerchief round her forehead, her hair hanging loose about her shoulders. Over her gown she wore a long light blue silk pelisse edged with fur, with half-sleeves; on her feet she had thin yellow-leather boots, with slippers which she left at the side of the sofa to put up her feet... Over her bosom she wore a thin fold of muslin which fastened under her cestus; and I assure you, though not of the première jeunnesse, it is difficult to imagine a more elegant figure.*[165]

This is a rather singular (though not unique) attention to fashion detail for a male observer of the time; and one is forced to conclude either that Morritt was determined to entertain his sister with the utmost precision in sartorial description, or that, for him, female fashion attracted the same attention to detail as did classical monuments. We assume the lady in question was Christian, because of the location, because Morritt would equate "Greek" with Christian, and because she personally entertained these male visitors while her husband was absent; but Morritt makes no mention of her religion. Here again, one notices that his distinctions among people tend to focus on ethnolinguistic identity and on cultural conventions.[166] He may well have been trying to present a more accurate portrait of female habit than his correspondents had available from visual representations (whether in engravings, theatricals, or material culture). But he certainly thought he was going Chandler one better when it came to interest in and attention to the mores of the people he encountered in his long journey through Ottoman space. That said, Morritt echoes Chandler in his admiration for Greek beauties,

---

[165] Morritt, *Letters*, 62–3.

[166] Greg Dening, "The Theatricality of Observing and Being Observed: Eighteenth-Century Europe 'Discovers' the ? Century 'Pacific,'" 451–83, in Stuart Schwartz, ed., *Implicit Understandings: Observing, Reporting, and Reflecting*, 458, also 264–5, notes the theatricality of ethnography and the inevitable effects of the "performance consciousness" which one detects to a greater or lesser degree in travel narratives.

his comparison of women's dress and seclusion across religious lines, and his commentary on patriarchal society. Morritt followed Chandler's route and noted that the women of Scio were "just as familiar as they were in Chandler's time."[167]

Angela Jianu has highlighted the difficulty inherent in pinning down dress styles by region and ethnicity, especially in Western representations of the lands designated as "Turkey in Europe."[168] Despite the burgeoning early modern literature on costume, the confusion Jianu alludes to is apparent in the narratives of various travelers whose characterizations of "Turk" or "Greek" dress might pay little heed to the specifics of locale or identity. These discrepancies are in part due to similarities in women's dress across ethnoreligious lines, and the varying levels of the travelers' experience; but they are also a function of the authors' ideologies and objectives (Figs. 7.8 and 7.9).[169] Alexandre-Maurice Blanc de Lanautte, Comte d'Hauterive (1754–1830), for example, a contemporary of Morritt's, was concerned with the moral implications of Ottoman sartorial style. De Lanautte, secretary to Alexandru Mavrocordat Phiraris, Governor of Moldova in 1785–6, claimed that "Turkish" dress damaged both the morals and health of the Moldavians.[170] For women it was revealing, and unbecoming for those over eighteen. For men it caused undue sweating and undue expense. And for both it was enervating and inclined one to illness.

Unlike d'Hauterive, Morritt conveys the particularities of dress without undue moralizing. And, as Jianu argues, when Morritt's sister was reading his letters home, she "must have been aware of the vogue for Turqueries that had reached its peak in England and in other parts of Western Europe around the 1770s."[171] Indeed, the devoted son promised his mother that on his return, he would "fit up the tea-room, *à la kiosk*, that is like a Turkish summer-house, for your own self, as I am sure it would suit you."[172] John Morritt would thus bring "Turkey" home to England. And Anne Morritt, with the help of her brother's curious eye, could compare the Turqueries of the English drawing room with those of the Wallachian county seat, just as she could "see" the Ottoman towns on her map in terms of comparable

---

[167] Morritt, *Letters*, 79, 132.
[168] Angela Jianu, "Women, Fashion, and Europeanization: The Romanian Principalities, 1750–1830," 201–30, in *Women in the Ottoman Balkans: Gender, Culture, and History*, Amıla Buturović and Irvin Schick, eds. (London: I.B. Tauris, 2007), 206–07.
[169] Chatelain, *Atlas Historique*, v. 5, plate 15 after page 40; also chart no. 7, after page 22, "Habillemens des Femmes de Smyrne des Greques et des Juifves de cette Ville." These images are based on Cornelis de Bruyn, *Voyage au Levant* (Delft: H. de Kroonevelt, 1700), page before 57 for women's turbans and janissary garb, page before 135 for women of Smyrne; French translation of Dutch original. Marie-Gabriel-Auguste-Florent Choiseul-Gouffier, *Voyage Pittoresque de la Grèce*, v. 1 (Paris, 1824), pl. 25.
[170] Jianu, "Women, Fashion, and Europeanization," 209–10.
[171] Jianu, "Women, Fashion, and Europeanization," 208. Alexander Bevilacqua and Helen Pfeifer, "Turquerie: Culture in Motion, 1650–1750," *Past and Present* 221 (November, 2013): 75–118, focus on a rather earlier period, arguing that these "intellectual, affective, and bodily experiences" of the Ottomans are notable for the "sheer variety and creativity of European responses to Ottoman culture (117)."
[172] Morritt, *Letters*, 99; Bevilacqua and Pfeifer, "Turquerie," 87, 103–4, 112.

Figure 7.8. Henri Chatelain, based on Cornelis de Bruyn, "Habillements Des Dames De Constantinople," *Atlas Historique*, v. 5, pl. 15, Amsterdam, 1739. Harvard Map Library, Harvard University, 29245.

towns in the English countryside. Her brother would lend his eyewitness authority (and his material acquisitions) to the accumulating pile of texts and knowledge that the English gentry had assembled back home.[173]

---

[173] Morritt, *Letters*, 179, was determined to bring various parts of the empire back home. At Ephesus he tried to bribe the Ağa to sell him a relief; and at Athens he settled into collecting with a vengeance. On the streets of Athens, "a perfect gallery of marbles," Morritt tells his family. "Some we steal, some we buy, and our court is much adorned with them."

DAMES DE L'ILE DE TINE.

A.P.D.R.

Figure 7.9. Marie-Gabriel-Auguste-Florent Choiseul-Gouffier, "Dames De L'Ile De Tine," *Voyage Pittoresque de la Grèce*, v. 1, pl. 25, Paris, 1824. John Hay Library, Brown University Library.

Moore

By Morritt's time the genre of travel collections was an old and familiar authority, a source of edification and amusement for adults and instruction for children. Thus John Hamilton Moore, in 1785, had published a collection of travels that matched and transcended the claims of the 1744 atlas assembled by Thomas Salmon and treated at the beginning of this chapter. Moore's collection, which Morritt could have seen, claimed to be the epitome of accurate representation in text and image:

> *A New and Complete Collection of Voyages and Travels: Containing All that have been remarkable from the earliest Period to the present Time... Describing, in the most accurate Manner, Every Place worthy of Notice, in Europe, Asia, Africa, and America... The whole exhibiting a View of the present State of the World... Being the result of unwearied Assiduity, assisted by the best Authorities. By John Hamilton Moore Master of the Academy at Brentford, and Author of the practical Navigator, &. c Assisted by several Persons who have made the Subjects of Voyages and Travels their particular Study. Embellished with the most superb and elegant Set of Copper-Plates, Maps, Charts, Plans, &c. (upwards of One Hundred in the Whole) that was ever given with a Work of this Kind...*[174]

The frontispiece of this collection makes it clear just how advanced travel knowledge of the Ottoman and other realms was perceived to be. It proposes that famous travelers have already been enshrined (as Morritt suggested) in the imaginations of state, sovereign, and subjects. On the page, a female in flowing gown leads four young boys, pointing out to them the portraits of the great explorers posted on four pillars. These columns front an imposing library, while in the foreground are piled books, charts, and instruments of measurement. The boys look attentively at their guide, the "Genius" of the collection (Fig. 7.10).[175] The travelers in this image are an exhibit, and Moore is the purveyor of authority, backed by the patronage of his king, who sees future glory in the education of English youth.[176]

Moore addresses his readers in the preface, pointing out their needs, their consumption of travel, and their classification of knowledge. He notes the conventional nature of the compendium of travel literature and the faults of his predecessors, who have proved lacking in restraint. He proposes that the weight of knowledge and text has become a burden. And he proposes to

---

[174] John Moore, *Voyages and Travels*... 2 vols., v. 1 (London: Printed for the Proprietors: And Sold by Alexander Hogg, [1785]), v.1, title page.

[175] Moore, *Voyages*, v. 1, frontispiece. The portraits echo (or play off of) those on the 1625 edition frontispiece of Samuel Purchas, *Hakluytus Posthumus or Purchas His Pilgrimes* (London: Henry Fetherston, 1625), which mingles the faces of explorers with those of historical and contemporary lords, as well as Biblical and classical figures.

[176] It is worth noting that the travels of such European explorers were also acknowledged by Ottoman authors, such as Piri Reis crediting Columbus as an authority for his now lost "world map," and Katib Çelebi highlighting Columbus and Magellan as critical figures in his geographical magnum opus, the *Cihannüma*. Gottfried Hagen, "Katip Çelebi's Discussion of European Expansion in the Cihânnümâ," paper presented at the Middle East Studies Association conference, 2009.

Figure 7.10. John Hamilton Moore, "Genius of the Work Instructing Youth," *A New and Complete Collection of Voyages and Travels*, v. 1, frontispiece, London [1785]. By permission of the Folger Shakespeare Library, Shelfmark: G160.M8 vi Cage.

rescue his readers from the "enormous dunghill" of narrative that has made the consumption of travel tedious.

> *Everyone knows that a collection of voyages and travels, merely consid-*
> *ered as such, has nothing in it of novelty; numbers of such compilations*
> *having been published from time to time: among the most remarkable,*
> *those of Hakluyt, Purchas, Harris, Churchill, . . . yet truth compels us*
> *to say, that on many accounts we cannot heartily approve of them: to*
> *present the public with a number of volumes, swelled to an enormous*
> *size, and filled with trivial circumstances, composed from the journals*
> *of seamen, or the memorandums of travelers, we do not conceive to be*
> *suited to the spirit of an undertaking of this sort, where much matter*
> *ought to be comprised in little space . . .* [177]

Despite these protestations, Moore's own *Voyages* is quite a weighty tome (indeed two tomes), their thickness illustrating his argument that the literature of travel had become unwieldy due to the dense matrix of description and commentary. In short, the foundations of knowledge, text, and observation that Rashid al-Din had proposed as necessary to achieve an understanding of the world were continually being augmented by new voyages and observations. This material needed an acute editorial eye and a strong editorial hand (Moore's hand) to separate the wheat from the chaff. Like Vernino, Soranzo, Freschot, and other earlier authors, Moore felt no compunction about criticizing his competitors and predecessors. But his work was unabashedly premised on theirs, its very success a function of his knowledge of, and access to, the piles upon piles of texts and maps that had constructed, shaped, and given a past and present to the Ottoman domains and the worlds (physical and mental) around them. It was to this heap of knowledge and text that our amiable traveler John Morritt proposed to add, assuming that his own wit and intellect would provide a new take on Ottoman space, without entirely discarding the old takes.

What had changed in the eighteenth century was familiarity: the scope of encounter, the perception that the magnitude of knowledge and text had grown burdensome, and a change in direction on the question of how knowing the Ottoman could be managed. In the processes of mapping the Ottoman empire, the antiquarian and touring impulses passed to a broader class of travelers. The consumption of antiquities was coupled to a broader range of commercial goods (such as Morritt's *à la Turque* salon). And the use of and reference to maps became conventional for a broader class of witnesses, actual and stay-at-home. The foundations of knowledge, text, and eyewitness authority remained in place, but assumed a wider audience that was engaged in more extensive ways.

Authors of the early modern era produced a vast array of narrative and imagery depicting the Ottoman realm. As suggested here, these accounts vary according to place; the knowledge, task, and personality of the authors; literary and visual conventions; and the demands of audiences, both formal and informal (among other factors). Such authors might be interested in the

---

[177] Moore, *Voyages and Travels*, first and second unnumbered pages of preface.

Ottomans, fearful of them, or little concerned with the current occupants of Ptolemy's "first part of Asia." They might present Ottoman space through comparison to their own domestic, historical, and imaginary landscapes, or treat it as indelibly foreign. They might privilege personal experience, and be reserved or lavish in their citation of previous myths, histories, travelers, and geographers. But most represented themselves as careful observers situated in a chain of authorities on Ottoman space reaching back into the recent and distant pasts. Those pasts, and their texts, were the bedrock on which early modern observers constituted their mapping of the Ottomans.

8

Afterword

Mapping the Fault Lines of Empire and Nation

In 1782, when the French ambassador to Constantinople, Marie-Gabriel-Florent-Auguste de Choiseul-Gouffier, published his travelogue, *Voyage Pittoresque*, he commented at length on the trajectory of mapping and geographic knowledge. Citing Voltaire (1694–1778), he wrote that Geography was "still of all the arts, that in greatest need of perfecting; and ambition has gone to great lengths to devastate the territory that Geography describes."[1] He illustrated this global ravishing using the examples of Pizarro and Cortez. Thus was the New World attached to the Old in the late-eighteenth-century author's vision of reality. And thus did Choiseul-Gouffier acknowledge the intimate connection between cartography and conquest, between the French mapping projects of his own time and the "innumerable armies hurled at the coasts of Asia" in times past by a "piously warlike Europe."[2] His own mission to Ottoman domains (1784–91) was directed both to the negotiation of a new 'world' order and to the observation and collection of a receding past. Both tasks found expression on the map. For Choiseul-Gouffier, mapping the "grand theatre" of the Mediterranean, in which the ambitions of the French and Ottomans were played out, had evolved from the lost charts of the ancients, the "too imperfect" cartographies of Ptolemy, and numerous error-filled itineraries, to a cartography that he proposed in his own time was "entirely different" from that which had come before.[3]

In the twenty-first century, when scholars and statesmen, news anchors and textbook writers struggle over the fault-lines of civilizations, we remain interested in maps, their evolution, and the messages they convey. The ends of empire have yet to be resolved; and nations (such as Kosovo, or Palestine/Israel) struggle for existence or sovereignty in some of the same spaces that bedeviled the lords and subjects of the early modern era. Turkey, in its

---

[1] Choiseul-Gouffier, *Voyage Pittoresque*, v. 2, pt. 1, 5, "La Geographie, dit Voltaire [1694–1778], est encore de tous les arts celui qui a le plus grand besoin d'etre perfectionné, et l'ambition a mis jusqu'ici plus de soins à dévaster la terre qu'à la décrire."

[2] Choiseul-Gouffier, *Voyage Pittoresque*, v.2, pt. 1, 6.

[3] Choiseul-Gouffier, *Voyage Pittoresque*, v. 2, pt. 1, 6–7, 9.

modern incarnation, its capital removed from the Straits into the interior of
Anatolia, has failed in its bid for admission to the European Union, while
Constantinople/Istanbul remains a continental bridge and one of the cultural
capitals of the world. Cyprus is split into Muslim and Christian 'halves,' the
nature of its attachment to the Greek and Turkish mainlands still unresolved.
And the "Holy Land" of the early modern era still holds sway, an enduring
object of devotion and bone of contention, though perhaps no longer envisioned as an appendage of Europe. The nations of Asia and of Europe no
longer rule unselfconsciously in the name of God; but divisions of religious
ethos and history play an ongoing and primary role in what they are and
how they represent themselves. And, for modern publics, identity-signifying
words and images manipulated by various interested parties continue to
problematize the boundaries of nation, culture, and faith.

Meanwhile, the scope of the information system has broadened substantially, and its pace has quickened dramatically, much as it quickened with the
advent and spread of print. The "enormous dunghill" of information that
Hamilton Moore bemoaned in his 1785 compendium of travel knowledge
has grown exponentially. And the ordinary citizen has become an eyewitness, in ways inconceivable in 1548, to almost every nook and cranny of
what once were Ottoman domains and the lands of the Christian kings.
But despite that level of access, to visual if not to textual knowledge, there
are still certain predictable and circumscribed avenues for formulating our
visions of one-time Ottoman spaces: the pronouncements of officials, school
texts, television shows, personal experience, or the websites and tweets of
traveling friends and strangers. Maps, through these venues and in multiple
formats, are readily accessible to all. Yet they have not escaped the rhetorical
dichotomies that characterized their early modern predecessors: similarity
and difference, war and peace, past and present, fear and conversation.

Nor have enduring notions of world order and global struggle disappeared
in the twenty-first century. The Ottomans and their imperial rivals claimed
the mantle of 'world' dominion certified through military and moral superiority. The sultan was thus *alempenah*, Refuge of the World, his presence (like
that of the Hapsburg emperor) purportedly guaranteeing a system of power,
protection, justice, punishment, and reward. That world order, embodied in
various types of map, was juxtaposed to the threats of chaos, terror, and
being engulfed by a foreign 'other.' So, too, the articulation of 'terror' in
the modern world has much to do with concepts of world power, faith,
ethnography, and the rights to certain spaces of 'proper' rulers over those
who challenge, resist, or rebel against them.

It may well be that the psychological impulse to transcend such boundaries
is more widespread or even more effective today than it was in the period
under discussion in this volume. There have always been boundary crossers
attracted to the transcultural experience. But what, in any given era, is the
scope of their operation and imagination? To what extent do they break
free of the constraints of the map? To what extent do they circumvent the
authority of knowledge, text, and experience?

And what of Choiseul-Gouffier's global devastation, "innumerable
armies," and the civilizational hierarchies that helped inspire them? One

question that stalks the historiography of the Ottoman empire is whether Ottoman rule represents relative tolerance or relative violence in the context of the early modern era. We have seen that violence played a central role in the cartographic imagination of early modern Europe as it explored the limits of Ottoman sovereignty, territory, and identity. And yet we know how much intercourse, conversation, and mingling of identities went on within the flexible borders of the empire. Indeed, the enduring nature of that empire was in part a function of its flexible and pragmatic administration, one capable of absorbing many of the people in between. One can argue that the Ottomans developed a system in which non-Muslim subjects and foreigners could be sorted into their assigned places in ways that were more tolerant or predictable than those employed in much of Christian Europe. But that does not mean that the Ottomans perceived no clear ethnoreligious borders dividing peoples and territories. Nor does it mean that violence and intimidation, as embodied in the taking of heads, for example, were not default modes of operation and of representation, just as they were for the Christian kingdoms. That default mode is clearly illustrated in the various kinds of mapping that characterized the era. The Ottoman polity was both violent and tolerant. It expected territories to "bow their heads," as the Mughul emperor Babur put it. So did its European Christian rivals, as illustrated in the engraving of Kaiser Leopold I by Giuseppe Mitelli that opens Ch. 4 of this volume. We cannot turn our gaze from that default condition of violence, in fact and in art. Simple rhetorics of difference, especially religious and cultural difference, do not translate into simple facts on the ground. But they do indicate that there are familiar, enduring, and predictable ways to demonstrate possession and show who is boss.

The map both affirms and violates our assumptions about visions of early modern space. The options for such visions are not limitless. Modes of telling and tropes of depiction repeat themselves over decades and centuries, defying the boundaries of state and culture. Thus the image of the fallen foe, minus his head or trodden beneath the feet of the warrior self, traces its way from our earliest histories into our twenty-first century arenas of battle. And the fortified city, perched at the crossroads or defining the limits between land and sea, remains the elemental marker of possession and sovereignty, despite the ways in which modern weapons and communications technologies have collapsed the space between one empire or one city and another. We still ask, "what cities does he hold, or can he hold, or can he take ... ?" These conventions might tempt us to homogenize the possessors of space and the makers and readers of maps, but as we have seen, there is always room for innovation in artistry; modes of seeing tend to shift over time; and the proliferation of image and text transforms audience expectations. Contemplating mapped space, its markers, its references, and its focus on a broad and sometimes amorphous ethno-imperial entity allows us to reexamine the "Turk" and "his" role in the early modern imagination. It illuminates our sense of narrative and visual modes, the genres of looking and telling, and the possibilities for incorporating Ottoman imagery into broader artistic rhetorics of space and power. As Thongchai Winichakul, in *Siam Mapped*, has shown for a later era and a more eastern territory, map, nation, language, sovereignty, border, and margin are complex formulations that reflect and challenge identities that evolve, contend, and overlap.[4] Unlike Winichakul's, our starting point here is not nation. It is empire: envisioned, encountered, and projected. Like Winichakul's Siam, however, our imperial entity was inscribed in its audiences' imaginations through a dynamic process of learning, physical contestation, and inscription in text and image.

Charles Press, in his 1950 study of the American political cartoon, provides us with a useful construct for understanding the power of that process of inscription: the notion of the "cherished community."[5] Press argues that the successful cartoon is one that deploys that which is familiar, enduring, and emotionally charged in order clearly to mark the boundaries of the readers' community. Visualizing what people cherish (faith, nation, history, 'home') through simple tropes or iconography prompts a predictable and sometimes visceral response, one that is heightened when the community is juxtaposed to some threatening foe. That paradigm also works for the map, which, like the cartoon, creates and records perceptions. Both translate worlds of textual knowledge, truth claims, and notions of possession into a bounded frame. Visions of graphic and geographic 'reality,' in both types of imagery, depend on what the viewer already 'knows' of history, place, class, costume, and custom. Thus, as they trace the limits of sovereignty and of space, their appeal to the cherished community (via eagle, lion, crescent, or cross) is hard to resist.

---

[4] Thongchai Winichakul, *Siam Mapped: A History of the Geo-body of a Nation* (Honolulu: University of Hawaii Press), 1994.
[5] Press, *The Political Cartoon*, 50–79.

Bibliography

HOC: J. B. Harley and David Woodward, eds. *The History of Cartography*, 3 vols. Chicago: University of Chicago Press, 1992–2007.

Abou El Fadl, Khaled. *Rebellion and Violence in Islamic Law*. Cambridge: Cambridge University Press, 2001.

Abu Lughod, Janet. *Before European Hegemony: The World System A.D. 1250–1350*. New York: Oxford University Press, 1989.

Abulafia, David. *The Great Sea: A Human History of the Mediterranean*. Oxford: Oxford University Press, 2011.

Ágoston, Gábor. "A Flexible Empire: Authority and Its Limits on the Ottoman Frontiers." In *Ottoman Borderlands: Issues, Personalities, and Political Changes*, Kemal Karpat with Robert Zens, eds., 15–31. Madison, Wisconsin: University of Wisconsin Press, 2003.

Guns for the Sultan: Military Power and the Weapons Industry in the Ottoman Empire. Cambridge: Cambridge University Press, 2005.

"Information, Ideology, and Limits of Imperial Policy: Ottoman Grand Strategy in the Context of Ottoman–Habsburg Rvalry." In *The Early Modern Ottomans: Remappping the Empire*, Virginia Aksan and Daniel Goffman, eds., 75–103. Cambridge: Cambridge University Press, 2007.

"Agria." [Rome?]: [1683?].

Akkach, Samer. "The Poetics of Concealment: Al-Nabulusi's Encounter with the Dome of the Rock." *Muqarnas* 22 (2005): 110–27.

Aksan, Virginia. "Choiseul-Gouffier at the Sublime Porte 1784–1792." In *Ottomans and Europeans: Contacts and Conflicts*, 59–65. Analecta Isisiana LXXV. İstanbul: Isis Press, 2004.

"The One-Eyed Fighting the Blind: Mobilization, Supply, and Command in the Russo-Turkish War of 1768–1774." In *Ottomans and Europeans: Contacts and Conflicts*, 173–90. Analecta Isisiana LXXV. İstanbul: Isis Press, 2004.

Ottoman Wars, An Empire Besieged 1700–1870. New York: Longman, 2007.

Aksan, Virginia, and Daniel Goffman, eds. *The Early Modern Ottomans: Remappping the Empire*. Cambridge: Cambridge University Press, 2007.

Alai, Cyrus. *General Maps of Persia 1477–1925*. Leiden: Brill, 2005.

Alam, Muzaffar, and Sanjay Subrahmanyam. *Indo Persian Travels in the Age of Discoveries, 1400–1800*. Cambridge: Cambridge University Press, 2007.

Alberi, Eugenio. *Relazioni degli Ambasciatori Veneti al Senato*, series III, v. 1. Florence: Tipografia all' Insegna di Clio, 1840; reprint, University of Michigan Library, n.d.

"Algeri." c. 1590. Newberry Library, Novacco 4F 398.

Allsen, Thomas. *Culture and Conquest in Mongol Eurasia*. Cambridge: Cambridge University Press, 2001.

Amalric, Jean Pierre. "Une géopolitique de bénédictin: la Turquie d'Europe dans la Géographie historique de Dom Vaissète (1755)." In *Byzance et ses périphéries: Hommage à Alain Ducellier*, 359–74. Toulouse: Université Toulouse, 2004.

Amanat, Abbas. *Imagining the End: Visions of Apocalypse from the Ancient Middle East to Modern America*. London: I. B. Tauris, 2001.

And, Metin. *Turkish Miniature Painting: The Ottoman Period*. İstanbul: Dost, 1987.

Andrews, Walter, and Mehmet Kalpaklı. *The Age of Beloveds: Love and the Beloved in Early-Modern Ottoman and European Culture and Society*. Durham, NC: Duke University Press, 2005.

Anonymous. "La dimostratione del luogo... Artha." [c. 1538].

[Anonymous]. "Nova di Corfu..." Rome, 1572.

Anonymous. *Fütuhat-ı Cemile*. [İstanbul: 1592]. Topkapı Sarayı Kütüphanesi, Hazine 1592.

Anonymous. "Clissa, Praecipuum Turcarum in Dalmatia popugnaculum." [c. 1596].

Anville, Jean Baptiste Bourguignon. "La Grece et les pays plus septentrionaux jusqu'au Danube: Pour l'Histoire Ancienne de Mr. Rollin." [Paris]: 1740.

Arbel, Benjamin. "The Port Towns of the Levant in Sixteenth-Century Travel Literature." In *Mediterranean Urban Culture, 1400–1700*, Alexander Cowan, ed., 151–64. Exeter: University of Exeter Press, 2000.

"Venetian Cyprus and the Muslim Levant, 1473–1570." In *Cyprus, the Franks, and Venetia, 13th to 16th Centuries*, Section XII. Variorum Collected Studies Series. Aldershot: Ashgate, 2000.

"Maps of the World for Ottoman Princes? Further Evidence and Questions Concerning 'The Mappamondo of Hajji Ahmed.'" *Imago Mundi* 54 (2002): 19–29.

Arblaster, Paul. "Posts, Newsletters, Newspapers: England in a European system of communication." In *News Networks in Seventeenth Century Britain and Europe*, Joad Raymond, ed., 19–34. London: Routledge, 2006.

Archer, John Michael. *Old Worlds: Egypt, Southwest Asia, India and Russia in Early Modern English Writing*. Stanford, CA: Stanford University, 2001.

Arifi Fethullah Çelebi. *Süleymanname*. İstanbul, 1558. Topkapı Sarayı Müzesi Kütüphanesi, Hazine 1517.

Armao, Ermanno. *Venezia in Oriente: La "Relatione dell'Isola et Città di Tine" di Pompeo Ferrari Gentil'huomo piacentino*. Rome: Dott. G. Bardi, 1938.

Vincenzo Coronelli: cenni sull'uomo e la sua vita. Firenze: Libreria Editrice, 1944.

Artan, Tülay. "Arts and Architecture." In *The Cambridge History of Turkey*, v. 3, *The Later Ottoman Empire, 1603–1839*, Suraiya Faroqhi, ed., 408–80. Cambridge: Cambridge University Press, 2006.

Astengo, Corradino. *La cartografia nautical mediterranea dei secoli XVI e XVII*. Genoa: Erga edizioni, 2000.

Atasoy, Nurhan. *Otağ-ı Hümayun: The Ottoman Imperial Tent Complex*. İstanbul: MEPA, 2000.

Atasoy, Nurhan, and Lale Uluç. *Impressions of Ottoman Culture in Europe: 1453–1699*. İstanbul: Turkish Cultural Foundation, 2012.

Atıl, Esin. *The Age of Sultan Süleyman the Magnificent*. Washington, DC: The National Gallery of Art, 1987.

"The Image of Süleymân in Ottoman Art." In *Süleymân the Second and His Time*, Halil İnalcık, and Cemal Kafadar, eds., 333–41. İstanbul: Isis Press, 1993.

Levni and the Surname: The Story of an Eighteenth-Century Ottoman Festival. İstanbul: Koçbank, 1999.

Austin, Michael, trans., Geoffrey Lewis, ed. *Domenico's Istanbul*. London: Gibb Memorial Trust, 2001.

Babur [Zahir ud-Din Muhammad]. *The Baburnama: Memoirs of Babur, Prince and Emperor*. Wheeler Thackston, ed. and trans. Washington D.C.: Freer Gallery of Art, 1996.

Bağci, Serpil. "From Translated Word to Translated Image: the Illustrated Şehnâme-i Türkî Copies." *Muqarnas* 17 (2000): 162–76.

Bağcı, Serpil, and Zeren Tanındı, "The Ottomans: From Mehmed II to Murad III." In *Turks: A Journey of a Thousand Years, 600–1600*, David Roxburgh, ed., 260–374. London: Royal Academy of Arts, 2005.

Balard, Michel. "The Genoese in the Aegean (1204–1566)." In *Latins and Greeks in the Eastern Mediterranean after 1204*, Benjamin Arbel, Bernard Hamilton, and David Jacoby, eds., 158–74. London: Frank Cass, 1989.

Balletto, Laura. "Ethnic Groups, Cross-Social and Cross-Cultural Contacts on Fifteenth Century Cyprus." In *Intercultural Contacts in the Medieval Mediterranean: Studies in Honour of David Jacoby*, Benjamin Arbel, ed., 35–48. London: Frank Cass, 1996.

Ballino, Giulio. *De' disegni delle piu illustri città, et fortezze del Mondo*. Venetia: Bolognino Zaltieri, 1569.

Banerjee, Pompa. "The White Othello: Turkey and Virginia in John Smith's True Travels." In *Envisioning the English Empire: Jamestown and the Emergence of the North Atlantic World*, Robert Applebaum and John Wood Sweet, eds., 135–51. Philadelphia: University of Pennsylvania Press, 2005.

"Postcards from the Harem: The Cultural Translation of Niccolao Manucci's Book of Travels." In *The 'Book' of Travels: Genre, Ethnology and Pilgrimage, 1250–1700*, Palmira Brummett, ed., 242–82. Leiden: Brill, 2009.

Barbarics-Hermanlik, Zsuzsa. "Handwritten Newsletters as Interregional Information Sources in Central and Southeastern Europe." In *The Dissemination of News and the Emergence of Contemporaneity in Early Modern Europe*, Brendan Dooley, ed., 155–78. Farnham, Surrey: Ashgate, 2011.

Barbarics-Hermanlik, Zsuzsa, and Renate Pieper, "Handwritten newsletters as a means of communication in early modern Europe." In *Cultural Exchange in Early Modern Europe*, v. 3, *Correspondence and Cultural Exchange in Europe, 1400–1700*, Francisco Bethencourt and Florike Egmond, eds., 53–79. Cambridge: Cambridge University Press, 2006.

Barber, Peter. "Mapmaking in England, ca. 1470–1650." In *HOC*, v. 3, part 2, 1589–1669.

Barbour, Philip L., ed. *The Complete Works of Captain John Smith (1580–1631)*, 3 vols. Chapel Hill, NC and London: University of North Carolina Press, 1986.

Bargrave, Robert. *The Travel Diary of Robert Bargrave Levant Merchant (1647–1656)*, Michael Brennan, ed. London: Hakluyt Society, 1999.

Barker, Thomas. *Double Eagle and Crescent: Vienna's Second Turkish Siege and Its Historical Setting*. Albany: S.U.N.Y. Press, 1967.

Barlieva, Slavia. "Two Venetians in Bulgaria in 1575." *Etudes Balkaniques* 2 (1996): 124–6.

Barta, Gábor. "The First Period of the Principality of Transylvania (1526–1606)." In *History of Transylvania*, v. 1, *From the Beginnings to 1606*, Béla Köpeczi, ed., 593–770. Boulder: Social Science Monographs, 2001.

Barzman, Karen. "Gregorio Lazzarini's Judith and Holofernes: Decapitation, Islam, and the Venetian State." In *Gifts in Return: Essays in Honour of Charles Dempsey*, Melinda Wilcox Schlitt, ed., 445–76. Toronto: Centre for Reformation and Renaissance Studies, 2012.

Bataillon, Marcel. "Mythe et connaissance de la Turquie en Occident au milieu du XVIe siècle." In *Venezia e l'Oriente fra tardo Medioevo e Rinascimento*, 451–70. [Firenze]: Sansoni, 1966.

Bayerle, Gustav. *Ottoman Diplomacy in Hungary: Letters from the Pashas of Buda 1590–1593*. Bloomington: Indiana University Press, 1972.

Ottoman Tributes in Hungary According to Sixteenth Century Tapu Registers of Novigrad. The Hague: Mouton, 1973.

Bayly, C. A. *Empire and information: Intelligence gathering and social communication in India, 1780–1870*. Cambridge: Cambridge University Press, 1996.

Béla, Szalai. "A tizenöt éves háború metszetábrázolásai a frankfurti vásári tudósításokban (1593–1606)." *Cartograhica Hungarica* 8 (May 2004): 18–39.

Beltrán, Cristina Borreguero. "Philip of Spain: The Spider's Web of News and Information." In *The Dissemination of News and the Emergence of Contemporaneity in Early Modern Europe*, Brendan Dooley, ed., 23–50. Farnham, Surrey: Ashgate, 2011.

Bembo, Ambrosio. *The Travels and Journal of Ambrosio Bembo*, Clara Bargellini, trans., Anthony Welch, ed. Berkeley: University of California Press, 2007.

   Il viaggio in Asia (1671–1675) nei manoscritti di Minneapolis e di Bergamo, Antonio Invernizzi, ed. Alessandria: Edizioni dell'Orso, 2012.

Bennassar, Bartolomé. "Malte, le traffic d'esclaves et l'inquisition." In *Hommage à Alain Ducellier: Byzance et ses périphéries*, Bernard Doumerc and Christophe Picard, eds., 375–81. Toulouse: CNRS, 2004.

Berey, N. "Carte de Haute et Basse Hongrie, Transylvanie, Sclavonie, Croatiae, et Dalmatie." Paris: 1663.

Bergogni, Gherardo. *Le Discordie christiane le quali causarono la Grandezza di Cassa ottomana*. Bergamo: Comino Ventura, 1590.

Bertelli, Sergio. *The King's Body*. University Park: Pennsylvania State University Press, 1995.

Berti, Marcello. *Nel Mediterraneo ed Oltre: Temi di storia e storiografia marittima Toscana (Secoli XIII–XVIII)*. Pisa: ETS, 2000.

Betzek, Jakob von. *Gesandtschaftsreise nach Ungarn und die Türkei im Jahre 1564/5*, Karl Nehring, ed. Munich: Veröffentlichungen des Finnisch-Ugrischen Seminars an der Universität München, 1979.

Bevilacqua, Alexander, and Helen Pfeifer. "Turquerie: Culture in Motion, 1650–1750." *Past and Present* 221 (November, 2013): 75–118.

Bevilacqua, Eugenia. *Le Immagini dell'Isola di Creta nella Cartografia Storica*. Venice: Istituto Veneto di Scienze, Lettere ed Arti, 1997.

Biedrońska-Słota, Beata. "The History of Turkish Textiles." In *War and Peace: Ottoman-Polish Relations in the 15th-19th Centuries*, 63–9. İstanbul: MAS, 1999.

Biggs, Michael. "Putting the State on the Map: Cartography, Territory, and European State Formation." *Comparative Studies in Society and History*, 41.2 (April, 1999): 374–405.

Bilici, Faruk. *XIV Louis ve İstanbul'u Fetih Tasarısı*. Ankara: Türk Tarih Kurumu, 2004.

Binney, Edwin. *Turkish Treasures From the Collection of Edwin Binney*. Portland, OR: Portland Art Museum, 1979.

Bisaha, Nancy. *Creating East and West: Renaissance Humanists and the Ottoman Turks*. Philadelphia: University of Pennsylvania Press, 2004.

Blome, Richard. *Cosmography and Geography*. London: S. Roycroft, 1684.

[Bodenehr, Gabriel]. *A collection of plans and views of fortified towns in Europe*. [Augsburg: c. 1730?]. British Library, Maps, C24.aa.18.

Bon, Ottaviano. *The Sultan's Seraglio: An Intimate Portrait of Life at the Ottoman Court (From the Seventeenth-Century Edition of John Withers)*, Godfrey Goodwin, ed. London: Saqi Books, 1996.

   Il seraglio del Gransignore, Bruno Basile, ed. Rome: Salerno Editrice, 2002.

The Book of Dede Korkut: A Turkish Epic. Faruk Sümer, Ahmet Uysal, and Warren Walker, eds. and trans. Austin: University of Texas Press, 1972.

Bordone, Benedetto. *Isolario*. Venetia: Nicolo d'Aristoile, 1534.

Borromeo, Elisabetta. *Voyageurs occidentaux dans l'empire ottoman (1600–1644)*, 2 vols. Paris: Maisonneuve & Larose, 2007.

Boschini, Marco. *L'Archipelago Con tutte le Isole, Scogli Secche, e Bassi Fondi, Con i Mari, Golfi, Seni, Porti, Citta, e Castelli; Nella Forma, Che si Vedono al Tempo Presente*. Venetia: Francesco Nicolini, 1658.

Bostan, İdris. *Kürekli ve Yelkenli Osmanlı Gemileri*. İstanbul: Bilge, 2005.

   "The establishment of the province of Cezayir-i Bahr-i Sefid." In *The Kapudan Pasha: His Office and His Domains*, Elizabeth Zachariadou, ed., 241–52. Rethymnon, Crete University Press, 2012.

Boyar, Ebru, and Kate Fleet. *A Social History of Ottoman Istanbul*. Cambridge: Cambridge University Press, 2010.

Brancaforte, Elio. *Visions of Persia: Mapping the Travels of Adam Olearius*. Cambridge: Harvard University Press, 2003.

Brauer, R. W. "Boundaries and Frontiers in Medieval Muslim Geography." *Transactions of the American Philosophical Society* 85, pt. 6 (1995).

Brentjes, Sonja. "The Interests of the Republic of Letters in the Middle East (1550–1700)." In *Travellers from Europe in the Ottoman and Safavid Empires, 16th–17th Centuries: Seeking, Transforming, Discarding Knowledge*, Section I, 435–68. Farnham, Surrey: Ashgate, Variorum Reprints, 2010.

"On the Relation between the Ottoman Empire and the West European Republic of Letters (17th–18th Centuries)." In *Travellers from Europe in the Ottoman and Safavid Empires, 16th–17th Centuries: Seeking, Transforming, Discarding Knowledge*, Section II, 121–48. Farnham, Surrey: Ashgate, Variorum Reprints, 2010.

"Pride and Prejudice: The Invention of a Historiography of Science in the Ottoman and Safavid Empires by European Travellers and Writers in the Sixteenth and Seventeenth Centuries." In *Travellers from Europe in the Ottoman and Safavid Empires, 16th–17th Centuries: Seeking, Transforming, Discarding Knowledge*, Section VI, 229–54.

Brentjes, Sonja, and Volkmar Schüller. "Pietro della Valle's Latin Geography of Safavid Iran (1624–1628): Introduction." *Journal of Early Modern History* 10.3 (2006): 169–219.

Briccio, Giovanni. *Successo della sollevatione de Gianizzeri, contra il Gran Turco Sultan Osman* . . . Bracciano and Rimino: Gio. Simbeni, 1622.

Brice, Martin. *A Chronicle History of Forts and Fortresses*. New York: Barnes and Noble, 2006.

Brotton, Jerry. *Trading Territories: Mapping the Early Modern World*. Ithaca, NY: Cornell University Press, 1998.

Brotton, Jerry, and Lisa Jardine. *Global Interests: Renaissance Art between East and West*. Ithaca, NY: Cornell University Press, 2000.

Brummett, Palmira. *Ottoman Seapower and Levantine Diplomacy in the Age of Discovery*. Albany: SUNY Press, 1994.

"The Myth of Shah Ismail Safavi: Political Rhetoric and 'Divine' Kingship." In *Medieval Christian Perceptions of Islam*, John Tolan, ed., 331–59. New York: Garland Publishing, 1996.

"The Early Modern Ottoman Campaign: Containing Violence, Commemorating Allegiance, and Securing Submission." *Eurasian Studies* III/I (2004): 1–19.

"A Kiss Is Just a Kiss: Rituals of Submission Along the East–West Divide." In *Cultural Encounters between East and West, 1453–1699*, Matthew Birchwood and Matthew Dimmock, eds., 107–31. Cambridge: Cambridge Scholars Press, 2005.

"'Turks' and 'Christians:' The Iconography of Possession in the Depiction of the Ottoman-Venetian-Hapsburg Frontiers, 1550–1689." In *The Religions of the Book: Co-existence and Conflict, 1400–1660*, Matthew Dimmock and Andrew Hadfield, eds., 110–39. Houndmills, Basingstoke: Palgrave, 2008.

"The Fortress: Defining & Mapping the Ottoman Frontier in the 16th–17th Centuries." In *The Frontiers of the Ottoman World*, 31–55. Oxford: Oxford University Press, 2009.

"Ottoman Expansion in Europe, 1453–1606." In *The Cambridge History of Turkey*, v. 2, *The Ottoman Empire as a World Power, 1453–1603*, Kate Fleet and Suraiya Faroqhi, eds., 44–73. Cambridge: Cambridge University Press, 2012.

"The Lepanto Paradigm Revisited: Knowing the Ottomans in the Sixteenth Century." In *The Renaissance and the Ottoman World*, Anna Contadini and Claire Norton, eds., 63–93. Farnham, Surrey: Ashgate, 2013.

Bruyn, Abraham de. *Omnium pene Europae, Asiae, Aphricae atque Americae gentium habitus*. Antwerp: Michel Colijn [1581].

Bruyn, Cornelis de. *Voyage au Levant*. Delft: H. de Kroonevelt, 1700.

Bry, Theodor de, workshop of. "Vetutissimi, Potentissimique Hungariae Regni . . . " Frankfort: 1596.

Buisseret, David. *The Mapmakers' Quest: Depicting New Worlds in Renaissance Europe*. Oxford: Oxford University Press, 2003.

Burke, Peter. "Early Modern Venice as a Center of Information and Communication." In *Venice Reconsidered: The History and Civilization of an Italian City-State, 1297–1797*, John Martin and Dennis Romano, eds., 389–419. Baltimore: Johns Hopkins University Press, 2000.

"Translations into Latin in Early Modern Europe." In *Cultural Translation in Early Modern Europe*, Peter Burke and R. Po-Chia Hsia, eds., 65–80. Cambridge: Cambridge University Press, 2007.

Burns, Robert I., and Paul Chevedden, with Míkel de Epalza. *Negotiating Cultures: Bilingual Surrender Treaties in Muslim–Crusader Spain under James the Conqueror*. Leiden: Brill, 1999.

Burton, Jonathan. *Traffic and Turning: Islam and English Drama, 1579–1624*. Newark: University of Delaware Press, 2005.

"Anglo-Ottoman Relations and the Image of the Turk in Tamburlaine." *Journal of Medieval and Early Modern Studies* 30.1 (2006): 125–56.

Busbecq, Ogier Ghiselin de. *The Turkish Letters of Ogier Ghiselin de Busbecq: Imperial Ambassador at Constantinople 1554–1562*, Edward Forster, trans. Oxford: Clarendon Press, 1968.

Bussemechers, Ioani [Johan Bussemacher]. "Sclavonia, Croatia, Bosnia & Dalmatiae Pars Maior." [Köln], 1596.

"Thracia Et Bulgaria Cum Viciniis." [Köln]: 1596.

Buzov, Snježana. "Ottoman Perceptions of Bosnia as Reflected in the World of Ottoman Authors who Visited or Lived in Bosnia." In *Ottoman Bosnia: A History in Peril*, Markus Koller and Kemal Karpat, eds., 83–91. Madison: University of Wisconsin Press, 2004.

Çagman, Filiz. "Portrait Series of Nakkaş Osman." In *The Sultan's Portrait: Picturing the House of Osman*, Selmin Kangal, ed., 164–87. İstanbul: İşbank, 1999.

Calabi, Donatella. "The Jews and the City in the Mediterranean Area." In *Mediterranean Urban Culture, 1400–1700*, Alexander Cowan, ed., 56–68. Exeter: University of Exeter Press, 2000.

Cambini, Andrea. *Two very notable commentaries [on the origins] of the Turcks and Empire of the house of Ottomanno, . . . and . . . the warres of the Turcke against George Scanderbeg, prince of Epiro, and of the great victories obteyned by the sayd George as well against the Emperour of Turkie, as other princes*. London: Humphrey Toye, 1562.

Camocio, Giovanni Francesco. *Isole famose, porti, fortezze, e terre maritime, sotto poste alla Sigma Sig.ria di Venetia, ad altri Principi Christiani, et al Sig.or Turco, novamente poste in luce*. Venetia: alla libraria de segno di S. Marco [1574].

Capponi, Niccolo. *Victory of the West: The Great Christian-Muslim Clash at the Battle of Lepanto*. Cambridge, MA: da Capo, 2008.

Cardini, Franco. *Europe and Islam*, Caroline Beamish, trans. Oxford: Blackwell, 1999.

Casale, Giancarlo. *The Ottoman Age of Exploration*. Oxford: Oxford University Press, 2010.

Cassola, Arnold. *The 1565 Ottoman Malta Campaign Register*. Malta: Publishers Enterprises Group, 1998.

Casti, Emanuela. *Reality as Representation: The Semiotics of Cartography and the Generation of Meaning*. Bergamo: Bergamo University Press, 2000.

Cavanaugh, Sheila. *Cherished Torment: The Emotional Geography of Lady Mary Wroth's Urania*. Pittsburgh, PA: Duquesne University Press, 2001.

Celalzade Mustafa. *Selim-Name*, Ahmet Uğur and Mustafa Çuhadar, ed. Ankara: Kültür Bakanlığı, 1990.

Çerci, Farıs. *Gelibolulu Mustafa Ali ve Künül-Ahbarında, II Selim, III Murat, ve III Mehmet Devrinleri*. Kayseri: Erciyes Üniversitesi, 2000.

Cervantes, Miguel de. *Novelas ejemplares I*, Harry Sieber, ed. Madrid: Ediciones Cátedra, 1980.

Chandler, Richard. *Travels in Asia Minor and Greece*, new edition, Nicholas Revett, ed., 2 vols. Oxford: Clarendon Press, 1825.

Chaney, Edward. *The Evolution of the Grand Tour: Anglo-Italian Cultural Relations since the Renaissance*. London: Frank Cass, 1998.

Chardin, Sir John. *Travels in Persia 1673–1677*, N.M Penzer and Sir Percy Sykes, preface and introduction. New York: Dover, 1988.

Chartier, Roger. "Foucault's Chiasmus." In *Scientific Authorship: Credit and Intellectual Property in Science*, Mario Biagiolo and Peter Galison, eds., 13–31. New York: Routledge, 2003.

Chassepol, François de. *Histoire des grand viziers…* Paris: E. Michalett, 1676.

[Chatelain, Henri Abraham], Mr. C. *Atlas Historique, ou Nouvelle Introduction à l'Histoire, à la Chronologie & à la Géographie Ancienne & Moderne; Représentëë dans de Nouvelles Cartes, Ou l'on remarque l'établissement des Etats & Empires du Monde, leur durée, leur chûte, & leurs differens Gouvernemens;…* 3rd ed., 4 vols. Amsterdam: Chez L'Honore & Chatelain, 1739.

Chew, Samuel. *The Crescent and the Rose: Islam and England during the Renaissance.* New York: Octagon Books, 1965.

Chiarello, Giovanni Battista. *Historia degl' avvenimenti dell' armi imperiali contro a' ribelli, et Ottomani.* Venetia: 1687.

Choiseul-Gouffier, Marie-Gabriel-Florent-Auguste. *Voyage Pittoresque,* 2 vols. Paris: 1782.

Choné, Paulette. "Le portrait du Turc: Les artistes devant le rêve héroïque de la maison de Lorraine (XVIe–XVIIe siècles)." In *Chrétiens et musulmans à la Renaissance,* Actes du 37e colloque international du CESR (1994), Bartolomé Bennassar and Robert Sauzet, eds., 61–74. Paris: Honoré Champion, 1998.

Clancy-Smith, Julia. *Mediterraneans: North Africa and Europe in an Age of Migration, c. 1800–1900.* Berkeley: University of California Press, 2012.

"Clissa," *The Molina Family Atlas,* Table 6, no. 5. [n.p.: mid-17th C.]. British Library, Maps K.Top. 78.31.b.

Cohen, Ada. "Art, Myth, and Travel in the Hellenistic World." In *Pausanias: Travel, Myth and Memory in Roman Greece,* Susan Alcock, John Cherry, and Jaś Elsner, eds., 93–126. Oxford: Oxford University Press, 2001.

Cohen, Amnon. *Economic Life in Ottoman Jerusalem.* Cambridge: Cambridge University Press, 2002.

Concina, Ennio, and Elisabetta Molteni. *La fabrica della fortezza: L'architettura militare di Venezia.* Verona: Banco Popolare di Verona, 2001.

Conley, Tom. *The Self-Made Map: Cartographic Writing in Early Modern France.* Minneapolis: University of Minnesota Press, 1996.

Connolly, Daniel. "Copying Maps by Matthew Paris: Itineraries Fit for a King." In *The 'Book' of Travels: Genre, Ethnology and Pilgrimage, 1250–1700,* Palmira Brummett, ed., 159–204. Leiden: Brill, 2009.

Cook, David. *Studies in Muslim Apocalyptic.* Princeton, NJ: Darwin Press, 2002.

Corbett, Margery, and Michael Norton. *Engraving in England In the Sixteenth and Seventeenth Centuries: A Descriptive Catalogue with Introductions,* Part III, *The Reign of Charles I.* Cambridge: Cambridge University Press, 1964.

Coronelli, Vincenzo. *Specchio del Mare.* Venetia: 1664.

    Conquiste della Serenissima Republica di Venezia nella Dalmazia, Epiro, e Morea. Venetia: Laboratorio del P.M. Coronelli, 1686.

    An historical and geographical account of the Morea, Negropont, and the maritime places. R.W. Gent. trans. London: Matth. Gillyflower, 1687.

    Atlante Veneto, nel quale si contiene la descrittione geografica, storica, sacra, profana, e politica, degl'imperij, regni, provincie, e stati dell'universo… Venetia: Appresso Domenico Padovani, 1690.

    "Fortezza di S. Maura." Venetia: [c. 1695]. British Library, Maps, C.27.g.16(.61).

    Isolario [dell'Atlante Veneto] descrittione geografico-historica, sacra-profana, antico-moderna, politica, naturale, e poetica… di tutte l'isole… del globo terracqueo… Venetia: a spese dell'autore, 1696.

    Isola di Rodi geografica-storica, antica e moderna: coll' altre adiacenti, gia possedute dà Cavalieri Hospitalieri di Giovanni di Gerusalemme. Venetia: [n.p.], 1702.

    Ships and Other Sort of Craft Used by the Various Nations of the World, Venice 1690. Mario M. Witt, ed. and trans. London: Francis Edwards, 1970.

[Cortano, Ludovico]. "Good Newes to Christendome." London: Printed [by G. Purslowe] for Nathanial Butter, 1620.

Cosgrove, Denis. "Global Illumination and Enlightenment in the Geographies of Vincenzo Coronelli and Athanasius Kircher." In *Geography and Enlightenment,* David Livingstone and Charles Withers, eds., 33–66. Chicago: University of Chicago Press, 1999.

Courmenin, Louis des Hayes [Deshayes] de. *Voyages*. Paris: Chez Pierre Promé, 1664.

Covel, John. *Voyages en Turquie 1675–1677*, Jean-Pierre Grélois, trans. *Réalités Byzantines* 6. Paris: Éditions P. Lethielleux, 1998.

Cowan, Alexander. "Foreigners and the City: The Case of the Immigrant Merchant." In *Mediterranean Urban Culture, 1400–1700*, Alexander Cowan, ed., 45–55. Exeter: University of Exeter Press, 2000.

   "Gossip and Street Culture in Early Modern Venice." *Journal of Early Modern History* 12 (2008): 313–33.

Crawford, Julie. *Marvelous Protestantism: Monstrous Births in Post-Reformation England*. Baltimore: Johns Hopkins University Press, 2005.

Crouzet-Pavan, Elisabeth. "Venice between Jerusalem, Byzantium, and Divine Retribution: the Origins of the Ghetto." In *Jews, Christians, and Muslims in the Mediterranean World after 1492*, Alisa Meyuhas Ginio, ed., 163–9. London: Frank Cass, 1992.

Cunningham, Andrew, and Ole Grell. *The Four Horsemen of the Apocalypse: Religion, War, Famine, and Death in Reformation Europe*. Cambridge: Cambridge University Press, 2004.

Cyriac of Ancona. *Later Travels*, Edward Bodnar, ed. and trans. London: Harvard University Press, 2003.

Danckerts (Dankers), C. "Danubius Fluvius Europae Maximus, A Fontibus as Ostia, Cum omnibus Flumnibus ab utroque latere. In illum defluentibus." Amsterdam: 1647.

Danckerts, D[ancker]. "Nova et Recens Emendata Totius Regni Ungariae." [Amsterdam]: 1663.

Danckerts, Justus. "Regni Hungariae, Graeciae, et Moreae." [Amsterdam]: [c. 1688?]. British Library, Maps 28195(.31).

Daniel, Norman. *Islam and the West: the Making of an Image*. Oxford: Reprint, Oneworld Publications, 2000.

Dankoff, Robert, ed. and trans. *The Intimate Life of an Ottoman Statesman: Melek Ahmed Pasha (1588–1662) As Portrayed in Evliya Çelebi's Book of Travels*. Albany: State University of New York Press, 1991.

Dapper, Olfert. *Description exacte des Isles de l'Archipel*. Amsterdam: Chez George Gallet, 1703.

Darling, Linda. "Mediterranean Borderlands: Early English Merchants in the Levant." In *The Ottoman Empire: Myths, Realities and 'Black Holes,'* Eugenia Kermeli and Oktay Özel, ed. 173–88. İstanbul: Isis Press, 2006.

Daston, Lorraine, and Katherine Park. *Wonders and the Order of Nature*. New York: Zone Books, 2001.

Dávid, Géza. "The Mühimme Defteri as a Source for Ottoman-Habsburg Rivalry in the Sixteenth Century." *Archivum Ottomanicum* 20 (2002): 167–209.

Davidson, Nicholas. "'As Much for its Culture as for its Arms,' The Cultural Relations of Venice and Its Dependent Cities, 1400–1700." In *Mediterranean Urban Culture, 1400–1700*, Alexander Cowan, ed., 197–214. Exeter: University of Exeter Press, 2000.

Davies, Norman. *Europe: A History*. Oxford: Oxford University Press, 1996.

De Groot, Alexander. "The Historical Development of the Capitulatory Regime in the Ottoman Middle East from the Fifteenth to the Nineteenth Centuries." *Oriente Moderno*, special edition, *The Ottoman Capitulations: Text and Context*, Maurits van den Boogert and Kate Fleet, eds., XXII (LXXXIII), n.s., 3 (2003): 575–604.

Debby, Nirit Ben-Aryeh. "Crusade Propaganda in Word and Image in Early Modern Italy Niccolò Guidalotto's Panorama of Constantinople (1662)." *Renaissance Quarterly* forthcoming, 2014.

Delano-Smith, Catherine. "Milieus of Mobility: Itineraries, Route Maps, and Road Maps." In *Cartographies of Travel and Navigation*, James R. Akerman, ed., 16–68. Chicago: University of Chicago Press, 2006.

   "Signs on Printed Topographical Maps, ca. 1470–ca. 1640." In *HOC*, v. 3, part 1, 529–590.

Dening, Greg. "The Theatricality of Observing and Being Observed: Eighteenth-Century Europe 'Discovers' the ? Century 'Pacific'." In *Implicit Understandings: Observing,*

Reporting, and Reflecting on the Encounters between European and Other Peoples in the Early Modern Era, Stuart Schwartz, ed., 451–83. Cambridge: Cambridge University Press, 1994.

Deslandes, André Daulier. *Les beautez de la Perse...* Paris: Gervais Clouzier, 1673.

Deutecum, Ioannes van, Lucas van Deutecum, and Matthias Zündt. "Hungariae Totius." [Nuremberg]: c. 1567.

Dew, Nicholas. *Orientalism in Louis XIV's France*. Oxford: Oxford University Press, 2009.

Dilke, O. A. W. "Itineraries and Geographical Maps in the Early and Late Roman Empires." In *HOC*, v. 1, 234–57.

Dimmock, Matthew. *New Turkes: Dramatizing Islam And The Ottomans In Early Modern England*. Houndmills: Ashgate, 2005.

"Disegno dell'Isola de Gerbi." [c. 1560]. Newberry Library, Novacco 2F 240.

Djelloul, Neji. *Les fortifications côtieres ottomanes de la régence de Tunis (XVIe–XIXe siècles)*. Zaghouan: Fondation Temimi pour la recherche scientifique et l'information, 1995.

Doggett, Rachel, ed. *New World of Wonders: European Images of the Americas 1492–1700*. Seattle: University of Washington Press, 1992.

Dooley, Brendan. "The Wages of War: Battles, Prints and Entrepreneurs in Late Seventeenth-Century Venice." *Word and Image* 17. 1–2 (Jan–June 2001): 7–24.

Morandi's Last Prophecy and the End of Renaissance Politics. Princeton, NJ: Princeton University Press, 2002.

Du Val, Pierre. "Itinéraire de Paris à Constantinople." In *Diverses Cartes et Tables pour la Géographie Ancienne, pour la Chronologie et pour les Itinéraires et voyages modernes*. Paris: 1665. British Library, Maps C.38.b.1 (.41).

[Du Vignau, Sieur des Joanots], Person of Quality. *A New Account of the Present Condition of Turkish Affairs*. London: Randall Taylor, 1688.

The Turkish Secretary, Containing The Art of Expressing ones Thoughts without Seeing, Speaking, or Writing to one another; With the Circumstances of a Turkish Adventure; As also A most Curious Relation of several particulars of the Serrail that have not before now ever been made publick. Translated by the Author of the Monthly Account. London: 1688.

Dubbini, Renzo. *Geography of the Gaze in Early Modern Europe*, Lydia Cochrane, trans. Chicago: University of Chicago Press, 2002.

Düriegl, Günter. "Geschichte der Belagerung Wiens." In *Die Türken vor Wien: Europa und die Entscheidung an der Donau, 1683*, 131–50. Salzburg and Vienna: Residenz, 1982.

Duffy, Christopher. *Siege Warfare: The Fortress in the Early Modern World*. New York: Barnes and Noble, 1979.

Dursteler, Eric. *Venetians in Constantinople: Nation, Identity, and Coexistence in the Early Modern Mediterranean*. Baltimore: Johns Hopkins University Press, 2006.

Renegade Women: Gender, Identity, and Boundaries in the Early Modern Mediterranean. Baltimore: Johns Hopkins University Press, 2011.

Duzer, Chet Van. "From Odysseus to Robinson Crusoe: A Survey of Early Western Island Literature." *Island Studies Journal* 1.1 (2006): 143–62.

Dym, Jordana. "The Familiar and the Strange: Western Travelers' Maps of Europe and Asia, ca. 1600–1800." *Philosophy and Geography* 7.2 (August 2004): 155–91.

Ebel, Kathryn. "City Views, Imperial Visions: Cartography and the Visual Culture of Urban Space in the Ottoman Empire, 1453–1603." Ph.D. thesis, Department of Geography, University of Texas, 2002.

"Representations of the Frontier in Ottoman Town Views of the Sixteenth Century." *Imago Mundi* 60.1 (2008): 1–22.

Eger, Asa. *The Spaces between the Teeth: A Gazetteer of Towns on the Islamic–Byzantine Frontier*. İstanbul: Isis, 2012.

Elden, Stuart. *The Birth of Territory*. Chicago: University of Chicago Press, 2013.

Emiralioğlu, M. Pinar. "Cartography and Geographical Consciousness in the Ottoman Empire (1453–1730)." In *European Cartographers and the Ottoman World, 1500–1750: Maps from the Collection of O.J. Sopranos*, 97–107. Chicago: Oriental Institute, 2010.

Geographical Knowledge and Imperial Culture in the Early Modern Ottoman Empire. Farnham, Surrey: Ashgate, 2014.

Evliya Çelebi. *Evliya Çelebi in Diyarbekir*, Martin van Bruinessen and Hendrik Boeschoten, ed. and trans. Brill: Leiden, 1988.

Evliya Çelebi in Albania and Adjacent Regions (Kosovo, Montenegro, Ohrid): The Relevant Sections of the Seyahatname, Robert Dankoff and Robert Elsie, ed. and trans. Brill: Leiden, 2000.

An Ottoman Traveller: Selections from the Book of Travels of Evliya Çelebi, Robert Dankoff and Sooyong Kim, ed. and trans. London: Eland, 2010.

Farhad, Massumeh, with Serpil Bağcı. *Falnama: The Book of Omens.* London: Thames and Hudson, 2010.

Faroqhi, Suraiya. "The Venetian Presence in the Ottoman Empire (1600–1630)." *Journal of European Economic History* 15.2 (Fall 1986): 345–83.

The Ottoman Empire and the World around It. London: I.B. Tauris, 2004.

Subjects of the Sultan: Culture and Daily Life in the Ottoman Empire. London: I.B. Tauris, 2007.

Faroqhi, Suraiya, and Christoph Neumann. *Ottoman Costumes From Textile to Identity.* İstanbul: Eren, 2004.

Favyn, André. *The Theater of Honor and Knight-Hood, or A Compendious Chronicle and Historie of the whole Christian World Containing The originall of all Monarchies, Kingdomes, and Estates, with their Emperours, Kings, Princes, and Governours, Their Beginnings, Continuance, and Successions, to this present Time*, [A.M.?, trans.]. London, Printed by William Iaggard, 1623.

Fehér, Géza. *Türkische Miniaturen aus den Chroniken der Ungarischen Feldzüge.* Budapest: Corvina Magyar Helikon, 1976.

Feliciano, María Judith. "Picturing the Ottoman Threat in Sixteenth-Century New Spain." In *The Turk and Islam in the Western Eye, 1450–1750: Visual Imagery before Orientalism*, James Harper, ed., 243–66. Farnham, Surrey: Ashgate, 2011.

Fenlon, Ian. *The Ceremonial City: History, Memory and Myth in Renaissance Venice.* New Haven: Yale University Press, 2007.

Fer, Nicolas de. "L'Asie, Ou tous les points Principaux sont placez sur les observations de Mrs. de l'Académie royale des sciences." Paris: 1696.

"Le Theatre De La Guerre Sur Les Frontieres Des Deux Empires de puis Vienne jusques à Constantinople." Paris: Chez l'Auteur, 1705.

Feridun Ahmet. *Nüshet ül-Esrar ul-Ahbar fi Sefer-i Szigetvar.* [İstanbul]. Topkapı Sarayı Müzesi, H. 1339.

Nüzhet-i Esrârü'l-Ahyâr Der-Ahbâr-ı Sefer-i Sigetvar: Sultan Süleyman'ın Son Seferi, H. Ahmet Arslantürk and Günhan Börekçi, eds. İstanbul: Zeytinburnu Belediyesi, 2012.

Fetvacı, Emine. "Viziers to Eunuchs: Transitions in Ottoman Manuscript Patronage, 1566–1617." Ph.D. thesis, Harvard University, Department of History of Art and Architecture, 2005.

"The Production of the Şehnāme-i Selīm Hān." *Muqarnas* 26 (2009): 263–315.

"Others and Other Geographies in the Şehnāme-i Selīm Hān." *Osmanlı Araştırmaları/Journal of Ottoman Studies* 40, (2012): 81–100.

"From Print to Trace: An Ottoman Imperial Portrait Book and Its Western European Models." *Art Bulletin* 95.2 (June 2013): 243–68.

Picturing History at the Ottoman Court. Bloomington: Indiana University Press, 2013.

Fielding, [John]. "Turky in Europe." [London]: 1783.

Finkel, Caroline. *The Administration of Warfare: The Ottoman Military Campaigns in Hungary, 1593–1606.* Vienna: VWGÖ, 1988.

Osman's Dream: The Story of the Ottoman Empire, 1300–1923. New York: Basic Books, 2005.

Fiorani, Francesca. *The Marvel of Maps: Art, Cartography, and Politics in Renaissance Italy.* New Haven, CT: Yale University Press, 2005.

Fischer-Galati, Stephen. *Ottoman Imperialism and German Protestantism.* Cambridge, MA: Harvard University Press, 1959.

Fisher, C. G., and A. Fisher. "Topkapı Sarayı in the Mid-Seventeenth Century: Bobovi's Description." *Archivum ottomanicum* 10 (1985–7): 5–81.

Fleet, Kate. "Turks, Italians and Intelligence in the Fourteenth and Fifteenth Centuries." In *The Balance of Truth: Essays in Honour of Geoffrey Lewis*, Çiğdem Balın-Harding and Colin Imber, eds., 98–112. İstanbul: Isis Press, 2000.

"Ottoman Expansion in the Mediterranean." In *The Cambridge History of Turkey*, v. 2, *The Ottoman Empire as a World Power, 1453–1603*, Suraiya Faroqhi and Kate Fleet, eds., 141–72. Cambridge: Cambridge University Press, 2013.

Fleischer, Cornell. "The Lawgiver as Messiah: The Making of the Imperial Image in the Reign of Süleiman." In *Soliman le Magnifique et son temps: Actes du Colloque de Paris, Galeries Nationales du Grand Palais, 7–10 mars 1990*, Gilles Veinstein, ed., 159–77. Paris: Ecole du Louvre, 1992.

"Shadows of Shadows: Prophecy in Politics in 1530s Istanbul." *International Journal of Turkish Studies* 13.1–2 (2007): 51–62.

Flood, Finbarr. *Objects of Translation: Material Culture and Medieval 'Hindu-Muslim' Encounter*. Princeton: Princeton University Press, 2009.

Fodor, Pál. "Who Should Obtain the Castle of Pankota (1565)?" *Turcica* 31 (1999): 67–86.

"An Anti-Semite Grand Vezier? The Crisis in Ottoman–Jewish Relations in 1589–1591 and its Consequences." In *In Quest of the Golden Apple: Imperial Ideology, Politics, and Military Administrations in the Ottoman Empire*, 191–205. *Analecta Isisiana XLV*. İstanbul: Isis Press, 2000.

"Making a Living on the Frontiers: Volunteers in the Sixteenth Century Ottoman Army." In *Ottomans, Hungarians, and Habsburgs in Central Europe: The Military Confines in the Era of Ottoman Conquest*, Géza Dávid and Pál Fodor, eds., 229–63. Leiden: Brill, 2000.

Forlani, Paolo. "Disegno particolare di Regni e Regioni che son da Venetia a Costantinopoli e da Costantinopoli a Vienna d'Austria, et da Vienna a Praga Citta regal di Boemia, et alla Citta regal di Polonia, et altri paesi fuori di detti viaggi, come si vede distintamente nel disegno." [Venetia]: [1566]. Newberry Novacco 4F 119.

Franco, G. *Effiggie naturali dei maggior prencipi et più valorosi capitani di questa età con l'arme loro*. Venetiis: Apud I. Francum, 1596.

Freschot, Casimiro. *Memorie historiche, e geografiche della Dalmazia*. Bologna, Giacomo Monti, 1687.

Fuchs, Barbara. *Passing for Spain: Cervantes and the Fictions of Identity*. Urbana: University of Illinois Press, 2003.

The Poetics of Piracy: Emulating Spain in English Literature. Philadelphia: University of Pennsylvania Press, 2013.

Fuller, Mary C. *English Travel to America, 1576–1624*. Cambridge: Cambridge University Press, 2007.

Fuller, Thomas. *Historie of the Holy Warre*. Oxford: Thomas Buck, 1639.

Fumée, Martin. *The Historie of the Troubles of Hungarie: Containing the Pitifull Losse and Ruine of that Kingdome, and the Warres Happened There, in That Time, betweene the Christians and Turkes*, R.C. Gentleman, trans. London: Felix Kyngston, 1600.

Fürst, Paulus. "Abbildung Des Königreich Ungarn Durch Türckey Bis Nach Constantinopel." Nuremberg: [c. 1658]. British Library, Maps 28195.34.

Gambi, Lucio, et al. *La Galleria delle Carte geographiche in Vaticano*, v. 1. Modena: Franco Cosimo Panini, 1994.

Garcés, María Antonia. *Cervantes in Algiers: A Captive's Tale*. Nashville: Vanderbilt University Press, 2002

Georgopoulou, Maria. *Venice's Mediterranean Colonies: Architecture and Urbanism*. Cambridge: Cambridge University Press, 2001.

Gerelyes, Ibolya, and Gyöngyi Kovács, ed. *Archaeology of the Ottoman Period in Hungary*. Budapest: Hungarian National Museum, 2003.

Gerlach, Stephan. *Türkiye Günlüğü 1573–1576*. Kemal Beydilli, ed., Türkis Noyan, trans., v. 1. İstanbul: Kitap Yayınevi, 2006.

Gerstenberg, Annette. *Thomaso Porcacchi's 'L'Isole piu famose del mondo,' Zur Text – und Wortgeschichte der Geographie im Cinquecento (mit Teiledition)*. Tübingen: Max Niemeyer Verlag, 2004.

Gertwagen, Ruth. "Venetian Modon and Its Port, 1358–1500." In *Mediterranean Urban Culture, 1400–1700*, Alexander Cowan, ed., 125–48. Exeter: University of Exeter Press, 2000.

Ghobrial, John-Paul. "The Secret Life of Elias of Babylon and the Uses of Global Microhistory." *Past and Present* 222.1 (2014): 51–93.

Gillies, John. *Shakespeare and the Geography of Difference*. Cambridge: Cambridge University Press, 1994.

Gilman, Ernest. "Madagascar on My Mind: The Earl of Arundel and the Arts of Colonization." In *Early Modern Visual Culture: Representation, Race, and Empire in Renaissance England*, Peter Erickson and Clark Hulse, ed., 284–314. Philadelphia: University of Pennsylvania Press, 2000.

Giovio, Paolo. *Commentario delle cose de' Turchi*. Venetia:1540.

Goffman, Daniel. *Izmir and the Levantine World, 1556–1650*. Seattle: University of Washington Press, 1990.

   Britons in the Ottoman Empire, 1642–1660. Seattle: University of Washington Press, 1998.

Gökbilgin, M. Tayyip. "Kanunî Sultan Süleiman'ın Macaristan ve Avrupa Siyasetinin Sebep ve Âmilleri Geçirdiği Safhalar." In *Kanunî Armağanı*, 5–40. Ankara: Türk Tarih Kurumu Basımevi, 1970.

Göllner, Carl. *Turcica: Die europäischen Türkendrucke des XVI. Jahrhunderts*, 3 vols. Baden-Baden: Verlag Valentin Koerner, 1994.

Goodman, Jennifer. *Chivalry and Exploration, 1298–1630*. Woodbridge, Suffolk: Boydell Press, 1998.

Goodrich, Thomas. *The Ottoman Turks and The New World: A Study of Tarih-i Hind-i Garbi and Sixteenth Century Ottoman Americana*. Wiesbaden: Otto Harrassowitz, 1990.

   "Better Directions at Sea: The Pîrî Reis Innovation," Foundation for Science, Technology and Civilization, 2007, http://www.muslimheritage.com/uploads/The_Piri_Reis_Innovation11.pdf.

Gouwens, Kenneth. "Perceiving the Past: Renaissance Humanism after the 'Cognitive Turn'." *American Historical Review* 103.1 (February 1998): 55–82.

Grabar, Oleg, and Sheila Blair. *Epic Images and Contemporary History: The Illustrations of the Great Mongol Shahnama*. Chicago: University of Chicago Press, 1980.

Gradeva, Rossitsa. "War and Peace along the Danube." In Rossitsa Gradeva, *Rumeli Under the Ottomans, 15th-18th Centuries: Institutions and Communities*, 107–32. İstanbul: Isis Press, 2004.

Grafton, Anthony. "The Humanist as Reader." In *A History of Reading in the West*, Guglielmo Cavallo and Roger Chartier, eds., Lydia Cochrane, trans., 180–211. Amherst: University of Massachusetts Press, 1997.

Grasselli, Margaret. "Color Printmaking before 1730." In *Colorful Impressions: The Printmaking Revolution in Eighteenth-Century France*, Margaret Grasseli, ed., 1–8. Washington, D.C.,: National Gallery of Art, 2003.

Green, Ian. "Orality, script, and print: the case of the English sermon c. 1530–1700." In *Cultural Exchange in Early Modern Europe*, v. 1, *Religion and Cultural Exchange in Europe, 1400–1700*, Heinz Schilling and István György Tóth, eds., 236–55. Cambridge: Cambridge University Press, 2006.

Greene, Molly. *Catholic Pirates and Greek Merchants: A Maritime History of the Mediterranean*. Princeton, NJ: Princeton University Press, 2010.

Griffiths, Anthony. *The Print in Stuart Britain 1603–1689*. London: The British Museum, 1998.

Guilmartin, John. *Gunpowder and Galleys: Changing Technology and Mediterranean Warfare at Sea in the 16th Century*. New York: Cambridge University Press, 1974.

Gülsoy, Ersin. "Bozcaada (Tenedos) before and after Its Capture by Venice in 1656." *II. National Aegean Islands Symposium, 2-3- July 2004, Gökçeada – Çanakkale*, İdris

Bostan and Sertaç Başeren, eds., 71–9. İstanbul: Turkish Marine Research Foundation, 2004.

Hadjikyriacou, S. Antonis. "Society and Economy on an Ottoman Island: Cyprus in the Eighteenth Century." Ph.D. thesis, University of London, School of African and Oriental Studies, Department of History, 2012.

Hagen, Gottfried. "The Traveller Mehmed Aşık." In *Essays on Ottoman Civilization: Proceedings of the XIIth Congress of the Comité international d'études pré-ottomanes et ottomans*, 145–54. Prague: Academy of Sciences of the Czech Republic, 1998.

"Some Considerations on the Study of Ottoman Geographical Writings." *Archivum Ottomanicum* 18 (2000): 183–93.

"Afterword: Ottoman Understandings of the World in the Seventeenth Century." In Robert Dankoff, *An Ottoman Mentality: The World of Evliya Çelebi*, 215–56. Leiden: Brill, 2004.

"Katip Çelebi's Discussion of European Expansion in the Cihânnümâ." Paper presented at the Middle East Studies Association conference, 2009.

Hagen, Gottfried, and Baki Tezcan, eds. *Essays in Honor of Thomas D. Goodrich*, special issues, *Osmanlı Araştırmaları/Journal of Ottoman Studies*, 39–40 (2012).

Hakluyt, Richard. *The principal navigations, voiages, traffiques and discoueries of the English nation...* 3 vols. London: 1598–1600.

Halasi-Kun, Tibor. "Ottoman Toponymic Data and Medieval Boundaries in Southeastern Hungary." In *From Hunyadi to Rákóczi, War and Society in Late Medieval and Early Modern Hungary*, János Bak and Béla Király, ed., 243–50. New York: Brooklyn College Press, 1982.

Hall, Kim F. *Things of Darkness: Economies of Race and Gender in Early Modern England*. Ithaca, NY, and New York: Cornell University Press, 1995.

Hamilton, Alastair. *Arab Culture and Ottoman Magnificence in Antwerp's Golden Age*. Oxford: Arcadian Library and Oxford University Press, 2001.

Harley, J. B. *The New Nature of Maps: Essays in the History of Cartography*. Baltimore: John's Hopkins Universty Press, 2001.

Harvey, P. D. A. "Local and Regional Cartography in Medieval Europe." In *HOC*, v. 1, 464–501.

Hegyi, Klára. *The Ottoman Empire in Europe*. Corvina, Budapest: Franklin Printing, 1989.

"Freed, Slaves as Soldiers in the Ottoman Fortresses in Hungary." In *Ransom Slavery along the Ottoman Borders (Early Fifteenth–Early Eighteenth Centuries)*, Géza Dávid and Pál Fodor, eds., 85–92. Leiden: Brill, 2007.

Heinz, Markus. "The Homan Family in the Eighteenth Century." *Imago Mundi* 49 (1997): 104–15.

Helms, Mary W. "Essay on Objects: Interpretations of Distance Made Tangible." In *Implicit Understandings: Observing, Reporting, and Reflecting on the Encounters between European and Other Peoples in the Early Modern Era*, Stuart Schwartz, ed., 355–77. Cambridge: Cambridge University Press, 1994.

Hess, Andrew. "The Battle of Lepanto and Its Place in Mediterranean History." *Past and Present* 57 (November, 1972): 53–73.

The Forgotten Frontier: A History of the Sixteenth Century Ibero-African Frontier. Chicago: University of Chicago Press, 1978.

Heyd, Uriel. *Ottoman Documents on Palestine, 1552–1615: A Study of the Firman According to the Mühimme Defteri*. Oxford: Clarendon Press, 1960.

Heywood, Colin. "Bosnia under Ottoman Rule, 1463–1800." In *The Muslims of Bosnia-Herzegovina: Their Historic Development from the Middle Ages to the Dissolution of Yugoslavia*, Mark Pinson, ed., 22–53. Cambridge, MA: Harvard University Press, 1993.

"The Frontier in Ottoman History: Old Ideas and New Myths." In *Frontiers in Question: Eurasian Borderlands 700–1700*, Daniel Power and Naomi Standen, ed., 228–50. Houndmills, Basingstoke: Macmillan, 1999.

"A Frontier without Archaeology? The Ottoman Maritime Frontier in the Western Mediterranean." In *The Ottoman World, the Mediterranean and North Africa 1660–1760*, Chapter XI. Variorum Collected Studies. Farnham, Surrey: Ashgate, 2013.

"Standing on Hasluck's Shoulders: Another Look at Francesco Lupazzolo and His Aegean Isolario (1638)." In *Archaeology Anthropology and Heritage in the Balkans and Anatolia: The Life and Times of F.W. Hasluck, 1878–1920*, David Shankland, ed., v. 1, 349–75. İstanbul: Isis Press, 2013.

"Ottoman Territoriality versus Maritime Usage. The Ottoman Islands and English Privateering in the Wars with France (1689–1714)." In *Insularités ottomanes*, Nicolas Vatin and Gilles Veinstein, eds., 145–76. Paris: Maisonneuve & Larose, n.d.

Hill, Tracey. *Anthony Munday and Civic Culture: Theatre, History and Power in Early Modern London, 1580–1633*. Manchester: Manchester University Press, 2004.

Hind, Arthur, and Margery Corbett. *Engraving in England in the Sixteenth and Seventeenth Centuries: a Descriptive Catalogue*, v. 2. Cambridge: Cambridge University Press, 1964.

Hoffman, Jacobus. "Archiducatus Austria Inferioris Geographicae et Noviter Emendata Accuratissima Descriptio." Vienna, 1697.

Hoffmann, Catherine. "Publishing and the Map Trade in France, 1470–1670." In *HOC*, v. 3, part 2, 1569–88.

Homann, Johann Baptist. "Danubii Fluminis (hic ab urbe Belgrado, per Mare Negrum . . .)." Nuremberg, 1720.

"Imperii Persici in Omnes Suas Provincias," Nuremberg, [c. 1720].

Homann heirs. "Bosniae Regnum. " [n.p.: n.d.]. British Library K.Top.113.54.

Hooghe, Romeyn de. ["The Defeat of Kara Mustafa Pasha"]. Amsterdam: 1684.

Les Indes Orientales et Occidentales, et autres lieux. Amsterdam: Van Hoeve; reprint of Leiden: c. 1685 edition.

Housley, Norman. "The Eschatological Imperative: Messianism and Holy War in Europe, 1260–1556." In *Crusading and Warfare in Medieval and Renaissance Europe*, part III, 123–50. Aldershot: Ashgate, Variorum Reprints, 2001.

Howard, Deborah. *Venice and the East: The Impact of the Islamic World on Venetian Architecture 1100–1500*. New Haven: Yale University Press, 2000.

"Cultural Transfer between Venice and the Ottomans in the Fifteenth and Sixteenth Centuries." In *Cultural Exchange in Early Modern Europe*, v. 4, *Forging European Identities, 1400–1700*, Heinz Schilling and István György Tóth, eds., 138–77. Cambridge: Cambridge University Press, 2006.

"The Role of the Book in the Transfer of Culture between Venice and the Eastern Mediterranean." In *The Renaissance and the Ottoman World*, Anna Contadini and Claire Norton, eds., 97–107. Farnham, Surrey: Ashgate, 2013.

Howell, James. *Instructions and directions for forreine travell*. London: W.W. for Humphrey Moseley, 1650.

Hrushevsky, Mykhailo. *History of the Ukraine-Rus*, v. 7, *The Cossack Age to 1625*, Bohdan Struminski, trans. Edmonton: Canadian Institute of Ukrainian Studies Press, 1999.

Hughes, Charles, ed., *Shakespeare's Europe: A Survey of the Condition of Europe at the End of the 16th Century, Being unpublished chapters of Fynes Moryson's Itinerary (1617)*. New York: Benjamin Blom, 1967; reprint of 1903 edition.

Husain, Adnan. "Mission and Imagination: Franciscan William Rubruck and Interreligious Encounters in the Mongol East," unpublished paper, 1999.

İhsanoğlu, Ekmelledin, ed., *Osmanlı Coğrafya Literatürü (History of Geographical Literature during the Ottoman Period)*, 2 vols. İstanbul: IRCICA, 2000.

Im Lichte des Halbmonds: Das Abendland und der türkische Orient. Leipzig: Edition Leipzig, 1995.

Imber, Colin. *The Ottoman Empire 1300–1481*. İstanbul: Isis Press, 1990.

The Ottoman Empire, 1300–1650: The Structure of Power. Houndmills: Palgrave Macmillan, 2002.

Imber, Colin, Keiko Kiyotake, and Rhoads Murphey, eds. *Frontiers of Ottoman Studies: State, Province, and the West*, v. 2. New York, I.B. Tauris, 2005.

İnalcık, Halil. "Lepanto in the Ottoman Documents." In *Il Mediterraneo nella seconda metà del '500 alla luce di Lepanto*, 185–92. Firenze: 1974.

Infelice, Mario. "The War, the News, and the Curious: Military Gazettes in Italy." In *The Politics of Information in Early Modern Europe*, Brendan Dooley and Sabrina Baron, ed., 216–36. London: Routledge, 2001.

"From Merchants' Letters to Handwritten Political Avvisi: Notes on the Origin of Public Information." In *Cultural Exchange in Early Modern Europe*, v. 3, *Correspondence and Cultural Exchange in Europe, 1400–1700*, Francisco Bethencourt and Florike Egmond, eds., 33–52. Cambridge: Cambridge University Press, 2006.

"News Networks between Italy and Europe." In *The Dissemination of News and the Emergence of Contemporaneity in Early Modern Europe*, Brendan Dooley, ed., 51–68. Farnham, Surrey: Ashgate, 2011.

Itzkowitz, Norman and Max Mote, eds. and trans. *Mubadele: An Ottoman–Russian Exchange of Ambassadors*. Chicago: University of Chicago Press, 1970.

Ivanics, Mária. "The March of the Imperial Relief Forces to Kanizsa in Contemporary Illustrations." In Hasan Güzel, et. al., ed., *The Turks*, v. 3, 351–8. Ankara: Yeni Türkiye, 2002.

Iyânî, Câfer. *Tevârîh-i Cedîd-i Vilâyet-i Üngürüs (Osmanlı-Macar Mücadelesi Tarihi, 1585–1595)*, Mehmet Kirişcioğlu, ed. İstanbul: Kitabevi, 2001.

J. S,. "Abris Der Vöstung Hadtwan, Von den Christen Belegert und Eröbert. Den. 2 Septemb: A: 1596." [Vienna]: [1596].

Jaillot, Hubert. "Estats del' Empire Du Grand Seigneur Des Turcs, en Europe, en Asie, et en Afrique, divisé en tous ses Beglerbeglicz, ou Gouvernements." Paris: 1708.

Jianu, Angela. "Women, Fashion, and Europeanization: The Romanian Principalities, 1750–1830." In *Women in the Ottoman Balkans: Gender, Culture, and History*, Amıla Buturović and Irvin Schick, eds., 201–30. London: I.B. Tauris, 2007.

Jode, Cornelis de [Cornelius de Iudaeis]. "Croatiae & circumiacentiu[m] Regionu[m] versus Turcam nova delineatio." Undated map, from Cornelis de Jode, *Speculum Orbis Terrae*. Antwerp: 1593.

Johns, Adrian. *The Nature of the Book: Print and Knowledge in the Making*. Chicago: University of Chicago Press, 1998.

   Piracy: The Intellectual Property Wars from Gutenberg to Gates. Chicago: University of Chicago Press, 2009.

Johnson, Lonnie. *Central Europe: Enemies, Neighbors, Friends*. New York: Oxford University Press, 1996.

Kaegi, Walter. "Initial Byzantine Reactions to the Arab Conquest." *Church History* 38.2 (June, 1969): 139–49.

Kafadar, Cemal. *Between Two Worlds: The Construction of the Ottoman State*. Berkeley: University of California Press, 1995.

Kangal, Selmin, ed. *The Sultan's Portrait: Picturing the House of Osman*. İstanbul: İşbank, 1999.

Kappel, Jutta. "Die Türkennot des Kaisers: Zu einigen Aspekten der Darstellung des Türkenkrieges (1593–1606) in der Hofkunst Rudolfs II." In *Im Lichte des Halbmonds: Das Abendland und der türkische Orient*, 124–33. Leipzig: Edition Leipzig, 1995.

Karamustafa, Ahmet. "Introduction to Ottoman Cartography." In *HOC*, v. 2, book 1, 206–8.

   "Military, Administrative, and Scholarly Maps and Plans." In *HOC*, v. 2, book 1, 209–27.

Karateke, Hakan. "Legitimizing the Ottoman Sultanate: A Framework for Historical Analysis." In *Legitimizing the Order: The Ottoman Rhetoric of State Power*, Hakan Karateke and Maurus Reinkowski, eds., 13–52. Leiden: Brill, 2005.

Karrow, Robert. *Mapmakers of the Sixteenth Century and Their Maps: Bio-bibliographies of the Cartographers of Abraham Ortelius, 1570*. Chicago: Newberry Library, 1993).

Kaske, Robert. *Medieval Christian Literary Imagery: A Guide to Interpretation*. Toronto: University of Toronto, 1988.

Kâtib Çelebi. *Tuhfet ül-kibar fi esfar ül-bihar*. [İstanbul]: Matbaa-ı Bahriye, 1911.

   Tuhfet ül-kibar fi esfar ül-bihar. [İstanbul]. Topkapı Sarayı Müzesi, R. 1192.

   Kitâb-ı Cihânnümâ, v. 1. Ankara: Türk Tarih Kurumu, 2009.

Kayvanian, Carla. "Maps and Wars: Charting the Mediterranean in the Sixteenth Century." In *Cities of the Mediterranean From the Ottomans to the Present Day*, Biray Kolluoğlu and Meltem Toksöz, eds., 38–60. London: I.B. Tauris, 2010.

Keere, Pieter van der (Petrus Kaerius). "Nova et Recens Emendata Totius Regni Ungariae Cum Adiacentibus Et Finitimis Regionibus Delineatio." [Amsterdam]: 1620.

Kelenik, József. "The Military Revolution in Hungary." In *Ottomans, Hungarians, and Habsburgs in Central Europe: The Military Confines in the Era of Ottoman Conquest*, Géza Dávid and Pál Fodor, eds., 117–59. Leiden: Brill, 2000.

Kemalpaşazade [İbn Kemâl]. *Tevarih-i Âl-i Osman X. Defter*. Şefaettin Severcan, ed. Ankara: Türk Tarih Kurumu, 1996.

   Tevârîh-i Âl-i Osmân, VIII Defter. Ahmet Uğur, ed. Ankara: Türk Tarih Kurumu, 1997.

Keulen, Ioannes van. "Paskaerte Vande Archipel en de Eylanden . . ." Amsterdam: [1680].

Kiel, Machiel. *Art and Society of Bulgaria in the Turkish Period*. Assen/Maastricht, the Netherlands: Van Gorcum, 1985.

Klusáková, Luud'a. *The Road to Constantinople: The Sixteenth-Century Ottoman Towns through Christian Eyes*. Prague: ISV, 2002.

Knolles, Richard. "The Prophesie of A Turk: concerning the Downfall of Mahometism And of the Setting up the Kingdom and Glory of Christ . . . Truly Related, as it was taken out of the Turkish History at Constantinople." In *Generall Historie of the Turkes*. London: Printed by Andrew Sowle, 1687.

Koeman, Cornelis. *The History of Abraham Ortelius and his Theatrum Orbis Terrarum*. Lausanne: Sequoia, 1964.

   Atlantes Neerlandici, v. 2. Amsterdam: Theatrum Orbis Terrarum, 1967.

   The Sea on Paper: The Story of the Van Keulens and Their 'Sea-torch'. Amsterdam: Theatrum Orbis Terrarum, 1972.

Koeman, Cornelis, Günter Schilder, Marco van Egmond, and Peter van derKrogt. "Commercial Cartography and Map Production in the Low Countries, 1500–ca. 1672." In *HOC*, v. 3, pt. 2, 1296–1383.

Kolodziejczyk, Dariusz. *Ottoman–Polish Diplomatic Relations (15th–18th Century): An Annotated Edition of 'Ahdnames and Other Documents*. Leiden: Brill, 2000.

   The Ottoman Survey Register of Podolia (ca. 1681): Defter-i Mufassal-ı Eyalet-i Kamaniçe. Cambridge, MA: Harvard Ukrainian Research Institute, 2003.

Kontje, Todd. *German Orientalisms*. Ann Arbor, MI: University of Michigan Press, 2007.

Konuk, Kader. "Ethnomasquerade in Ottoman–European Encounters: Reenacting Lady Mary Wortley Montagu." *Criticism* 46.3 (summer, 2004): 393–414.

Köseoğlu, Cengiz. *The Topkapı Saray Museum: The Treasury*, translated, expanded, and edited by J.M. Rogers. Boston: Little, Brown and Co., 1987.

Kozličić, Midhat. *Kartografski Spomenici Hrvatskoga Jadrana: Izbor karata, planova i veduta do kraja 17 stoljeća*. Zagreb: AGM, 1995.

Krekić, Bariša. *Dubrovnik in the 14th and 15th Centuries: A City Between East and West*. Norman: University of Oklahoma Press, 1972.

   "Courier Traffic between Dubrovnik, Constantinople and Thessalonika in the First Half of the Fourteenth Century." In *Dubrovnik, Italy, and the Balkans in the Late Middle Ages*, XI, 1–8. London: Variorum Reprints, 1980.

Krokar, James. "The Ottoman Presence in Southeastern Europe, 16th–19th Centuries: A View in Maps." Slide set text. Chicago: Newberry Library, 1997.

Kumrular, Özlem. *Las Relaciones entre el Imperio Otomano y la Monarquía Católica entre los años 1520–1535 y el papel de los Estados satélites*. İstanbul: Isis Press, 2003.

   The Ottoman World, Europe and the Mediterranean. İstanbul, Isis Press, 2012.

Kütükoğlu, Bekir. *Osmanlı-İran Siyâsî Münâsebetleri (1578–1612)*. İstanbul: İstanbul Fethi Cemiyeti, 1993.

Kyle, Chris, and Jason Peacey. *Breaking News: Renaissance Journalism and the Birth of the Newspaper*. Washington, DC: Folger Shakespeare Library, 2008.

L. P., "Agria, Fortezza nel paese di Ongheria nel modo che al presente si trova." [Venetia?], 1568.

La Naissance de L'Antechrist en Babillonee. Paris: Laurent Lacquehay, 1623.

Lach, Donald. *Asia in the Making of Europe*, vol. 2, *A Century of Wonder*. Chicago: University of Chicago Press, 1970.

Lafreri, Antonio. "La Vera ritratto de Zighet." Rome: 1566.

   "Ordine con il quale l'esercito Turchesco suole presentarsi in Campagna contro de Christiani, o Persiani . . ." Rome: 1566.

Lavezzo, Kathy. *Angels on the Edge of the World: Geography, Literature, and English Community, 1000–1534*. Ithaca, NY: Cornell University Press, 2006.

Lehne, Inge, and Lonnie Johnson. *Vienna: The Past in the Present, A Historical Survey*, 2nd ed. Vienna: Österreichischer Bundesverlag, 1995.

Lellouch, Benjamin, and Stéphane Yerasimos, eds. *Les Traditions apocalyptiques au tournant de la chute de Constantinople, Actes de la Table Ronde d'Istanbul (13–14 avril 1996)*. Paris and Montreal: l'Harmattan, 1999.

Lemay, J. A. Leo. *Did Pocahontas Save Captain John Smith?* Athens, GA: University of Georgia Press, 1992.

Leth, Hendrik de. "De stad Algiers." Amsterdam: [n.d.]. British Library, Maps C.2491.02.

Levi, Scott, and Ron Sela, eds. *Islamic Central Asia: An Anthology of Historical Sources*. Bloomington: Indiana University Press, 2010.

Linschoten, Jan Huyghen van. *John Huighen Van Linschoten, his Discourse of Voyages into East and West Indies*. London by John Wolfe Printer, [1598].

Locatelli, Alessandro. *Racconto historico della Veneta guerra in Levante*. Venetia: Girolamo Albrizzi, 1691.

Lokman, Seyyid. *Hünername*. İstanbul: c. 1588. Topkapı Sarayı Müzesi Kütüphanesi, Hazine 1523.

Lucas, Paul. *Troisième voyage du sieur Paul Lucas: fait en MDCCXIV... dans la Turquie, l'Asie, la Sourie, la Palestine, la Haute et la Basse Egypte, &c.*, v. 1. Rouen: Chez Robert Machuel le jeune, 1719.

Luchini, Vincenzo. "Totius Graeciae Descriptio," Rome: 1558. British Library, Maps. C.7.e.2.(.29).

Luebbers, Leslie. "Documenting the Invisible: European Images of Ottoman Women, 1567–1867." *The Print Collector's Newsletter* 24.1 (March–April 1993): 2–7.

Luther, Martin. "On War against the Turk, 1529" (*Vom Kriege wider die Türken*), Charles Jacobs, trans., 5. Libronix Digital Library, http://www.libronix.com.

"Appeal for Prayer against the Turks, 1541" (*Vermahnung zum Gebet wider den Türcken*), Paul Moessner, trans., 4. Libronix Digital Library, http://www.libronix.com.

Luttrell, Anthony. "The Latins and Life on the Smaller Aegean Islands, 1204–1453." In *Latins and Greeks in the Eastern Mediterranean after 1204*, Benjamin Arbel, Bernard Hamilton, and David Jacoby, eds., 146–57. London: Frank Cass, 1989.

MacEvitt, Christopher. *The Crusades and the Christian World of the East: Rough Tolerance*. Philadelphia: University of Pennsylvania Press, 2008.

MacLean, Gerald. *The Rise of Oriental Travel: English Visitors to the Ottoman Empire, 1580–1720*. Houndmills: Palgrave Macmillan, 2004.

Looking East: English Writing and the Ottoman Empire before 1800. Houndmills, Basingstoke: Palgrave, 2007.

MacLean, Gerald, and William Dalrymple, eds. *Re-Orienting the Renaissance: Cultural Exchange with the East*. London: Palgrave, 2005.

Madunić, Domagog. "Frontier Elites of the Ottoman Empire during the War for Crete (1645–1669): The Case of Ali-Pasha Čengić." In *Europe and the Ottoman World: Exchanges and Conflicts*, 47–82. İstanbul: Isis Press, 2013.

Magocsi, Paul Robert. *Historical Atlas of East Central Europe*. Seattle: University of Washington Press, 1993.

Maier, Alexander. "Iavarinum sive Raab à Christianis captum 29 die Martij Anno Christi 1598." [Augsburg]: [1598]. British Library, Maps 28335.(.5).

Maier, Jessica. "A 'True Likeness': The Renaissance City Portrait." *Renaissance Quarterly* 65 (2012): 711–52.

Maire, F. I. "Carte. De la partie d'Albanie occupée par le Bacha de Scutari. le District des Montenegrins, et partie des Territoires des Rep.ques de Venise, et de Raguse." Vienna: 1788.

"Carte générale des Limites entre les trois Empires et leurs variations successives depuis l'année 1718 jusqu'à ce jour, ou Théâtre de la Guerre présente." Vienna: 1788.

Majer, Hans Georg. "Europäische und osmanische Sultansporträts." In *Im Lichte des Halbmonds: Das Abendland und der türkische Orient*, 37–42. Leipzig: Edition Leipzig, 1995.

Maltezou, Chryssa. "From Crete to Jerusalem: The Will of a Cretan Jew (1626)." In *Inter-cultural Contacts in the Medieval Mediterranean: Studies in Honour of David Jacoby*, Benjamin Arbel, ed., 189–201. London: Frank Cass, 1996.

Mancall, Peter. "Introduction: What Fynes Moryson Knew." *Journal of Early Modern History* 10.1–2 (2006): 1–9.

  Hakluyt's Promise: An Elizabethan's Obsession for an English America. New Haven: Yale University Press, 2007.

Manners, Ian, ed., with M. Pinar Emiralioğlu. *European Cartographers and the Ottoman World, 1500–1750: Maps from the Collection of O.J. Sopranos*. Chicago: Oriental Institute, 2010.

"Map of Asia Minor Designed to Illustrate the Third Volume of Union Questions." *Union Questions, on select portions of Scripture from the Old and New Testaments*. Philadelphia: American Sunday School Union, 1830.

"Map of Assyria, Asia Minor, &c." In *Sacred Geography*. Philadelphia: American Sunday School Union, c. 1830.

Marlowe, Christopher. *Tamburlaine*. Mineola, NY: Dover Books, 2002.

Marshall, P. J., and Glyndwr Williams. *The Great Map of Mankind: British Perceptions of the World in the Age of Enlightenment*. London: J.M. Dent & Sons, 1982.

Matar, Nabil. *Turks, Moors, and Englishmen in the Age of Discovery*. New York: Columbia University Press, 1999.

  Islam in Britain, 1558–1685. Cambridge: Cambridge University Press, 2004.

  Europe through Arab Eyes, 1578–1727. New York: Columbia University Press, 2009.

Matrakçı Nasuh. *Fethname-i Karabuğdan*. İstanbul: [c. 1538].

  Tarih-i Feth-i Şikloş ve Estergon ve Estolnibelgrad (History of the Conquest of Siklos, Esztérgom and Székesfehérvar). İstanbul: c. 1545. Topkapı Sarayı Müzesi Kütüphanesi, H.1608.

  Nasūhü's-Silāhī (Matrākçī), Beyān-ı Menāzil-i Sefer-i 'Irākeyn. H.G. Yurdaydın, ed. Ankara: Türk Tarih Kurumu Basımevi, 1976.

Matthee, Rudi. "The Safavid-Ottoman Frontier: Iraq-ı Arab as Seen by the Safavids." In *Ottoman Borderlands: Issues, Personalities, and Political Changes*, Kemal Karpat with Robert Zens, eds., 157–73. Madison, WI: University of Wisconsin Press, 2003.

Matthew, K. M. *History of the Portuguese Navigations in India*. Delhi: Mittal Publications, 1988.

Mayhew, Tea. *Dalmatia between Ottoman and Venetian Rule: contado di Zara 1645–1718*. Rome: Viella, 2008.

McGowen, Bruce. "Defter-i mufassal-ı liva-ı Sirem: An Ottoman Revenue Survey Dating from the Reign of Selim II." Ph.D. thesis, Columbia University, 1967.

McJannet, Linda. *The Sultan Speaks: Dialogue in English Plays and Histories about the Ottoman Turks*. Houndmills: Palgrave, 2006.

McLean, Matthew. *The Cosmographia of Sebastian Münster: Describing the World in the Reformation*. Houndmills: Ashgate, 2007.

Mehmed Hurşid [Paşa]. *Seyâhatnâme-i Hudûd*. Alâattin Eser, ed. İstanbul: Simurg, 1997.

Mehmed Neşri, *Kitâb-ı Cihan-nümâ: Neşri Tarihi*, Faik Reşit Unat and Mehmed Köymen, eds., v. 2. Ankara: Türk Tarih Kurumu, 1995.

Membré, Michele. *Mission to the Lord Sophy of Persia*, A.H. Morton, ed. and trans. London: School of Oriental and African Studies, 1993.

"Il Meraviglioso Ordine de Gran Esercito Turchesco." [n.p.: n.d.].

Meserve, Margaret. "News from Negroponte." *Renaissance Quarterly* 59.2 (Summer 2006): 440–80.

  Empires of Islam in Renaissance Historical Thought. Cambridge, MA: Harvard University Press, 2008.

Michaud, Claude. "Les Turcs dans l'Histoire universelle de Jacques-Auguste de Thou [1553–1617]." In *Chrétiens et musulmans à la Renaissance, Actes du 37e colloque international du CESR (1994)*, Bartolomé Bennassar and Robert Sauzet, eds., 241–54. Paris: Honoré Champion, 1998.

Minadoi da Rovigo, Giovanni Tommaso. *Historia della Guerra fra Turchi et Persiani*. Venetia: Andrea Muschio & Barezzo Barezzi, 1588.

Miquel, André. *La géographie humaine du monde musulman jusqu'au milieu du 11e siècle: Géographie arabe et représentation du monde: la terre et l'étranger.* Paris: Éditions de l'École des Hautes Études en Sciences Sociales, 2001.

Mitchell, Colin. *The Practice of Politics in Safavid Iran: Power, Religion and Rhetoric.* London: I.B. Tauris, 2009.

Mitelli, Giuseppe. "Allegorie auf die Größe Kaiser Leopold I." Bologna: 1687.

Mittman, Asa. *Maps and Monsters in Medieval England.* New York: Routledge, 2006.

Moačanin, Nenad. *Town and Country on the Middle Danube, 1526–1690.* Leiden: Brill, 2006.

Moll, Herman. *The Compleat Geographer of the Earth,* 4th ed. London: J. Knapton, 1723.

Monaco, Angelo Maria. "'Qui sunt et unde venerunt?' Topoi iconografici per il consenso agiografico nel culto degli ottocento Martiri di Otranto." In *La conquista turca di Otranto (1480) tra storia e mito, Atti del convegno internazionale di studio Otranto-Muro Leccese, 28–31 marzo 2007,* Hubert Houben, ed., v.2, 157–95. Galatina: Congedo Editor, 2008.

Moore, John Hamilton. *A New and Complete Collection of Voyages and Travels...* 2 vols. London: Printed for the Proprietors, [1785].

Morden, Robert. *Geography Rectified; or, a description of the world, in all its kingdoms provinces, countries...* London: R. Morden and T. Cockerill.

Morritt, John B. S. *The Letters of John B. S. Morritt of Rokeby, Descriptive of Journeys in Europe and Asia Minor in the Years 1794–1796,* G. E. Marindin, ed. London: John Murray, 1914.

Murphey, Rhoads. *Ottoman Warfare 1500–1700.* New Brunswick, NJ: Rutgers University Press, 1999.

"The Cultural and Political Meaning of Ottoman Rituals of Welcome: A Text-Linked Analysis Based on Accounts by Three Key Ottoman Historians." In *Acta Viennensis Ottomanica, Akten des 13 CIEPO – Symposiums (Comité international des études pré-ottomanes et ottomanes), vom 21 bis 25 September, 1998,* Markus Köhback, Gisela Procházka-Eisl, and Claudia Römer, eds., 247–55. Vienna: Selbstverlag des Instituts für Orientalistik, 1999.

"Evolving Versus Static Elements in Ottoman Geographical Writing Between 1598 and 1729, Perspectives and Real Life Experience of 'The Northern Lands' (Taraf al-Shimali) over 130 Years." In *Ottoman Bosnia: A History in Peril,* Markus Koller and Kemal Karpat, eds., 73–82. Madison, WI: University of Wisconsin Press, 2004.

Exploring Ottoman Sovereignty: Tradition, Image and Practice in the Ottoman Imperial Household, 1400–1800. London: Continuum, 2008.

Mustafa Naima, *Annals of the Turkish Empire from 1591 to 1659 of the Christian Era,* Charles Fraser, trans., v. 1. New York: Arno Press, 1973; reprint of London: Oriental Translation Fund, 1832.

Tarih-i Na'ima. Mehmet İpşirli, ed., v. 1. Ankara: T.T.K., 2007.

Nasir-i Khusraw. *Nāser-e Khosraw's Book of Travels (Safarnāma),* W.M. Thackston, trans. New York: Bibliotheca Persica, 1986.

Naughton, James. "Czech and Slovak Literature Resources: Renaissance and Humanism," http://users.ox.ac.uk/~tayloo10/lit_renais.htm.

Navari, Leonora. "Gasparo Tentivo's Il Nautica Ricercato. The Manuscripts." In *Eastern Mediterranean Cartographies,* George Tolias and Dimitris Loupis, eds., 135–55. Athens: Institute for Neohellenic Research, 2004.

"Mapping the Mediterranean in the Gennadius Library." *New Griffon* 8 (2006): 8–21.

Necipoğlu, Gülru. *Architecture, Ceremonial, and Power: The Topkapı Palace in the Fifteenth and Sixteenth Centuries.* Cambridge, MA: MIT Press, 1991.

Nefedova, Olga. *A Journey into the World of the Ottomans: The Art of Jean-Baptiste Vanmour (1671–1737).* Milan: Skira, 2009.

Nefedova, Olga, Sara Al Mana, and Farhad Al Faihani. "The Travel Album of Bartholomäus Schachman." In *Bartholomäus Schachman (1559–1614), The Art of Travel,* 63–90. Milan: Skira, 2012.

Nevitt, Marcus. "Ben Johnson and the Serial Publication of News." In *News Networks in Seventeenth Century Britain and Europe,* Joad Raymond, ed., 51–66. London: Routledge, 2006.

New and Universal History of Voyages and Travels Collected from the most authentic Authors in all Languages . . . London: W. Owen, 1754.

Newton, Charles. *Images of the Ottoman Empire.* London: V and A Publications, 2007.

Niccoli, Ottavia. *Prophecy and People in Renaissance Italy*, Lydia Cochrane, trans. Princeton, NJ: Princeton University Press, 1990.

Nicolay, Nicolas de. *Les quatre premiers livres des navigations et peregrinations orientales de N. de Nicolay.* Lyon: 1567.

  The Nauigations, Peregrinations and Voyages Made into Turkie. London: Thomas Dawson, 1585.

Norton, Claire. "Smack-Head Hasan: Why Are All Turkic Superheroes Intemperate, Treacherous, or Stupid?" In *Super/heroes: From Hercules to Superman*, Wendy Haslem, Angela Ndalianis, and C. J. Mackie, eds., 263–274. Washington, DC: New Academia Press, 2007.

Norwich, John J. *Venice: The Greatness and the Fall.* London: Penguin Books, 1981.

Novak, Drago, Miljenko Lapaine, and Dubravka Mlinarić, eds. *Five Centuries of Maps and Charts of Croatia / Pet stoljeća geografskih i pomorskih karata Hrvatske.* Zagreb: Školska Knjiga, 2005.

Onians, Richard. *The Origins of European Thought: About the Body, the Mind, the Soul, the World, Time, and Fate.* Cambridge: Cambridge University Press, 1954.

Orhonlu, Cengiz. "Hint Kaptanlığı ve Pîrî Reis." *Belleten* 34 (1970): 234–54.

Özdemir, Kemal. *Ottoman Nautical Charts and the Atlas of Ali Macar Reis.* İstanbul: Creative Yayıncılık, 1992.

Özpınar, Şükrü, et. al., eds. *Türk Deniz Müzesi, Harita Kataloğu/Chart and Map Catalogue of Turkish Naval Museum.* Ankara: Kültür Yayınları Tarih Dizisi, 2001.

Padrón, Ricardo. "Mapping Imaginary Worlds." In *Maps: Place in the World*, James R. Ackerman and Robert Karrow, eds., 255–88. Chicago: University of Chicago Press, 2007.

Pagan, Matteo. "La Processione del Corteo Ducale in Piazza San Marco, c. 1559." Museo Correr, n. 5933.

Palace of Gold and Light: Treasures from the Topkapı, Istanbul. Washington, DC: Palace Arts Foundation, 2000.

Paleotti, Gabriele. *Discorso Intorno alle Immagini Sacre e Profane (1582).* Vatican City: Libreria Editrice Vaticana, 2002.

Pálffy, Géza. "The Origins and Development of the Border Defense System against the Ottoman Empire in Hungary (Up to the Early Eighteenth Century)." In *Ottomans, Hungarians, and Habsburgs in Central Europe: The Military Confines in the Era of Ottoman Conquest*, Géza Dávid and Pál Fodor, eds., 3–70. Leiden: Brill, 2000.

Pamuk, Şevket. *A Monetary History of the Ottoman Empire.* Cambridge: Cambridge University Press, 2000.

Panaite, Viorel. *The Ottoman Law of War and Peace: The Ottoman Empire and Tribute Payers.* Boulder, CO: East European Monographs, 2000.

  "Wallachia and Moldavia from the Ottoman Juridical and Political Viewpoint, 1774–1829." In *Ottoman Rule and the Balkans, 1760–1850: Conflict, Transformation, Adaptation*, Proceedings of an international conference Rethymno, Greece, 13–14 December 2003, Antonis Anastasopoulos and Elias Kolovos, eds., 21–44. Rethymnon: University of Crete, 2007.

Panzac, Daniel. *La Caravane maritime: Marins européens et marchands ottomans en Méditerranée.* Paris: CNRS, 2004.

Patterson, W. B. "Fuller, Thomas (1607/8–1661)," in H. Matthew and Brian Harrison, eds. *Oxford Dictionary of National Biography*, v. 21, 159–63. Oxford: Oxford University Press, 2004.

Paul, Benjamin. " 'And the moon has started to bleed': Apocalypticism and Religious Reform in Venetian Art at the Time of the Battle of Lepanto," in *The Turk and Islam in the Western Eye, 1450–1750*, James G. Harper, ed., 67–94. Farnham, Surrey: Ashgate, 2011.

Payne, Anthony. " ' Strange, remote, and farre distant countreys': The Travel Books of Richard Hakluyt," 1–38, in *Journeys Through the Market: Travel, Travellers, and the Book Trade*, Robin Myers and Michael Harris, ed. Newcastle: Oak Knoll Press, 1999.

Peacock, Andrew, ed. *The Frontiers of the Ottoman World*. Oxford: Oxford University Press, 2009.

Peck, Linda Levy. *Consuming Splendor: Society and Culture in Seventeenth-Century England*. Cambridge: Cambridge University Press, 2005.

Pedani (Fabris), Maria Pia, ed. *Relazioni di Ambasciatori Veneti al Senato*, v. XIV, *Costantinopoli Relazioni Inedite (1512–1789)*. Padova: Bottega d'Erasmo, 1996.

Dalla frontiera al confine, Quaderni di studi Arabi. Studi e testi 5. Venice: Università Ca' Foscari, Herder Editrice, 2002.

"Christiani e Musulmani nel Mediterraneo." In *La mobilité des personnes en Méditerranée de l'antiquité à L'èpoque moderne*, Claudie Moatti, ed., 239–51. Rome: Éçole Française de Rome, 2004.

"Venetians in the Levant in the Age of Selim I." In *Conquête ottomane de l'Égypte (1517)*, Benjamin Lellouch and Nicolas Michel, eds., 99–112. Leiden: Brill, 2013.

Pedley, Mary. *The Commerce of Cartography: Making and Marketing Maps in Eighteenth-Century France and England*. Chicago: University of Chicago Press, 2005.

Pelletier, Monique. "National and Regional Mapping in France." In *HOC*, v. 3, pt. 2, 1480–1503.

Pennell, C. R., ed. *Piracy and Diplomacy in Seventeenth-Century North Africa: The Journal of Thomas Baker, English Consul in Tripoli 1677–1685*. Rutherford, NJ: Fairleigh Dickinson University Press, 1989.

Perjés, Géza. *The Fall of the Medieval Kingdome of Hungary: Mohács 1526 – Buda 1541*, Márió Fenyö, trans. Boulder, CO: Social Science Monographs, 1989.

Petitjean, Johann. "On His Holiness' Secret Service: How Ragusa became an Intelligence Agency after Lepanto." In *Europe and the 'Ottoman World': Exchanges and Conflicts (Sixteenth to Seventeenth Centuries)*, Gábor Kárman and Radu Păun, eds., 83–106. İstanbul: Isis Press, 2013.

Petkov, Kiril. *Infidels, Turks, and Women: The South Slavs in the German Mind, ca. 1400–1600*. Frankfurt: Peter Lang, 1997.

Pettegree, Andrew. "Translation and Migration of Texts." In *Borders and Travellers in Early Modern Europe*, Thomas Betteridge, ed., 113–25. Aldershot, Hampshire: Ashgate, 2007.

Philliou, Christine. "Communities on the Verge: Unraveling the Phanariot Ascendancy in Ottoman Governance." *Comparative Studies in Society and History* 51.1 (2009): 151–81.

Phillips, Carla Rahn. *Spain's Golden Fleece: Wool Production and the Wool Trade from the Middle Ages to the Nineteenth Century*. Baltimore: Johns Hopkins University Press, 1997.

Phillips, J. R. S. *The Medieval Expansion of Europe*, 2nd ed. Oxford: Clarendon Press, 1998.

Pinargenti, Simon. *Isole che son da Venetia nella Dalmatia, et per tutto l'Archipelago, fino a Costantinopoli*. Venetia: 1573.

Pincombe, Mike. "Life and Death on the Hapsburg-Ottoman Frontier: Bálint Balassi's 'In Laudem Confiniorum' and Other Soldier-Songs." In *Borders and Travellers in Early Modern Europe*, Thomas Betteridge, ed., 74–86. Aldershot, Hampshire: Ashgate, 2007.

Pinto, Karen. "The Maps Are the Message: Mehmet II's Patronage of an 'Ottoman Cluster.'" *Imago Mundi* 63. 2 (2011): 155–79.

"Searchin' His Eyes, Lookin' for Traces: Piri Reis' World Map of 1513 & Its Islamic Iconographic Connections (A Reading through Baghdat 334 and Proust)." *Osmanlı Araştırmaları/The Journal of Ottoman Studies* 39 (2012): 63–94.

Pippidi, Andrei. *Visions of the Ottoman World in Renaissance Europe*. London: Hurst, 2012.

Pirovano, Carlo, ed. *Venezia e i Turchi: Scontri e confronti di due civiltà*. Milan: Electa Editrice, 1985.

Pius II, Pope. *Epistola ad Morbisanum Turcarum Principe[m] . . . .* Coloniae: Ex officina Eucharij Ceruicorni, 1532.

Piwocka, Magdalena. "Turkish Tents in Poland." In *War and Peace: Ottoman–Polish Relations in the 15th–19th Centuries*, 52–61. İstanbul: MAS, 1999.

Pix, Mary. *Ibrahim, The Thirteenth Emperour of the Turks: A Tragedy As it is Acted By His Majesties Servants*. London, John Harding and Richard Wilkin, 1696.

Pollak, Martha. "Military Architecture and Cartography in the Design of the Early Modern City." In *Envisioning the City: Six Studies in Urban Cartography*, David Buisseret, ed., 109–24. Chicago: University of Chicago Press, 1998.

Porfyriou, Heleni. "The Cartography of Crete in the First Half of the 17th Century: A Collective Work of a Generation of Engineers." In *Eastern Mediterranean Cartographies*, George Tolias and Dimitris Loupis, eds., 65–92. Athens: Institute for Neohellenic Research, 2004.

Postel, Guillaume. *Le thresor des prophéties de l'univers*. François Secret, ed. La Haye: Martinus Nijhoff, 1969.

Press, Charles. *The Political Cartoon*. Rutherford, NJ: Fairleigh Dickinson University Press, 1981.

Ptolemy, Claudius. *Géographie de Ptolémée*, Jacopo D'Angiolo, trans. Paris: Catala Frères, [1926?].

Purchas, Samuel. *Purchas his pilgrimage, or Relations of the world and the religions obserued in all ages and places discouered, from the Creation vnto this present*. London: William Stansby for Henry Fetherstone, 1613.

    Hakluytus Posthumus or Purchas His Pilgrimes, 2 vols. London: Henry Fetherston, 1625.

Pust, Klemen. "The Image of the 'Turk' in the Christian Countries of the Adriatic Basin in Modern Age," 4 (English abstract), http://www.zrs.kp.si/konferenca/retorika_dev/avtorji/Klemen_P.html.

Quiclet, M. *Les voyages de M. Quiclet a Constantinople par terre*. Paris: Chez Pierre Prome, 1664.

Raby, Julian. *Venice, Dürer, and the Oriental Mode*. Totawa, N.J.: Islamic Art Publications, 1982.

    "From Europe to Istanbul." In *The Sultan's Portrait: Picturing the House of Osman*, Selmin Kangal, ed., 136–63. İstanbul: İşbank, 2000.

Rahimi, Babak. "The Rebound Theater State: The Politics of the Safavid Camel Sacrifice Rituals, 1598–1695 C.E." *Iranian Studies* 37.3 (September 2004): 1–28.

Ramberti, Benedetto. *Libri tre delle cose de Turchi*. Venetia: In casa de' figlioli di Aldo, 1539.

    The order of the great Turckes courte, of hys mene of warre, and of all hys conquests, with the summe of Mahumetes doctryne. Trans. from the French. [London]: Ricardus Grafton, 1542.

Ramusio, Giovanni Battista. *Delle Navigationi et Viaggi*, v. 2. Venetia: I Giunti, 1583.

    Navigationi et viaggi, v. 2. Amsterdam: Theatrum Orbis Terrarum, 1968; reprint of Venetia: I Giunti, 1583.

Randolph, Bernard. *The Present State of the Morea, called anciently Peloponnesus: Together with a Description of the City of Athens, Islands of Zant, Strafades, and Serrigo...* 3rd ed. London: Will. Notts, Tho. Basset; and Thomas Bennet, 1689.

Rashīd al-Dīn, *The Successors of Genghis Khan*, John Andrew Boyle, trans. New York: Columbia University Press, 1971.

Reindl, Hedda. "Zu einigen Miniaturen und Karten aus Handschriften Matraqči Nasuh's." *Islamkundliche Abhandlungen, Beiträge zur Kenntnis Südosteuropas und des Nahen Orients*, XVII band. Munich: Institut für Geschichte und Kultur des Nahen Orients, Universität München, 1974.

Reinink, G. J. "Ps. Methodius: A Concept of History in Response to the Rise of Islam." In *The Byzantine and Early Islamic Near East: Problems in the Literary Source Material*, Averil Cameron and Lawrence Conrad, eds., v. 1, 149–87. Princeton, NJ: Darwin Press, 1992.

Reitan, E. A. "Expanding Horizons: Maps in the Gentleman's Magazine, 1731–1754." *Imago Mundi* 37 (1985): 54–62.

Relihan, Constance. *Cosmographical Glasses: geographic discourse, gender, and Elizabethan fiction*. Kent, Ohio: Kent State University Press, 2004

Renda, Günsel. "The Ottoman Empire and Europe in the 17th Century: Changing Images." In *Image of the Turks in the 17th century Europe*, 44–55. İstanbul: Sabancı University, 2005.

Rijksmuseum Amsterdam: Highlights from the Collection. Amsterdam: Rijksmuseum, 1995.

Roberts, Sean. *Printing a Mediterranean World: Florence, Constantinople, and the Renaissance of Geography*. Cambridge: Harvard University Press, 2013.

Rogers, J. M. "Itineraries and Town Views in Ottoman Histories." In *HOC*, v. 2, book 1, 228–55.

Empire of the Sultans: Ottoman Art from the Khalili Collection. London: Nour Foundation, 2000.

Roider, Karl, Jr. *Austria's Eastern Question, 1700–1790*. Princeton, NJ: Princeton University Press, 1982.

Römer, Claudia. "An Ottoman Copyist Working for Sebastian Tengnagel, Librarian at the Vienna Hofbibliothek, 1608–1636." In *Essays on Ottoman Civilization; Proceedings of the XIIth Congress of the Comité international d'études pré-ottomanes et ottomanes*, 331–50. Prague: Essays on Ottoman Civilization, 1998.

"A Firman of Süleyman the Magnificent to the King of France Preserved in an Exercise Book of the 'K.K. Akademie Orientalischer Sprachen' in Vienna, 1831." *Turcica* 31 (1999): 461–70.

Rosaccio, Giuseppe. *Viaggio da Venetia a Costantinopoli*. Venetia: Giacomo Franco, 1598.

Rossi, M. G. "Dimostratione de confini delle principale Città dell' Austria et Ungaria (Vienna assediata dal Turco nel mese di Luglio, 1683)." [Rome]: [c. 1583]. Bayerische Staatsbibliothek, Abteilung Karten & Bilder.

Rothenberg, Gunther Erich. *The Austrian Military Border in Croatia, 1522–1747*. Urbana, IL: University of Illinois Press, 1960.

Rothman, Natalie. "Self-Fashioning in the Mediterranean Contact Zone: Giovanni Battista Salvago and His *Africa Overo Barbaria* (1625)." In *Renaissance Medievalisms*, Konrad Eisenbichler, ed., 123–43. Toronto: Centre for Reformation and Renaissance Studies, 2009.

"Conversion, Convergence, and Commensuration in the Venetian–Ottoman Borderlands." *Journal of Medieval and Early Modern Studies* 41.3 (Fall, 2011): 601–33.

Brokering Empire: Trans-imperial Subjects between Venice and Istanbul. Ithaca: Cornell University Press, 2012.

Roxburgh, David. *Prefacing the Image: The Writing of Art History in Sixteenth-Century Iran*. Leiden: Brill, 2001.

Rubiés, Joan-Pau. *Travel and Ethnology in the Renaissance: South India through European Eyes, 1250–1625*. Cambridge: Cambridge University Press, 2000.

Rycaut, Paul. *Istoria dello stato presente dell'imperio ottomano*. Venetia: Combi & La Noù, 1672.

Sacks, David Harris. "Richard Hakluyt and his Publics, c. 1580–1620." In *Making Publics in Early Modern Europe: People, Things, Forms of Knowledge*, Bronwen Wilson and Paul Yachnin, eds., 160–76. New York: Routledge, 2010.

Sadettin, *The Reign of sultan Orchan Second King of the Turks, Translated out of Hojah Effendi, an eminent Turkish Historian*, William Seaman, trans. London: 1652.

Sahillioğlu, Halil. "Dördüncü Muradın Bağdat Seferi Menzilnamesi." *Belgeler* 2.3–4 (1965): 1–36.

Said, Edward. *Orientalism*. New York: Vintage, 1979.

[Salamanca, Antonio], A. S. "Algeri." [Rome]: 1541.

Salmon, Thomas. *Modern History or the Present State of All Nations Describing their respective Situations, Persons, Habits, and Buildings; Manners, Laws and Customs, Religion, and Policy; Arts and Sciences, Trades, Manufactures, and Husbandry; Plants, Animals, and Minerals*, 3rd ed., 3 vols., v. 1. London: T. Longman, T. Osborne, J. Shuckburgh, C. Hitch, S. Austen, and J. Rivington [1744].

Salzmann, Ariel. *Tocqueville in the Ottoman Empire: Rival Paths to the Modern State*. Leiden: Brill, 2004.

Sanderson, John. *The Travels of John Sanderson in the Levant, 1584–1602*, William Foster, ed., Series 2, LXVII. London: Hakluyt Society, 1931.

Sandys, George. *A Relation of a Journey begun An: Dom: 1610. Containing a Description of the Turkish Empire of Aegypt, of the Holy Land, of the Remote parts of Italy and Ilands ad ioyning*, 2nd ed. Amsterdam: Theatrum Orbis Terrarum, 1973; reprint of London: W. Barren, 1615.

Sanson, Nicolas. "Estats De L'Empire Du Grand Seigneur des Turqs ou Sultan des Ottomans en Asie, en Afrique, et en Europe." Paris: 1654.

Scafi, Alessandro. *Mapping Paradise: A History of Heaven on Earth*. Chicago: University of Chicago Press, 2006.

Scardassa, Egidio. *Relatione delle felici successi giorno per giorno dopò la mossa dell'armi della Sereniss. Republica di Venetia contro Turchi nella Dalmatia*. Rome: Franco Moneta, 1647.

Schick, Leslie Meral. "Ottoman Costume Albums in a Cross-Cultural Context." *Art Turc / Turkish Art: 10th International congress of Turkish Art, Geneva, 17–23 September 1995, Proceedings*, 625–8. Geneva: Fondation Max Van Berchem, 1999.

Schienerl, Peter W. "Süleyman der Prächtige (1520–1566)." In *Im Lichte des Halbmonds: Das Abendland und der türkische Orient*, 62–7. Leipzig: Edition Leipzig, 1995.

Schmidt, Jan. *The Joys of Philology: Studies in Ottoman Literature, History and Orientalism (1500–1923)*, 2 vols. Analecta Isisiana 60. İstanbul: Isis Press, 2002.

Schwarz, Klaus. "Vom Krieg zum Frieden: Berlin, das Kurfürstentum Brandenburg, das Reich und die Türken." In *Europa und der Orient 800–1900*, Sievernich, Gereon, and Hendrik Budde, eds., 245–78. Berlin: Bertelsmann Lexikon Verlag, 1989.

Schweigger, Salomon. *Ein newe reyssbeschreibung auss Teutschland nach Constantinopel und Jerusalem...* Rudolf Neck, ed. Graz: Akademische Druck v. Verlagsanstalt, 1964; reprint of Nürnberg: Casper Fulden, 1619.

Scolari, Stefano. "Viagio Da Vienna Sino Petro Varadino, Con La Distanza Di Miglia Da Una Citta Al Altra. Viagio Da Carlovitz Sino A Costantinopoli Con La Sua Distanza Di Miglia Da Una Citta Al Altra." Venetia: 1590. Newberry Library, Novacco 2F 184.

Senex, John, and G. de l'Isle. "A Map of Turky, Arabia, and Persia: Corrected from the latest Travels and from ye Observations of ye Royal Society's [sic.] of London and Paris." London: c. 1721.

Setton, Kenneth. "Lutheranism and the Turkish Peril." *Balkan Studies* 3 (1962): 133–68.
    Western Hostility to Islam and Prophecies of Turkish Doom. Series: *Memoirs*, 201. Philadelphia: American Philosophical Society, 1992.

Seutter [Seuttero], Georg Matthäus, Johann Baptist Homann [et al.], "Nova et Accurata Hungariae cum Adiacentib. Regni." [*Weltatlas*]. [Augsburg]: [17–], map 98. Knanstvena knjižnica Zadar, GA10421A.
    "Peloponnesus hodie Morea." [*Weltatlas*]. [Augsburg]: [17–], map 102. Knanstvena knjižnica Zadar, GA10421A.

Shaw, Stanford. *History of the Ottoman Empire and Modern Turkey*, v. 1, *Empire of the Gazis: the Rise and Decline of the Ottoman Empire 1280–1808*. Cambridge: Cambridge University Press, 1976.

Sievernich, Gereon, and Hendrik Budde, eds. *Europa und der Orient 800–1900*. Berlin: Bertelsmann Lexikon Verlag, 1989.

Silver, Larry. "East is East: Images of the Turkish Nemesis in the Hapsburg World." In *The Turk and Islam in the Western Eye, 1450–1750: Visual Imagery before Orientalism*, James Harper, ed., 185–215. Farnham, Surrey: Ashgate, 2011.

Singer, Amy. *Constructing Ottoman Beneficence: An Imperial Soup Kitchen in Jerusalem*. Albany: State University of New York Press, 2002.

Skilliter, Susan. *William Harborne And The Trade With Turkey 1578–1582. A Documentary Study of The First Anglo-Ottoman Relations*. Oxford: Oxford University Press, 1977.

Smail, Daniel. *Imaginary Cartographies: Possession and Identity in Late Medieval Marseille*. Ithaca: Cornell University Press, 1999)

Smith, John. *The True Travels, Adventures, and Observations of Captain John Smith in Europe, Affrica, and America, from Anno Domini 1593 to 1629*. London: Printed by I[ohn]. H[aviland] for Thomas Slater, 1630.

Sohrweide, H. "Lukman b. Sayyid Husayn." In *Encyclopedia of Islam*, CD-ROM ed., v.1.0. Leiden: Brill, 1999.

Sönmez, Ebru. *İdris-i Bidlisi: Ottoman Kurdistan and Islamic Legitimacy*. İstanbul: Libra Kitapçılık, 2012.

Soranzo, Lazzaro. *L'ottomano*. Ferrara: Vittorio Baldini, 1598.

L'ottomano. Napoli, Nella stamperia à Porta Reale, per Costantino Vitale, 1600.

Sotheby's, "Natural History, Travel, Atlases and Maps." Catalog: London, Thursday 18 November, 2004, 110–23.

Soucek, Svat. "Islamic Charting in the Mediterranean." In *HOC*, v. 2, book 1, 265–87.

Piri Reis and Turkish Mapmaking after Columbus: The Khalili Portolan Atlas. London: Nour Foundation, 1996.

Studies in Ottoman Naval History and Maritime Geography. İstanbul: Isis Press, 2008.

Soykut, Mustafa. *Image of the "Turk" in Italy*. Berlin: Islamkundliche Untersuchungen, 2001.

Sparke, M. *Crumms of Comfort And godly Prayers with Thankful Remembrance of Gods wonderful deliverances of this Land*. [London]: Printed for Charles Brome, [1708].

Speed, John. "The Turkish Empire." [London]: 1626.

Prospect of the Most Famous Parts of the World. London: By M.F. for W. Humble, 1646.

Spon, Jacob. *Voyage d'Italie, de Dalmatie, de Grèce et du Levant, 1678*. Paris: Honoré Champion, 2004.

Springborg, Patricia. *Western Republicanism and the Oriental Prince*. Cambridge: Polity, 1992.

Stackhouse, T. *A New Universal Atlas*, 2nd ed. London: For Mrs. Stackhouse, 1785

Stein, Mark. *Guarding the Frontier: Ottoman Border Forts and Garrisons in Europe*. London: I.B. Tauris, 2007.

Stoye, John. *Marsigli's Europe 1680–1730: The Life and Time of Luigi Ferdinando Marsigli, Soldier and Virtuoso*. New Haven: Yale University Press, 1994.

STRANGE fearful & true newes, which happened at CARLSTADT, in the kingdome of CROATIA. DECLARING HOW THE Sunne did shine like Bloude nine dayes together, and how two Armies were seene in the Ayre, the one encountering the other . . . London: Printed by R.B. for G. Vincent and W. Blackwall, [1606].

Strauss, Walter. *The German Single-Leaf Woodcut 1550–1600*, v. 1: A-J. New York: Abaris Books, 1975.

Striker, Laura Polanyi. "Appendix I: Captain John Smith's Hungary and Transylvania." In Bradford Smith. *Captain John Smith, His Life and Legend*, 311–42. Philadelphia: J.B. Lippincott Co., 1953.

Strunck, Christina. "The Barbarous and Noble Enemy: Pictorial Representations of the Battle of Lepanto." In *The Turk and Islam in the Western Eye, 1450–1750: Visual Imagery before Orientalism*, James Harper, ed., 217–42. Farnham, Surrey: Ashgate, 2011.

Szakály, Ferenc. "The Early Ottoman Period, Including Royal Hungary, 1526–1606." In *A History of Hungary*, Peter Sugar, et al., eds., 83–99. Bloomington: Indiana University Press, 1994.

"The Ransom of Ali Bey of Koppány: The Impact of Capturing Slaves on Trade in Ottoman Hungary." In *Ransom Slavery along the Ottoman Borders (Early Fifteenth-Early Eighteenth Centuries)*, Géza Dávid and Pál Fodor, eds., 93–114. Brill: Leiden, 2007.

Szántai, Louis. "The Riddle of de l'Isle's 1703 Map of Hungary." *Cartograhica Hungarica* 8 (May 2004): 7.

Tadayoshi, Miyoshi. "Japanese Map Screens." In *Encounters: The Meeting of Asia and Europe, 1500–1800*, Anna Jackson and Amin Jaffer, eds., 326–9. London: V & A Publications, [2004].

Tanındı, Zeren. "Bibliophile Aghas (Eunuchs) at Topkapı Palace." In *Muqarnas 2, Essays in Honor of Michael Rogers* (2004): 333–43.

Tarnowski, Christaforo. "Castelnovo." [n.p.]: 1605.

"Clissa." [n.p.]: 1605.

Tassy, [Jacques Philippe] Laugier de. *Histoire du royaume d'Alger, Avec l'etat de son gouvernement de ses forces de terre & de mer, de ses revenus, police, justice politique, & commerce*. n.p.: Elibron Classics, 2007; reprint of Amsterdam: Chez Henri du Sauzet, 1725.

Taylor, E. G. R. *Tudor Geography 1485–1583*. New York: Octagon Books, 1968.

Tenenti, Alberto. "Profilo di un conflitto secolare." In *Venezia e i Turchi: Scontri e confronti di due civiltà*, Carlo Pirovano, ed. Milan: Electa Editrice, 1985.

Teunissen, Harrie, and John Steegh, *Balkan in kaart: Vijf eeuwen strijd om identiteit*. Catalogus bij een tentoonstelling in de Universiteitsbibliotheek Leiden, 4 September–16 Oktober 2003. Leiden: Universiteitsbibliotheek, 2003.

Tezcan, Baki. "The Frank in the Ottoman Eye of 1583." In *The Turk and Islam in the Western Eye, 1450–1750: Visual Imagery before Orientalism*, James Harper, ed., 267–96. Farnham, Surrey: Ashgate, 2011.

Tezcan, Nurhan, and Semih Tezcan, eds. *Evliyâ Çelebi: Doğumunun 40. Yılında*. Ankara: T.C. Kültür ve Turizm Bakanlığı, 2011.

Theunissen, Hans. *Ottoman–Venetian Diplomatics: the 'ahd-names: The Historical Background and the Development of a Category of Political–Commercial Instruments Together with an Annotated Edition of a Corpus of Relevant Documents*, in *Electronic Journal of Oriental Studies*, or reprint, 2. vols. Utrecht: Universiteit Utrecht, 1998.

Thevet, André. *Cosmographie de Levant*, Frank Lestringant, ed. Geneva: Librairie Droz, 1985.

Thompson, Stith. *Motif-index of Folk Literature; A Classification of Narrative Elements in Folktales, Fables, Mediaeval Romances, Exempla, Fabliaux, Jest-Books, and Local Legends*, 6 vols., v. 6. Bloomington: University of Indiana Press, 1956–8.

Thys-Şenocak, Lucienne. *Ottoman Women Builders: The Architectural Patronage of Hadice Turhan Sultan*. Aldershot: Ashgate, 2006.

Tishby, Ariel, ed. *Holy Land in Maps*. Jerusalem: The Israel Museum, 2001.

Tissol, Garth. *The Face of Nature: Wit, Narrative, and Cosmic Origins in Ovid's Metamorphoses*. Princeton, NJ: Princeton University Press, 1997.

Todorova, Maria. *Imagining the Balkans*. New York: Oxford University Press, 1997.

Todorova-Pirgova, Iveta. "Cultural Images of the Ethnic Groups and Ethnic Interrelations in the Balkans." *Ethnologies* 21. 2 (1999): 147–75.

Todorović, Jelena. *An Orthodox Festival Book in the Habsburg Empire: Zaharija Orfelin's 'Festive Greeting to Mojsej Putnik' (1757)*. Aldershot, Hampshire: Ashgate, 2006.

Tolan, John V. *Saracens: Islam in the Medieval European Imagination*. New York: Columbia University Press, 2002.

  Saint Francis and the Sultan: The Curious History of a Christian–Muslim Encounter. Oxford: Oxford University Press, 2009.

Tolias, George. "Isolarii, Fifteenth to Seventeenth Centuries." In *HOC*, v. 3, part 1, 263–84.

  "Nikolaos Sophianos's *Totius Graeciae Descriptio*: The Resources, Diffusion, and Function of a Sixteenth Century Antiquarian Map of Greece." *Imago Mundi* 58.2 (July 2006): 150–82.

Tooley, R. V. "Maps in Italian Atlases of the Sixteenth Century, Being a Comparative List of the Italian Maps Issued by Lafreri, Forlani, Duchetti, Bertelli, and Others, Found in Atlases." *Imago Mundi*, 3 (1939): 12–47.

Tóth, István György. "Missionaries as cultural intermediaries in religious borderlands: Habsburg Hungary and Ottoman Hungary in the seventeenth century." In *Cultural Exchange in Early Modern Europe*, v. 1, *Religion and Cultural Exchange*, Heinz Schilling and István György Tóth, eds., 88–108. Cambridge: Cambridge University Press, 2006.

Tour, Brion de la. "Perse, Turquie Asiatique, et Arabie." Paris: 1766.

Traub, Valerie. "Mapping the Global Body." In *Early Modern Visual Culture: Representation, Race, and Empire in Renaissance England*, Peter Erickson and Clark Hulse, eds., 43–97. Philadelphia: University of Pennsylvania Press, 2000.

Trigault, Nicolas. "Tripoli Citta di Barberia." c. 1570. Newberry Library, Novacco 4F 404.

  De Christiana Expeditione apud Sinas. Augsburg: 1615.

Tubach, Frederic. *Index Exemplorum: A Handbook of Medieval Religious Tales*. Helsinki: Suomalainen Tiedeakatemia, 1981.

Tudebode, Peter. *Historia de Hierosolymitano Itinere*, John Hill and Laurita Hill, eds. and trans. Philadelphia: American Philosophical Society, 1974.

Turri, Eugenio. "Gli isolario ovvero l'idealizzazione cartografica." In *Navigare e descrivere: Isolari e portolani del Museo Correr di Venezia XV–XVIII secolo*, Camillo Tonini and Piero Lucchi, eds., 19–36. Venice: Marsilio, 2001.

Tütüncü, Mehmet. *Cezair'de Osmanlı İzleri (1516–1830)*. İstanbul: Çamlıca Basım, 2013.

Ullrich, Heinrich. "Der Christen Belägerung Der Vesten Raab: in dem 1597 iar." [Nuremberg?]: [1600?].

Valensi, Lucette. *The Birth of the Despot: Venice and the Sublime Porte*, Arthur Denner, trans. Ithaca, NY: Cornell University Press, 1993.

Vatican Museum. http://www.vaticanstate.va/EN/Monuments/The_Vatican_Museums/Gallery_of_Maps.htm.

Vaughan, Alden T. "John Smith Satirized: The Legend of Captaine Iones." *William and Mary Quarterly*, 3rd series, 45.4 (Oct. 1988): 712–32.

Vecellio, Cesare. *Vecellio's Renaissance Costume Book*. New York: Dover, 1977; reprint of *Degli habiti antiche, et moderni di tutto il mondo*. Venetia: Giovanni Bernardo Sessa, 1598.

Veinstein, Gilles. "L'Occupation ottomane d'Očakov et le problème de la frontière lituano-tartare 1538–1544." In *Passé Turco-Tatar présente soviétique: Études offertes à Alexandre Bennigsen*, 123–55. Louvain-Paris: Éditions Peeters, 1986.

"Some Views of Provisioning in the Hungarian Campaigns of Suleyman the Magnificent. In *Osmanistische Studien zur Wirschafts- und Sozialgeschichte: in memoriam Vančo Boškov*, H.S. Majer, ed., 177–85. Wiesbaden: 1986.

"Le Législateur ottoman face à l'insularité. L'enseignement des kânûnnâme." In *Insularités ottomanes*, Nicolas Vatin and Gilles Veinstein, eds., 91–110. Paris: Maisonneuve & Larose, n.d.

Velkov, Asparuch, and Evgeniy Radushev. *Ottoman Garrisons on the Middle Danube: Based on Austrian National Library MS MXT 562 of 956/1549–1550*. Budapest: Akadémiai Kiadó, 1996.

"La vera descrittione del sita della città de Tunisi." [1574].

Verberckmoes, Johan. "The imaginative recreation of overseas cultures in western European pageants in the sixteenth to seventeenth centuries." In *Cultural Exchange in Early Modern Europe*, v. 4, *Forging European Identities, 1400–1700*, Heinz Schilling and István György Tóth, eds., 361–80. Cambridge: Cambridge University Press, 2006.

Vernino, Alessandro. *Della historia delle guerre di Dalmatia sotto il generalato di Leonardo Foscolo*. Venetia: G.G. Herz, 1648.

Viero, Monica, and Yoo Omi Serena Campagnol. " Opera a Stampa." In *Navigare e descrivere: Isolari e portolani del Museo Correr di Venezia XV–XVIII secolo*, Camillo Tonini and Piero Lucchi, eds., 84–152. Venice: Marsilio, 2001.

Visscher, Nicolas. "Magni Turcarum Domini Imperium in Europa, Asia, et Africa." [Amsterdam]: [c. 1680].

Vitkus, Daniel, ed. *Three Turk Plays from Early Modern England: Selimus, A Christian Turned Turk, and The Renegado*. New York: Columbia University Press, 2000.

Turning Turk: English Theater and the Multicultural Mediterranean, 1570–1630. New York: Palgrave, 2003.

Vivo, Filippo de. "Paolo Sarpi and the Uses of Information in Seventeenth Century Venice." In *News Networks in Seventeenth Century Britain and Europe*, Joad Raymond, ed., 35–49. London: Routledge, 2006.

Vratislav z Mitrovic, Václav. *Adventures of Baron Wenceslas Wratislaw*. n.p.: Bibliobazar, n.d.; reprint of London: Bell and Daldy, 1862.

Příhody. Milada Nedvědová, ed. Prague: M.F., 1976.

Walsham, Alexandra. "Miracles and the Counter-Reformation Mission to England." *The Historical Journal* 46.4 (2003): 779–815.

Wansborough, John. *Lingua Franca in the Mediterranean*. Richmond, Surrey: Curzon Press, 1996.

Watson, Burton, ed. and trans. *Record of the Grand Historian of China, Translated from the Shih chi of Ssu-ma Ch'ien*, v. 2, *The Age of Emperor Wu, 140 to circa 100 B.C.* New York: Columbia University Press, 1961.

Weber, Johannes. "The Early German Newspaper – A Medium of Contemporaneity." In *The Dissemination of News and the Emergence of Contemporaneity in Early Modern Europe*, Brendan Dooley, ed., 69–79. Farnham, Surrey: Ashgate, 2011.

Wells, Edward. "A New Map of the Eastern Parts of Asia Minor." Included in his *A Sett of Maps*, 1700.

Westerberg, Sten. "Claes Rålamb: Statesman, scholar and ambassador." In *The Sultan's Procession: The Swedish Embassy to Sultan Mehmed IV in 1657–1658*, Karin Ådahl, ed., 26–57. İstanbul: Swedish Research Institute in Istanbul, 2006.

Wheler, George. *A journey into Greece, by George Wheler Esq; in company of Dr Spon of Lyons*. London: William Cademan, Robert Kettlewell, and Awnsham Churchill, 1682.

An account of the churches, or places of assembly, of the primitive Christians; from the churches of Tyre, Jerusalem, and Constantinople. Described by Eusebius. London: S. Roycroft, for R. Clavell, 1689.

Whitfield, Peter. *The Charting of the Oceans: Ten Centuries of Maritime Maps*. London: British Library, 1996.

Williams, Wes. " 'A mirrour of mis-haps, / A Mappe of Miserie': Dangers, Strangers, and Friends in Renaissance Pilgrimage." In *The 'Book' of Travels: Genre, Ethnology and Pilgrimage, 1250–1700*, Palmira Brummett, ed., 205–41. Leiden: Brill, 2009.

Wilson, Bronwen. *The World of Venice: Print, the City, and Early Modern Identity*. Toronto: University of Toronto Press, 2005.

"Foggie diverse di vestire de' Turchi: Turkish Costume Illustration and Cultural Translation." *Journal of Medieval and Early Modern Studies* special issue *Mapping the Mediterranean*, Valeria Finucci, ed., 37.1 (Winter 2007): 97–140.

"Francesco Lupazolo's *Isolario* and the Rewriting of the Mediterranean." In *Festschrift for Patricia Fortini Brown*, Blake de Maria and Tracy Cooper, eds. Milan: Five Continents, in press.

Winichakul, Thongchai. *Siam Mapped: A History of the Geo-body of a Nation*. Honolulu: University of Hawaii Press, 1994.

Wintle, Michael. *The Image of Europe: Visualizing Europe in Cartography and Iconography throughout the Ages*. Cambridge, Cambridge University Press, 2009.

Wit, F. de. "Regnum Hungaria in Omnes suos Comitatus." [Amsterdam]: [1680].

Witcombe, Christopher. *Copyright in the Renaissance: Prints and Privilegio in Sixteenth Century Venice and Rome*. Leiden: Brill, 2004.

Withers, Charles. "Place and the 'Spatial Turn' in Geography and in History." *Journal of the History of Ideas* 70.4 (October, 2009): 637–58.

Wittmann, Reinhard. "Was There a Reading Revolution at the End of the Eighteenth Century?" In *A History of Reading in the West*, Guglielmo Cavallo and Roger Chartier, eds., Lydia Cochrane, trans., 284–312. Amherst: University of Massachusetts Press, 1997.

Woodhead, Christine. *Ta'līkī-zāde's şehnāme-i hümāyūn: A History of the Ottoman Campaign into Hungary 1593–94*. Islamkundliche Untersuchungen, band 82. Berlin: Klaus Schwarz Verlag, 1983.

"Environment, Communications and Economy in the Ottoman Balkans and Eastern Mediterranean." *International Journal of Turkish Studies* 14, 1–2 (Fall, 2008):117–23.

Woodward, David. "Medieval Mappaemundi." In *HOC*, v. 1, 286–370.

"Cartography and the Renaissance: Continuity and Change." In *HOC*, v. 3, part 1, 3–24.

"The Italian Map Trade, 1480–1650." In *HOC*, v. 3, part 1, 773–803.

The Maps and Prints of Paolo Forlani: A Descriptive Bibliography. Chicago: Newberry Library, 1990.

Maps as Prints in the Italian Renaissance: Makers, Distributors, and Consumers. London: The British Library, 1997.

"Mapping the World." In *Encounters: The Meeting of Asia and Europe, 1500–1800*, Anna Jackson and Amin Jaffer, eds., 14–31. London: V & A Publications, [2004].

Worms, Laurence. "The London Map Trade to 1640." In *HOC*, v. 3, book 2, 1693–1721.

Wright, Diana Gilliland, and John Melville-Jones. "Bartolomeo Minio: Dispacci 1479–1483 from Nauplion," online extracts, "Stato da Mar" section, 10 February 1479 and 14 August 1480. In *The Greek Correspondence of Bartolomeo Minio*, v. 1: *Dispacci from Nauplion, 1479–83*, 4–13. Padua: Unipress, 2008.

Wunder, Amanda. "Western Travelers, Eastern Antiquities, and the Image of the Turk in Early Modern Europe." *Journal of Early Modern History* 7.1–2 (2003): 90–119.

Yerasimos, Stephane. *Les voyageurs dans l'empire ottoman (XIVe–XVIe siècles)*. Ankara: Société turque d'histoire, 1991.

Yoltar-Yıldırım, Ayşin. "A 1498–99 *Khusraw va Shīrīn*: Turning the Pages of an Ottoman Illustrated Manuscript." *Muqarnas* 22 (2005): 95–109.

Zachariadou, Elizabeth, ed. *The Via Egnatia under Ottoman Rule (1380–1699)*. Rethymnon: Crete University Press, 1996.

Zarinebaf, Fariba. *Crime and Punishment in Istanbul 1700–1800*. Berkeley: University of California Press, 2010.

Zarinebaf, Fariba, and Jack Davis. *A Historical and Economic Geography of Ottoman Greece*. Athens: American School of Classical Studies, 2004.

Zenoi, Domenico. "L'Ultimo disegno de l'isola di Malta. " Venetia: 1565.

Zilfi, Madeline. *Women and Slavery in the Late Ottoman Empire*. Cambridge: Cambridge University Press, 2010.

Zlatar, Zdenko. *Dubrovnik's Merchants and Capital in the Ottoman Empire (1520–1620): A Quantitative Study*. İstanbul: Isis Press, 2010.

Zukas, Alex. "The British Imperial Imagination in the Maps of Herman Moll, 1700–1730." *Proceedings of the American Historical Association, 2009*. Ann Arbor, MI: National Archive Publishing Company, 2009.

Żygulski, Zdzisław. *Ottoman Art in the Service of Empire*. New York: New York University, 1992.

Index